Yamada-kun and the Seven Witches

19

MIKI YOSHIKAWA

FLUSTERED
はわわわわ

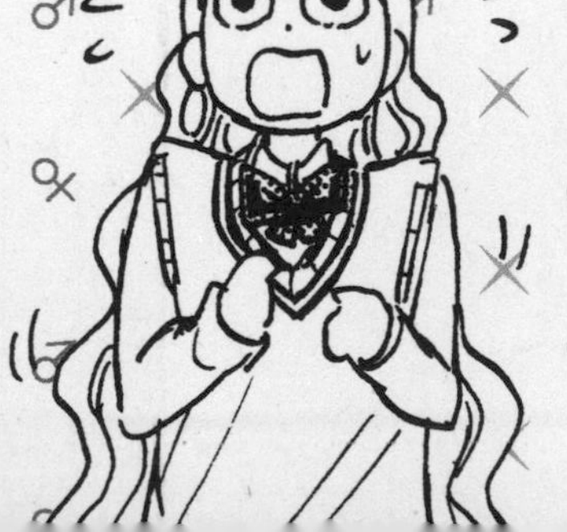

Yamada-kun and the Seven Witches

Cast of Characters

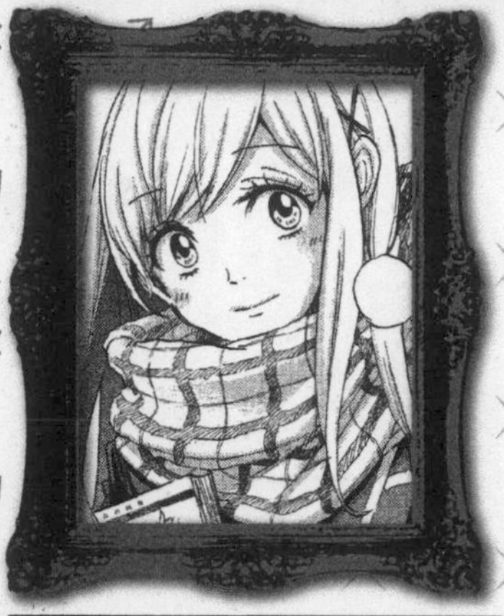

Urara Shiraishi

A second-year at Suzaku High School and president of the Supernatural Studies Club. She used to be known as the "Switch Witch" and she is Yamada's girlfriend. She was under Masamune Ichijo's "Incitement" spell, but she's currently free from its power.

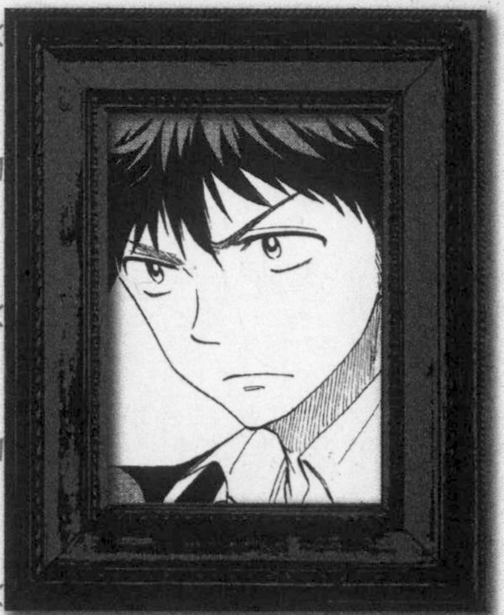

Ryu Yamada

A second-year at Suzaku High School. He's known as the "Copy Guy" and possesses the ability to copy the power of whichever witch he kisses. He's decided to perform a ceremony to retrieve his memories that got erased by Nancy.

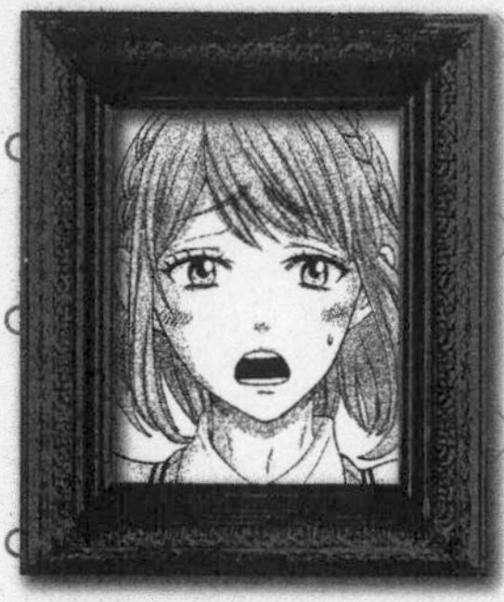

Nene Odagiri

A second-year at Suzaku High School and clerk for the Student Council. She used to be the "Charm Witch" and worked with Igarashi when she was a witch. She likes Yamada.

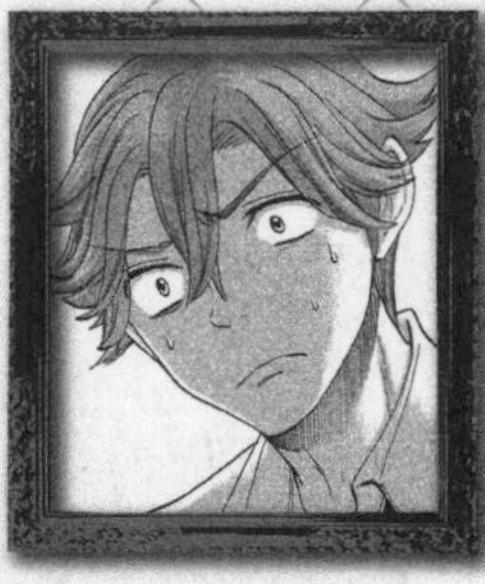

Shinichi Tamaki

A second-year at Suzaku High School and treasurer for the Student Council. He's known as the "Capture Guy" and steals the power of the witch whom he kisses. He's running to become the next Student Council president and he's giving it his all to win.

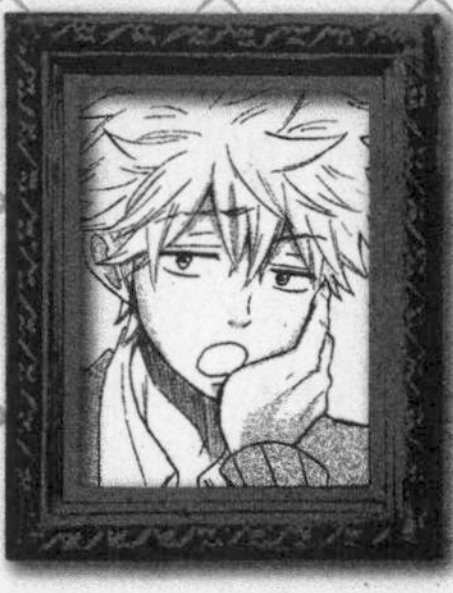

Toranosuke Miyamura

A second-year at Suzaku High School and president of the Student Council. Friendly, approachable, and a reliable leader. A plot by the Shogi Club resulted in a re-election, but he won't be in the running.

Noa Takigawa

A first-year at Suzaku High School and formerly a witch with the power to see into the past. She's a mischievous girl who's smitten with Yamada. She's getting better at messing with Yamada along with Miyamura.

Jin Kurosaki

A first-year at Suzaku High School and one of the vice-presidents of the Student Council. People thought he was a cheeky kohai, but he was just a slightly stupid, good-looking guy who's a bit of a disappointment.

Midori Arisugawa

A first-year at Suzaku High School and one of the vice-presidents of the Student Council. While she has a carefree personality, she also displays a calculating side at times…

Kotori Moegi

A second-year at Suzaku High School and a witch. She had her mind-reading power stolen by Igarashi. Performing the ceremony to get her power back is of the utmost urgency!

Sora Himekawa

A second-year at Suzaku High School and member of the Handicrafts Club. She's a klutzy and good-natured person who has an extremely "unique" sense of handcraftsmanship. She shares a past connection with Yamada…

Nancy

A second-year at Suzaku High School and a member of the Light Music Club. As the seventh witch, she has been hiding the fact that she erased Yamada and Himekawa's memories.

Yuri Miura

A first-year Suzaku High School student who belongs to the Shogi Club. He's a witch who has the power to manipulate others. He knows about Yamada and Himekawa's past…

Mikoto Asuka

A third-year at Suzaku High School and former vice-president of the student council. She used to be the "Invisible Witch" and now serves as the president of the Shogi Club. What's her goal in getting the recall…?

Ushio Igarashi

A second-year at Suzaku High School and vice-president of the Shogi Club. He used to be Yamada's friend. He has the same power as Tamaki and has stolen Kotori's power.

CONTENTS

CHAPTER 156: This is a toy gun.

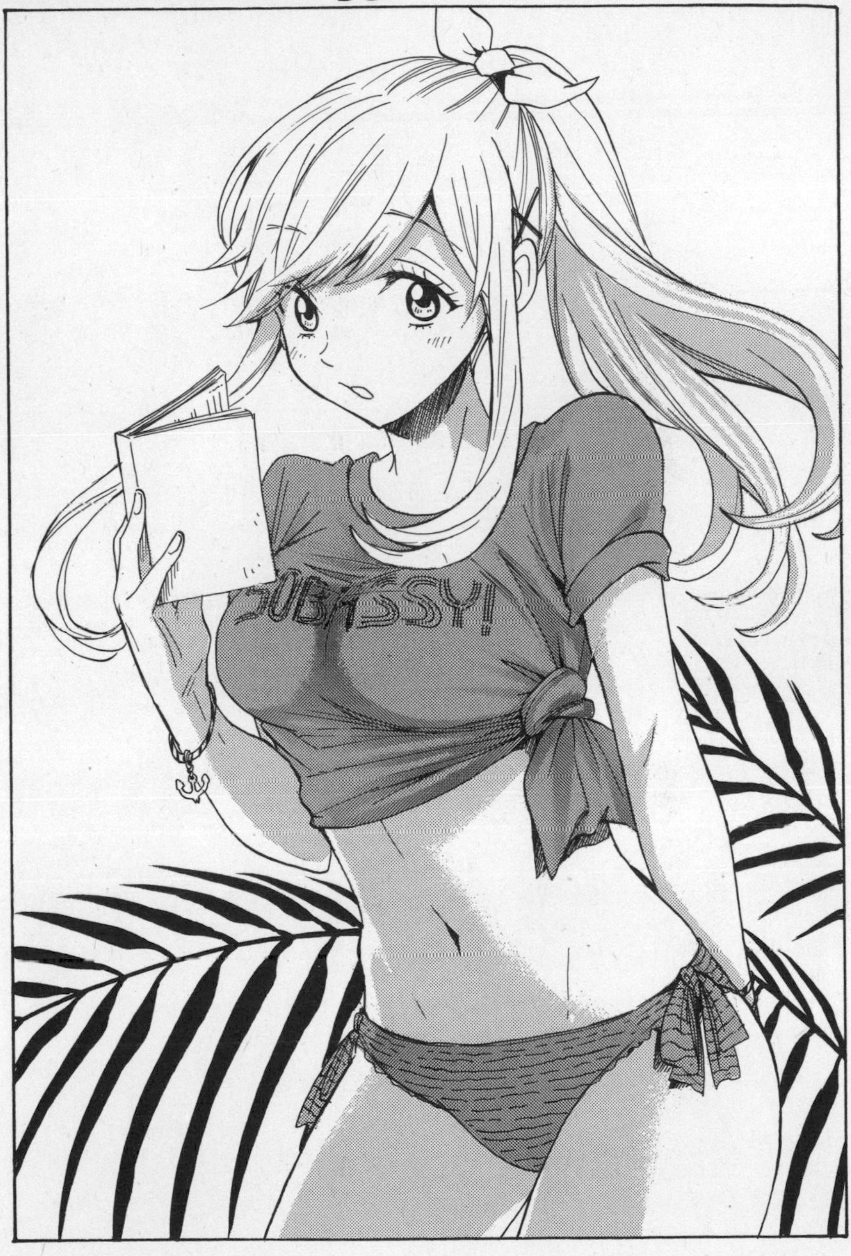

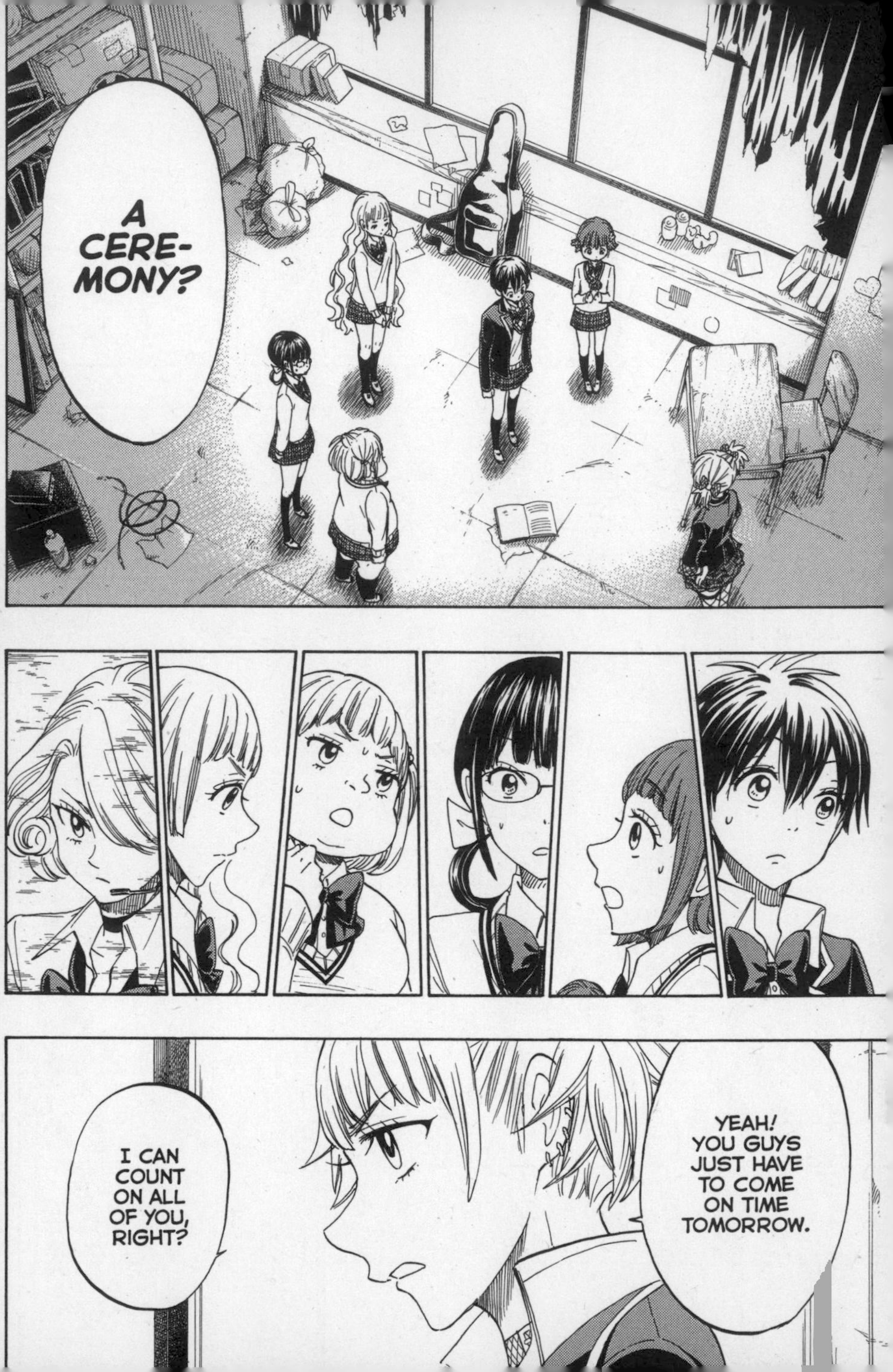
A CERE-MONY?
YEAH! YOU GUYS JUST HAVE TO COME ON TIME TOMORROW.
I CAN COUNT ON ALL OF YOU, RIGHT?

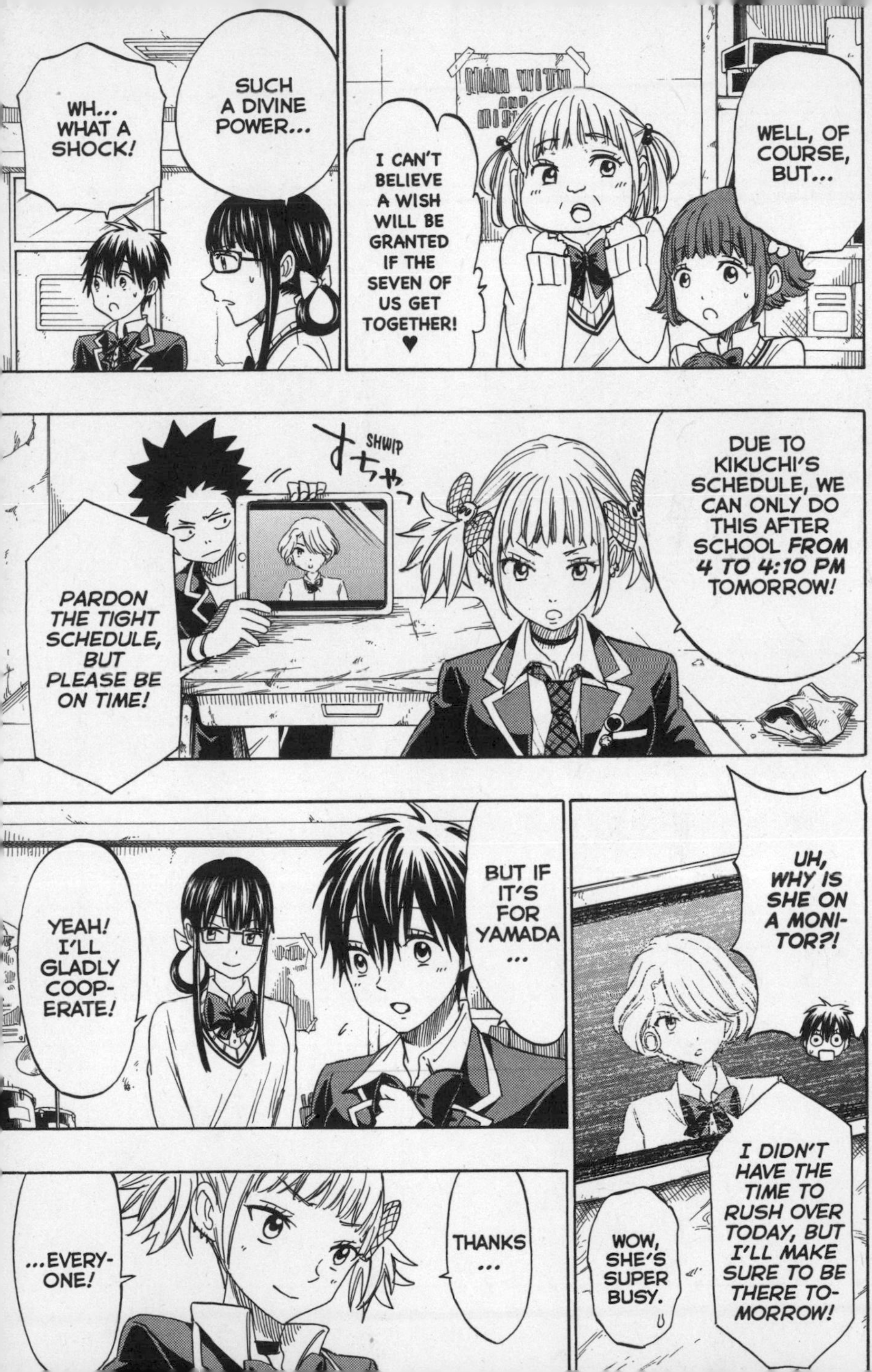
WELL, OF COURSE, BUT...
I CAN'T BELIEVE A WISH WILL BE GRANTED IF THE SEVEN OF US GET TOGETHER! ♥
SUCH A DIVINE POWER...
WH... WHAT A SHOCK!
DUE TO KIKUCHI'S SCHEDULE, WE CAN ONLY DO THIS AFTER SCHOOL FROM 4 TO 4:10 PM TOMORROW!
すちゃっ SHWIP
PARDON THE TIGHT SCHEDULE, BUT PLEASE BE ON TIME!
UH, WHY IS SHE ON A MONITOR?!
I DIDN'T HAVE THE TIME TO RUSH OVER TODAY, BUT I'LL MAKE SURE TO BE THERE TOMORROW!
WOW, SHE'S SUPER BUSY.
BUT IF IT'S FOR YAMADA...
YEAH! I'LL GLADLY COOPERATE!
THANKS...
...EVERYONE!

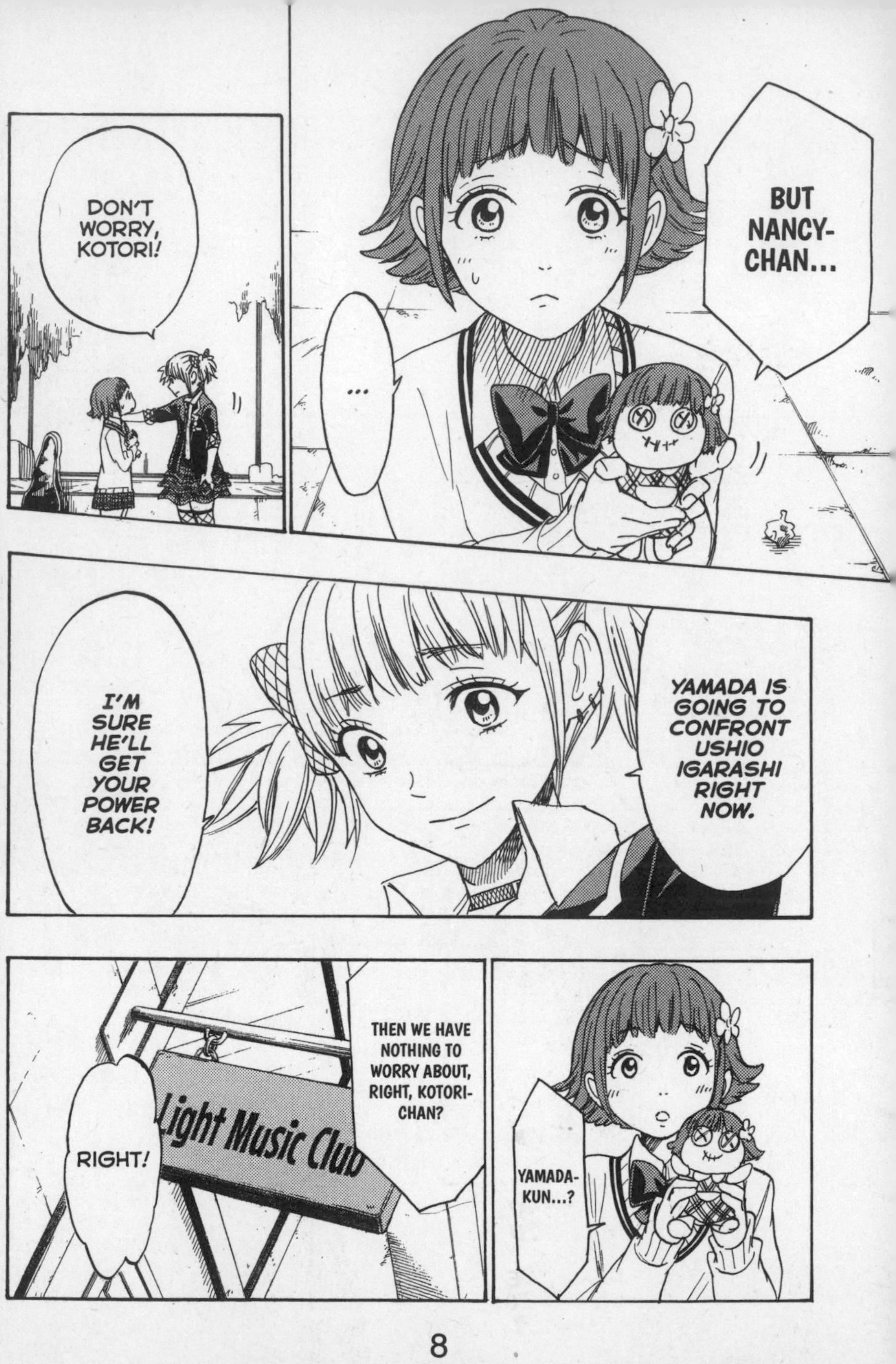
BUT NANCY-CHAN...
...
DON'T WORRY, KOTORI!
YAMADA IS GOING TO CONFRONT USHIO IGARASHI RIGHT NOW.
I'M SURE HE'LL GET YOUR POWER BACK!
YAMADA-KUN...?
THEN WE HAVE NOTHING TO WORRY ABOUT, RIGHT, KOTORI-CHAN?
Light Music Club
RIGHT!

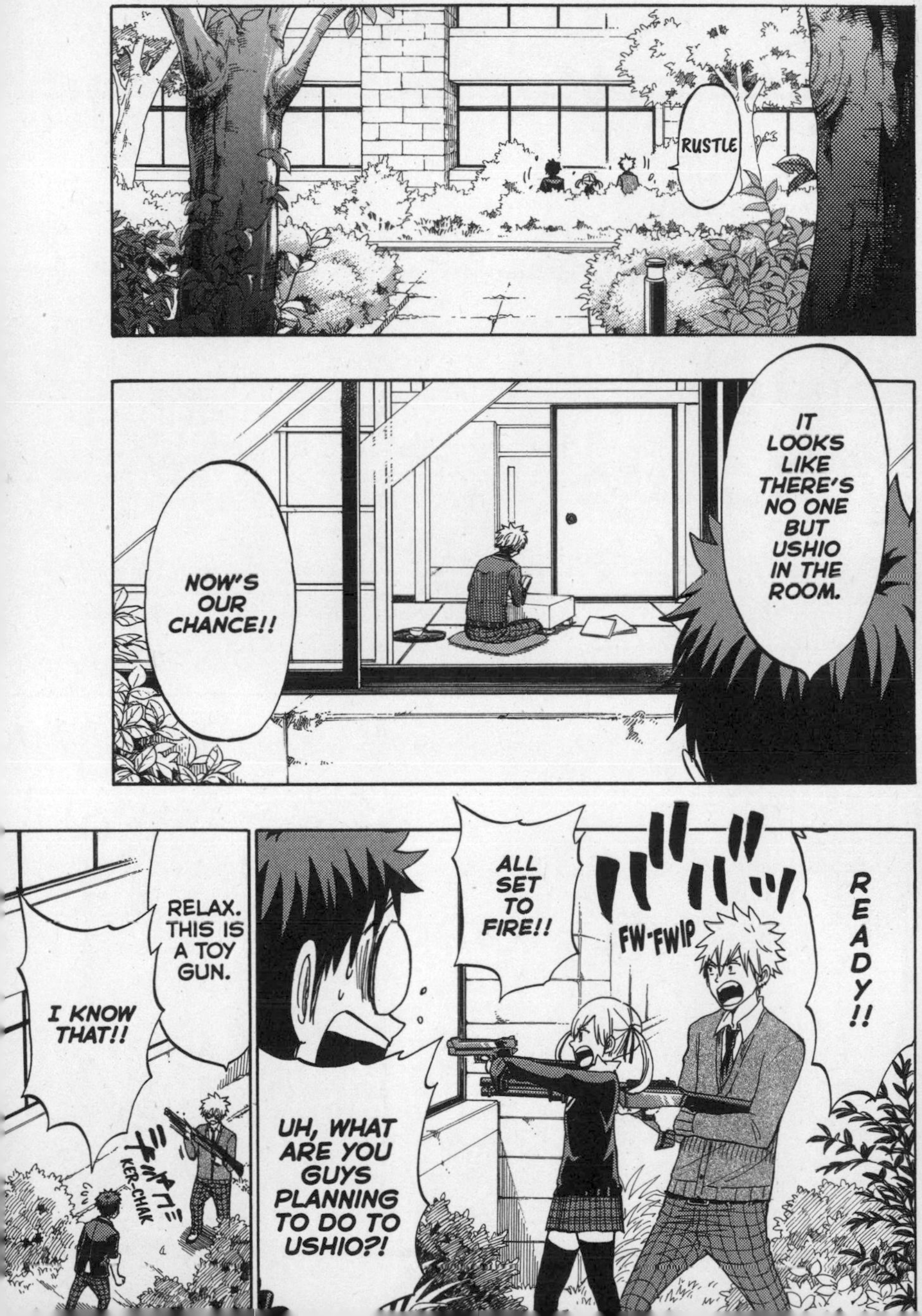
RUSTLE
IT LOOKS LIKE THERE'S NO ONE BUT USHIO IN THE ROOM.
NOW'S OUR CHANCE!!
READY!!
FW-FWIP
ALL SET TO FIRE!!
UH, WHAT ARE YOU GUYS PLANNING TO DO TO USHIO?!
RELAX. THIS IS A TOY GUN.
I KNOW THAT!!
KER-CHAK

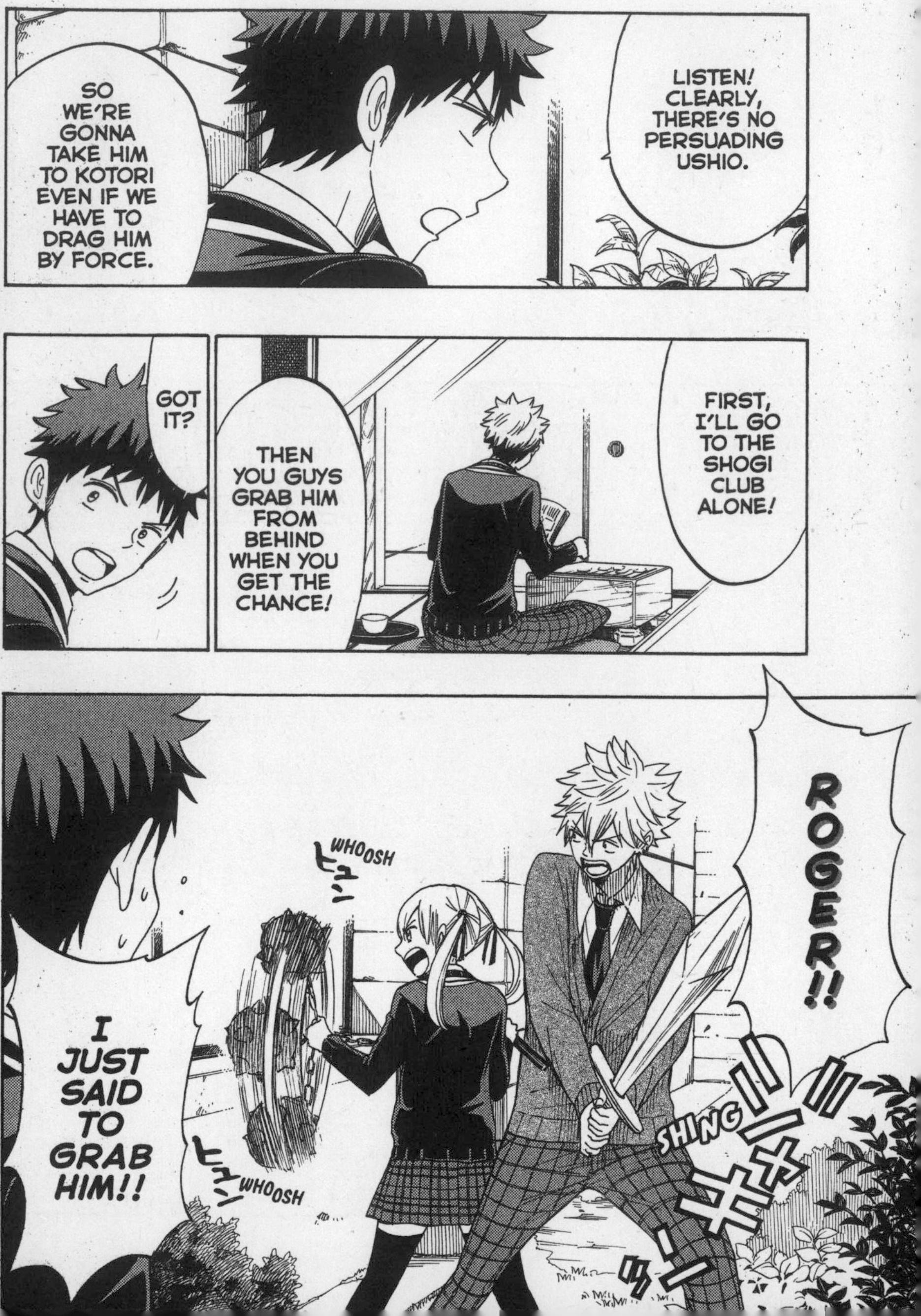
LISTEN! CLEARLY, THERE'S NO PERSUADING USHIO.
SO WE'RE GONNA TAKE HIM TO KOTORI EVEN IF WE HAVE TO DRAG HIM BY FORCE.
FIRST, I'LL GO TO THE SHOGI CLUB ALONE!
THEN YOU GUYS GRAB HIM FROM BEHIND WHEN YOU GET THE CHANCE!
GOT IT?
ROGER!!
SHING
WHOOSH
WHOOSH
I JUST SAID TO GRAB HIM!!

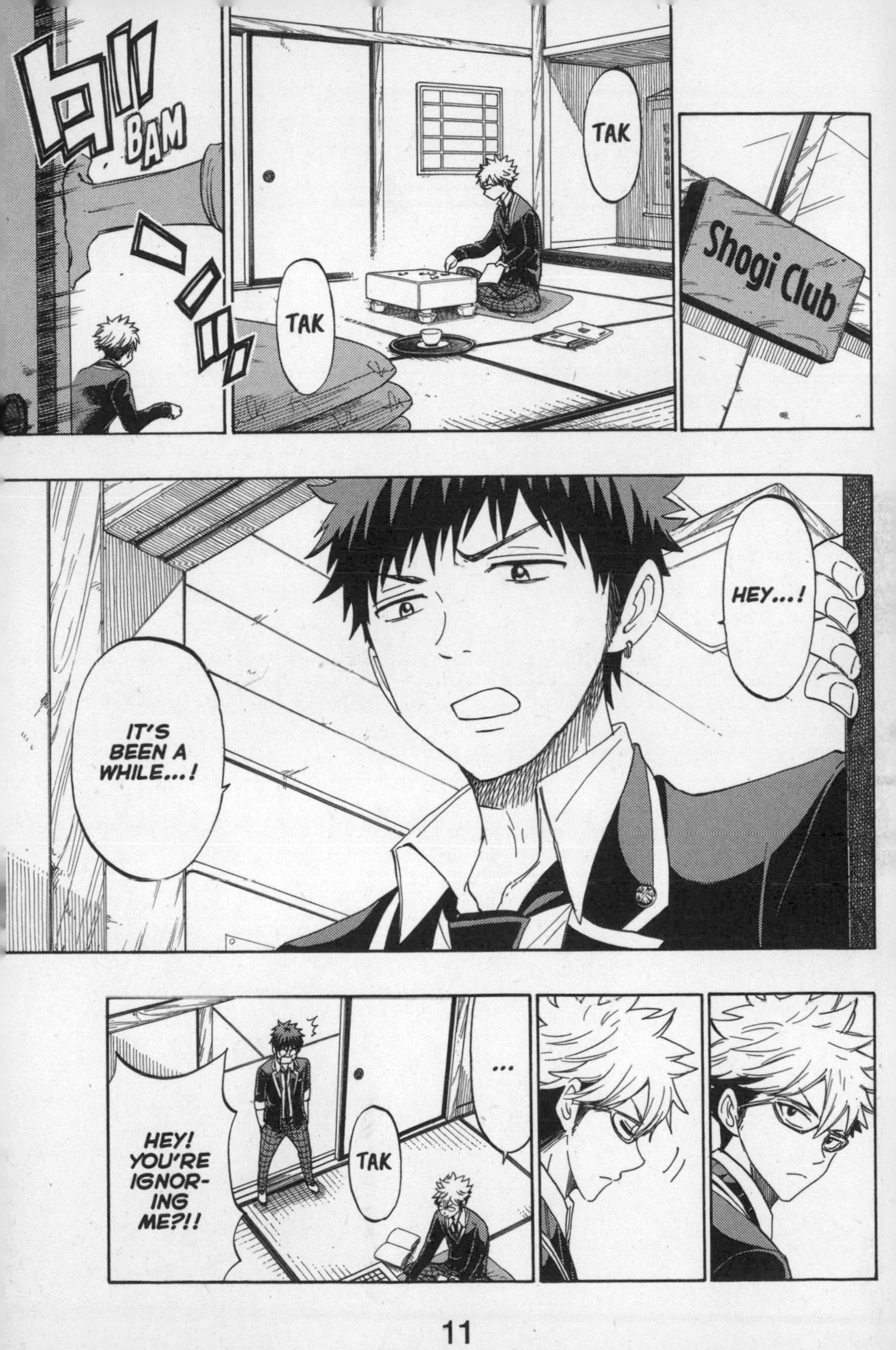
Shogi Club
TAK
TAK
BAM
HEY...!
IT'S BEEN A WHILE...!
...
TAK
HEY! YOU'RE IGNOR-ING ME?!!

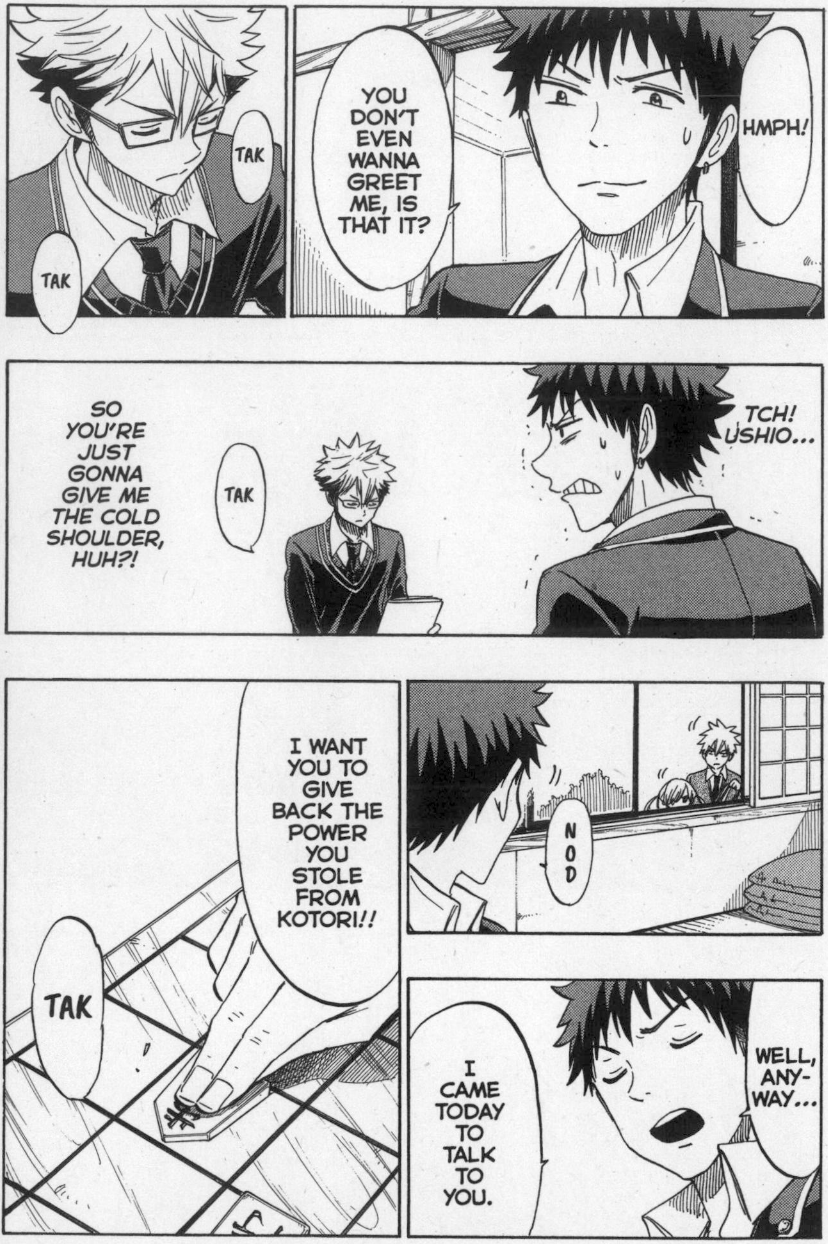
HMPH!
YOU DON'T EVEN WANNA GREET ME, IS THAT IT?
TAK
TAK
TCH! USHIO...
TAK
SO YOU'RE JUST GONNA GIVE ME THE COLD SHOULDER, HUH?!
NOD
WELL, ANY-WAY...
I CAME TODAY TO TALK TO YOU.
I WANT YOU TO GIVE BACK THE POWER YOU STOLE FROM KOTORI!!
TAK

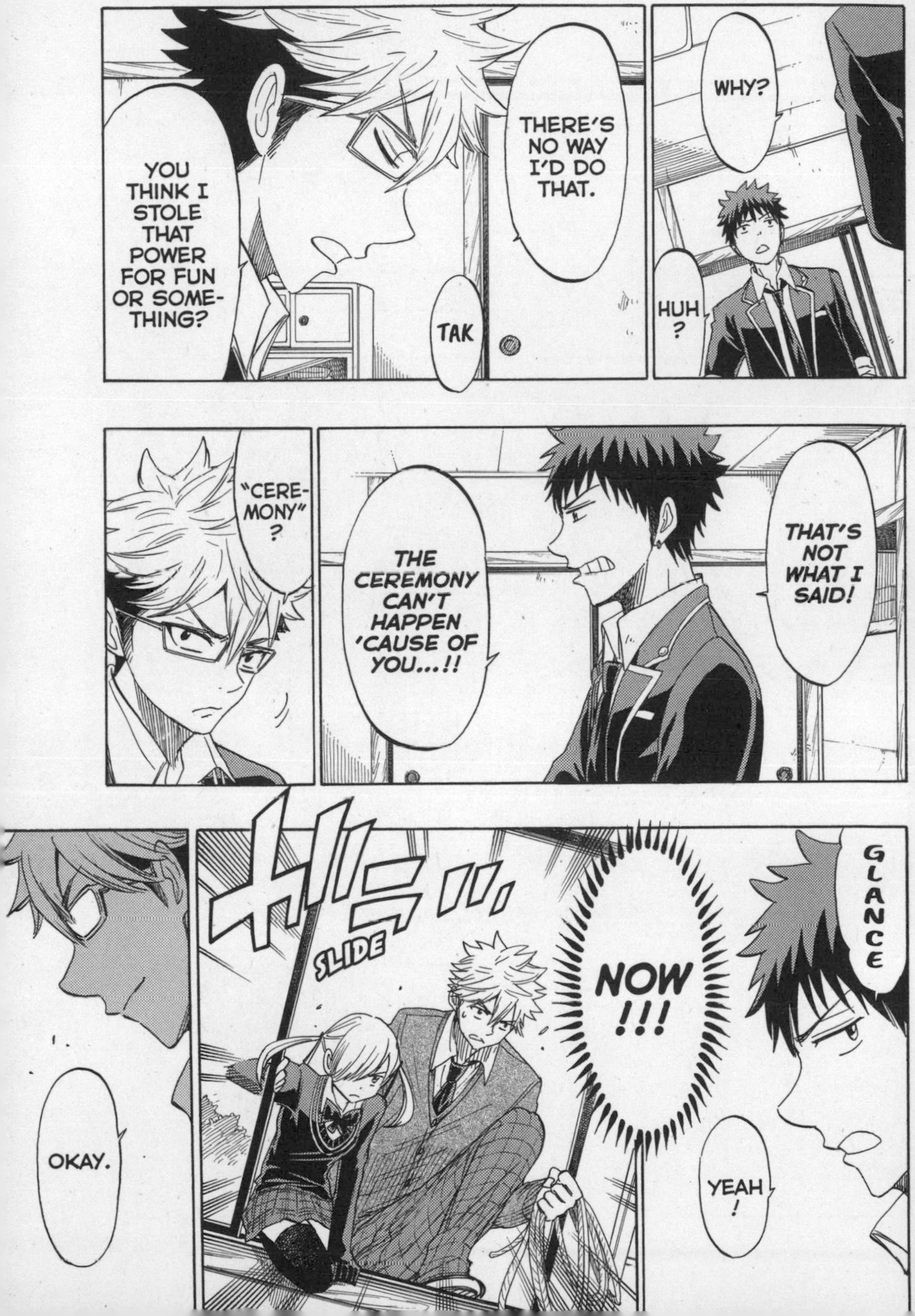
WHY?
HUH?
THERE'S NO WAY I'D DO THAT.
YOU THINK I STOLE THAT POWER FOR FUN OR SOME-THING?
TAK
THAT'S NOT WHAT I SAID!
THE CEREMONY CAN'T HAPPEN 'CAUSE OF YOU...!!
"CERE-MONY"?
GLANCE
YEAH!
NOW!!!
SLIDE
OKAY.

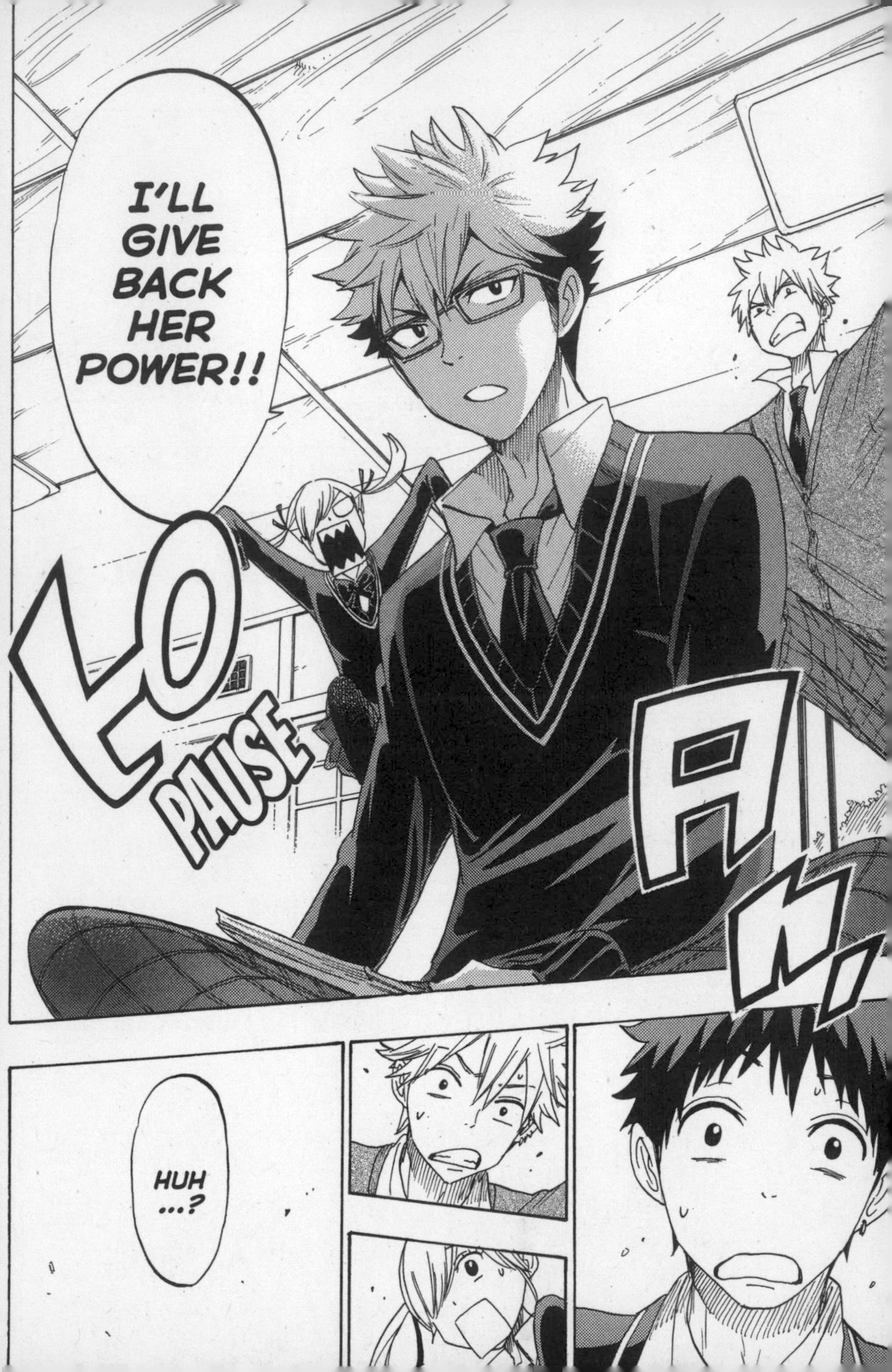
I'LL GIVE BACK HER POWER!!
ZO
PAUSE
A
N
HUH ...?

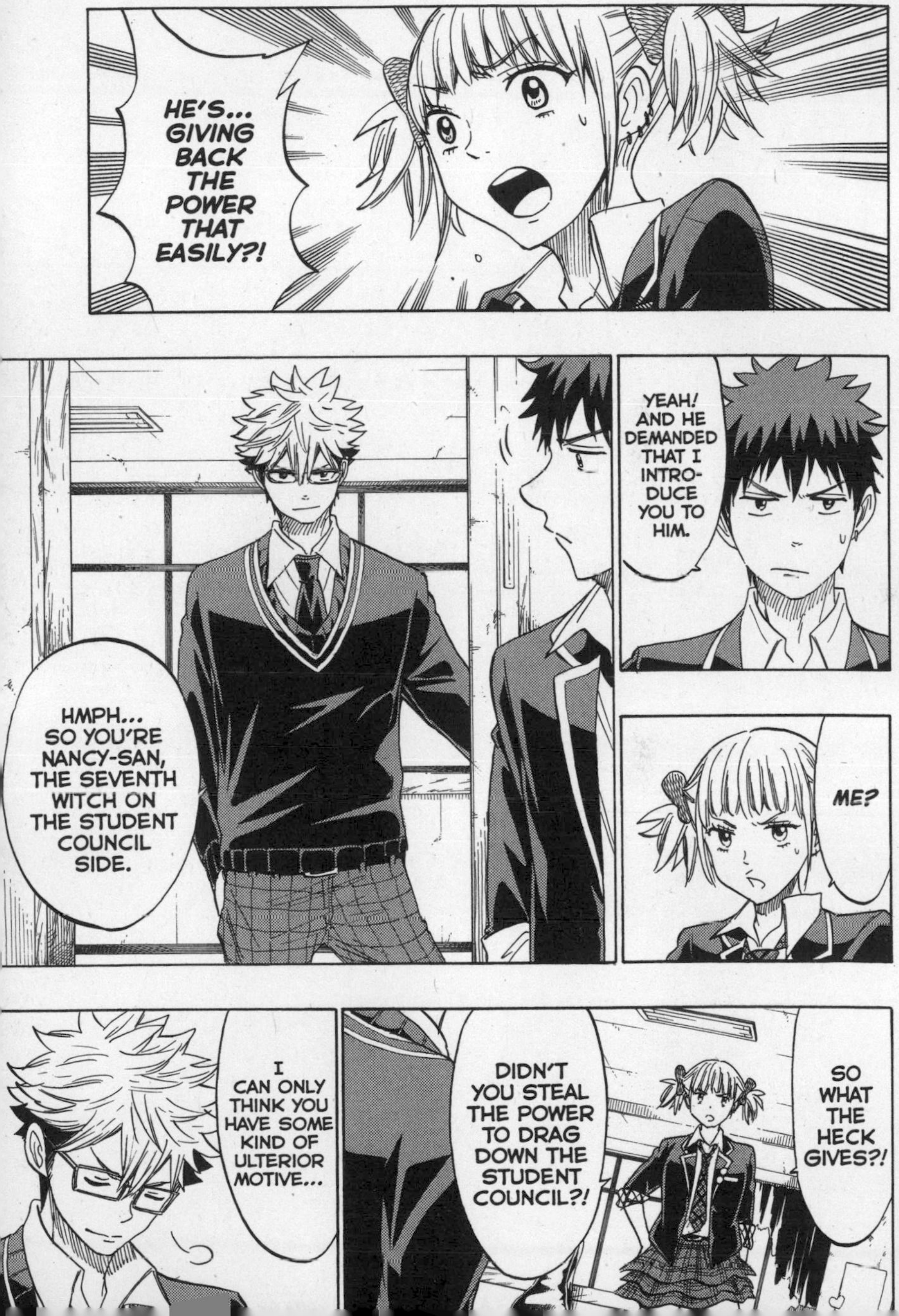
HE'S... GIVING BACK THE POWER THAT EASILY?!
YEAH! AND HE DEMANDED THAT I INTRODUCE YOU TO HIM.
ME?
HMPH... SO YOU'RE NANCY-SAN, THE SEVENTH WITCH ON THE STUDENT COUNCIL SIDE.
SO WHAT THE HECK GIVES?!
DIDN'T YOU STEAL THE POWER TO DRAG DOWN THE STUDENT COUNCIL?!
I CAN ONLY THINK YOU HAVE SOME KIND OF ULTERIOR MOTIVE...

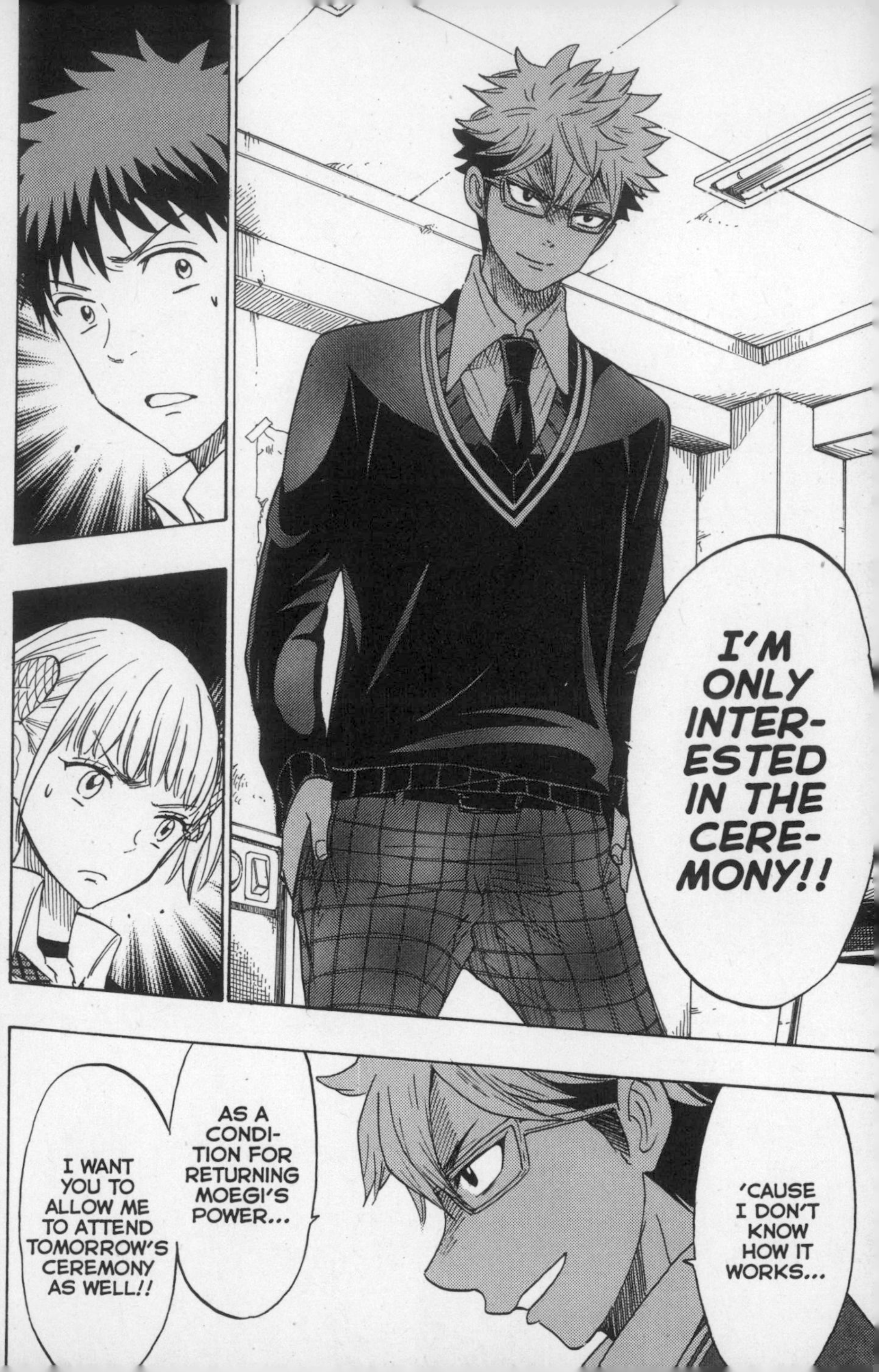
I'M ONLY INTER-ESTED IN THE CERE-MONY!!
'CAUSE I DON'T KNOW HOW IT WORKS...
AS A CONDITION FOR RETURNING MOEGI'S POWER...
I WANT YOU TO ALLOW ME TO ATTEND TOMORROW'S CEREMONY AS WELL!!

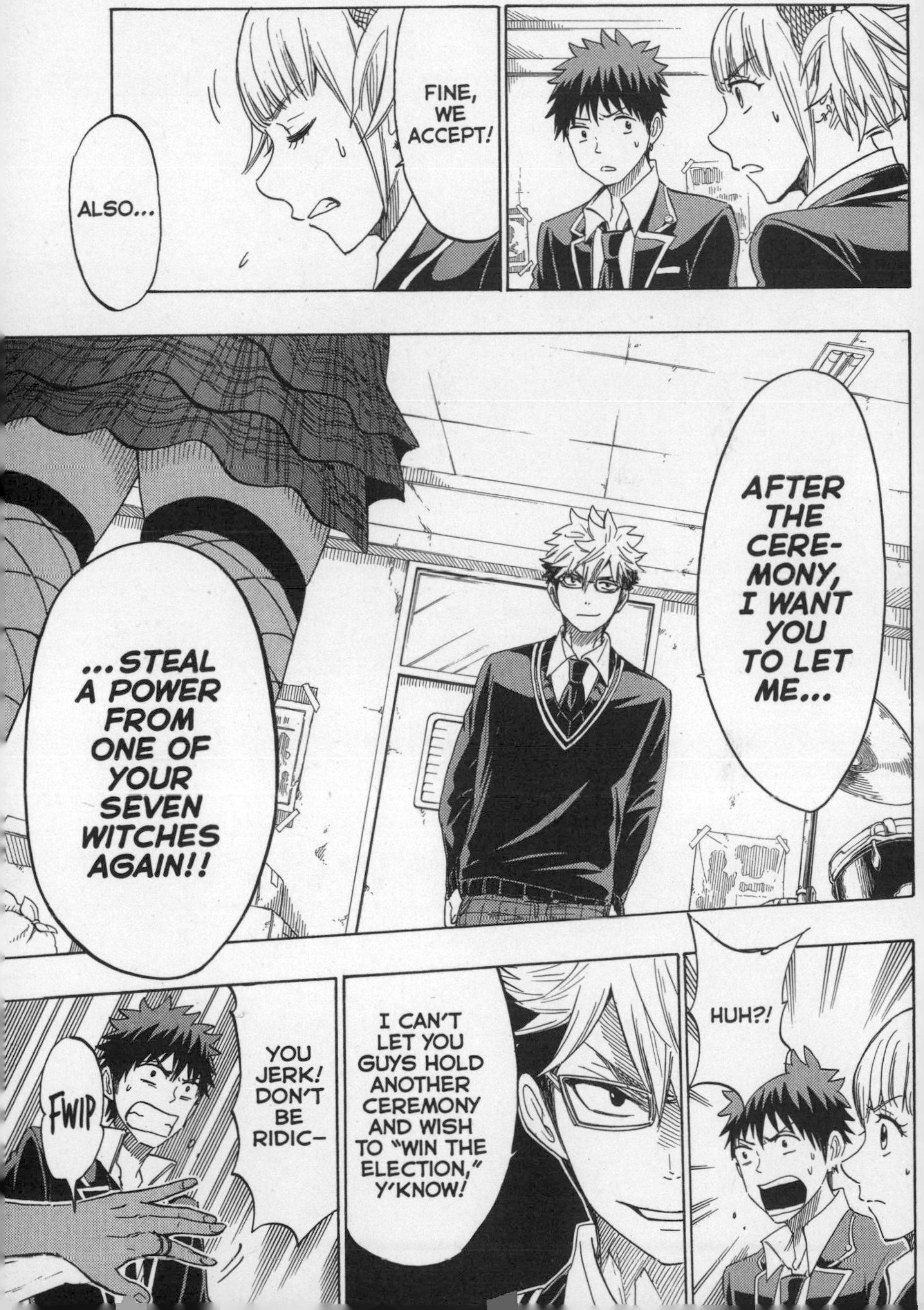
FINE, WE ACCEPT!
ALSO...
AFTER THE CERE-MONY, I WANT YOU TO LET ME...
...STEAL A POWER FROM ONE OF YOUR SEVEN WITCHES AGAIN!!
HUH?!
I CAN'T LET YOU GUYS HOLD ANOTHER CEREMONY AND WISH TO "WIN THE ELECTION," Y'KNOW!
YOU JERK! DON'T BE RIDIC—
FWIP

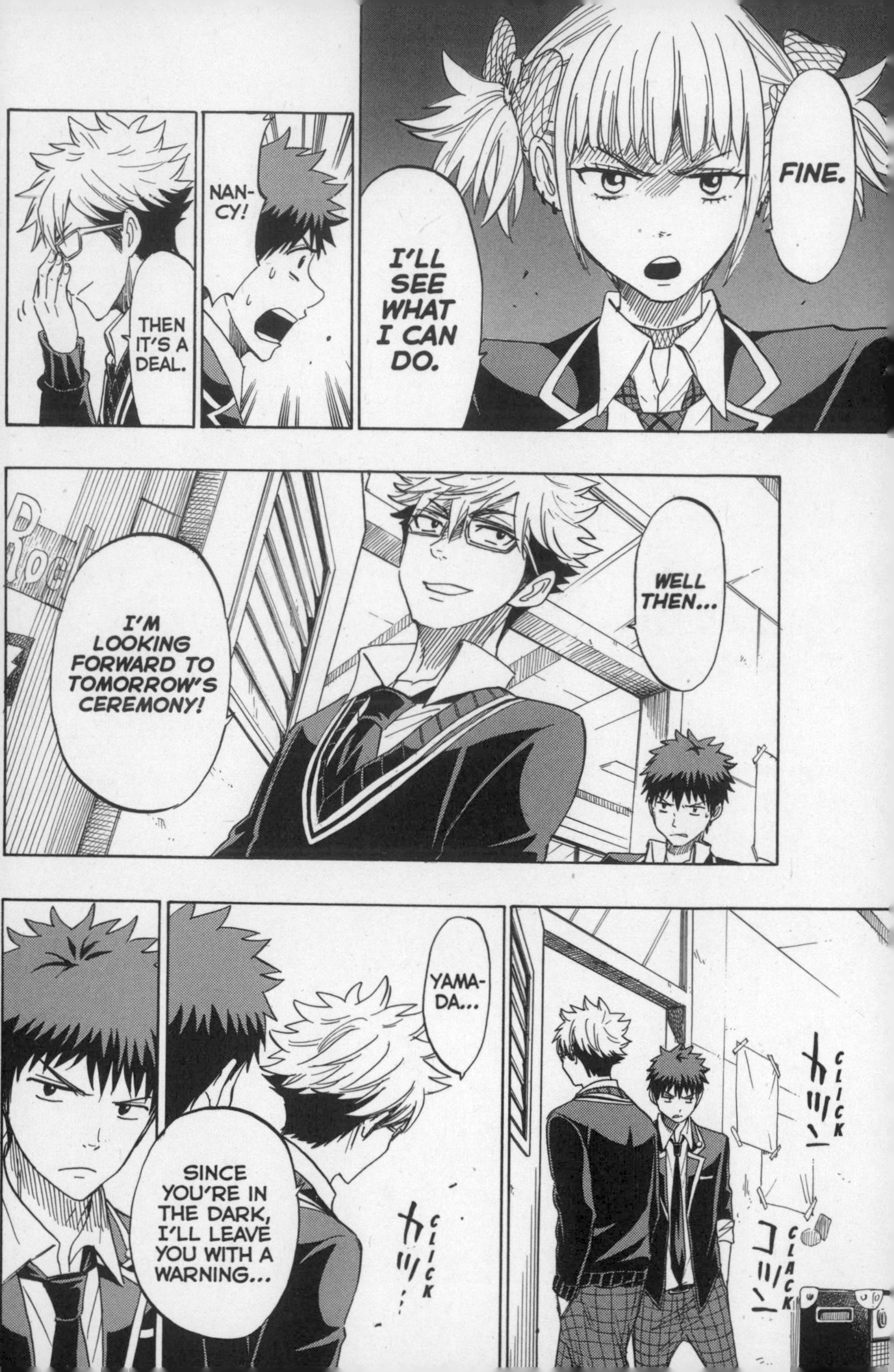
FINE.
I'LL SEE WHAT I CAN DO.
NAN-CY!
THEN IT'S A DEAL.
WELL THEN...
I'M LOOKING FORWARD TO TOMORROW'S CEREMONY!
CLICK
CLACK
YAMA-DA...
CLICK
SINCE YOU'RE IN THE DARK, I'LL LEAVE YOU WITH A WARNING...

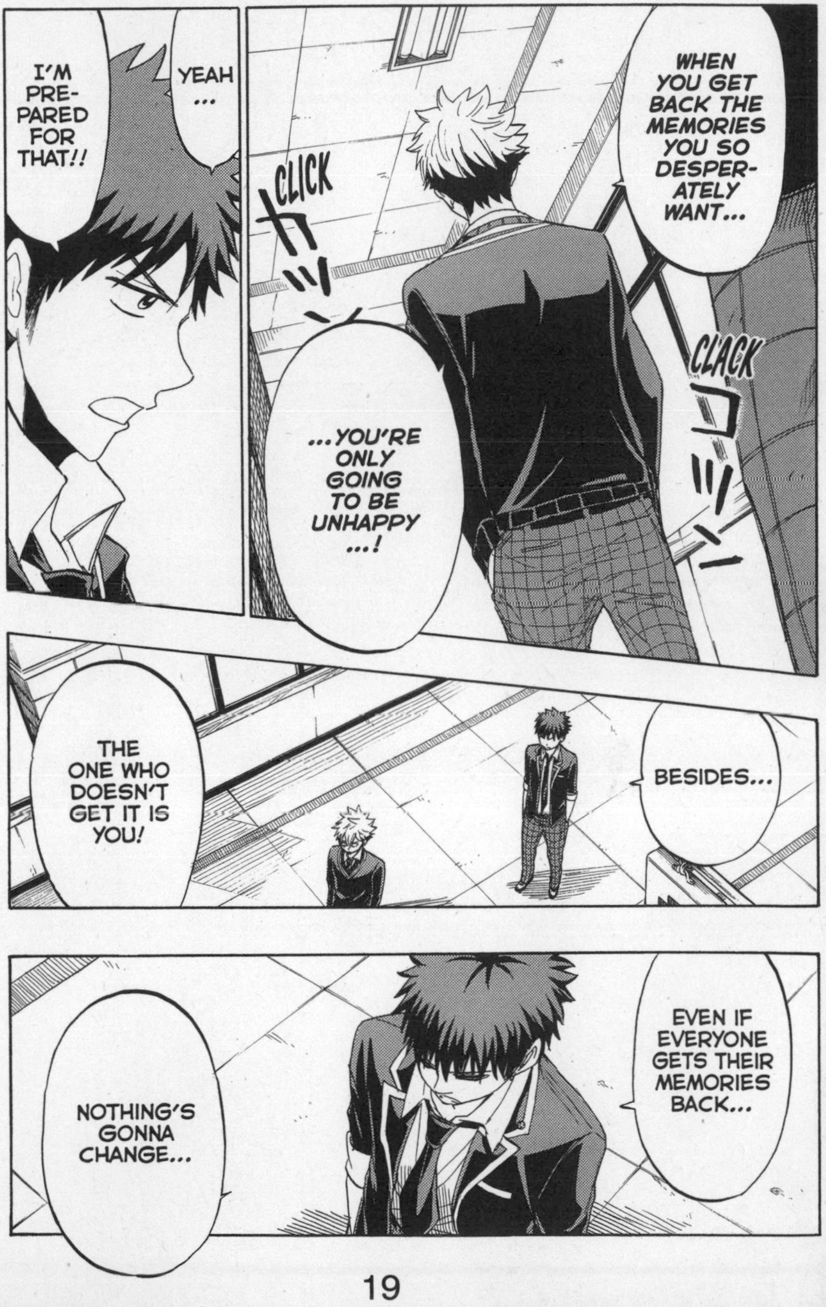
WHEN YOU GET BACK THE MEMORIES YOU SO DESPER-ATELY WANT...
CLACK
CLICK
...YOU'RE ONLY GOING TO BE UNHAPPY ...!
YEAH ...
I'M PRE-PARED FOR THAT!!
BESIDES...
THE ONE WHO DOESN'T GET IT IS YOU!
EVEN IF EVERYONE GETS THEIR MEMORIES BACK...
NOTHING'S GONNA CHANGE...

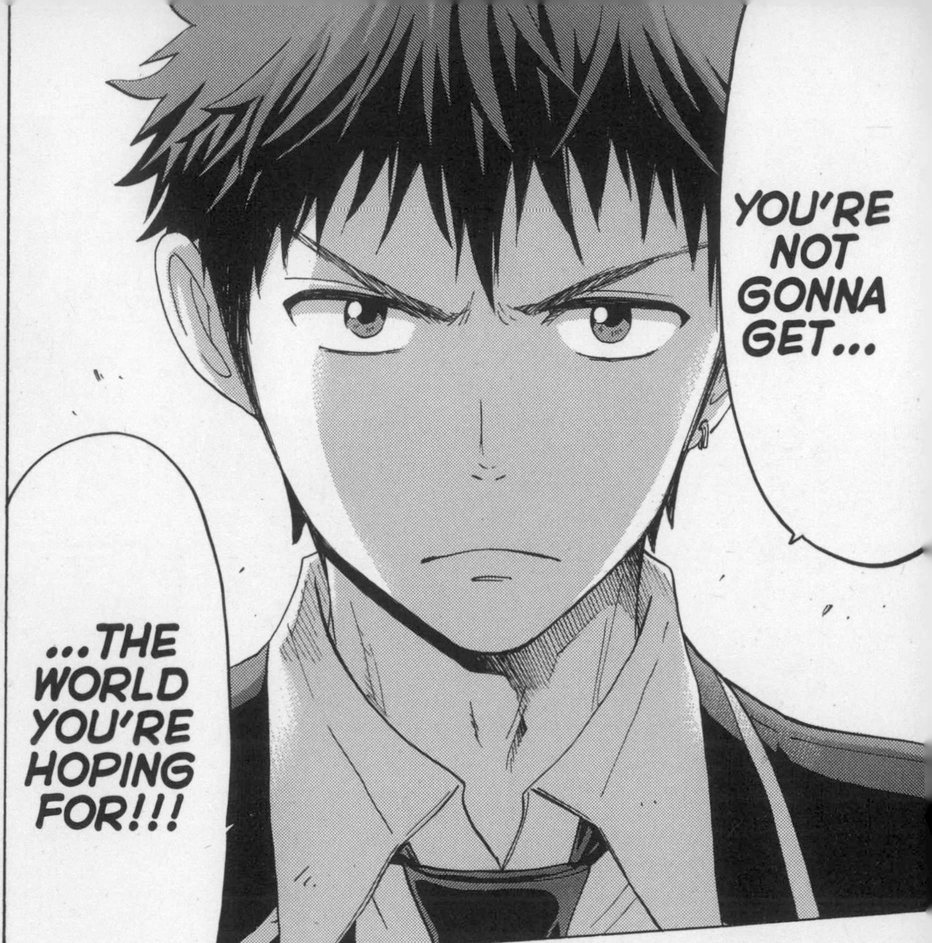
YOU'RE NOT GONNA GET...
...THE WORLD YOU'RE HOPING FOR!!!
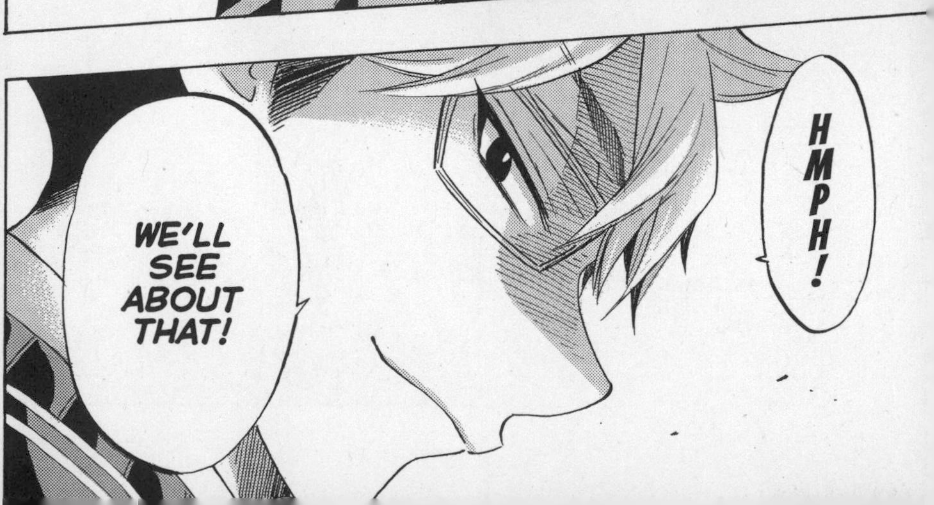
HMPH!
WE'LL SEE ABOUT THAT!

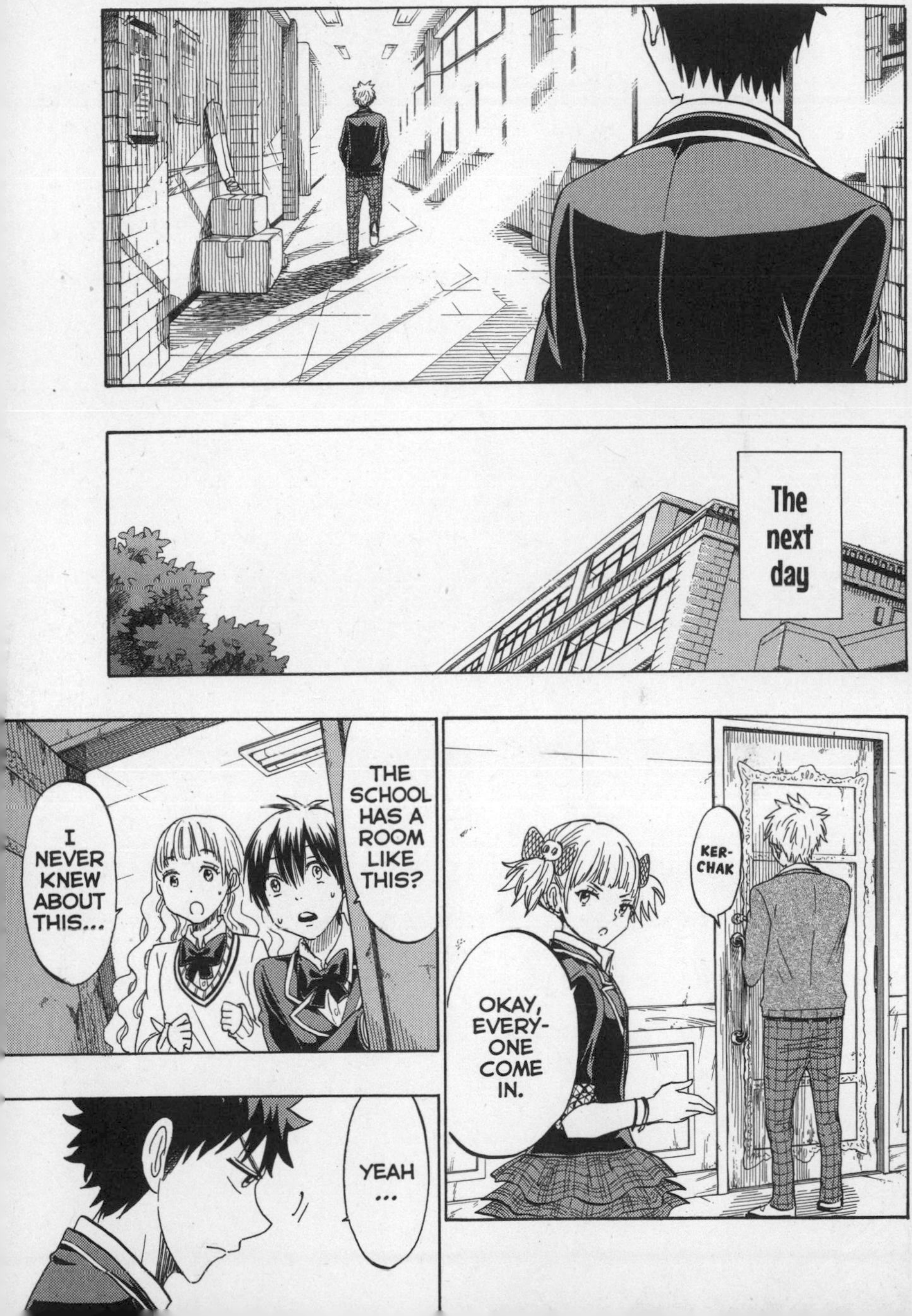
The next day
KER-CHAK
OKAY, EVERYONE COME IN.
THE SCHOOL HAS A ROOM LIKE THIS?
I NEVER KNEW ABOUT THIS...
YEAH...

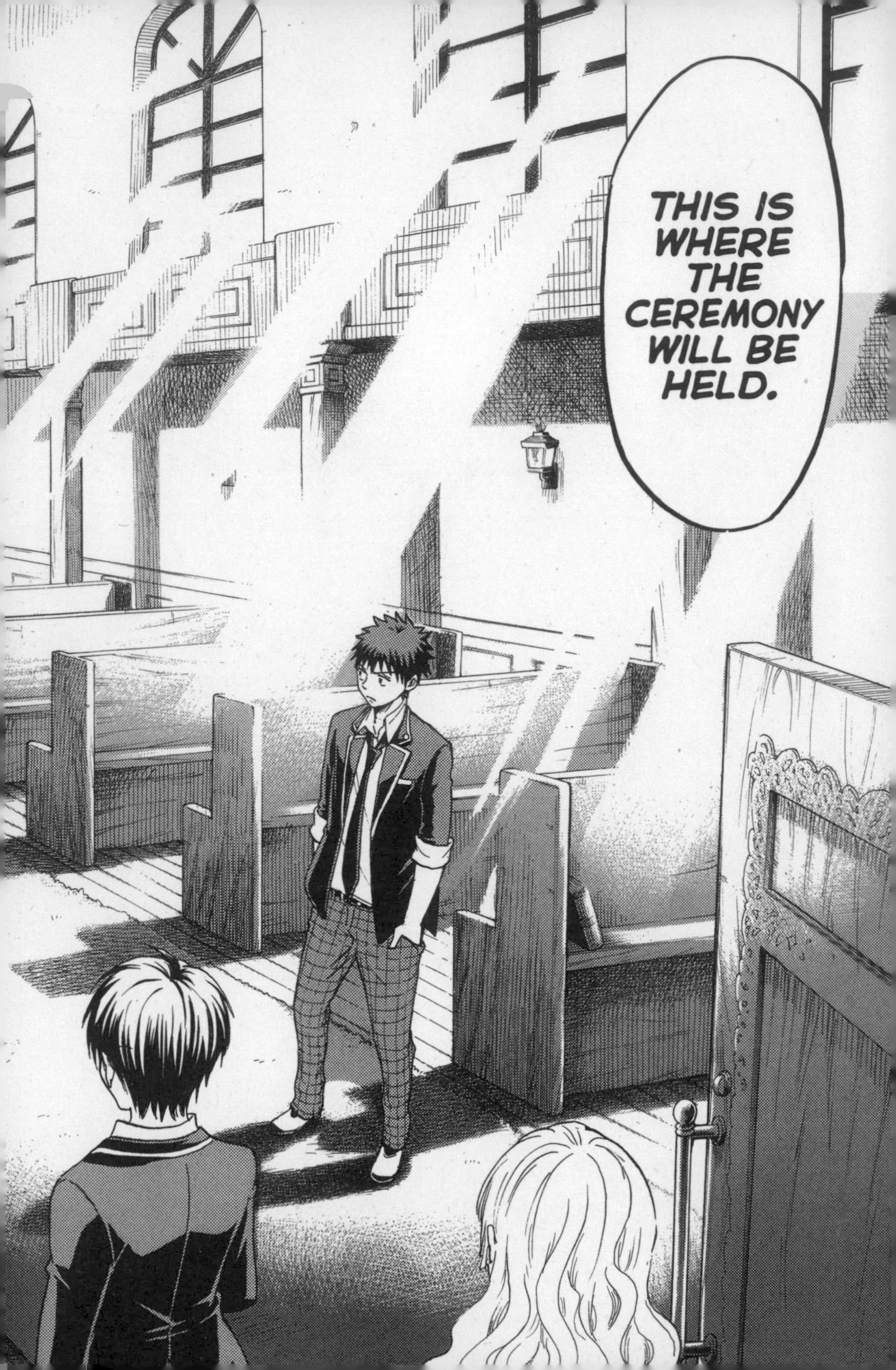
THIS IS WHERE THE CEREMONY WILL BE HELD.

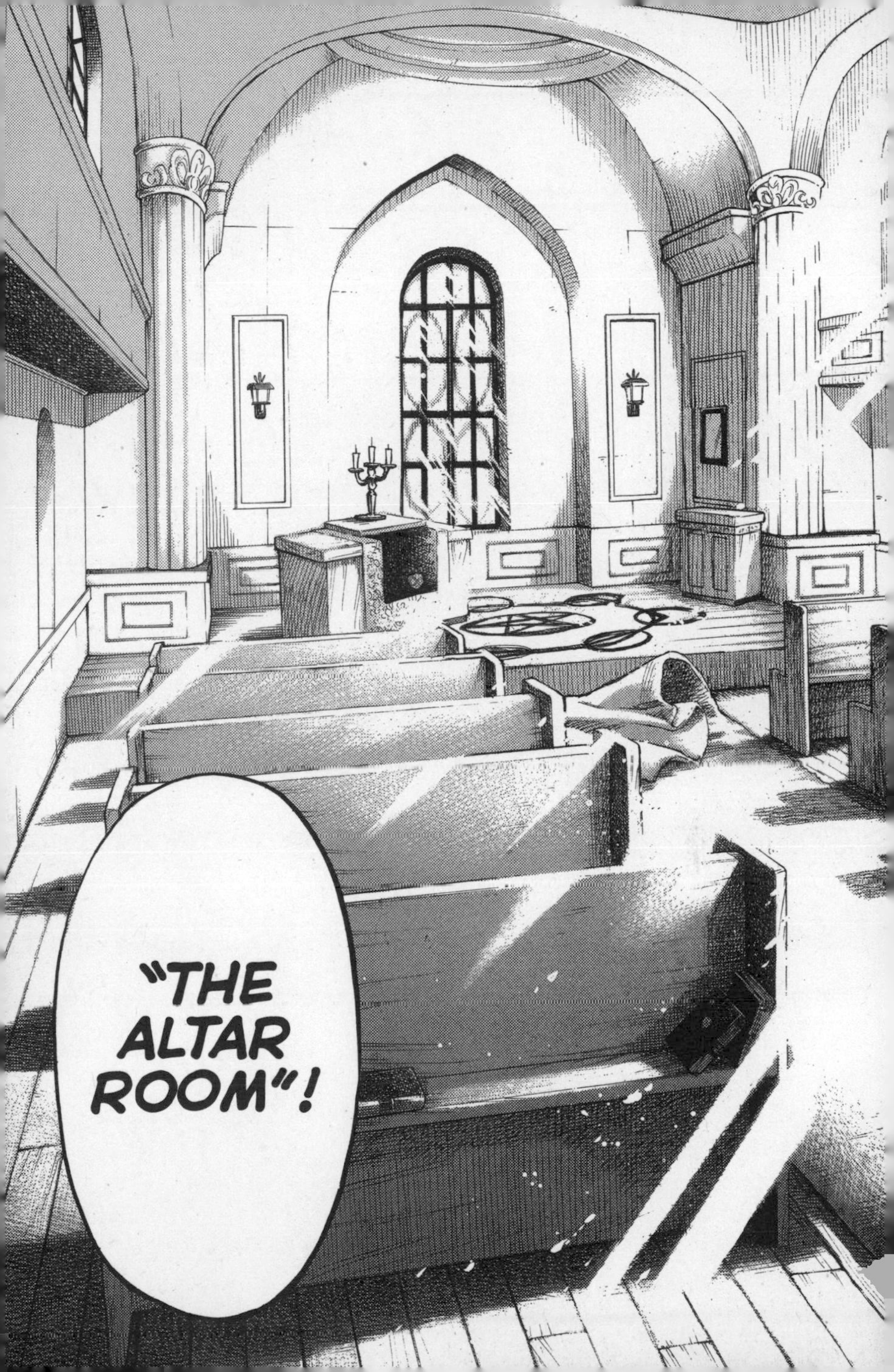
"THE ALTAR ROOM"!

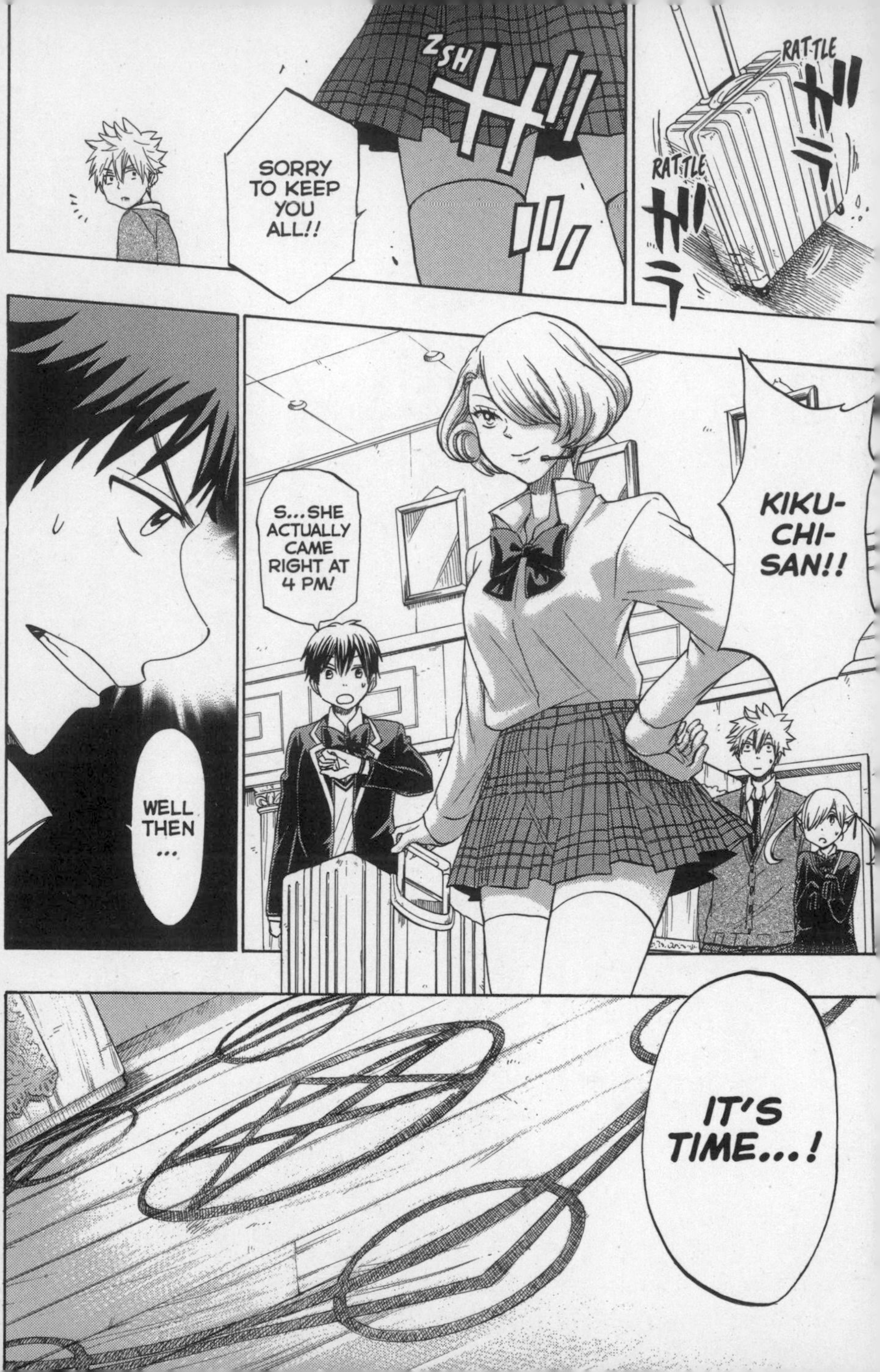
RATTLE
RATTLE
ZSH
SORRY TO KEEP YOU ALL!!
KIKU-CHI-SAN!!
S...SHE ACTUALLY CAME RIGHT AT 4 PM!
WELL THEN...
IT'S TIME...!

CHAPTER 157: Show no mercy!!

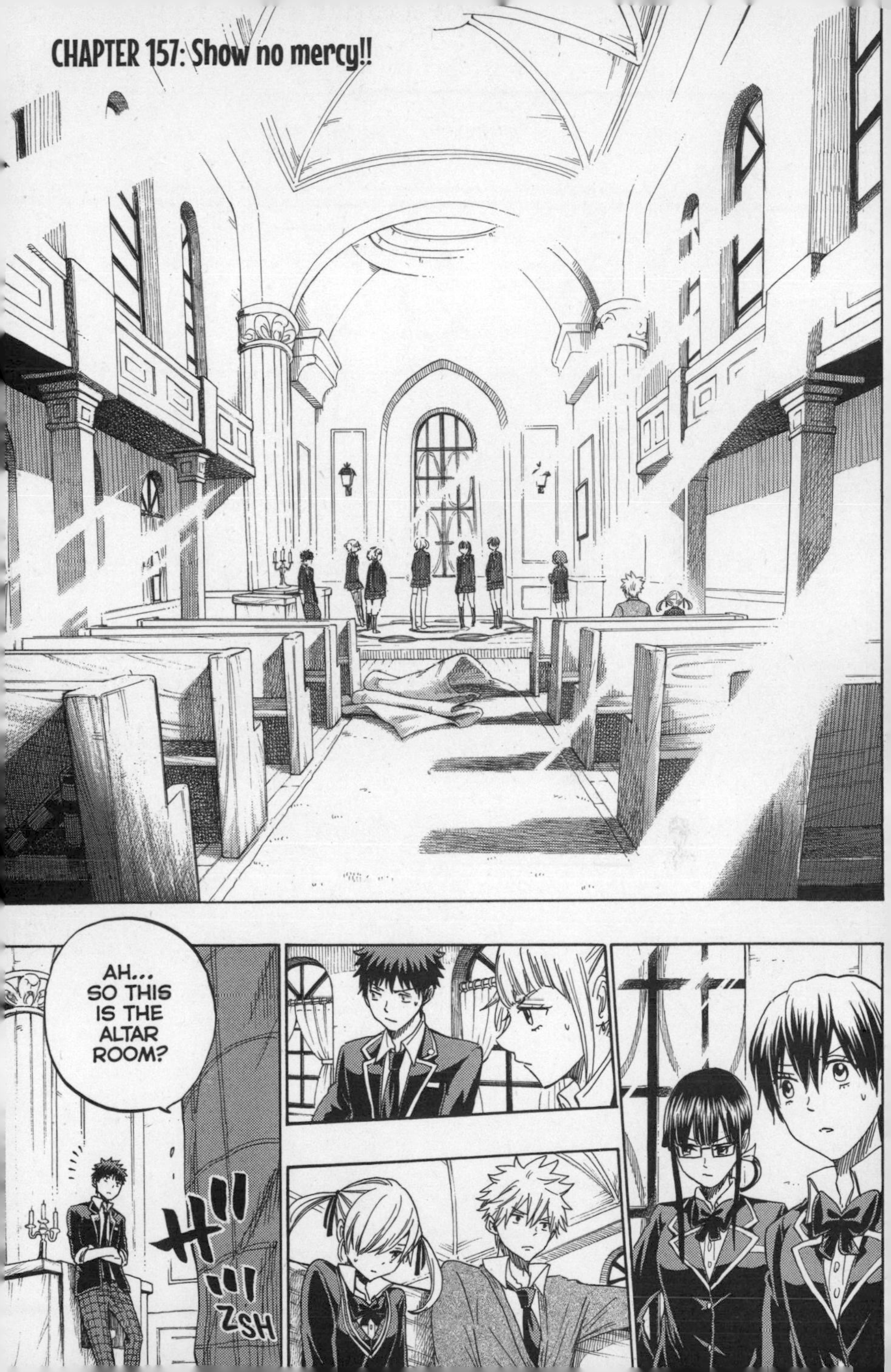
AH... SO THIS IS THE ALTAR ROOM?
ZSH

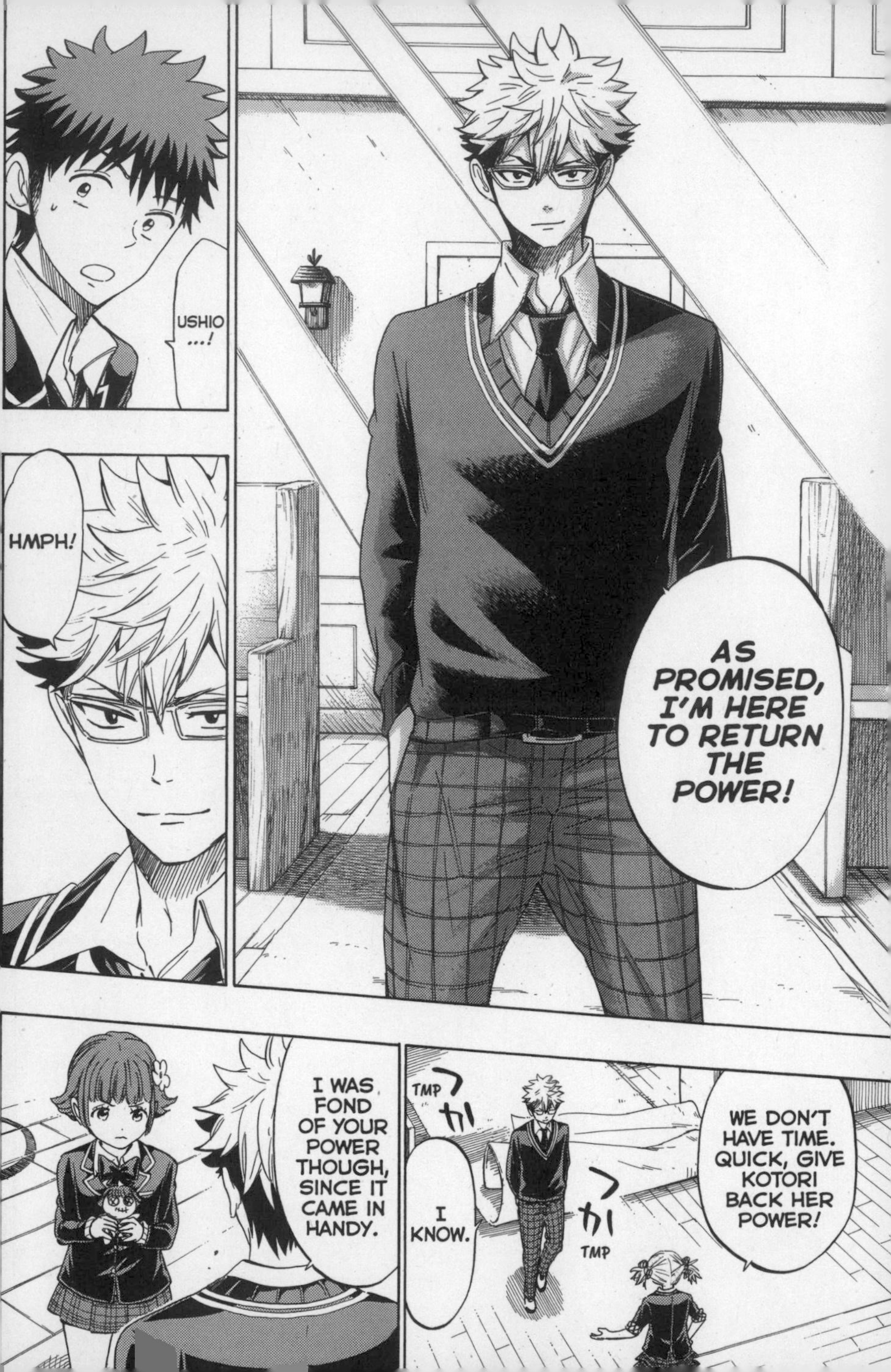
AS PROMISED, I'M HERE TO RETURN THE POWER!
USHIO ...!
HMPH!
WE DON'T HAVE TIME. QUICK, GIVE KOTORI BACK HER POWER!
TMP
TMP
I KNOW.
I WAS FOND OF YOUR POWER THOUGH, SINCE IT CAME IN HANDY.

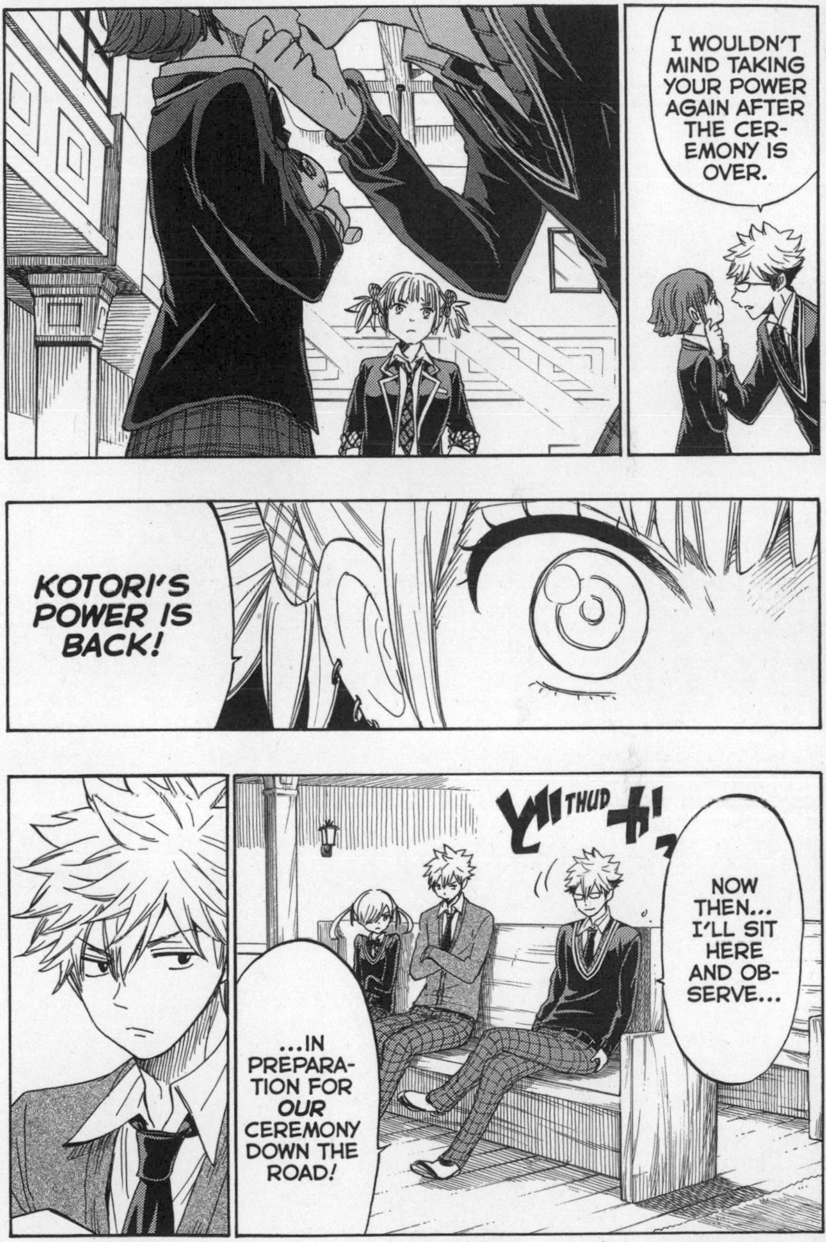
I WOULDN'T MIND TAKING YOUR POWER AGAIN AFTER THE CEREMONY IS OVER.
KOTORI'S POWER IS BACK!
THUD
NOW THEN... I'LL SIT HERE AND OBSERVE...
...IN PREPARATION FOR *OUR* CEREMONY DOWN THE ROAD!

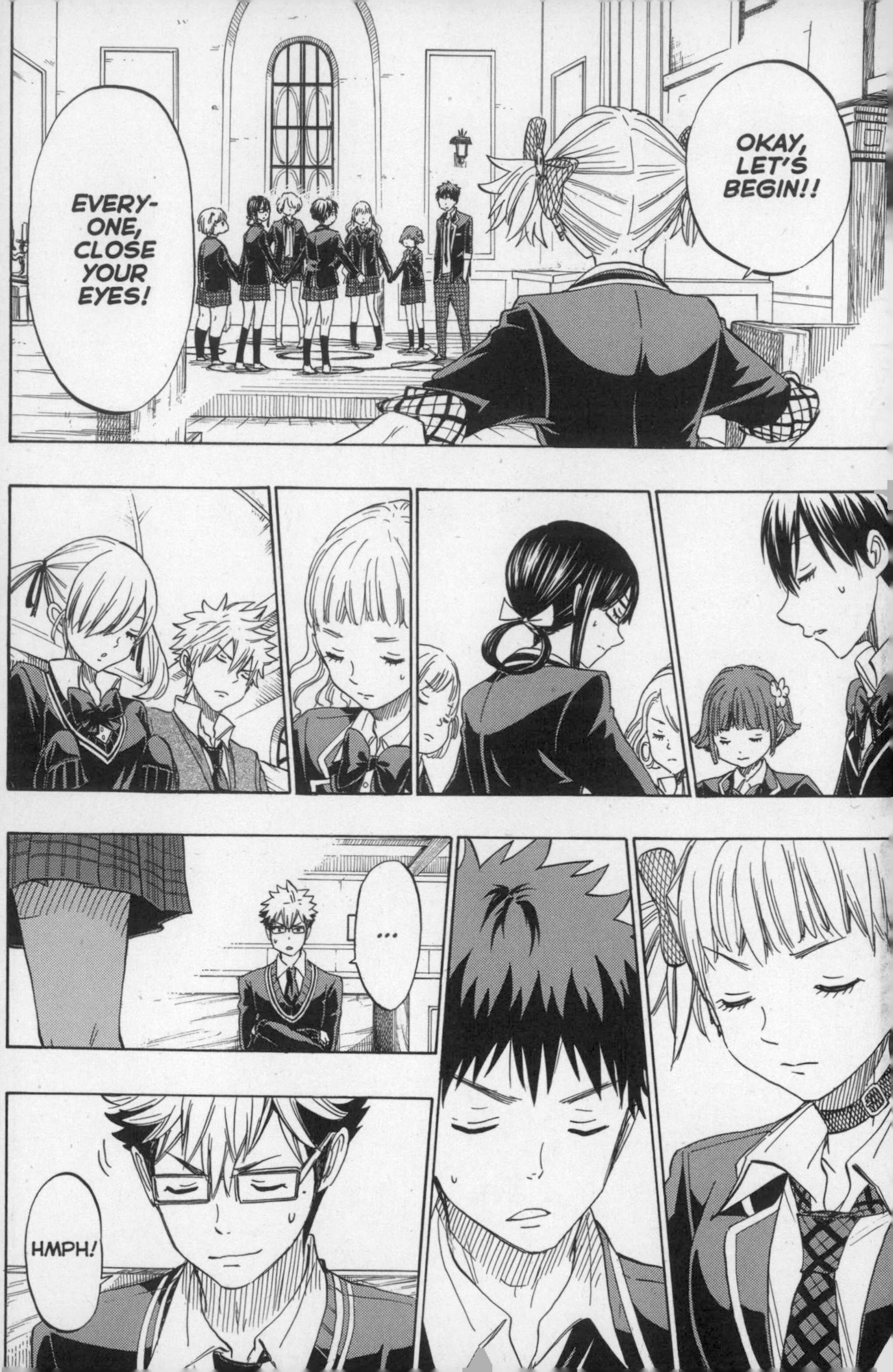
OKAY, LET'S BEGIN!!
EVERY-ONE, CLOSE YOUR EYES!
...
HMPH!

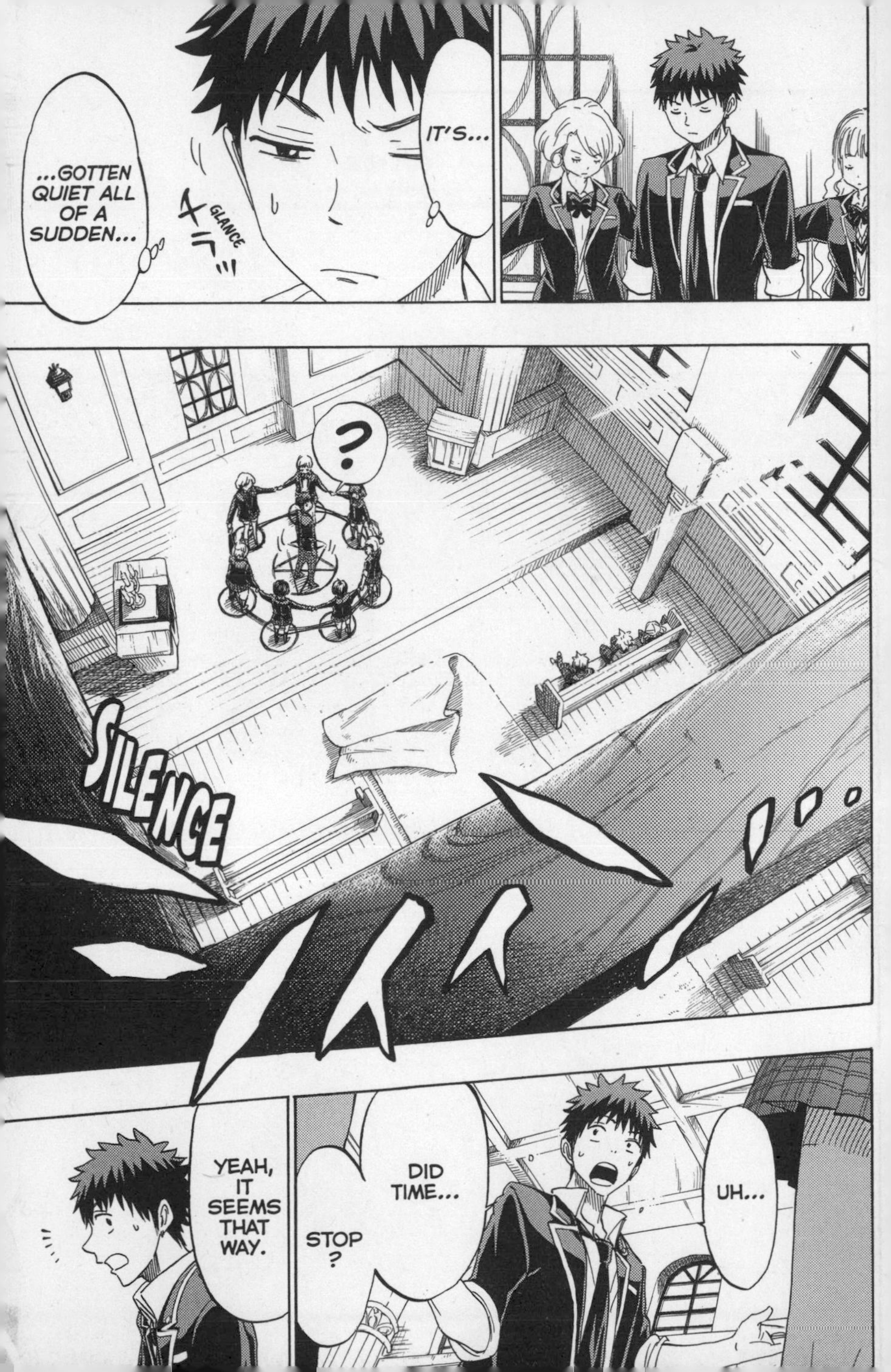
IT'S...
GLANCE
...GOTTEN QUIET ALL OF A SUDDEN...
?
SILENCE
...
UH...
DID TIME... STOP?
YEAH, IT SEEMS THAT WAY.

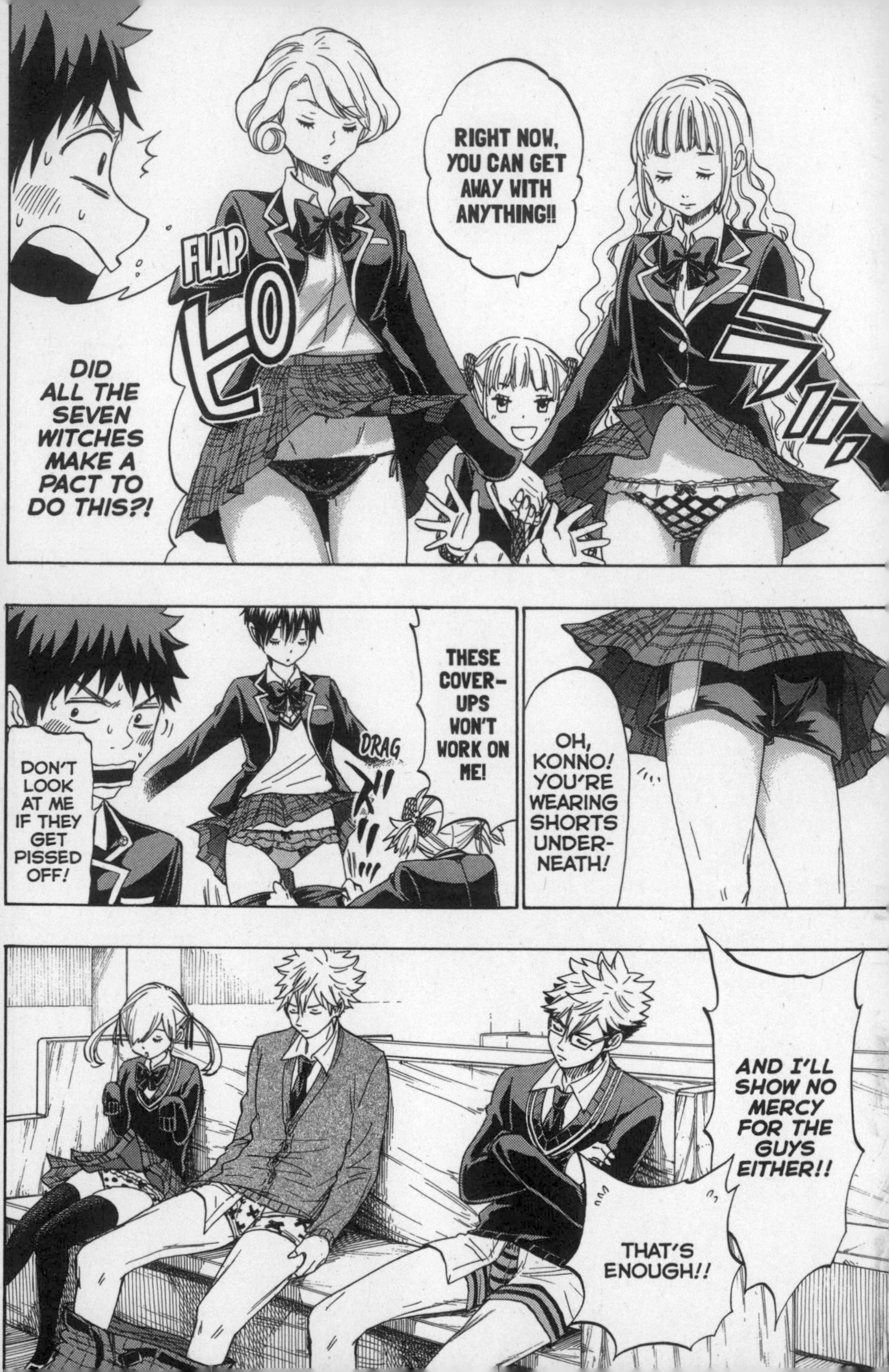
RIGHT NOW, YOU CAN GET AWAY WITH ANYTHING!!
FLAP
DID ALL THE SEVEN WITCHES MAKE A PACT TO DO THIS?!
OH, KONNO! YOU'RE WEARING SHORTS UNDERNEATH!
THESE COVER-UPS WON'T WORK ON ME!
DRAG
DON'T LOOK AT ME IF THEY GET PISSED OFF!
AND I'LL SHOW NO MERCY FOR THE GUYS EITHER!!
THAT'S ENOUGH!!

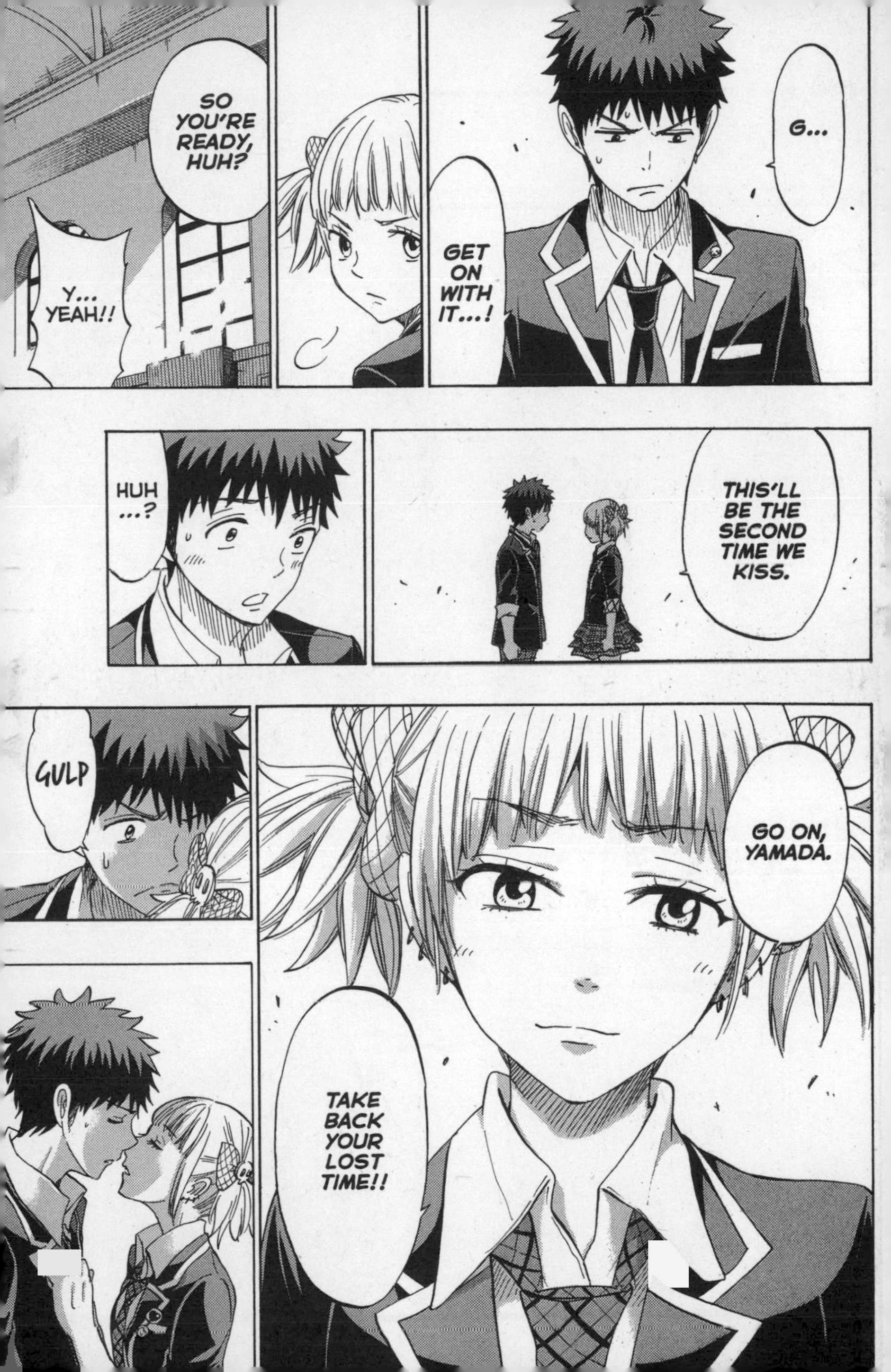
G...
GET ON WITH IT...!
SO YOU'RE READY, HUH?
Y... YEAH!!
THIS'LL BE THE SECOND TIME WE KISS.
HUH ...?
GO ON, YAMADA.
TAKE BACK YOUR LOST TIME!!
GULP

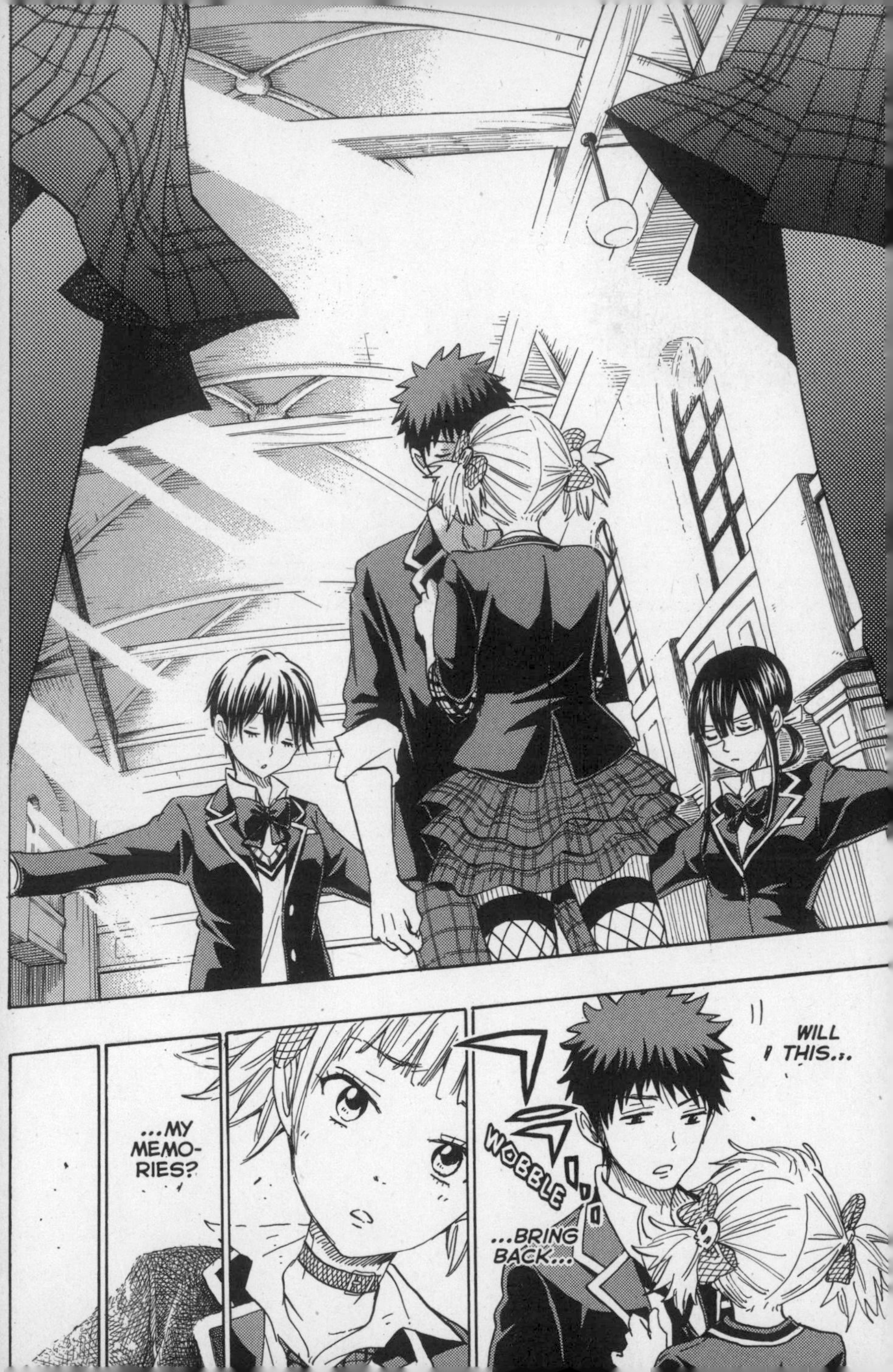
WILL THIS...
WOBBLE
...BRING BACK...
...MY MEMORIES?

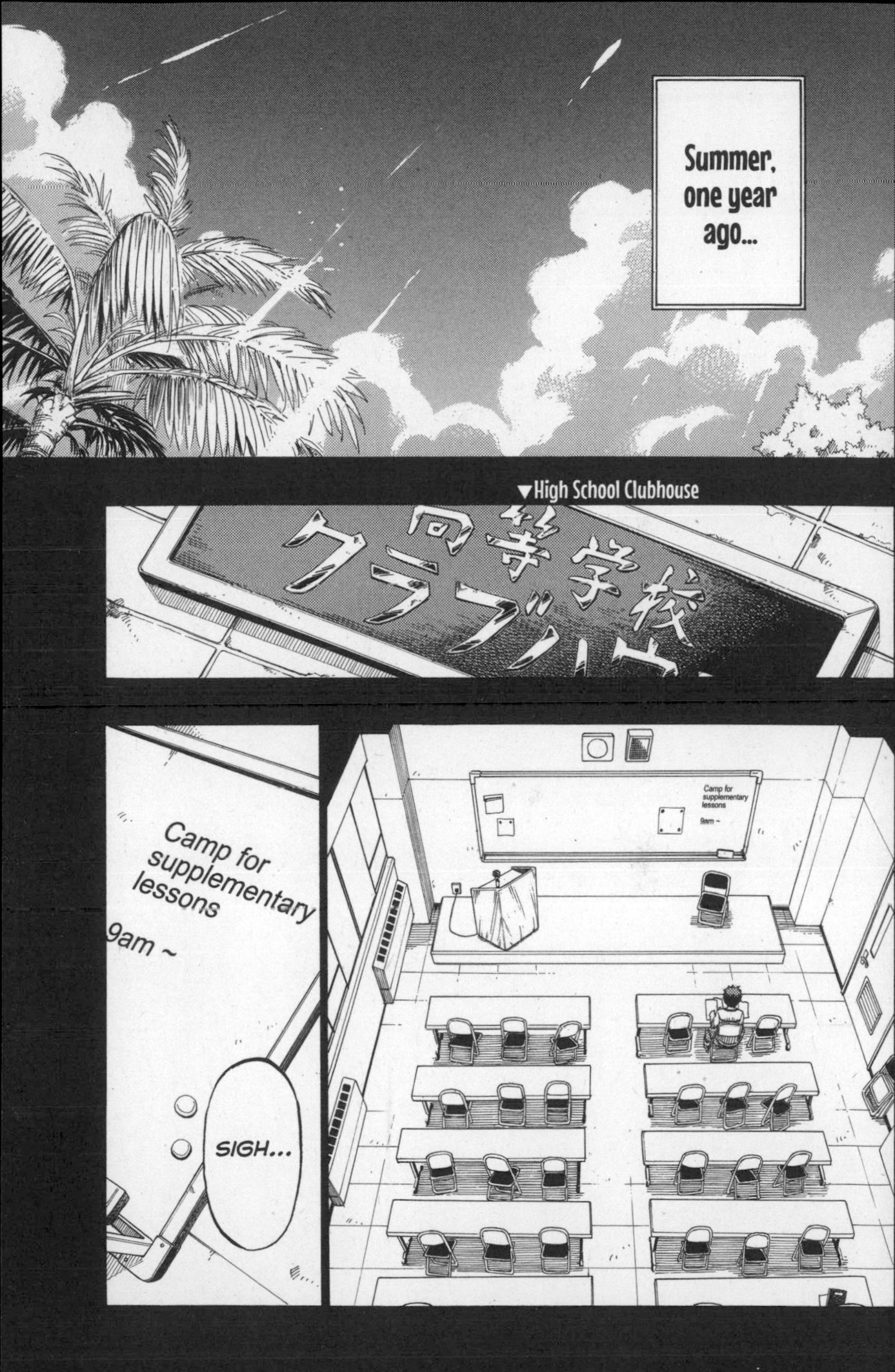
Summer, one year ago...
▼High School Clubhouse
Camp for supplementary lessons
9am ~
Camp for supplementary lessons
9am ~
SIGH...

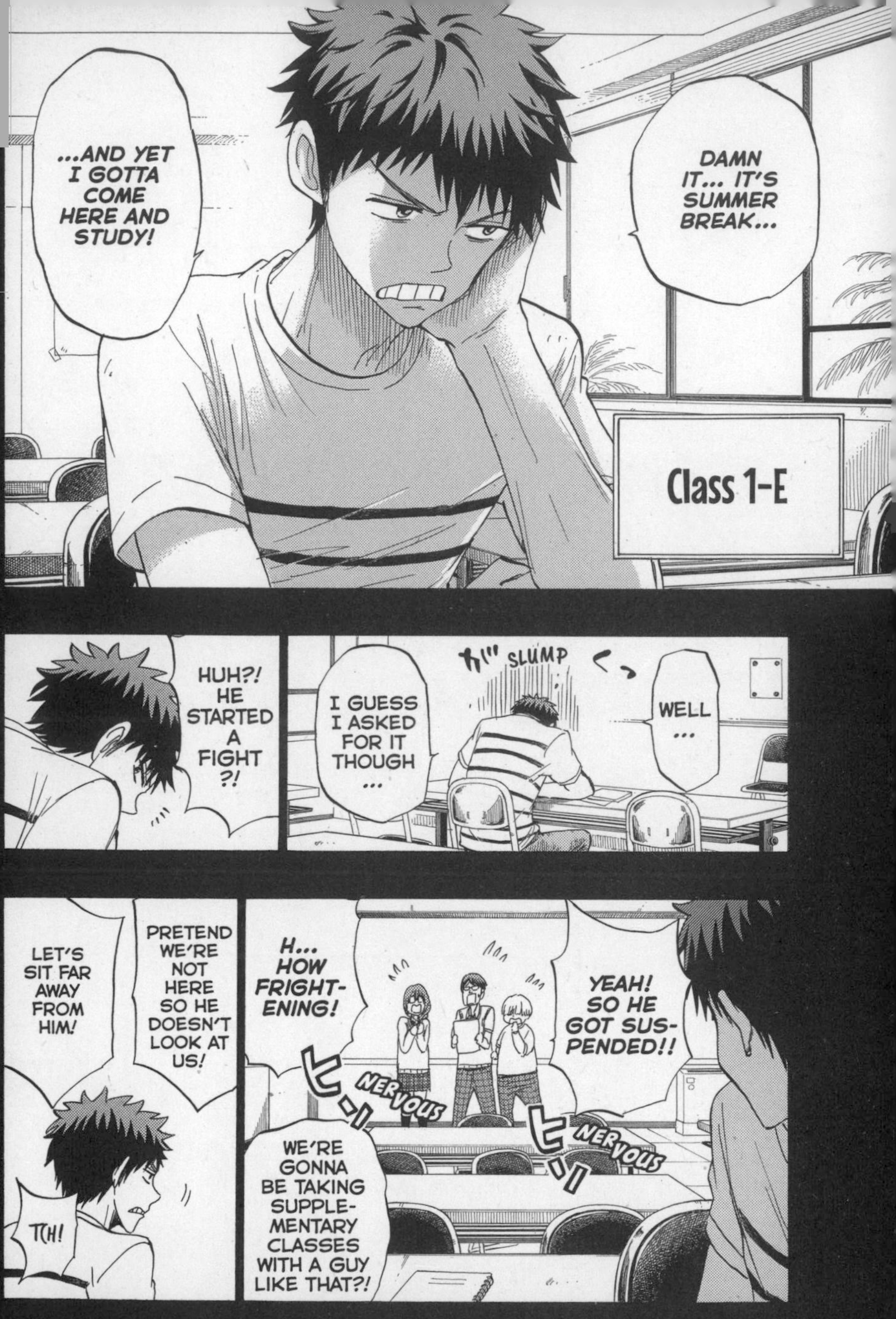
DAMN IT... IT'S SUMMER BREAK...
...AND YET I GOTTA COME HERE AND STUDY!
Class 1-E
WELL...
SLUMP
I GUESS I ASKED FOR IT THOUGH...
HUH?! HE STARTED A FIGHT?!
YEAH! SO HE GOT SUS-PENDED!!
H... HOW FRIGHT-ENING!
NERVOUS
NERVOUS
WE'RE GONNA BE TAKING SUPPLE-MENTARY CLASSES WITH A GUY LIKE THAT?!
PRETEND WE'RE NOT HERE SO HE DOESN'T LOOK AT US!
LET'S SIT FAR AWAY FROM HIM!
TCH!

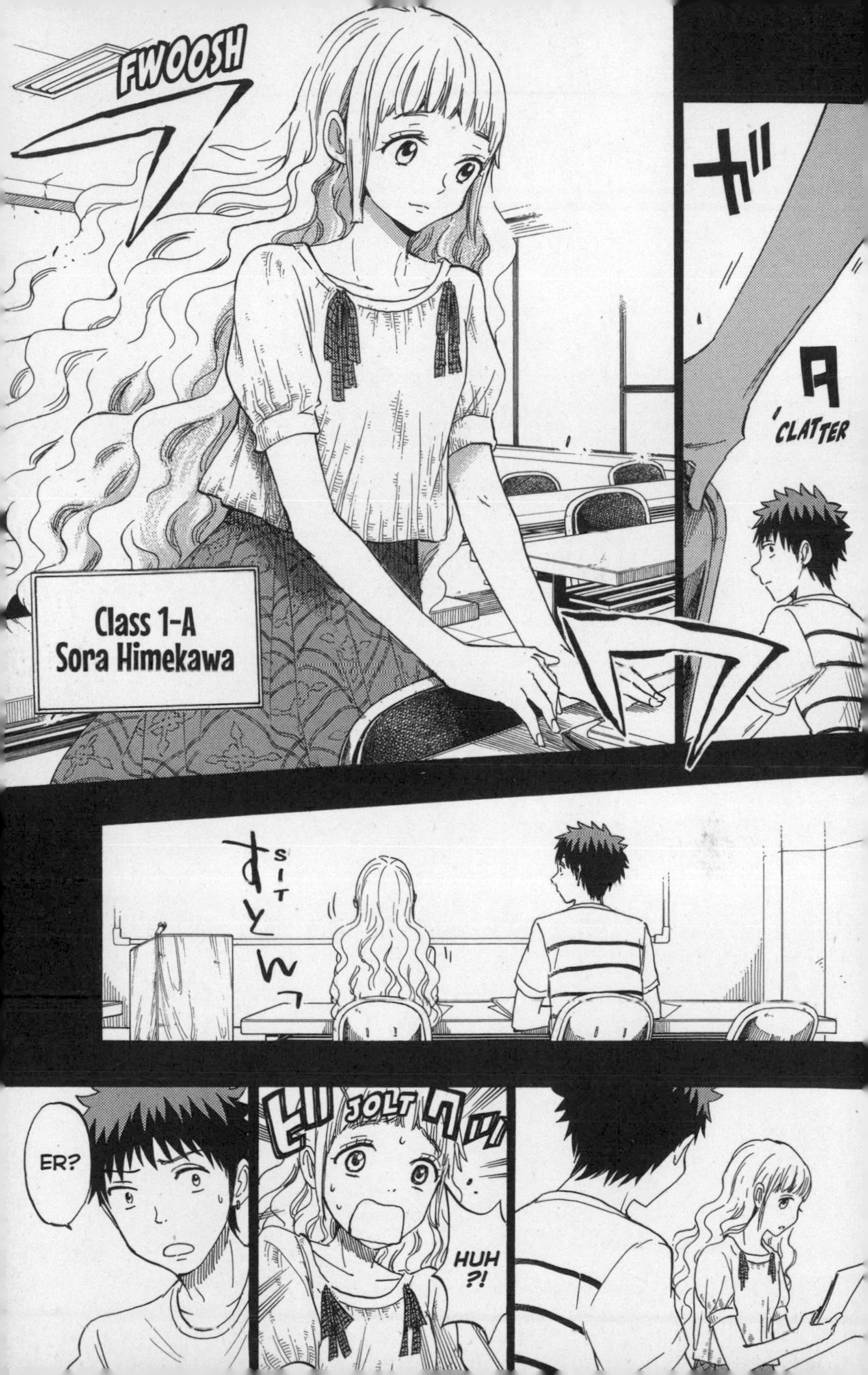

CLATTER
FWOOSH
Class 1-A
Sora Himekawa
SIT
JOLT
HUH?!
ER?

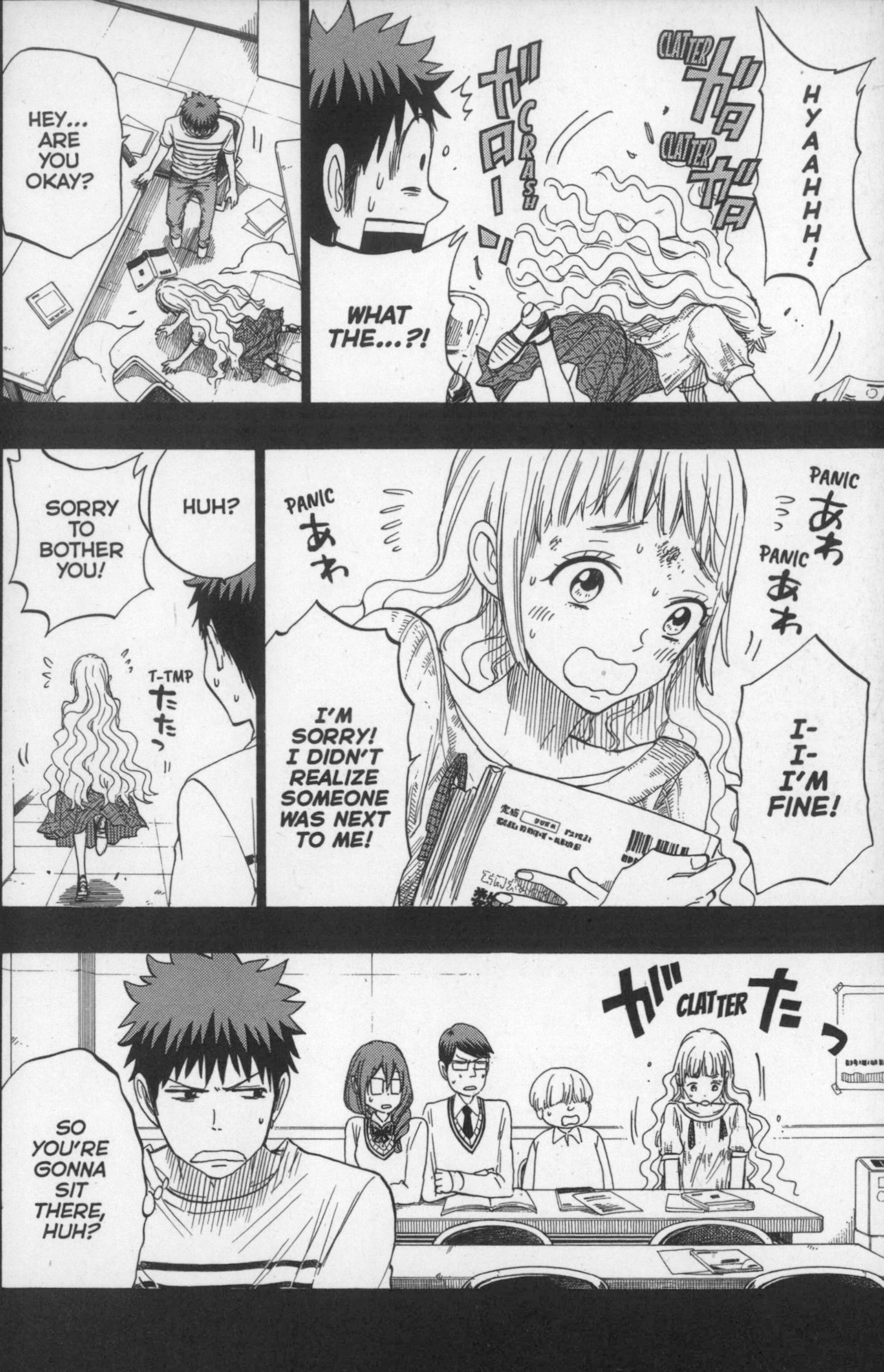

HYAAHHH!
CLATTER ガタ
CLATTER ガタ
CRASH ガロー
WHAT THE...?!
HEY... ARE YOU OKAY?
PANIC あわ
PANIC あわ
I- I- I'M FINE!
PANIC あわ
I'M SORRY! I DIDN'T REALIZE SOMEONE WAS NEXT TO ME!
HUH?
SORRY TO BOTHER YOU!
T-TMP たたっ
ガ CLATTER たっ
SO YOU'RE GONNA SIT THERE, HUH?

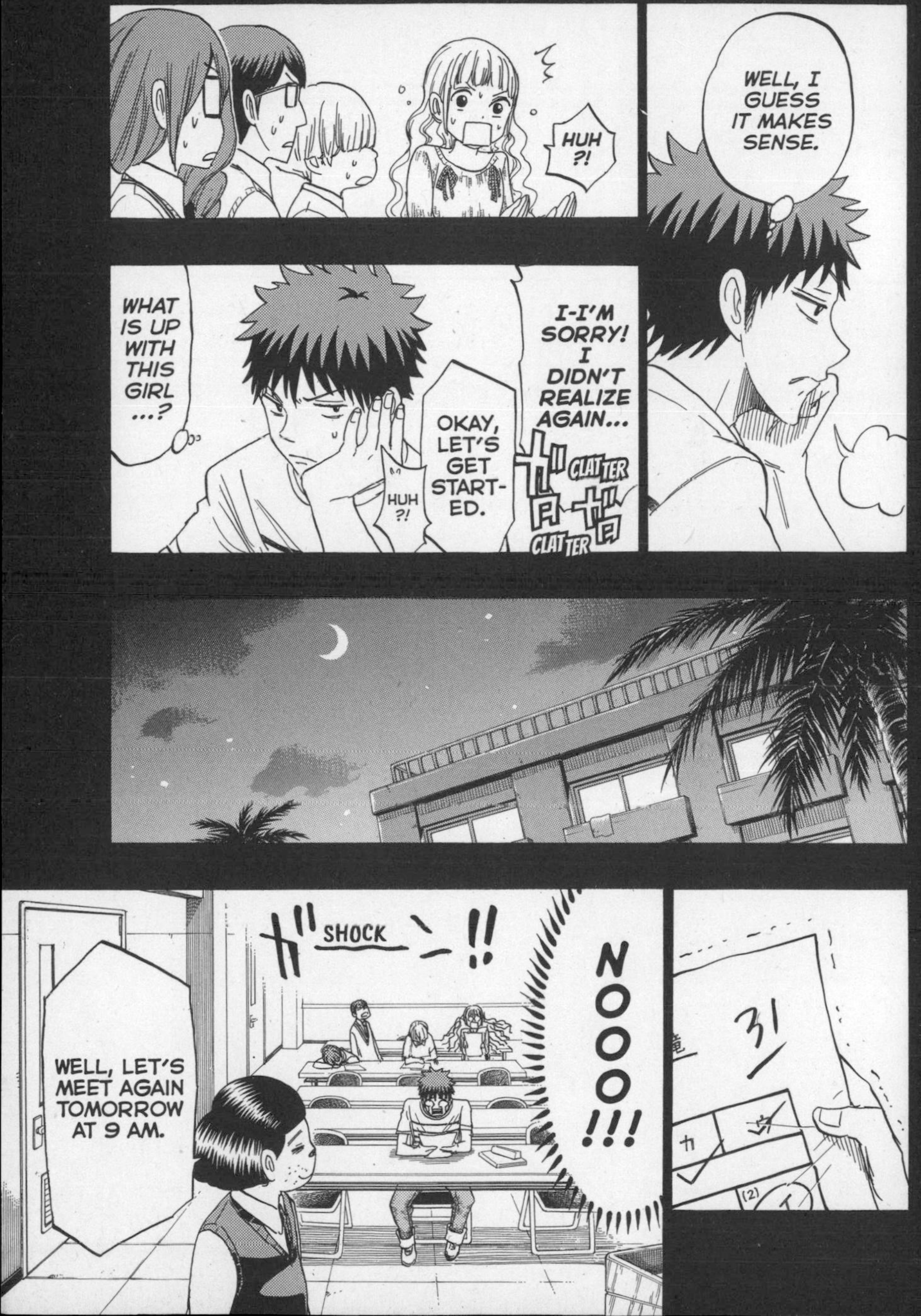
WELL, I GUESS IT MAKES SENSE.
HUH ?!
I-I'M SORRY! I DIDN'T REALIZE AGAIN...
CLATTER
CLATTER
WHAT IS UP WITH THIS GIRL ...?
OKAY, LET'S GET STARTED.
HUH ?!
31
NOOOO!!!
SHOCK
WELL, LET'S MEET AGAIN TOMORROW AT 9 AM.

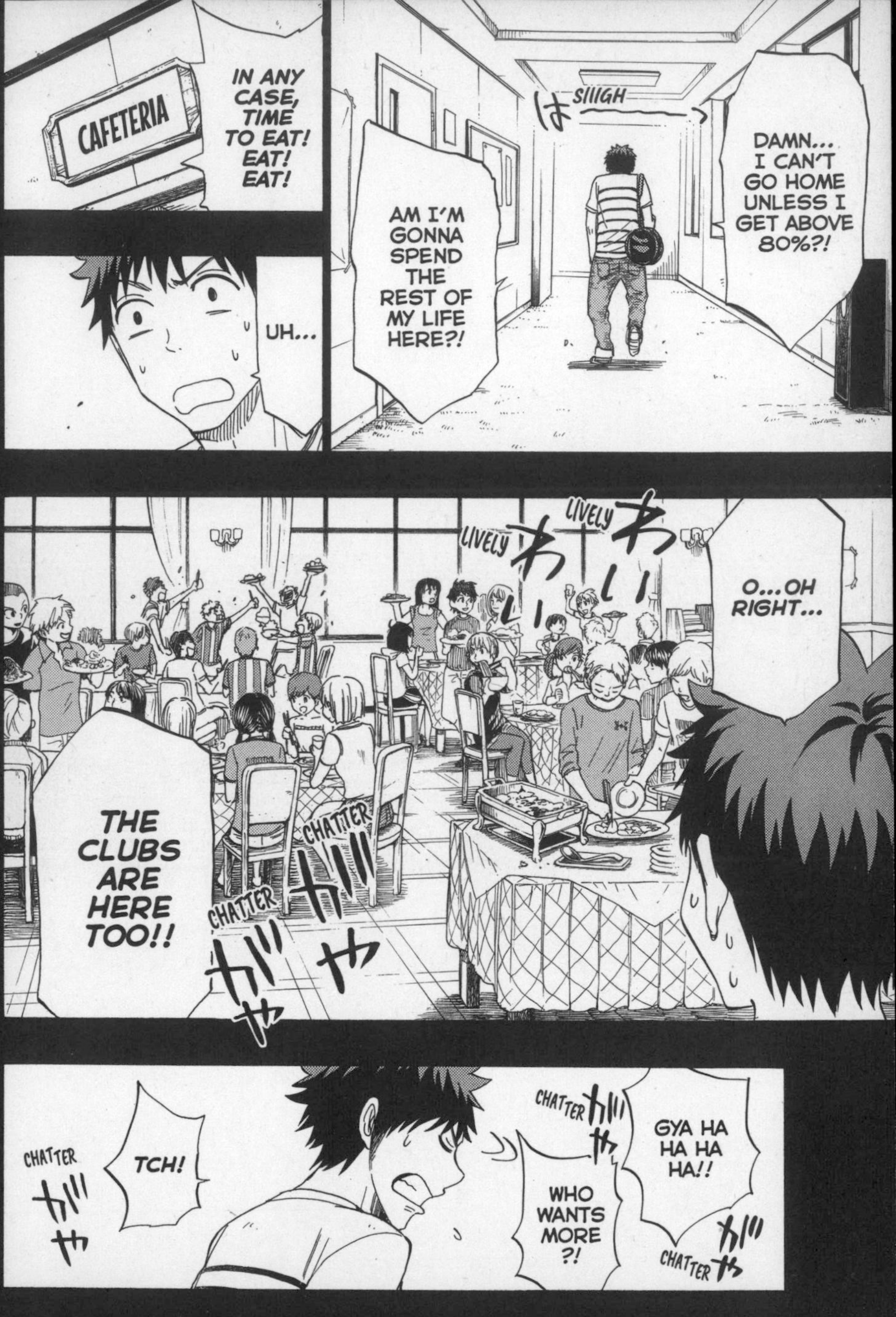
は SIIIGH
DAMN... I CAN'T GO HOME UNLESS I GET ABOVE 80%?!
AM I'M GONNA SPEND THE REST OF MY LIFE HERE?!
CAFETERIA
IN ANY CASE, TIME TO EAT! EAT! EAT!
UH...
O...OH RIGHT...
LIVELY わい
LIVELY わい
CHATTER ガヤ
CHATTER ガヤ
THE CLUBS ARE HERE TOO!!
GYA HA HA HA HA!!
CHATTER ガヤ
CHATTER ガヤ
WHO WANTS MORE?!
TCH!
CHATTER ガヤ

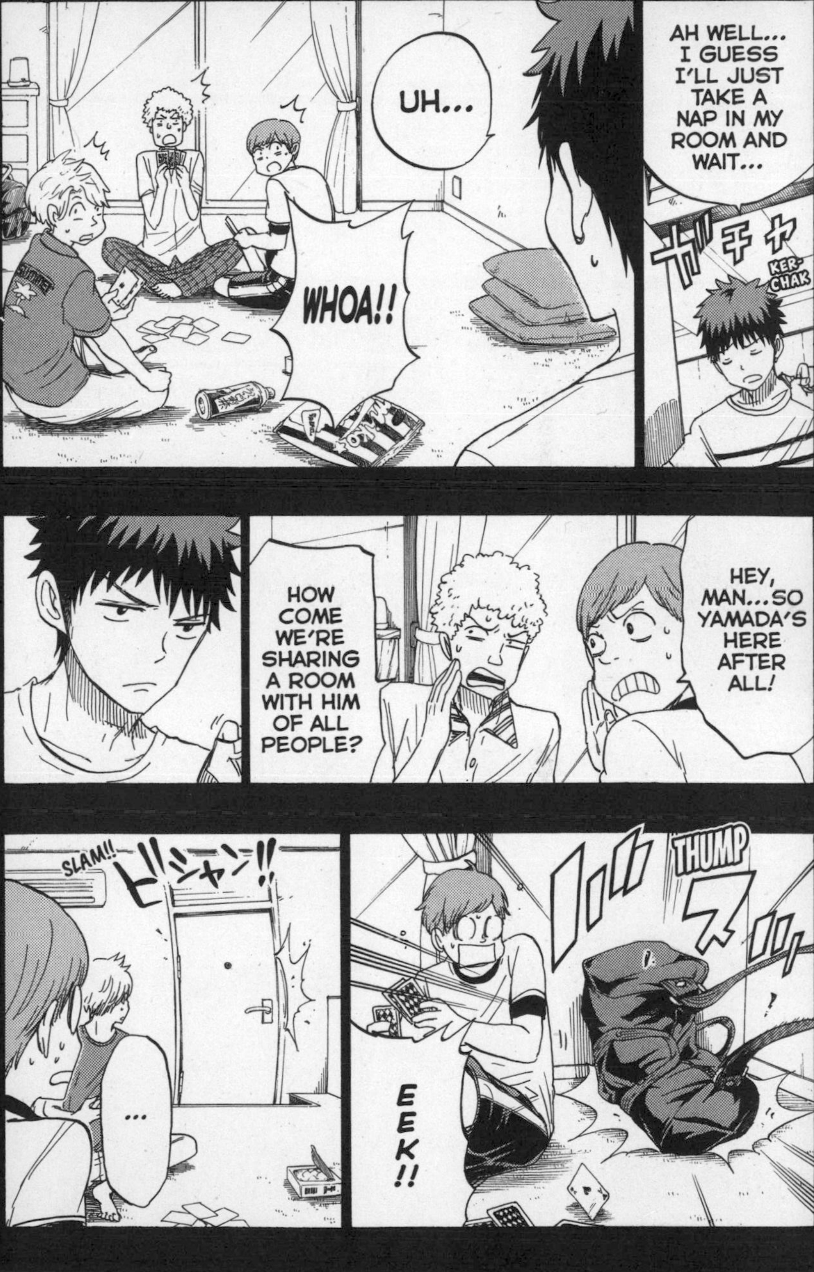
AH WELL... I GUESS I'LL JUST TAKE A NAP IN MY ROOM AND WAIT...
KER-CHAK
UH...
WHOA!!
HEY, MAN...SO YAMADA'S HERE AFTER ALL!
HOW COME WE'RE SHARING A ROOM WITH HIM OF ALL PEOPLE?
THUMP
EEK!!
SLAM!!
...

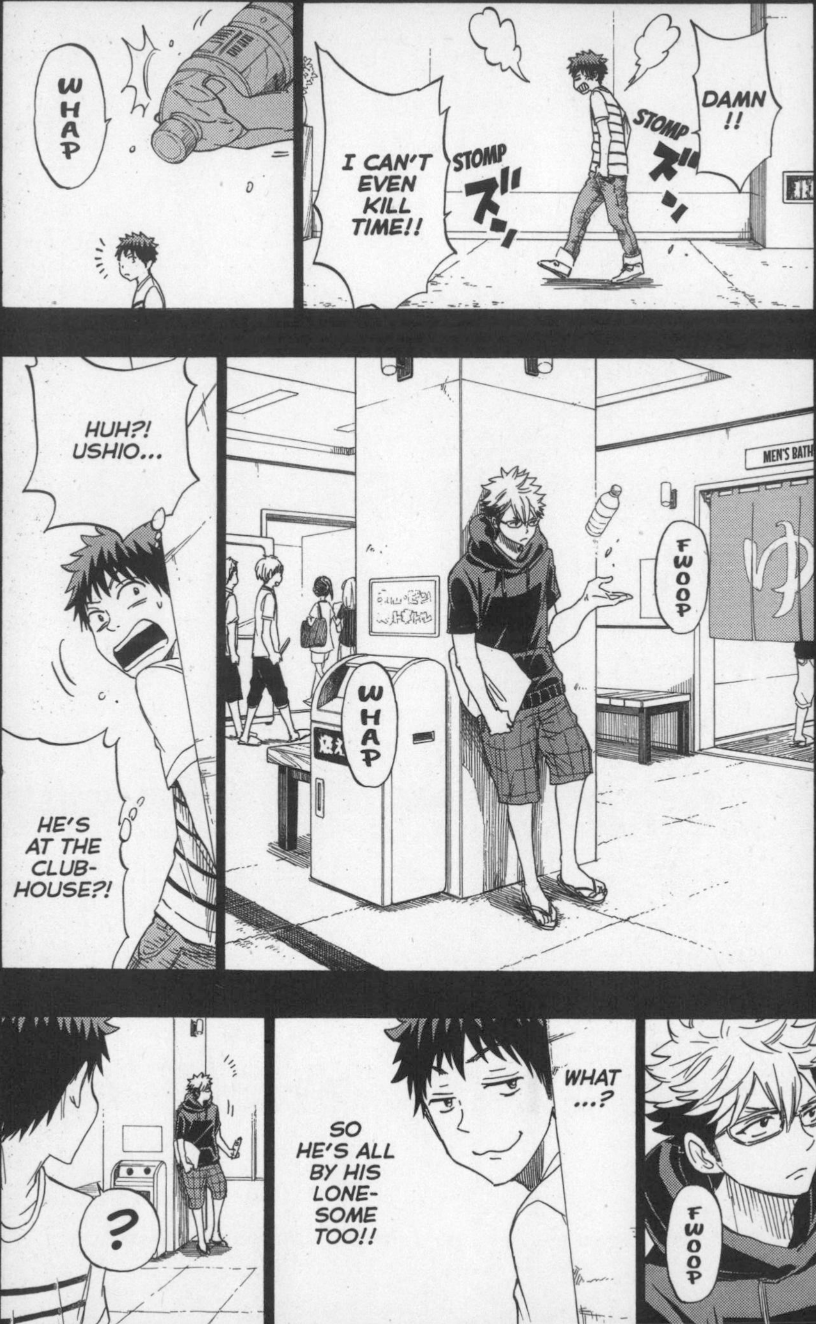
DAMN !!
STOMP
STOMP
I CAN'T EVEN KILL TIME!!
WHAP
MEN'S BATH
FWOOP
WHAP
HUH?! USHIO...
HE'S AT THE CLUB-HOUSE?!
FWOOP
WHAT ...?
SO HE'S ALL BY HIS LONE-SOME TOO!!
?

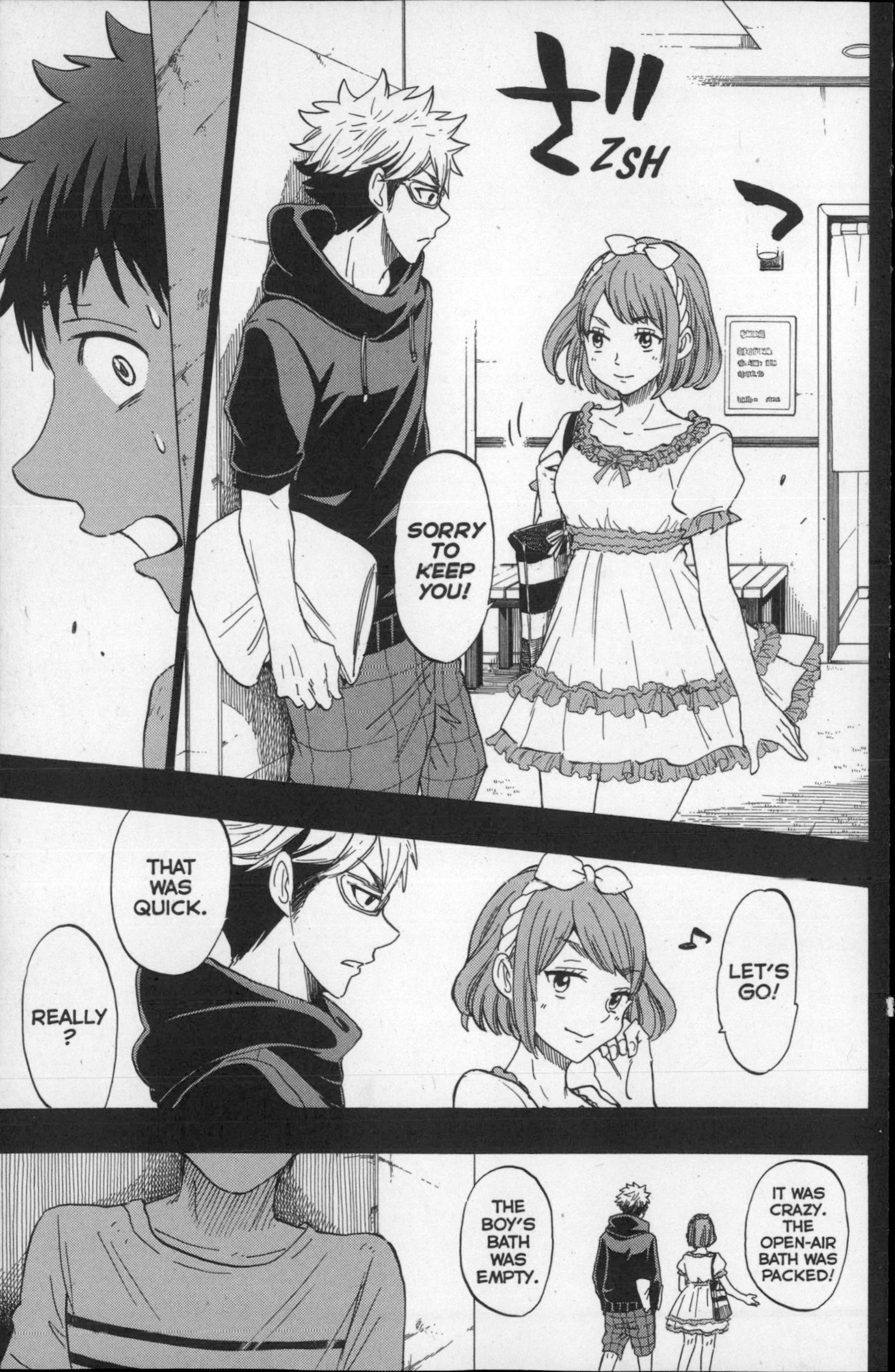
ZSH
?
SORRY TO KEEP YOU!
LET'S GO!
THAT WAS QUICK.
REALLY?
IT WAS CRAZY. THE OPEN-AIR BATH WAS PACKED!
THE BOY'S BATH WAS EMPTY.

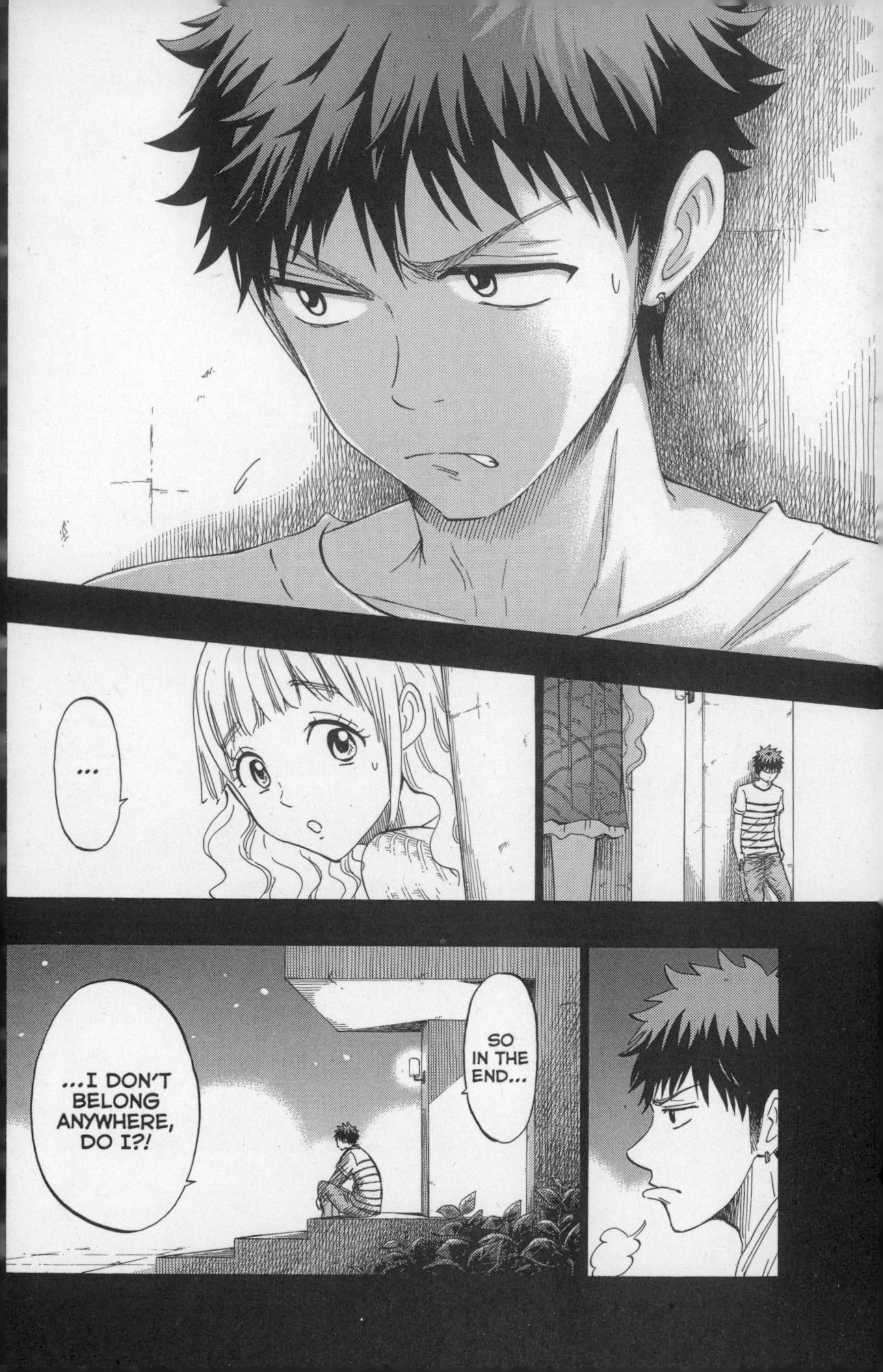
...
SO IN THE END...
...I DON'T BELONG ANYWHERE, DO I?!

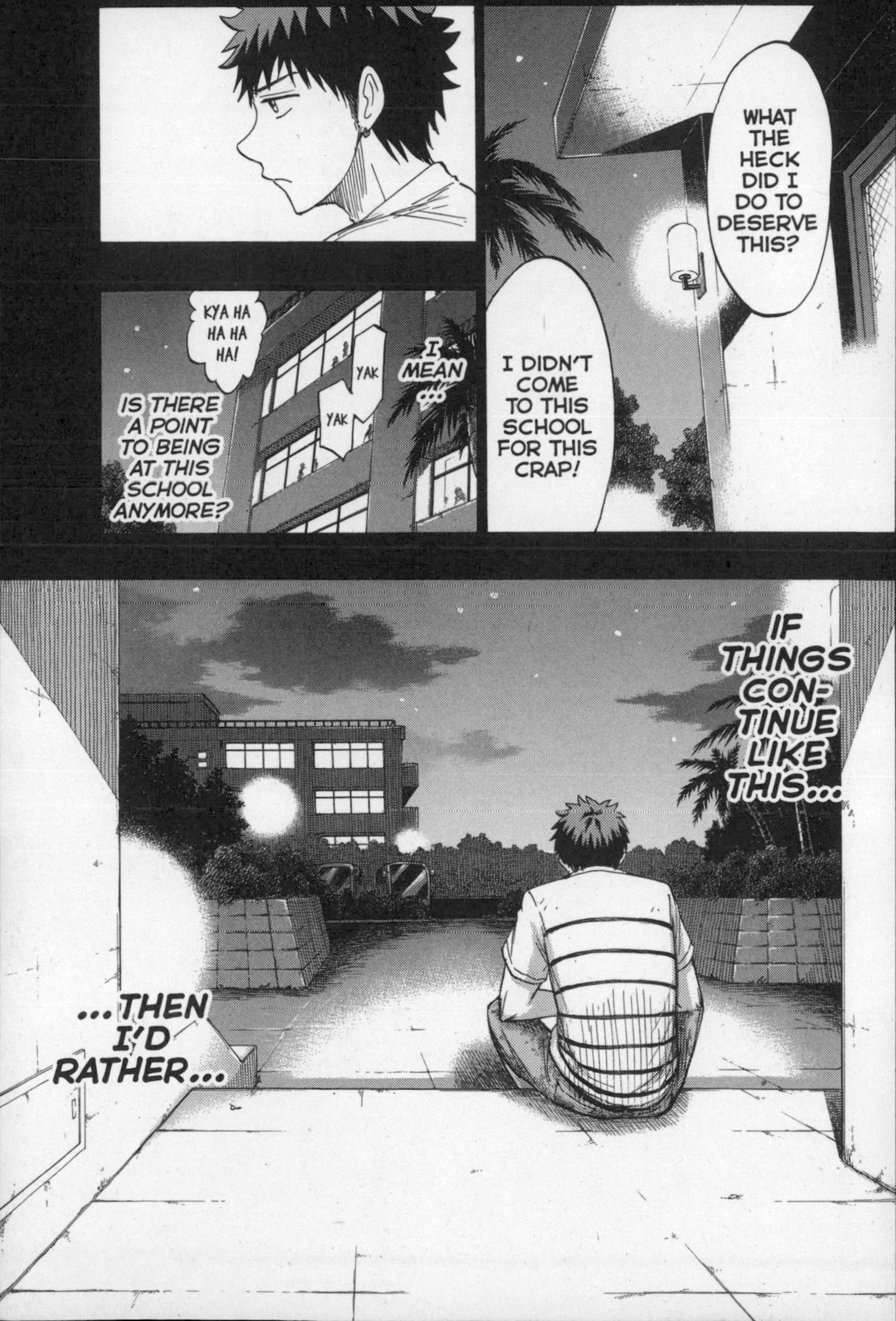
WHAT THE HECK DID I DO TO DESERVE THIS?
I DIDN'T COME TO THIS SCHOOL FOR THIS CRAP!
I MEAN...
YAK
YAK
KYA HA HA HA HA!
IS THERE A POINT TO BEING AT THIS SCHOOL ANYMORE?
IF THINGS CONTINUE LIKE THIS...
...THEN I'D RATHER...

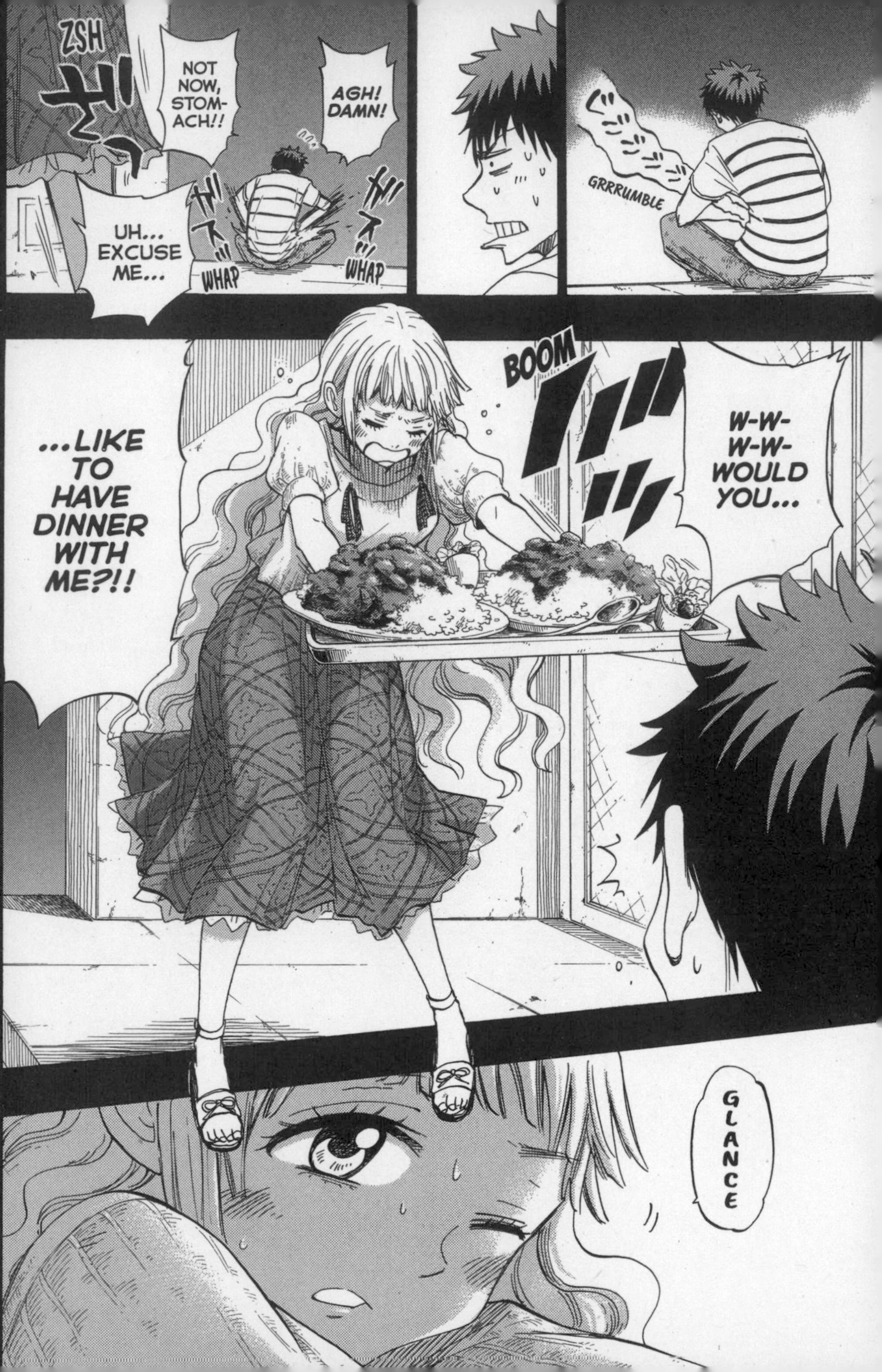
GRRRUMBLE
AGH! DAMN!
NOT NOW, STOMACH!!
WHAP
WHAP
ZSH
UH... EXCUSE ME...
BOOM
W-W-W-W-WOULD YOU...
...LIKE TO HAVE DINNER WITH ME?!!
GLANCE

CHAPTER 158: Haruko-chan!

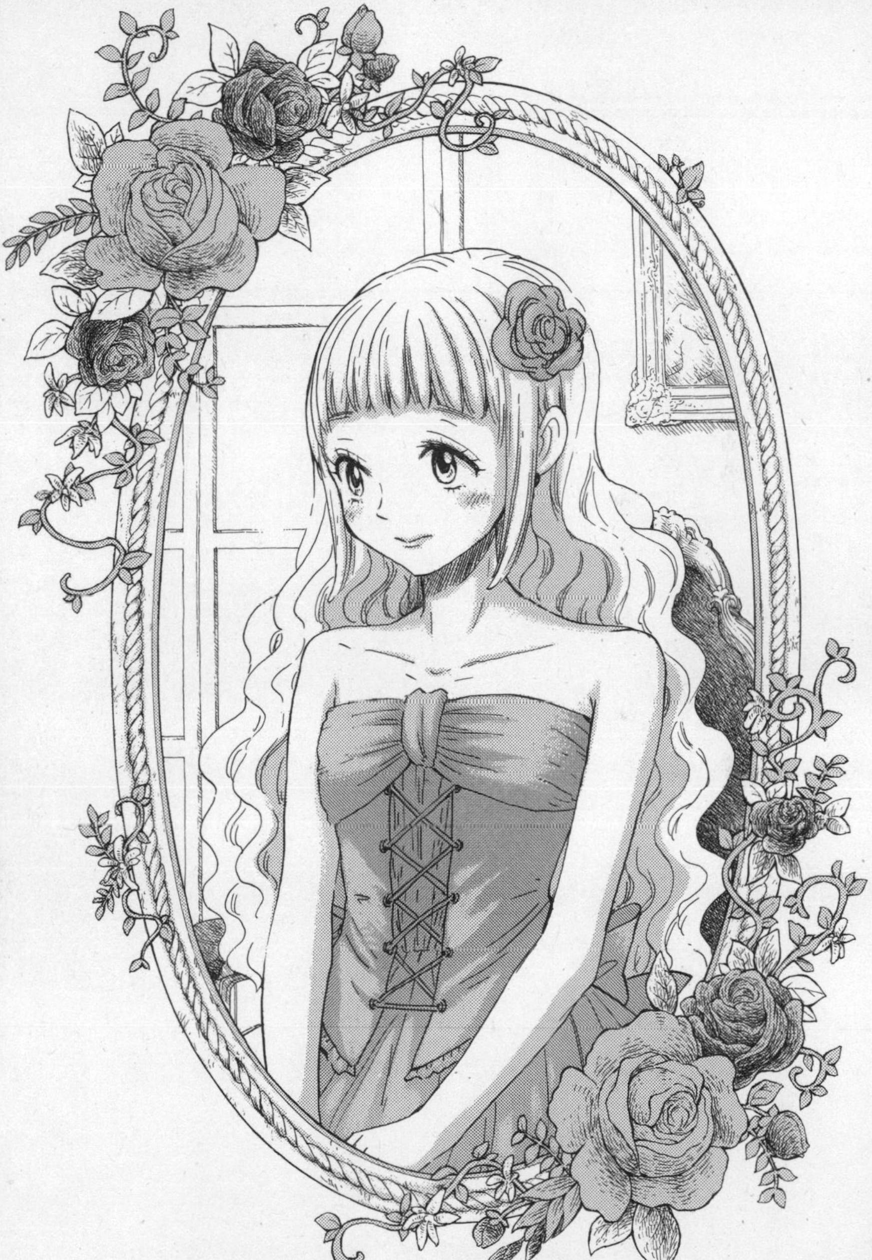

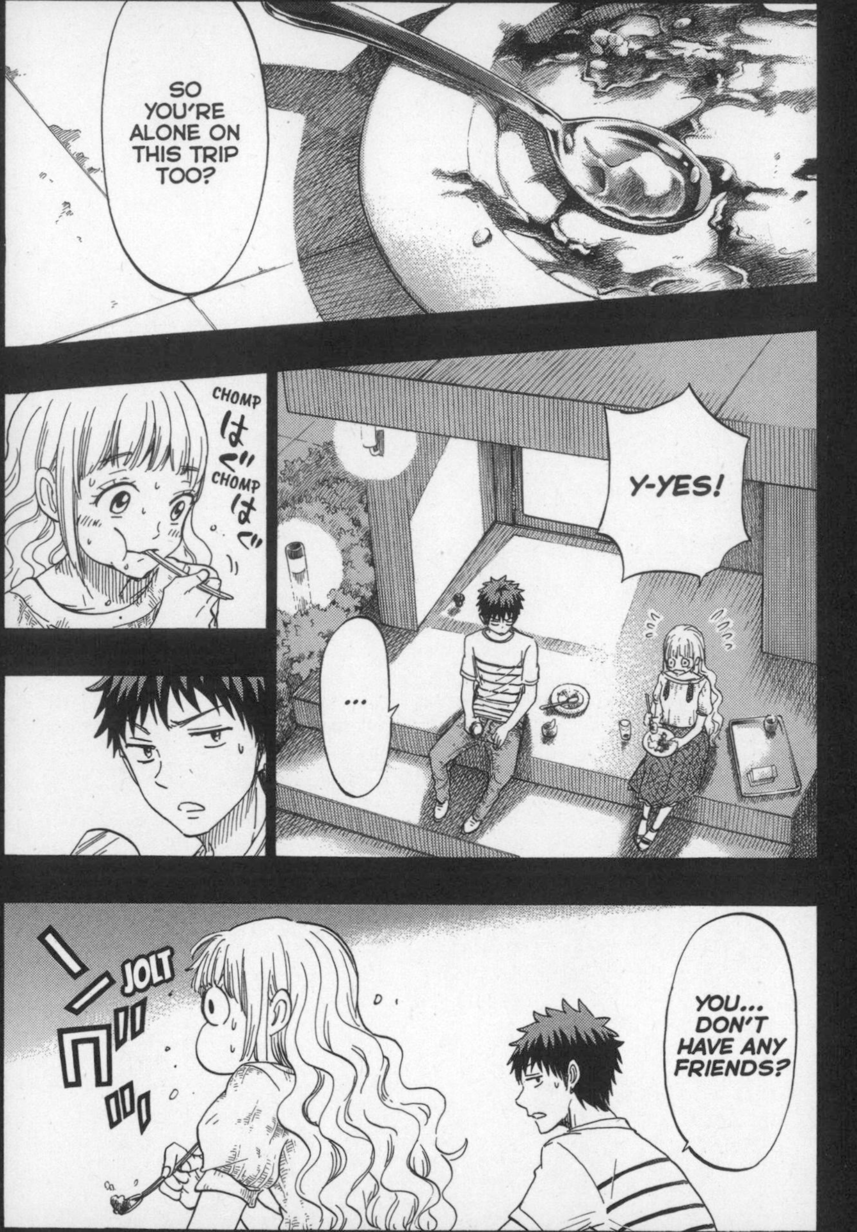
SO YOU'RE ALONE ON THIS TRIP TOO?
Y-YES!
...
CHOMP
はぐ
CHOMP
はぐ
YOU... DON'T HAVE ANY FRIENDS?
JOLT

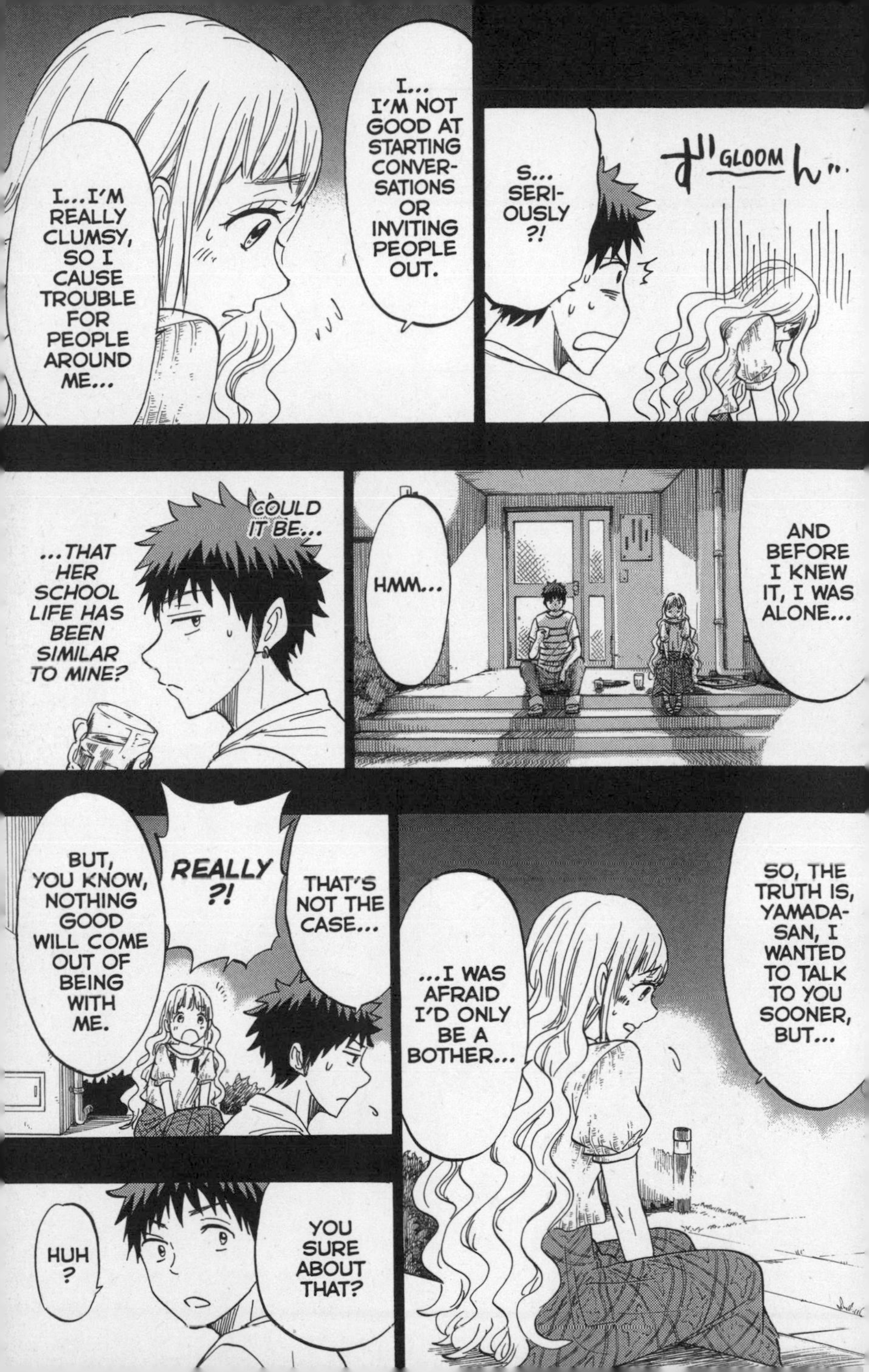
ず GLOOM ん…
S... SERIOUSLY ?!
I... I'M NOT GOOD AT STARTING CONVERSATIONS OR INVITING PEOPLE OUT.
I...I'M REALLY CLUMSY, SO I CAUSE TROUBLE FOR PEOPLE AROUND ME...
AND BEFORE I KNEW IT, I WAS ALONE...
HMM...
COULD IT BE...
...THAT HER SCHOOL LIFE HAS BEEN SIMILAR TO MINE?
SO, THE TRUTH IS, YAMADA-SAN, I WANTED TO TALK TO YOU SOONER, BUT...
...I WAS AFRAID I'D ONLY BE A BOTHER...
THAT'S NOT THE CASE...
REALLY ?!
BUT, YOU KNOW, NOTHING GOOD WILL COME OUT OF BEING WITH ME.
YOU SURE ABOUT THAT?
HUH ?

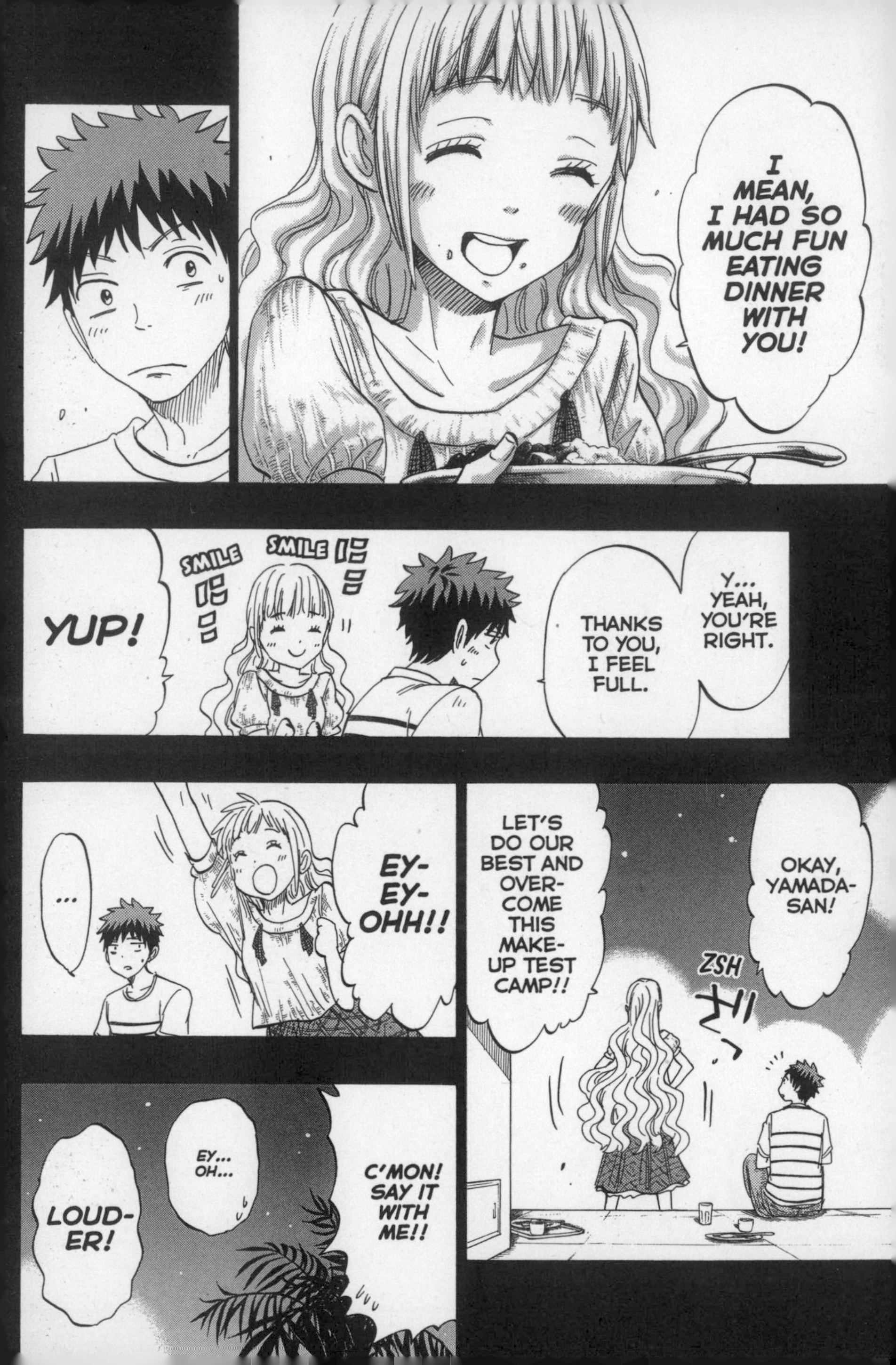
I MEAN, I HAD SO MUCH FUN EATING DINNER WITH YOU!
Y... YEAH, YOU'RE RIGHT.
THANKS TO YOU, I FEEL FULL.
SMILE
SMILE
YUP!
OKAY, YAMADA-SAN!
ZSH
LET'S DO OUR BEST AND OVER-COME THIS MAKE-UP TEST CAMP!!
EY-EY-OHH!!
...
C'MON! SAY IT WITH ME!!
EY... OH...
LOUDER!

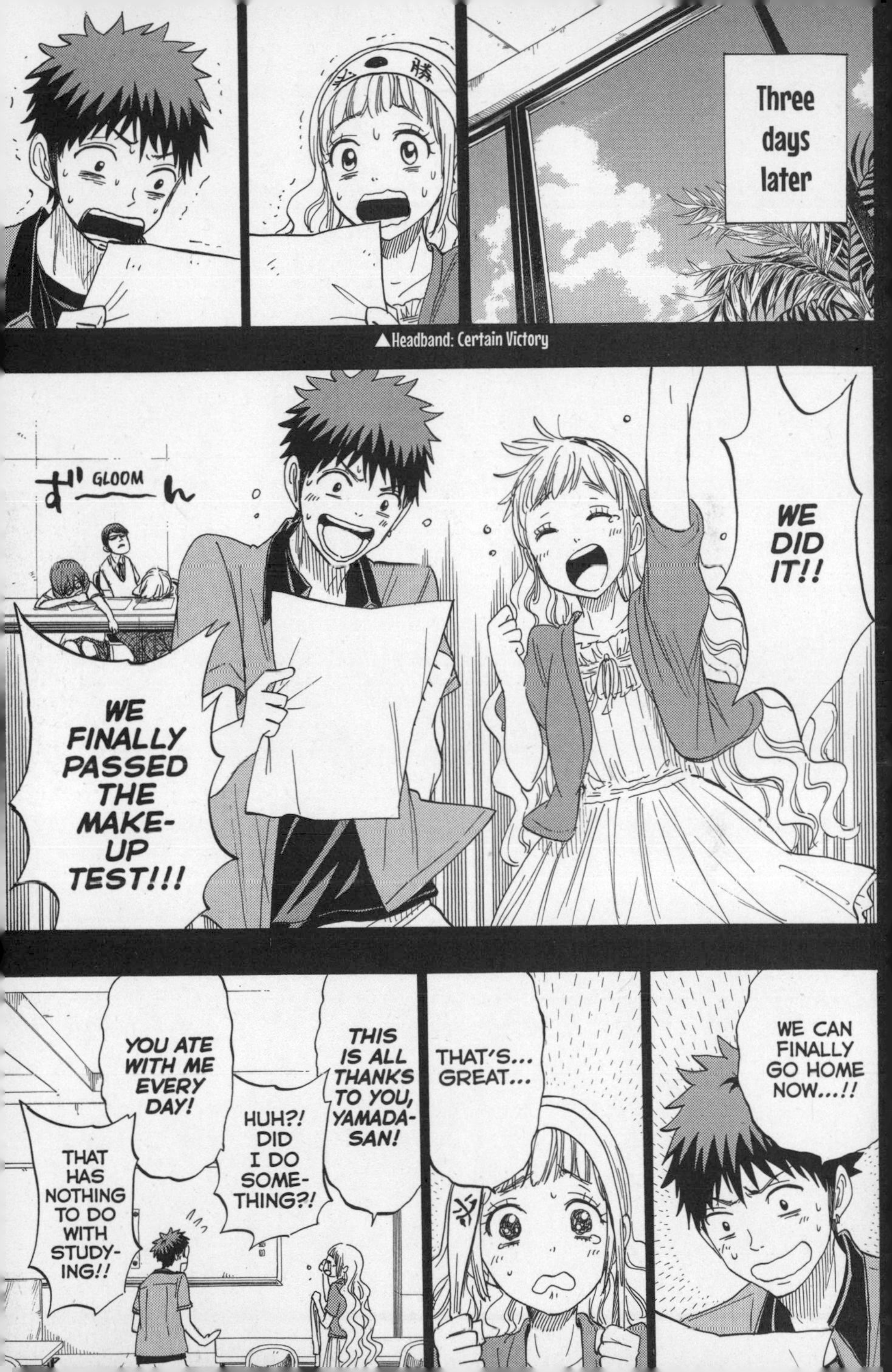
Three days later
▲Headband: Certain Victory
WE DID IT!!
WE FINALLY PASSED THE MAKE-UP TEST!!!
ずーん GLOOM
WE CAN FINALLY GO HOME NOW...!!
THAT'S... GREAT...
THIS IS ALL THANKS TO YOU, YAMADA-SAN!
HUH?! DID I DO SOMETHING?!
YOU ATE WITH ME EVERY DAY!
THAT HAS NOTHING TO DO WITH STUDYING!!

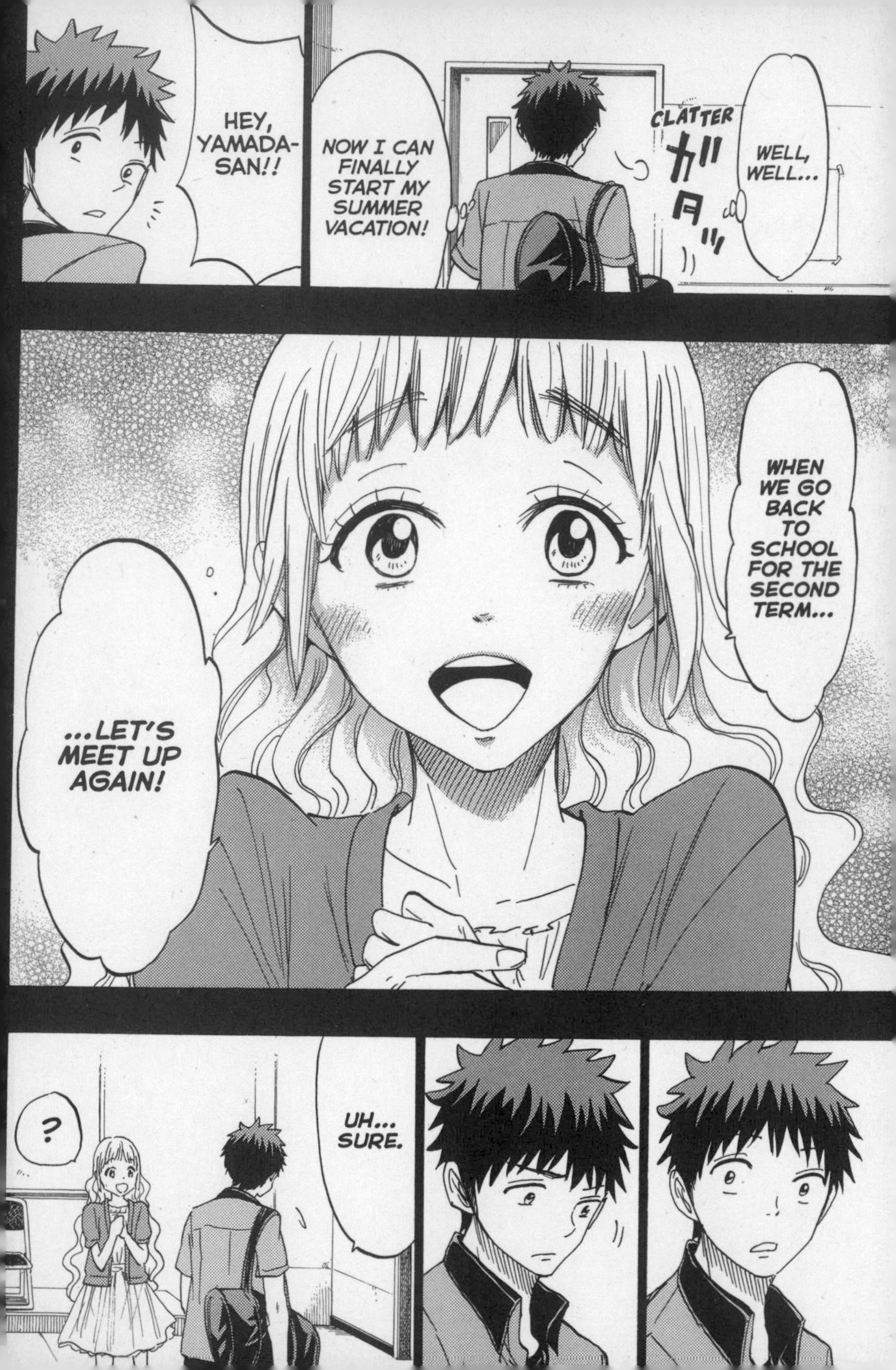
WELL, WELL...
CLATTER
ガタッ
NOW I CAN FINALLY START MY SUMMER VACATION!
HEY, YAMADA-SAN!!
WHEN WE GO BACK TO SCHOOL FOR THE SECOND TERM...
...LET'S MEET UP AGAIN!
UH... SURE.
?

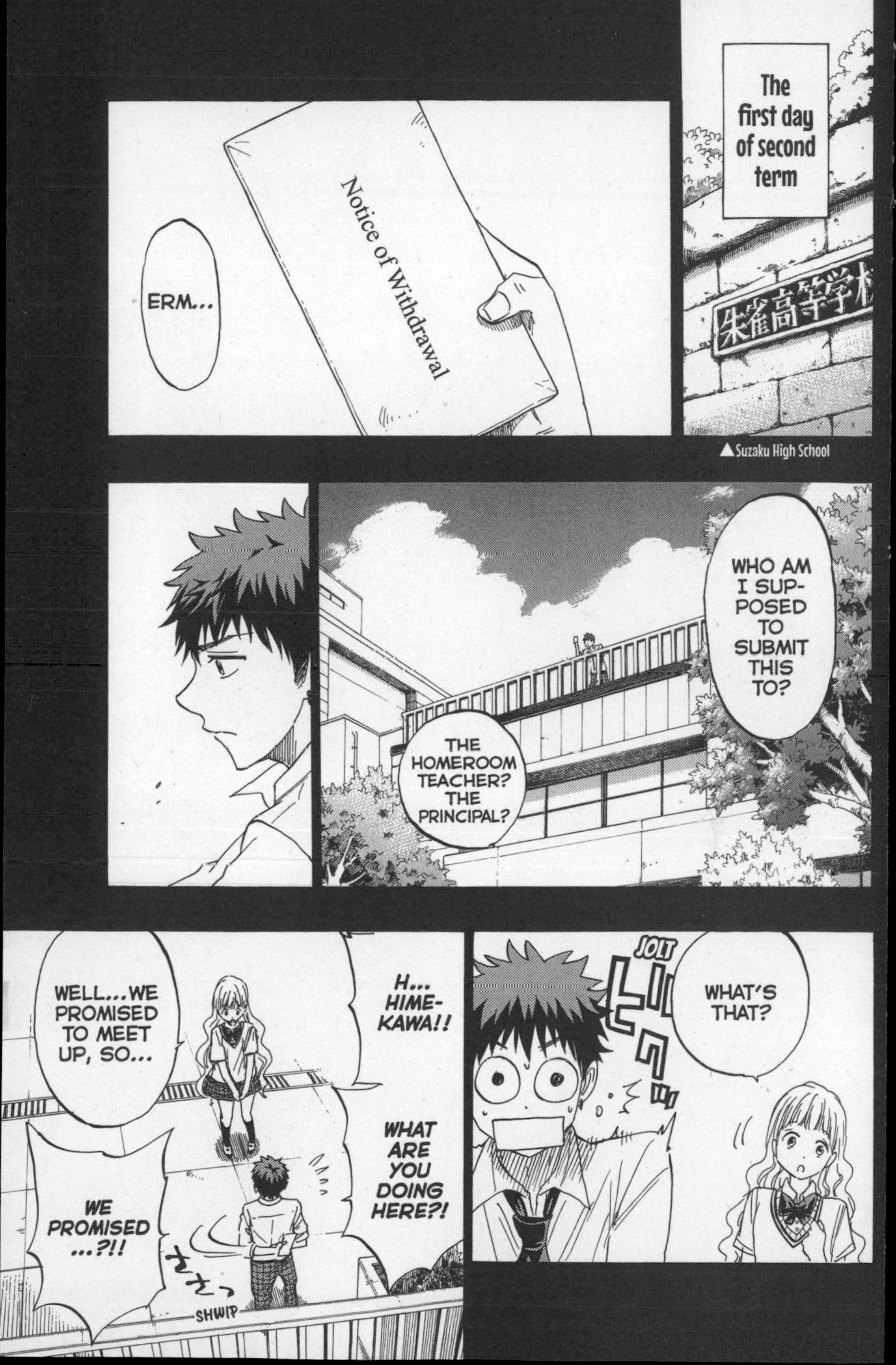
The first day of second term
朱雀高等学校
▲Suzaku High School
Notice of Withdrawal
ERM...
WHO AM I SUP-POSED TO SUBMIT THIS TO?
THE HOMEROOM TEACHER? THE PRINCIPAL?
WHAT'S THAT?
JOLT
H... HIME-KAWA!!
WHAT ARE YOU DOING HERE?!
WELL...WE PROMISED TO MEET UP, SO...
WE PROMISED ...?!!
SHWIP

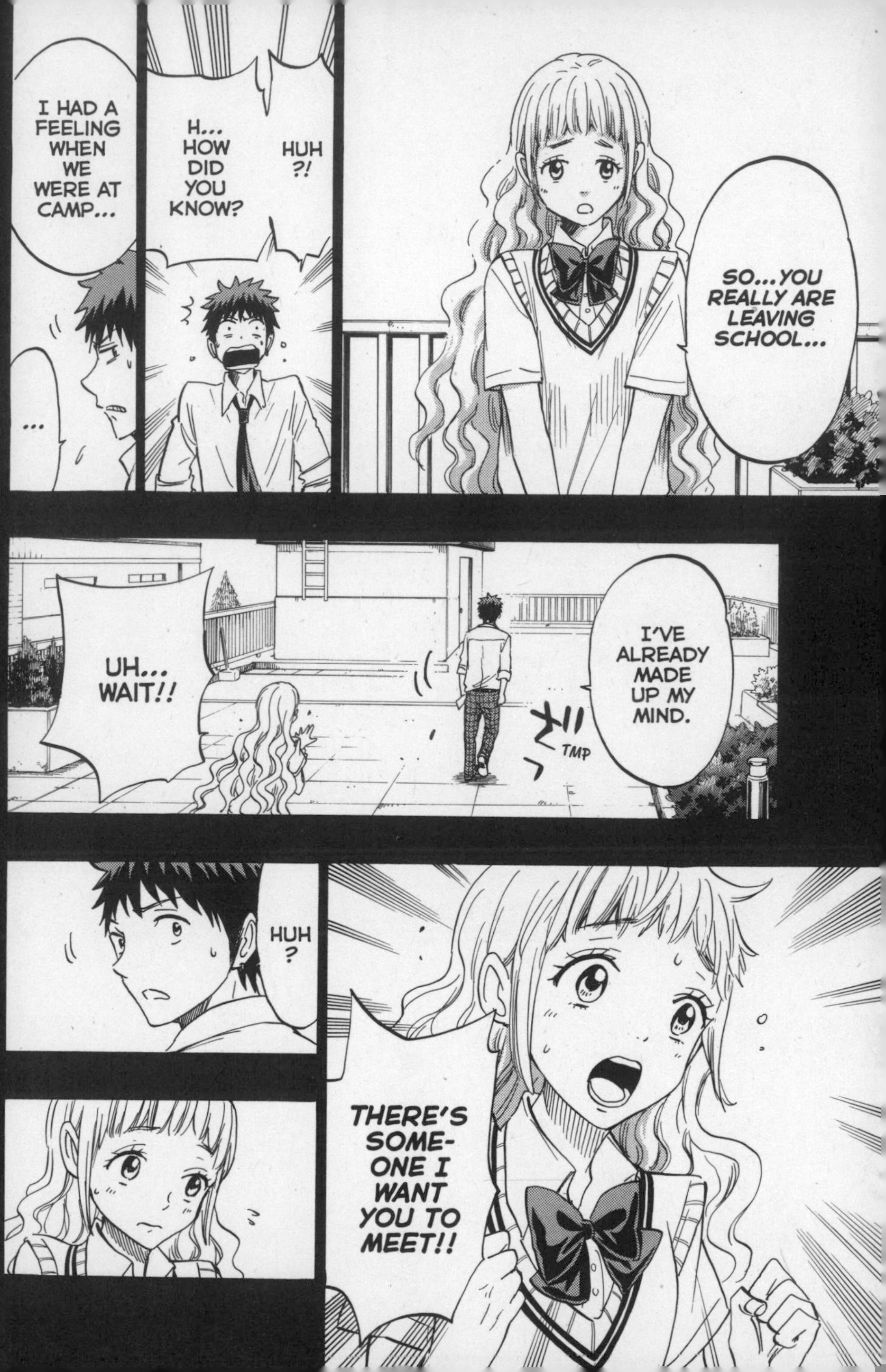
SO...YOU REALLY ARE LEAVING SCHOOL...
HUH ?!
H... HOW DID YOU KNOW?
I HAD A FEELING WHEN WE WERE AT CAMP...
...
I'VE ALREADY MADE UP MY MIND.
TMP
UH... WAIT!!
THERE'S SOME-ONE I WANT YOU TO MEET!!
HUH ?

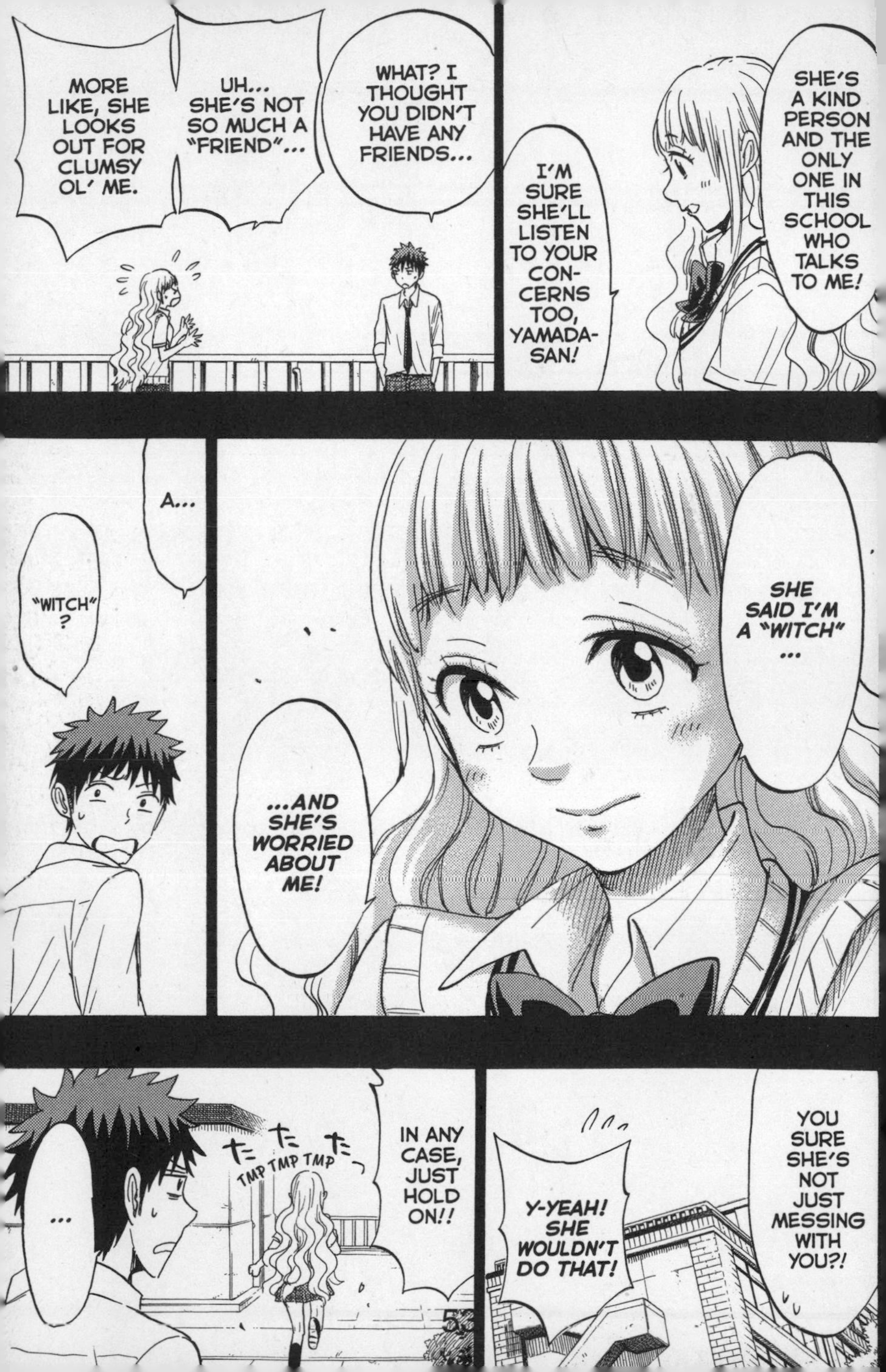
SHE'S A KIND PERSON AND THE ONLY ONE IN THIS SCHOOL WHO TALKS TO ME!
I'M SURE SHE'LL LISTEN TO YOUR CONCERNS TOO, YAMADA-SAN!
WHAT? I THOUGHT YOU DIDN'T HAVE ANY FRIENDS...
UH... SHE'S NOT SO MUCH A "FRIEND"...
MORE LIKE, SHE LOOKS OUT FOR CLUMSY OL' ME.
SHE SAID I'M A "WITCH" ...
...AND SHE'S WORRIED ABOUT ME!
A...
"WITCH"?
YOU SURE SHE'S NOT JUST MESSING WITH YOU?!
Y-YEAH! SHE WOULDN'T DO THAT!
IN ANY CASE, JUST HOLD ON!!
TMP TMP TMP
...

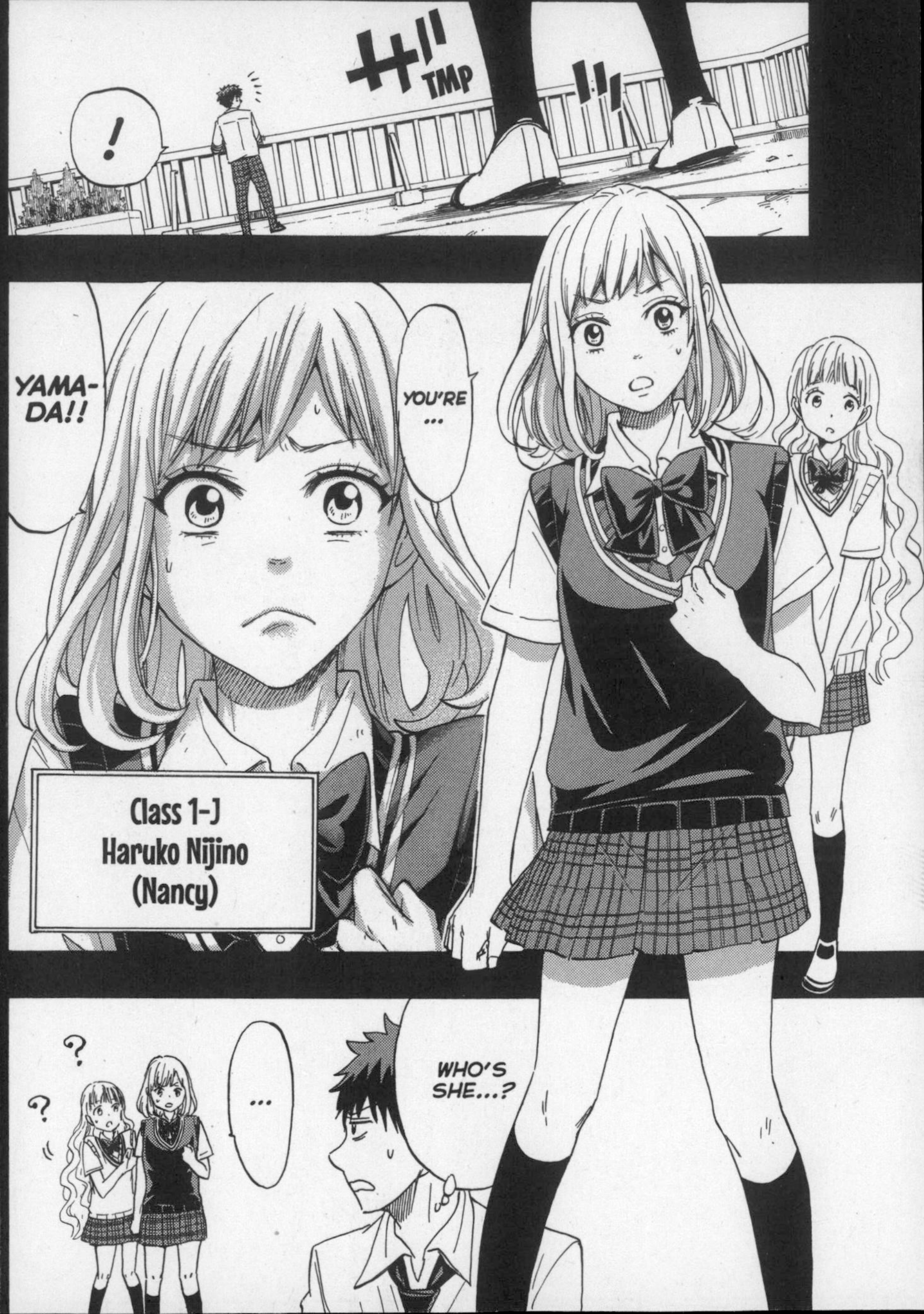
TMP
!
YAMA-DA!!
YOU'RE ...
Class 1-J
Haruko Nijino
(Nancy)
WHO'S SHE...?
...
?
?

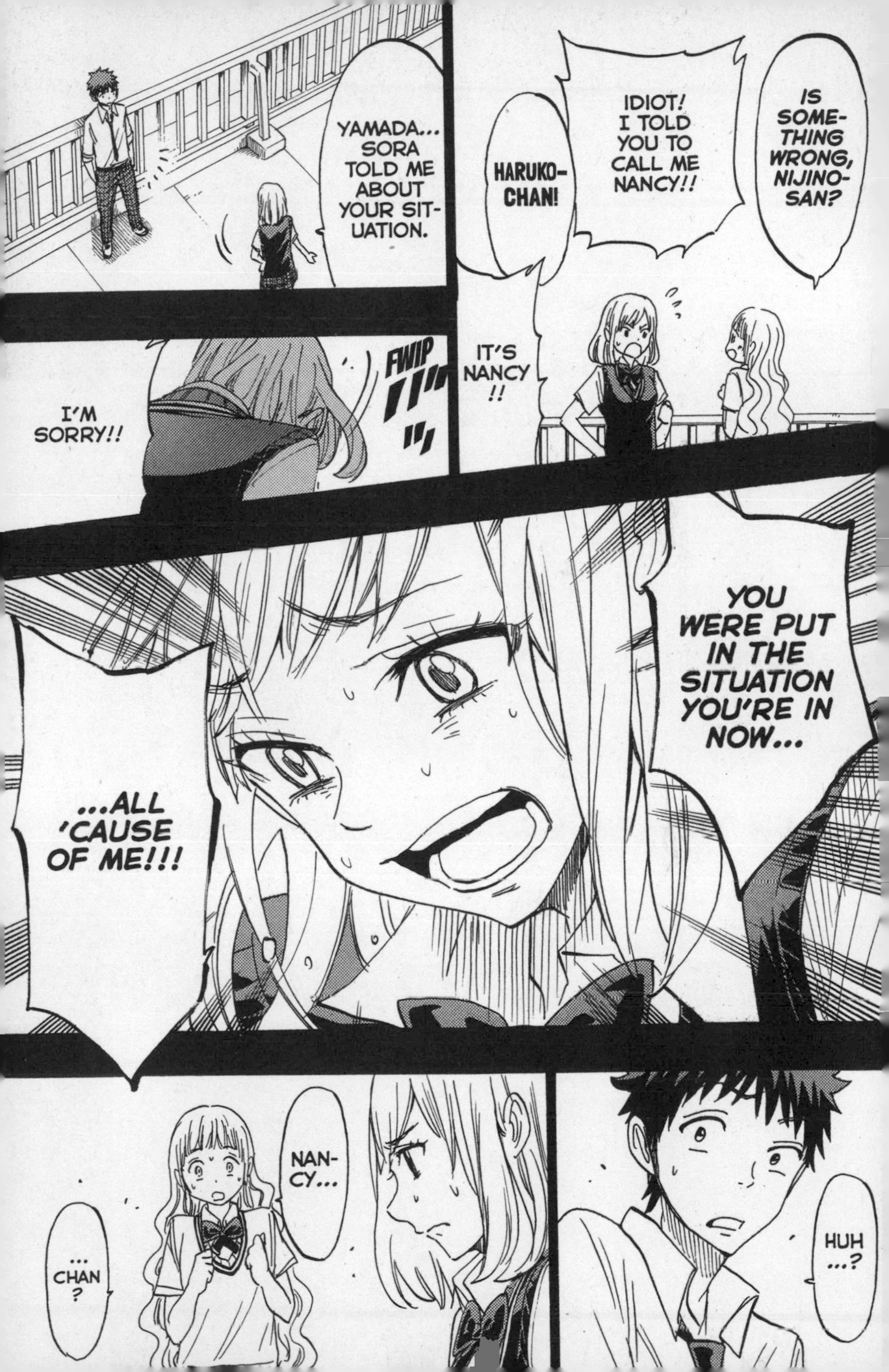
IS SOMETHING WRONG, NIJINO-SAN?
IDIOT! I TOLD YOU TO CALL ME NANCY!!
HARUKO-CHAN!
IT'S NANCY!!
YAMADA... SORA TOLD ME ABOUT YOUR SITUATION.
FWIP
I'M SORRY!!
YOU WERE PUT IN THE SITUATION YOU'RE IN NOW...
...ALL 'CAUSE OF ME!!!
HUH...?
NANCY...
...CHAN?

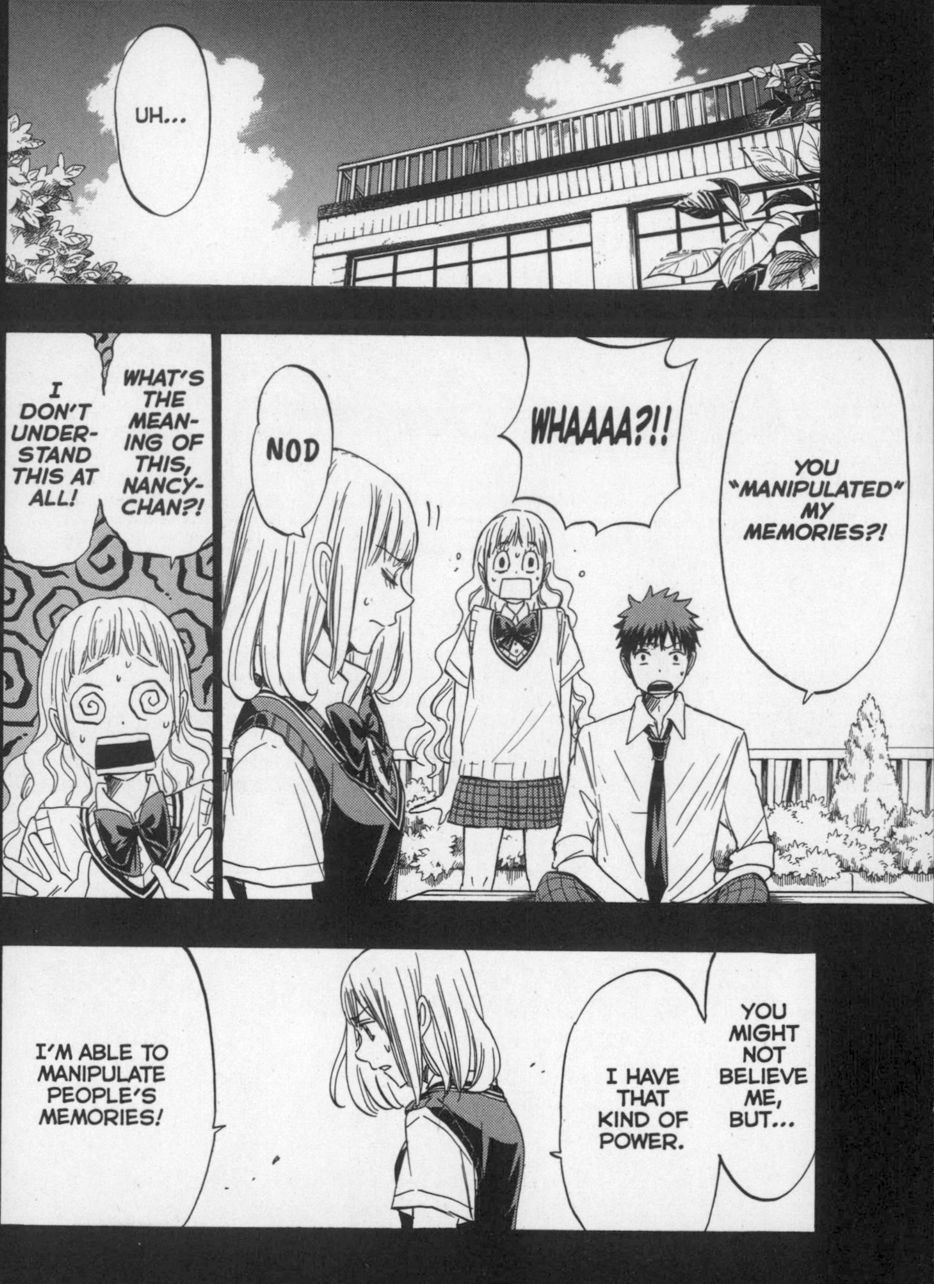
UH...
YOU "MANIPULATED" MY MEMORIES?!
WHAAAA?!!
NOD
WHAT'S THE MEANING OF THIS, NANCY-CHAN?!
I DON'T UNDER-STAND THIS AT ALL!
YOU MIGHT NOT BELIEVE ME, BUT...
I HAVE THAT KIND OF POWER.
I'M ABLE TO MANIPULATE PEOPLE'S MEMORIES!

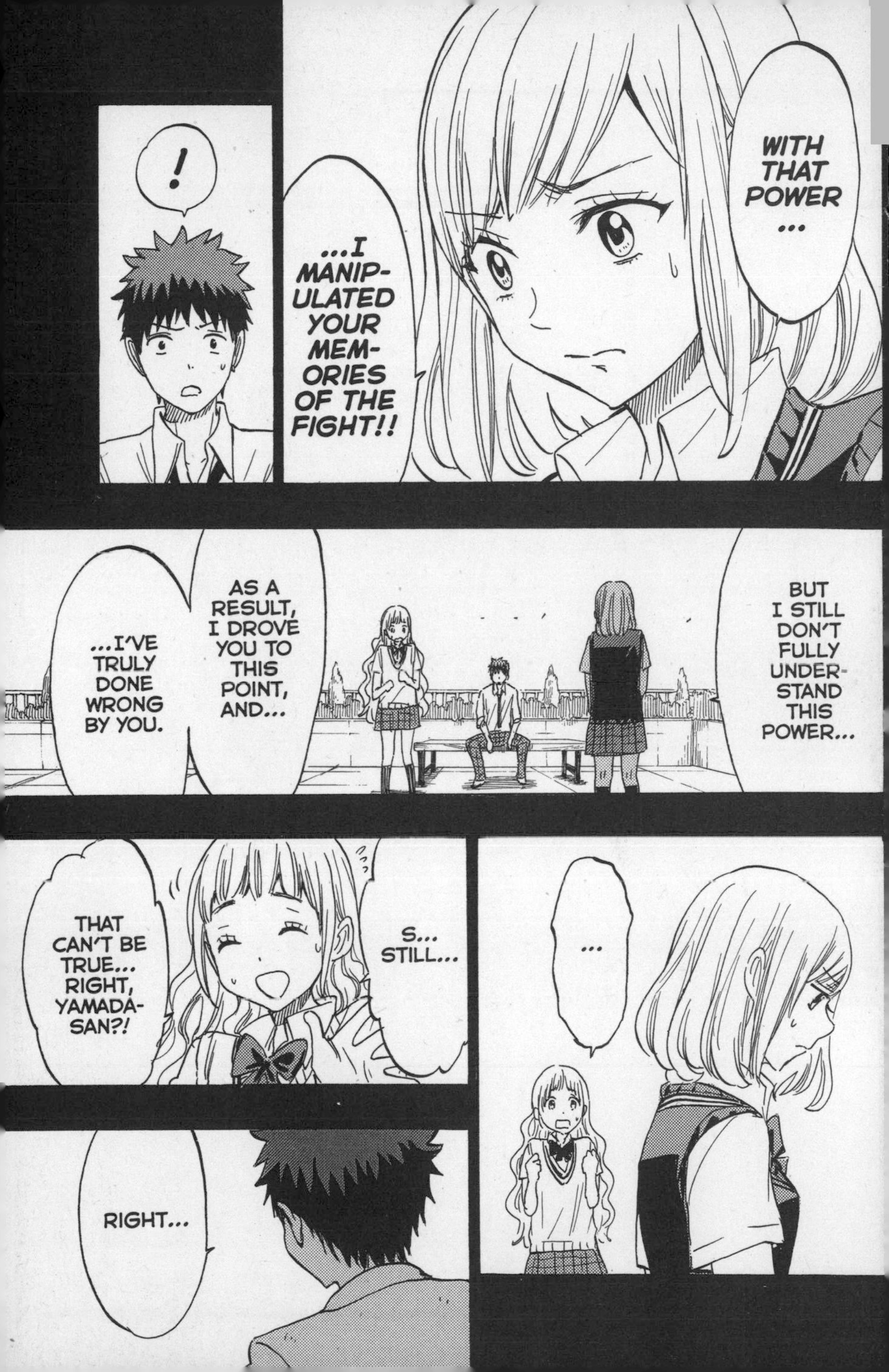
WITH THAT POWER...
...I MANIPULATED YOUR MEMORIES OF THE FIGHT!!
!
BUT I STILL DON'T FULLY UNDERSTAND THIS POWER...
AS A RESULT, I DROVE YOU TO THIS POINT, AND...
...I'VE TRULY DONE WRONG BY YOU.
...
S... STILL...
THAT CAN'T BE TRUE... RIGHT, YAMADA-SAN?!
RIGHT...

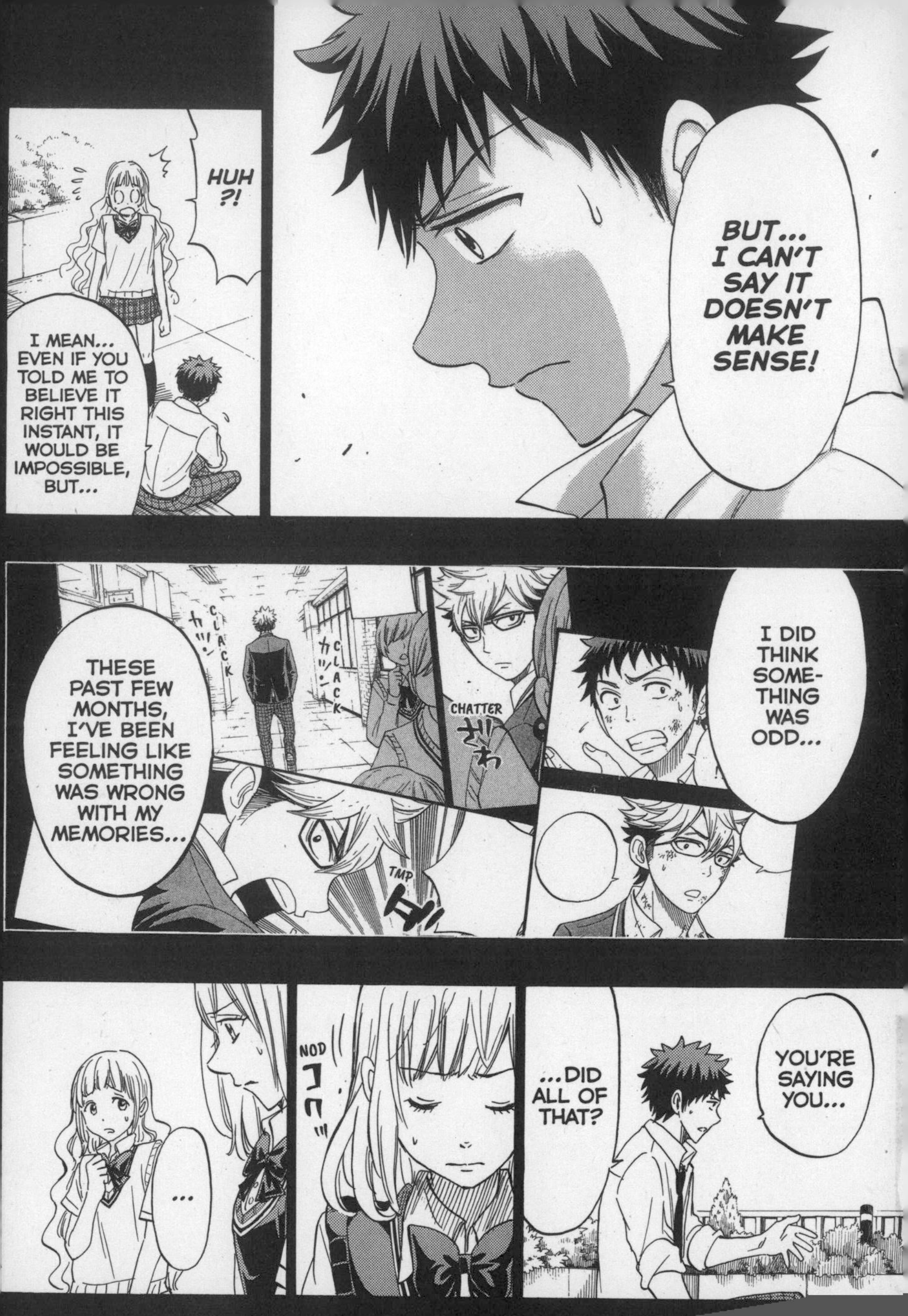
BUT... I CAN'T SAY IT DOESN'T MAKE SENSE!
HUH ?!
I MEAN... EVEN IF YOU TOLD ME TO BELIEVE IT RIGHT THIS INSTANT, IT WOULD BE IMPOSSIBLE, BUT...
I DID THINK SOME-THING WAS ODD...
CHATTER
CLACK
CLACK
THESE PAST FEW MONTHS, I'VE BEEN FEELING LIKE SOMETHING WAS WRONG WITH MY MEMORIES...
TMP
YOU'RE SAYING YOU...
...DID ALL OF THAT?
NOD
...

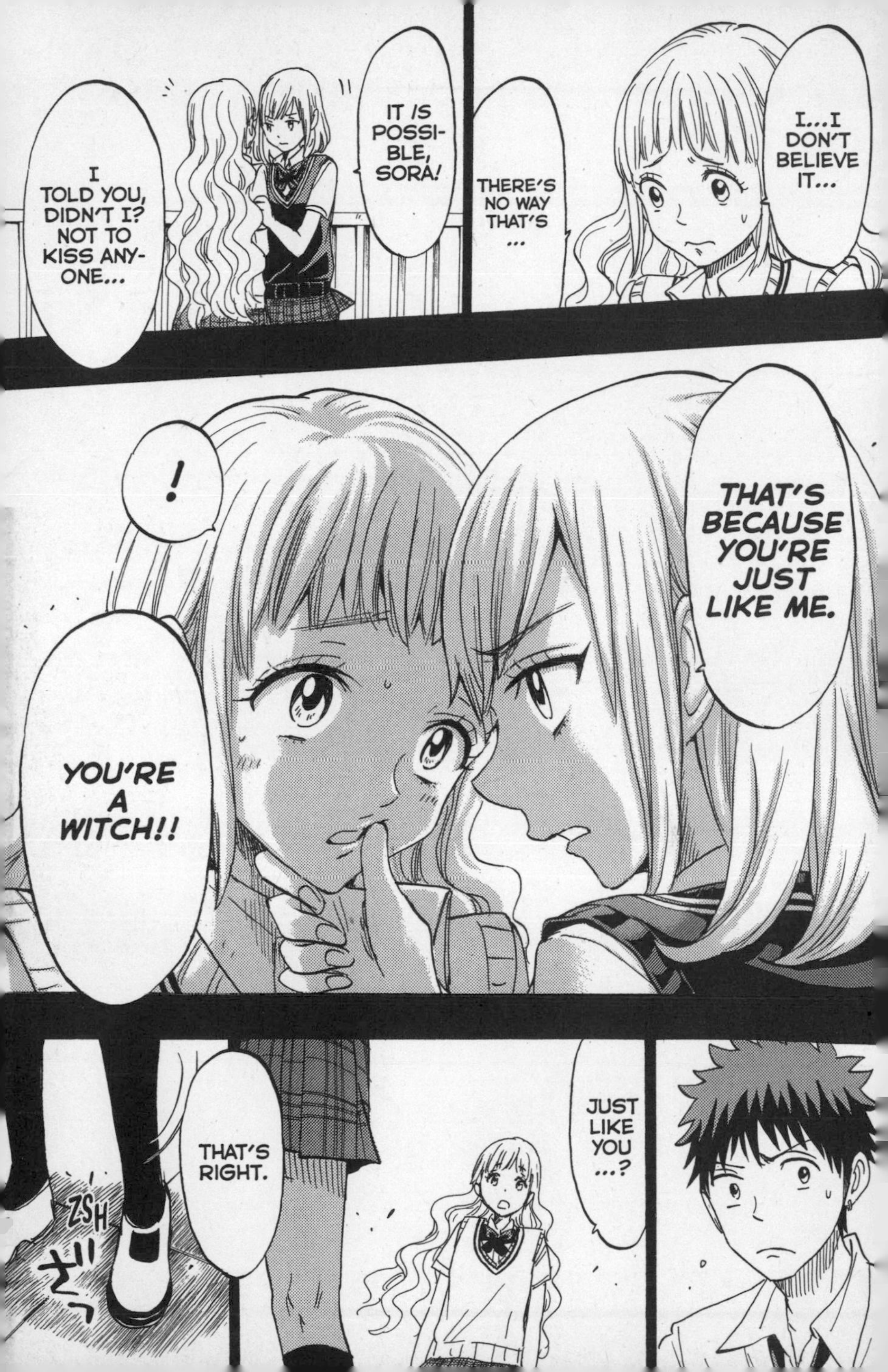
I...I DON'T BELIEVE IT...
THERE'S NO WAY THAT'S ...
IT IS POSSIBLE, SORA!
I TOLD YOU, DIDN'T I? NOT TO KISS ANYONE...
THAT'S BECAUSE YOU'RE JUST LIKE ME.
!
YOU'RE A WITCH!!
JUST LIKE YOU ...?
THAT'S RIGHT.
ZSH
ざっ

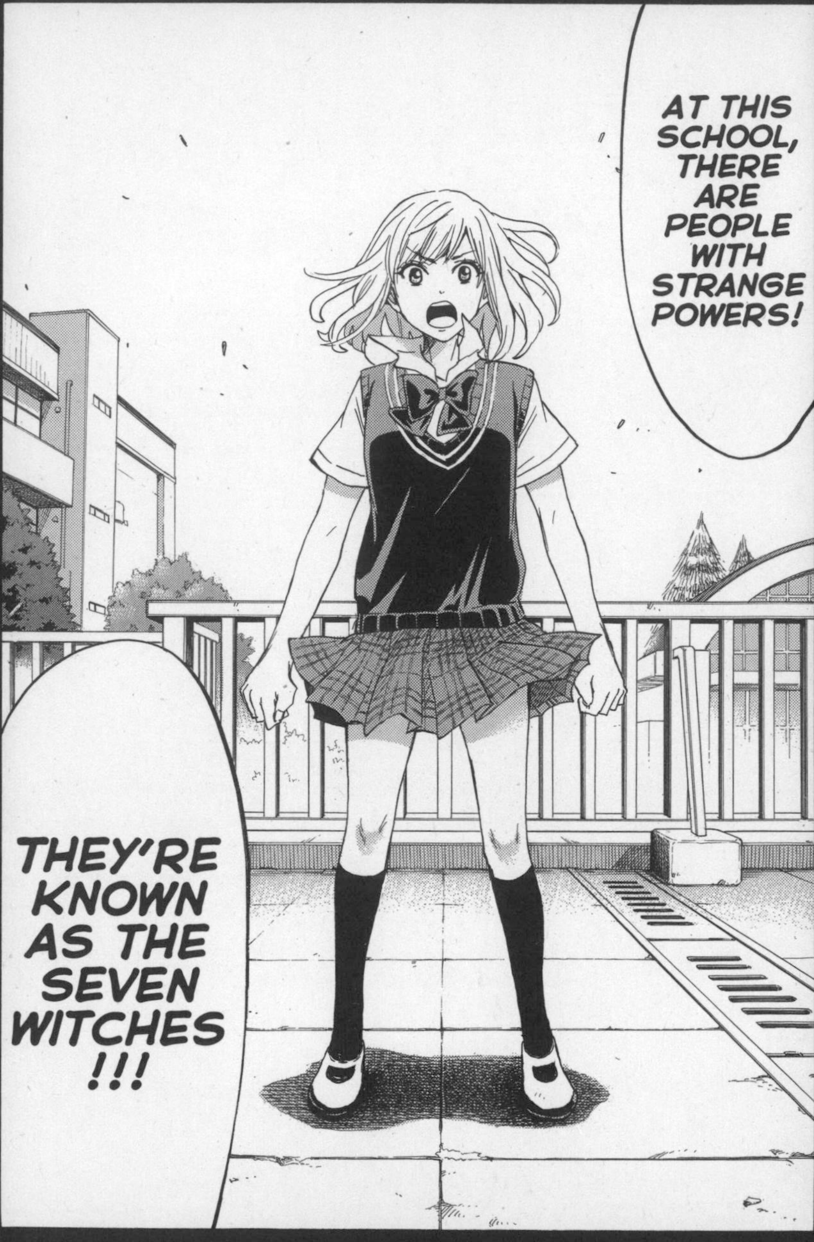
AT THIS SCHOOL, THERE ARE PEOPLE WITH STRANGE POWERS!
THEY'RE KNOWN AS THE SEVEN WITCHES!!!

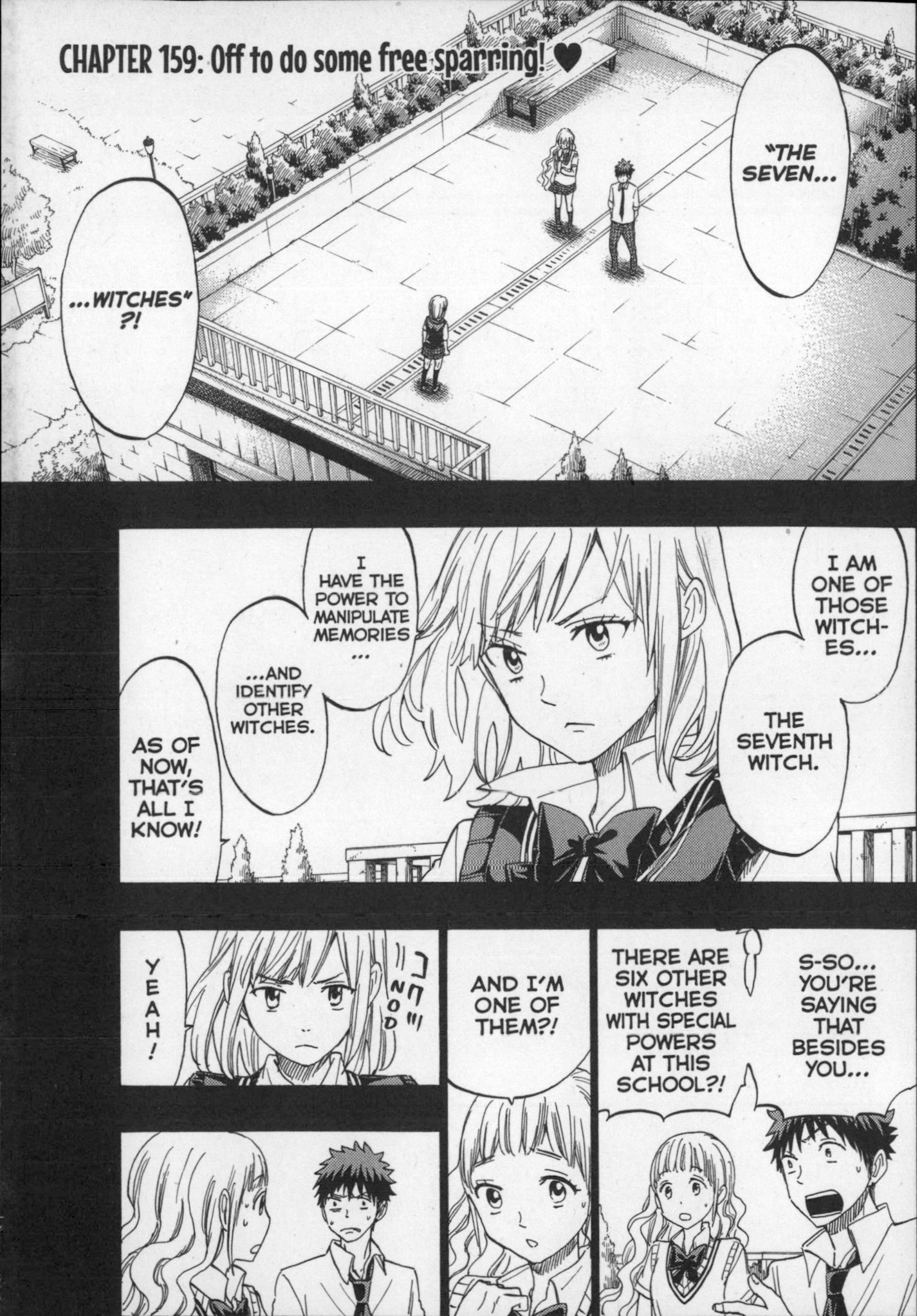
CHAPTER 159: Off to do some free sparring! ♥
"THE SEVEN...
...WITCHES" ?!
I AM ONE OF THOSE WITCHES...
THE SEVENTH WITCH.
I HAVE THE POWER TO MANIPULATE MEMORIES...
...AND IDENTIFY OTHER WITCHES.
AS OF NOW, THAT'S ALL I KNOW!
S-SO... YOU'RE SAYING THAT BESIDES YOU...
THERE ARE SIX OTHER WITCHES WITH SPECIAL POWERS AT THIS SCHOOL?!
AND I'M ONE OF THEM?!
NOD
YEAH!

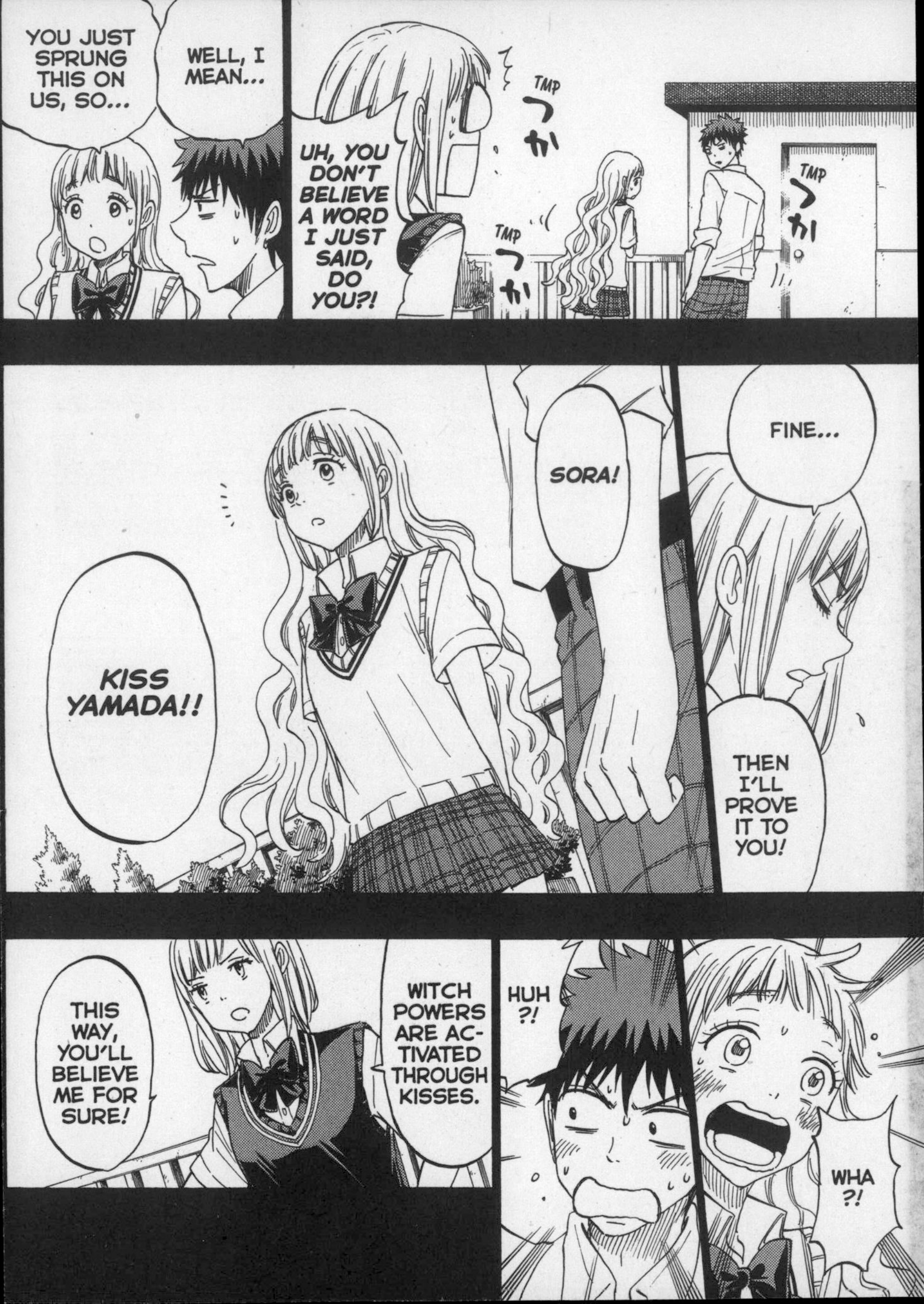
TMP
つか
TMP
つか
TMP
つか
UH, YOU DON'T BELIEVE A WORD I JUST SAID, DO YOU?!
WELL, I MEAN...
YOU JUST SPRUNG THIS ON US, SO...
FINE...
THEN I'LL PROVE IT TO YOU!
SORA!
KISS YAMADA!!
HUH ?!
WHA ?!
WITCH POWERS ARE ACTIVATED THROUGH KISSES.
THIS WAY, YOU'LL BELIEVE ME FOR SURE!

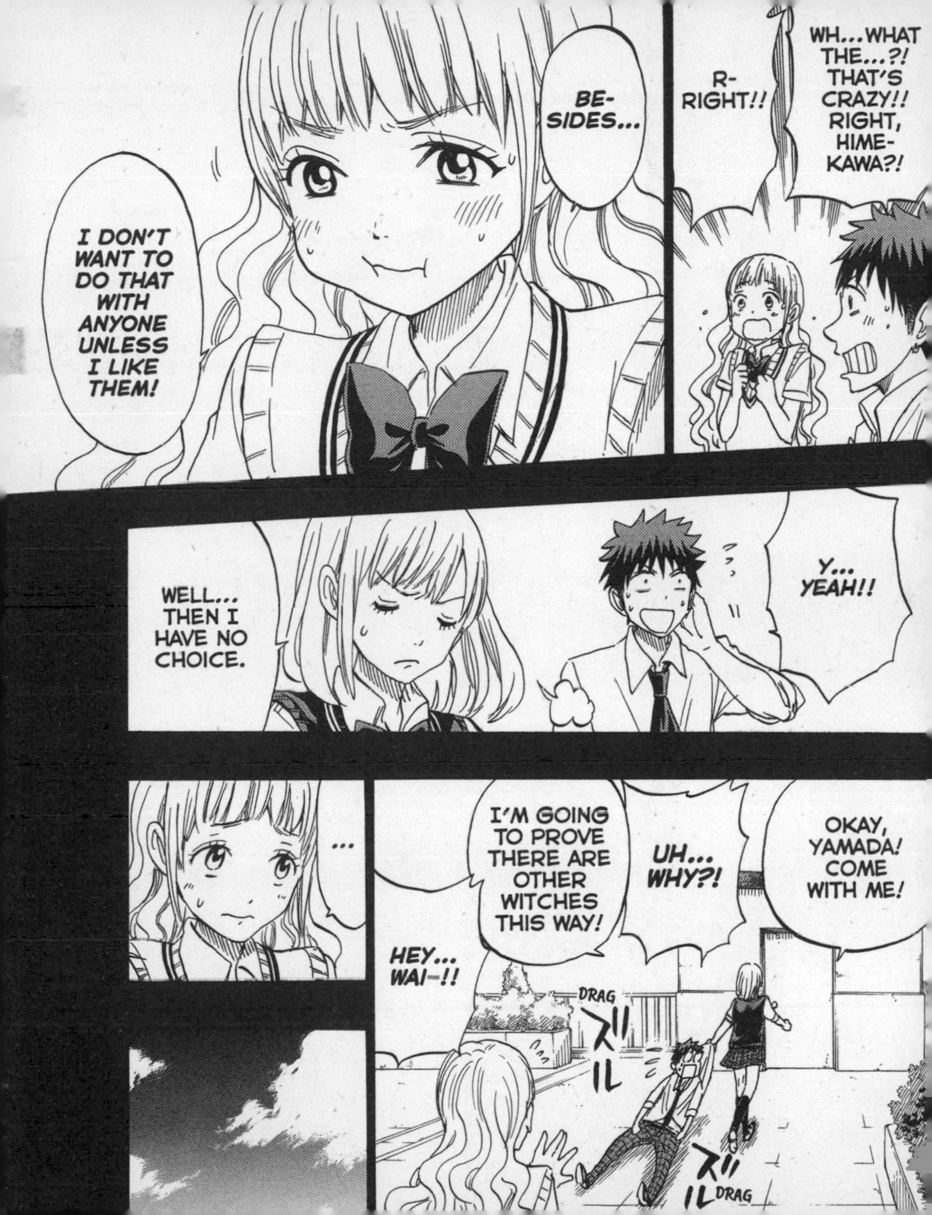
WH...WHAT THE...?! THAT'S CRAZY!! RIGHT, HIME-KAWA?!
R-RIGHT!!
BE-SIDES...
I DON'T WANT TO DO THAT WITH ANYONE UNLESS I LIKE THEM!
Y... YEAH!!
WELL... THEN I HAVE NO CHOICE.
OKAY, YAMADA! COME WITH ME!
UH... WHY?!
I'M GOING TO PROVE THERE ARE OTHER WITCHES THIS WAY!
HEY... WAI-!!
ズル
DRAG
ズル
DRAG
...

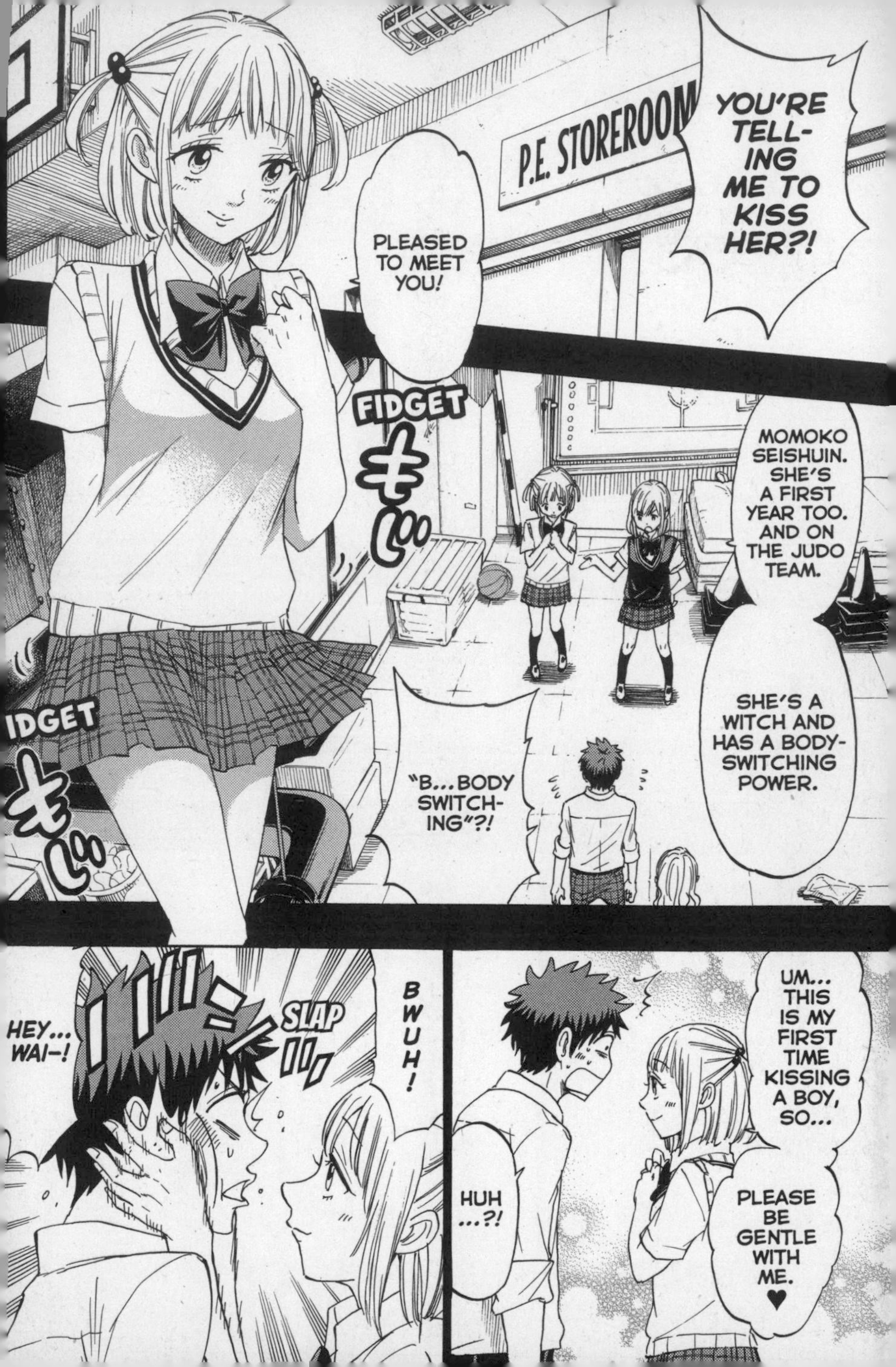
YOU'RE TELLING ME TO KISS HER?!
P.E. STOREROOM
MOMOKO SEISHUIN. SHE'S A FIRST YEAR TOO. AND ON THE JUDO TEAM.
SHE'S A WITCH AND HAS A BODY-SWITCHING POWER.
"B...BODY SWITCHING"?!
PLEASED TO MEET YOU!
FIDGET
もじ
IDGET
もじ
UM... THIS IS MY FIRST TIME KISSING A BOY, SO...
PLEASE BE GENTLE WITH ME. ♥
HUH ...?!
BWUH!
SLAP
HEY... WAI-!

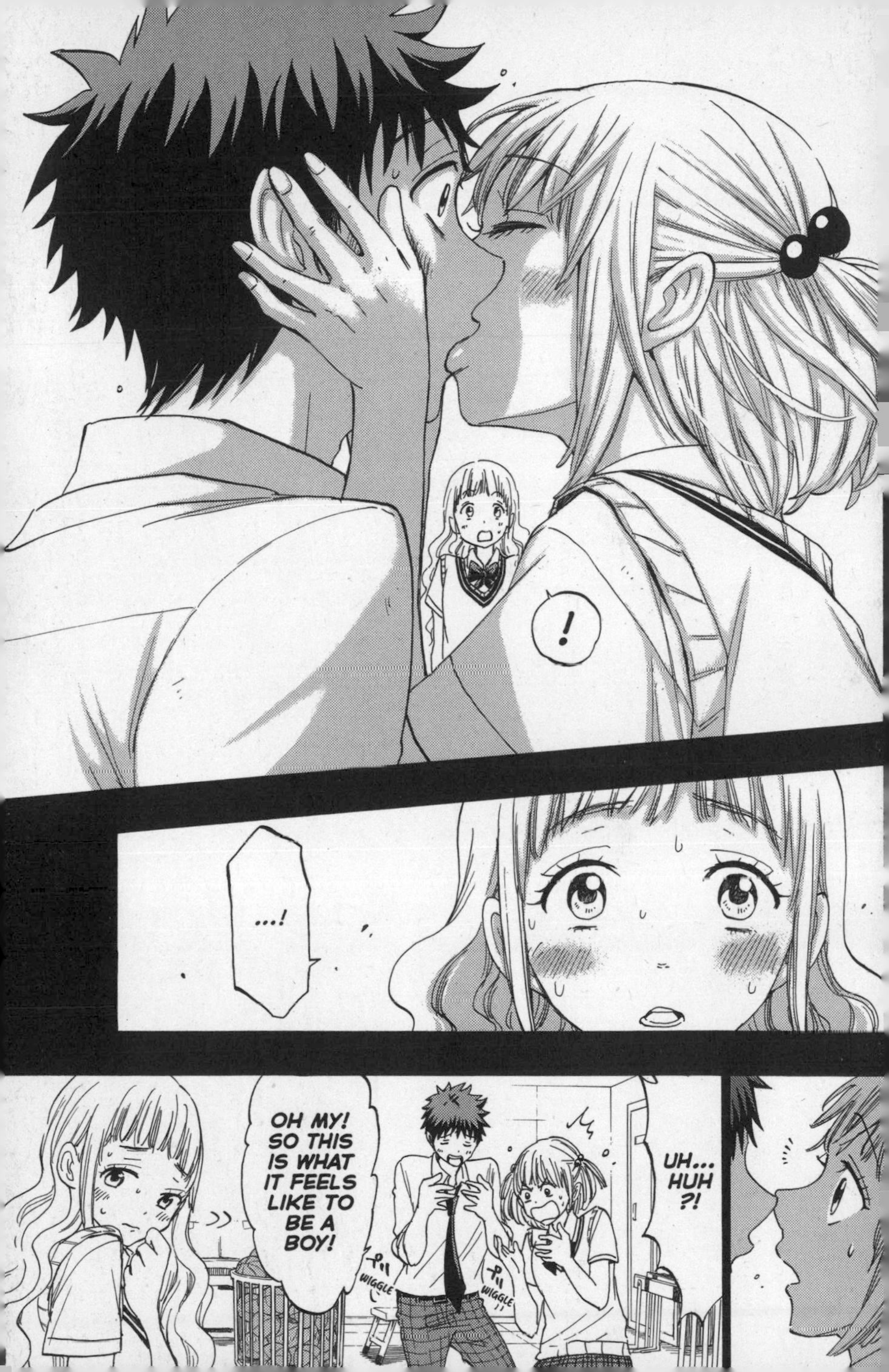
!
...!
UH... HUH ?!
OH MY! SO THIS IS WHAT IT FEELS LIKE TO BE A BOY!
WIGGLE
WIGGLE

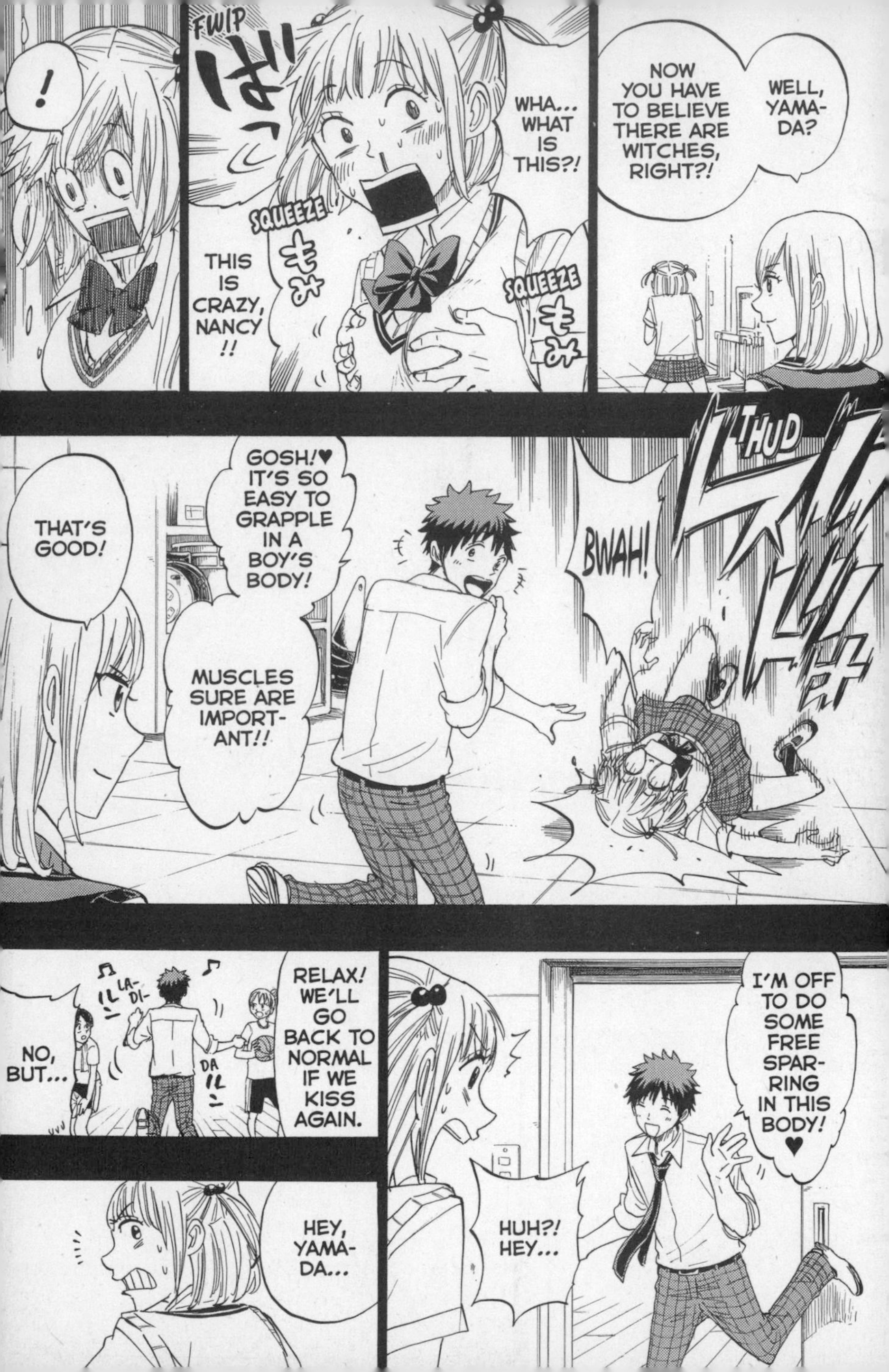

WELL, YAMA-DA?
NOW YOU HAVE TO BELIEVE THERE ARE WITCHES, RIGHT?!
FWIP
ぱっ
WHA... WHAT IS THIS?!
SQUEEZE
もみ
THIS IS CRAZY, NANCY!!
SQUEEZE
もみ
!
THUD
BWAH!
GOSH!♥ IT'S SO EASY TO GRAPPLE IN A BOY'S BODY!
MUSCLES SURE ARE IMPORTANT!!
THAT'S GOOD!
I'M OFF TO DO SOME FREE SPARRING IN THIS BODY! ♥
HUH?! HEY...
RELAX! WE'LL GO BACK TO NORMAL IF WE KISS AGAIN.
LA-DI-
DA
NO, BUT...
HEY, YAMA-DA...

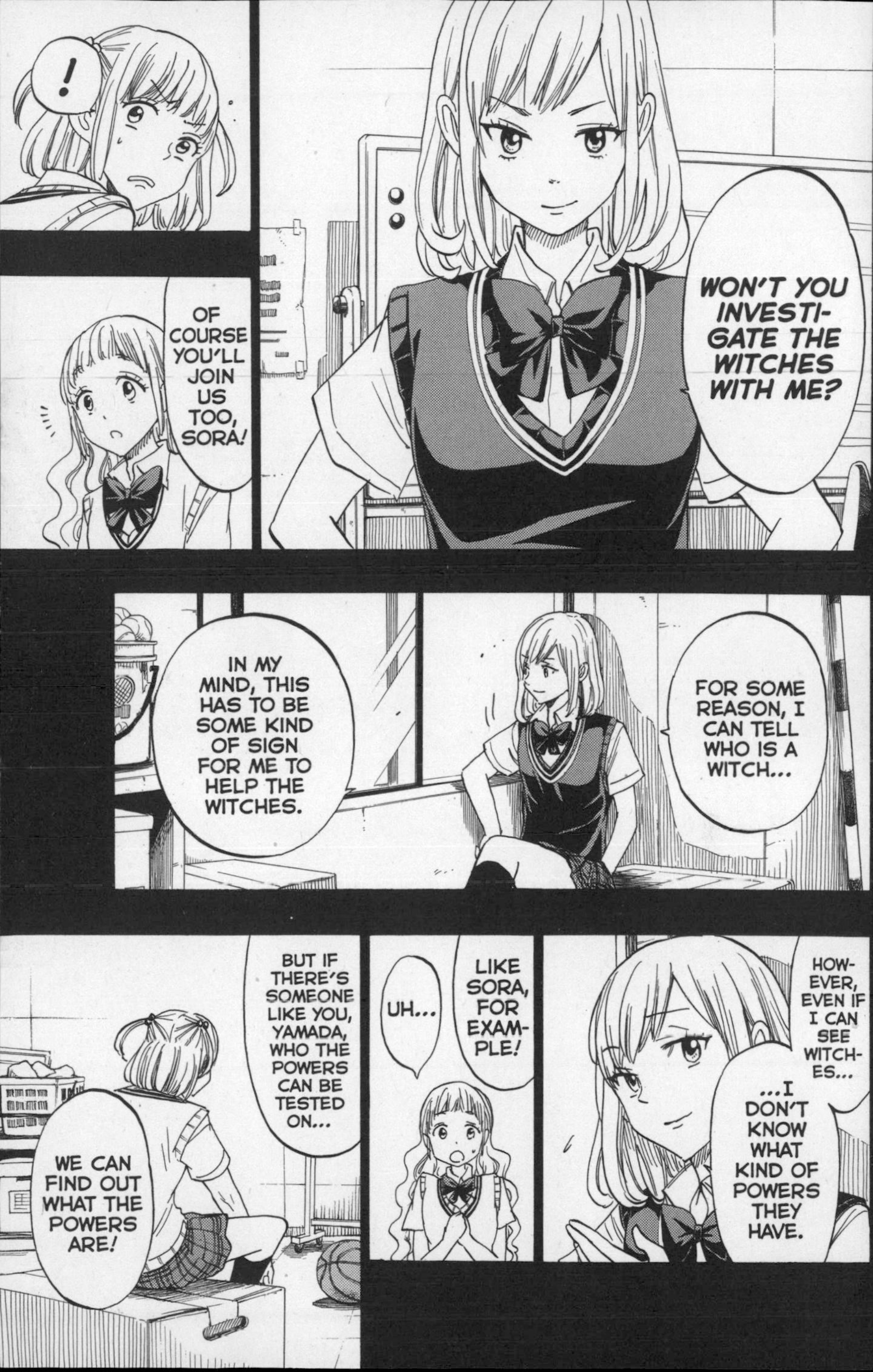
WON'T YOU INVESTI-GATE THE WITCHES WITH ME?
!
OF COURSE YOU'LL JOIN US TOO, SORA!
FOR SOME REASON, I CAN TELL WHO IS A WITCH...
IN MY MIND, THIS HAS TO BE SOME KIND OF SIGN FOR ME TO HELP THE WITCHES.
HOW-EVER, EVEN IF I CAN SEE WITCH-ES...
...I DON'T KNOW WHAT KIND OF POWERS THEY HAVE.
LIKE SORA, FOR EXAM-PLE!
UH...
BUT IF THERE'S SOMEONE LIKE YOU, YAMADA, WHO THE POWERS CAN BE TESTED ON...
WE CAN FIND OUT WHAT THE POWERS ARE!

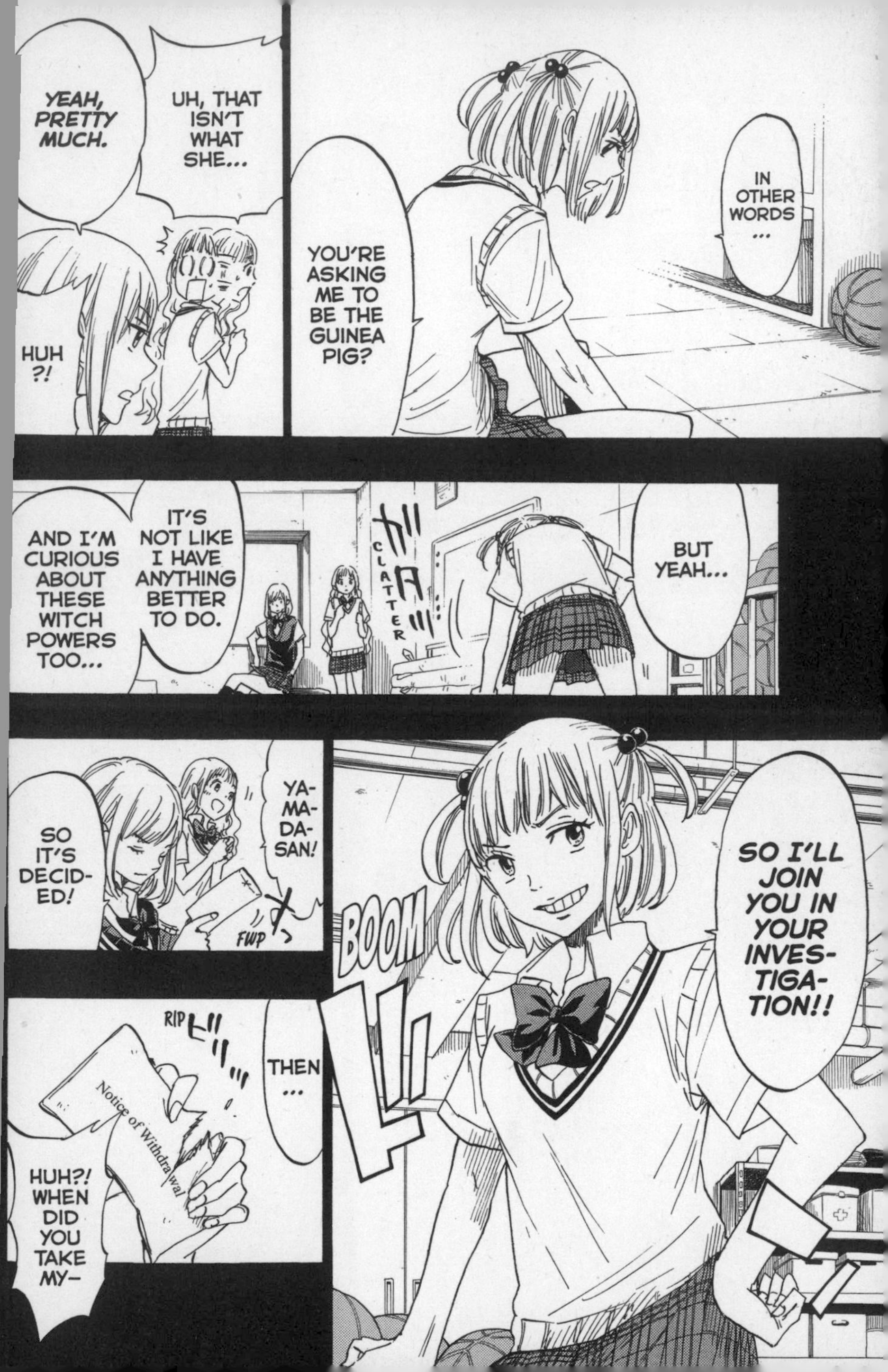
IN OTHER WORDS...
YOU'RE ASKING ME TO BE THE GUINEA PIG?
UH, THAT ISN'T WHAT SHE...
YEAH, PRETTY MUCH.
HUH?!
BUT YEAH...
CLATTER
IT'S NOT LIKE I HAVE ANYTHING BETTER TO DO.
AND I'M CURIOUS ABOUT THESE WITCH POWERS TOO...
SO I'LL JOIN YOU IN YOUR INVESTIGATION!!
BOOM
YAMADA-SAN!
SO IT'S DECIDED!
FWP
THEN...
RIP
Notice of Withdrawal
HUH?! WHEN DID YOU TAKE MY—

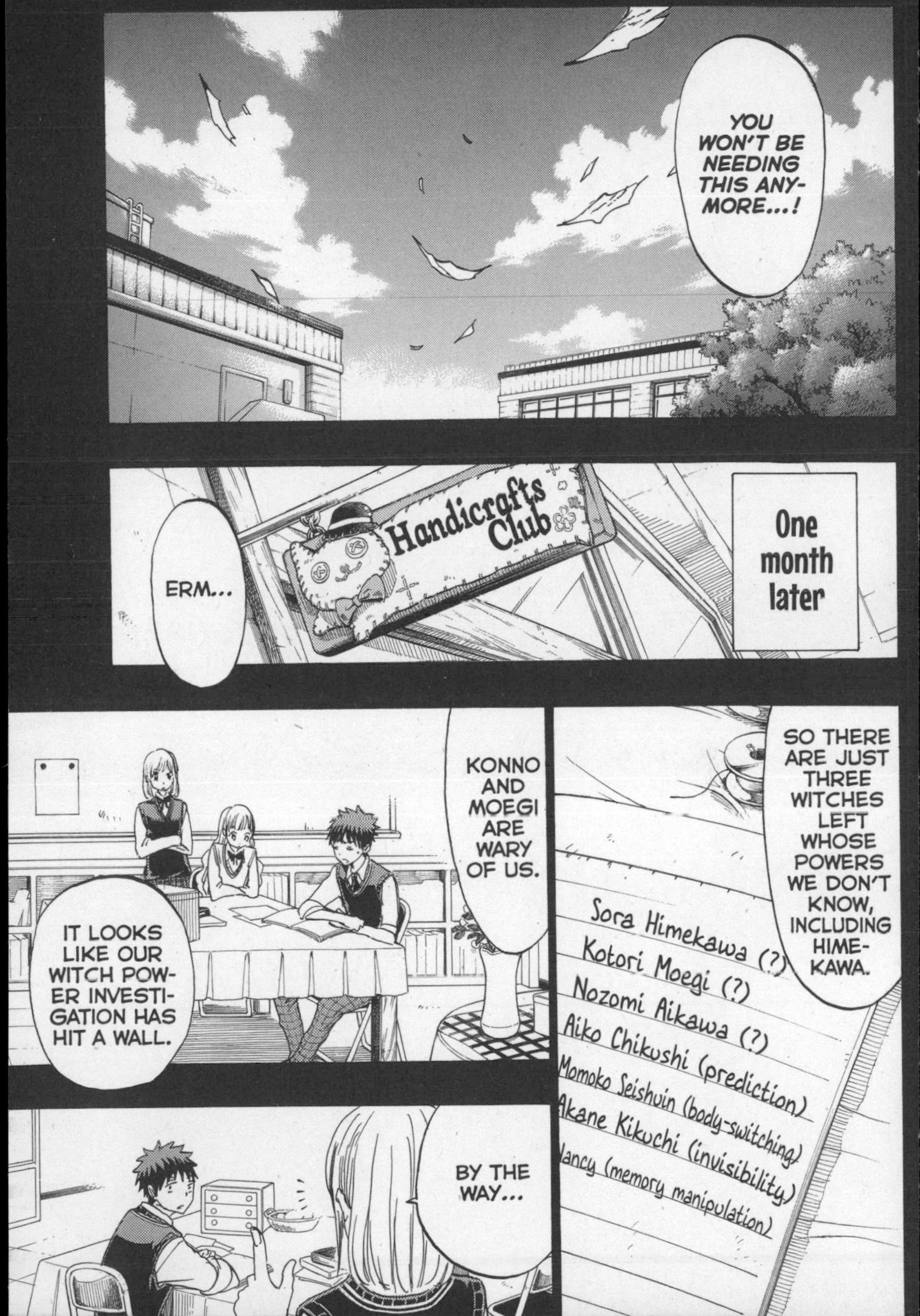

YOU WON'T BE NEEDING THIS ANY-MORE...!
One month later
Handicrafts Club
ERM...
SO THERE ARE JUST THREE WITCHES LEFT WHOSE POWERS WE DON'T KNOW, INCLUDING HIME-KAWA.
Sora Himekawa (?)
Kotori Moegi (?)
Nozomi Aikawa (?)
Aiko Chikushi (prediction)
Momoko Seishuin (body-switching
Akane Kikuchi (invisibility)
ancy (memory manipulation)
KONNO AND MOEGI ARE WARY OF US.
IT LOOKS LIKE OUR WITCH POW-ER INVESTI-GATION HAS HIT A WALL.
BY THE WAY...

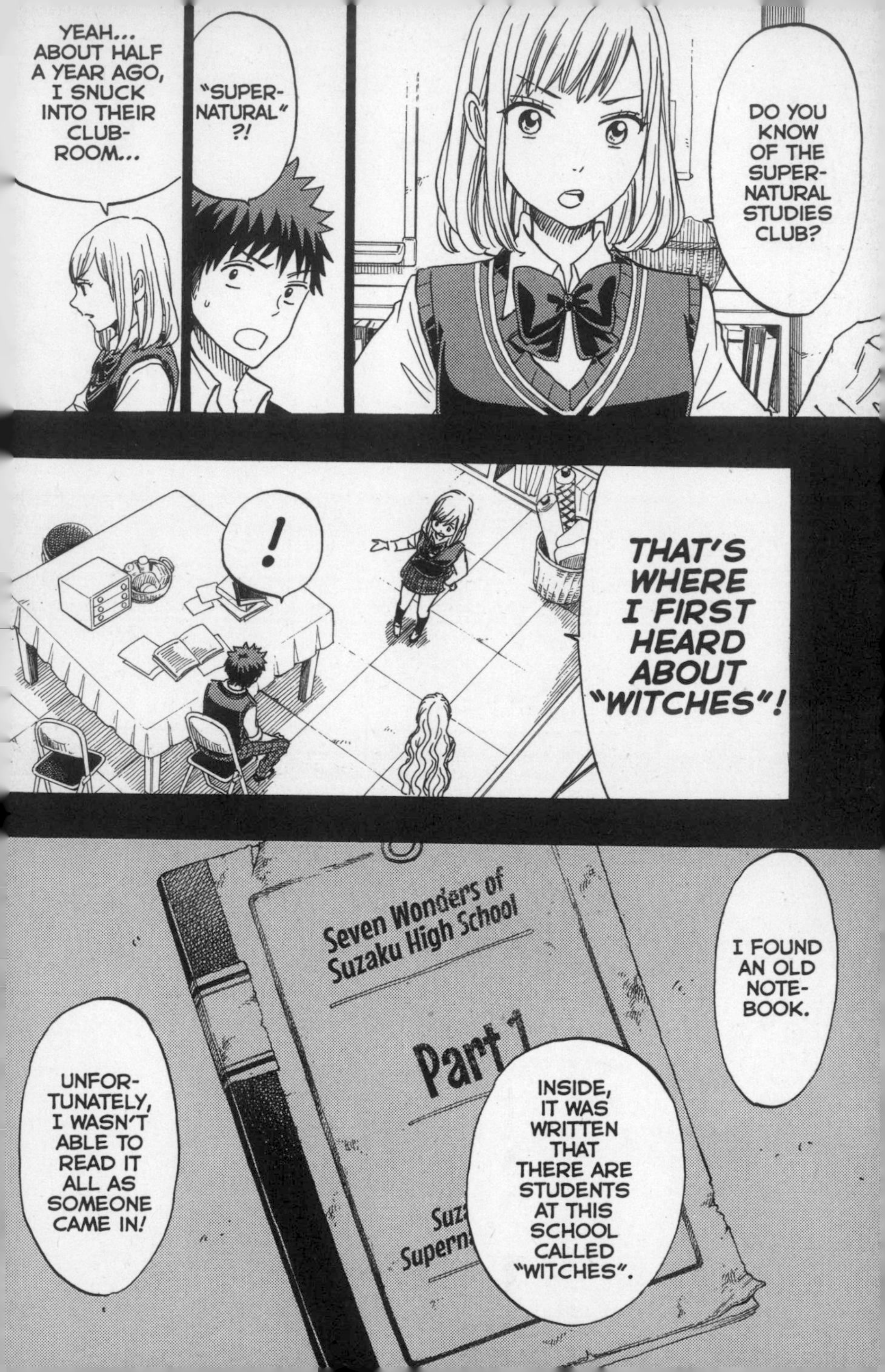
DO YOU KNOW OF THE SUPER-NATURAL STUDIES CLUB?
"SUPER-NATURAL"?!
YEAH... ABOUT HALF A YEAR AGO, I SNUCK INTO THEIR CLUB-ROOM...
THAT'S WHERE I FIRST HEARD ABOUT "WITCHES"!
!
I FOUND AN OLD NOTE-BOOK.
Seven Wonders of Suzaku High School
Part 1
INSIDE, IT WAS WRITTEN THAT THERE ARE STUDENTS AT THIS SCHOOL CALLED "WITCHES".
UNFORTUNATELY, I WASN'T ABLE TO READ IT ALL AS SOMEONE CAME IN!

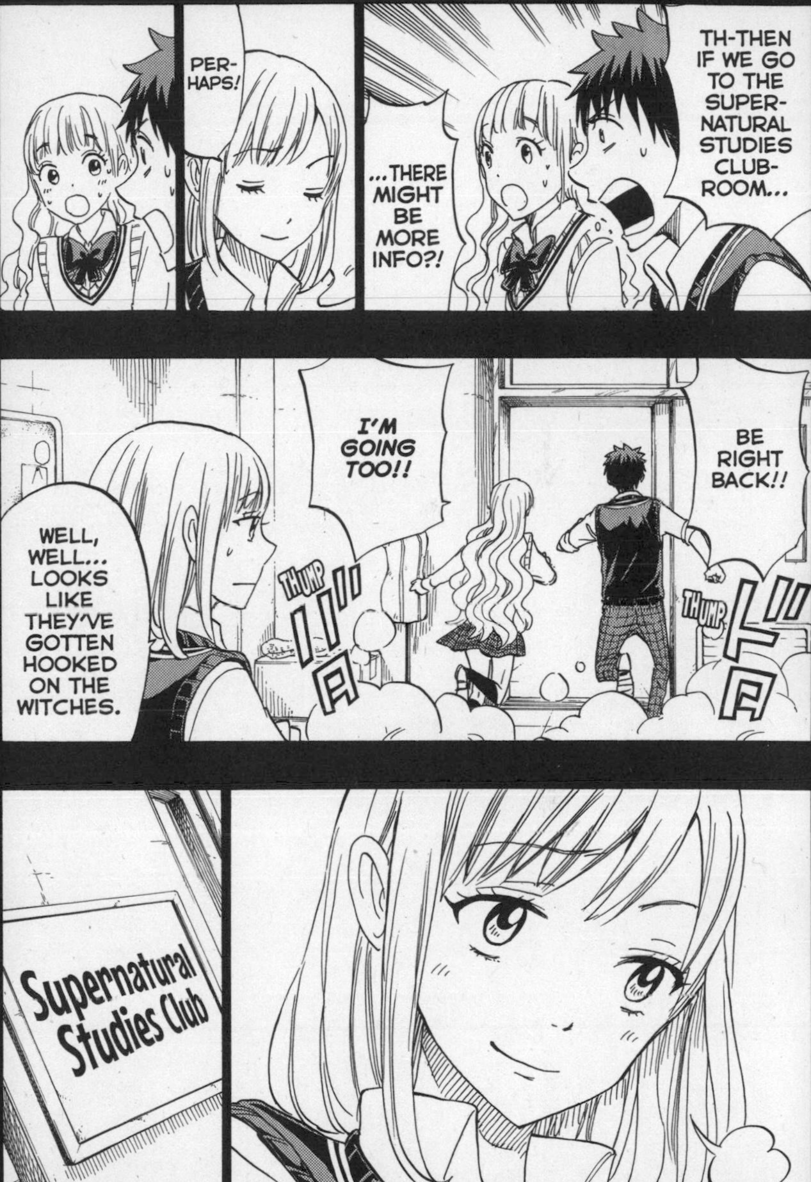
TH-THEN IF WE GO TO THE SUPER-NATURAL STUDIES CLUB-ROOM...
...THERE MIGHT BE MORE INFO?!
PER-HAPS!
BE RIGHT BACK!!
THUMP
I'M GOING TOO!!
THUMP
WELL, WELL... LOOKS LIKE THEY'VE GOTTEN HOOKED ON THE WITCHES.
Supernatural Studies Club

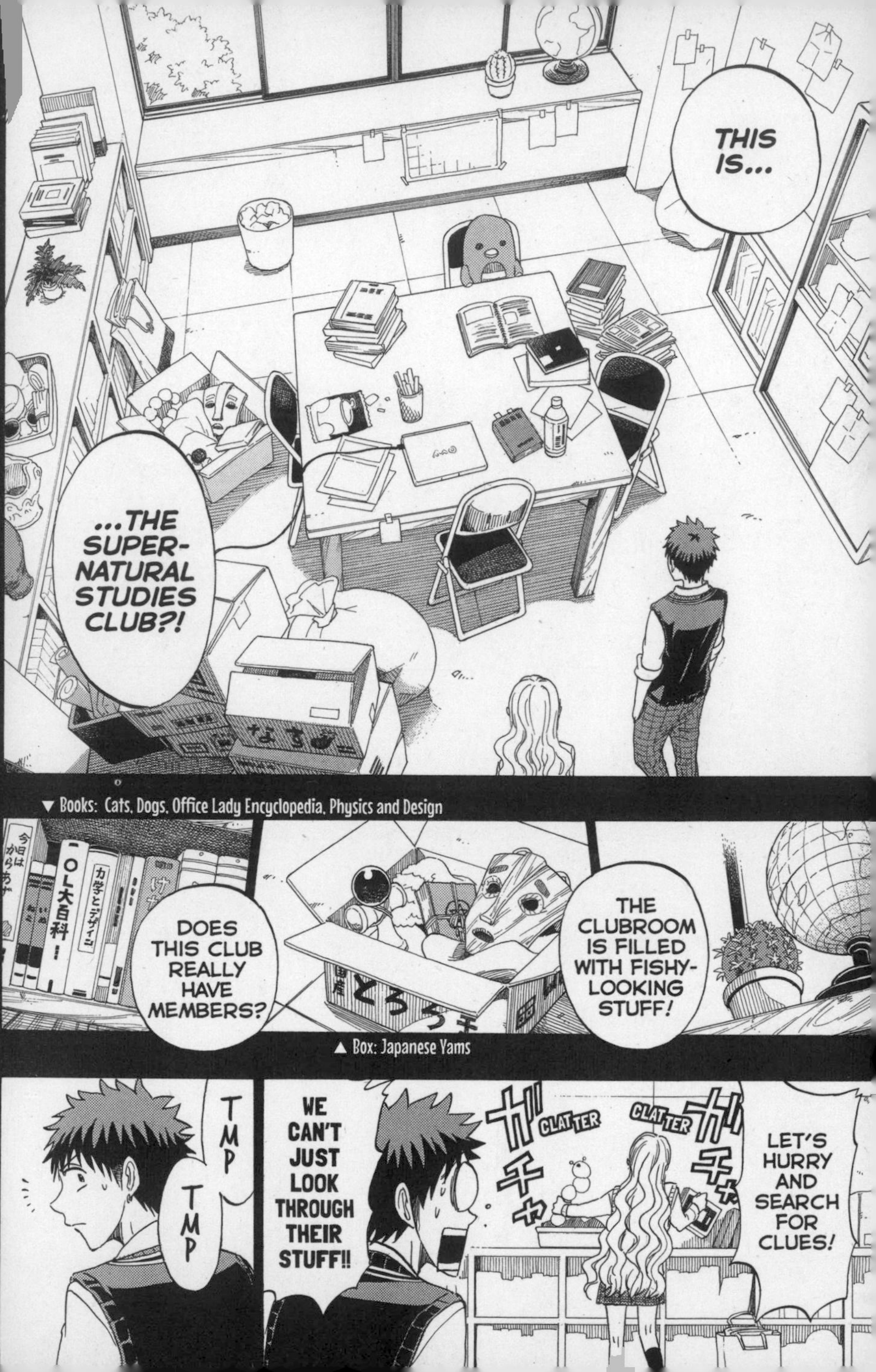
THIS IS...
...THE SUPER-NATURAL STUDIES CLUB?!
▼ Books: Cats, Dogs, Office Lady Encyclopedia, Physics and Design
THE CLUBROOM IS FILLED WITH FISHY-LOOKING STUFF!
DOES THIS CLUB REALLY HAVE MEMBERS?
▲ Box: Japanese Yams
LET'S HURRY AND SEARCH FOR CLUES!
CLATTER
CLATTER
WE CAN'T JUST LOOK THROUGH THEIR STUFF!!
TMP
TMP

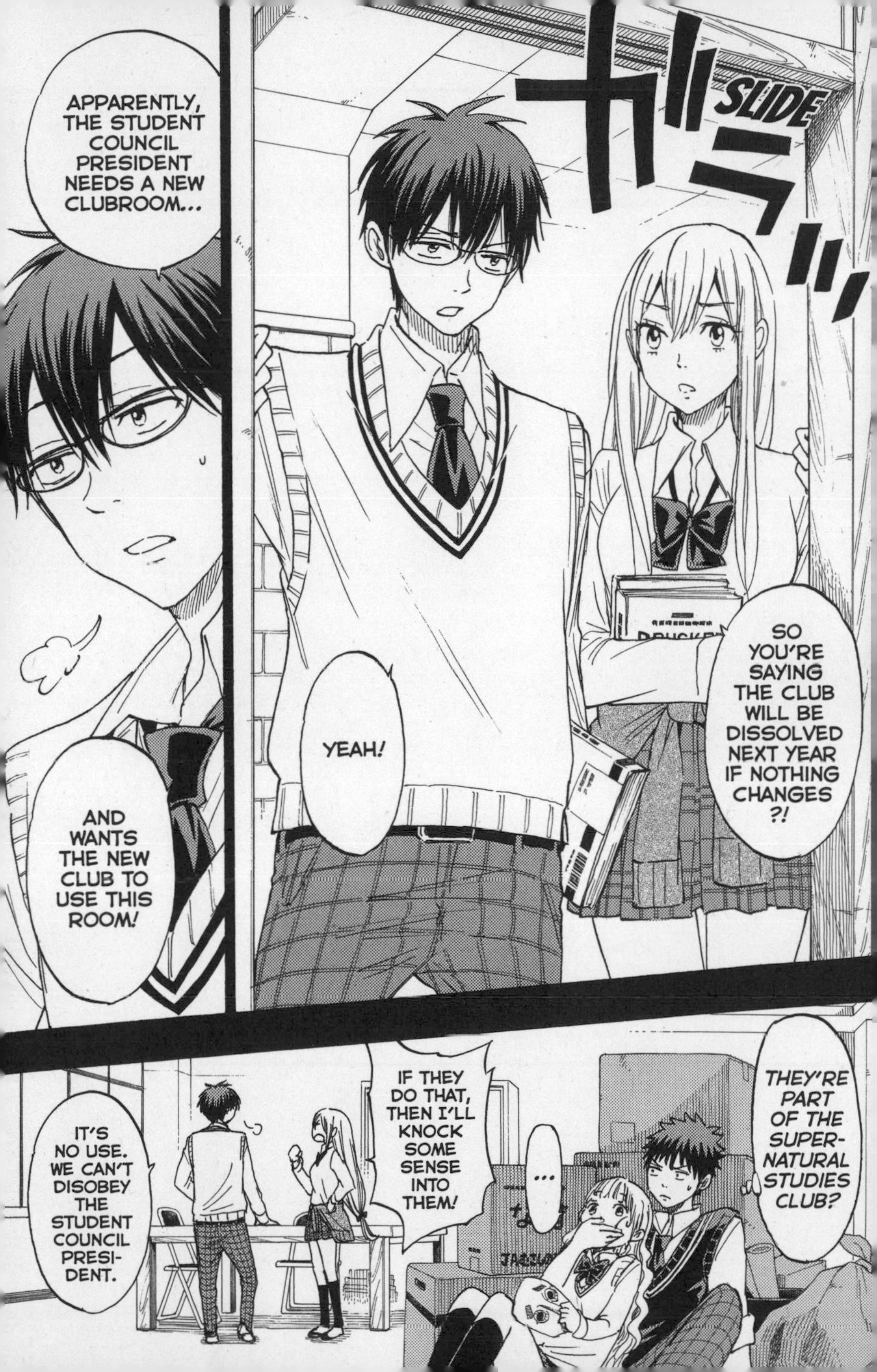
SLIDE
SO YOU'RE SAYING THE CLUB WILL BE DISSOLVED NEXT YEAR IF NOTHING CHANGES?!
YEAH!
APPARENTLY, THE STUDENT COUNCIL PRESIDENT NEEDS A NEW CLUBROOM...
AND WANTS THE NEW CLUB TO USE THIS ROOM!
THEY'RE PART OF THE SUPER-NATURAL STUDIES CLUB?
...
IF THEY DO THAT, THEN I'LL KNOCK SOME SENSE INTO THEM!
IT'S NO USE. WE CAN'T DISOBEY THE STUDENT COUNCIL PRESI-DENT.

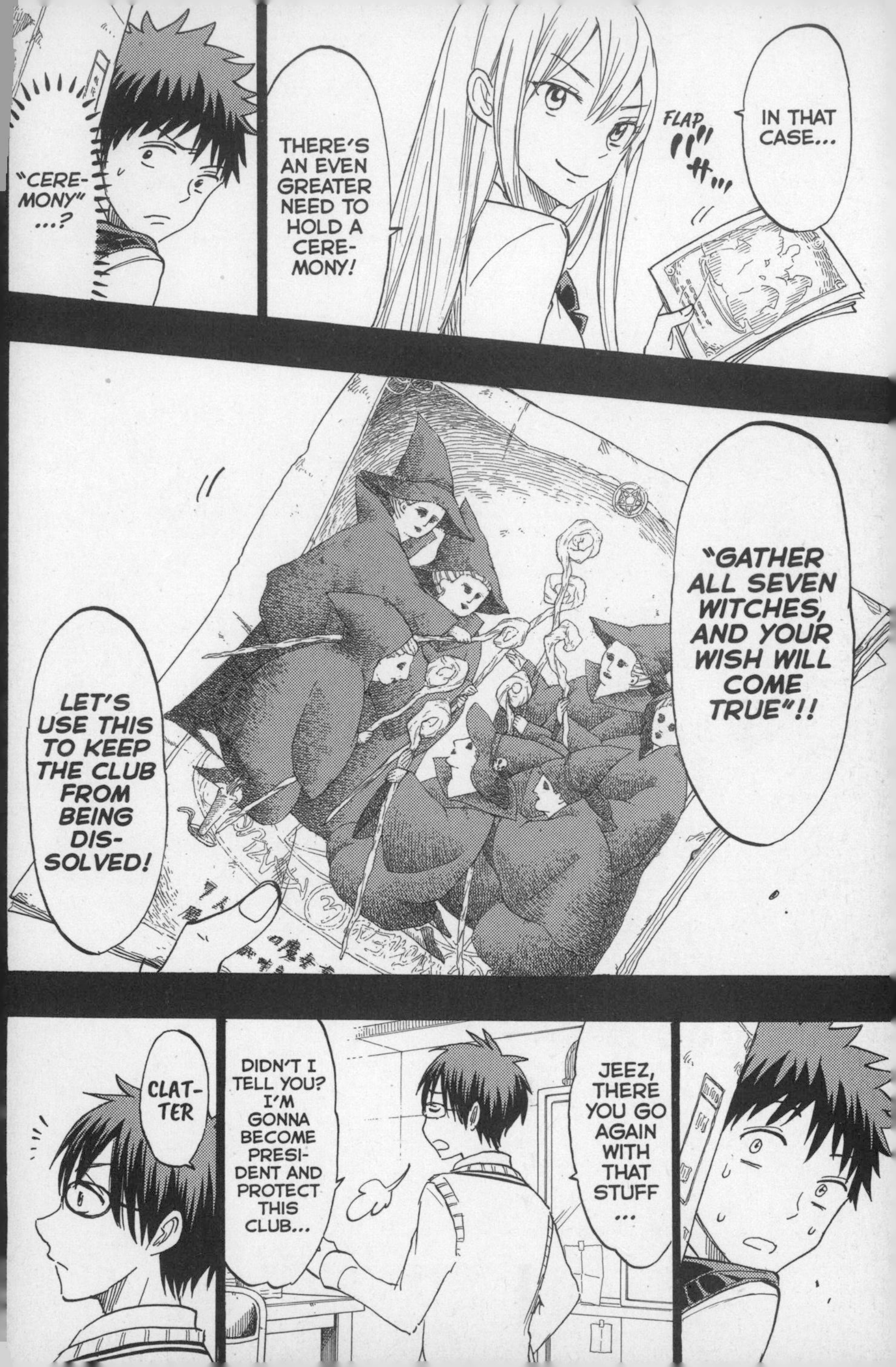
IN THAT CASE...
FLAP
THERE'S AN EVEN GREATER NEED TO HOLD A CERE-MONY!
"CERE-MONY"...?
"GATHER ALL SEVEN WITCHES, AND YOUR WISH WILL COME TRUE"!!
LET'S USE THIS TO KEEP THE CLUB FROM BEING DIS-SOLVED!
JEEZ, THERE YOU GO AGAIN WITH THAT STUFF...
DIDN'T I TELL YOU? I'M GONNA BECOME PRESI-DENT AND PROTECT THIS CLUB...
CLAT-TER

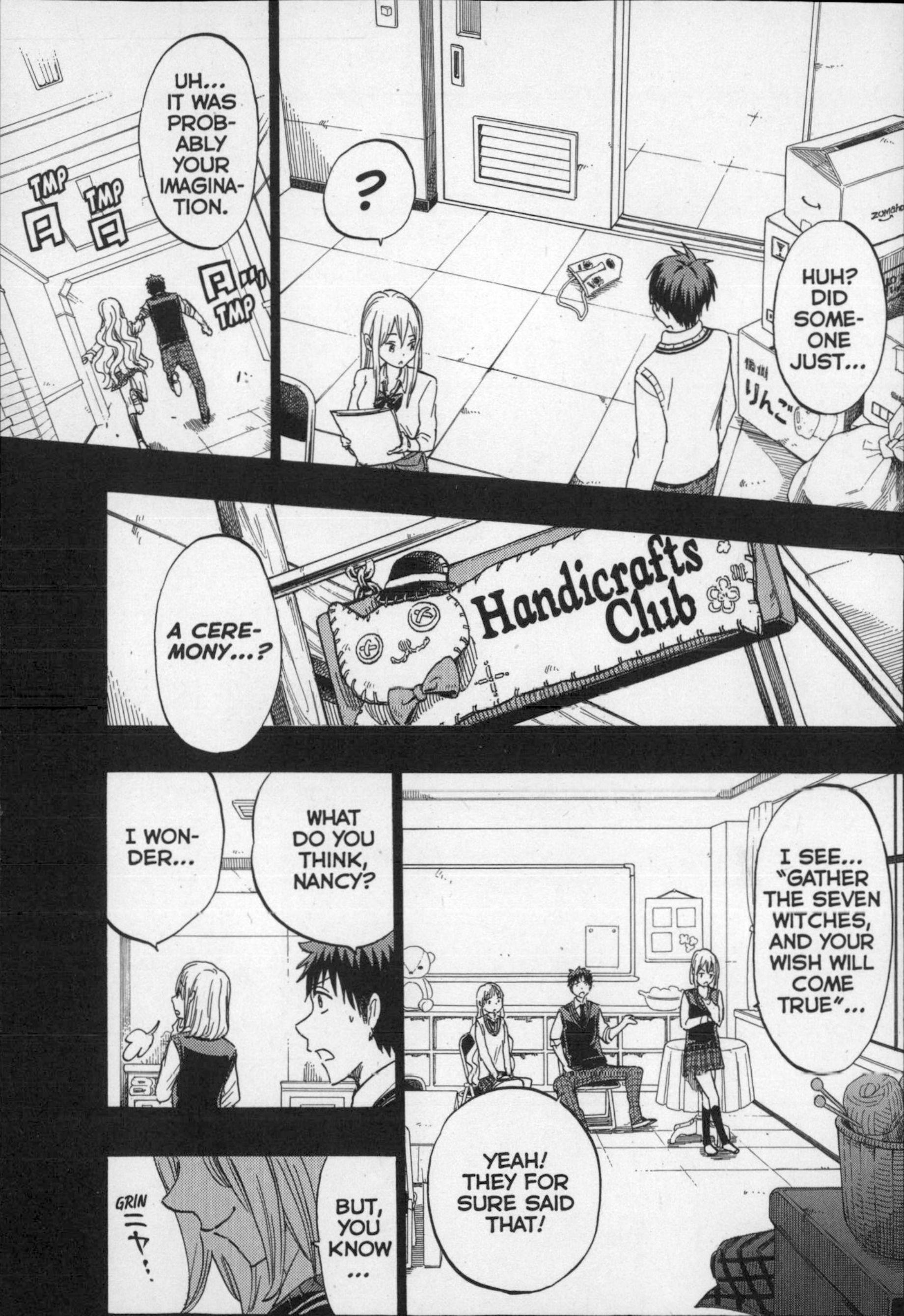
HUH? DID SOME-ONE JUST...
?
UH... IT WAS PROB-ABLY YOUR IMAGINA-TION.
TMP TMP TMP
Handicrafts Club
A CERE-MONY...?
I SEE... "GATHER THE SEVEN WITCHES, AND YOUR WISH WILL COME TRUE"...
YEAH! THEY FOR SURE SAID THAT!
WHAT DO YOU THINK, NANCY?
I WON-DER...
BUT, YOU KNOW ...
GRIN
ニヤ...

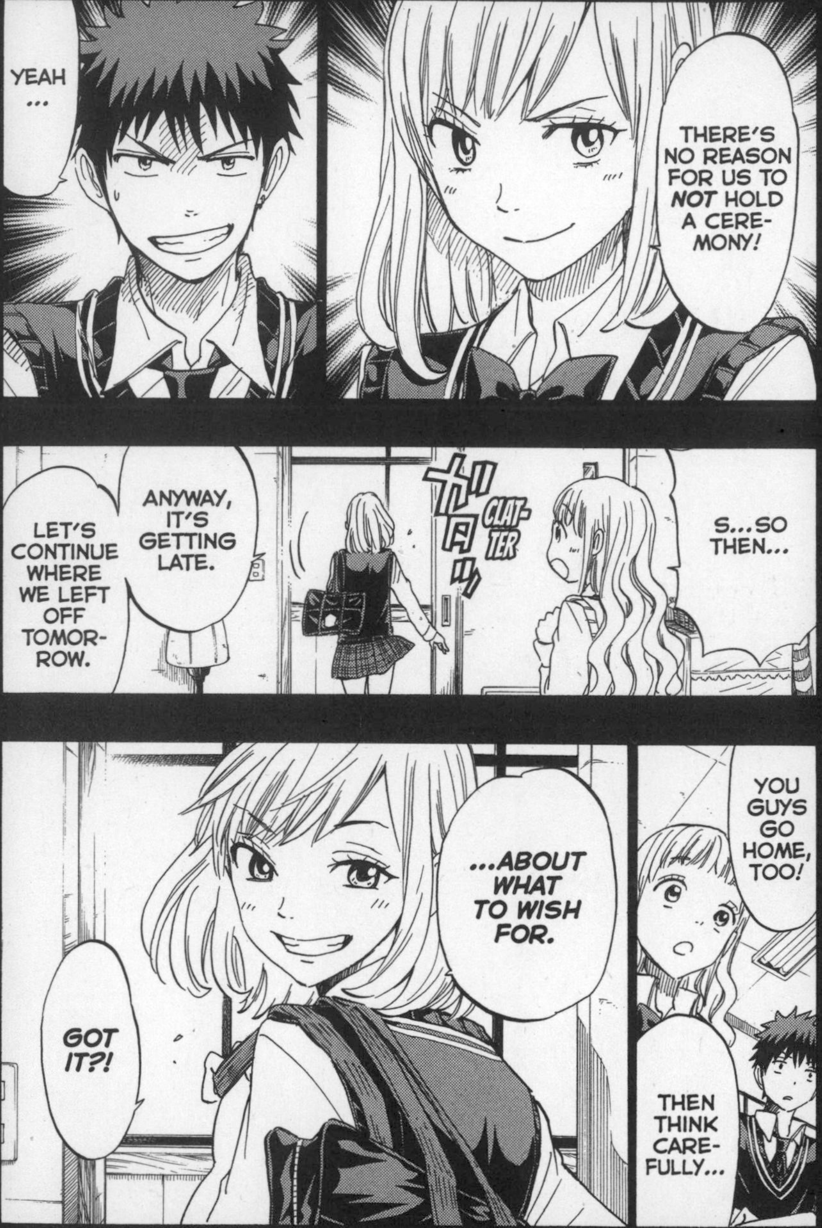
THERE'S NO REASON FOR US TO *NOT* HOLD A CEREMONY!
YEAH ...
S...SO THEN...
CLATTER
ANYWAY, IT'S GETTING LATE.
LET'S CONTINUE WHERE WE LEFT OFF TOMORROW.
YOU GUYS GO HOME, TOO!
THEN THINK CAREFULLY...
...ABOUT WHAT TO WISH FOR.
GOT IT?!

▼ Page titles: Magic, Witches, Fortune telling, Ceremonies

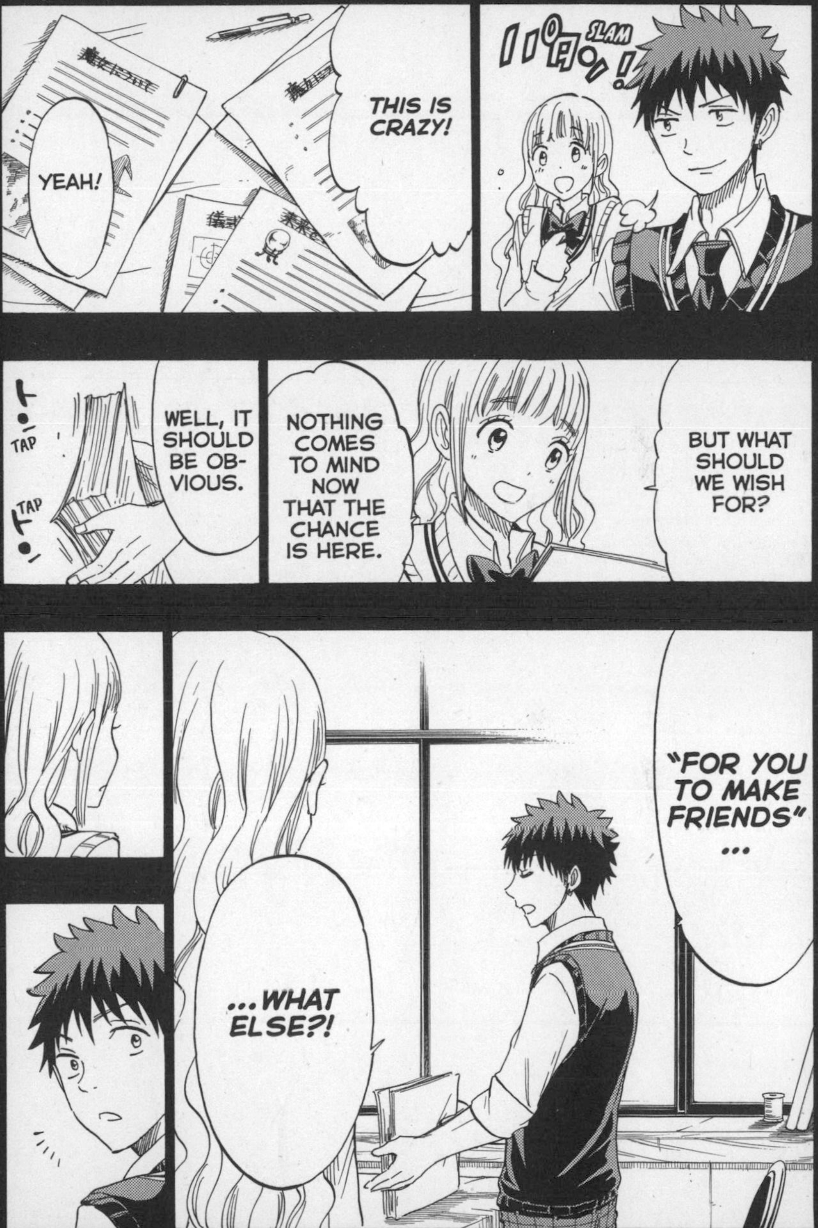
SLAM
THIS IS CRAZY!
YEAH!
BUT WHAT SHOULD WE WISH FOR?
NOTHING COMES TO MIND NOW THAT THE CHANCE IS HERE.
WELL, IT SHOULD BE OBVIOUS.
TAP
TAP
"FOR YOU TO MAKE FRIENDS" ...
...WHAT ELSE?!

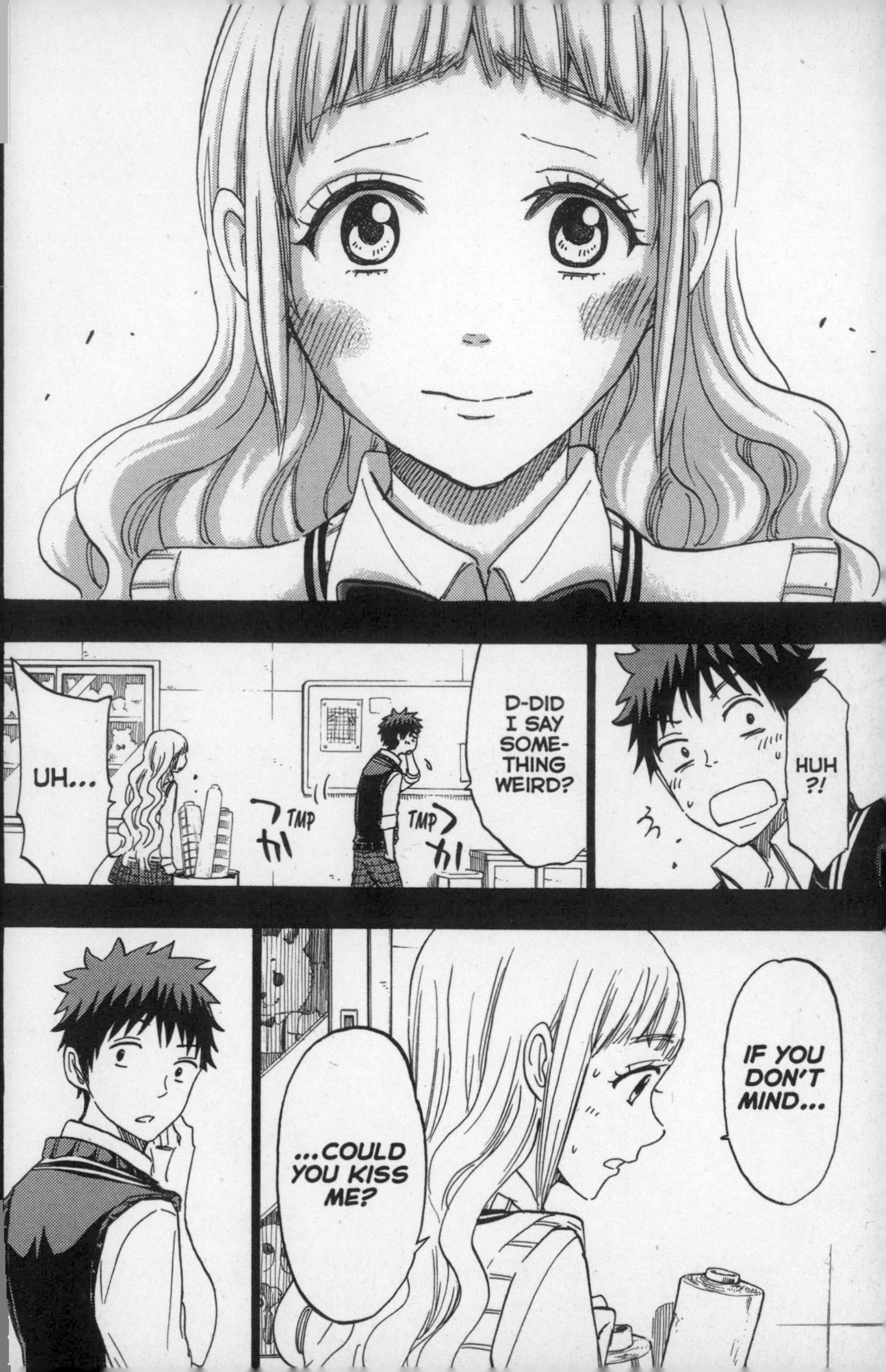
HUH ?!
D-DID I SAY SOME-THING WEIRD?
TMP
TMP
UH...
IF YOU DON'T MIND...
...COULD YOU KISS ME?

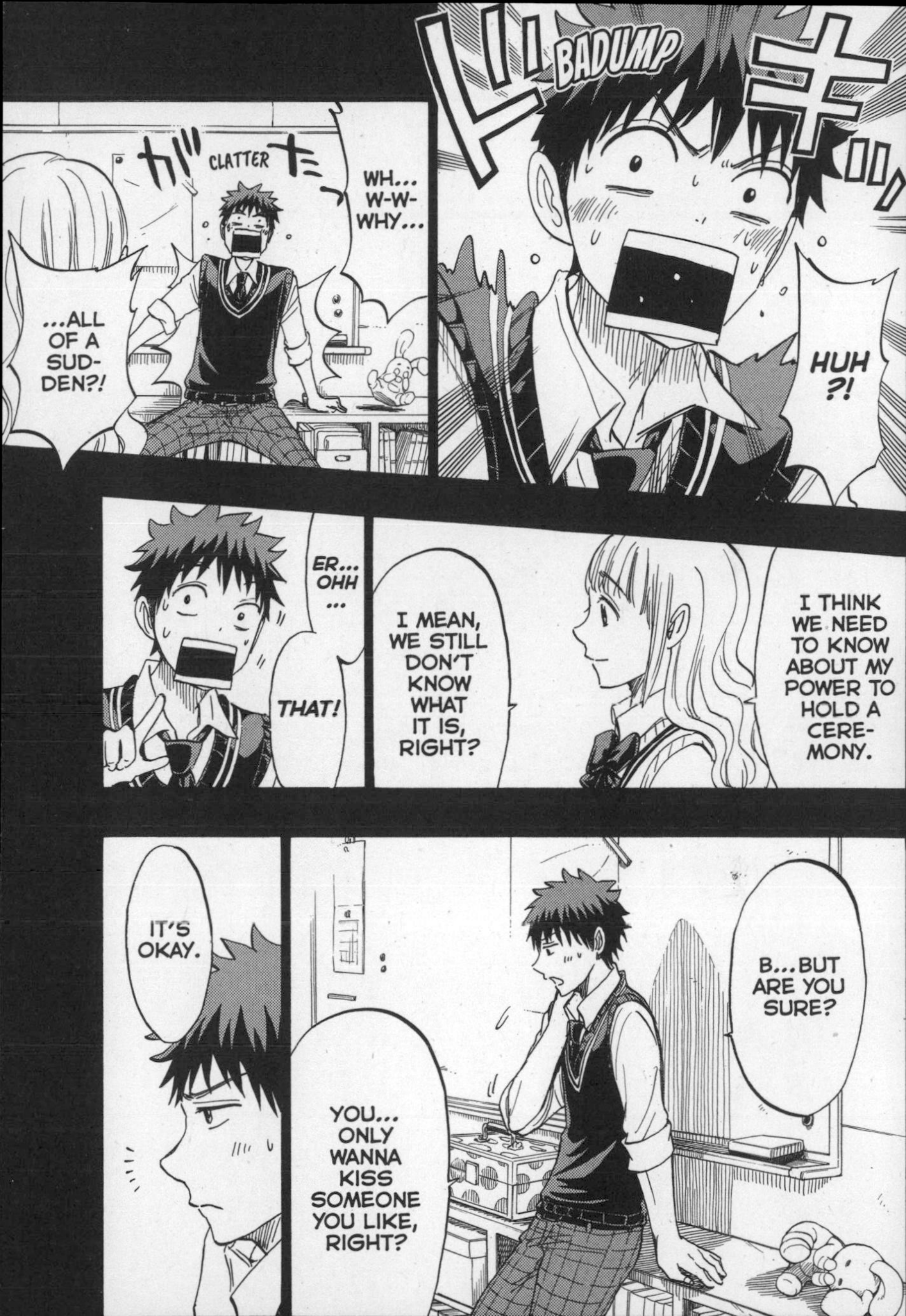
BADUMP
HUH ?!
CLATTER
WH... W-W-WHY...
...ALL OF A SUD-DEN?!
I THINK WE NEED TO KNOW ABOUT MY POWER TO HOLD A CERE-MONY.
I MEAN, WE STILL DON'T KNOW WHAT IT IS, RIGHT?
ER... OHH ... THAT!
B...BUT ARE YOU SURE?
YOU... ONLY WANNA KISS SOMEONE YOU LIKE, RIGHT?
IT'S OKAY.

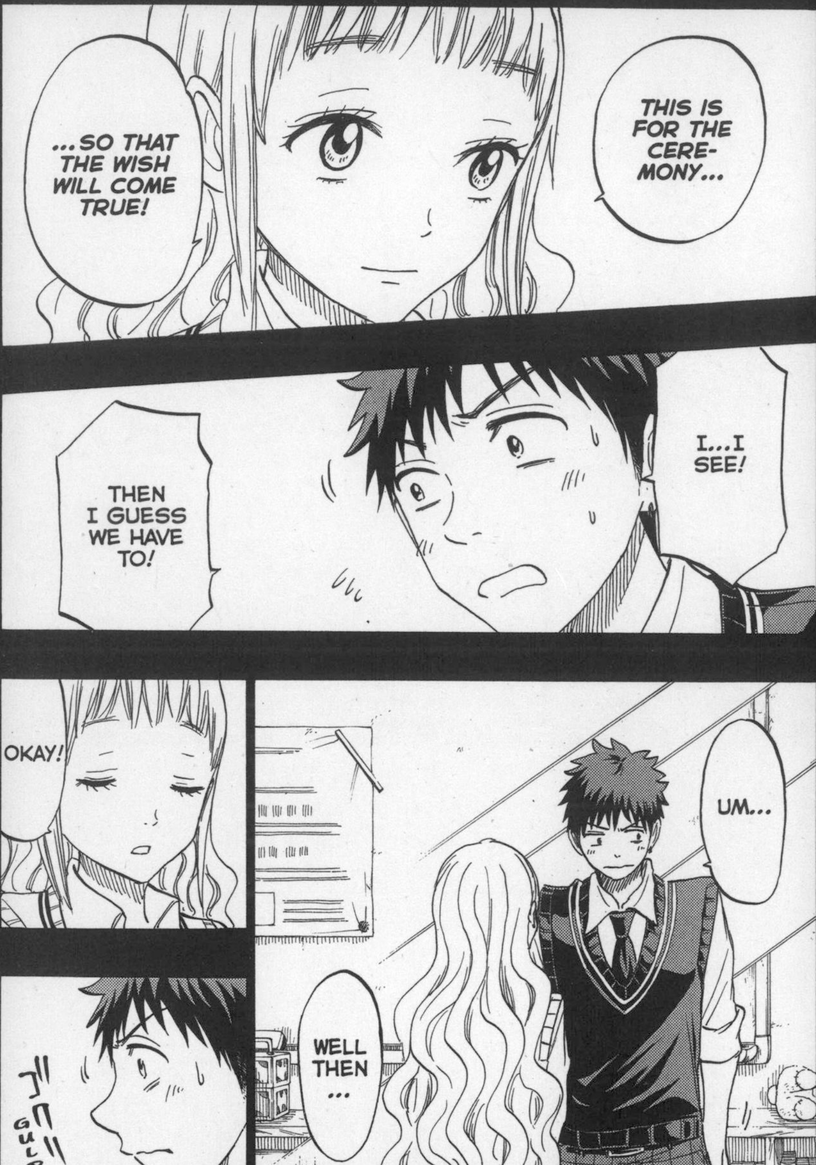
THIS IS FOR THE CERE-MONY...
...SO THAT THE WISH WILL COME TRUE!
I...I SEE!
THEN I GUESS WE HAVE TO!
UM...
WELL THEN ...
OKAY!
GULP

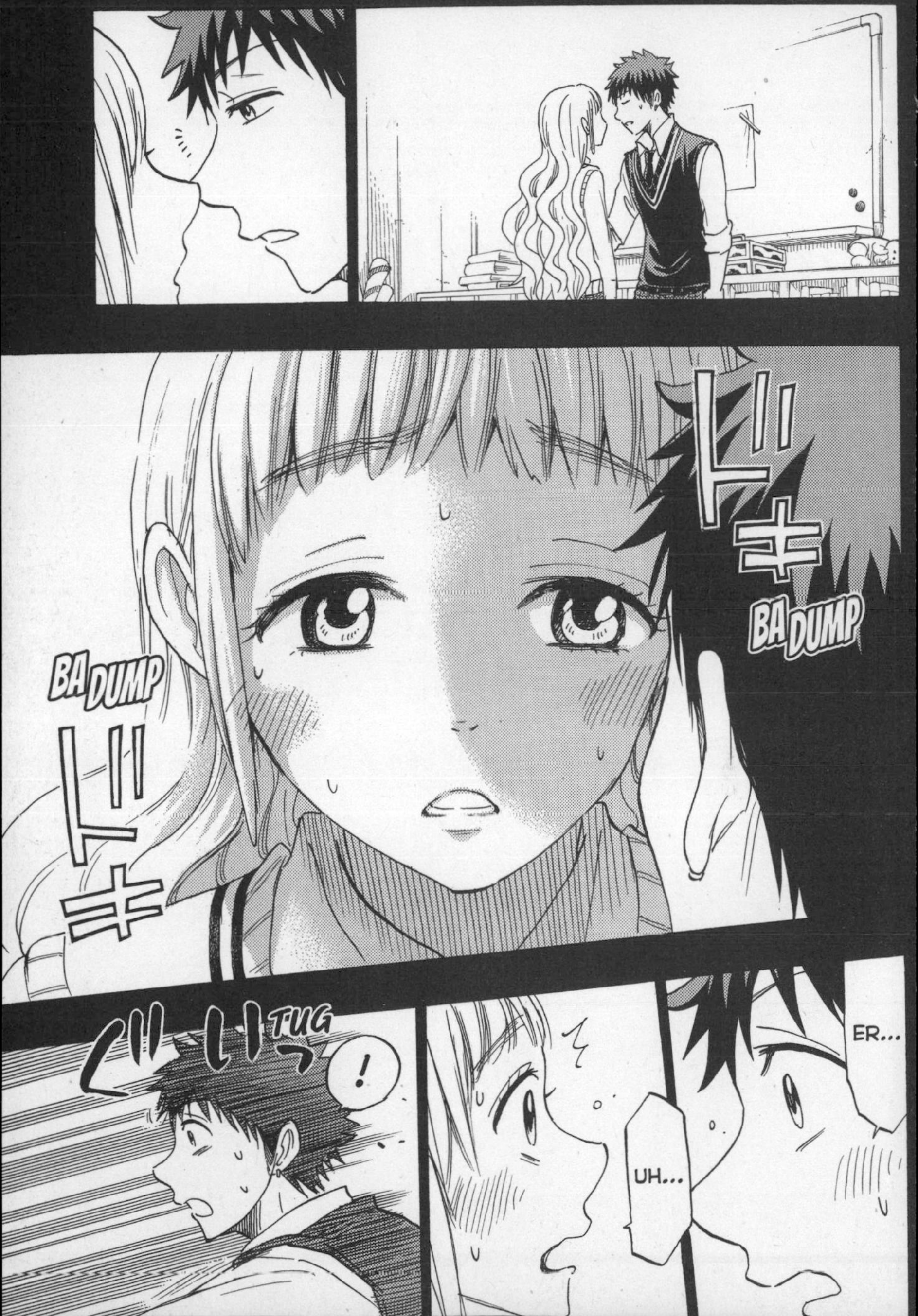
ドキ
BA DUMP
BA DUMP
ドキ
ER...
UH...
ぐいっ
TUG
!

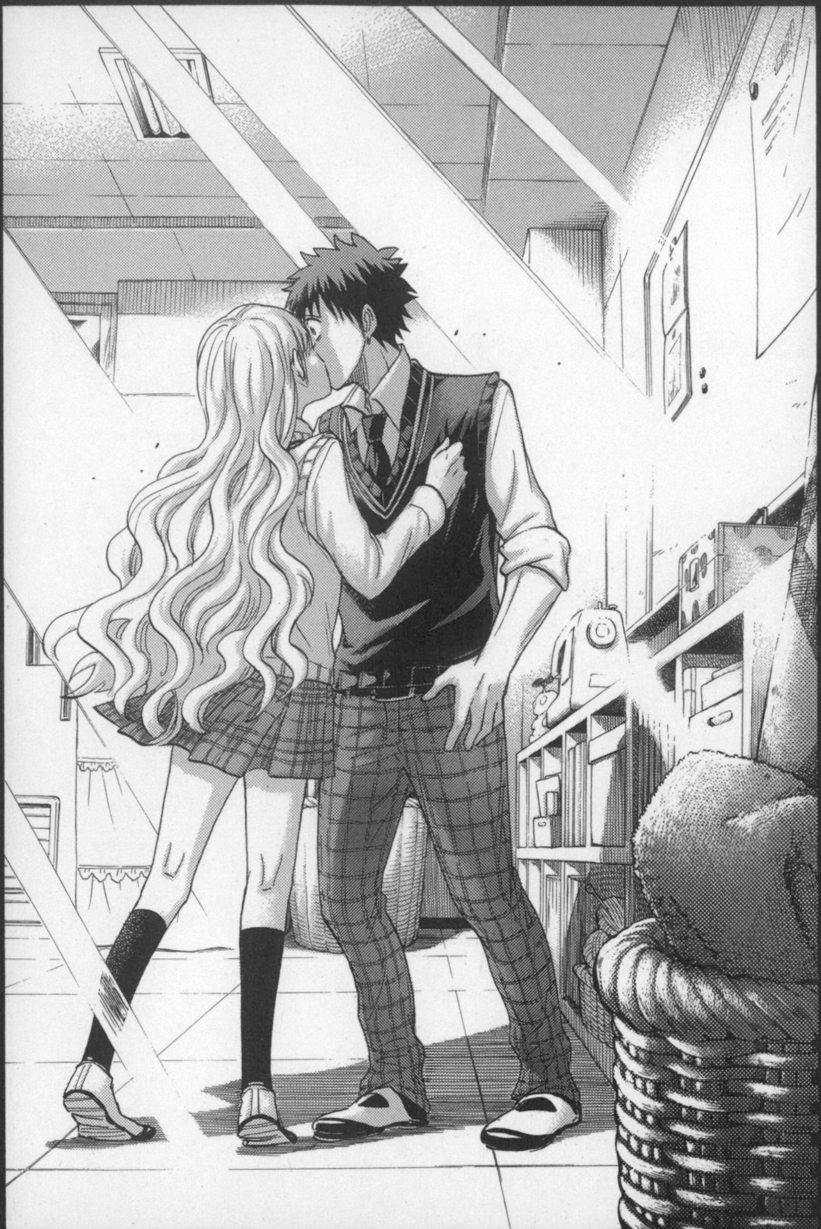

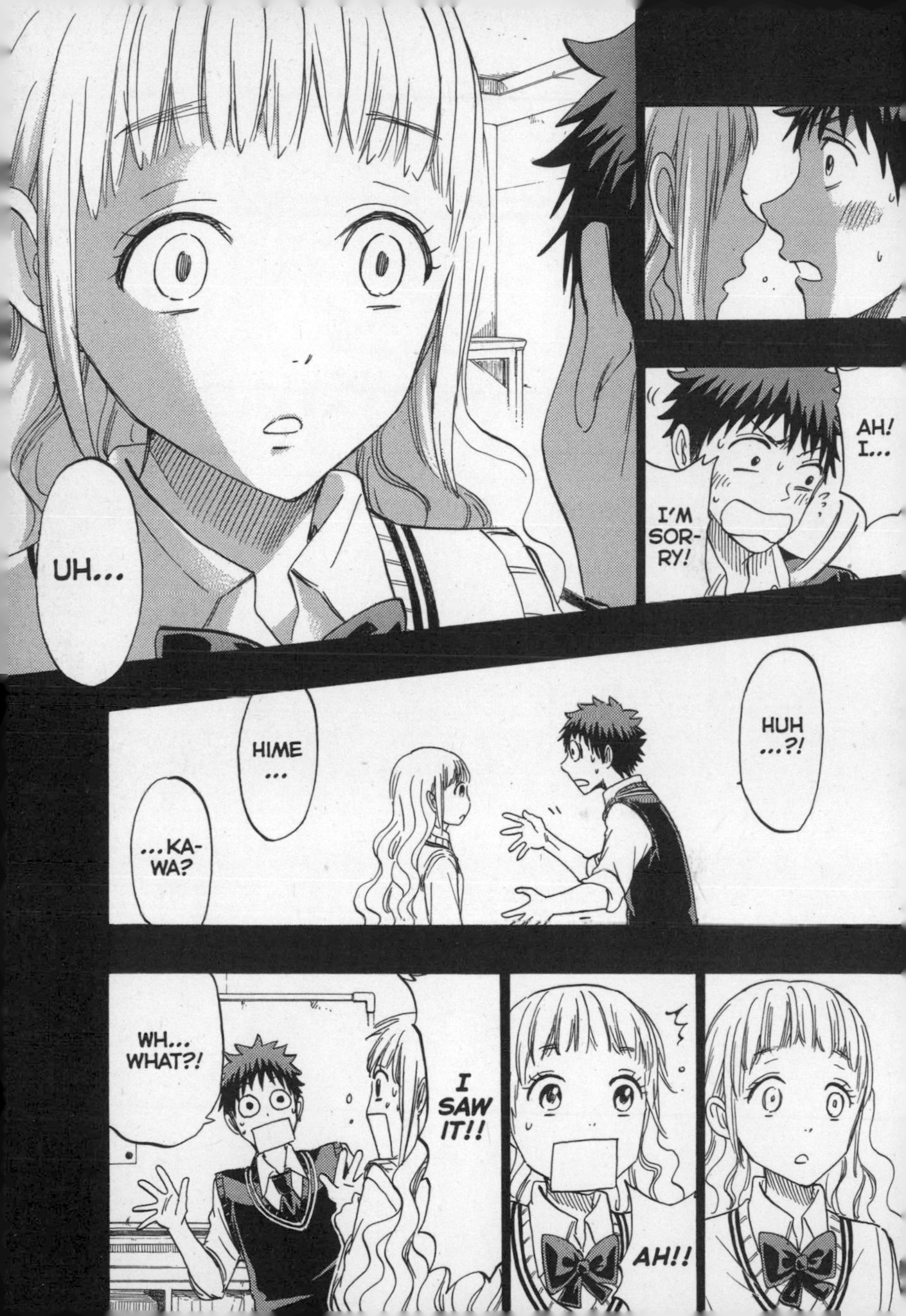
AH! I...
I'M SORRY!
UH...
HUH...?!
HIME...
...KAWA?
AH!!
I SAW IT!!
WH... WHAT?!

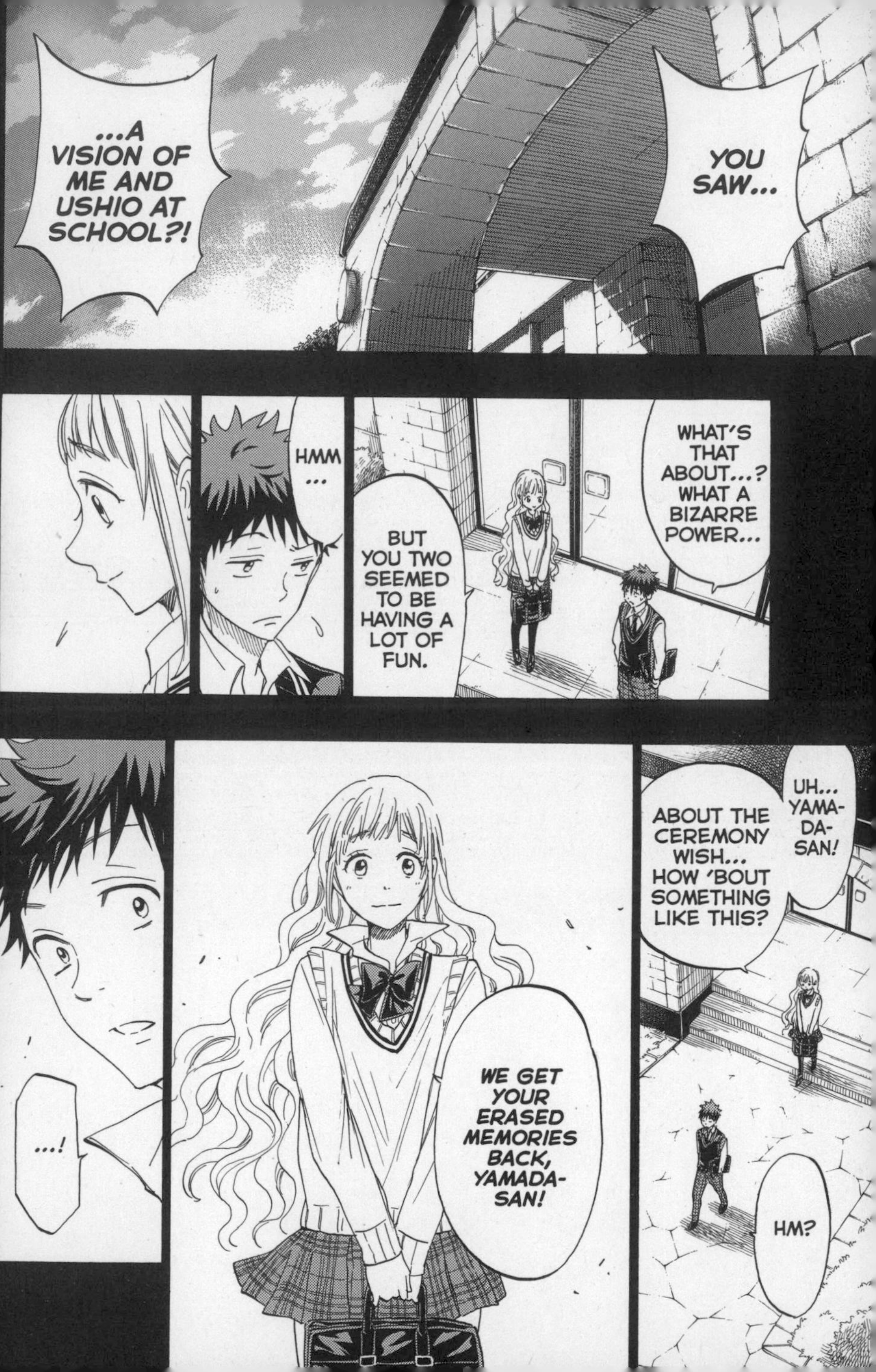
YOU SAW...
...A VISION OF ME AND USHIO AT SCHOOL?!
WHAT'S THAT ABOUT...? WHAT A BIZARRE POWER...
BUT YOU TWO SEEMED TO BE HAVING A LOT OF FUN.
HMM ...
UH... YAMADA-SAN!
ABOUT THE CEREMONY WISH... HOW 'BOUT SOMETHING LIKE THIS?
HM?
WE GET YOUR ERASED MEMORIES BACK, YAMADA-SAN!
...!

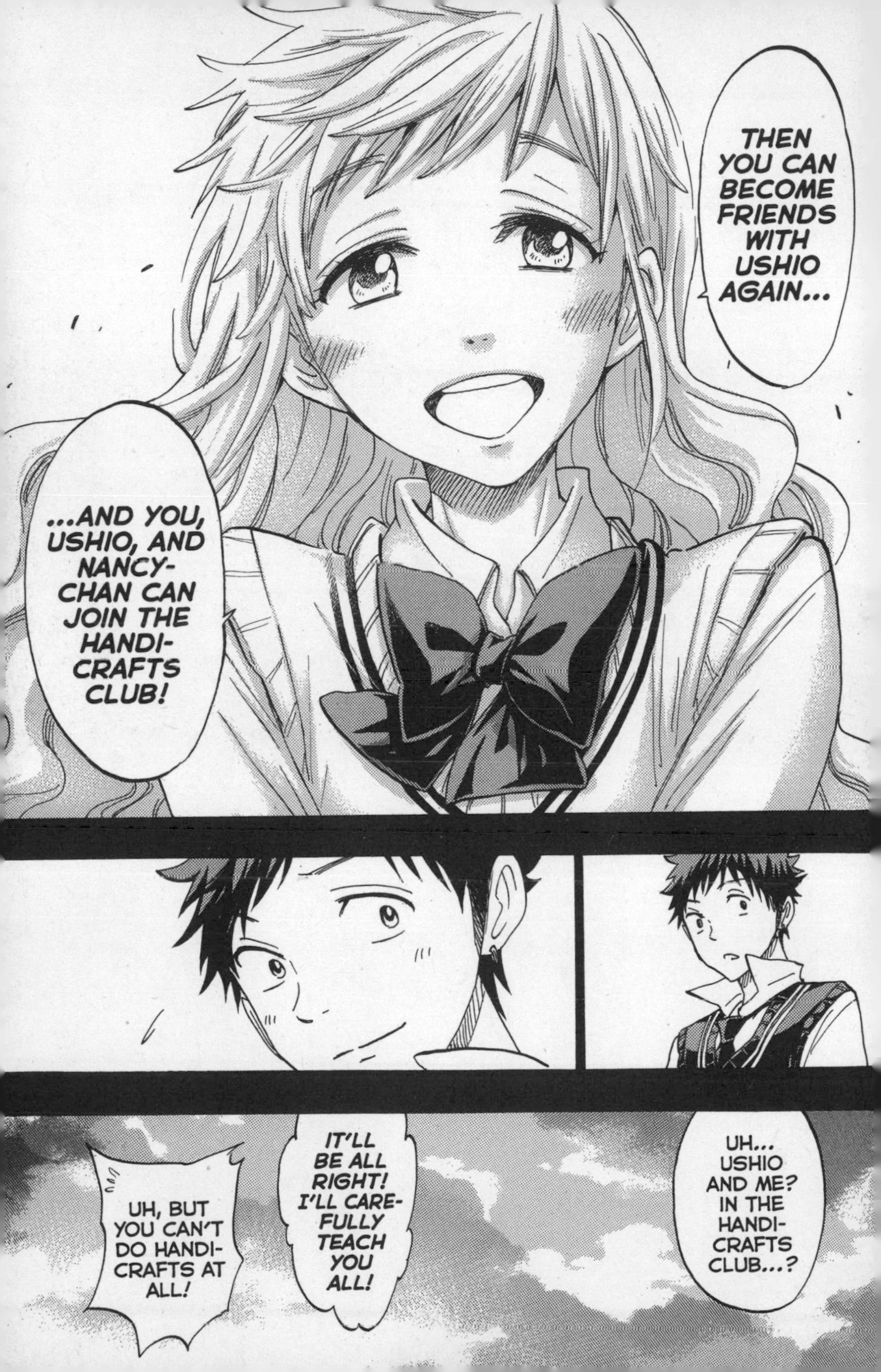
THEN YOU CAN BECOME FRIENDS WITH USHIO AGAIN...
...AND YOU, USHIO, AND NANCY-CHAN CAN JOIN THE HANDI-CRAFTS CLUB!
UH... USHIO AND ME? IN THE HANDI-CRAFTS CLUB...?
IT'LL BE ALL RIGHT! I'LL CARE-FULLY TEACH YOU ALL!
UH, BUT YOU CAN'T DO HANDI-CRAFTS AT ALL!

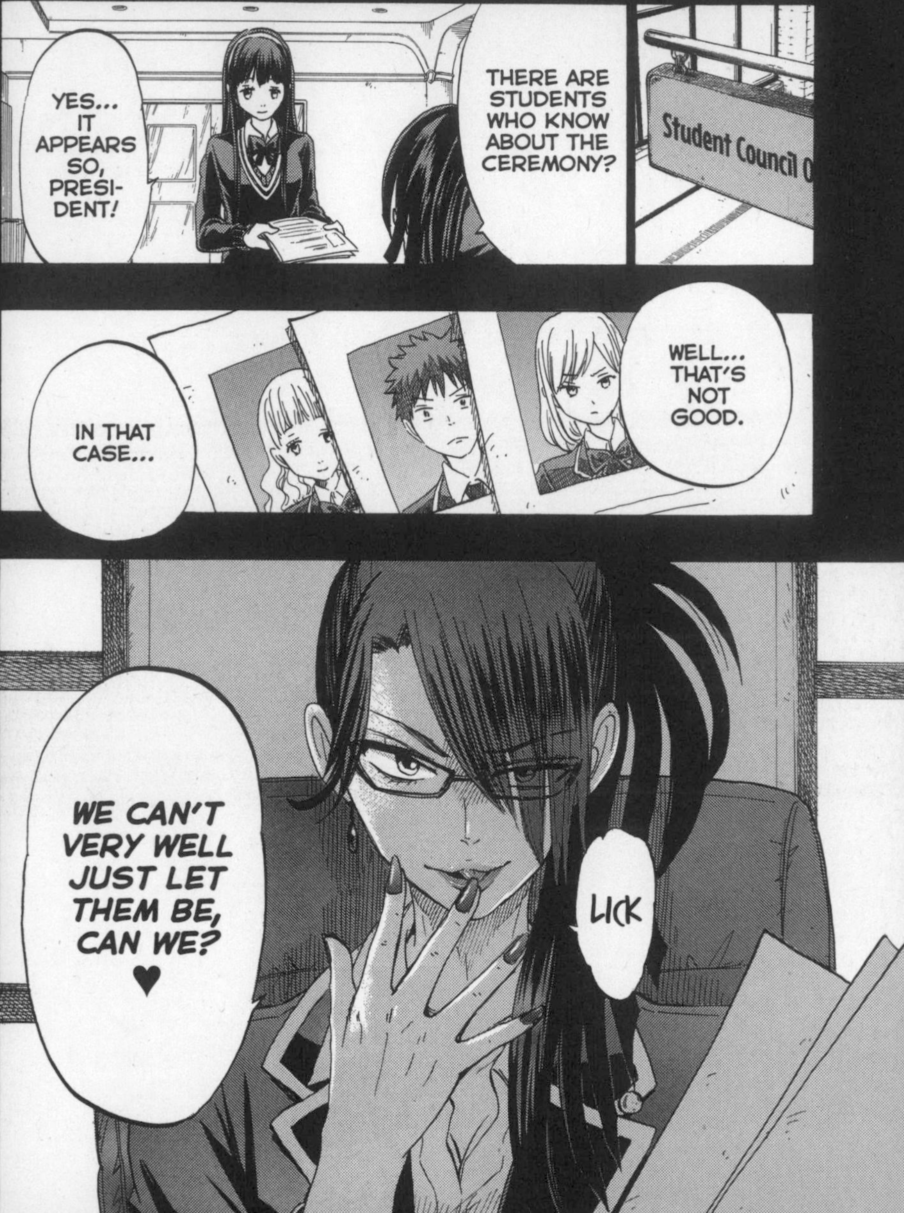
Student Council
THERE ARE STUDENTS WHO KNOW ABOUT THE CEREMONY?
YES... IT APPEARS SO, PRESI-DENT!
WELL... THAT'S NOT GOOD.
IN THAT CASE...
WE CAN'T VERY WELL JUST LET THEM BE, CAN WE? ♥
LICK

CHAPTER 160: I...I don't believe it!!

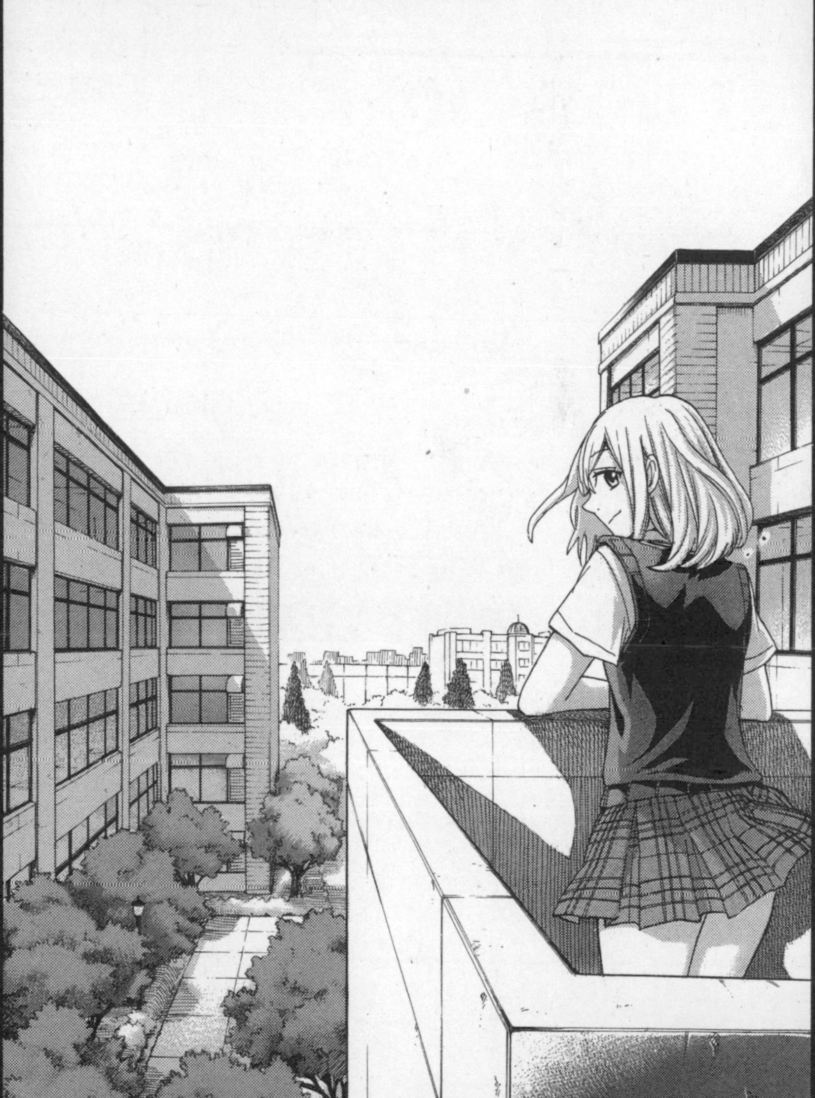

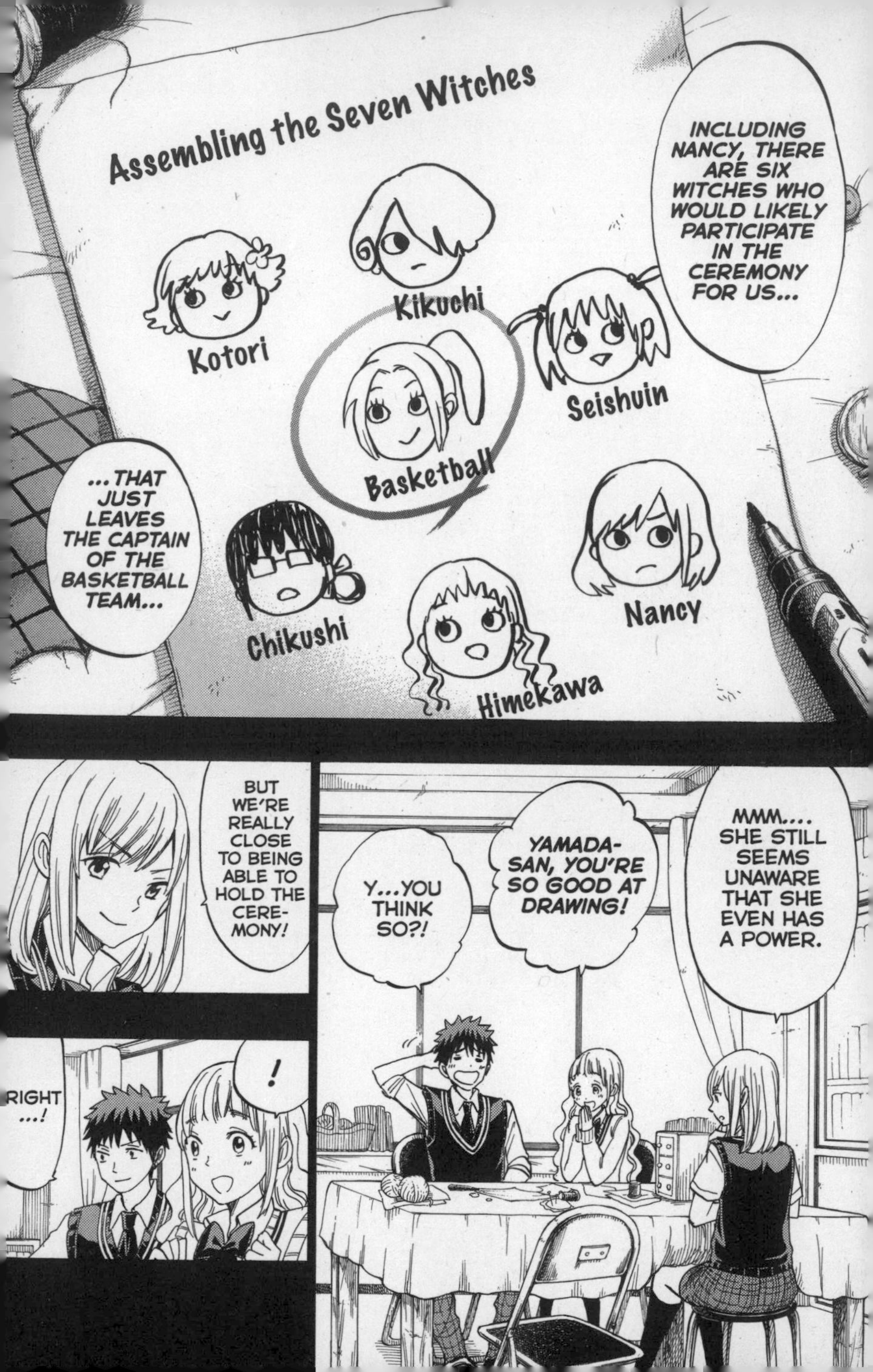
Assembling the Seven Witches
Kikuchi
Kotori
Seishuin
Basketball
Nancy
Chikushi
Himekawa
INCLUDING NANCY, THERE ARE SIX WITCHES WHO WOULD LIKELY PARTICIPATE IN THE CEREMONY FOR US...
...THAT JUST LEAVES THE CAPTAIN OF THE BASKETBALL TEAM...
MMM.... SHE STILL SEEMS UNAWARE THAT SHE EVEN HAS A POWER.
YAMADA-SAN, YOU'RE SO GOOD AT DRAWING!
Y...YOU THINK SO?!
BUT WE'RE REALLY CLOSE TO BEING ABLE TO HOLD THE CERE-MONY!
!
RIGHT ...!

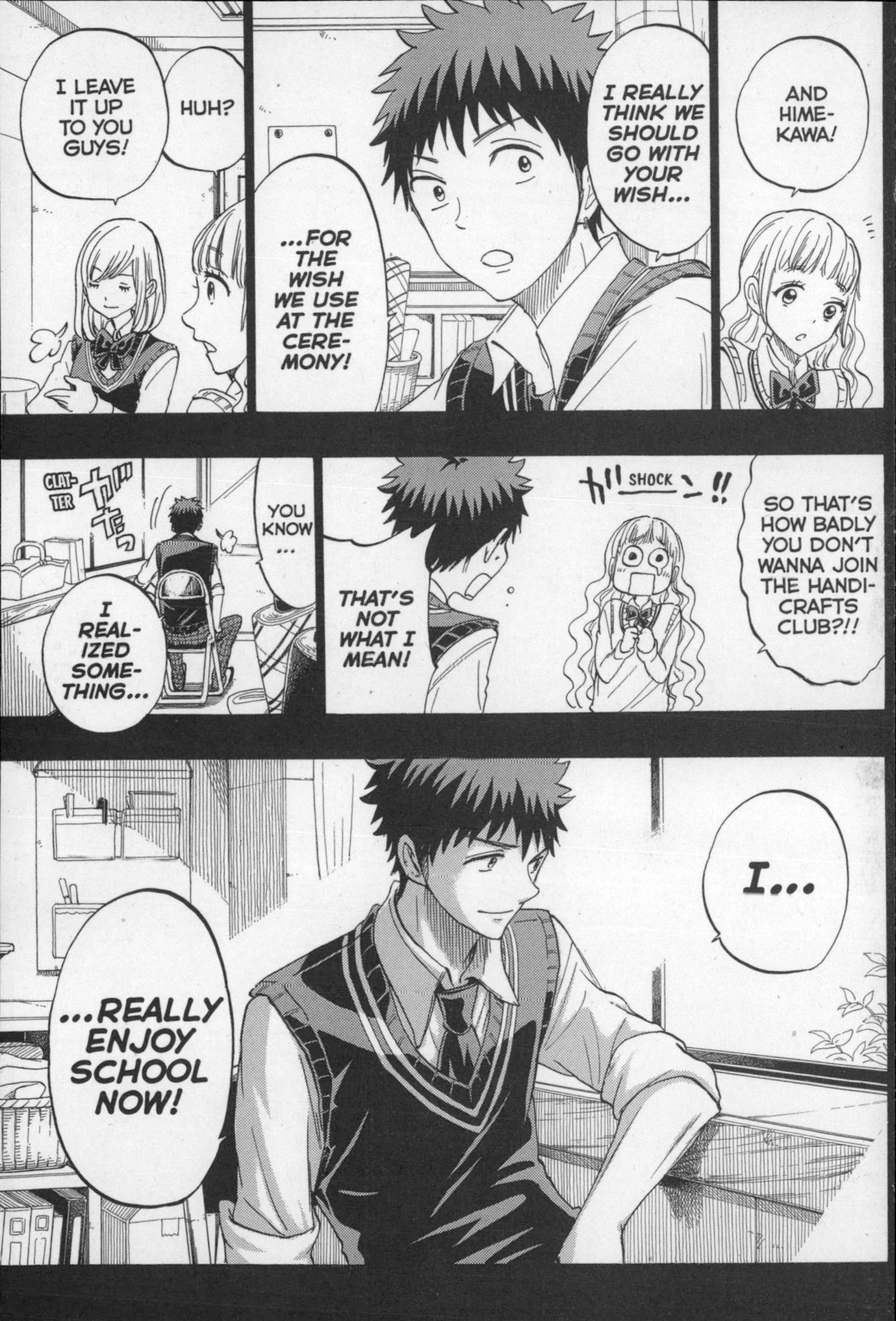
AND HIME-KAWA!
I REALLY THINK WE SHOULD GO WITH YOUR WISH...
...FOR THE WISH WE USE AT THE CEREMONY!
I LEAVE IT UP TO YOU GUYS!
HUH?
SO THAT'S HOW BADLY YOU DON'T WANNA JOIN THE HANDICRAFTS CLUB?!!
SHOCK
THAT'S NOT WHAT I MEAN!
YOU KNOW...
CLATTER
I REALIZED SOMETHING...
I...
...REALLY ENJOY SCHOOL NOW!

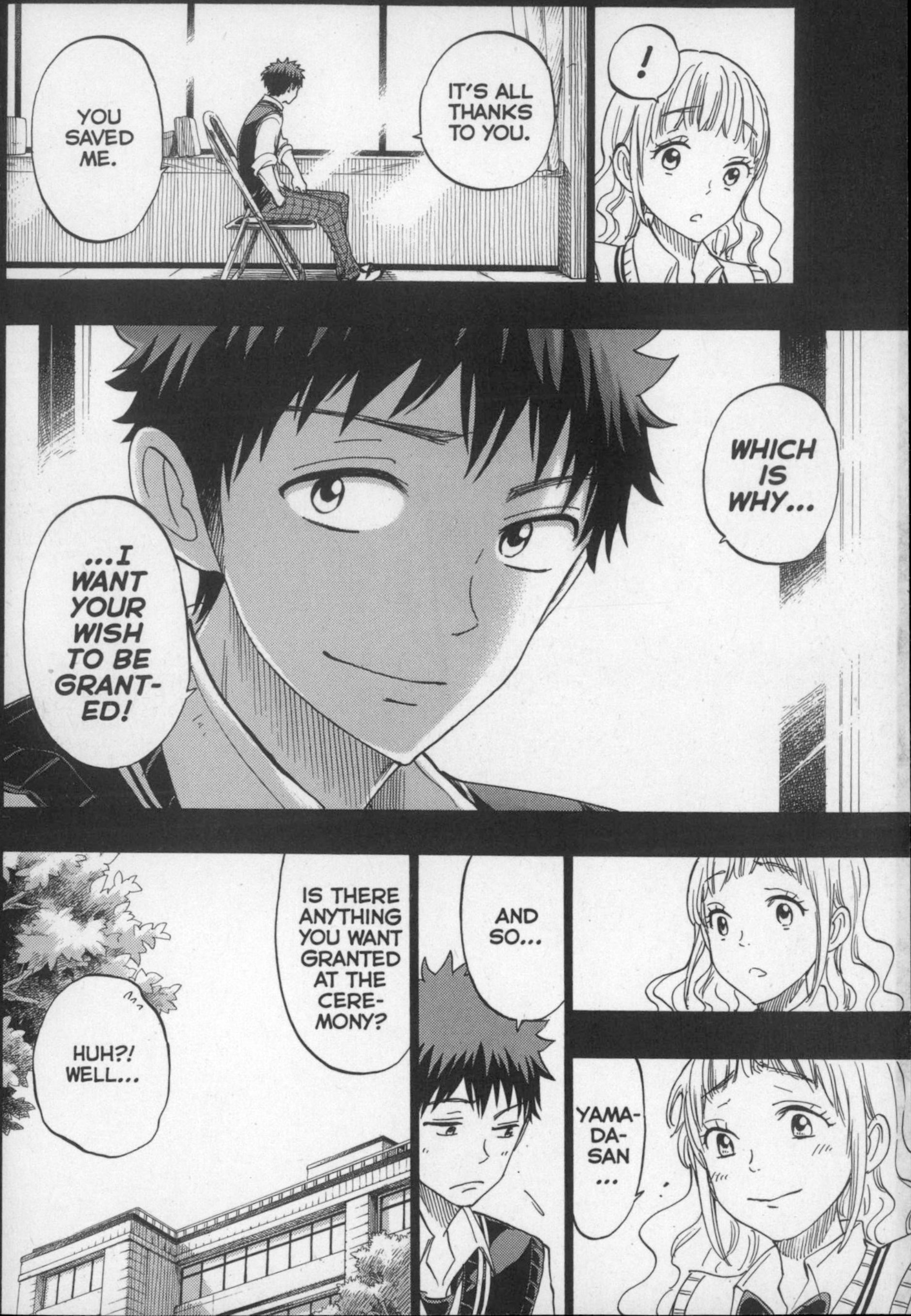
!
IT'S ALL THANKS TO YOU.
YOU SAVED ME.
WHICH IS WHY...
...I WANT YOUR WISH TO BE GRANT-ED!
YAMA-DA-SAN ...
AND SO...
IS THERE ANYTHING YOU WANT GRANTED AT THE CERE-MONY?
HUH?! WELL...

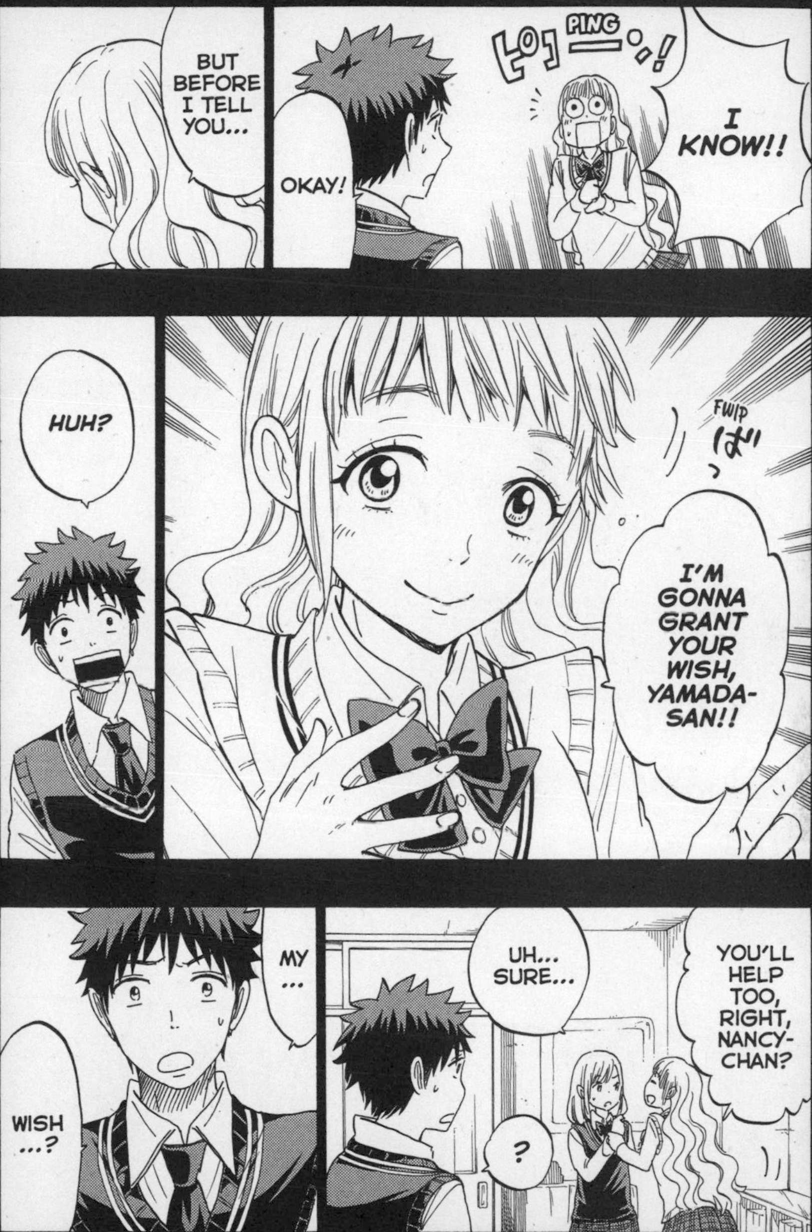
I KNOW!!
PING
OKAY!
BUT BEFORE I TELL YOU...
FWIP
I'M GONNA GRANT YOUR WISH, YAMADA-SAN!!
HUH?
YOU'LL HELP TOO, RIGHT, NANCY-CHAN?
UH... SURE...
?
MY ...
WISH ...?

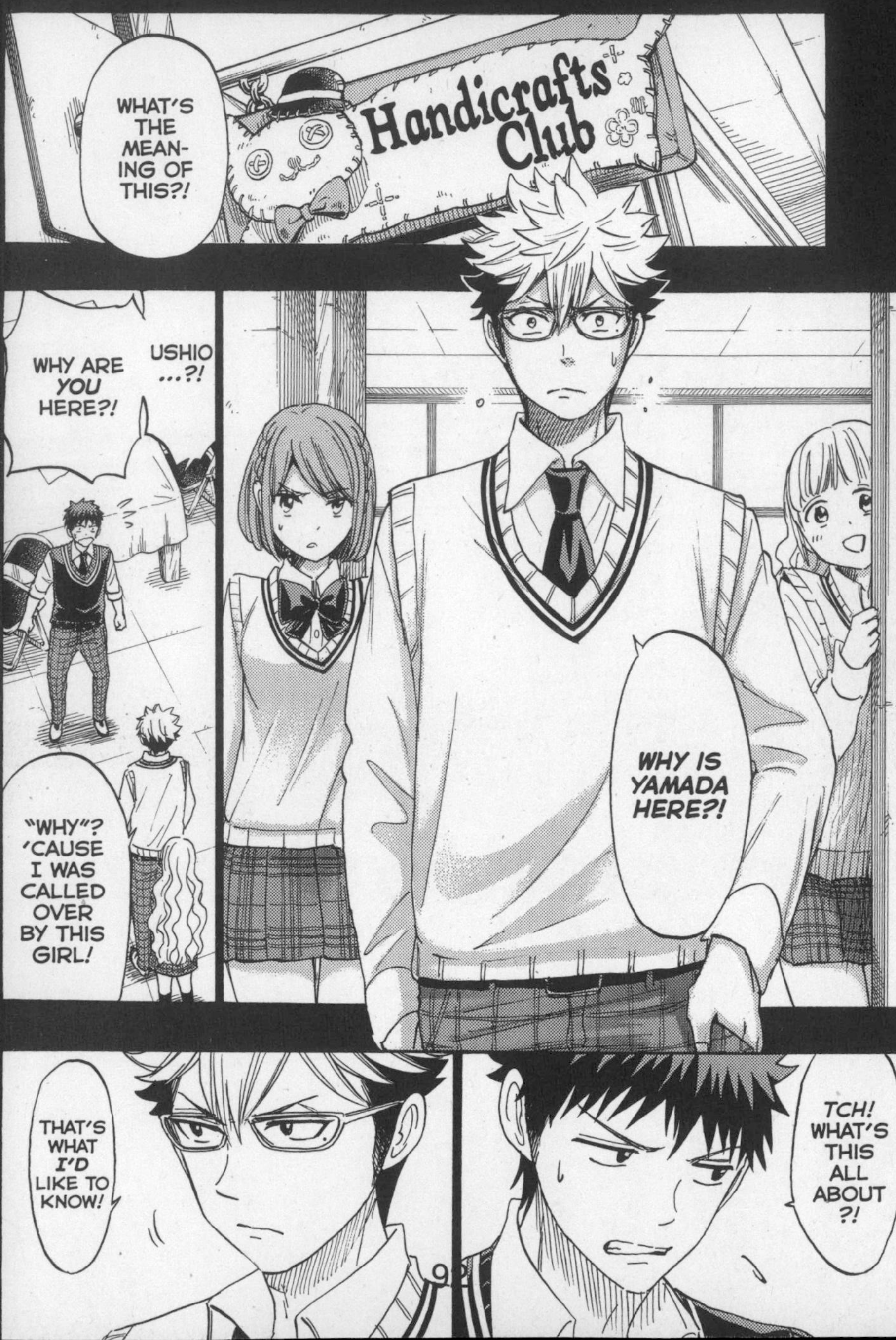
Handicrafts Club
WHAT'S THE MEANING OF THIS?!
WHY IS YAMADA HERE?!
USHIO ...?!
WHY ARE *YOU* HERE?!
"WHY"? 'CAUSE I WAS CALLED OVER BY THIS GIRL!
TCH! WHAT'S THIS ALL ABOUT ?!
THAT'S WHAT *I'D* LIKE TO KNOW!

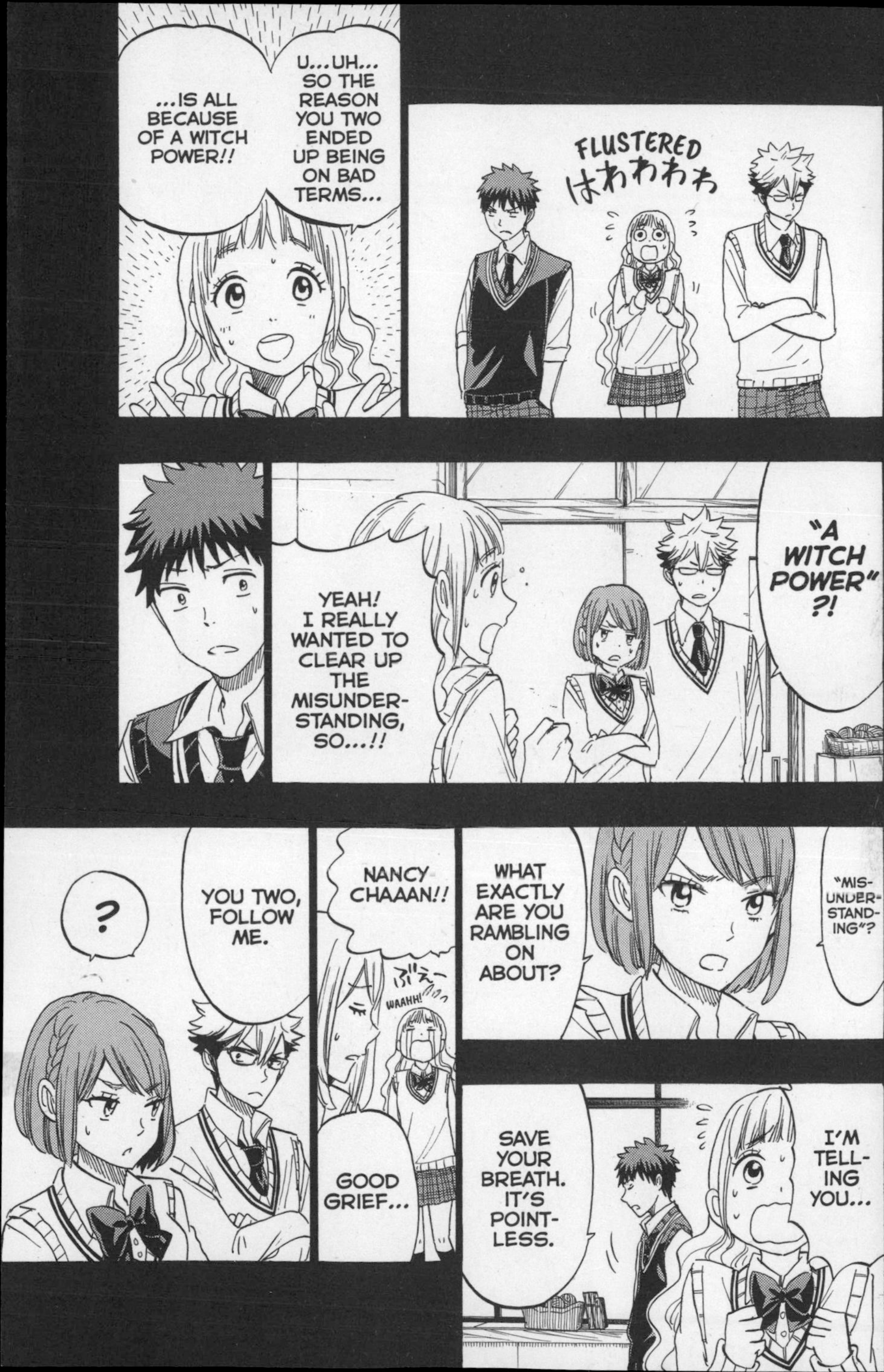
FLUSTERED
はわわわわ
U...UH... SO THE REASON YOU TWO ENDED UP BEING ON BAD TERMS...
...IS ALL BECAUSE OF A WITCH POWER!!
"A WITCH POWER"?!
YEAH! I REALLY WANTED TO CLEAR UP THE MISUNDER-STANDING, SO...!!
"MIS-UNDER-STAND-ING"?
WHAT EXACTLY ARE YOU RAMBLING ON ABOUT?
I'M TELL-ING YOU...
SAVE YOUR BREATH. IT'S POINT-LESS.
NANCY-CHAAAN!!
ぶえ～
WAAHH!
GOOD GRIEF...
YOU TWO, FOLLOW ME.
?

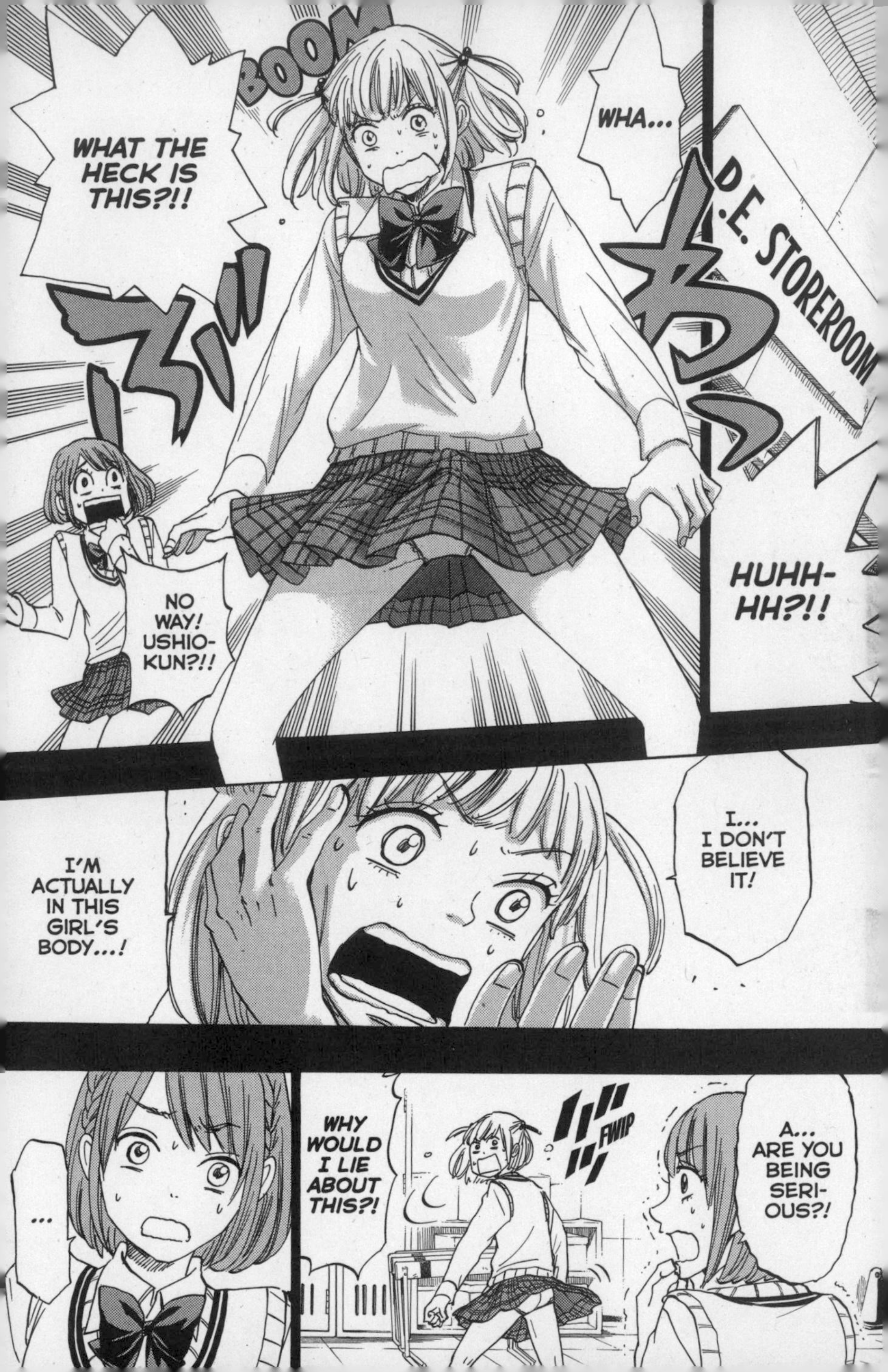

WHA...
P.E. STOREROOM
HUHH-HH?!!
BOOM
WHAT THE HECK IS THIS?!!
NO WAY! USHIO-KUN?!!
I... I DON'T BELIEVE IT!
I'M ACTUALLY IN THIS GIRL'S BODY...!
A... ARE YOU BEING SERI-OUS?!
FWIP
WHY WOULD I LIE ABOUT THIS?!
...

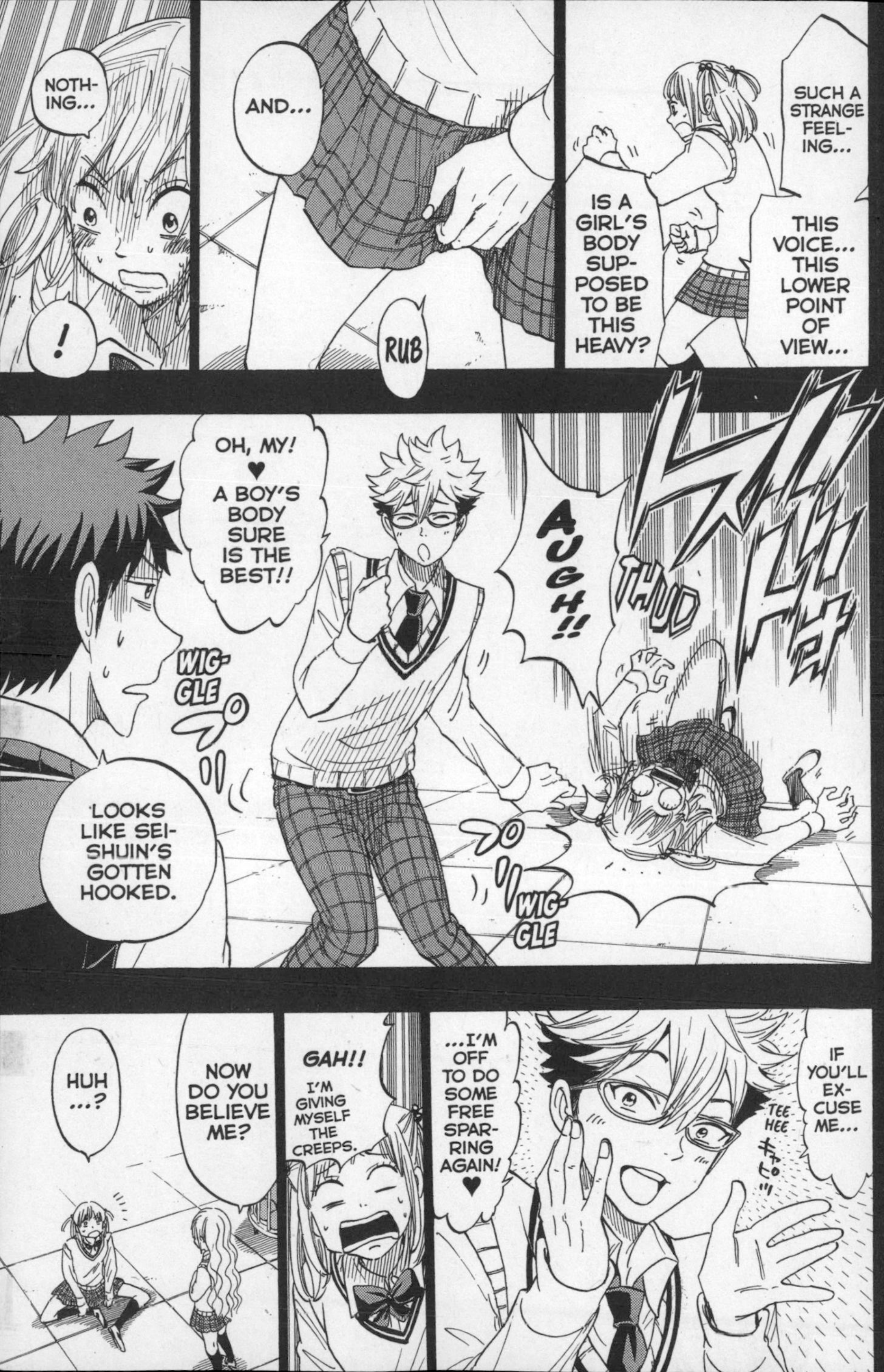
SUCH A STRANGE FEEL-ING...
THIS VOICE... THIS LOWER POINT OF VIEW...
IS A GIRL'S BODY SUP-POSED TO BE THIS HEAVY?
AND...
RUB
NOTH-ING...
!
AUGH!!
THUD
OH, MY! ♥ A BOY'S BODY SURE IS THE BEST!!
WIG-GLE
WIG-GLE
LOOKS LIKE SEI-SHUIN'S GOTTEN HOOKED.
IF YOU'LL EX-CUSE ME...
TEE HEE
...I'M OFF TO DO SOME FREE SPAR-RING AGAIN! ♥
GAH!!
I'M GIVING MYSELF THE CREEPS.
NOW DO YOU BELIEVE ME?
HUH ...?

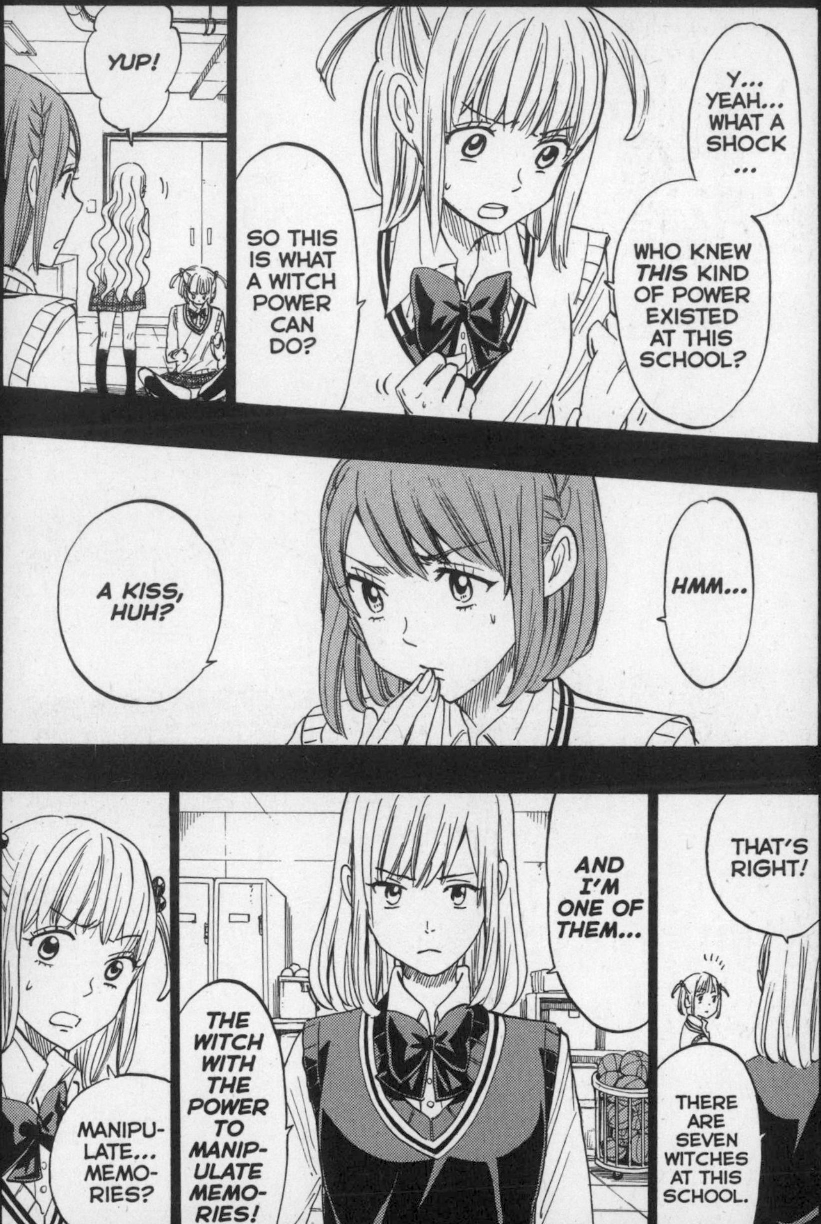
Y... YEAH... WHAT A SHOCK...
WHO KNEW *THIS* KIND OF POWER EXISTED AT THIS SCHOOL?
SO THIS IS WHAT A WITCH POWER CAN DO?
YUP!
HMM...
A KISS, HUH?
THAT'S RIGHT!
THERE ARE SEVEN WITCHES AT THIS SCHOOL.
AND I'M ONE OF THEM...
THE WITCH WITH THE POWER TO MANIPULATE MEMORIES!
MANIPULATE... MEMORIES?

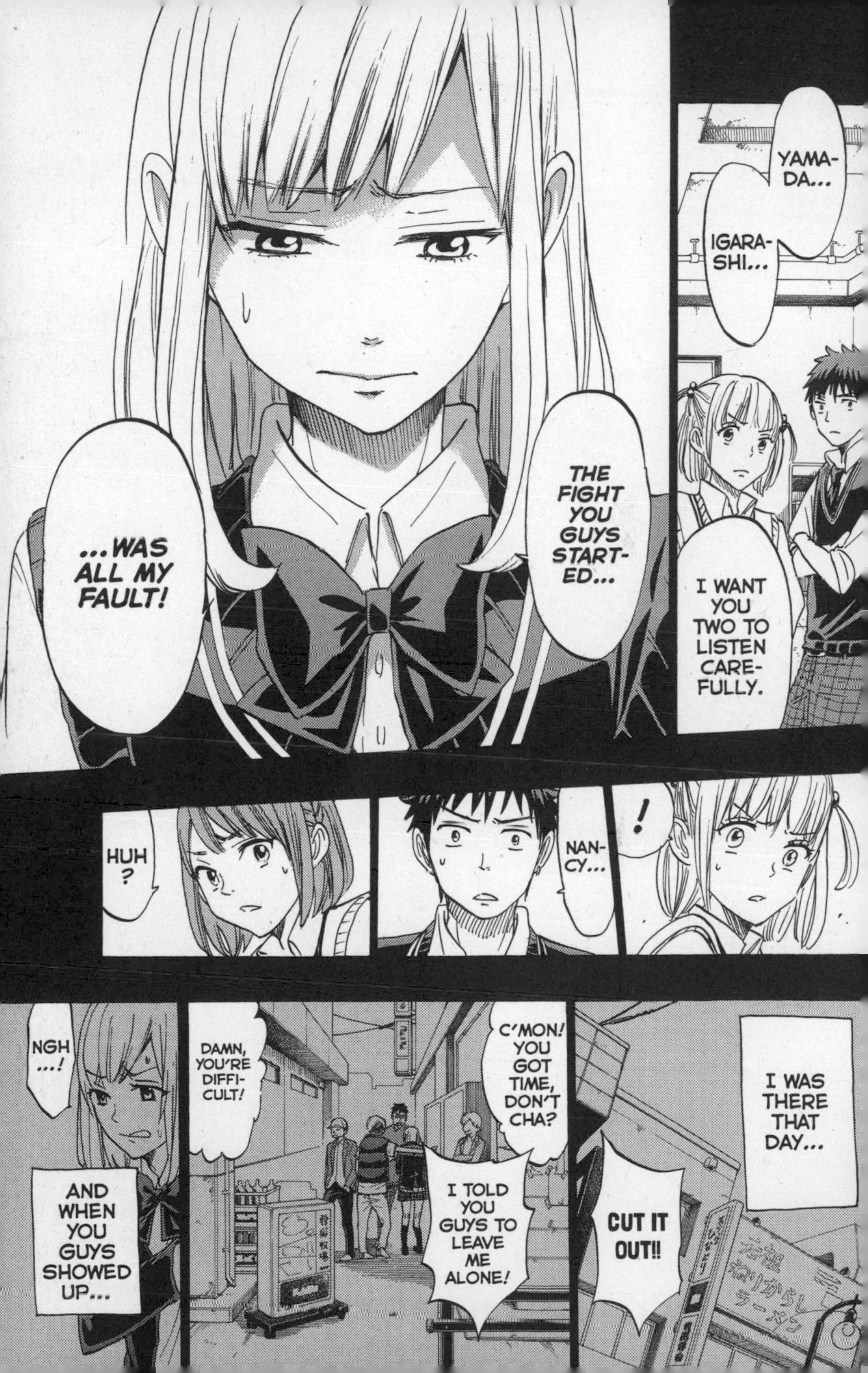

YAMADA...
IGARASHI...
I WANT YOU TWO TO LISTEN CAREFULLY.
THE FIGHT YOU GUYS STARTED...
...WAS ALL MY FAULT!
!
NANCY...
HUH?
I WAS THERE THAT DAY...
CUT IT OUT!!
C'MON! YOU GOT TIME, DON'T CHA?
I TOLD YOU GUYS TO LEAVE ME ALONE!
DAMN, YOU'RE DIFFICULT!
NGH...!
AND WHEN YOU GUYS SHOWED UP...

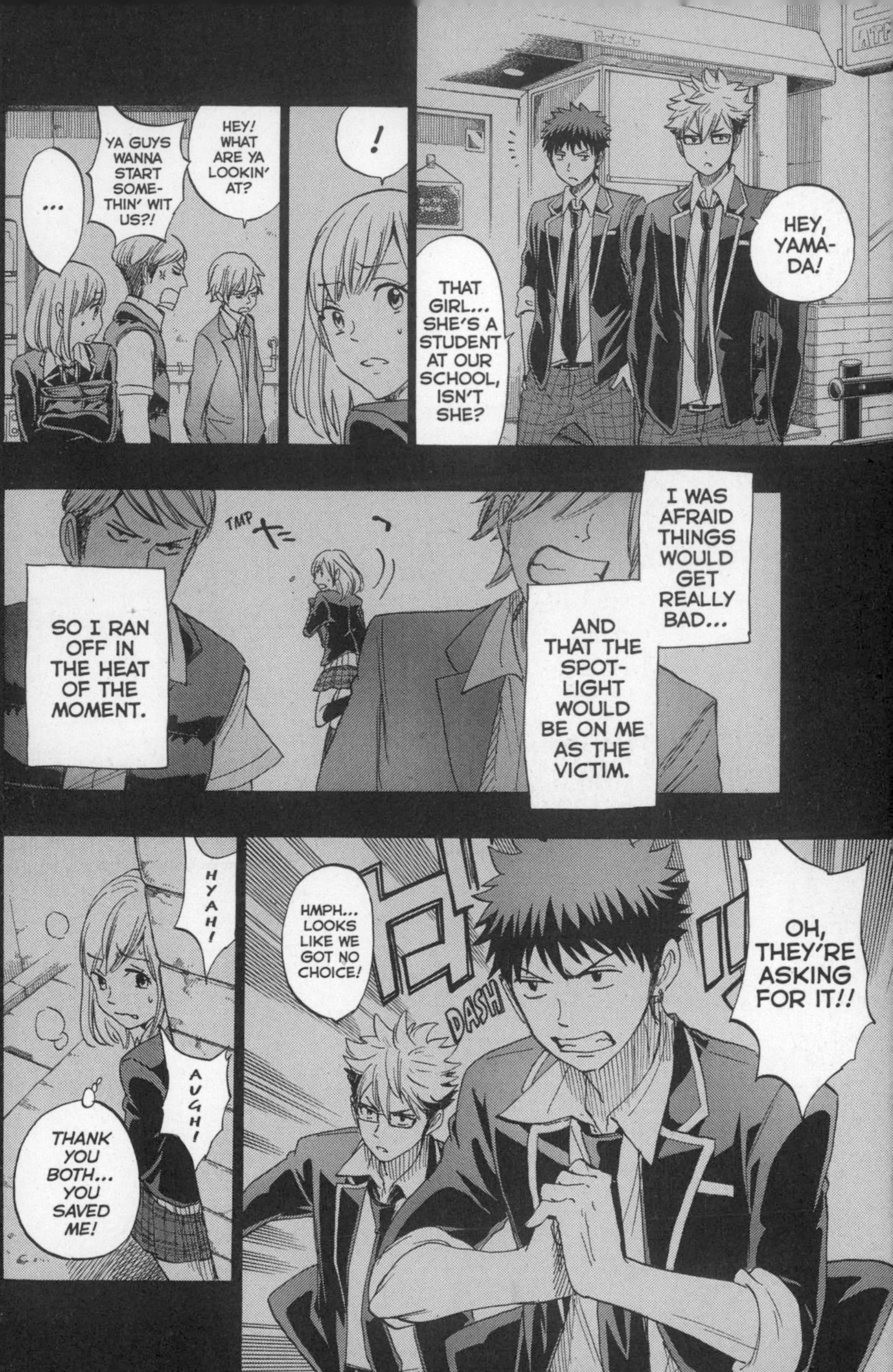
HEY, YAMADA!
THAT GIRL... SHE'S A STUDENT AT OUR SCHOOL, ISN'T SHE?
!
HEY! WHAT ARE YA LOOKIN' AT?
YA GUYS WANNA START SOME-THIN' WIT US?!
...
I WAS AFRAID THINGS WOULD GET REALLY BAD...
AND THAT THE SPOT-LIGHT WOULD BE ON ME AS THE VICTIM.
TMP
SO I RAN OFF IN THE HEAT OF THE MOMENT.
OH, THEY'RE ASKING FOR IT!!
DASH
HMPH... LOOKS LIKE WE GOT NO CHOICE!
HYAH!
AUGH!
THANK YOU BOTH... YOU SAVED ME!

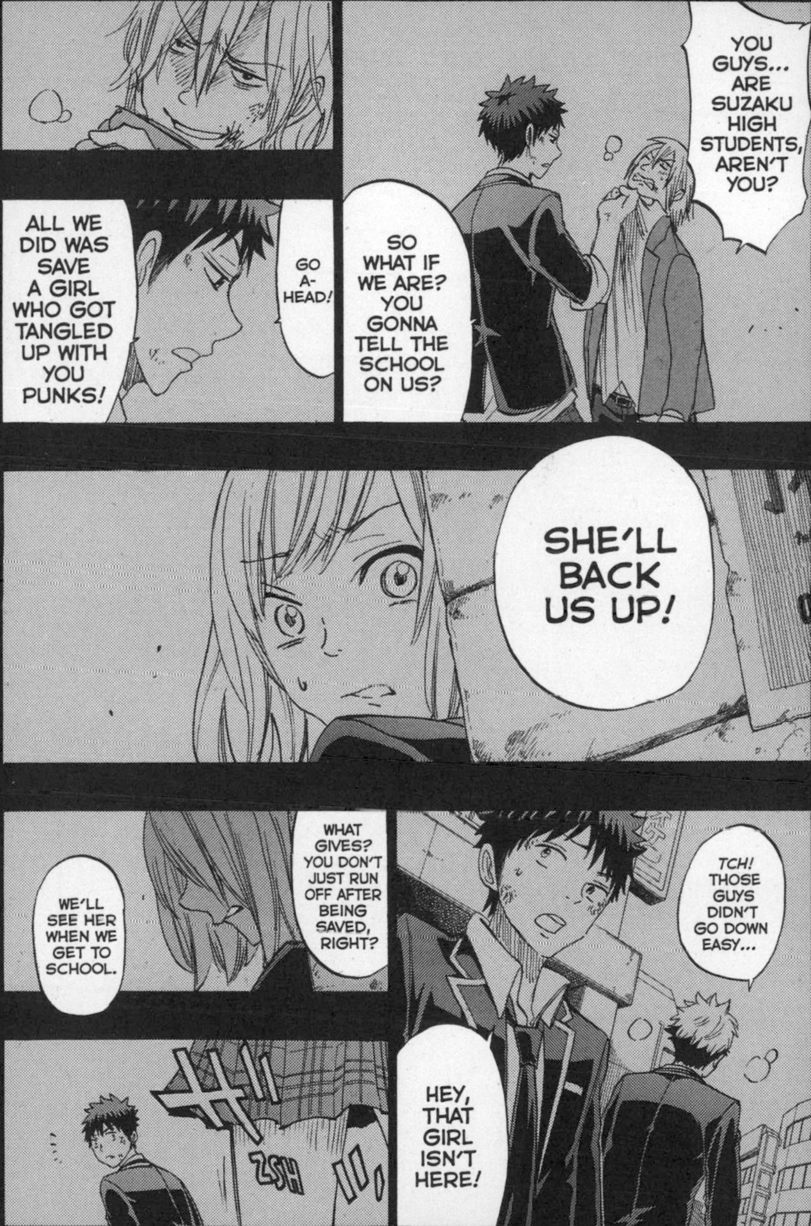

YOU GUYS... ARE SUZAKU HIGH STUDENTS, AREN'T YOU?
SO WHAT IF WE ARE? YOU GONNA TELL THE SCHOOL ON US?
GO A-HEAD!
ALL WE DID WAS SAVE A GIRL WHO GOT TANGLED UP WITH YOU PUNKS!
SHE'LL BACK US UP!
TCH! THOSE GUYS DIDN'T GO DOWN EASY...
HEY, THAT GIRL ISN'T HERE!
WHAT GIVES? YOU DON'T JUST RUN OFF AFTER BEING SAVED, RIGHT?
WE'LL SEE HER WHEN WE GET TO SCHOOL.
ZSH

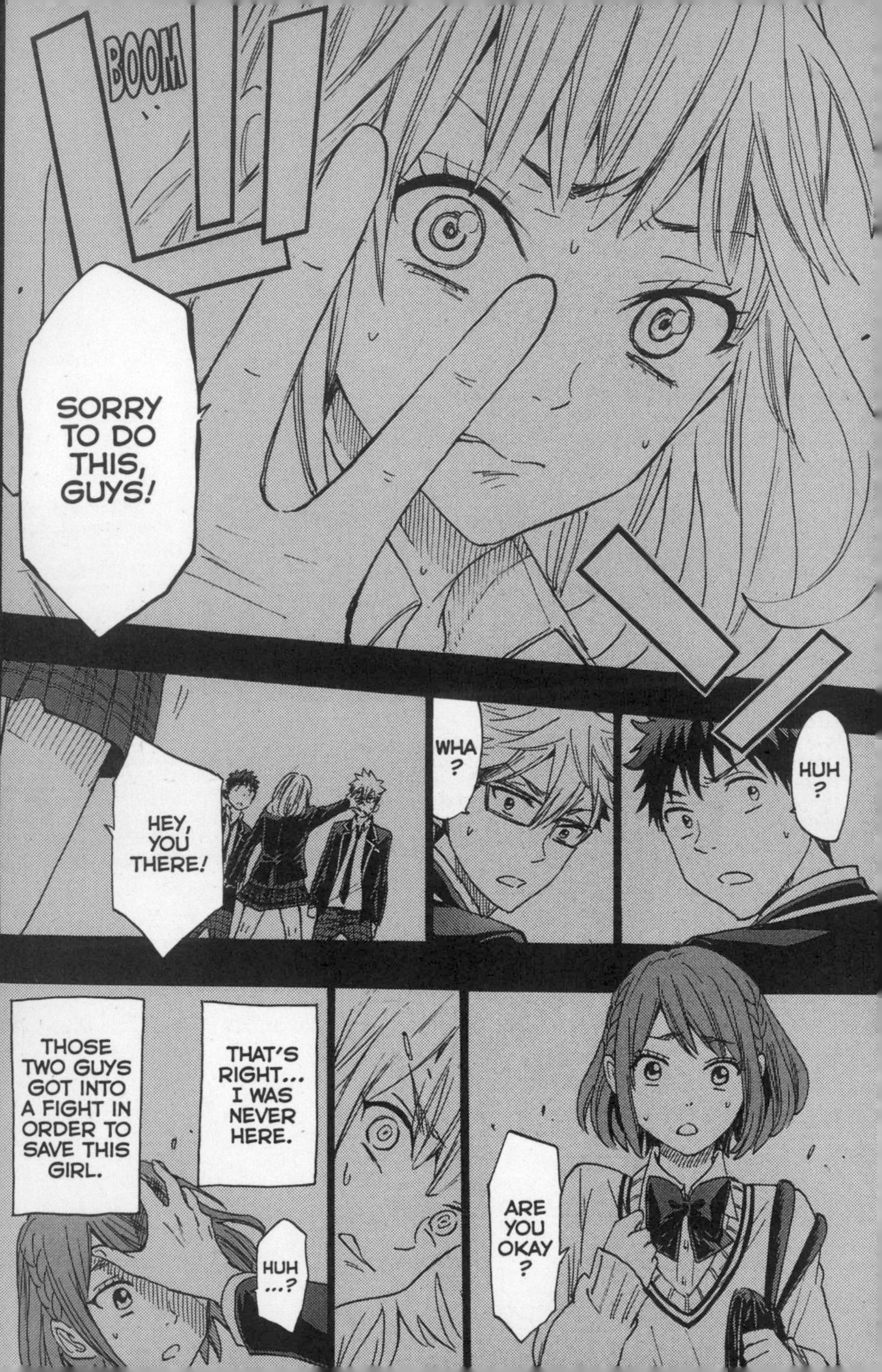

BOOM
SORRY TO DO THIS, GUYS!
HUH?
WHA?
HEY, YOU THERE!
ARE YOU OKAY?
HUH...?
THAT'S RIGHT... I WAS NEVER HERE.
THOSE TWO GUYS GOT INTO A FIGHT IN ORDER TO SAVE THIS GIRL.

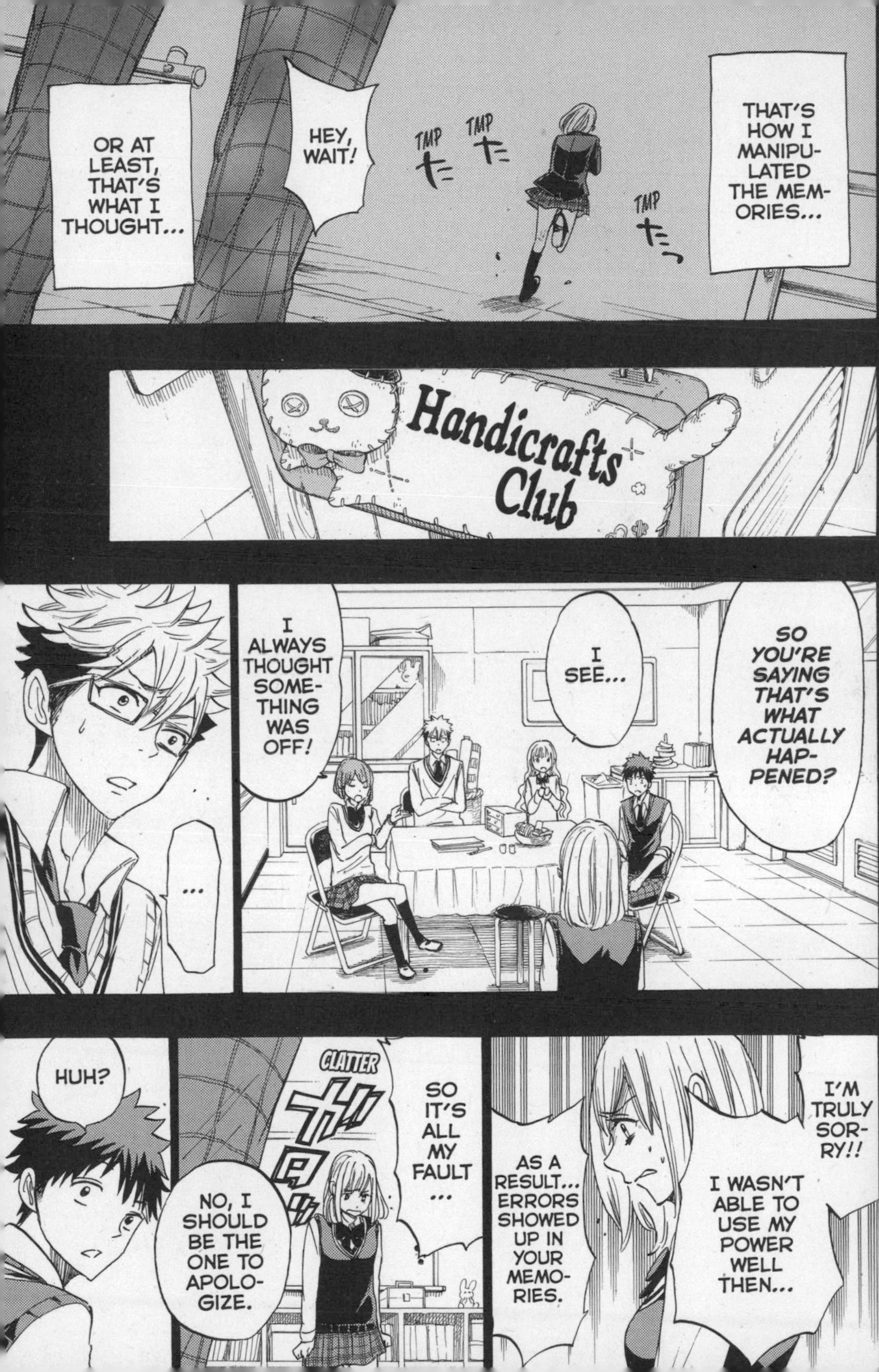
THAT'S HOW I MANIPULATED THE MEMORIES...
TMP
TMP
TMP
HEY, WAIT!
OR AT LEAST, THAT'S WHAT I THOUGHT...
Handicrafts Club
SO YOU'RE SAYING THAT'S WHAT ACTUALLY HAPPENED?
I SEE...
I ALWAYS THOUGHT SOMETHING WAS OFF!
...
I'M TRULY SORRY!!
I WASN'T ABLE TO USE MY POWER WELL THEN...
AS A RESULT... ERRORS SHOWED UP IN YOUR MEMORIES.
SO IT'S ALL MY FAULT...
CLATTER
NO, I SHOULD BE THE ONE TO APOLOGIZE.
HUH?

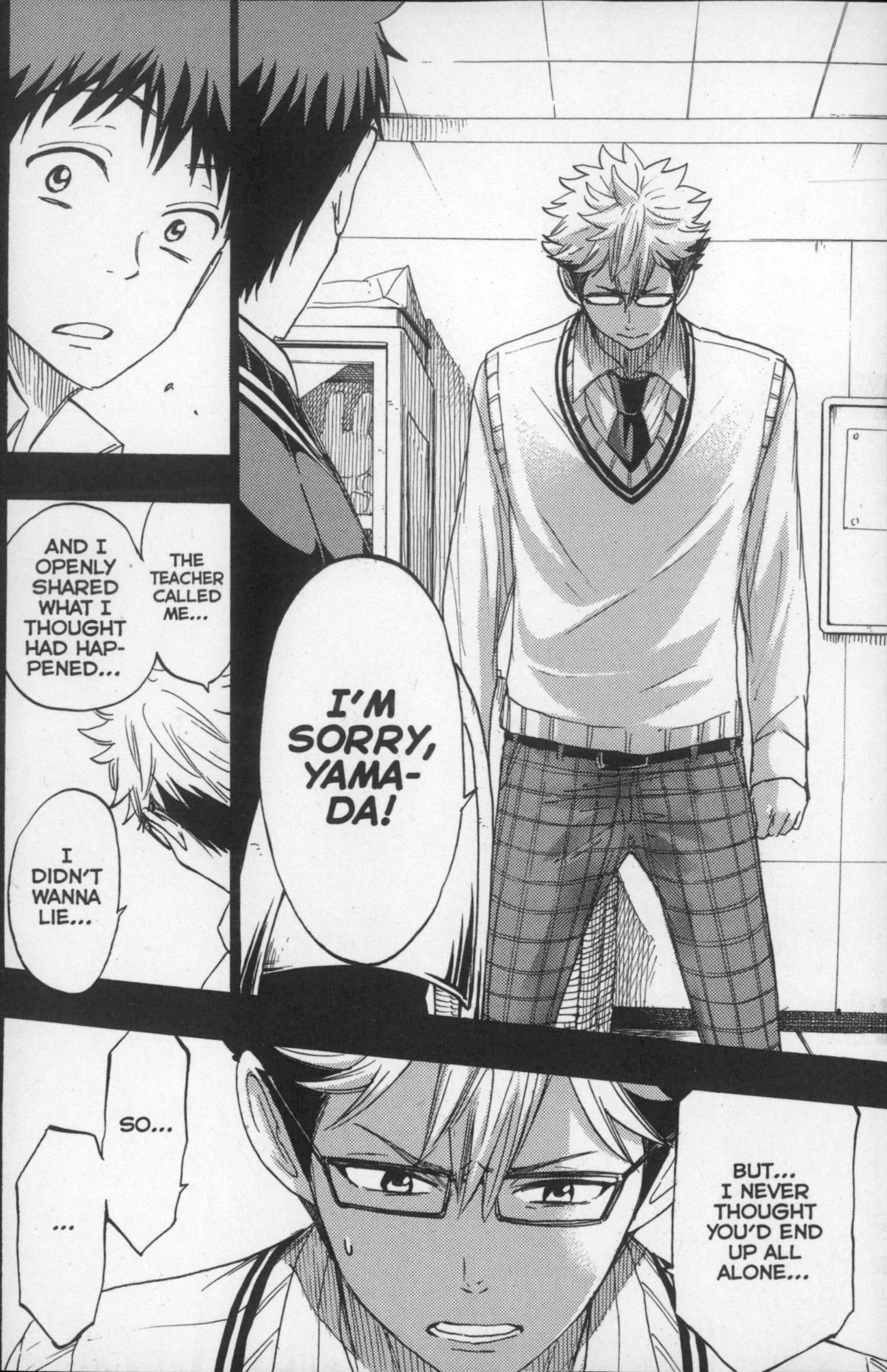
I'M SORRY, YAMADA!
THE TEACHER CALLED ME...
AND I OPENLY SHARED WHAT I THOUGHT HAD HAPPENED...
I DIDN'T WANNA LIE...
BUT... I NEVER THOUGHT YOU'D END UP ALL ALONE...
SO...
...

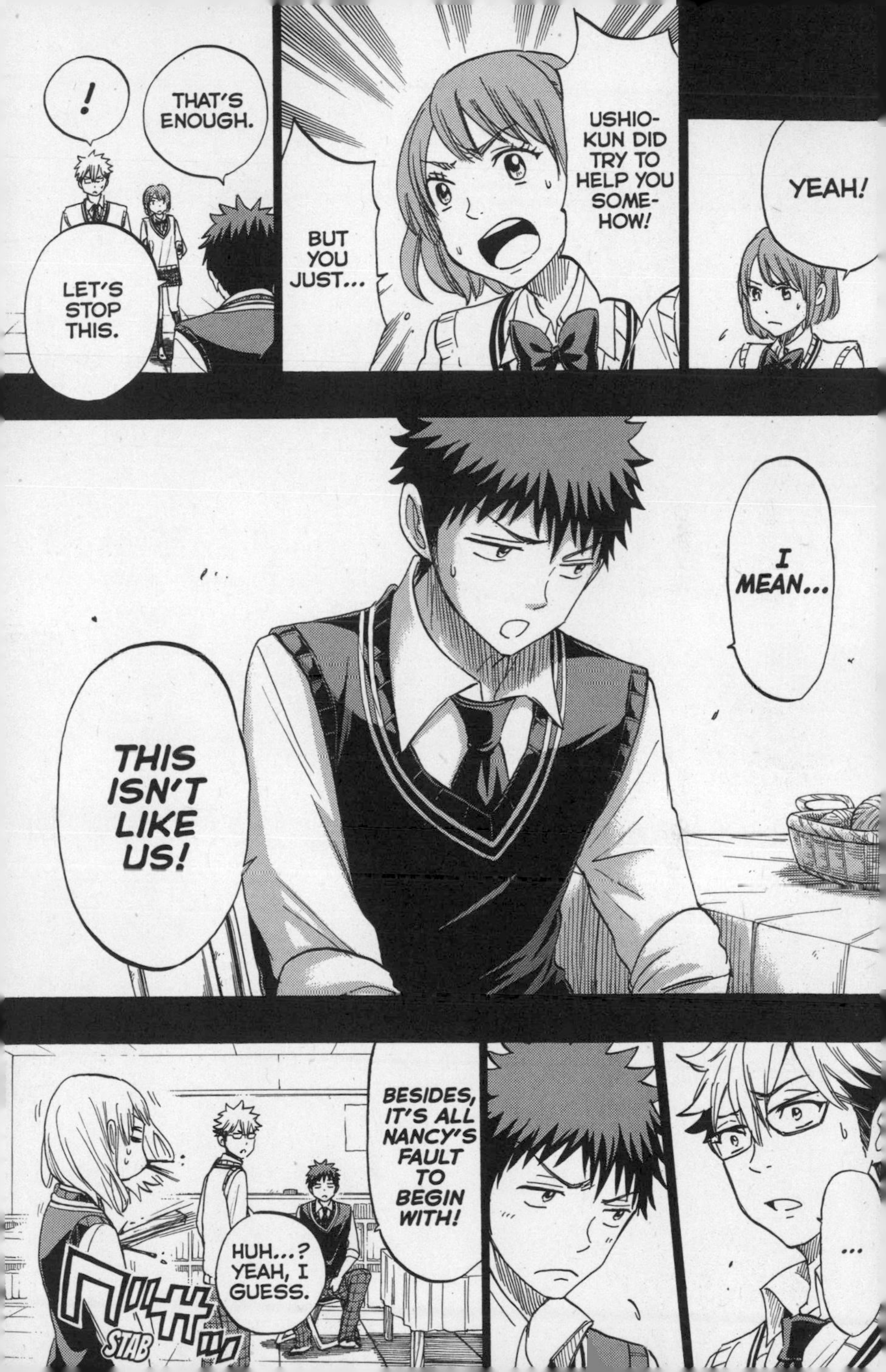
YEAH!
USHIO-KUN DID TRY TO HELP YOU SOMEHOW!
BUT YOU JUST...
THAT'S ENOUGH.
!
LET'S STOP THIS.
I MEAN...
THIS ISN'T LIKE US!
...
BESIDES, IT'S ALL NANCY'S FAULT TO BEGIN WITH!
HUH...? YEAH, I GUESS.
STAB

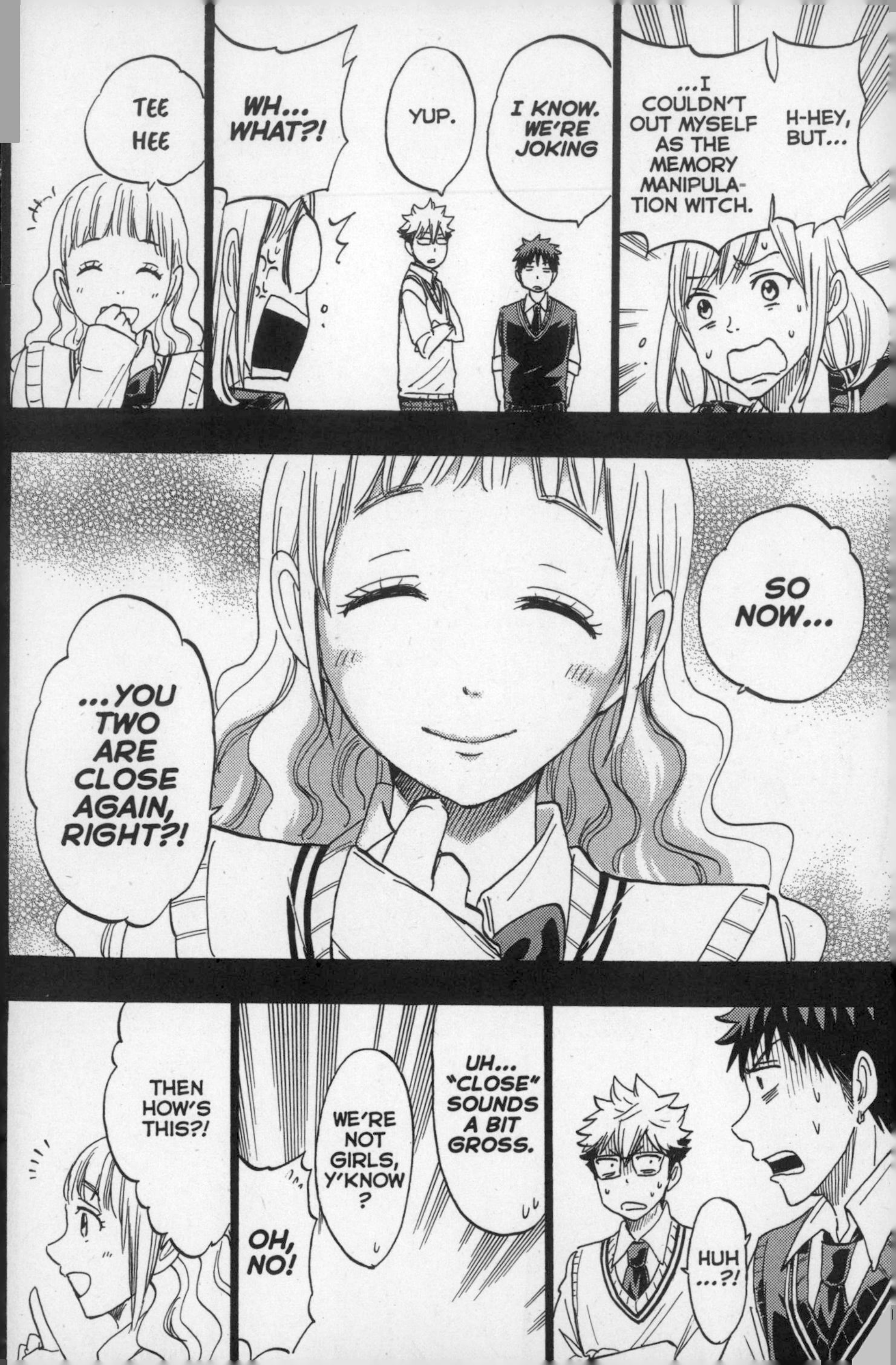
H-HEY, BUT...
...I COULDN'T OUT MYSELF AS THE MEMORY MANIPULATION WITCH.
I KNOW. WE'RE JOKING
YUP.
WH... WHAT?!
TEE HEE
SO NOW...
...YOU TWO ARE CLOSE AGAIN, RIGHT?!
HUH ...?!
UH... "CLOSE" SOUNDS A BIT GROSS.
WE'RE NOT GIRLS, Y'KNOW?
OH, NO!
THEN HOW'S THIS?!

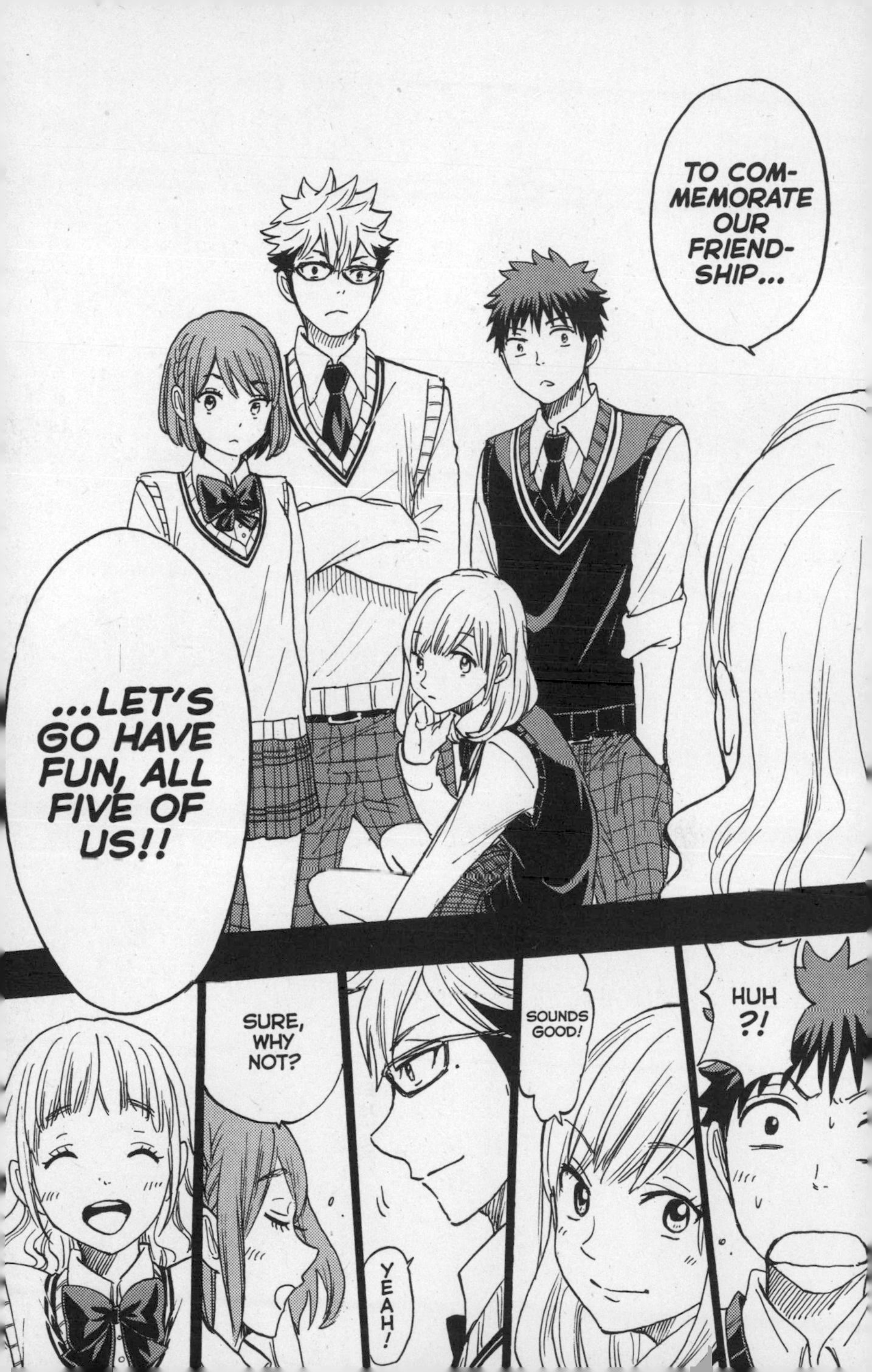
TO COM-MEMORATE OUR FRIEND-SHIP...
...LET'S GO HAVE FUN, ALL FIVE OF US!!
HUH ?!
SOUNDS GOOD!
YEAH!
SURE, WHY NOT?

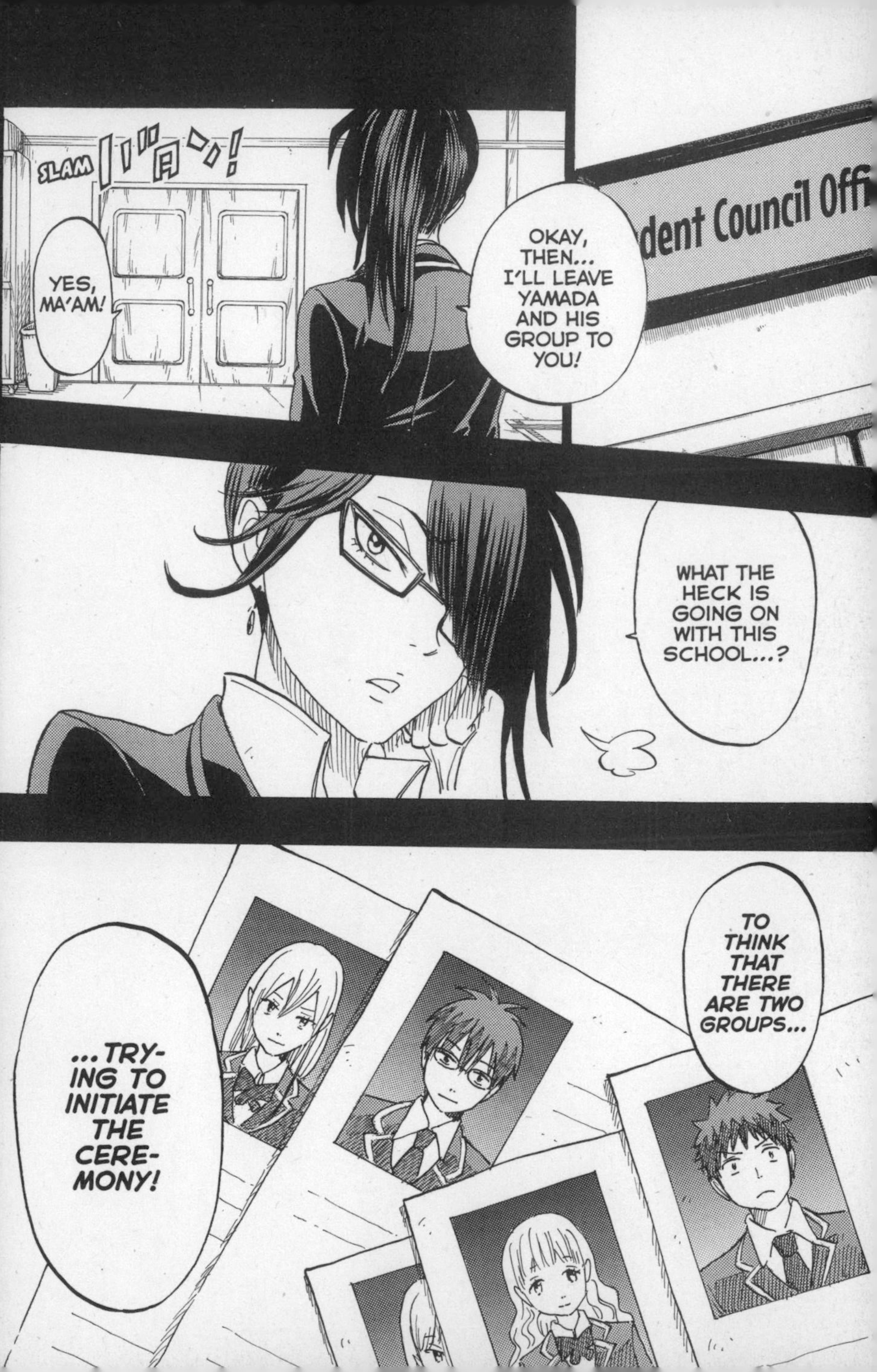
dent Council Offi
OKAY, THEN... I'LL LEAVE YAMADA AND HIS GROUP TO YOU!
YES, MA'AM!
SLAM
WHAT THE HECK IS GOING ON WITH THIS SCHOOL...?
TO THINK THAT THERE ARE TWO GROUPS...
...TRY-ING TO INITIATE THE CERE-MONY!

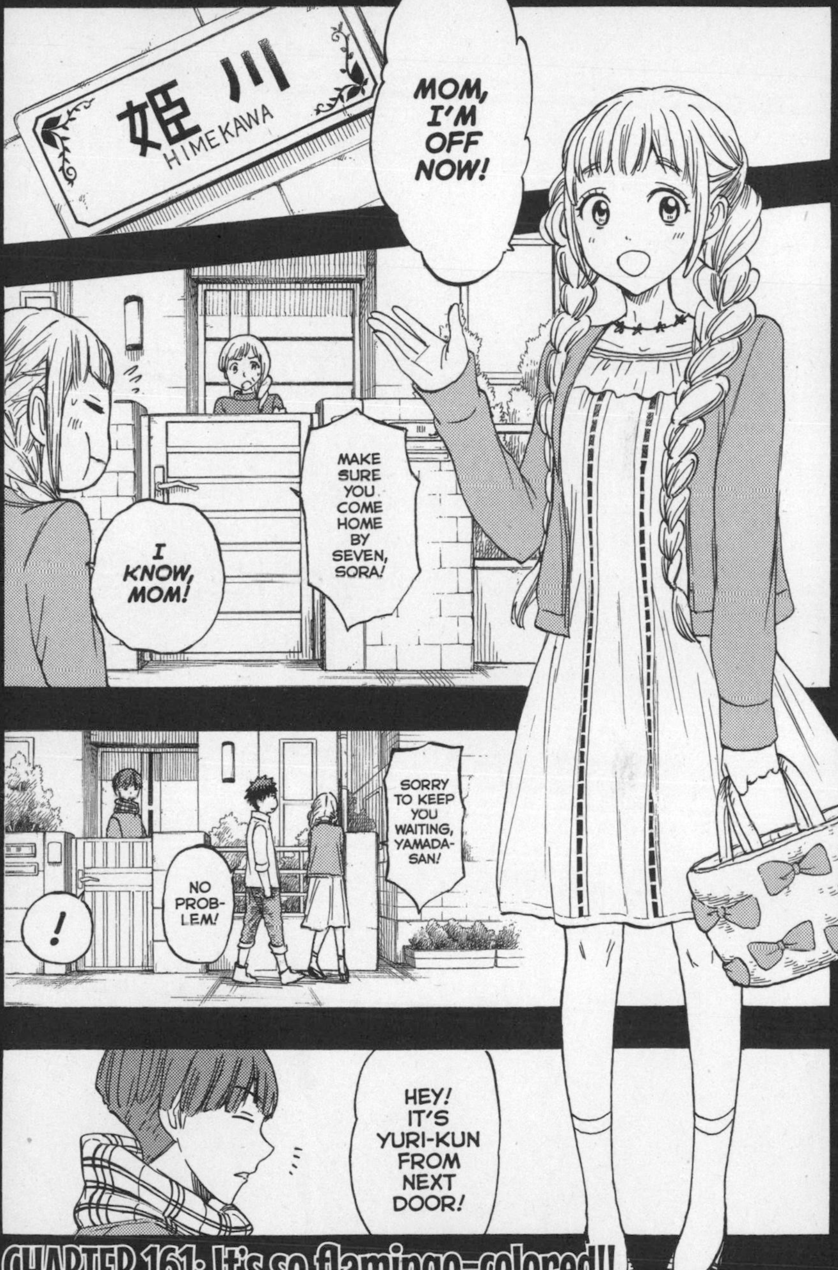
MOM, I'M OFF NOW!
姫川
HIMEKAWA
MAKE SURE YOU COME HOME BY SEVEN, SORA!
I KNOW, MOM!
SORRY TO KEEP YOU WAITING, YAMADA-SAN!
NO PROB-LEM!
!
HEY! IT'S YURI-KUN FROM NEXT DOOR!
...

CHAPTER 161: It's so flamingo-colored!!

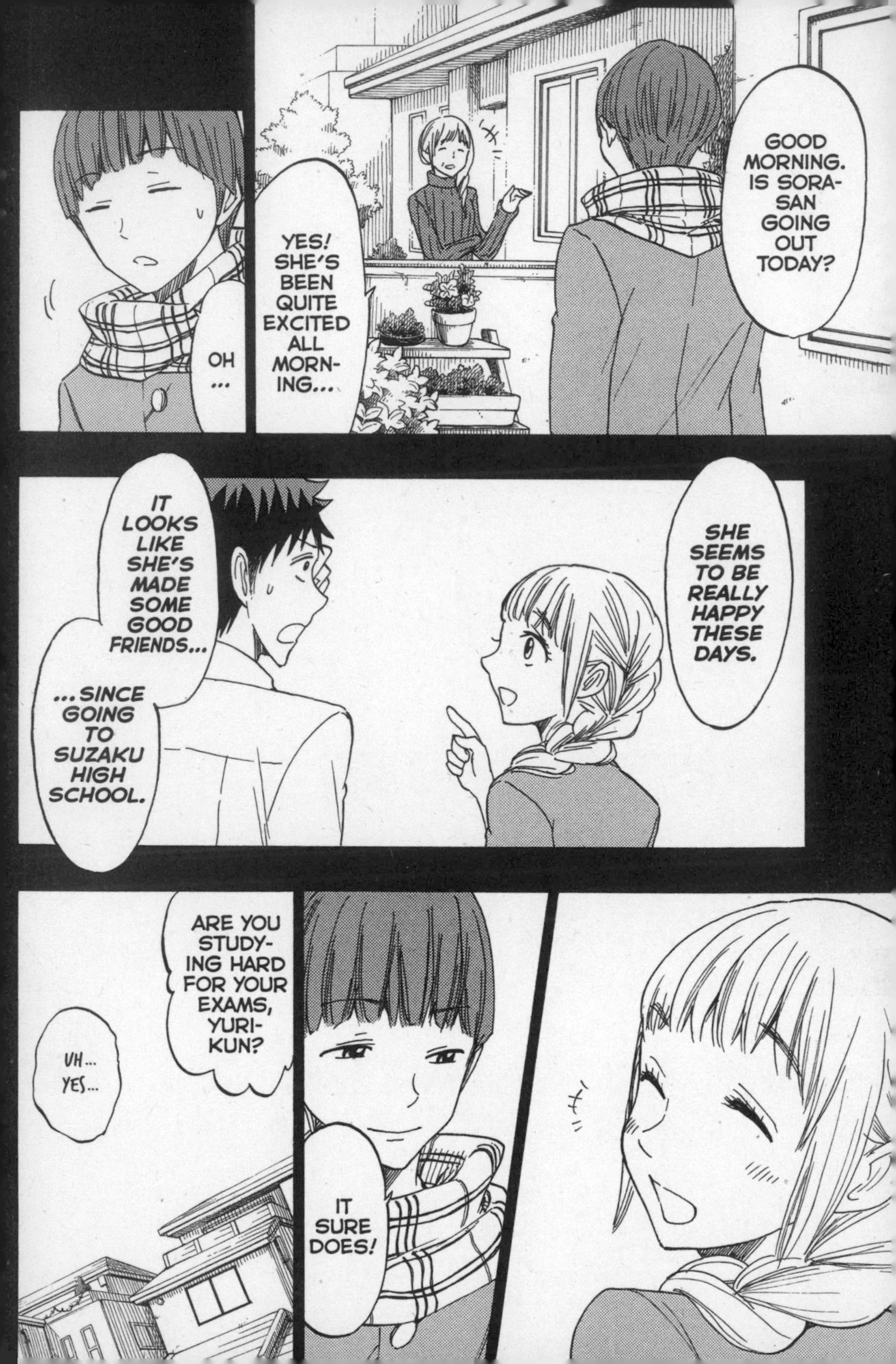
GOOD MORNING. IS SORA-SAN GOING OUT TODAY?
YES! SHE'S BEEN QUITE EXCITED ALL MORNING...
OH ...
SHE SEEMS TO BE REALLY HAPPY THESE DAYS.
IT LOOKS LIKE SHE'S MADE SOME GOOD FRIENDS...
...SINCE GOING TO SUZAKU HIGH SCHOOL.
IT SURE DOES!
ARE YOU STUDYING HARD FOR YOUR EXAMS, YURI-KUN?
UH... YES...

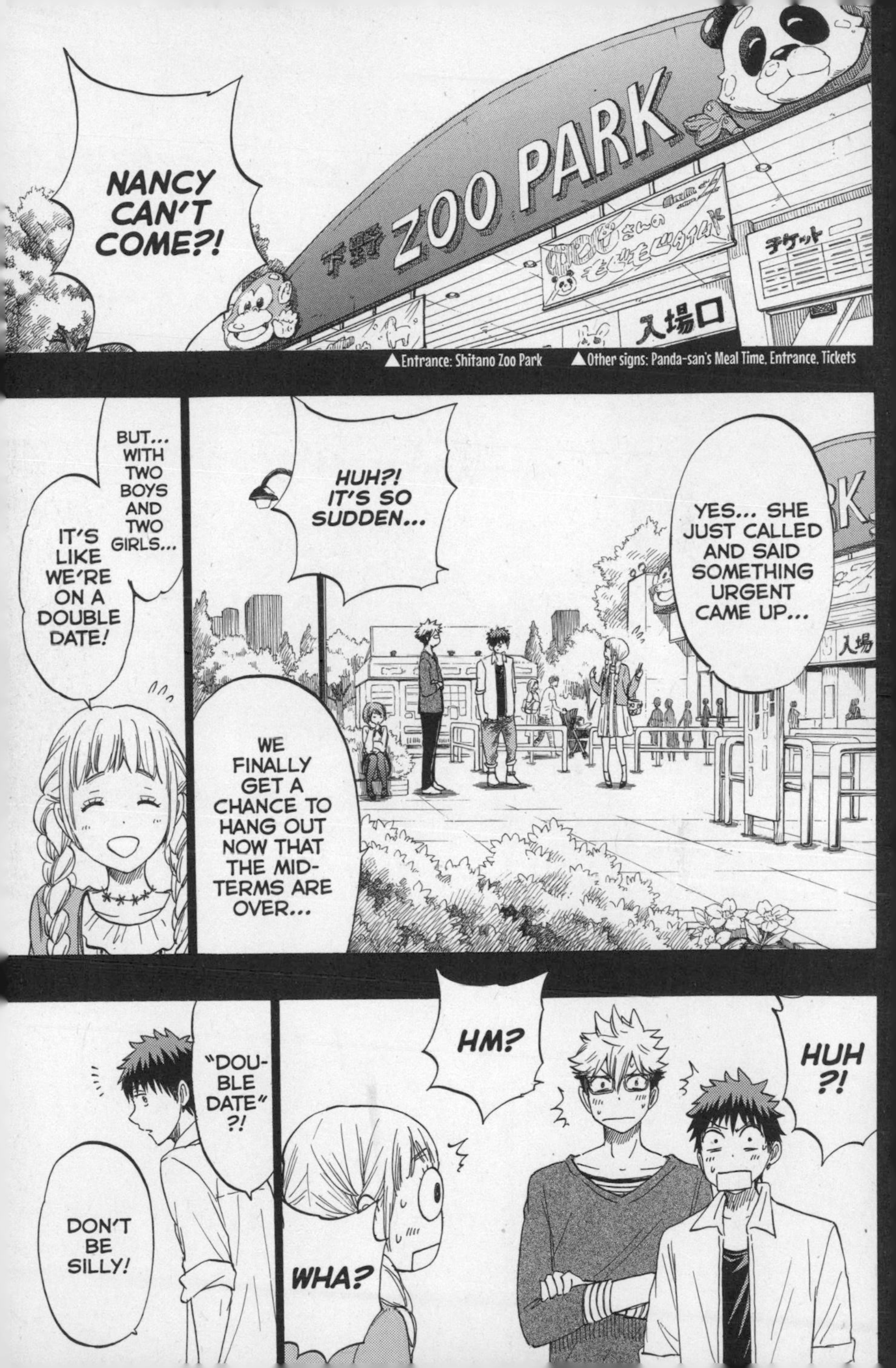
ZOO PARK
NANCY CAN'T COME?!
▲Entrance: Shitano Zoo Park
▲Other signs: Panda-san's Meal Time, Entrance, Tickets
YES... SHE JUST CALLED AND SAID SOMETHING URGENT CAME UP...
HUH?! IT'S SO SUDDEN...
WE FINALLY GET A CHANCE TO HANG OUT NOW THAT THE MID-TERMS ARE OVER...
BUT... WITH TWO BOYS AND TWO GIRLS...
IT'S LIKE WE'RE ON A DOUBLE DATE!
HUH?!
HM?
WHA?
"DOUBLE DATE"?!
DON'T BE SILLY!

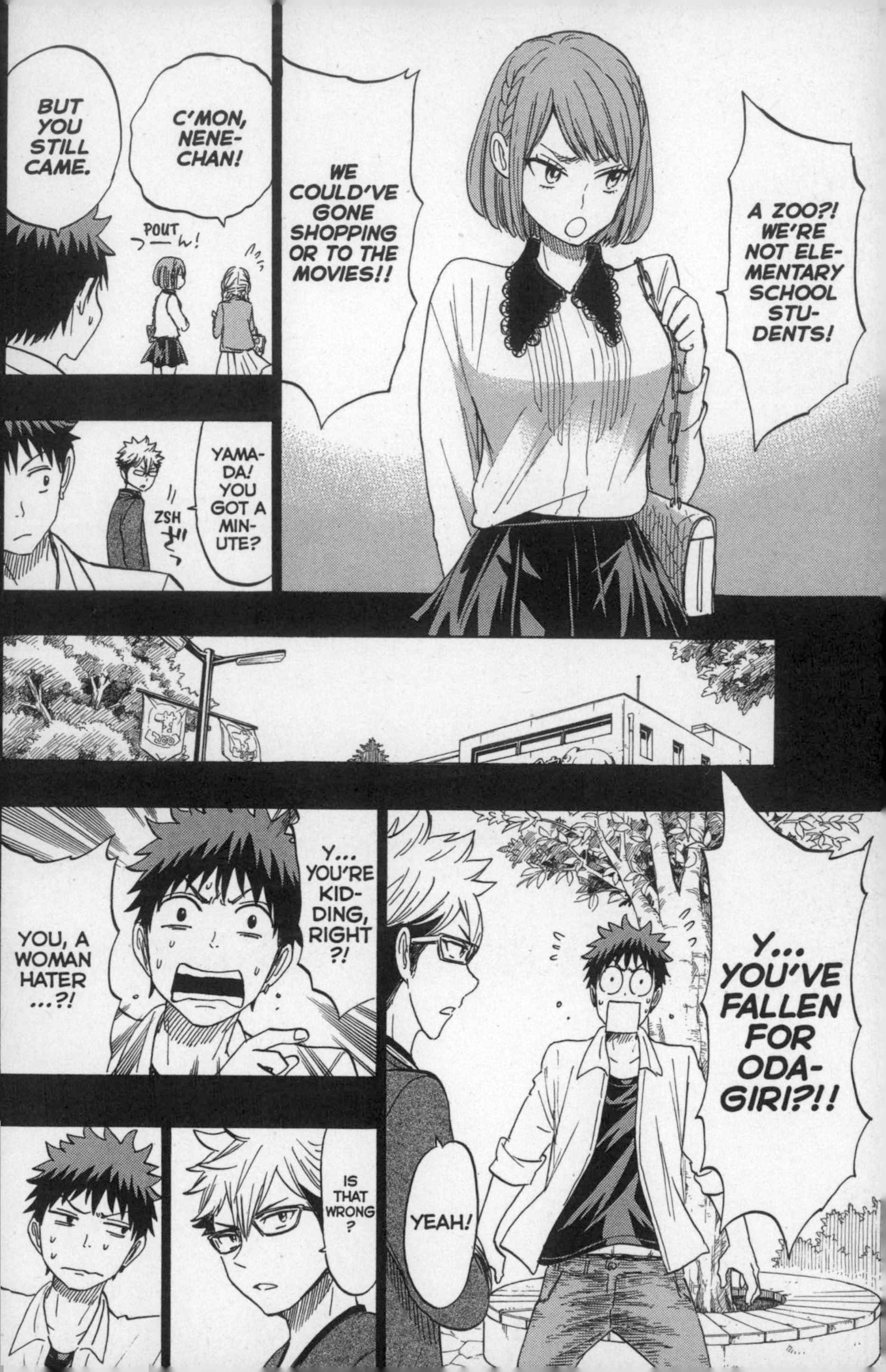
A ZOO?! WE'RE NOT ELEMENTARY SCHOOL STUDENTS!
WE COULD'VE GONE SHOPPING OR TO THE MOVIES!!
C'MON, NENE-CHAN!
POUT
BUT YOU STILL CAME.
YAMADA! YOU GOT A MINUTE?
ZSH
Y... YOU'VE FALLEN FOR ODAGIRI?!!
YEAH!
Y... YOU'RE KIDDING, RIGHT?!
YOU, A WOMAN HATER...?!
IS THAT WRONG?

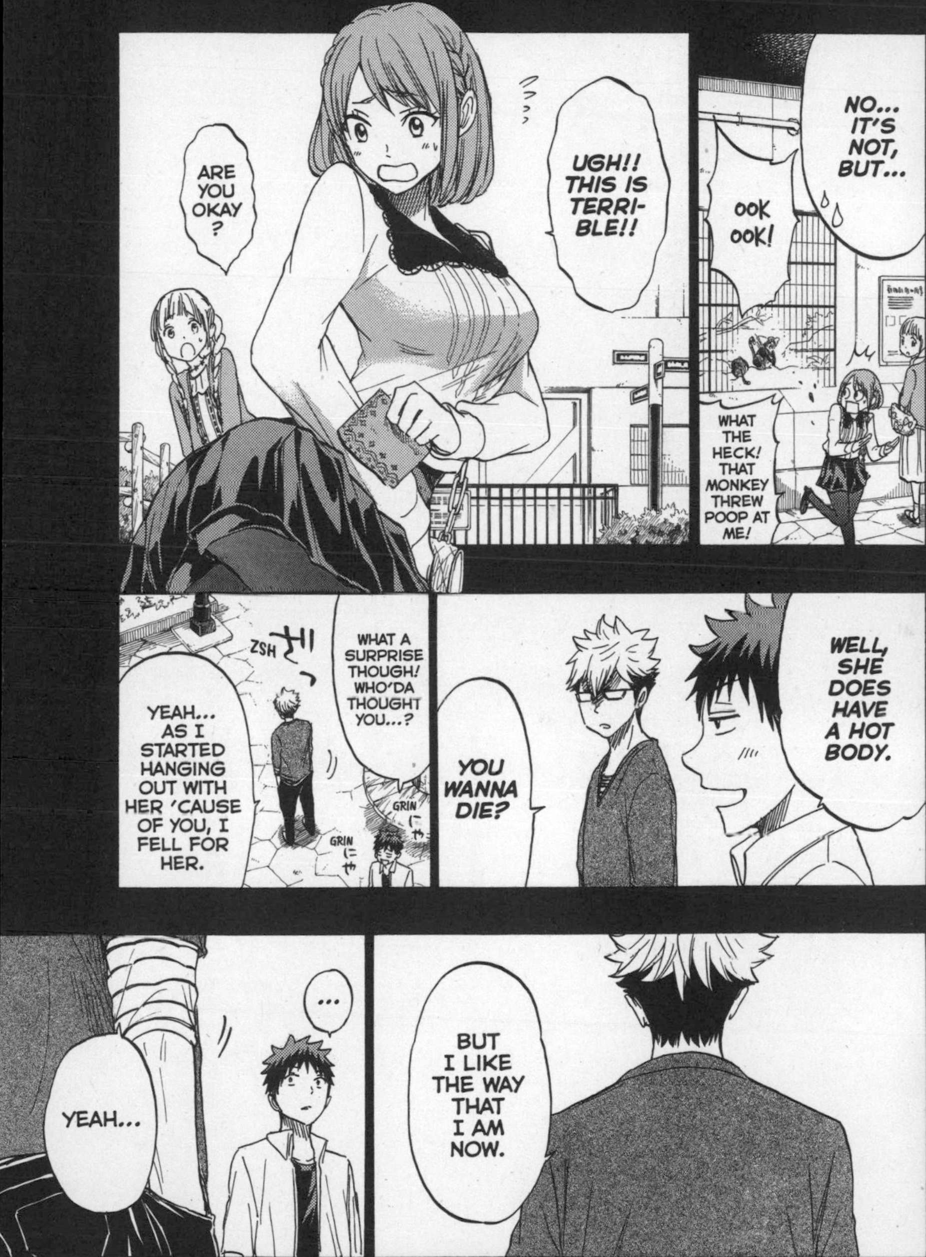

NO... IT'S NOT, BUT...
OOK OOK!
WHAT THE HECK! THAT MONKEY THREW POOP AT ME!
UGH!! THIS IS TERRI-BLE!!
ARE YOU OKAY?
WELL, SHE DOES HAVE A HOT BODY.
YOU WANNA DIE?
WHAT A SURPRISE THOUGH! WHO'DA THOUGHT YOU...?
ZSH
YEAH... AS I STARTED HANGING OUT WITH HER 'CAUSE OF YOU, I FELL FOR HER.
GRIN
GRIN
BUT I LIKE THE WAY THAT I AM NOW.
...
YEAH...

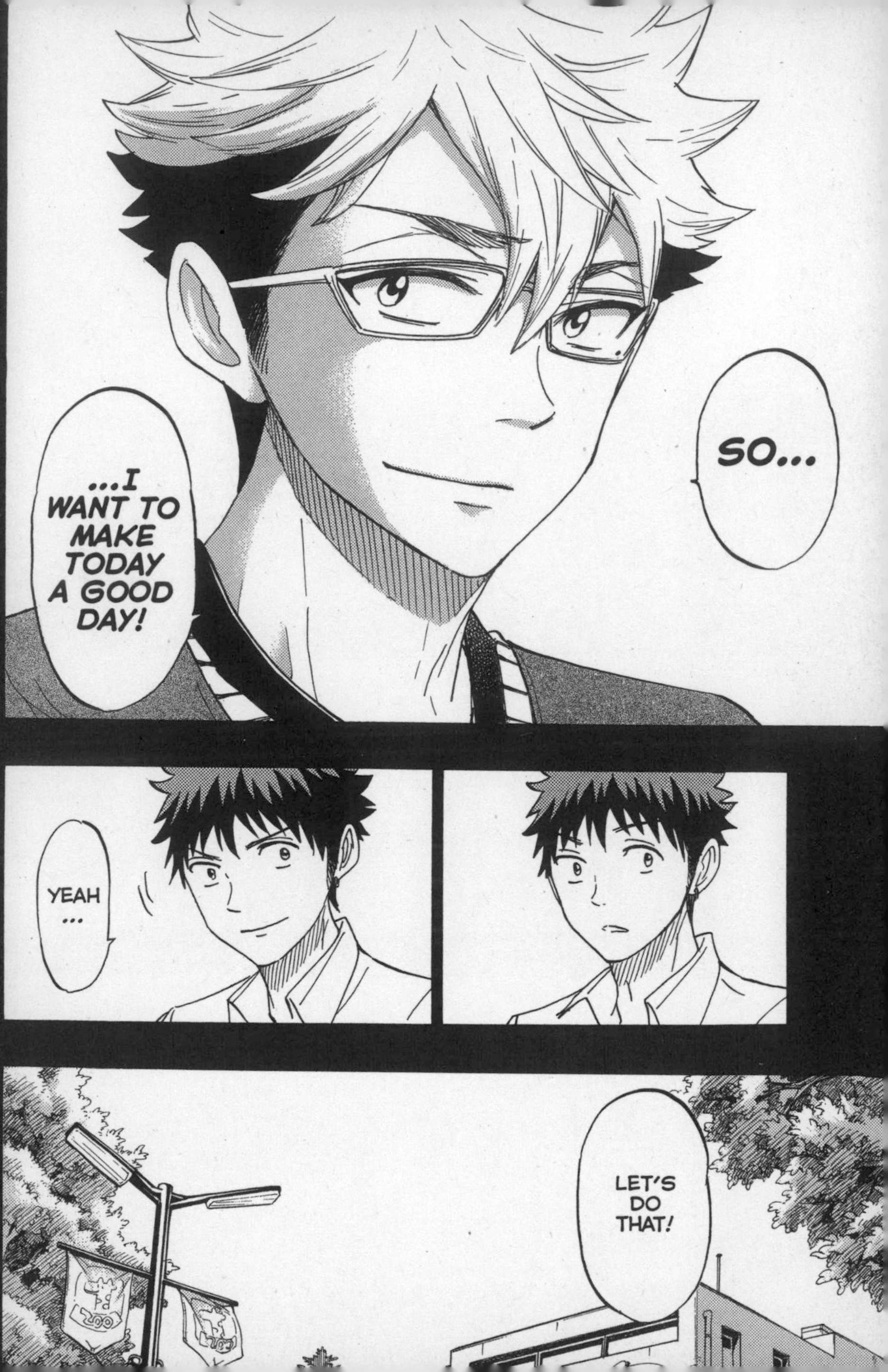
SO...
...I WANT TO MAKE TODAY A GOOD DAY!
YEAH ...
LET'S DO THAT!

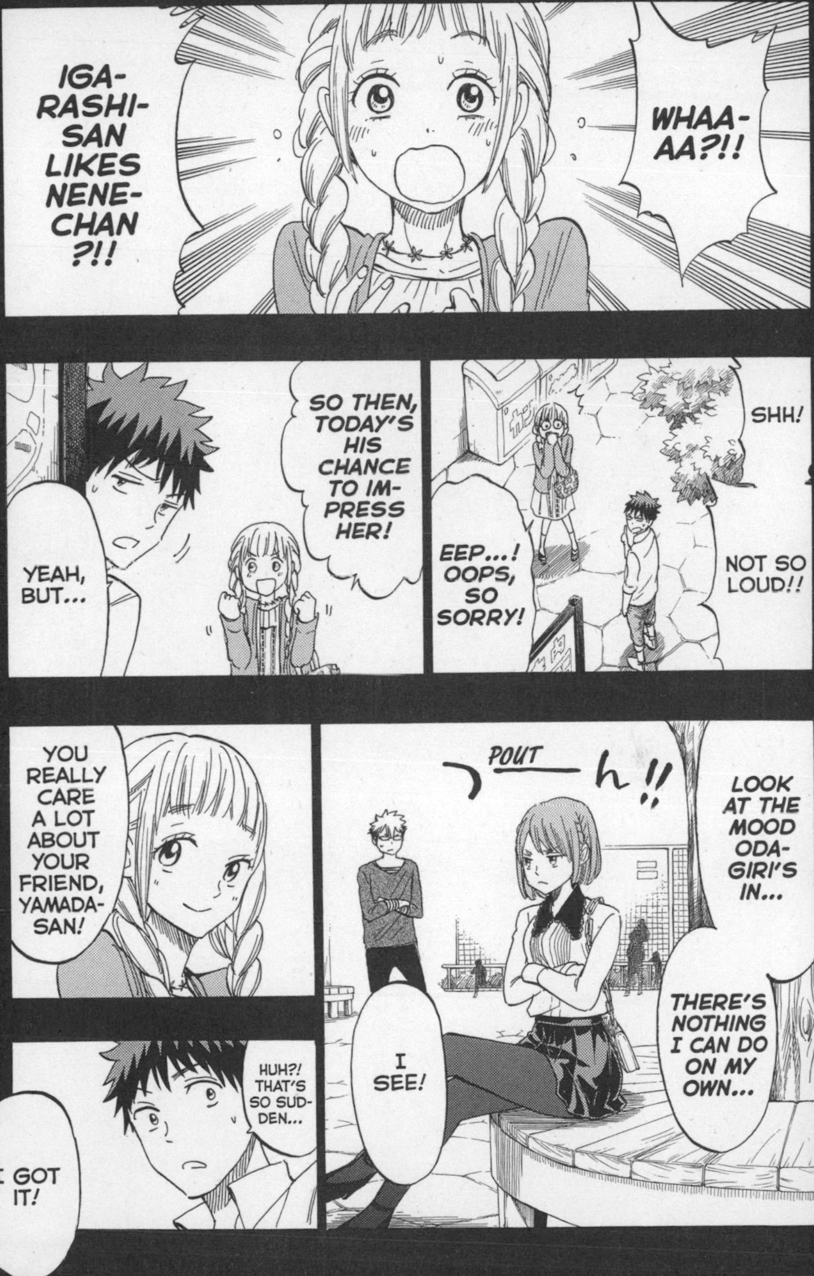
WHAAA-AA?!!
IGA-RASHI-SAN LIKES NENE-CHAN?!!
SHH!
NOT SO LOUD!!
EEP...! OOPS, SO SORRY!
SO THEN, TODAY'S HIS CHANCE TO IM-PRESS HER!
YEAH, BUT...
POUT
つーん!!
LOOK AT THE MOOD ODA-GIRI'S IN...
THERE'S NOTHING I CAN DO ON MY OWN...
I SEE!
YOU REALLY CARE A LOT ABOUT YOUR FRIEND, YAMADA-SAN!
HUH?! THAT'S SO SUD-DEN...
I GOT IT!

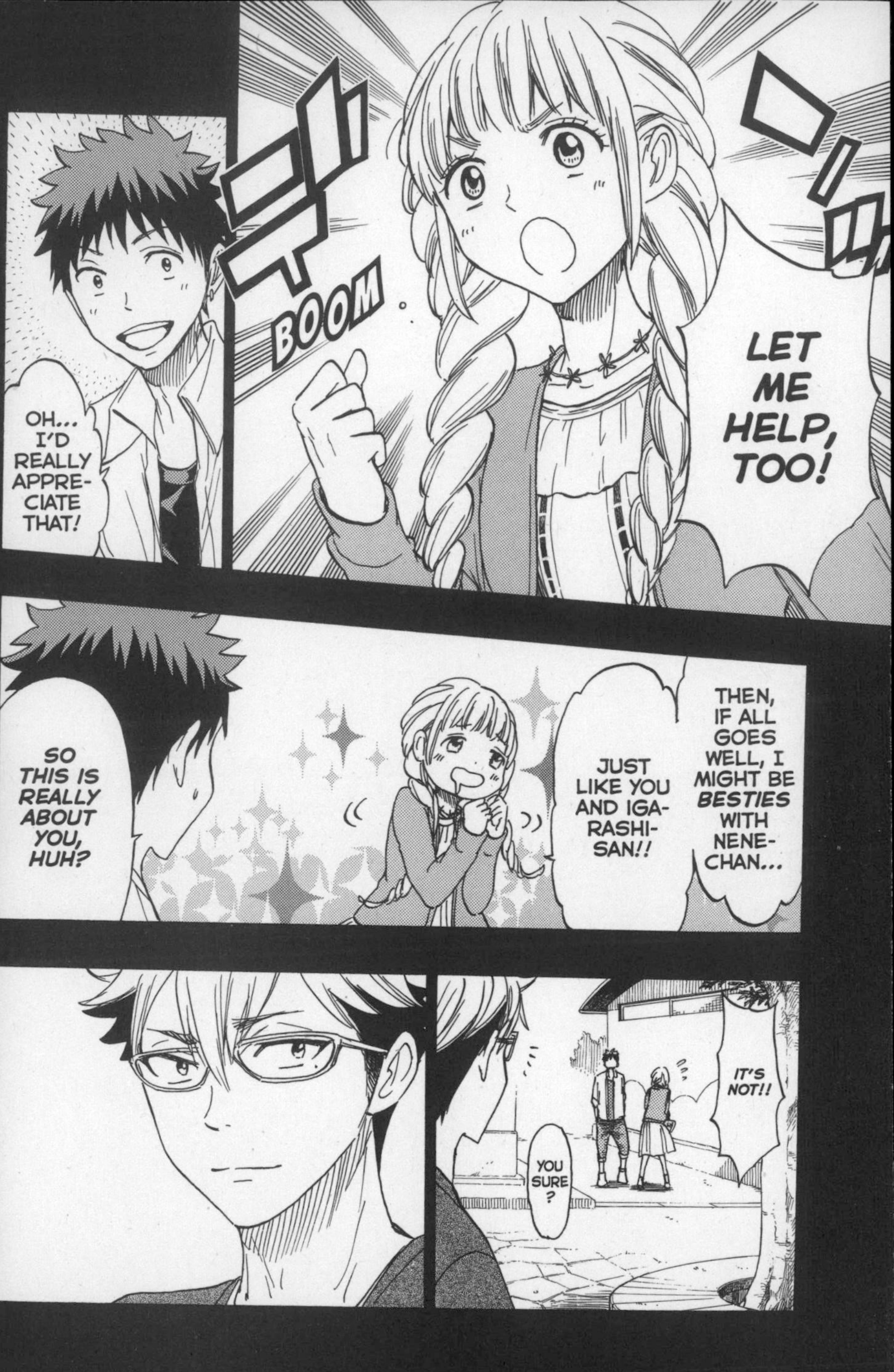
BOOM
LET ME HELP, TOO!
OH... I'D REALLY APPRE-CIATE THAT!
THEN, IF ALL GOES WELL, I MIGHT BE BESTIES WITH NENE-CHAN...
JUST LIKE YOU AND IGA-RASHI-SAN!!
SO THIS IS REALLY ABOUT YOU, HUH?
IT'S NOT!!
YOU SURE?

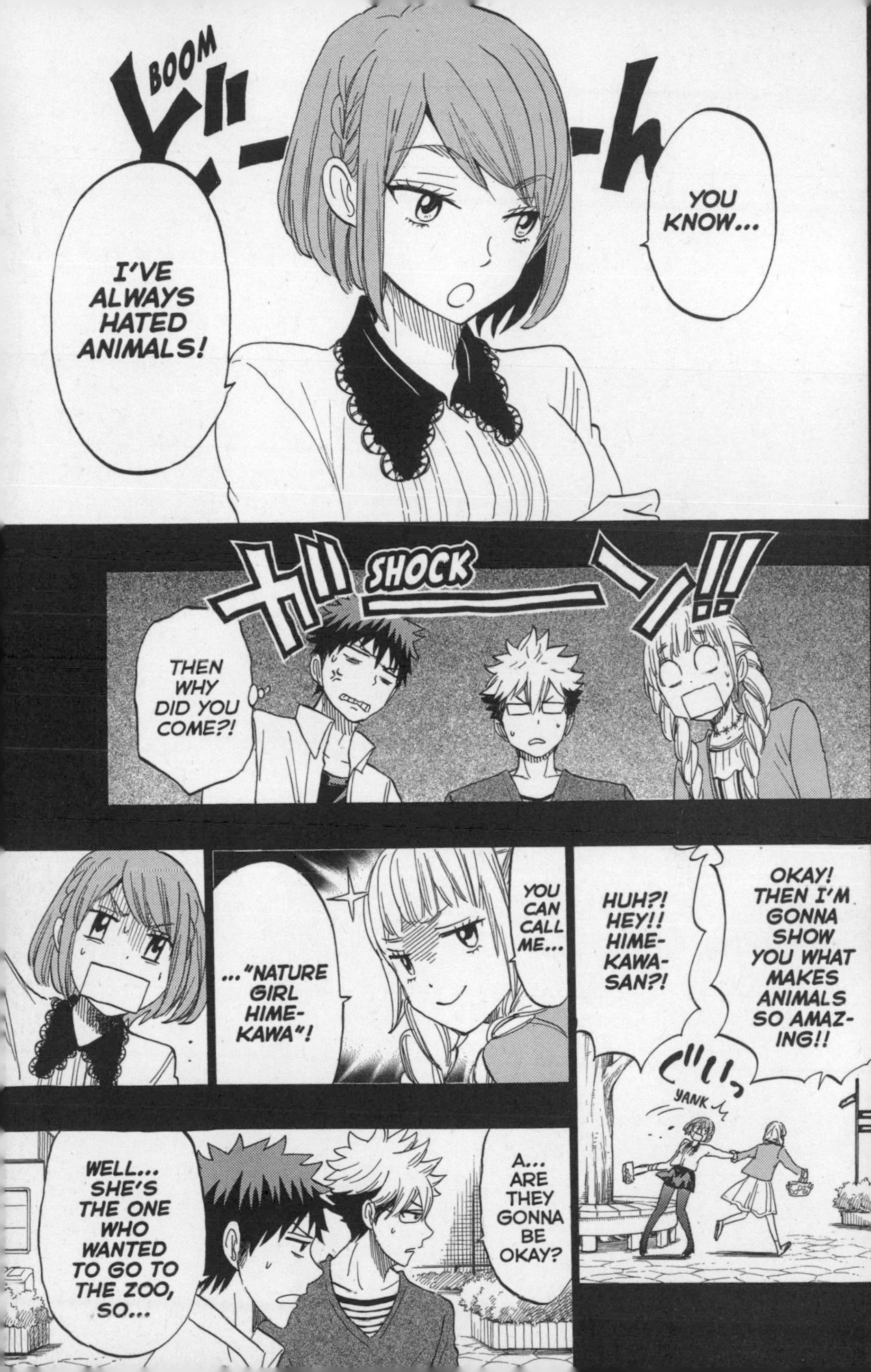
BOOM
YOU KNOW...
I'VE ALWAYS HATED ANIMALS!
SHOCK
THEN WHY DID YOU COME?!
OKAY! THEN I'M GONNA SHOW YOU WHAT MAKES ANIMALS SO AMAZ-ING!!
HUH?! HEY!! HIME-KAWA-SAN?!
YANK
YOU CAN CALL ME...
..."NATURE GIRL HIME-KAWA"!
A... ARE THEY GONNA BE OKAY?
WELL... SHE'S THE ONE WHO WANTED TO GO TO THE ZOO, SO...

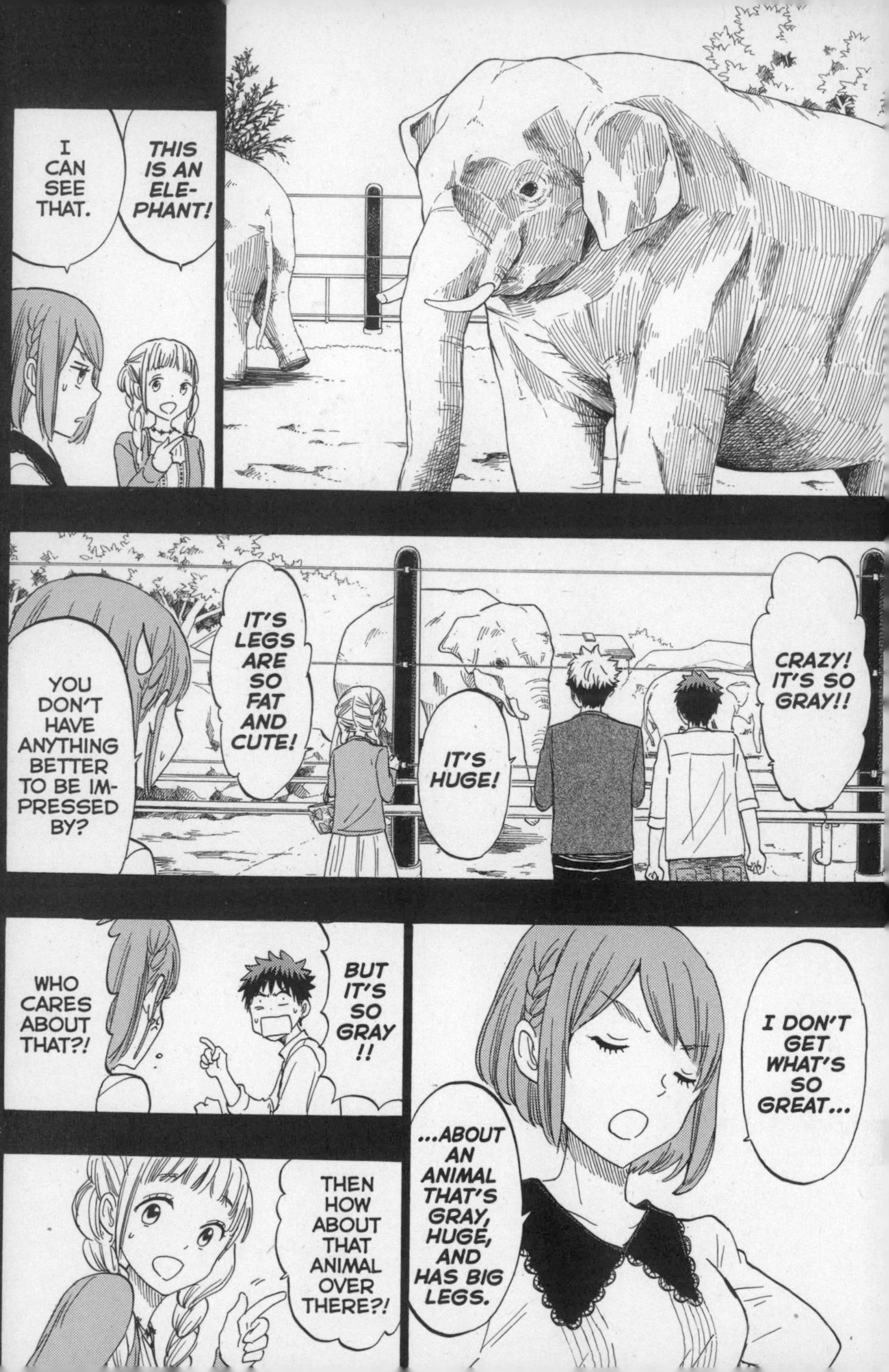
THIS IS AN ELE-PHANT!
I CAN SEE THAT.
CRAZY! IT'S SO GRAY!!
IT'S HUGE!
IT'S LEGS ARE SO FAT AND CUTE!
YOU DON'T HAVE ANYTHING BETTER TO BE IM-PRESSED BY?
I DON'T GET WHAT'S SO GREAT...
...ABOUT AN ANIMAL THAT'S GRAY, HUGE, AND HAS BIG LEGS.
BUT IT'S SO GRAY!!
WHO CARES ABOUT THAT?!
THEN HOW ABOUT THAT ANIMAL OVER THERE?!

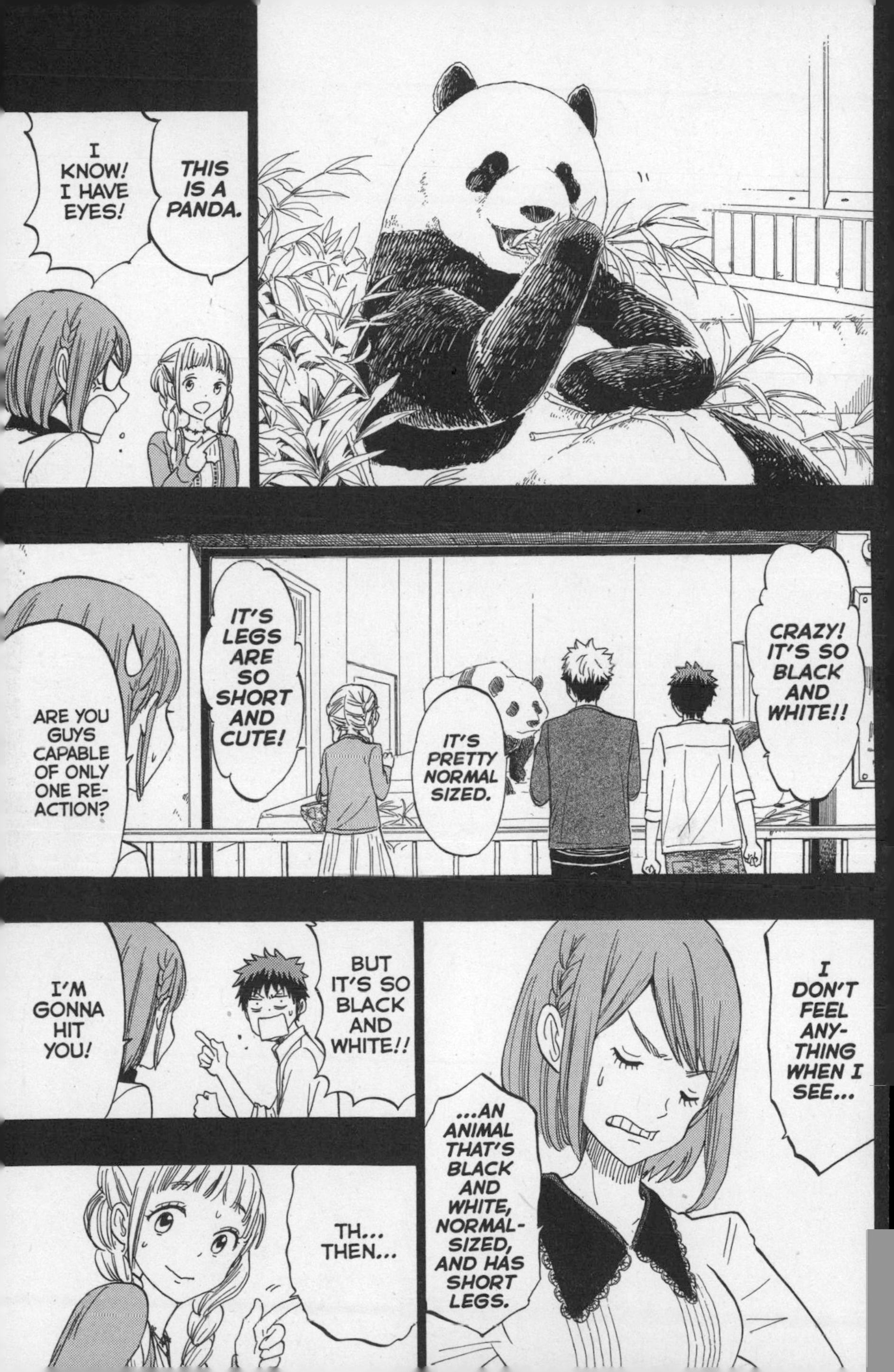
THIS IS A PANDA.
I KNOW! I HAVE EYES!
CRAZY! IT'S SO BLACK AND WHITE!!
IT'S PRETTY NORMAL SIZED.
IT'S LEGS ARE SO SHORT AND CUTE!
ARE YOU GUYS CAPABLE OF ONLY ONE RE-ACTION?
I DON'T FEEL ANY-THING WHEN I SEE...
...AN ANIMAL THAT'S BLACK AND WHITE, NORMAL-SIZED, AND HAS SHORT LEGS.
BUT IT'S SO BLACK AND WHITE!!
I'M GONNA HIT YOU!
TH... THEN...

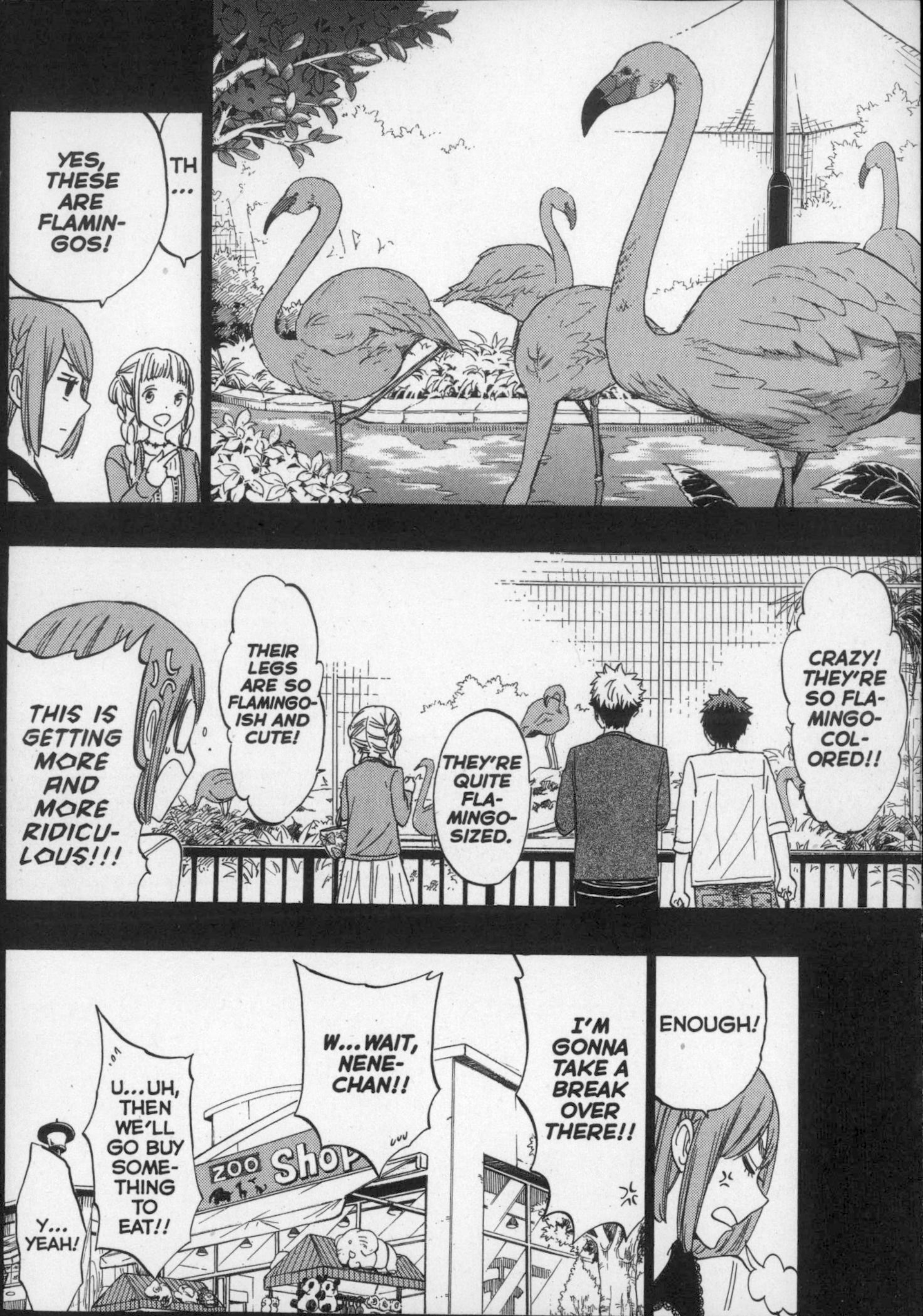
TH...
YES, THESE ARE FLAMIN-GOS!
CRAZY! THEY'RE SO FLA-MINGO-COL-ORED!!
THEY'RE QUITE FLA-MINGO-SIZED.
THEIR LEGS ARE SO FLAMINGO-ISH AND CUTE!
THIS IS GETTING MORE AND MORE RIDICU-LOUS!!!
ENOUGH!
I'M GONNA TAKE A BREAK OVER THERE!!
W...WAIT, NENE-CHAN!!
ZOO Shop
U...UH, THEN WE'LL GO BUY SOME-THING TO EAT!!
Y... YEAH!

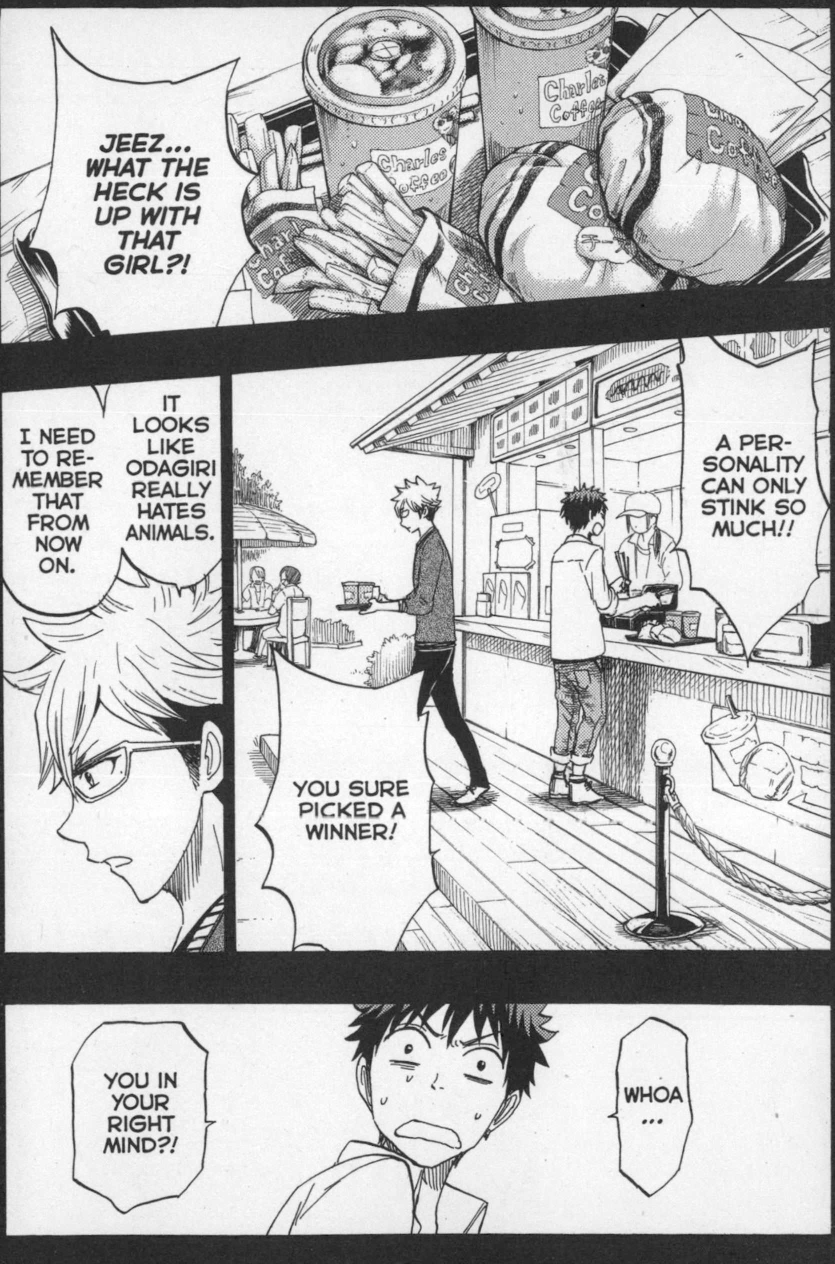
JEEZ... WHAT THE HECK IS UP WITH THAT GIRL?!
A PER-SONALITY CAN ONLY STINK SO MUCH!!
YOU SURE PICKED A WINNER!
IT LOOKS LIKE ODAGIRI REALLY HATES ANIMALS.
I NEED TO RE-MEMBER THAT FROM NOW ON.
WHOA ...
YOU IN YOUR RIGHT MIND?!

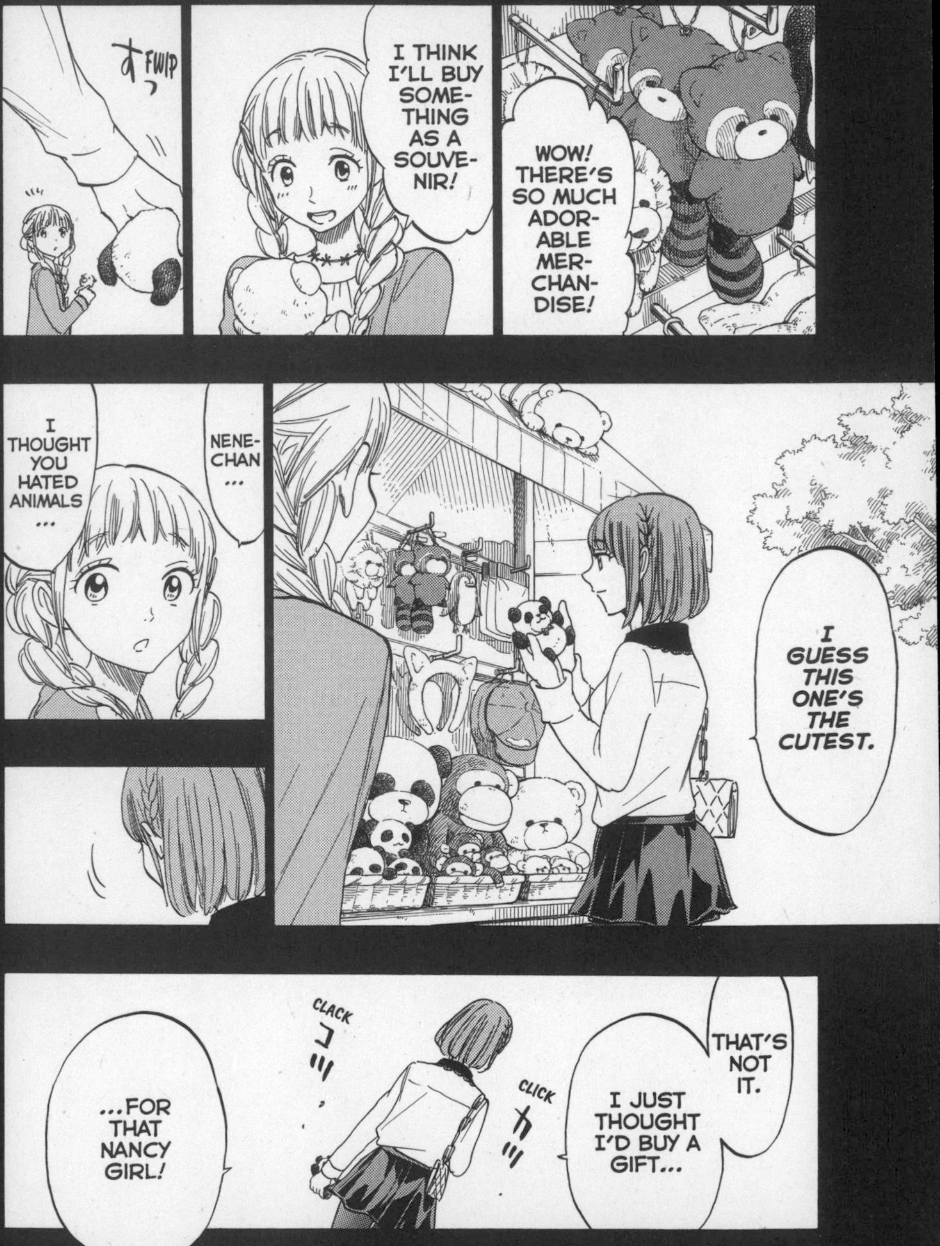
WOW! THERE'S SO MUCH ADORABLE MERCHANDISE!
I THINK I'LL BUY SOMETHING AS A SOUVENIR!
す FWIP
I GUESS THIS ONE'S THE CUTEST.
NENE-CHAN...
I THOUGHT YOU HATED ANIMALS...
THAT'S NOT IT.
I JUST THOUGHT I'D BUY A GIFT...
CLICK
CLACK
...FOR THAT NANCY GIRL!

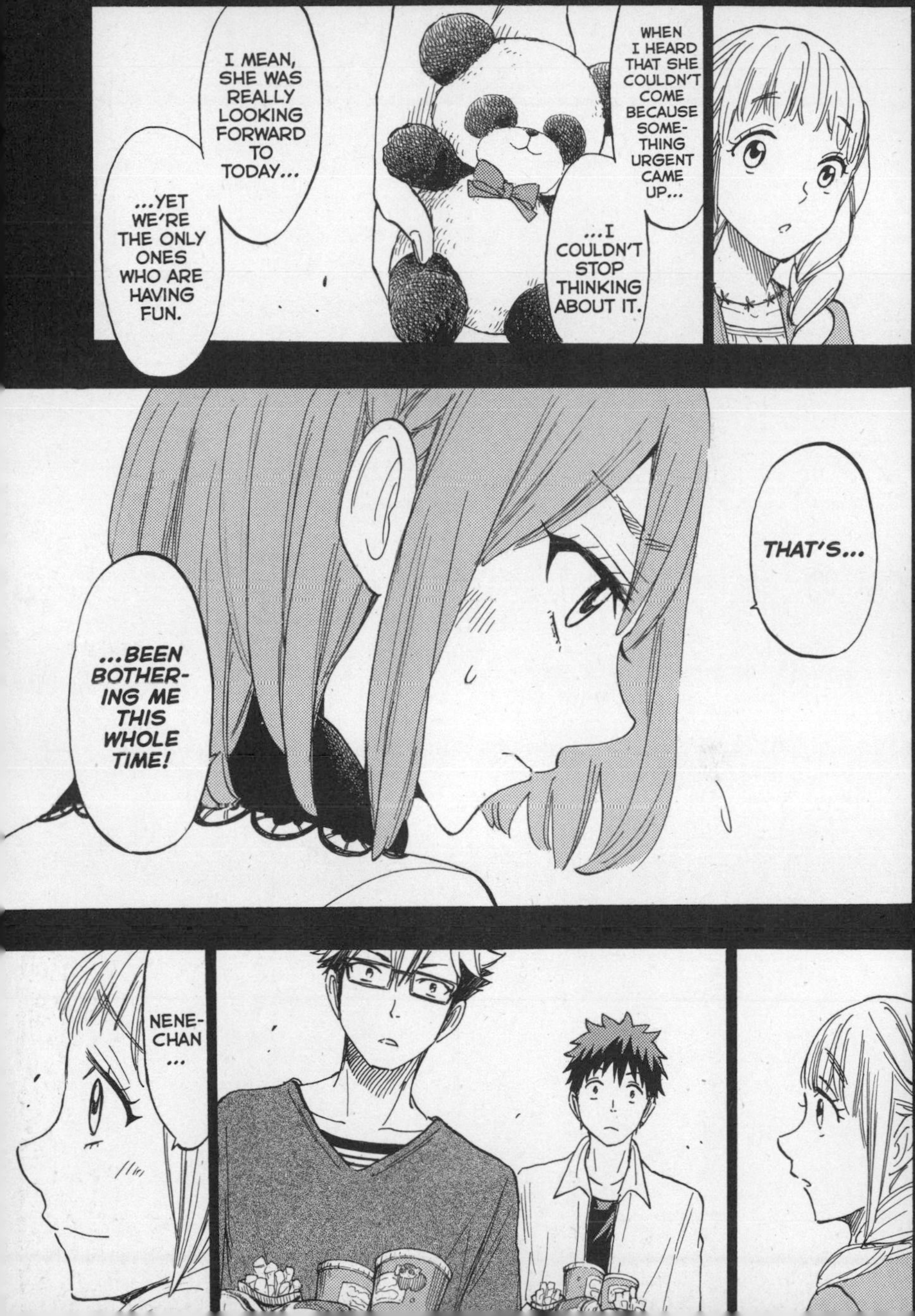
WHEN I HEARD THAT SHE COULDN'T COME BECAUSE SOME-THING URGENT CAME UP...
...I COULDN'T STOP THINKING ABOUT IT.
I MEAN, SHE WAS REALLY LOOKING FORWARD TO TODAY...
...YET WE'RE THE ONLY ONES WHO ARE HAVING FUN.
THAT'S...
...BEEN BOTHERING ME THIS WHOLE TIME!
NENE-CHAN...

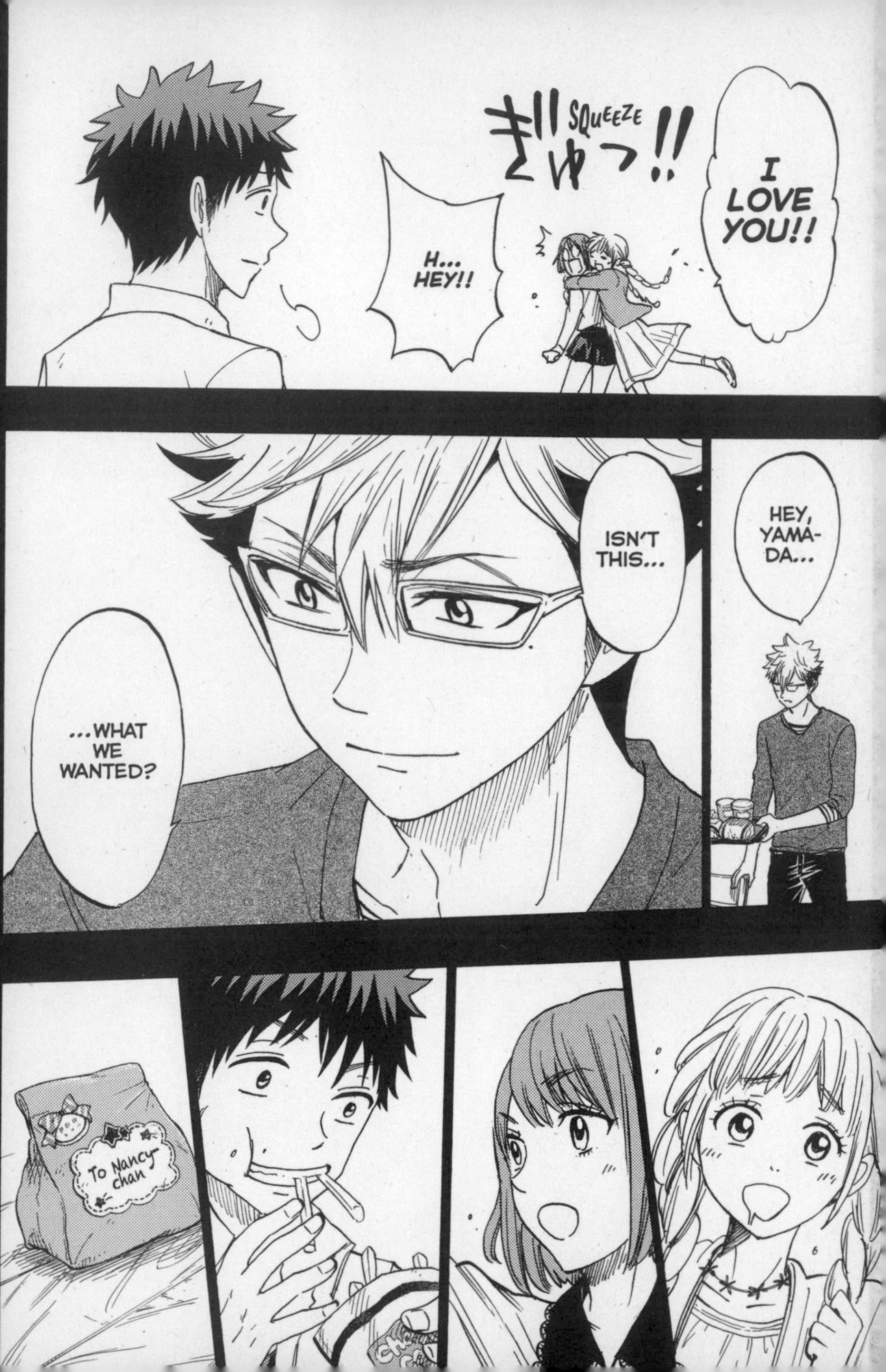
I LOVE YOU!!
きゅっ!!
SQUEEZE
H... HEY!!
HEY, YAMA-DA...
ISN'T THIS...
...WHAT WE WANTED?
To Nancy-chan

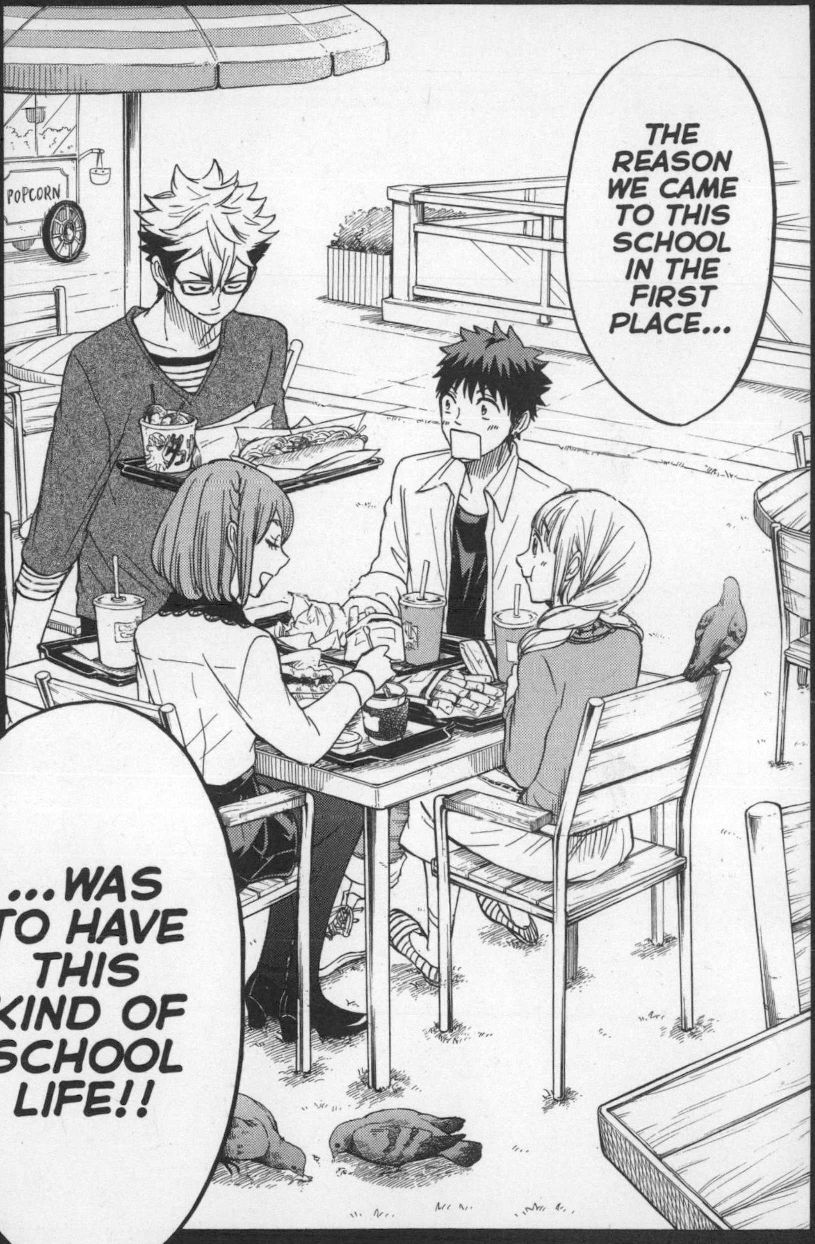
THE REASON WE CAME TO THIS SCHOOL IN THE FIRST PLACE...
...WAS TO HAVE THIS KIND OF SCHOOL LIFE!!
POPCORN

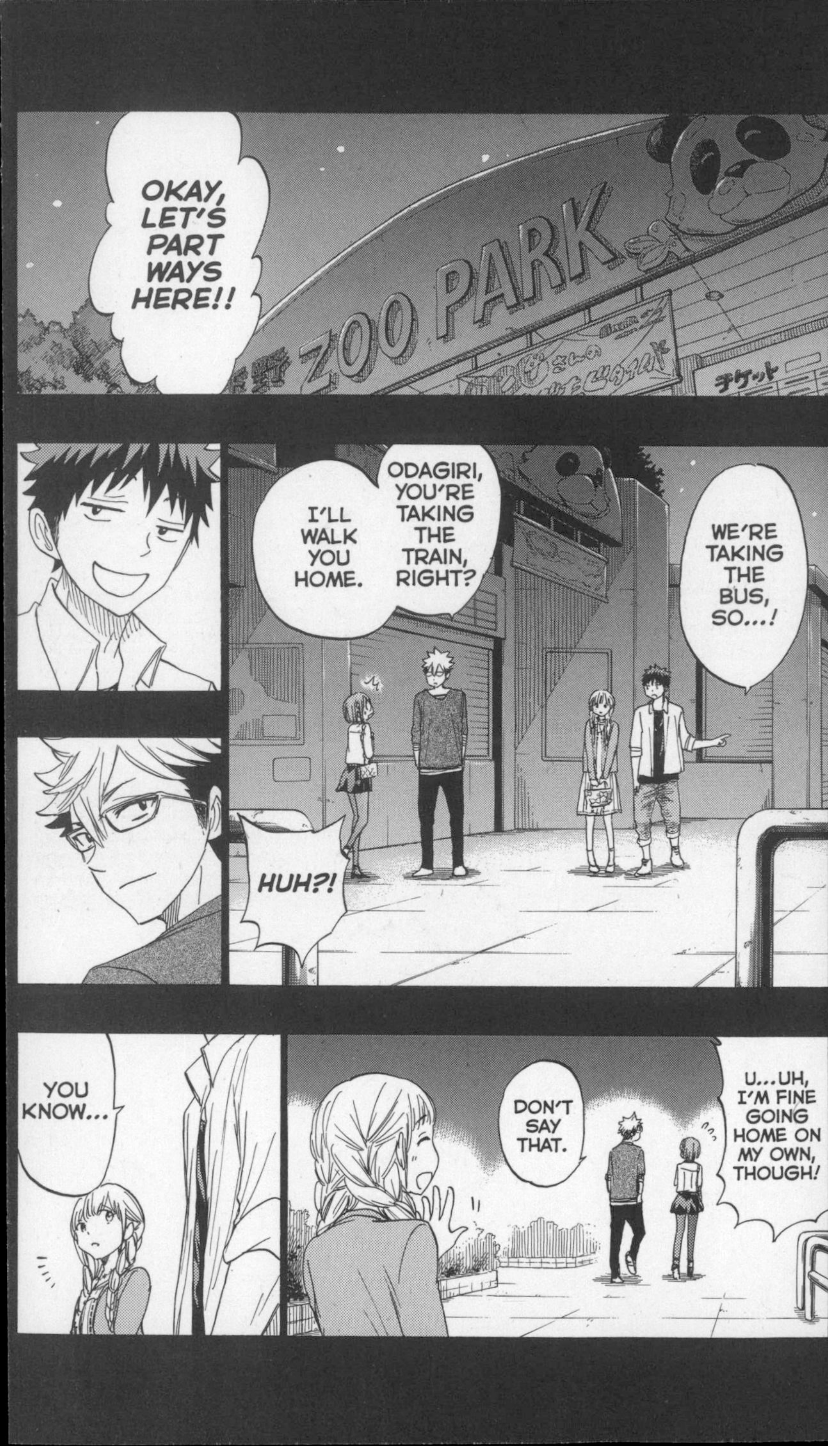
OKAY, LET'S PART WAYS HERE!!
ZOO PARK
WE'RE TAKING THE BUS, SO...!
ODAGIRI, YOU'RE TAKING THE TRAIN, RIGHT?
I'LL WALK YOU HOME.
HUH?!
U...UH, I'M FINE GOING HOME ON MY OWN, THOUGH!
DON'T SAY THAT.
YOU KNOW...

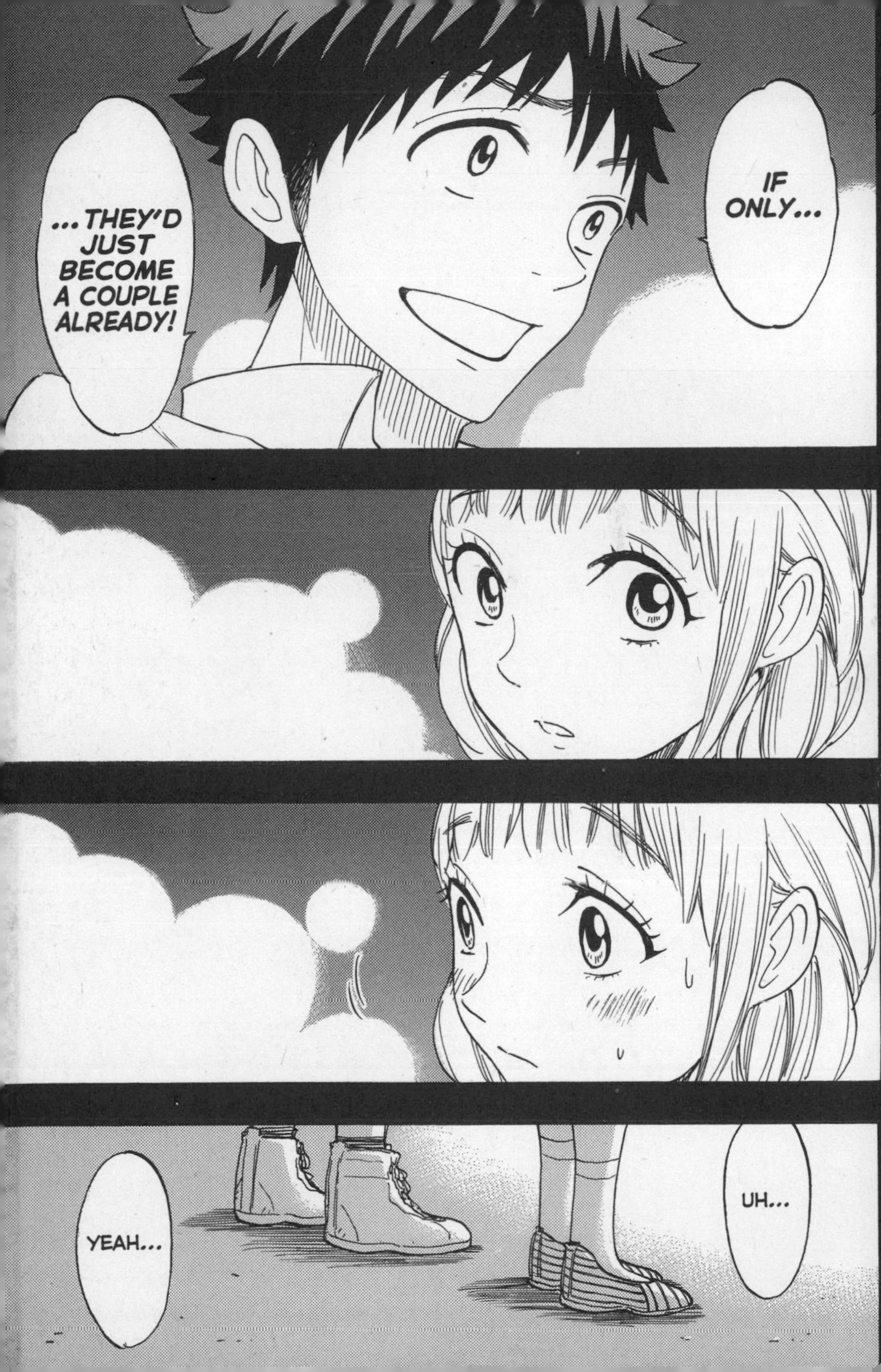
IF ONLY...
...THEY'D JUST BECOME A COUPLE ALREADY!
UH...
YEAH...

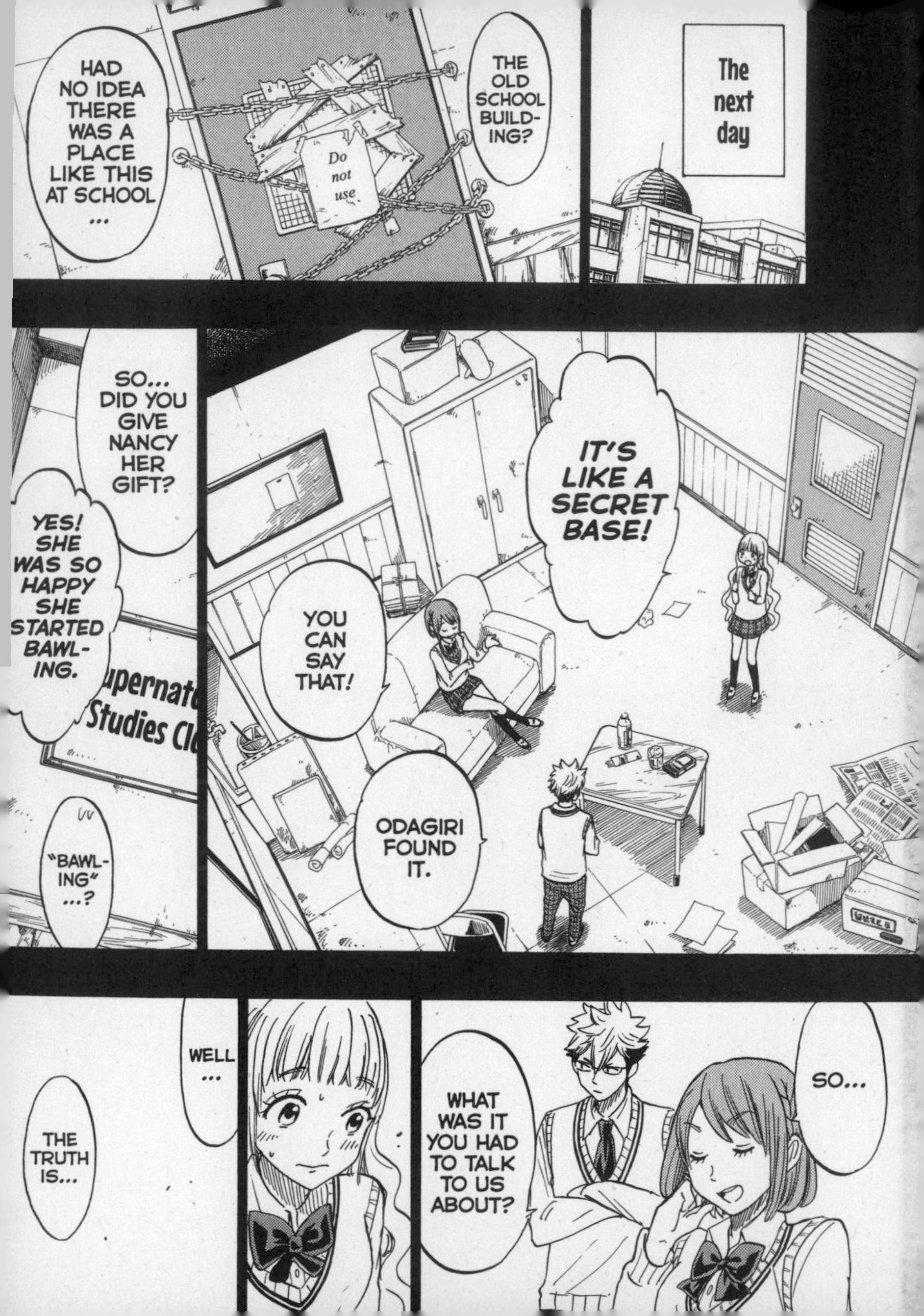
The next day
THE OLD SCHOOL BUILDING?
Do not use
HAD NO IDEA THERE WAS A PLACE LIKE THIS AT SCHOOL...
IT'S LIKE A SECRET BASE!
YOU CAN SAY THAT!
ODAGIRI FOUND IT.
SO... DID YOU GIVE NANCY HER GIFT?
YES! SHE WAS SO HAPPY SHE STARTED BAWLING.
"BAWLING"...?
SO...
WHAT WAS IT YOU HAD TO TALK TO US ABOUT?
WELL...
THE TRUTH IS...

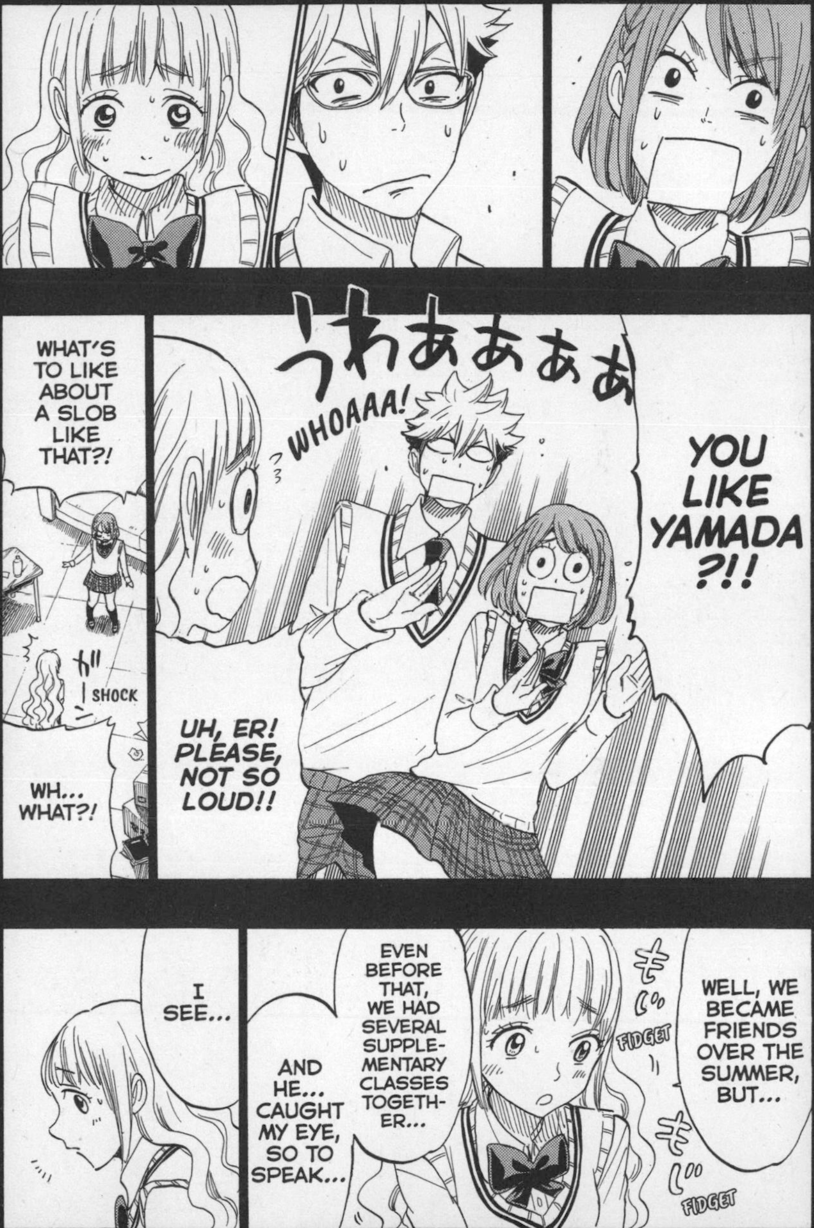
YOU LIKE YAMADA ?!!
うわああああ
WHOAAA!
UH, ER! PLEASE, NOT SO LOUD!!
WHAT'S TO LIKE ABOUT A SLOB LIKE THAT?!
ガ
SHOCK
WH... WHAT?!
WELL, WE BECAME FRIENDS OVER THE SUMMER, BUT...
もじ
FIDGET
もじ
FIDGET
EVEN BEFORE THAT, WE HAD SEVERAL SUPPLE-MENTARY CLASSES TOGETH-ER...
AND HE... CAUGHT MY EYE, SO TO SPEAK...
I SEE...

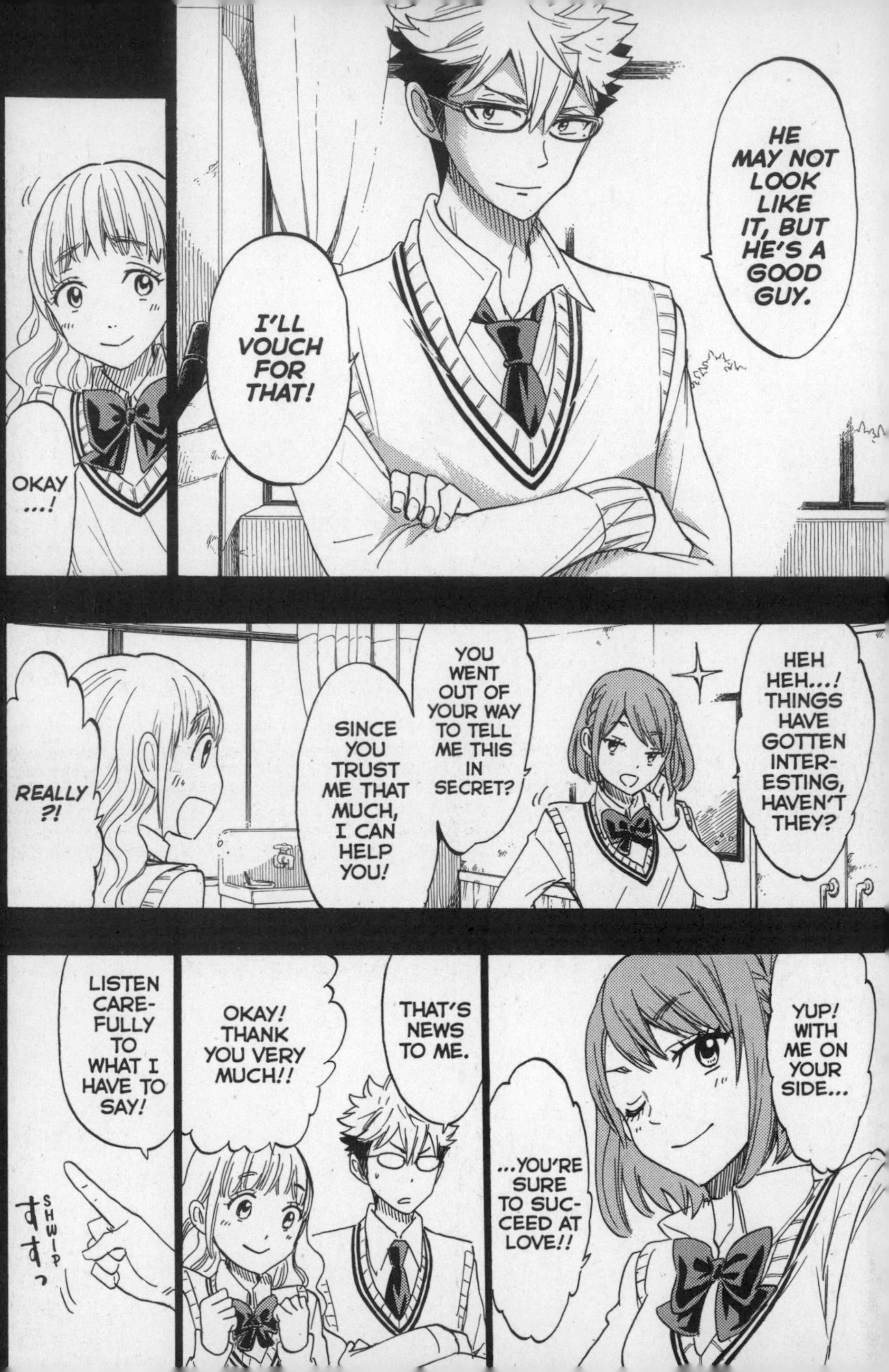
HE MAY NOT LOOK LIKE IT, BUT HE'S A GOOD GUY.
I'LL VOUCH FOR THAT!
OKAY ...!
HEH HEH...! THINGS HAVE GOTTEN INTER-ESTING, HAVEN'T THEY?
YOU WENT OUT OF YOUR WAY TO TELL ME THIS IN SECRET?
SINCE YOU TRUST ME THAT MUCH, I CAN HELP YOU!
REALLY?!
YUP! WITH ME ON YOUR SIDE...
...YOU'RE SURE TO SUC-CEED AT LOVE!!
THAT'S NEWS TO ME.
OKAY! THANK YOU VERY MUCH!!
LISTEN CARE-FULLY TO WHAT I HAVE TO SAY!
すすっ SHWIP

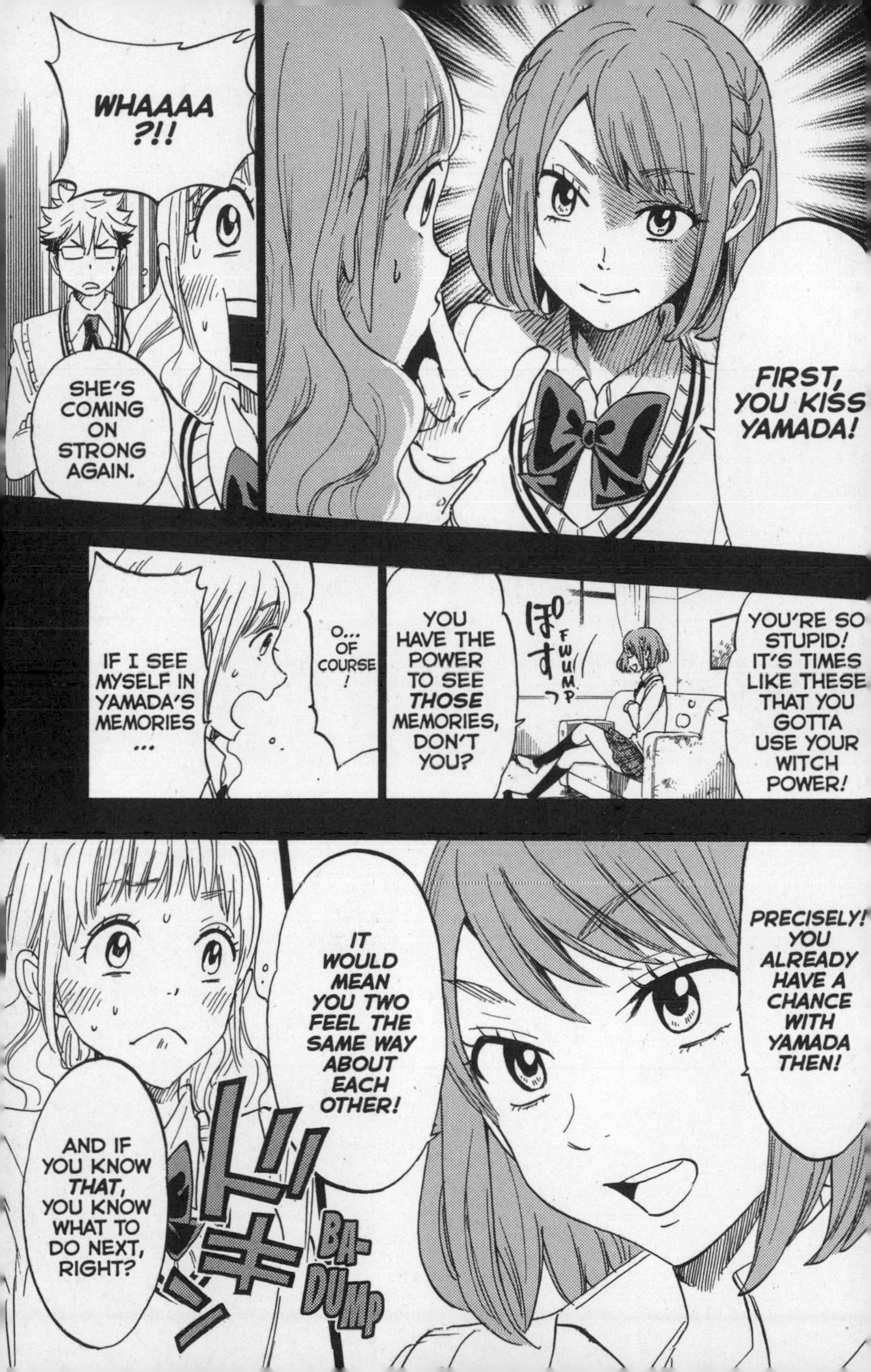
FIRST, YOU KISS YAMADA!
WHAAAA?!!
SHE'S COMING ON STRONG AGAIN.
YOU'RE SO STUPID! IT'S TIMES LIKE THESE THAT YOU GOTTA USE YOUR WITCH POWER!
ぽす
FWUMP
YOU HAVE THE POWER TO SEE *THOSE* MEMORIES, DON'T YOU?
O... OF COURSE!
IF I SEE MYSELF IN YAMADA'S MEMORIES...
PRECISELY! YOU ALREADY HAVE A CHANCE WITH YAMADA THEN!
IT WOULD MEAN YOU TWO FEEL THE SAME WAY ABOUT EACH OTHER!
ドキン
BA-DUMP
AND IF YOU KNOW *THAT*, YOU KNOW WHAT TO DO NEXT, RIGHT?

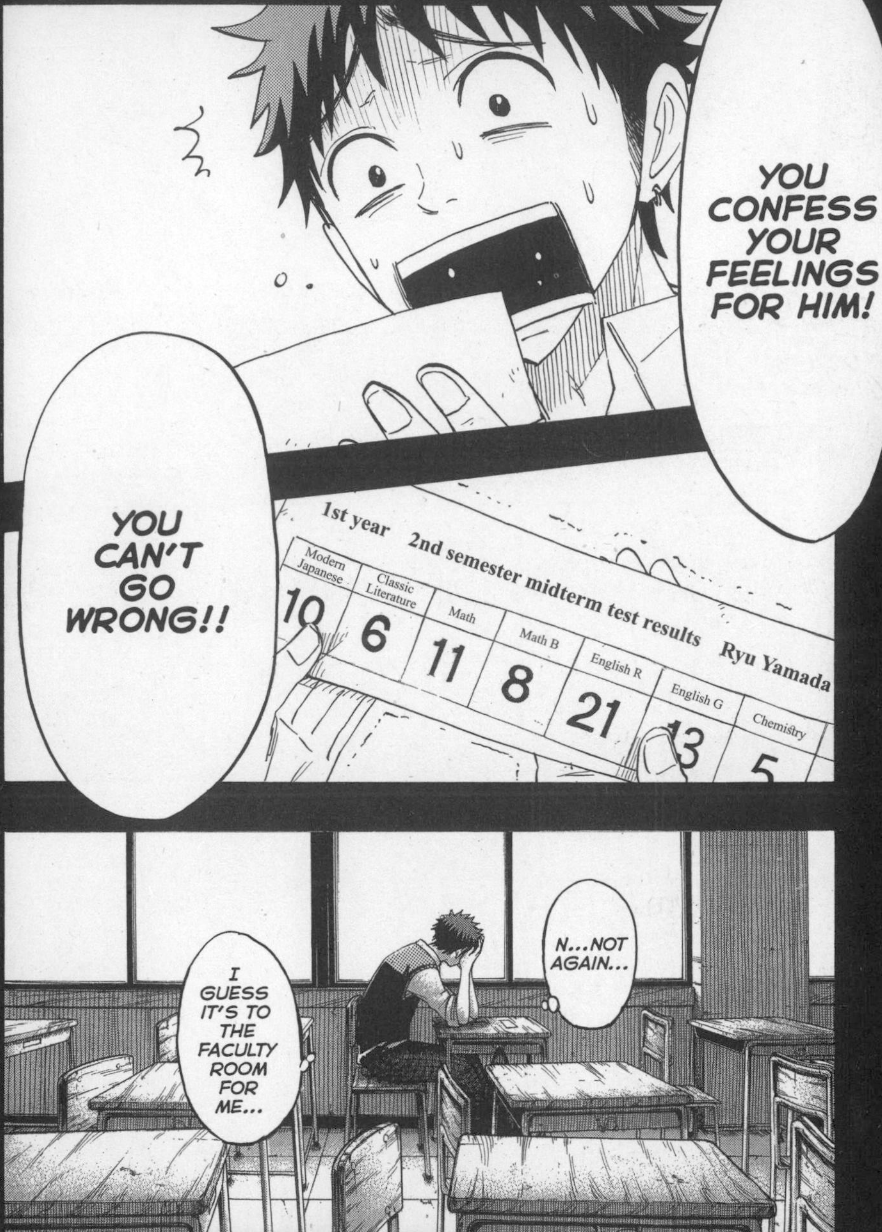
YOU CONFESS YOUR FEELINGS FOR HIM!
YOU CAN'T GO WRONG!!
1st year 2nd semester midterm test results Ryu Yamada
Modern Japanese 10
Classic Literature 6
Math 11
Math B 8
English R 21
English G 13
Chemistry 5
N...NOT AGAIN...
I GUESS IT'S TO THE FACULTY ROOM FOR ME...

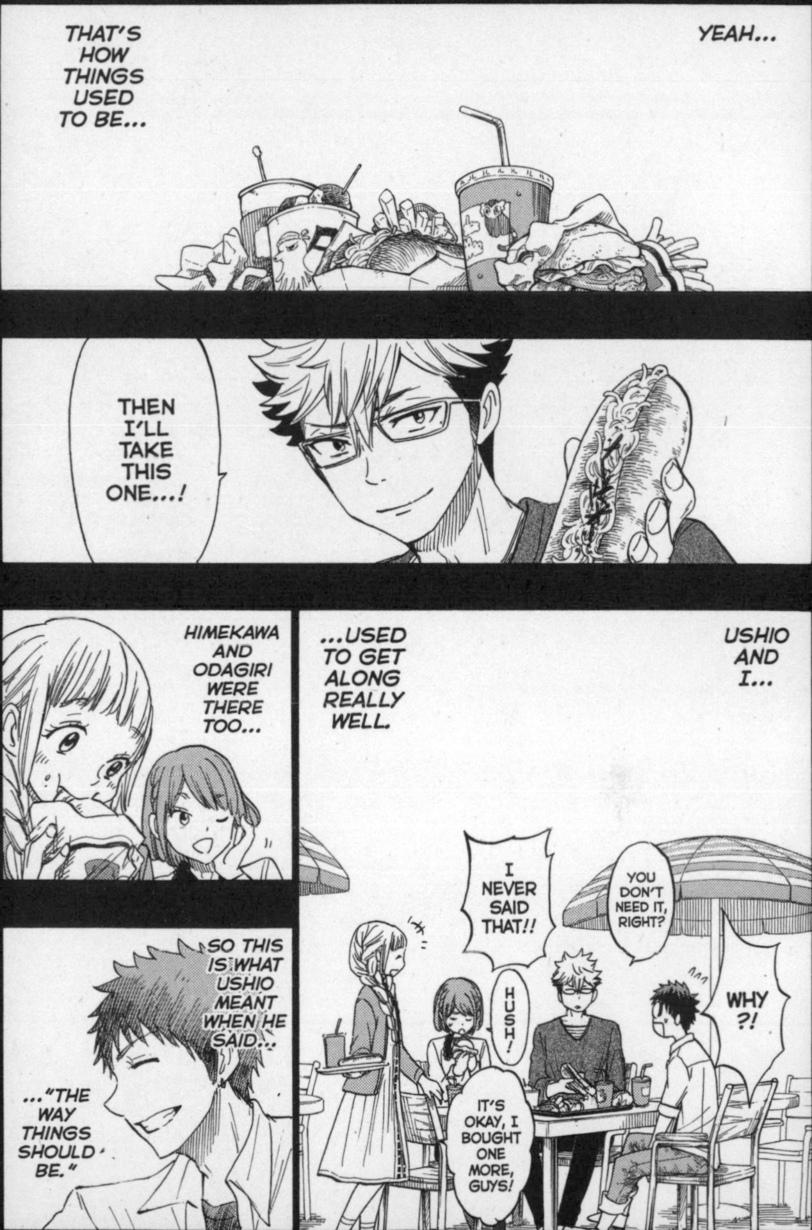
YEAH...
THAT'S HOW THINGS USED TO BE...
THEN I'LL TAKE THIS ONE...!
USHIO AND I...
...USED TO GET ALONG REALLY WELL.
YOU DON'T NEED IT, RIGHT?
I NEVER SAID THAT!!
WHY?!
HUSH!
IT'S OKAY, I BOUGHT ONE MORE, GUYS!
HIMEKAWA AND ODAGIRI WERE THERE TOO...
SO THIS IS WHAT USHIO MEANT WHEN HE SAID...
..."THE WAY THINGS SHOULD BE."

CHAPTER 162: Blamed me for the whole underwear thing!!

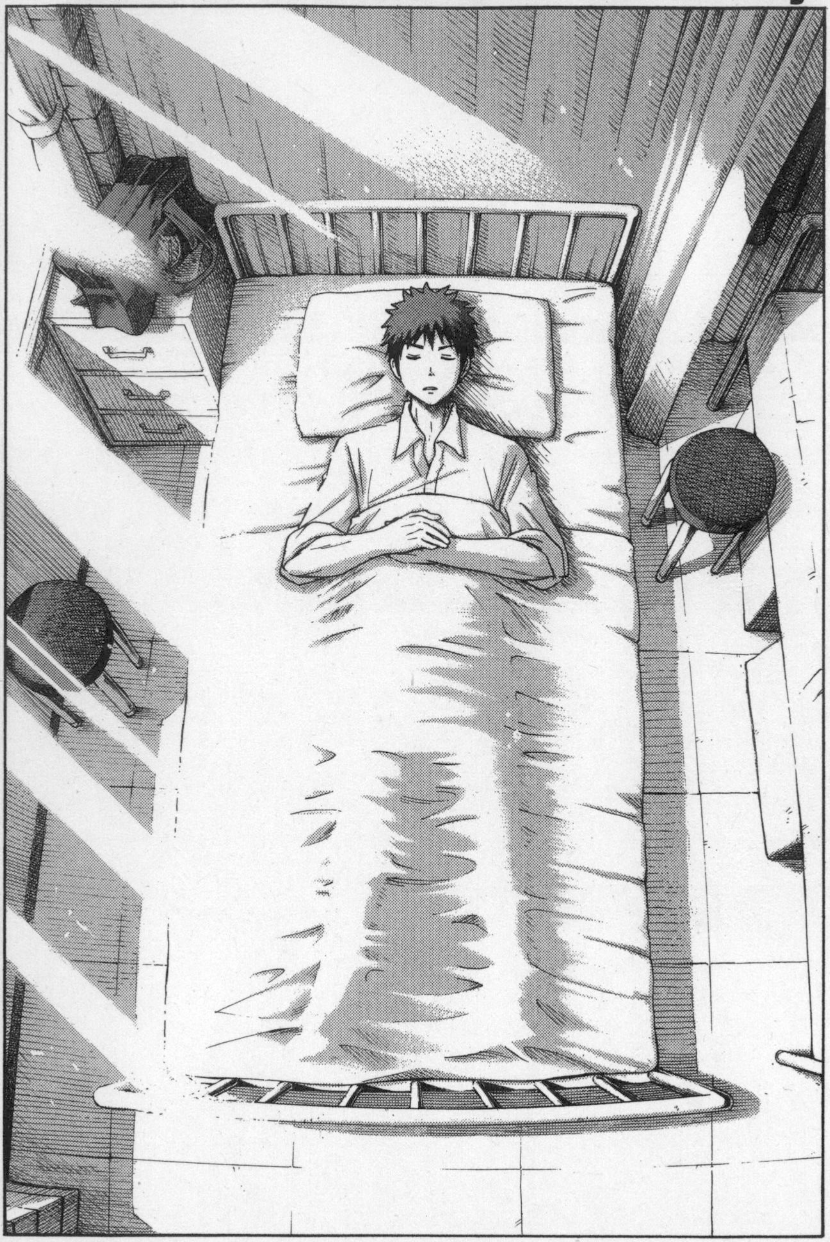

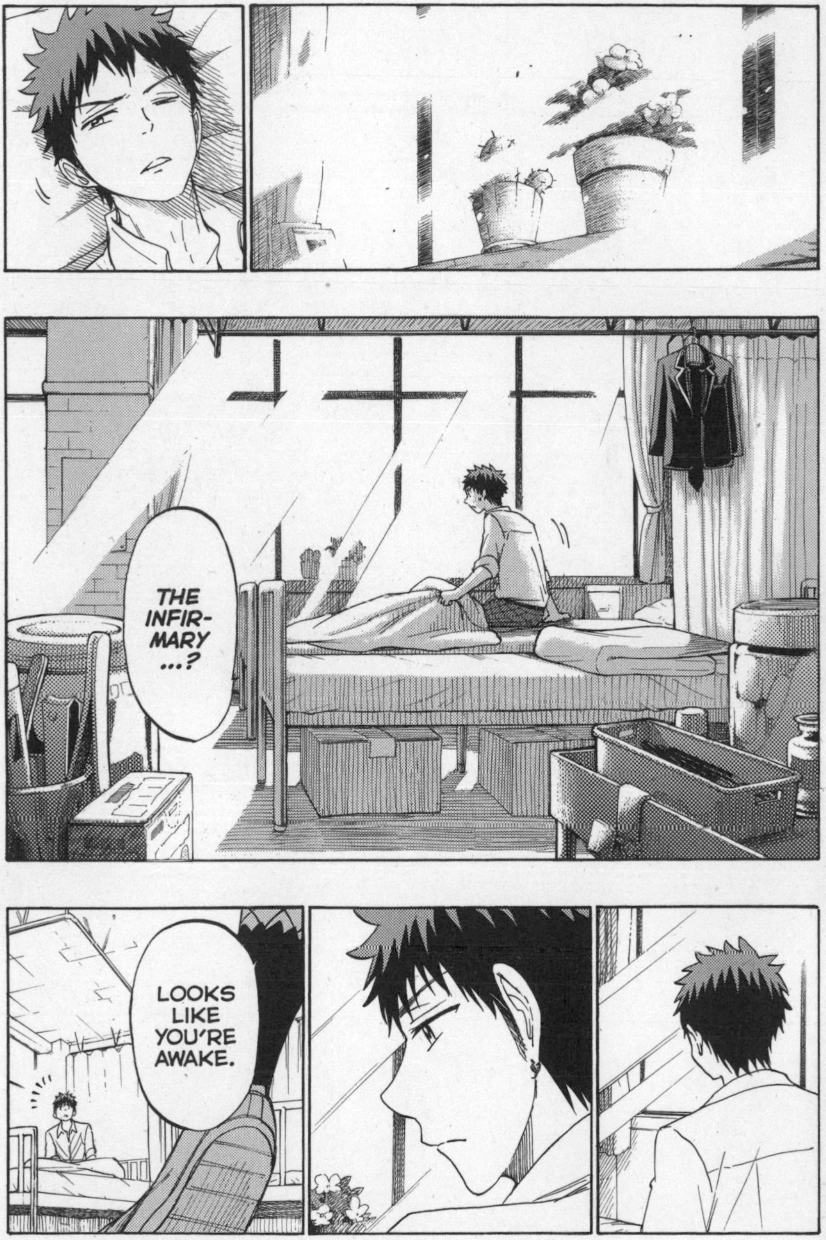
THE INFIR-MARY ...?
LOOKS LIKE YOU'RE AWAKE.

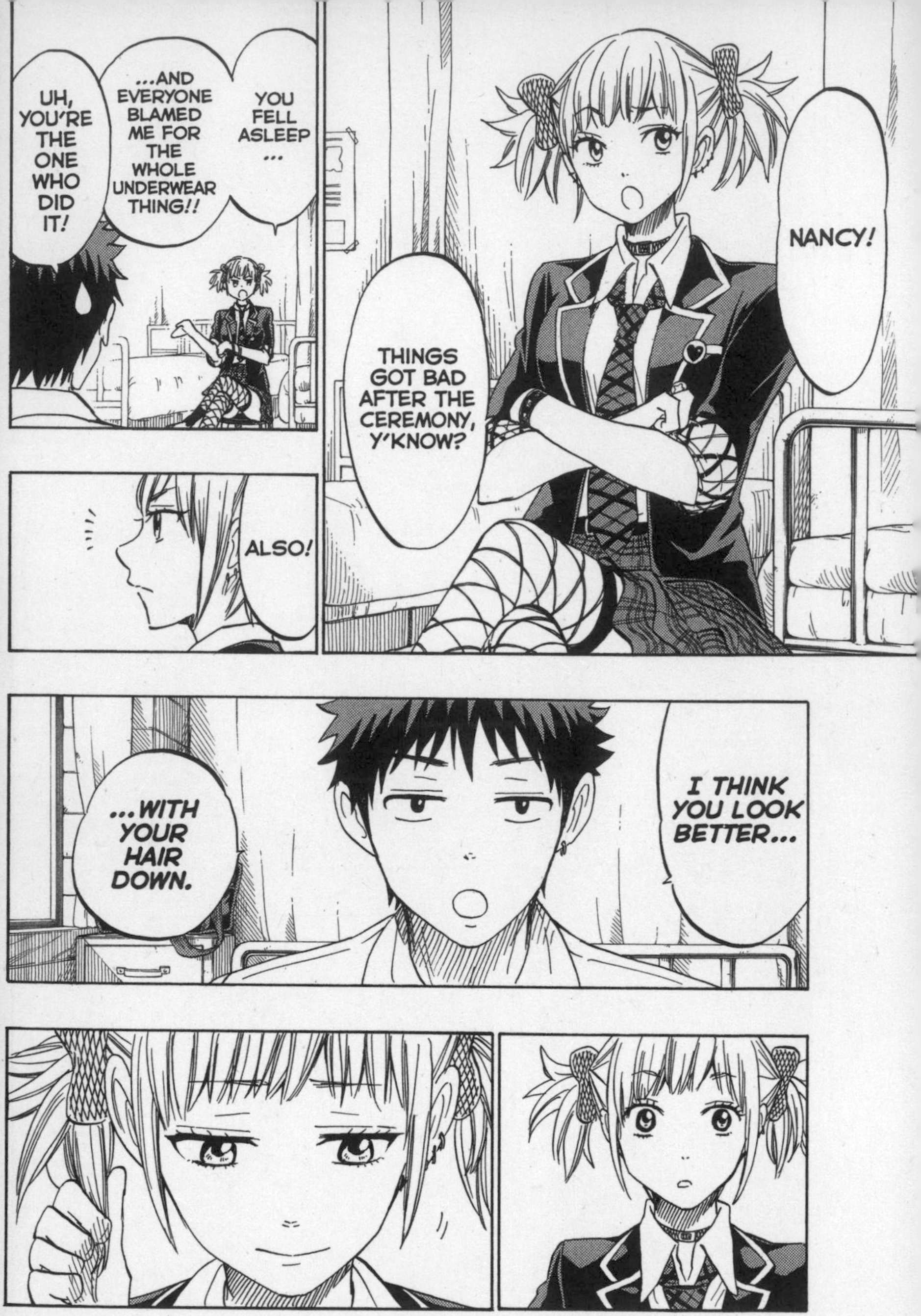
NANCY!
THINGS GOT BAD AFTER THE CEREMONY, Y'KNOW?
YOU FELL ASLEEP ...
...AND EVERYONE BLAMED ME FOR THE WHOLE UNDERWEAR THING!!
UH, YOU'RE THE ONE WHO DID IT!
ALSO!
I THINK YOU LOOK BETTER...
...WITH YOUR HAIR DOWN.

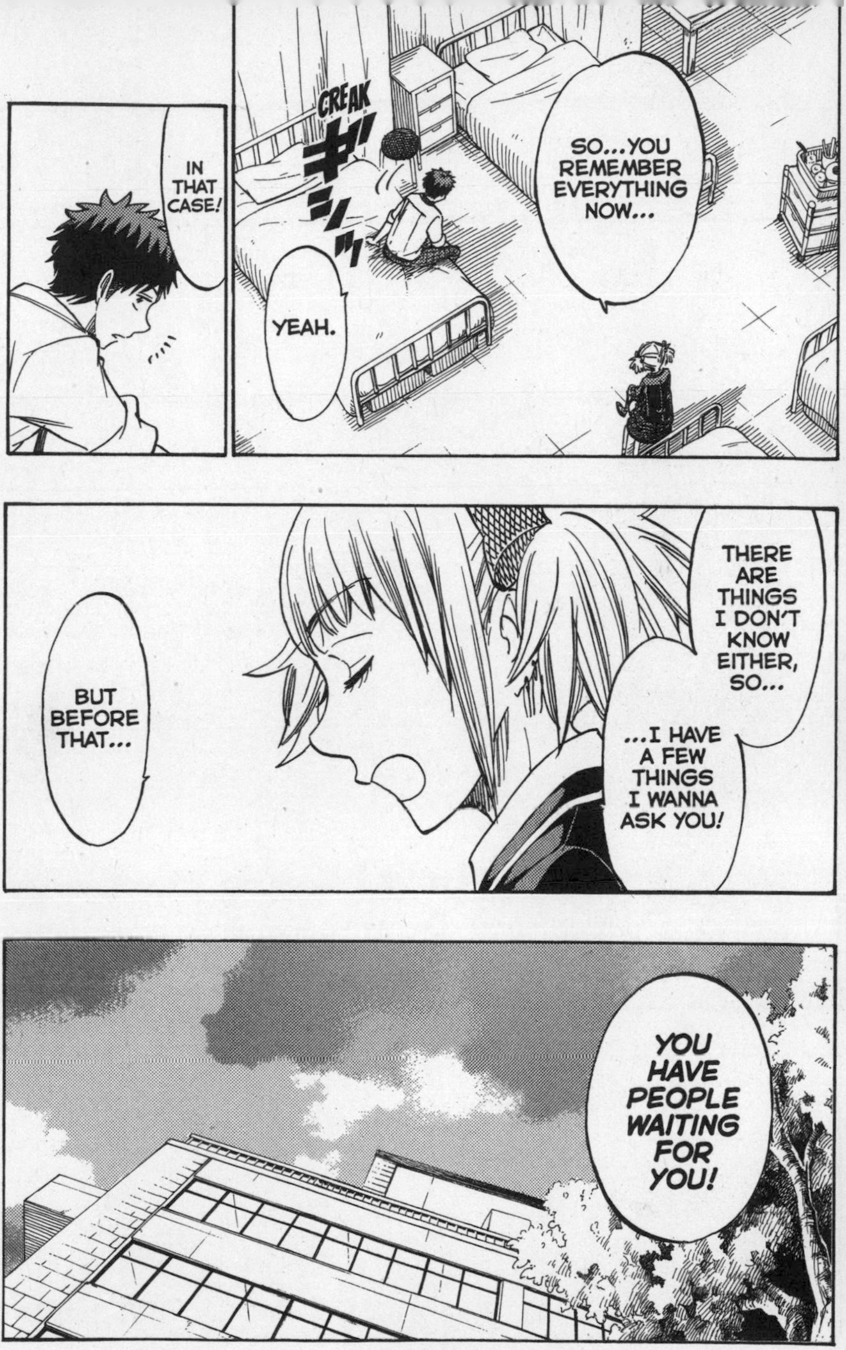
CREAK
SO...YOU REMEMBER EVERYTHING NOW...
YEAH.
IN THAT CASE!
THERE ARE THINGS I DON'T KNOW EITHER, SO...
...I HAVE A FEW THINGS I WANNA ASK YOU!
BUT BEFORE THAT...
YOU HAVE PEOPLE WAITING FOR YOU!

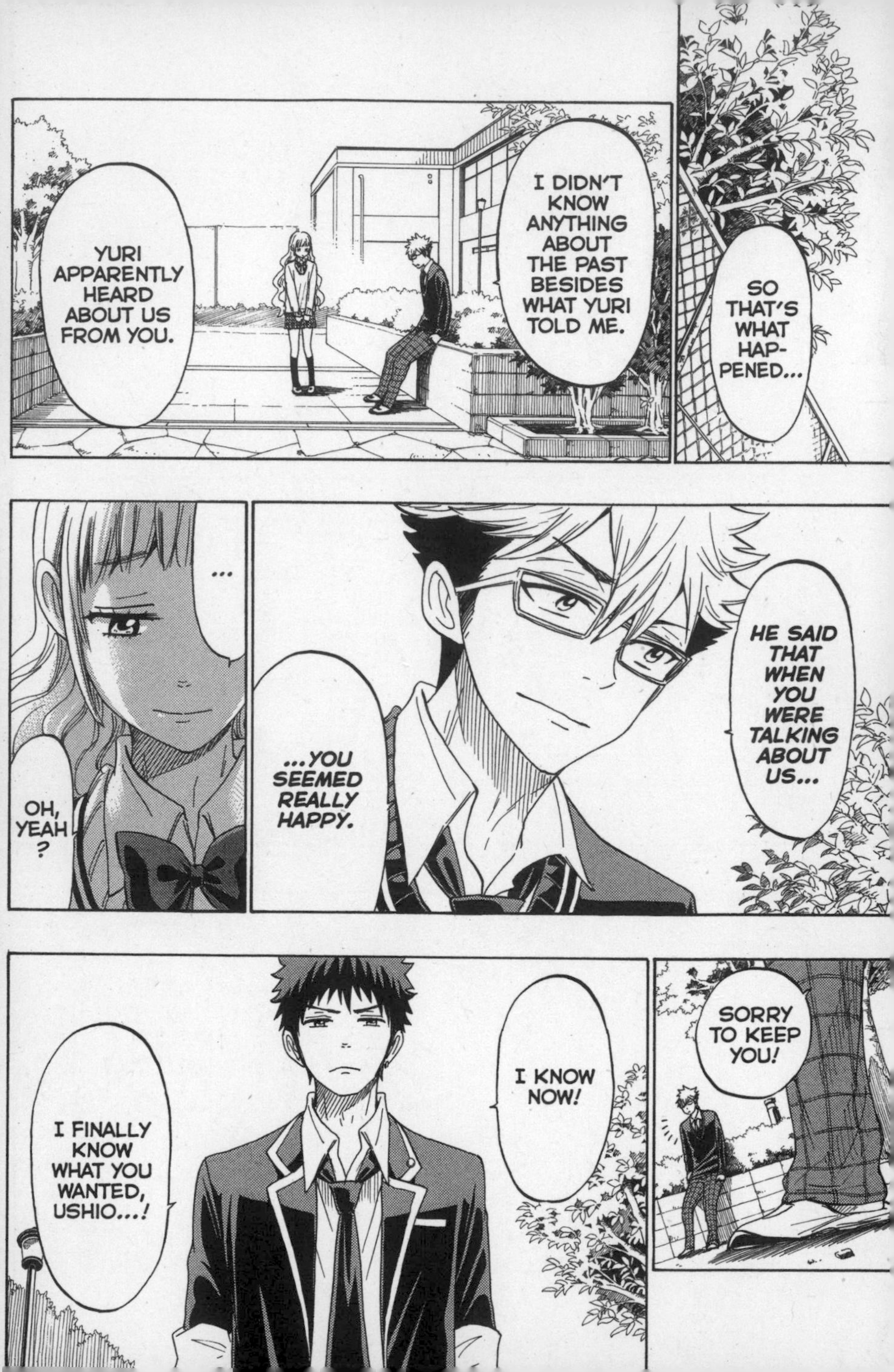
SO THAT'S WHAT HAP-PENED...
I DIDN'T KNOW ANYTHING ABOUT THE PAST BESIDES WHAT YURI TOLD ME.
YURI APPARENTLY HEARD ABOUT US FROM YOU.
HE SAID THAT WHEN YOU WERE TALKING ABOUT US...
...YOU SEEMED REALLY HAPPY.
...
OH, YEAH?
SORRY TO KEEP YOU!
I KNOW NOW!
I FINALLY KNOW WHAT YOU WANTED, USHIO...!

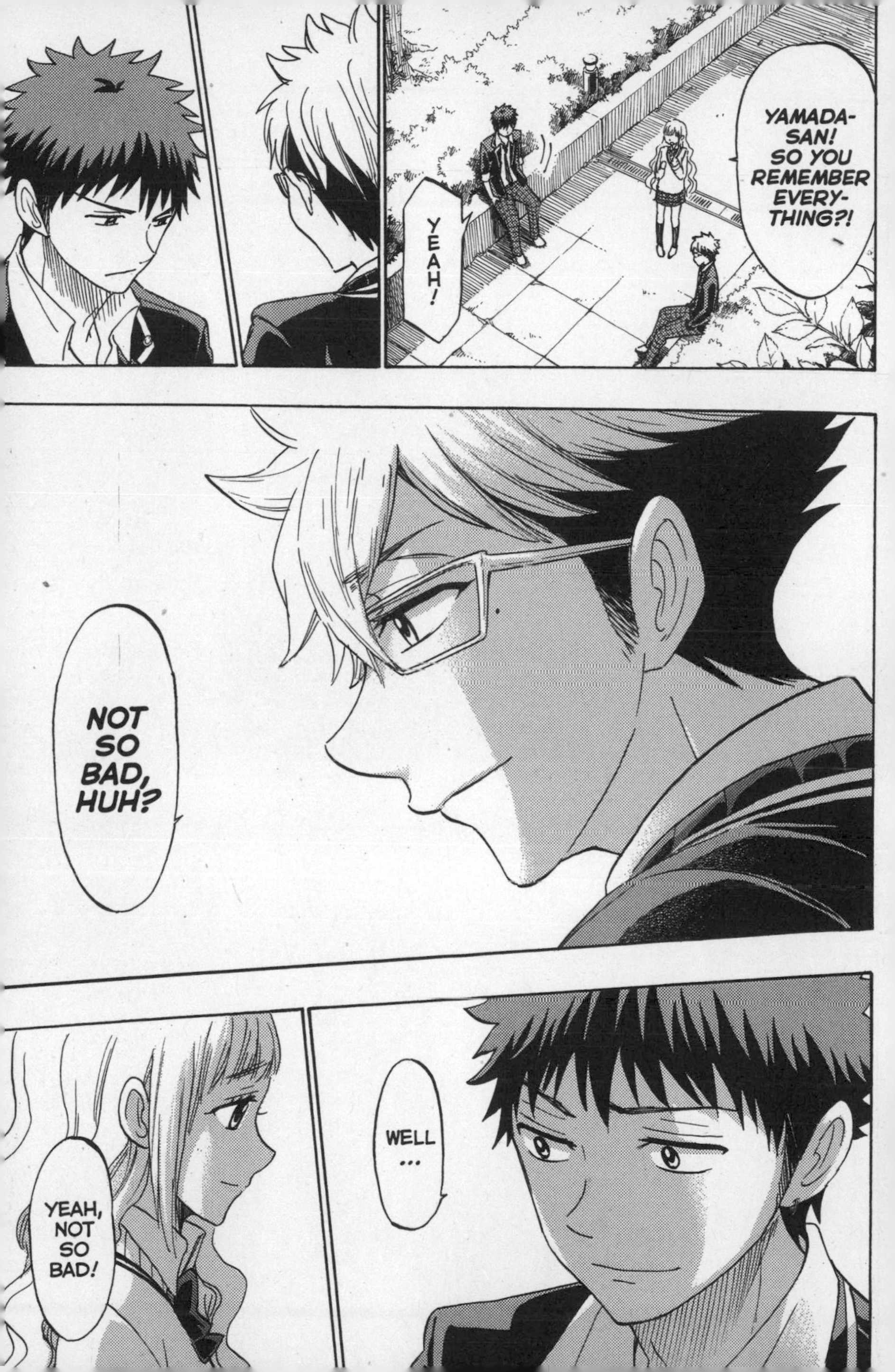
YAMADA-SAN! SO YOU REMEMBER EVERY-THING?!
YEAH!
NOT SO BAD, HUH?
WELL ...
YEAH, NOT SO BAD!

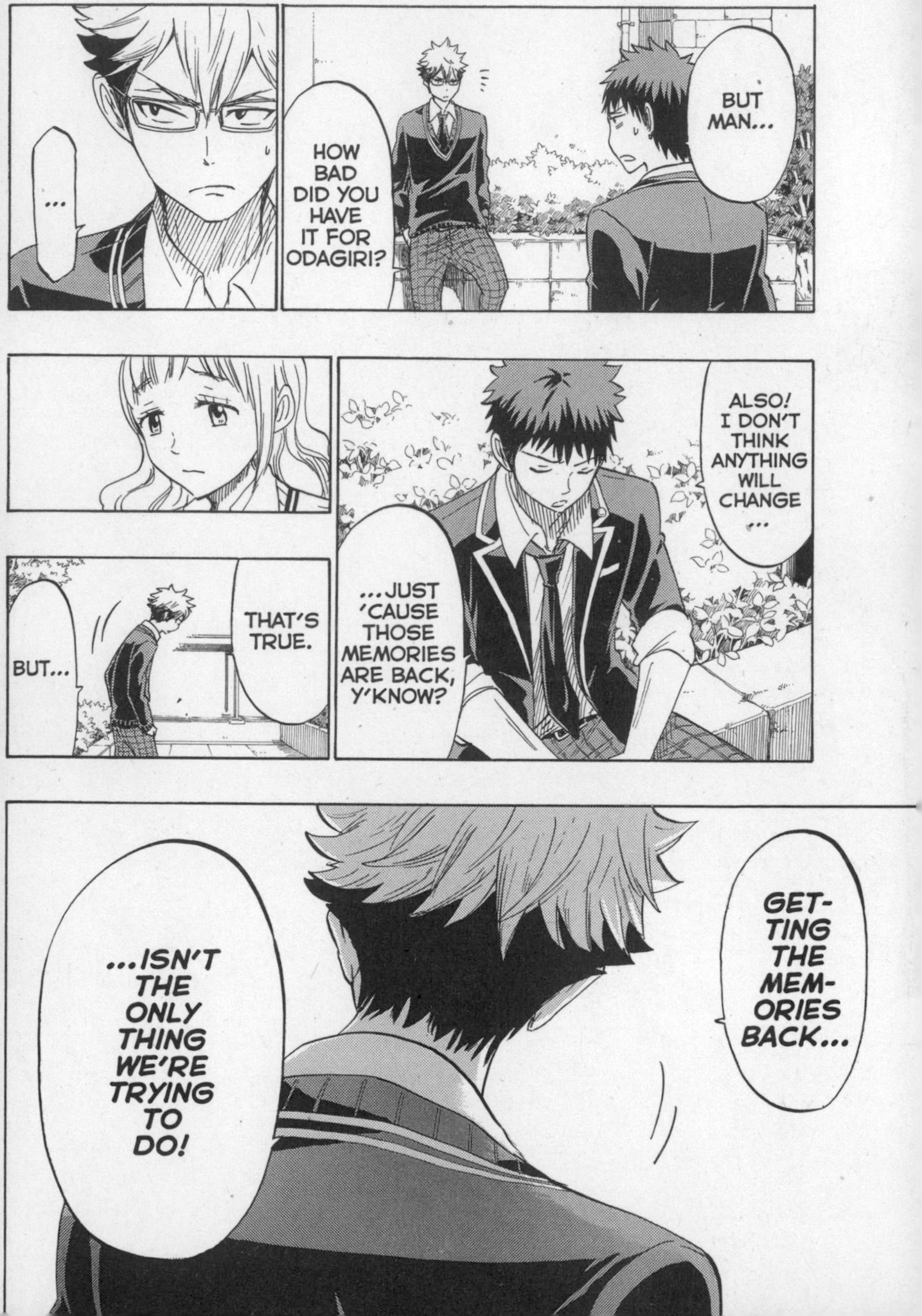
BUT MAN...
HOW BAD DID YOU HAVE IT FOR ODAGIRI?
...
ALSO! I DON'T THINK ANYTHING WILL CHANGE ...
...JUST 'CAUSE THOSE MEMORIES ARE BACK, Y'KNOW?
THAT'S TRUE.
BUT...
GETTING THE MEMORIES BACK...
...ISN'T THE ONLY THING WE'RE TRYING TO DO!

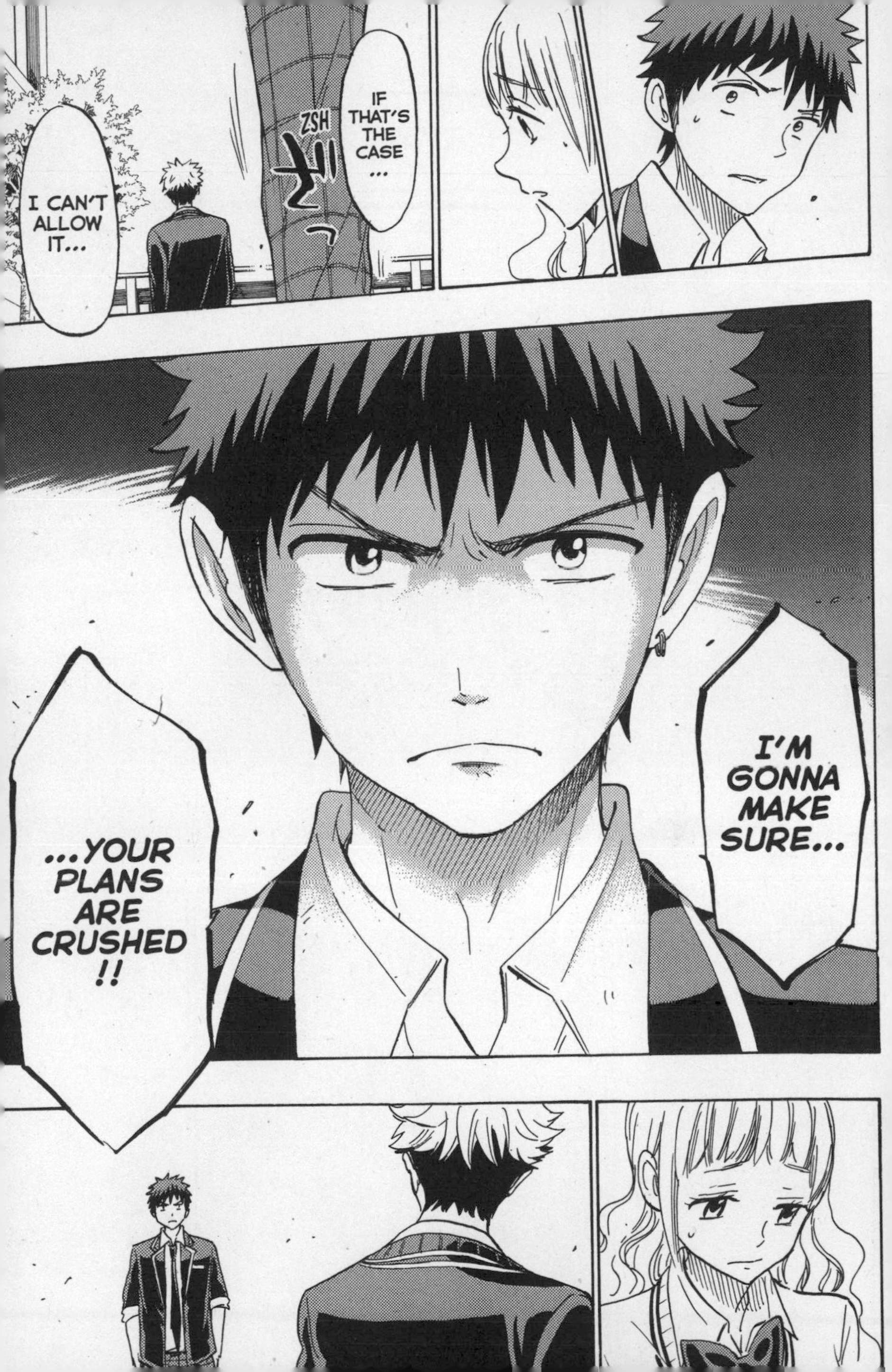
IF THAT'S THE CASE...
ZSH
I CAN'T ALLOW IT...
I'M GONNA MAKE SURE...
...YOUR PLANS ARE CRUSHED!!

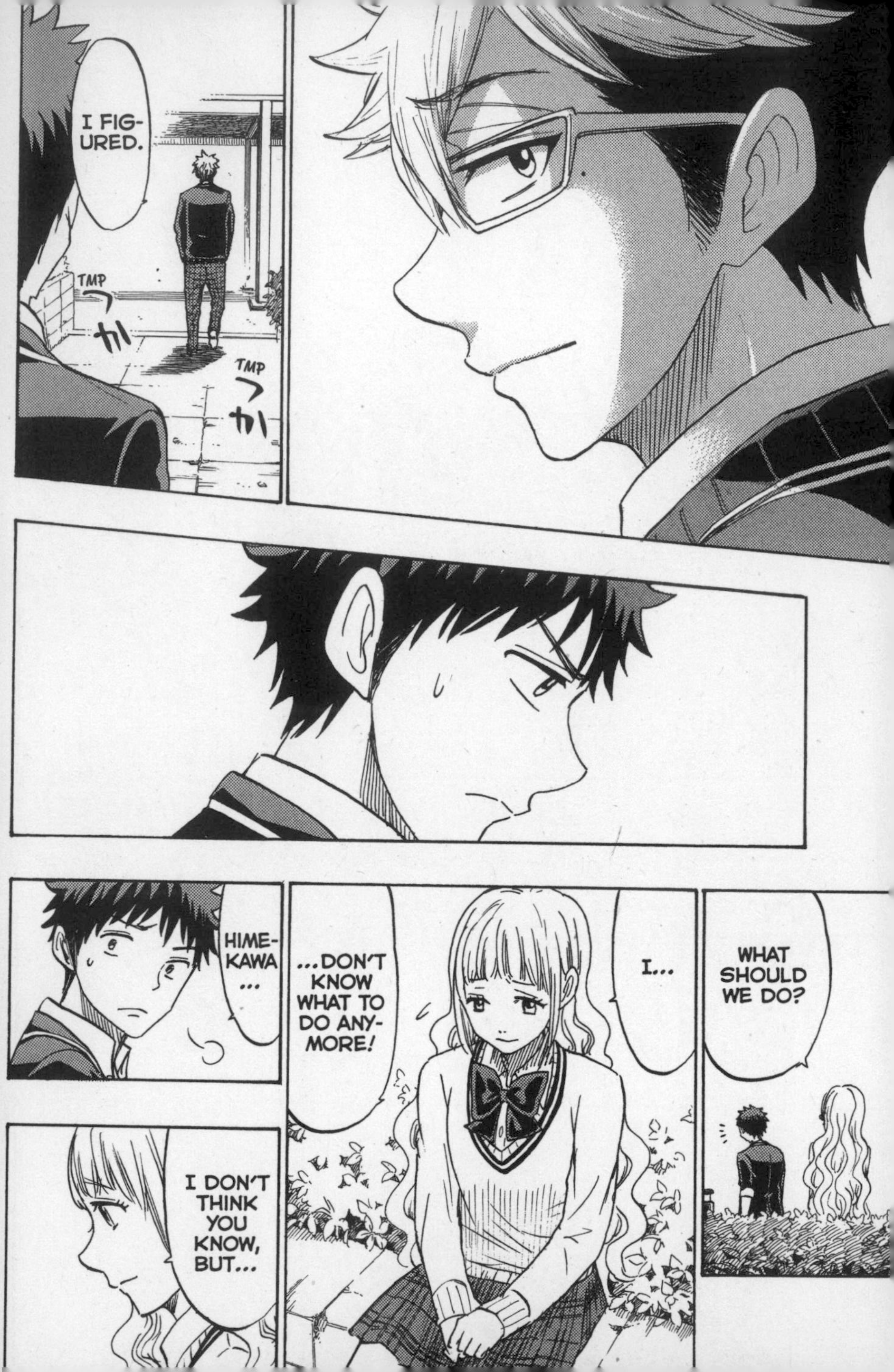

I FIG-URED.
TMP
つか
TMP
つか
WHAT SHOULD WE DO?
I...
...DON'T KNOW WHAT TO DO ANY-MORE!
HIME-KAWA...
I DON'T THINK YOU KNOW, BUT...

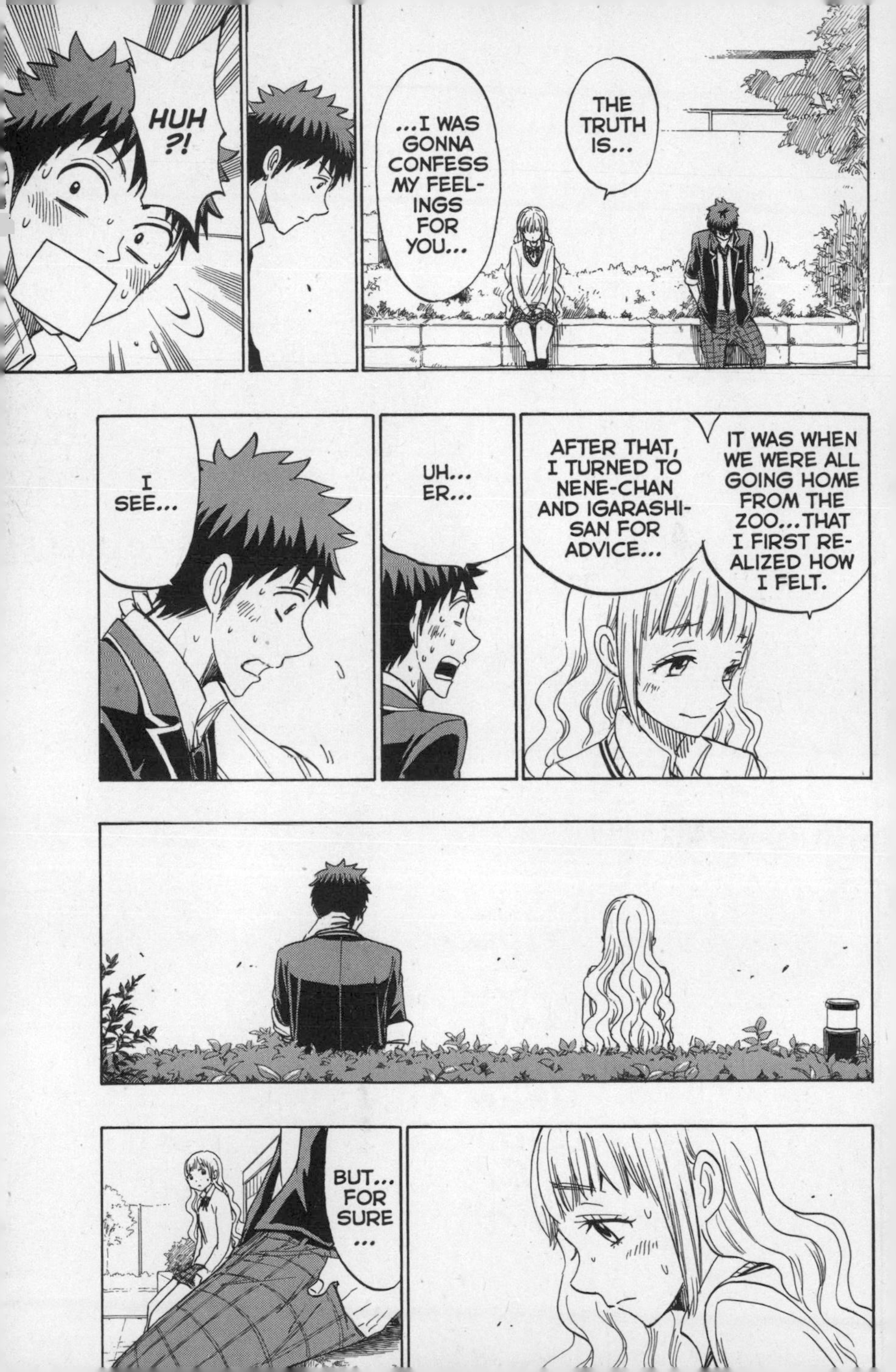
THE TRUTH IS...
...I WAS GONNA CONFESS MY FEELINGS FOR YOU...
HUH ?!
IT WAS WHEN WE WERE ALL GOING HOME FROM THE ZOO...THAT I FIRST REALIZED HOW I FELT.
AFTER THAT, I TURNED TO NENE-CHAN AND IGARASHI-SAN FOR ADVICE...
UH... ER...
I SEE...
BUT... FOR SURE ...

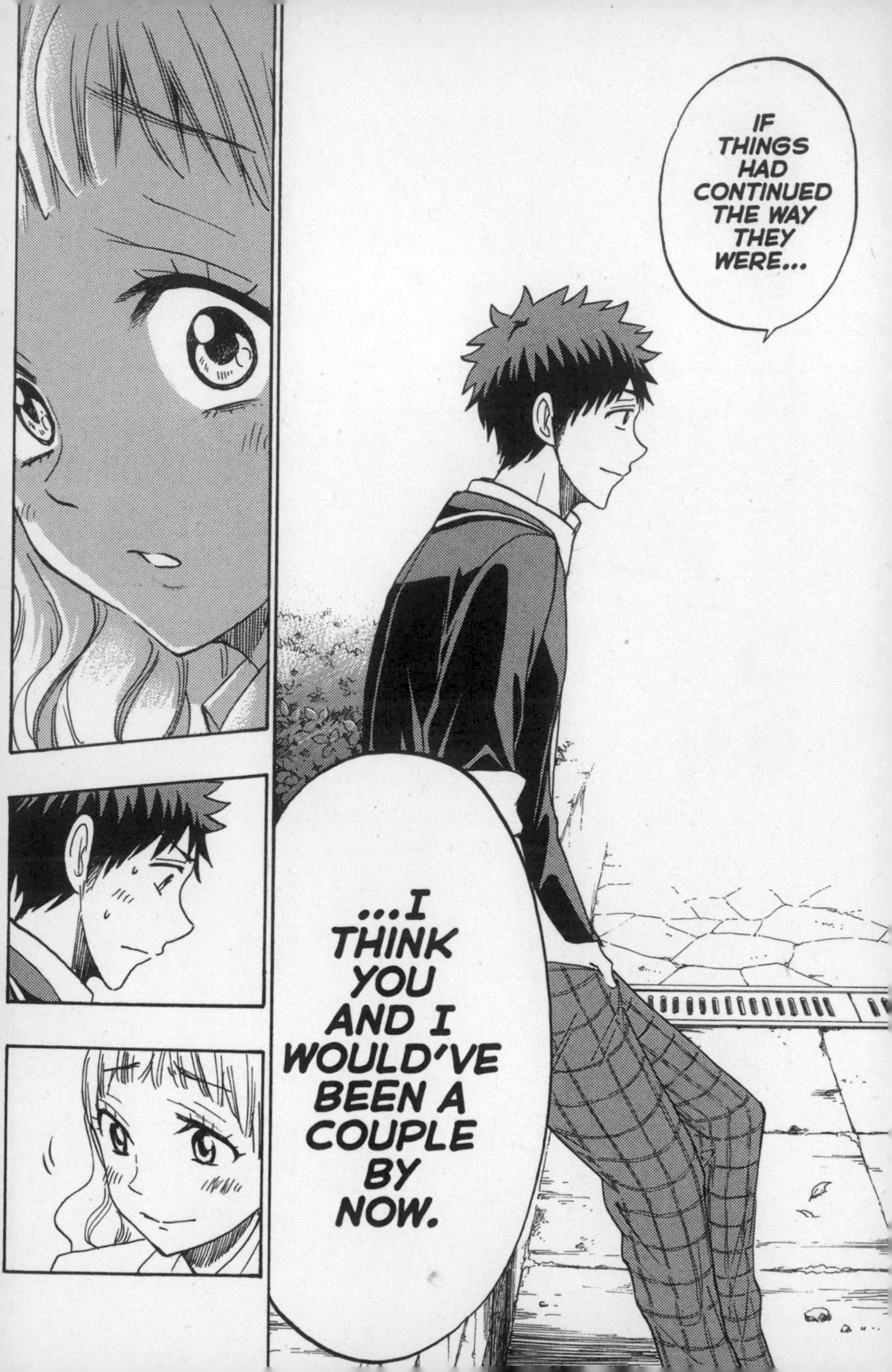
IF THINGS HAD CONTINUED THE WAY THEY WERE...
...I THINK YOU AND I WOULD'VE BEEN A COUPLE BY NOW.

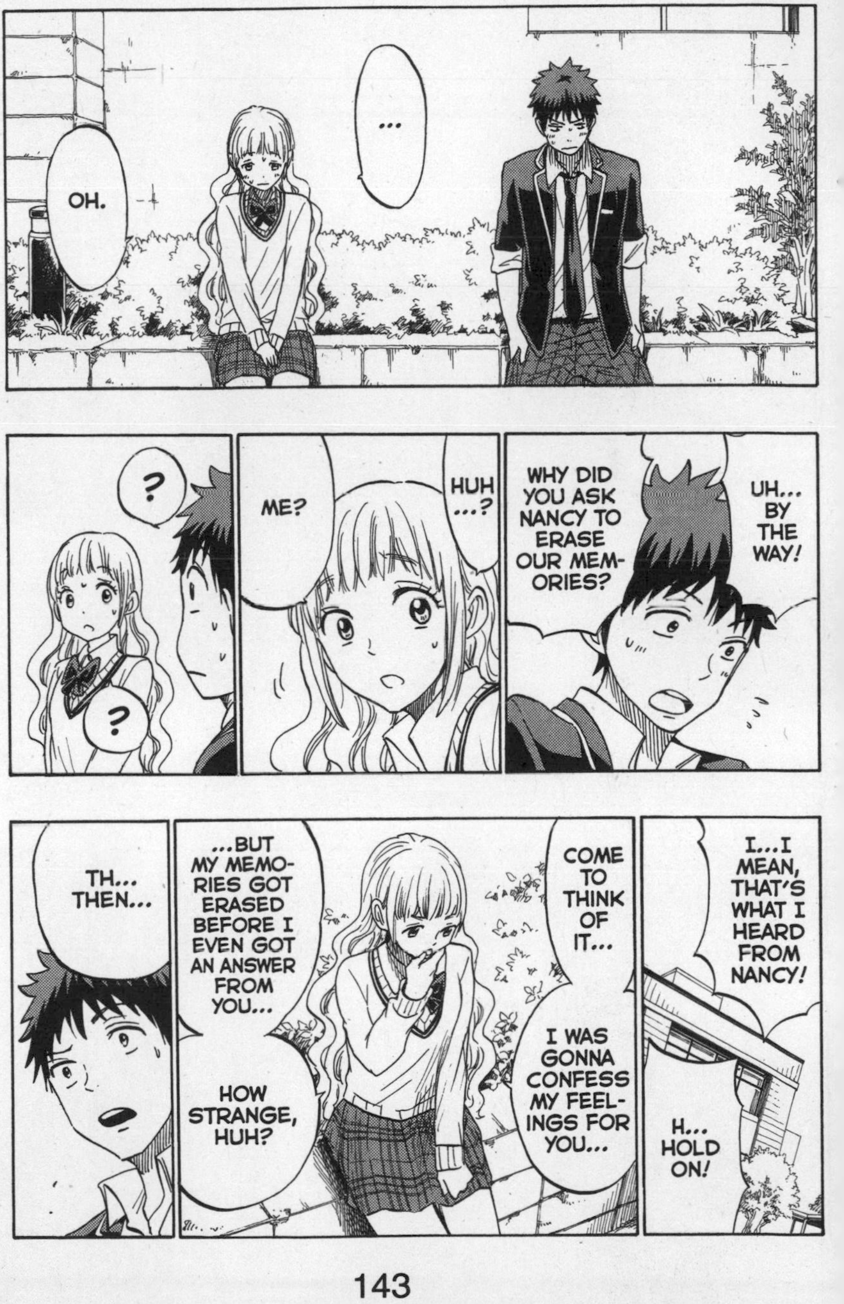
...
OH.
UH... BY THE WAY!
WHY DID YOU ASK NANCY TO ERASE OUR MEMORIES?
HUH ...?
ME?
?
?
I...I MEAN, THAT'S WHAT I HEARD FROM NANCY!
H... HOLD ON!
COME TO THINK OF IT...
I WAS GONNA CONFESS MY FEELINGS FOR YOU...
...BUT MY MEMORIES GOT ERASED BEFORE I EVEN GOT AN ANSWER FROM YOU...
HOW STRANGE, HUH?
TH... THEN...

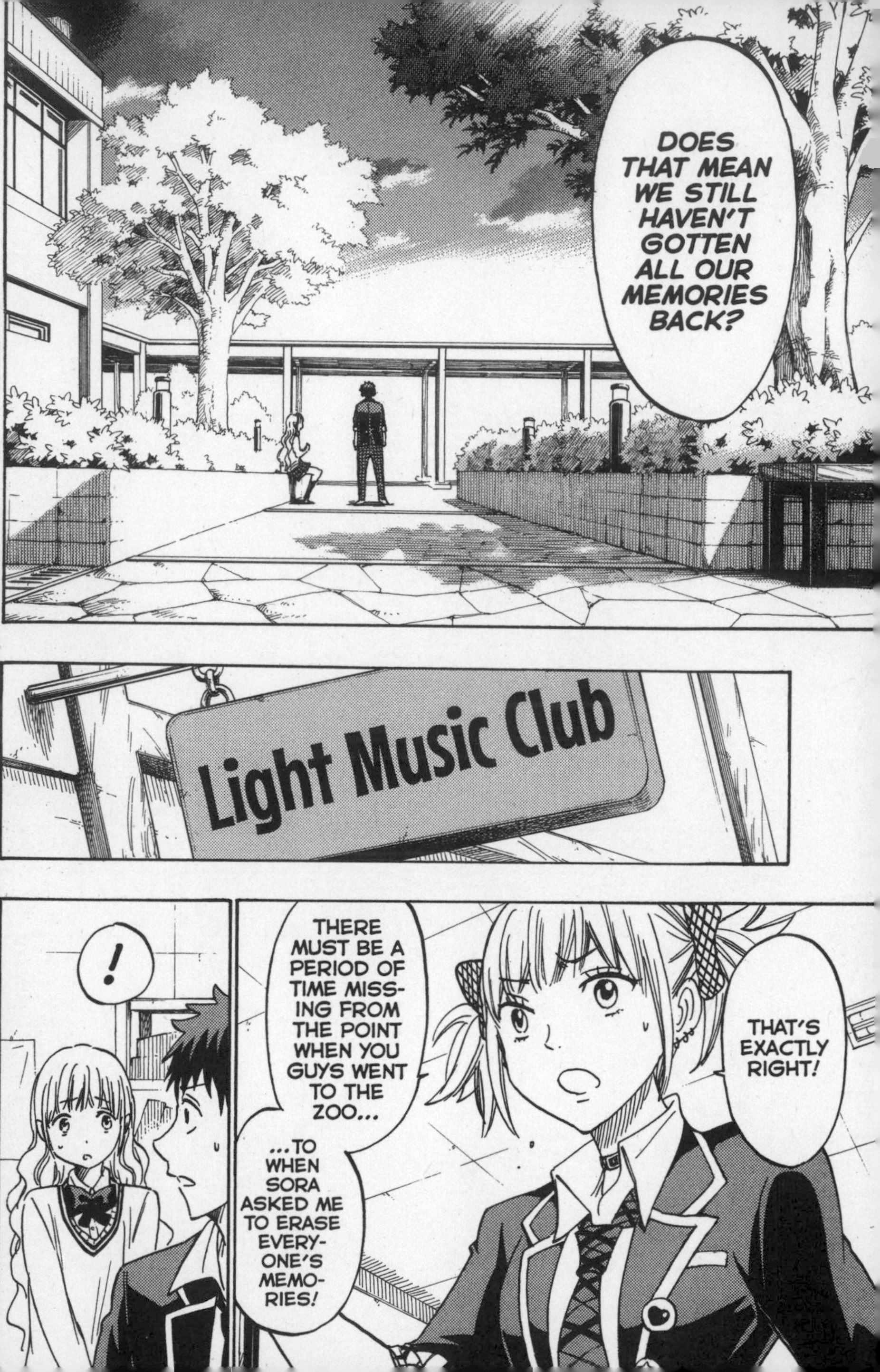
DOES THAT MEAN WE STILL HAVEN'T GOTTEN ALL OUR MEMORIES BACK?
Light Music Club
THAT'S EXACTLY RIGHT!
THERE MUST BE A PERIOD OF TIME MISS-ING FROM THE POINT WHEN YOU GUYS WENT TO THE ZOO...
...TO WHEN SORA ASKED ME TO ERASE EVERY-ONE'S MEMO-RIES!
!

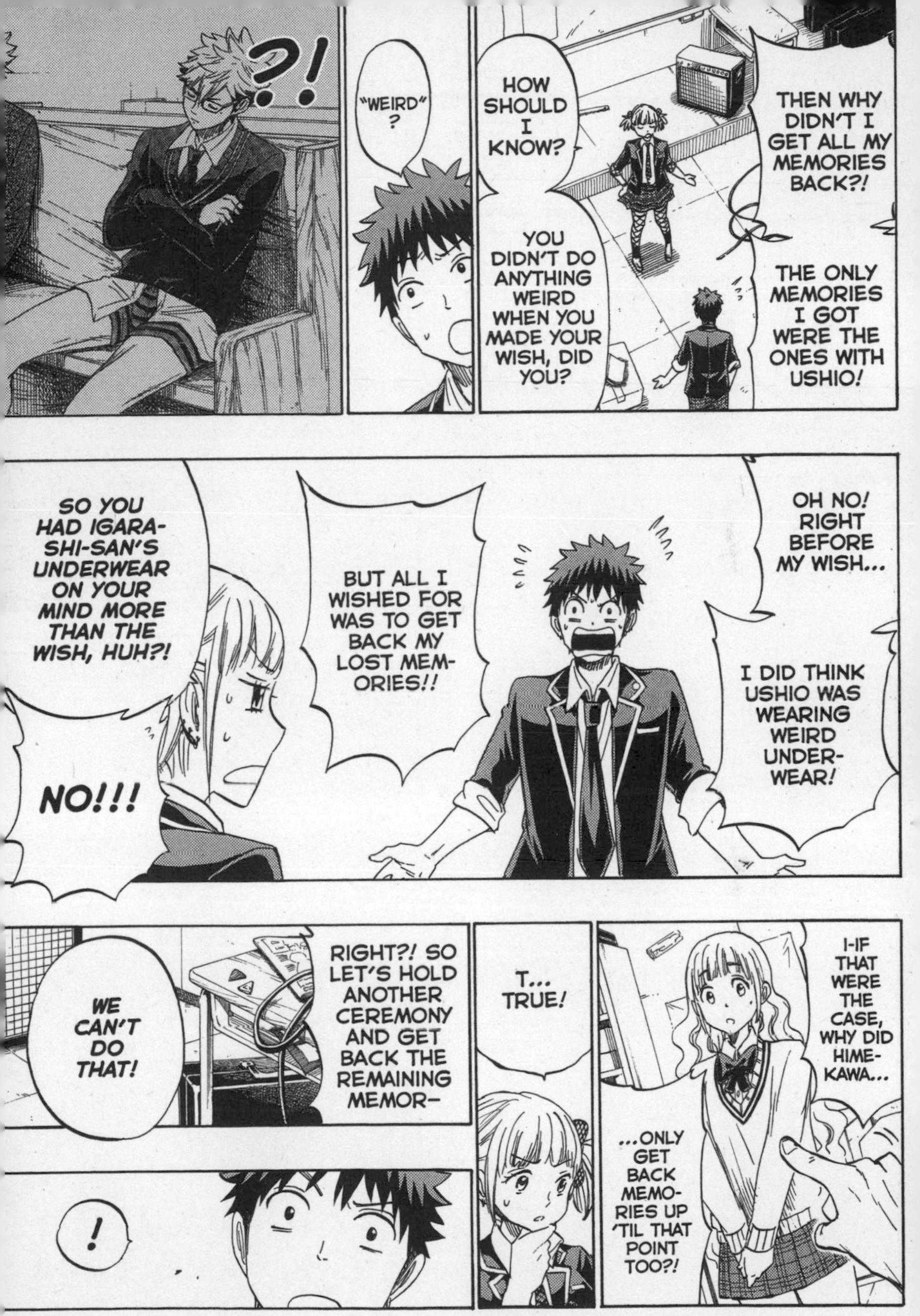
THEN WHY DIDN'T I GET ALL MY MEMORIES BACK?!
THE ONLY MEMORIES I GOT WERE THE ONES WITH USHIO!
HOW SHOULD I KNOW?
YOU DIDN'T DO ANYTHING WEIRD WHEN YOU MADE YOUR WISH, DID YOU?
"WEIRD"?
?!
OH NO! RIGHT BEFORE MY WISH...
I DID THINK USHIO WAS WEARING WEIRD UNDERWEAR!
BUT ALL I WISHED FOR WAS TO GET BACK MY LOST MEMORIES!!
SO YOU HAD IGARASHI-SAN'S UNDERWEAR ON YOUR MIND MORE THAN THE WISH, HUH?!
NO!!!
I-IF THAT WERE THE CASE, WHY DID HIMEKAWA...
...ONLY GET BACK MEMORIES UP 'TIL THAT POINT TOO?!
T... TRUE!
RIGHT?! SO LET'S HOLD ANOTHER CEREMONY AND GET BACK THE REMAINING MEMOR–
WE CAN'T DO THAT!
!

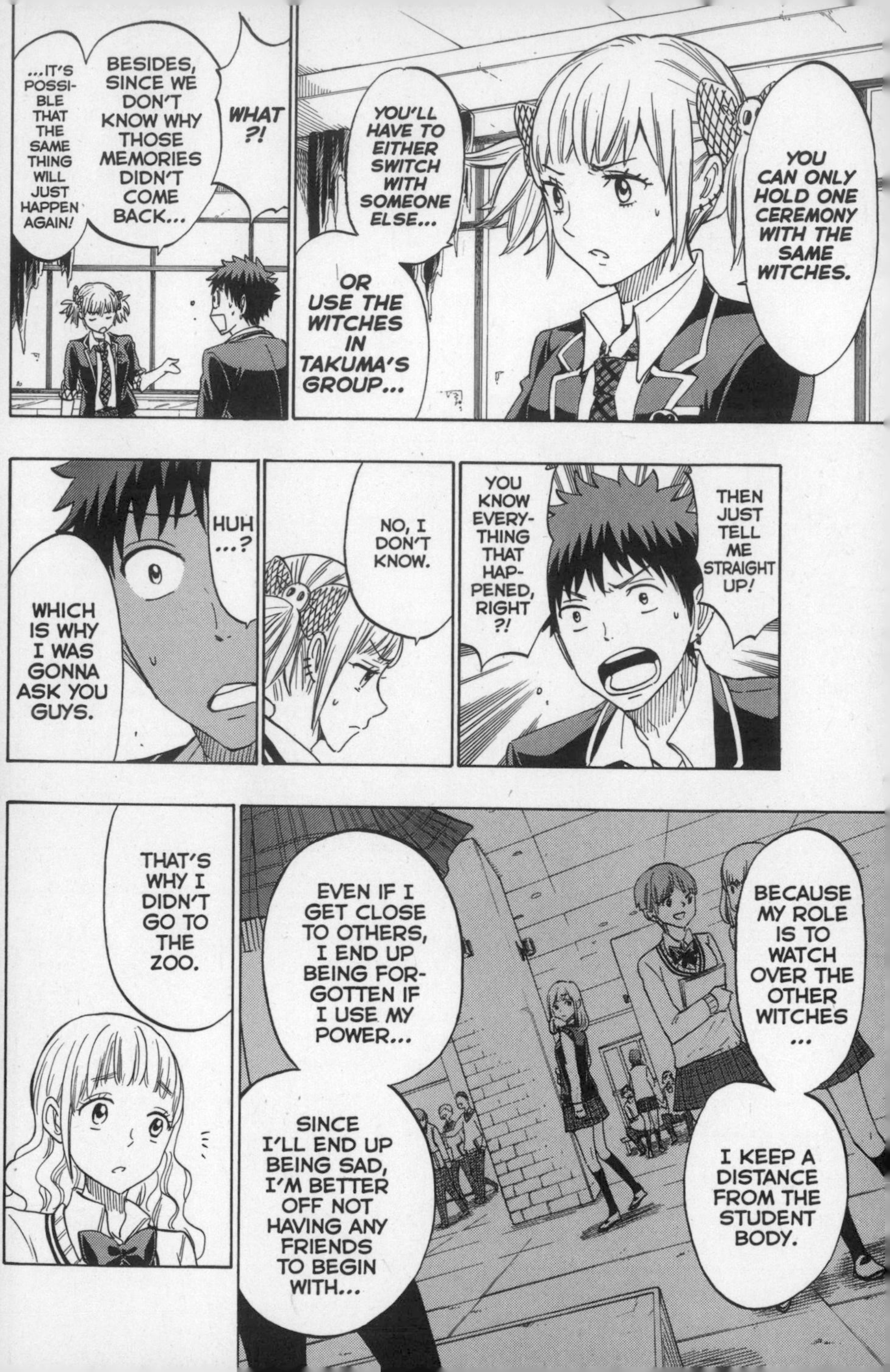
YOU CAN ONLY HOLD ONE CEREMONY WITH THE SAME WITCHES.
YOU'LL HAVE TO EITHER SWITCH WITH SOMEONE ELSE...
OR USE THE WITCHES IN TAKUMA'S GROUP...
WHAT?!
BESIDES, SINCE WE DON'T KNOW WHY THOSE MEMORIES DIDN'T COME BACK...
...IT'S POSSIBLE THAT THE SAME THING WILL JUST HAPPEN AGAIN!
THEN JUST TELL ME STRAIGHT UP!
YOU KNOW EVERYTHING THAT HAPPENED, RIGHT?!
NO, I DON'T KNOW.
HUH...?
WHICH IS WHY I WAS GONNA ASK YOU GUYS.
BECAUSE MY ROLE IS TO WATCH OVER THE OTHER WITCHES...
I KEEP A DISTANCE FROM THE STUDENT BODY.
EVEN IF I GET CLOSE TO OTHERS, I END UP BEING FORGOTTEN IF I USE MY POWER...
SINCE I'LL END UP BEING SAD, I'M BETTER OFF NOT HAVING ANY FRIENDS TO BEGIN WITH...
THAT'S WHY I DIDN'T GO TO THE ZOO.

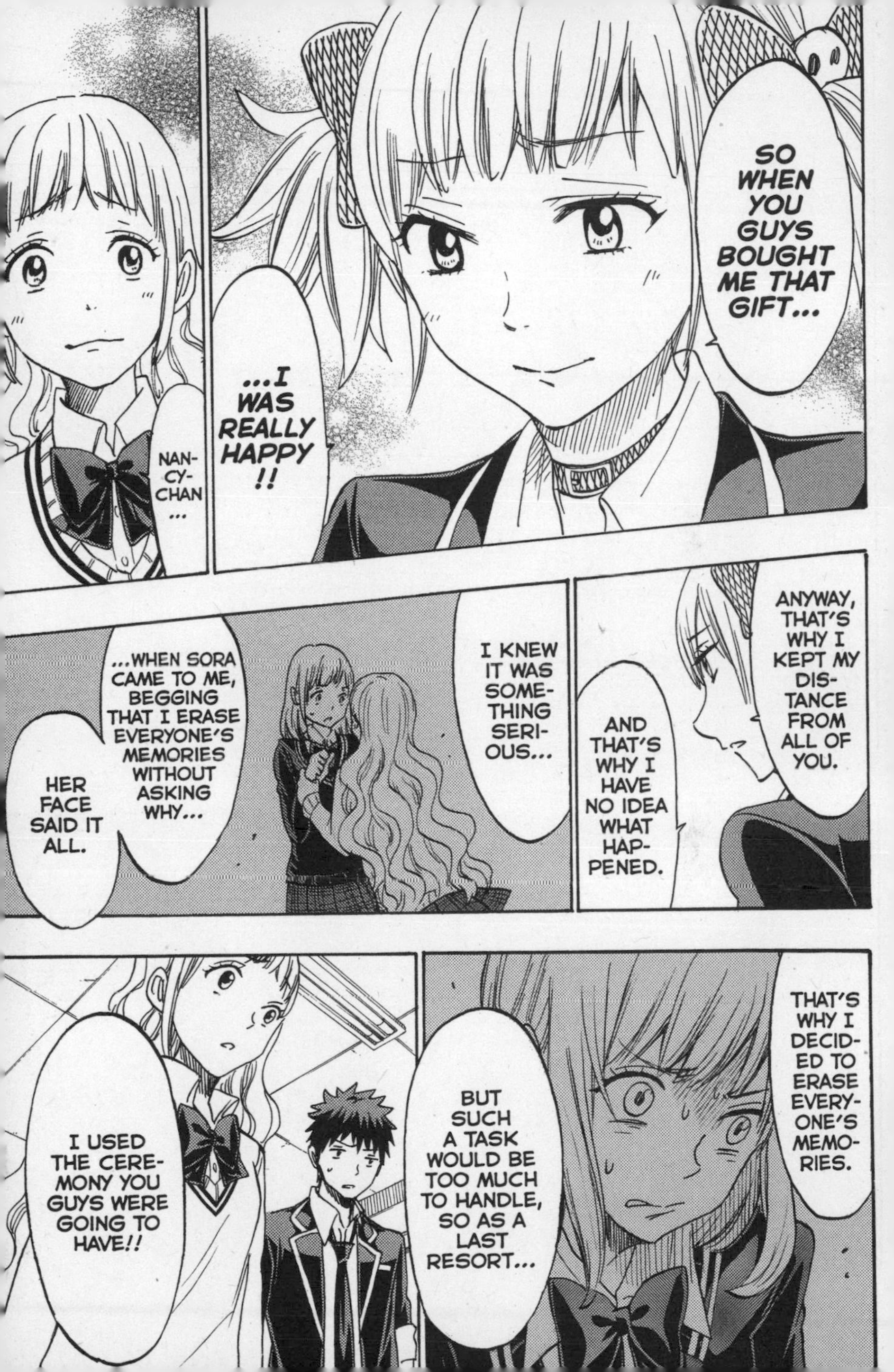
SO WHEN YOU GUYS BOUGHT ME THAT GIFT...
...I WAS REALLY HAPPY!!
NAN-CY-CHAN...
ANYWAY, THAT'S WHY I KEPT MY DIS-TANCE FROM ALL OF YOU.
AND THAT'S WHY I HAVE NO IDEA WHAT HAP-PENED.
I KNEW IT WAS SOME-THING SERI-OUS...
...WHEN SORA CAME TO ME, BEGGING THAT I ERASE EVERYONE'S MEMORIES WITHOUT ASKING WHY...
HER FACE SAID IT ALL.
THAT'S WHY I DECID-ED TO ERASE EVERY-ONE'S MEMO-RIES.
BUT SUCH A TASK WOULD BE TOO MUCH TO HANDLE, SO AS A LAST RESORT...
I USED THE CERE-MONY YOU GUYS WERE GOING TO HAVE!!

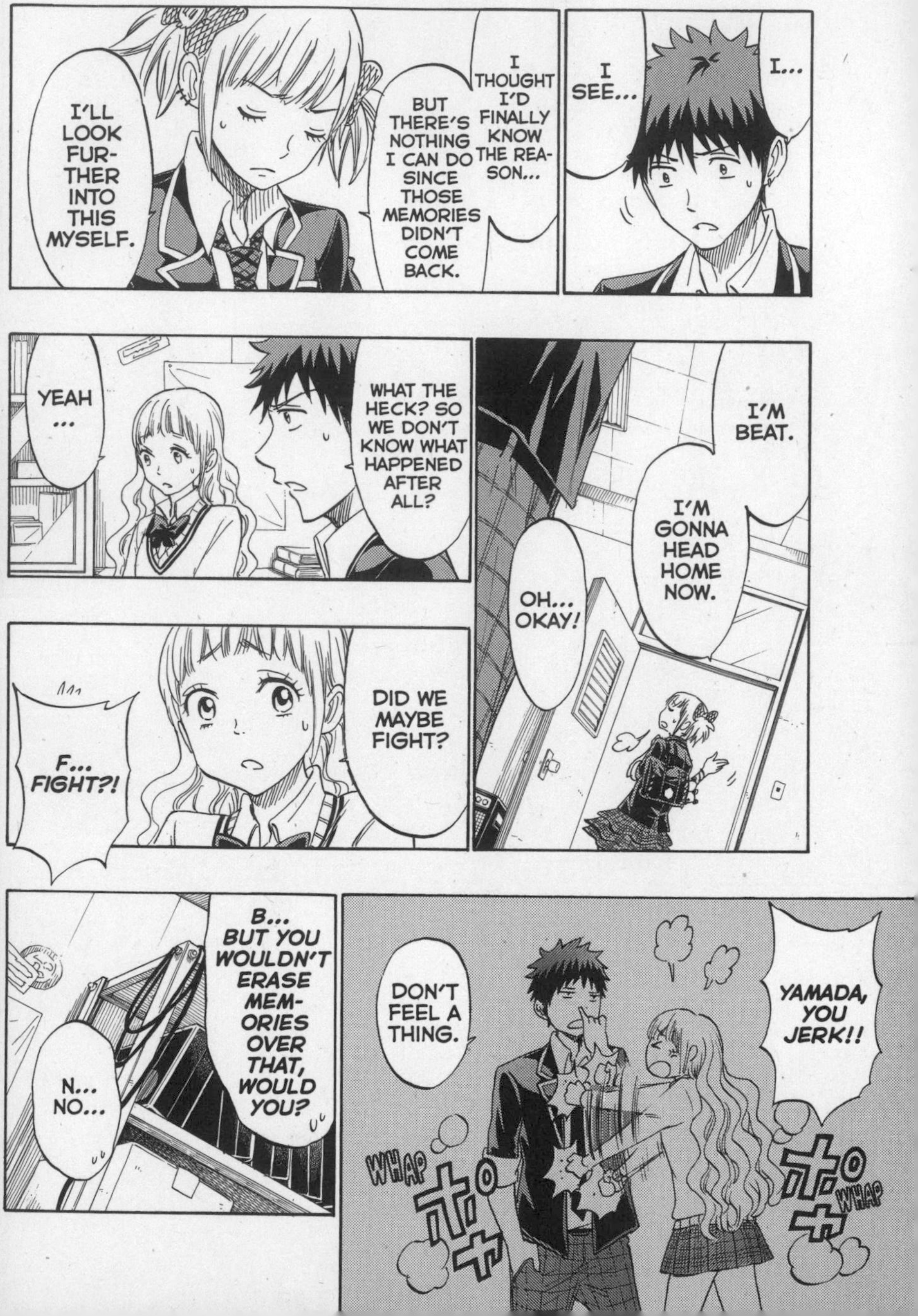
I...
I SEE...
I THOUGHT I'D FINALLY KNOW THE REA-SON...
BUT THERE'S NOTHING I CAN DO SINCE THOSE MEMORIES DIDN'T COME BACK.
I'LL LOOK FUR-THER INTO THIS MYSELF.
I'M BEAT.
I'M GONNA HEAD HOME NOW.
OH... OKAY!
WHAT THE HECK? SO WE DON'T KNOW WHAT HAPPENED AFTER ALL?
YEAH ...
DID WE MAYBE FIGHT?
F... FIGHT?!
YAMADA, YOU JERK!!
DON'T FEEL A THING.
WHAP
WHAP
B... BUT YOU WOULDN'T ERASE MEM-ORIES OVER THAT, WOULD YOU?
N... NO...

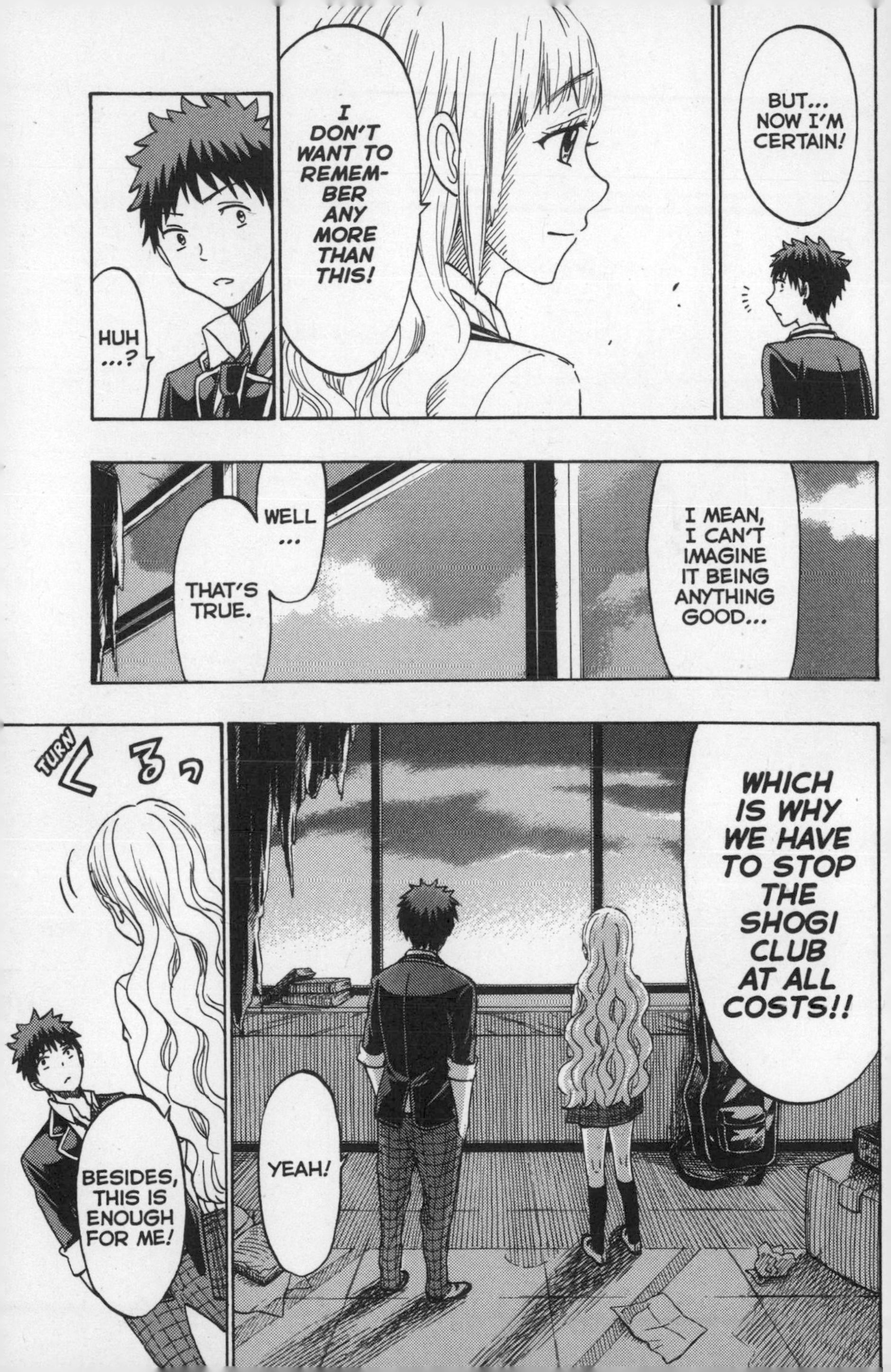
BUT... NOW I'M CERTAIN!
I DON'T WANT TO REMEMBER ANY MORE THAN THIS!
HUH ...?
I MEAN, I CAN'T IMAGINE IT BEING ANYTHING GOOD...
WELL ... THAT'S TRUE.
WHICH IS WHY WE HAVE TO STOP THE SHOGI CLUB AT ALL COSTS!!
YEAH!
TURN くるっ
BESIDES, THIS IS ENOUGH FOR ME!

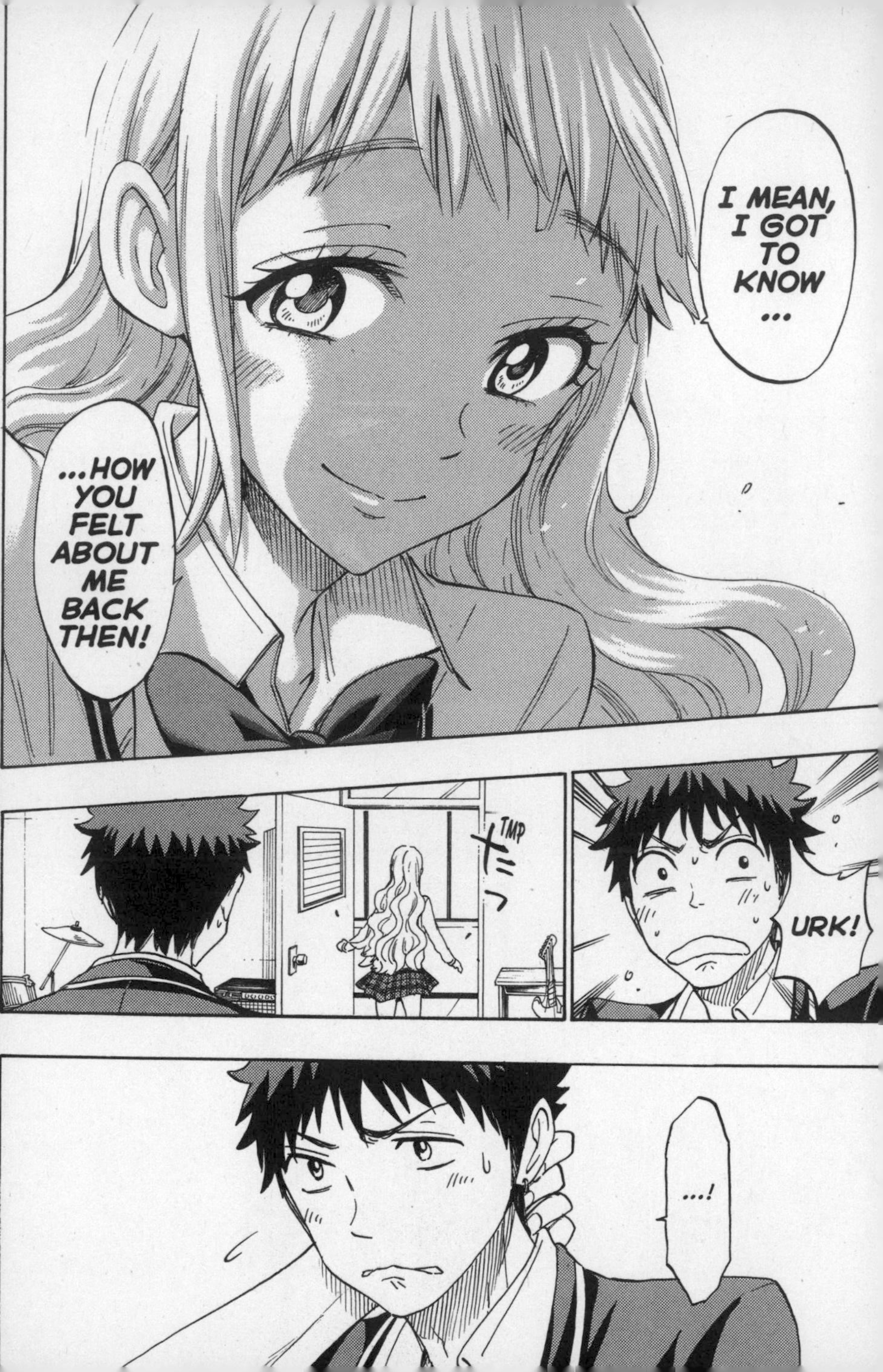
I MEAN, I GOT TO KNOW ...
...HOW YOU FELT ABOUT ME BACK THEN!
URK!
TMP
...!

CHAPTER 163: I might get dumped, huh?

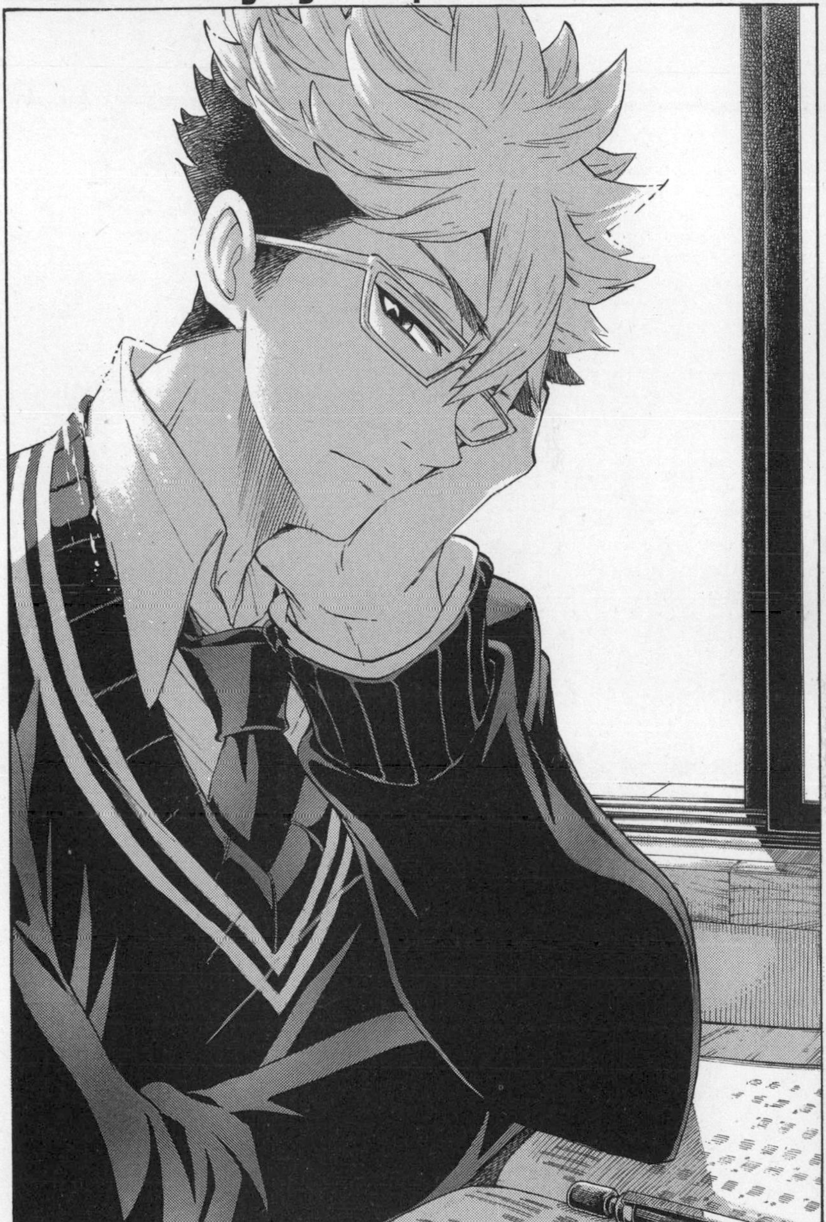

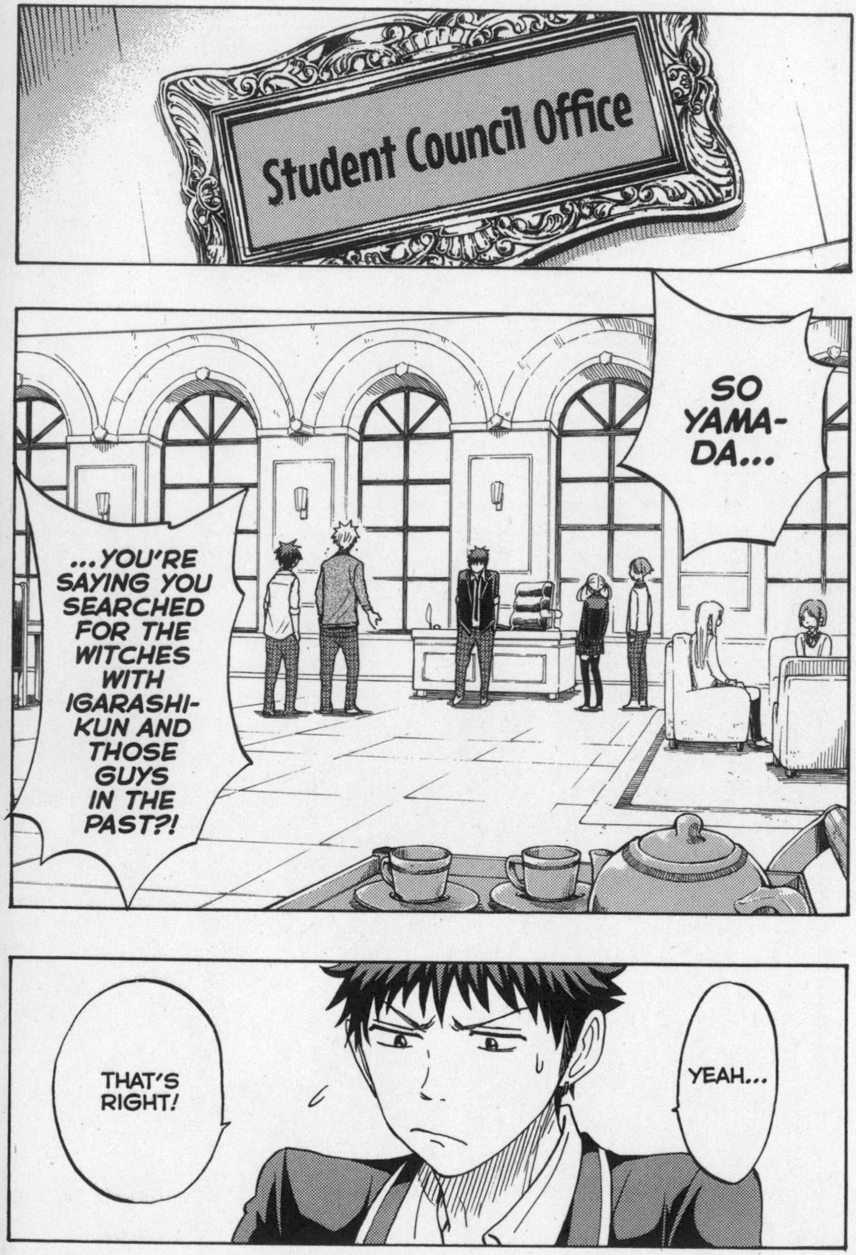
Student Council Office
SO YAMADA...
...YOU'RE SAYING YOU SEARCHED FOR THE WITCHES WITH IGARASHI-KUN AND THOSE GUYS IN THE PAST?!
YEAH...
THAT'S RIGHT!

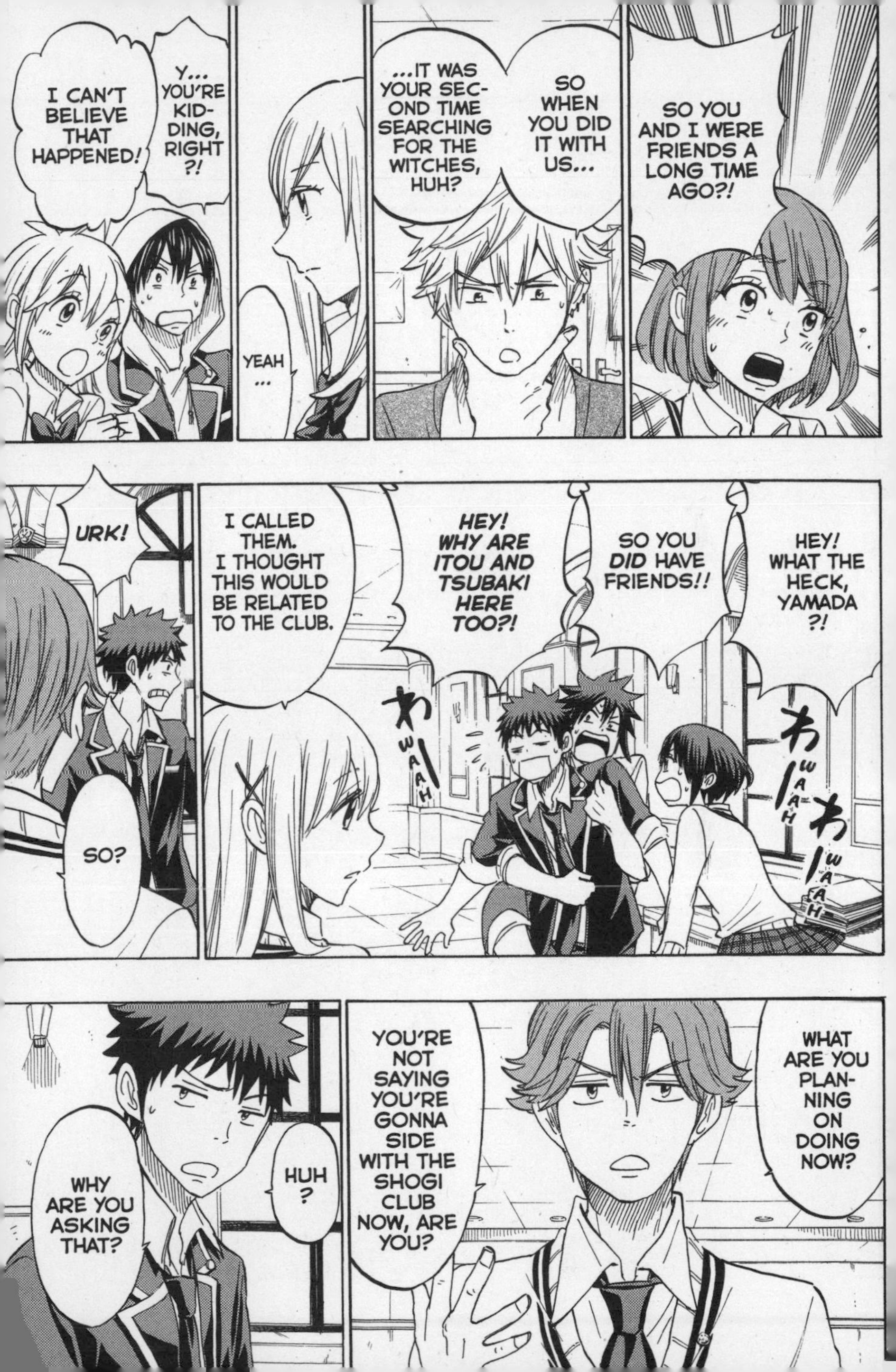
SO YOU AND I WERE FRIENDS A LONG TIME AGO?!
SO WHEN YOU DID IT WITH US...
...IT WAS YOUR SECOND TIME SEARCHING FOR THE WITCHES, HUH?
YEAH...
Y... YOU'RE KIDDING, RIGHT?!
I CAN'T BELIEVE THAT HAPPENED!
HEY! WHAT THE HECK, YAMADA?!
WAAH
SO YOU *DID* HAVE FRIENDS!!
WAAH
HEY! WHY ARE ITOU AND TSUBAKI HERE TOO?!
WAAH
I CALLED THEM. I THOUGHT THIS WOULD BE RELATED TO THE CLUB.
URK!
SO?
WHAT ARE YOU PLANNING ON DOING NOW?
YOU'RE NOT SAYING YOU'RE GONNA SIDE WITH THE SHOGI CLUB NOW, ARE YOU?
HUH?
WHY ARE YOU ASKING THAT?

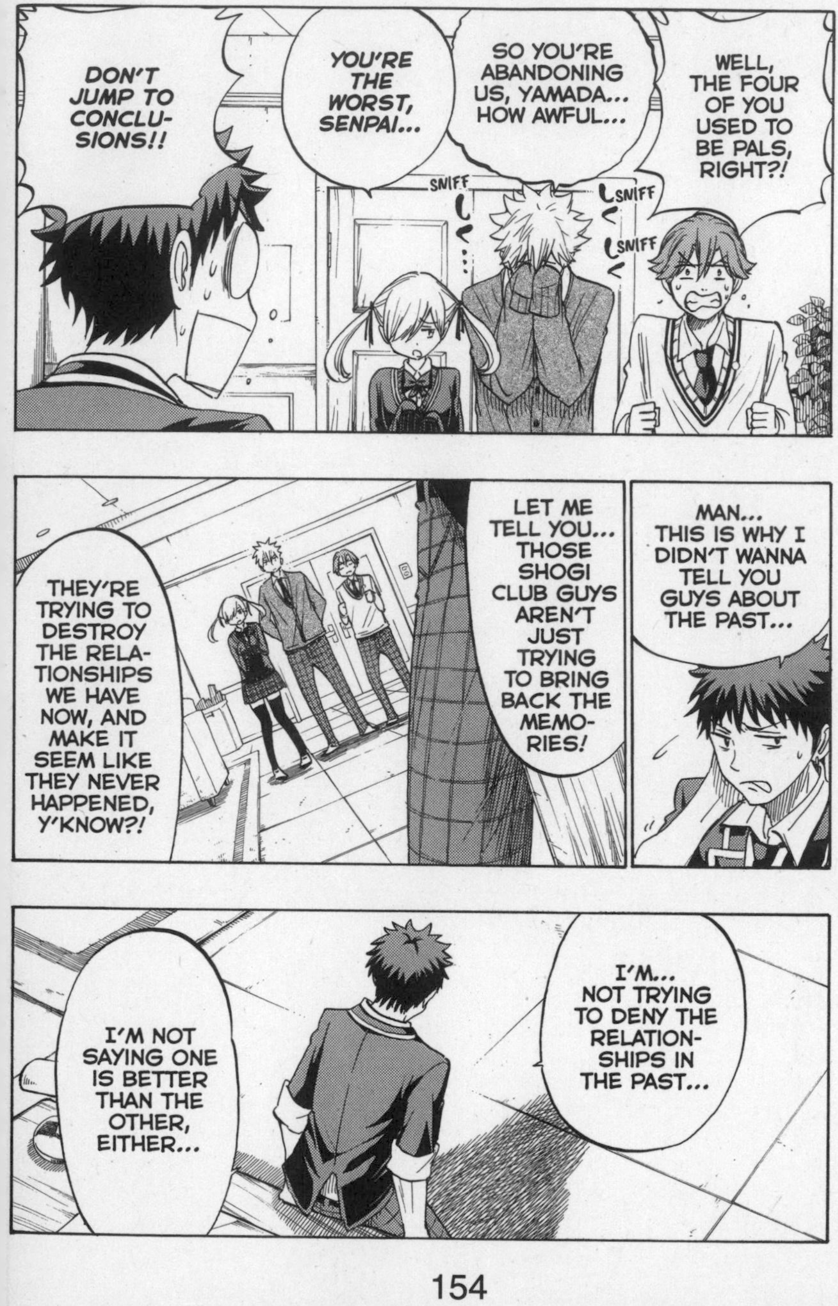
WELL, THE FOUR OF YOU USED TO BE PALS, RIGHT?!
SO YOU'RE ABANDONING US, YAMADA... HOW AWFUL...
YOU'RE THE WORST, SENPAI...
SNIFF
SNIFF
SNIFF
DON'T JUMP TO CONCLUSIONS!!
MAN... THIS IS WHY I DIDN'T WANNA TELL YOU GUYS ABOUT THE PAST...
LET ME TELL YOU... THOSE SHOGI CLUB GUYS AREN'T JUST TRYING TO BRING BACK THE MEMORIES!
THEY'RE TRYING TO DESTROY THE RELATIONSHIPS WE HAVE NOW, AND MAKE IT SEEM LIKE THEY NEVER HAPPENED, Y'KNOW?!
I'M... NOT TRYING TO DENY THE RELATIONSHIPS IN THE PAST...
I'M NOT SAYING ONE IS BETTER THAN THE OTHER, EITHER...

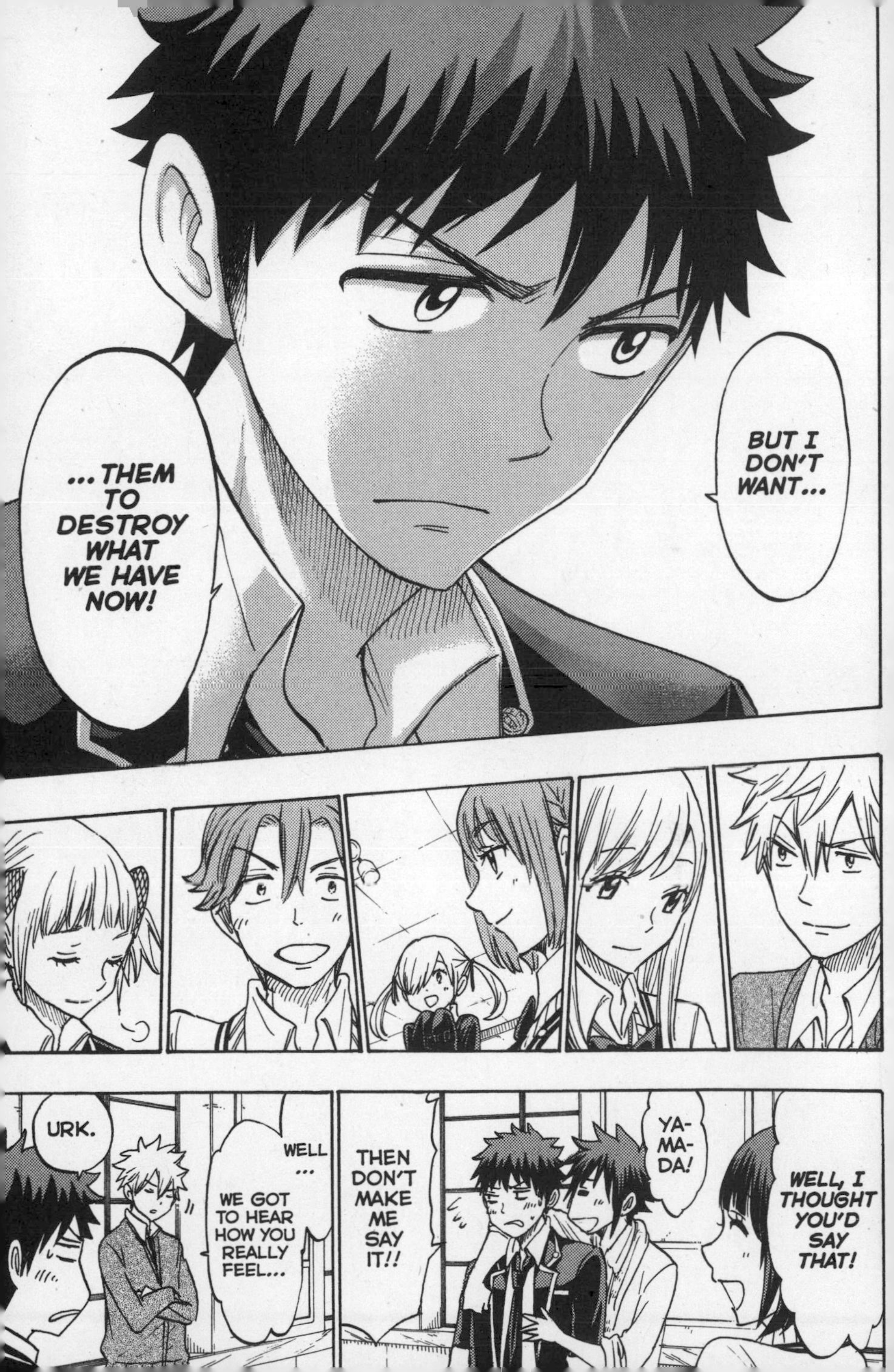
BUT I DON'T WANT...
...THEM TO DESTROY WHAT WE HAVE NOW!
WELL, I THOUGHT YOU'D SAY THAT!
YA-MA-DA!
THEN DON'T MAKE ME SAY IT!!
WELL ...
WE GOT TO HEAR HOW YOU REALLY FEEL...
URK.

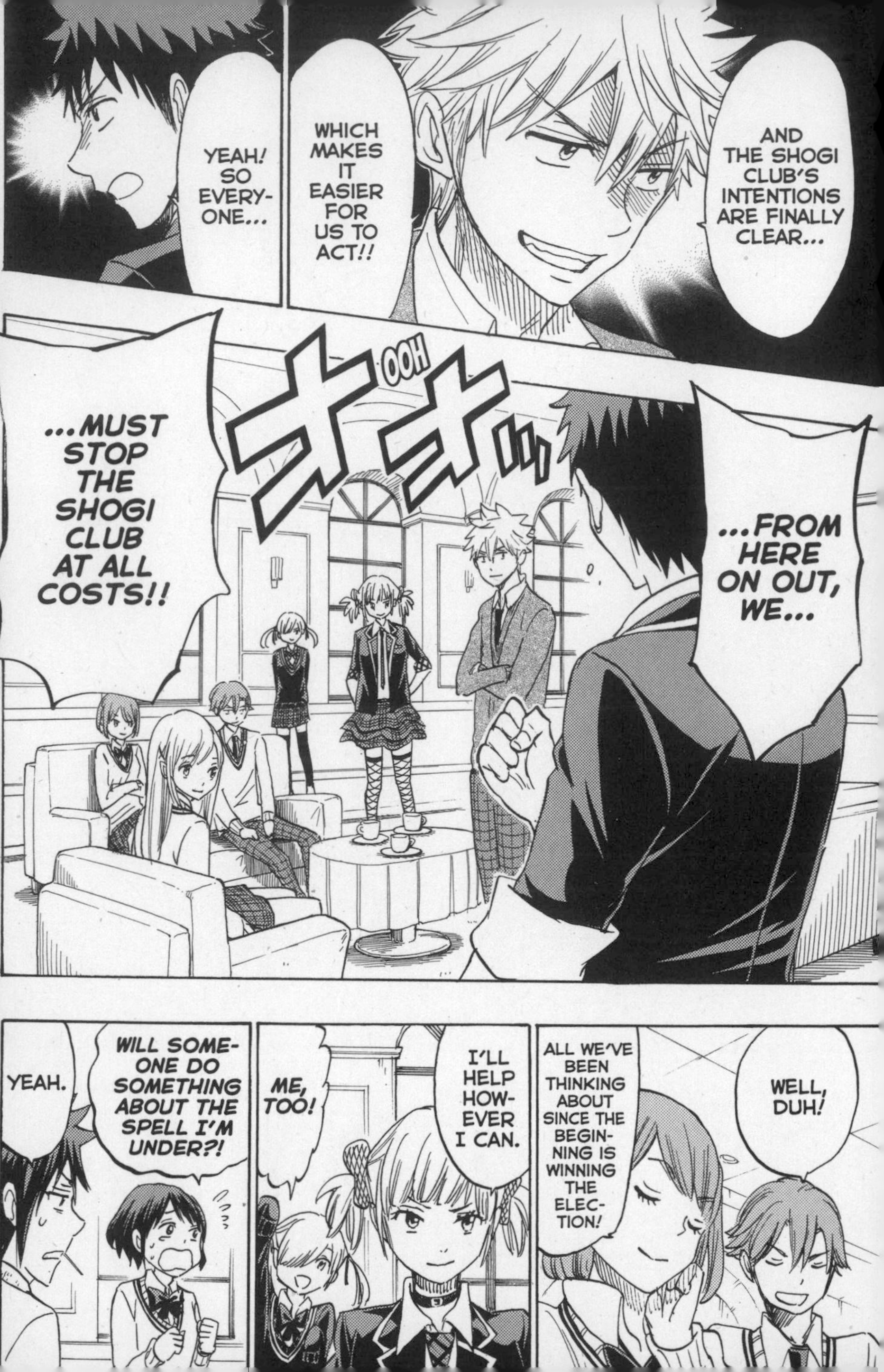
AND THE SHOGI CLUB'S INTENTIONS ARE FINALLY CLEAR...
WHICH MAKES IT EASIER FOR US TO ACT!!
YEAH! SO EVERYONE...
...FROM HERE ON OUT, WE...
OOH
...MUST STOP THE SHOGI CLUB AT ALL COSTS!!
WELL, DUH!
ALL WE'VE BEEN THINKING ABOUT SINCE THE BEGINNING IS WINNING THE ELECTION!
I'LL HELP HOWEVER I CAN.
ME, TOO!
WILL SOMEONE DO SOMETHING ABOUT THE SPELL I'M UNDER?!
YEAH.

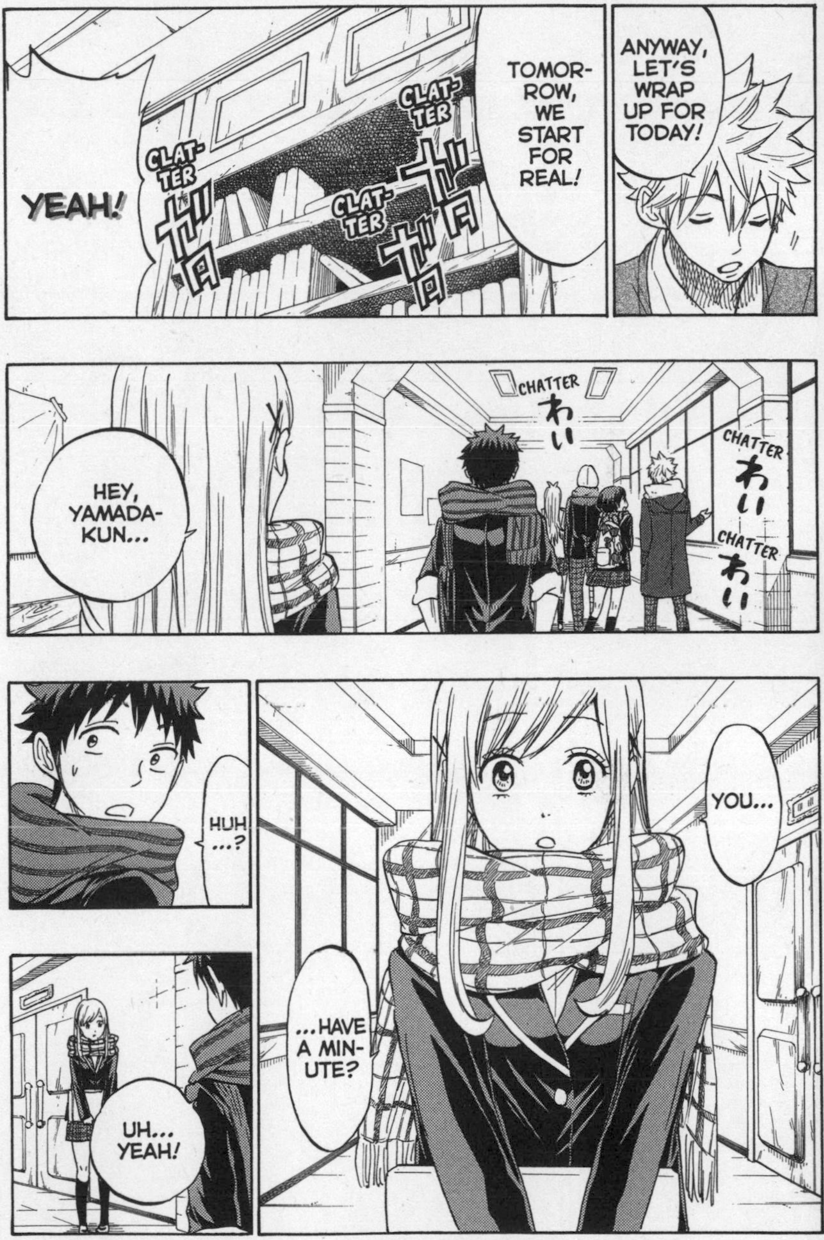
ANYWAY, LET'S WRAP UP FOR TODAY!
TOMOR-ROW, WE START FOR REAL!
CLAT-TER
ガタ
CLAT-TER
ガタ
CLAT-TER
ガタ
YEAH!
CHATTER
わい
CHATTER
わい
CHATTER
わい
HEY, YAMADA-KUN...
YOU...
...HAVE A MIN-UTE?
HUH ...?
UH... YEAH!

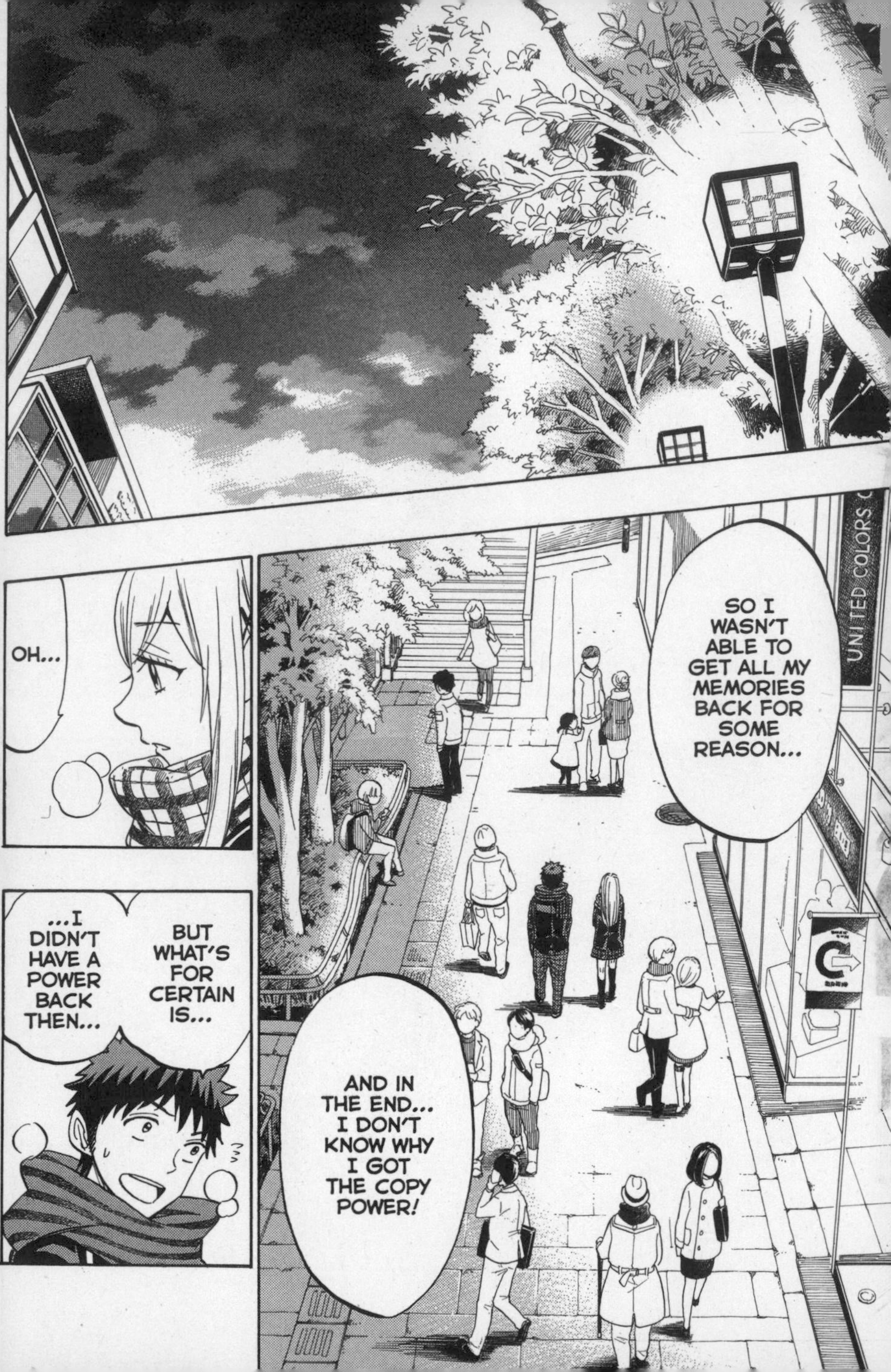
UNITED COLORS
SO I WASN'T ABLE TO GET ALL MY MEMORIES BACK FOR SOME REASON...
AND IN THE END... I DON'T KNOW WHY I GOT THE COPY POWER!
OH...
BUT WHAT'S FOR CERTAIN IS...
...I DIDN'T HAVE A POWER BACK THEN...

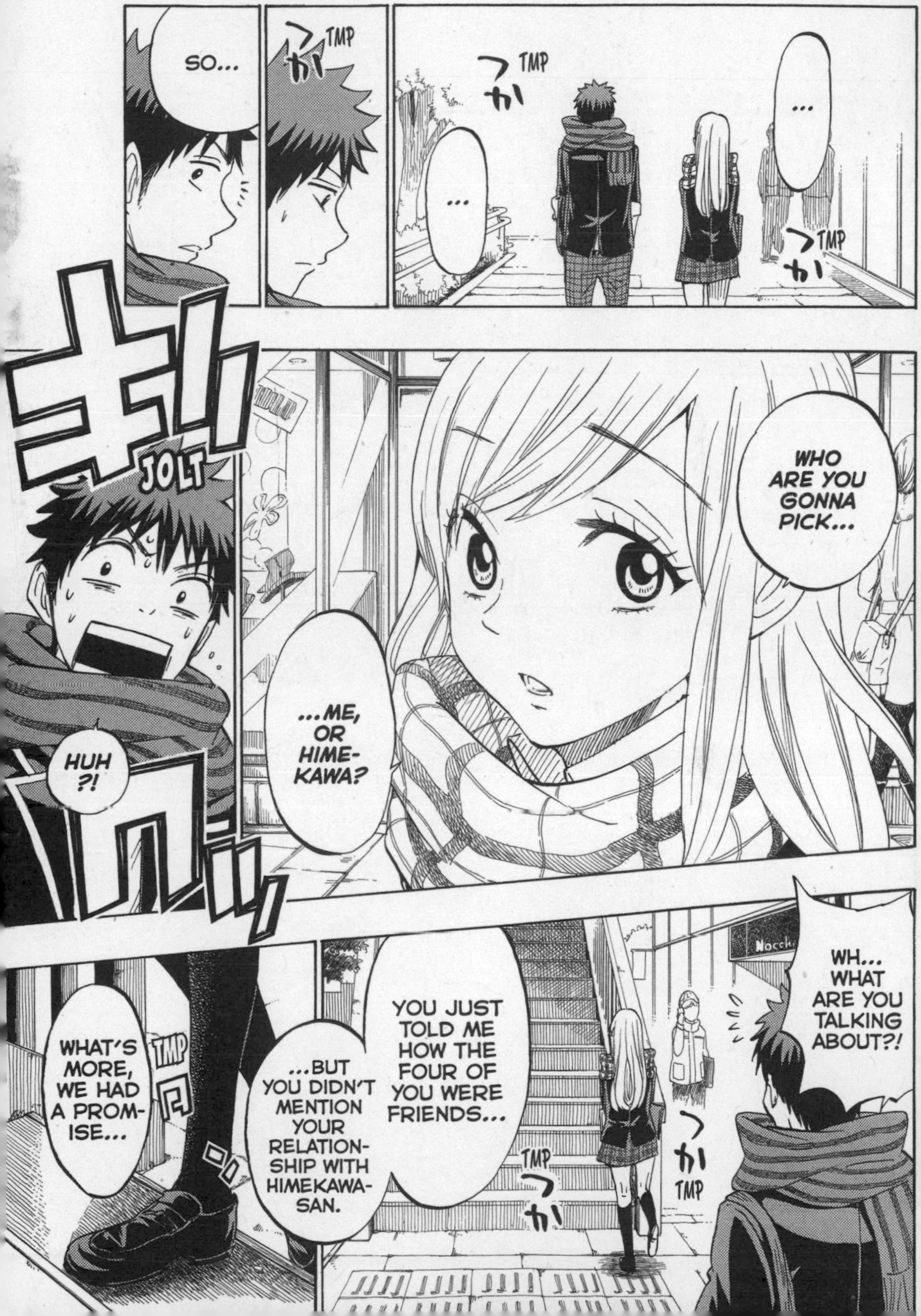
TMP
...
TMP
...
TMP
SO...
WHO ARE YOU GONNA PICK...
...ME, OR HIME-KAWA?
JOLT
HUH ?!
WH... WHAT ARE YOU TALKING ABOUT?!
TMP
TMP
YOU JUST TOLD ME HOW THE FOUR OF YOU WERE FRIENDS...
...BUT YOU DIDN'T MENTION YOUR RELATION-SHIP WITH HIMEKAWA-SAN.
TMP
WHAT'S MORE, WE HAD A PROM-ISE...

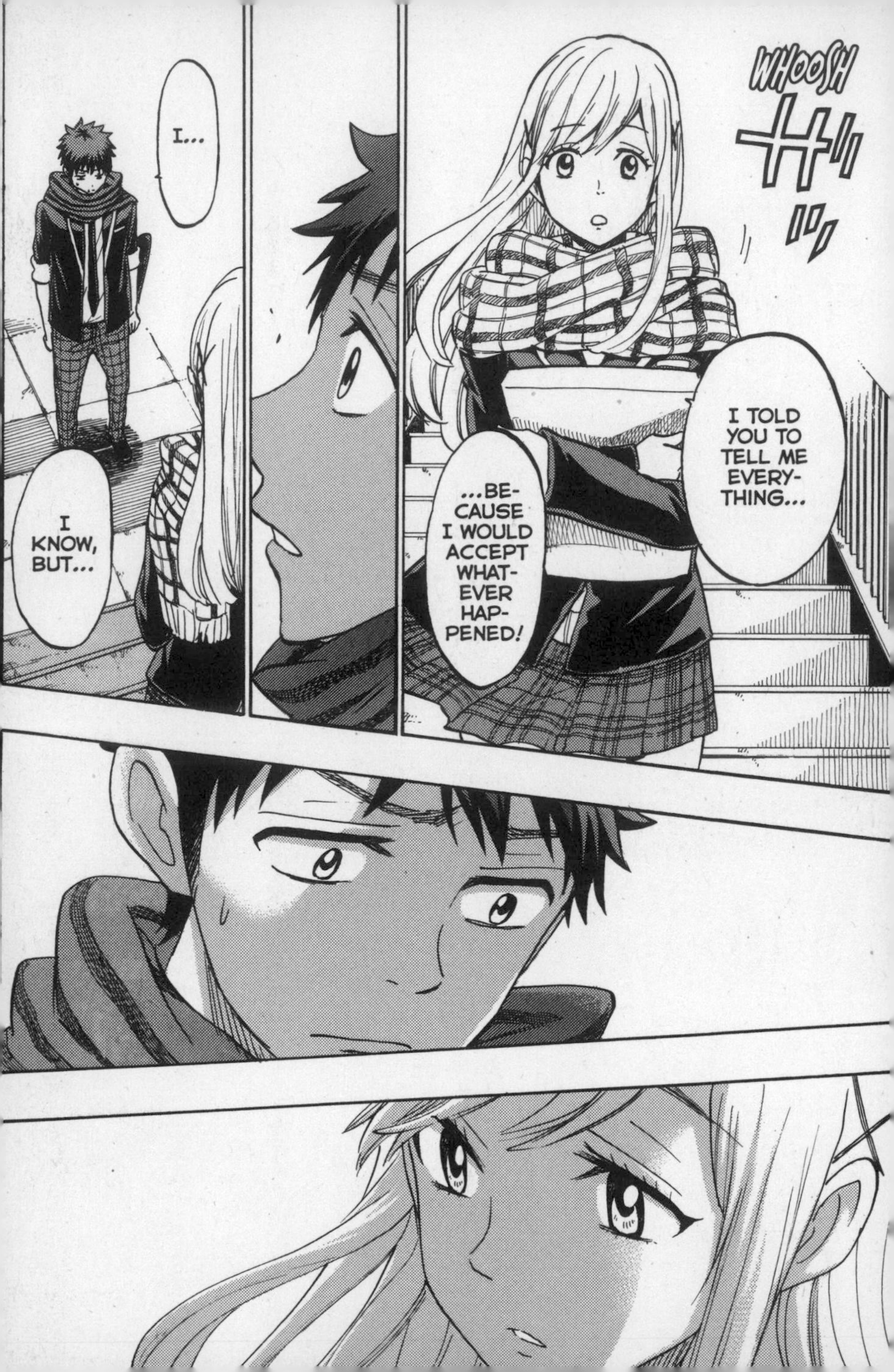
WHOOSH
I TOLD YOU TO TELL ME EVERY-THING...
...BE-CAUSE I WOULD ACCEPT WHAT-EVER HAP-PENED!
I...
I KNOW, BUT...

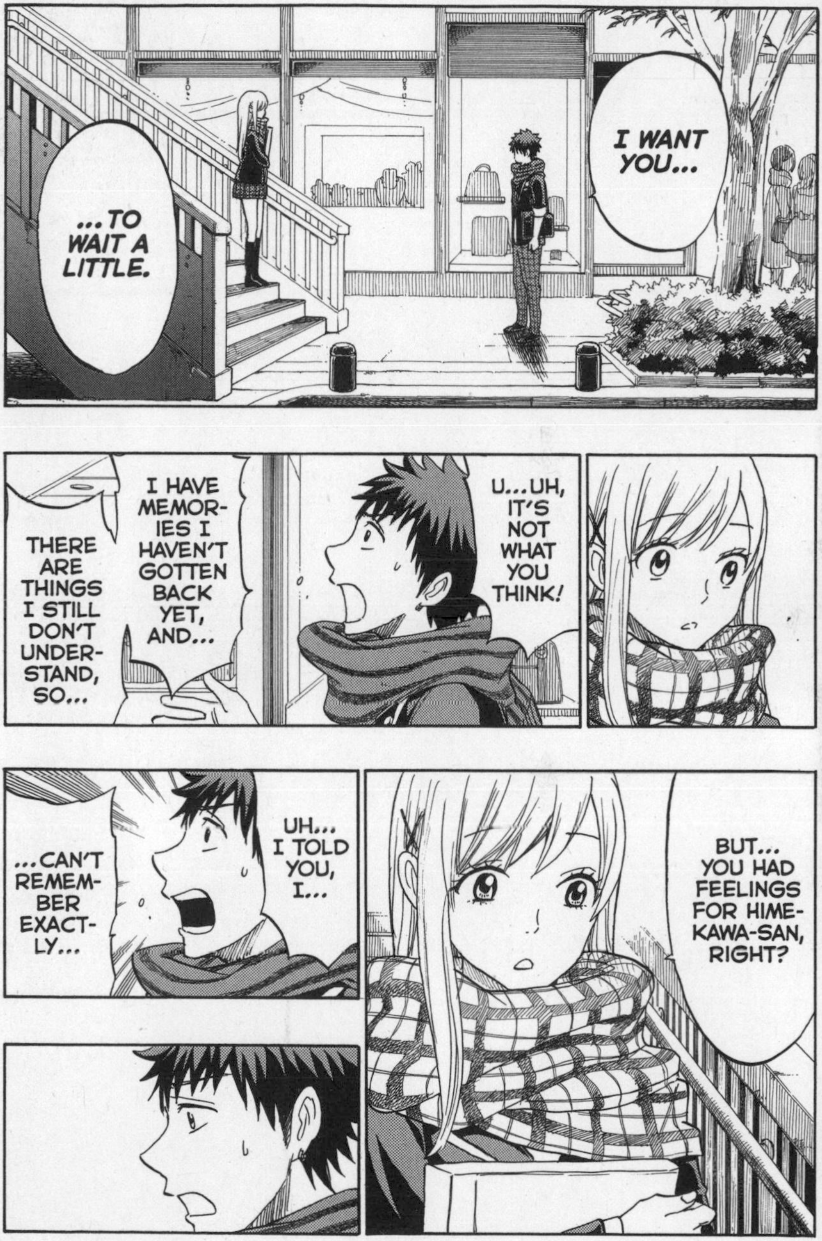
I WANT YOU...
...TO WAIT A LITTLE.
U...UH, IT'S NOT WHAT YOU THINK!
I HAVE MEMORIES I HAVEN'T GOTTEN BACK YET, AND...
THERE ARE THINGS I STILL DON'T UNDERSTAND, SO...
BUT... YOU HAD FEELINGS FOR HIME-KAWA-SAN, RIGHT?
UH... I TOLD YOU, I...
...CAN'T REMEMBER EXACTLY...

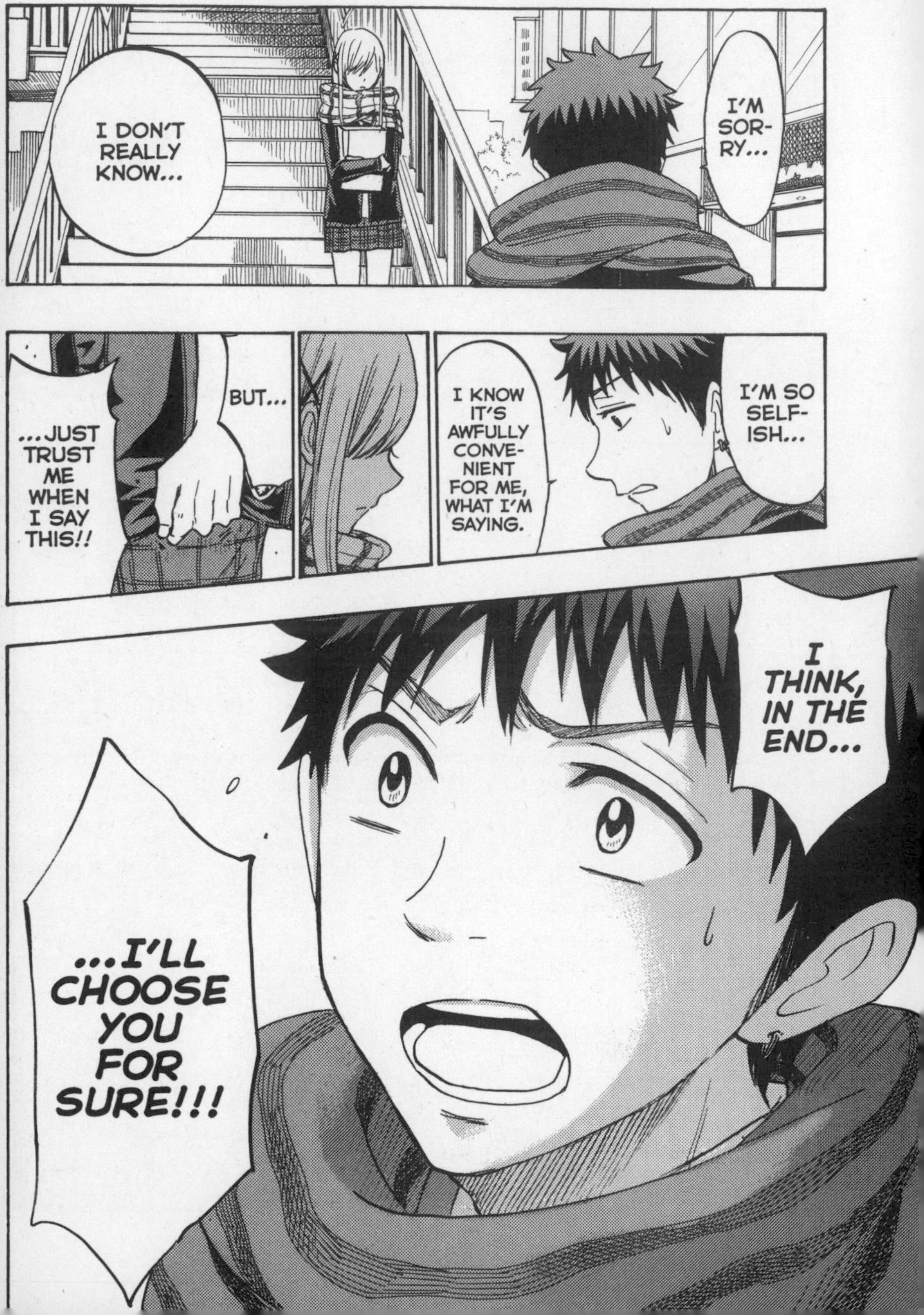
I'M SORRY...
I DON'T REALLY KNOW...
I'M SO SELFISH...
I KNOW IT'S AWFULLY CONVENIENT FOR ME, WHAT I'M SAYING.
BUT...
...JUST TRUST ME WHEN I SAY THIS!!
I THINK, IN THE END...
...I'LL CHOOSE YOU FOR SURE!!!

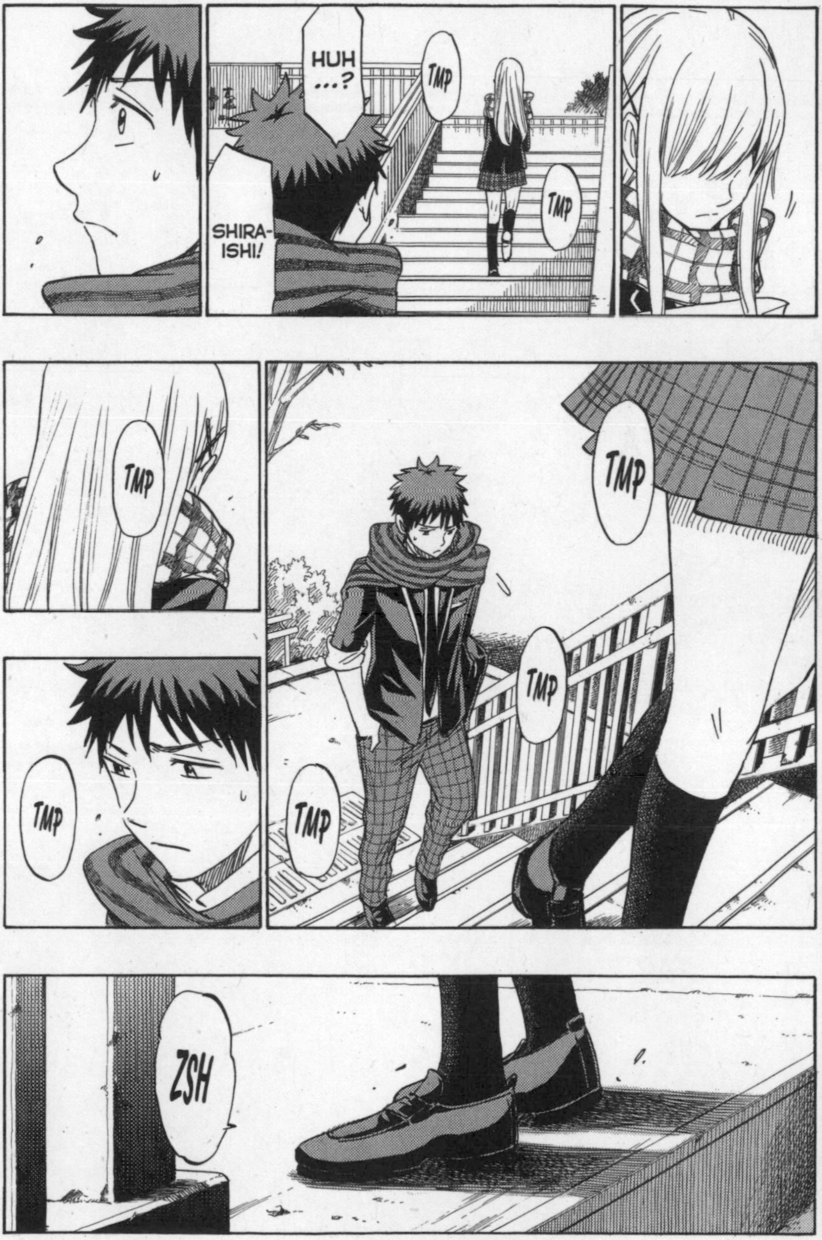
HUH ...?
TMP
TMP
SHIRA-ISHI!
TMP
TMP
TMP
TMP
TMP
ZSH

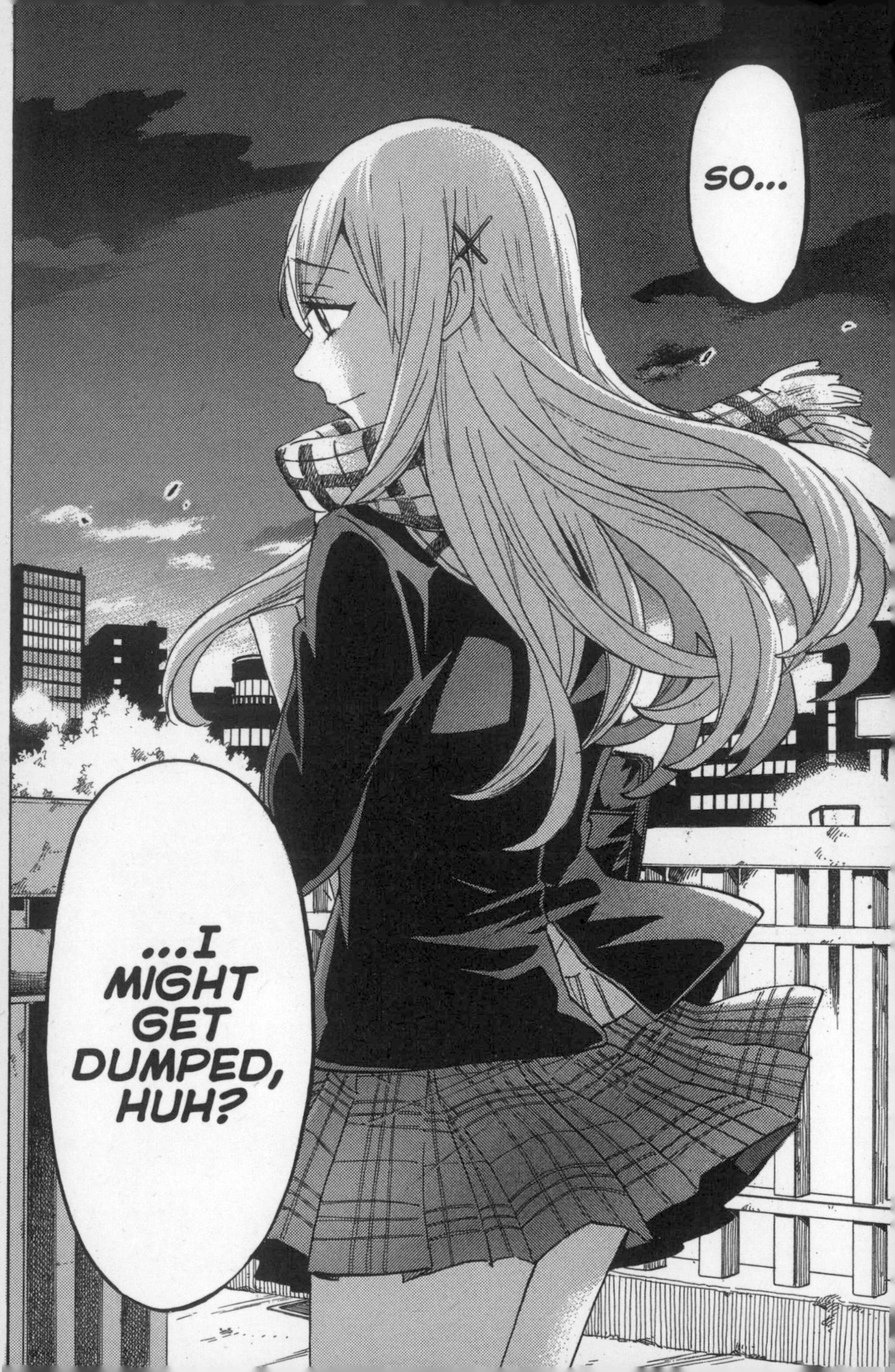
SO...
...I MIGHT GET DUMPED, HUH?

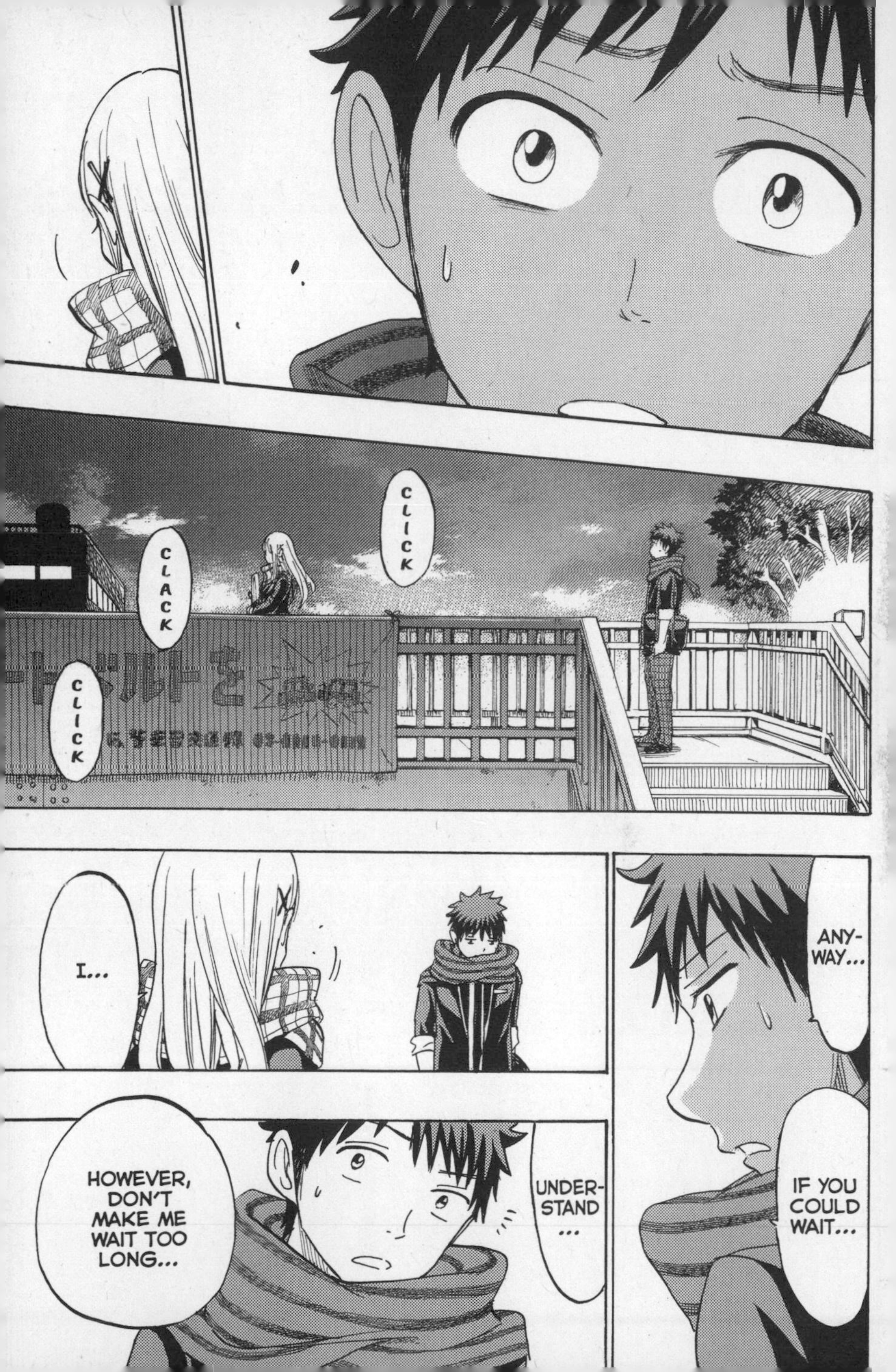
CLICK
CLACK
CLICK
ANY-WAY...
IF YOU COULD WAIT...
I...
UNDER-STAND...
HOWEVER, DON'T MAKE ME WAIT TOO LONG...

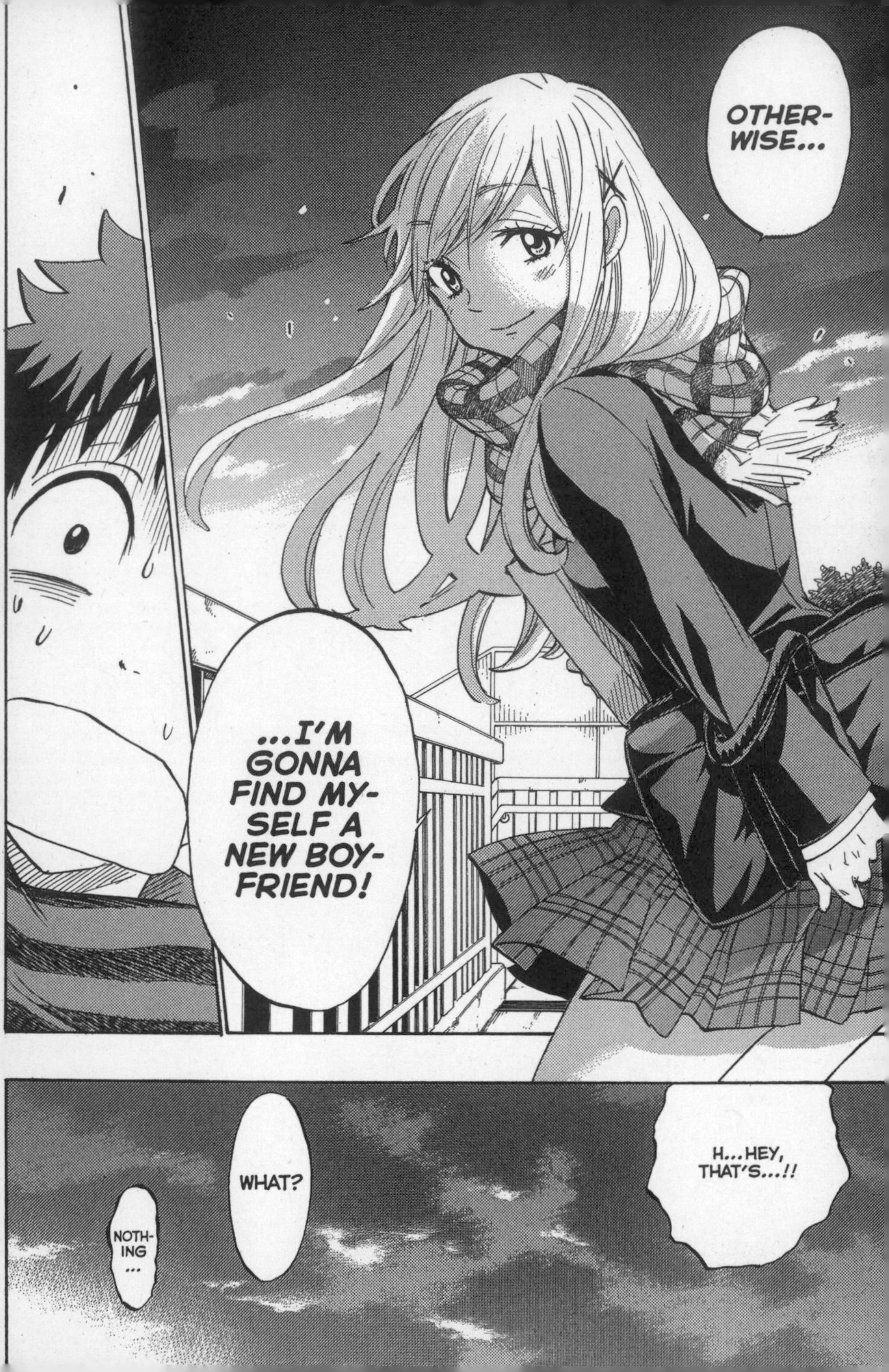
OTHER-WISE...
...I'M GONNA FIND MY-SELF A NEW BOY-FRIEND!
H...HEY, THAT'S...!!
WHAT?
NOTH-ING ...

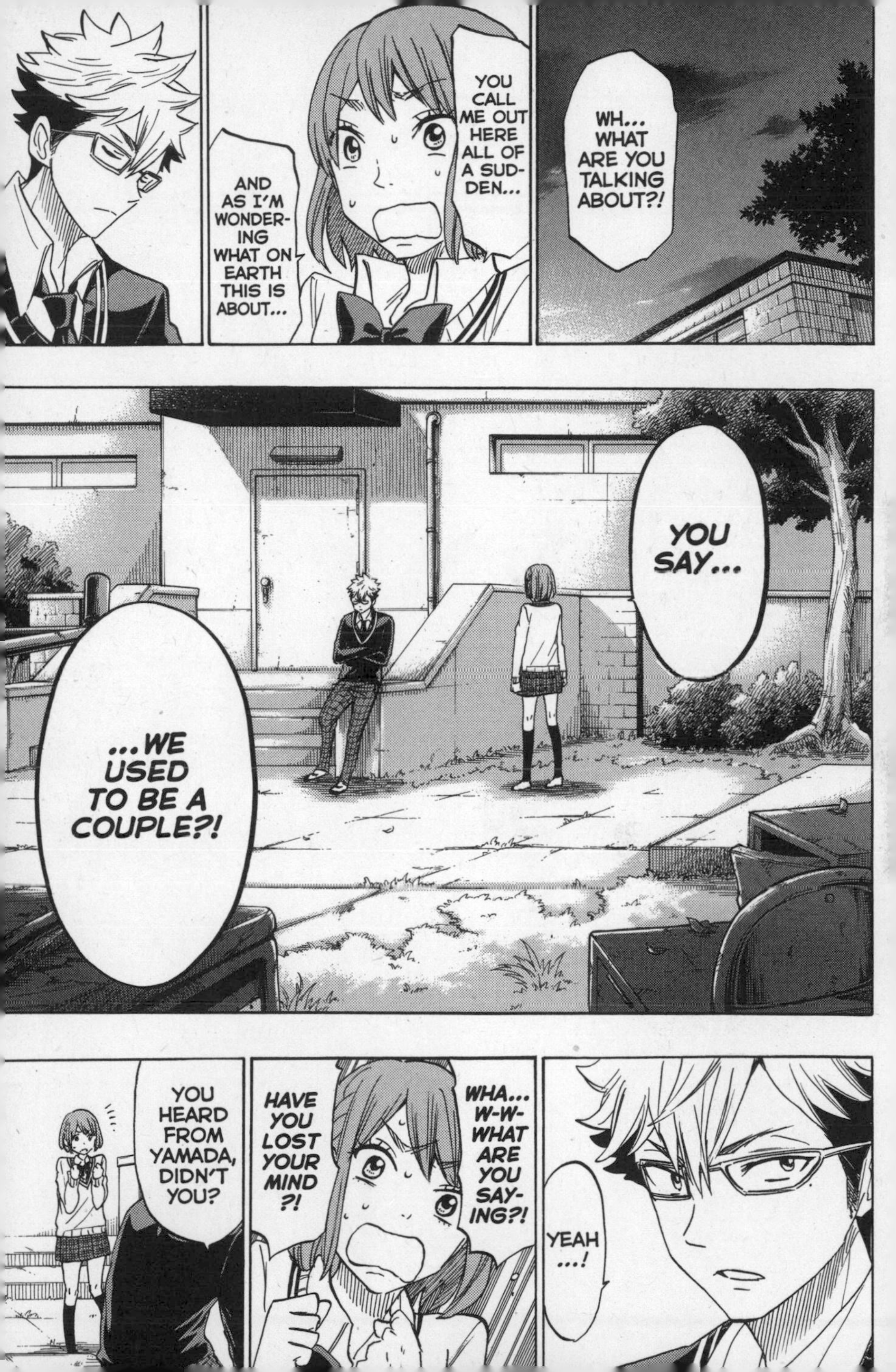
WH... WHAT ARE YOU TALKING ABOUT?!
YOU CALL ME OUT HERE ALL OF A SUD-DEN...
AND AS I'M WONDER-ING WHAT ON EARTH THIS IS ABOUT...
YOU SAY...
...WE USED TO BE A COUPLE?!
YEAH...!
WHA... W-W-WHAT ARE YOU SAY-ING?!
HAVE YOU LOST YOUR MIND?!
YOU HEARD FROM YAMADA, DIDN'T YOU?

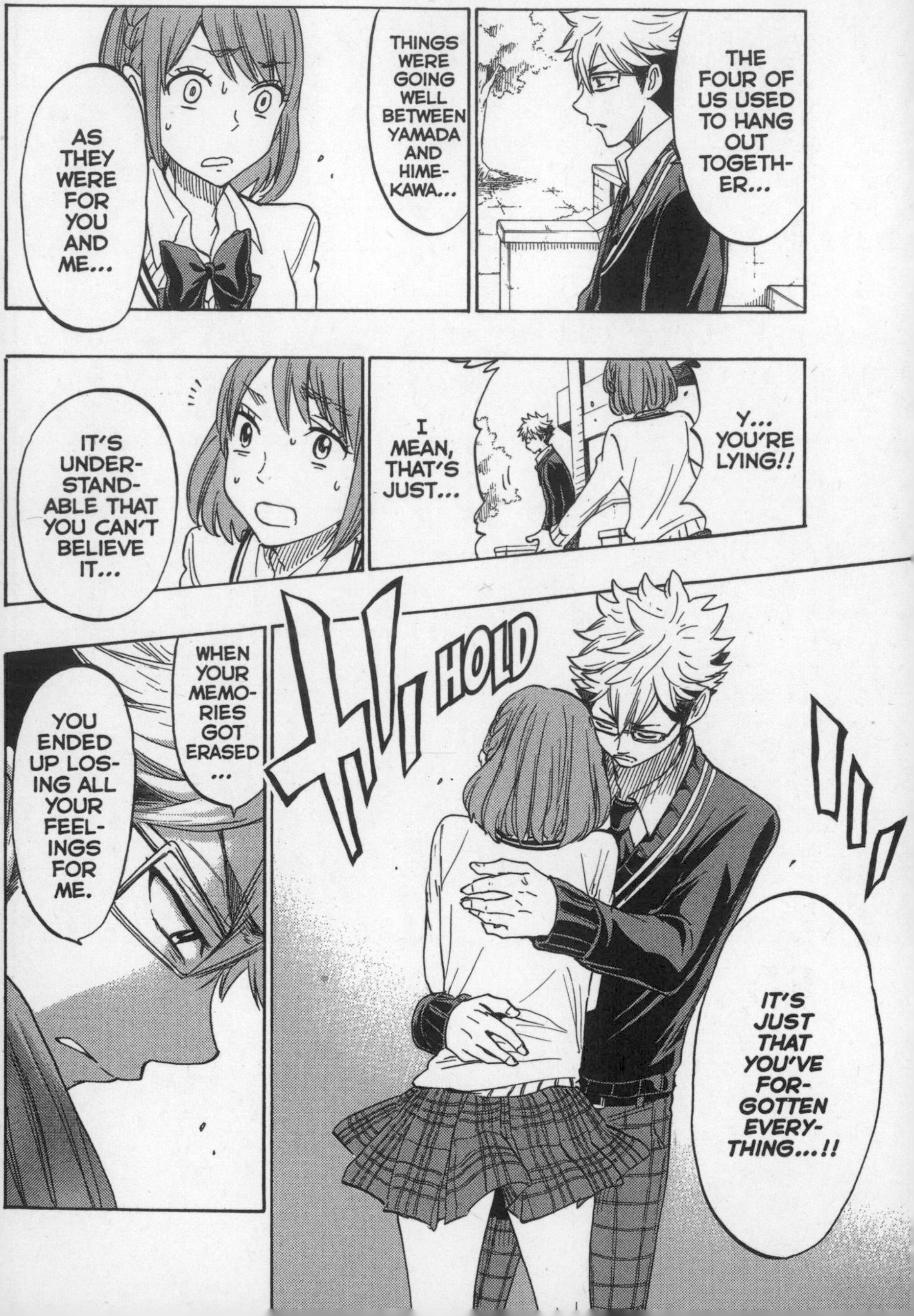
THE FOUR OF US USED TO HANG OUT TOGETH-ER...
THINGS WERE GOING WELL BETWEEN YAMADA AND HIME-KAWA...
AS THEY WERE FOR YOU AND ME...
Y... YOU'RE LYING!!
I MEAN, THAT'S JUST...
IT'S UNDER-STAND-ABLE THAT YOU CAN'T BELIEVE IT...
HOLD
IT'S JUST THAT YOU'VE FOR-GOTTEN EVERY-THING...!!
WHEN YOUR MEMO-RIES GOT ERASED...
YOU ENDED UP LOS-ING ALL YOUR FEEL-INGS FOR ME.

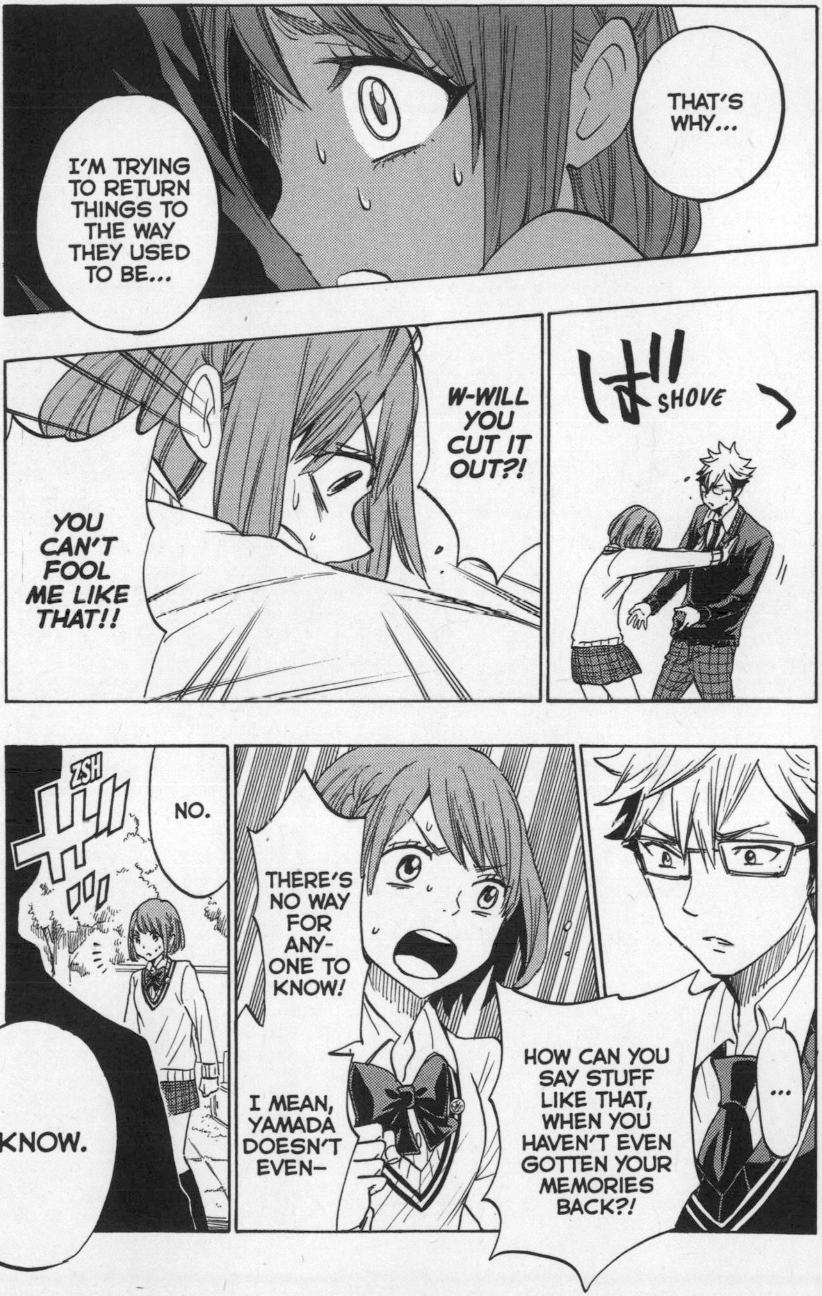

THAT'S WHY...
I'M TRYING TO RETURN THINGS TO THE WAY THEY USED TO BE...
ばっ SHOVE
W-WILL YOU CUT IT OUT?!
YOU CAN'T FOOL ME LIKE THAT!!
...
HOW CAN YOU SAY STUFF LIKE THAT, WHEN YOU HAVEN'T EVEN GOTTEN YOUR MEMORIES BACK?!
THERE'S NO WAY FOR ANY-ONE TO KNOW!
I MEAN, YAMADA DOESN'T EVEN—
ZSH
NO.
I KNOW.

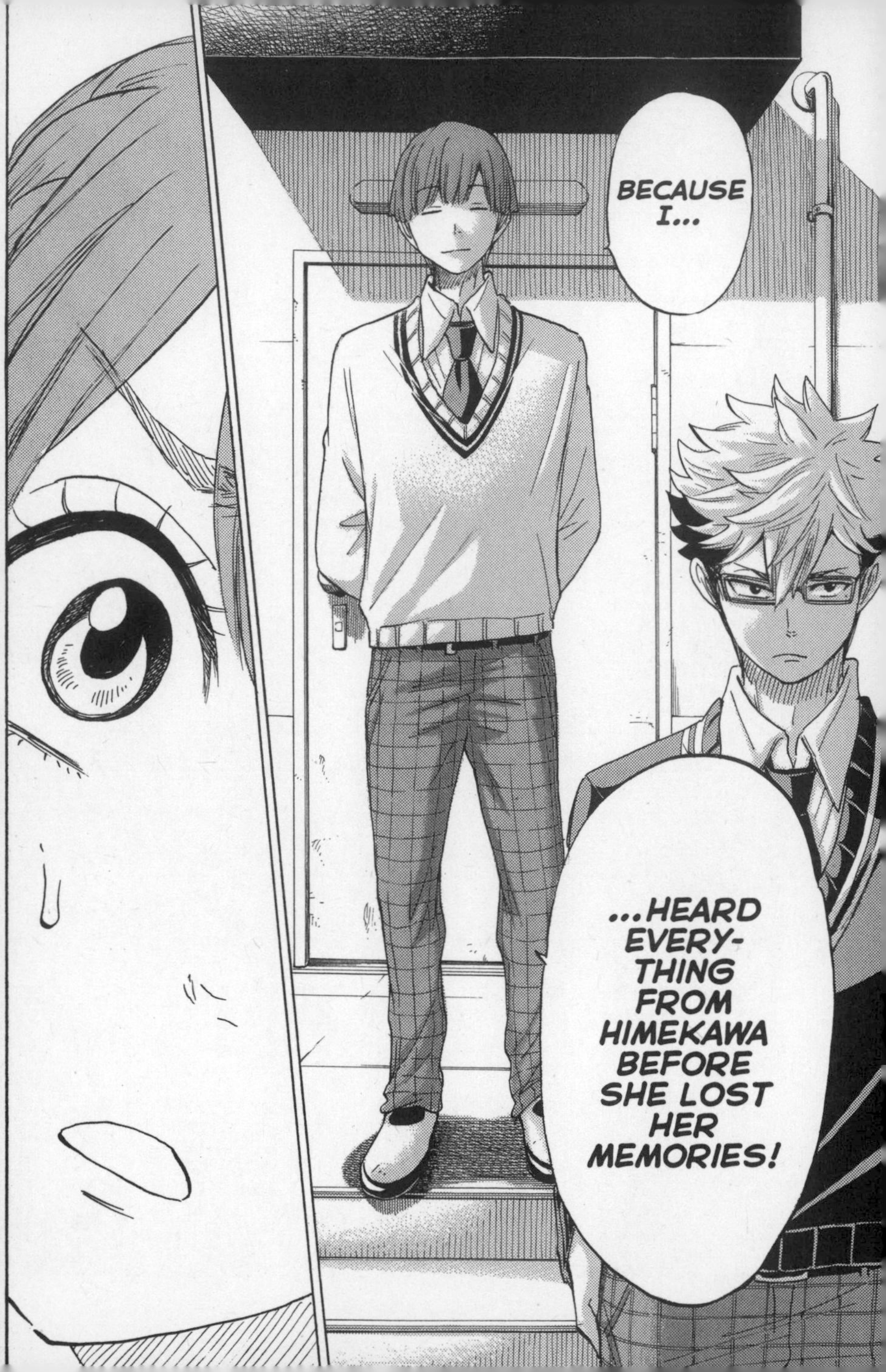
BECAUSE I...
...HEARD EVERY-THING FROM HIMEKAWA BEFORE SHE LOST HER MEMORIES!

CHAPTER 164: I want you to touch me... ♥

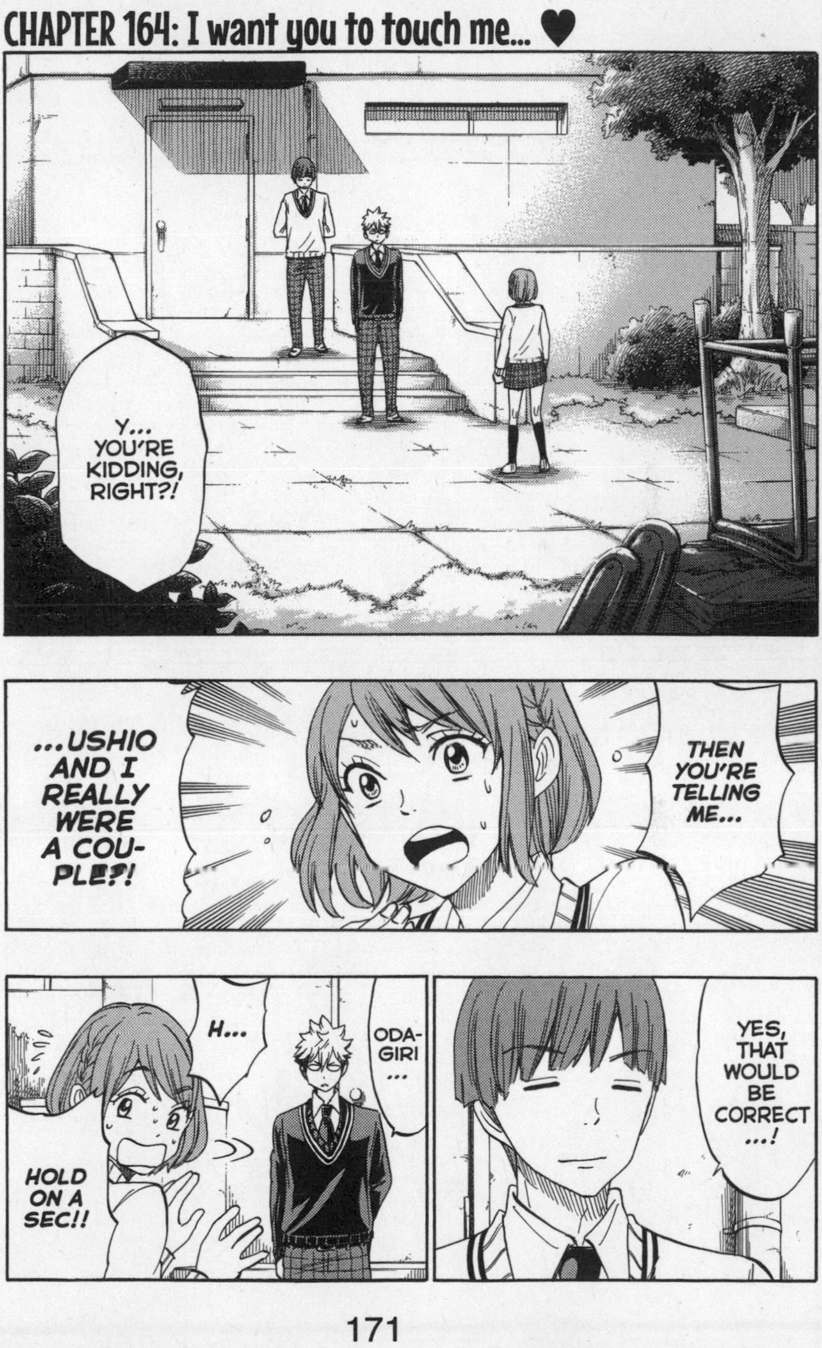

Y... YOU'RE KIDDING, RIGHT?!
THEN YOU'RE TELLING ME...
...USHIO AND I REALLY WERE A COU-PLE?!
YES, THAT WOULD BE CORRECT ...!
ODA-GIRI ...
H...
HOLD ON A SEC!!

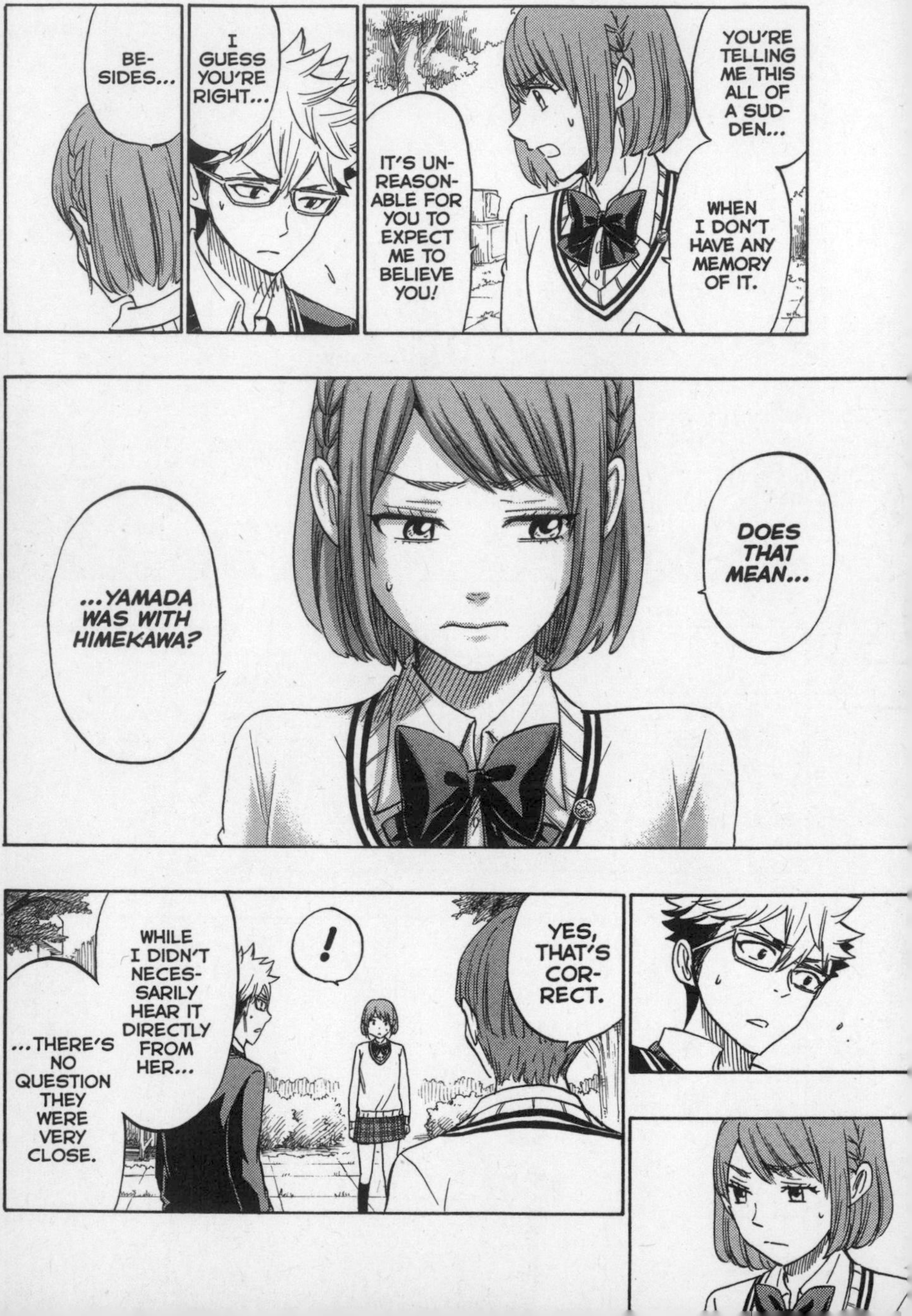
YOU'RE TELLING ME THIS ALL OF A SUDDEN...
WHEN I DON'T HAVE ANY MEMORY OF IT.
IT'S UNREASONABLE FOR YOU TO EXPECT ME TO BELIEVE YOU!
I GUESS YOU'RE RIGHT...
BESIDES...
DOES THAT MEAN...
...YAMADA WAS WITH HIMEKAWA?
YES, THAT'S CORRECT.
!
WHILE I DIDN'T NECESSARILY HEAR IT DIRECTLY FROM HER...
...THERE'S NO QUESTION THEY WERE VERY CLOSE.

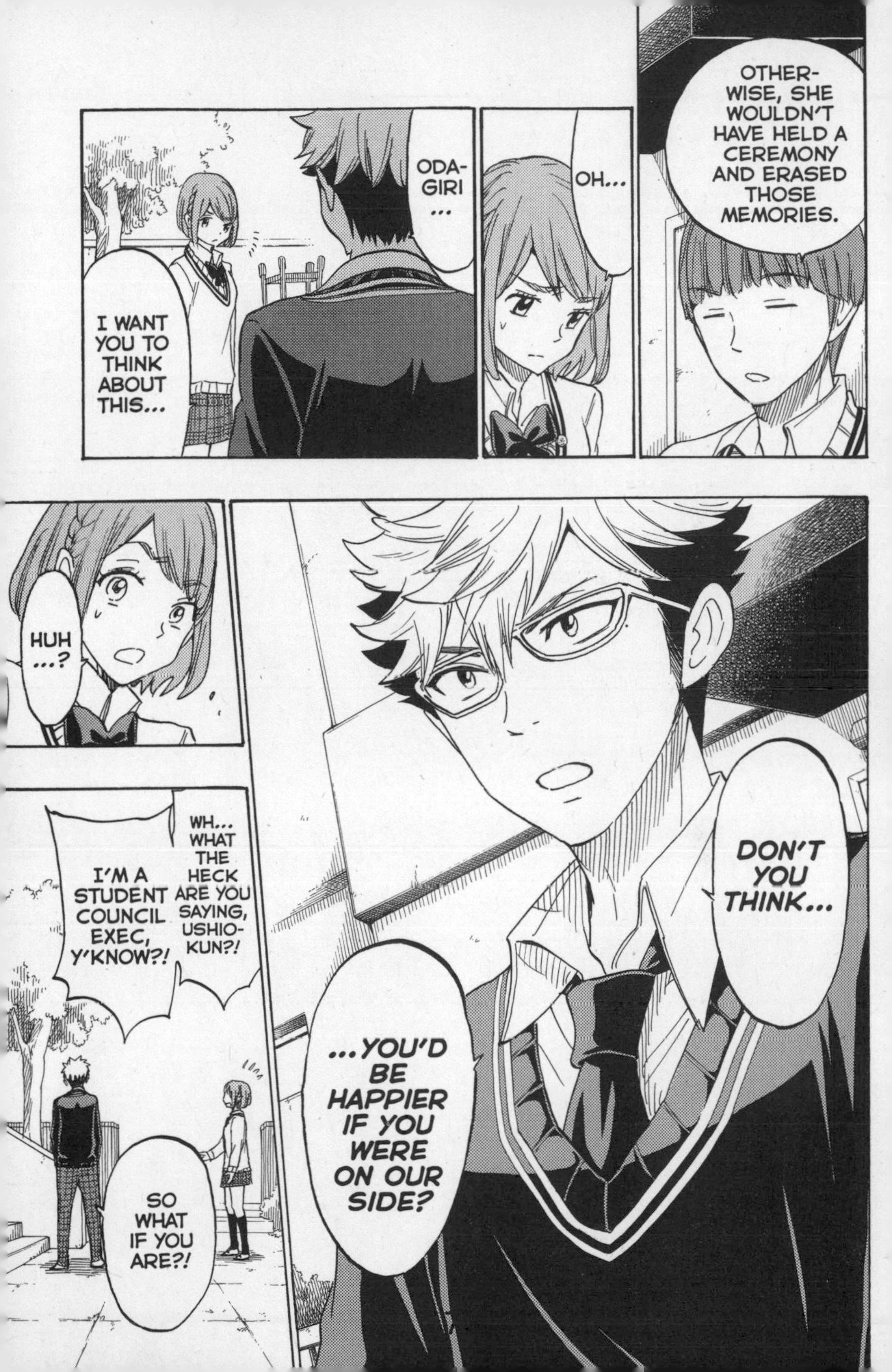
OTHER-WISE, SHE WOULDN'T HAVE HELD A CEREMONY AND ERASED THOSE MEMORIES.
OH...
ODA-GIRI...
I WANT YOU TO THINK ABOUT THIS...
DON'T YOU THINK...
...YOU'D BE HAPPIER IF YOU WERE ON OUR SIDE?
HUH...?
WH... WHAT THE HECK ARE YOU SAYING, USHIO-KUN?!
I'M A STUDENT COUNCIL EXEC, Y'KNOW?!
SO WHAT IF YOU ARE?!

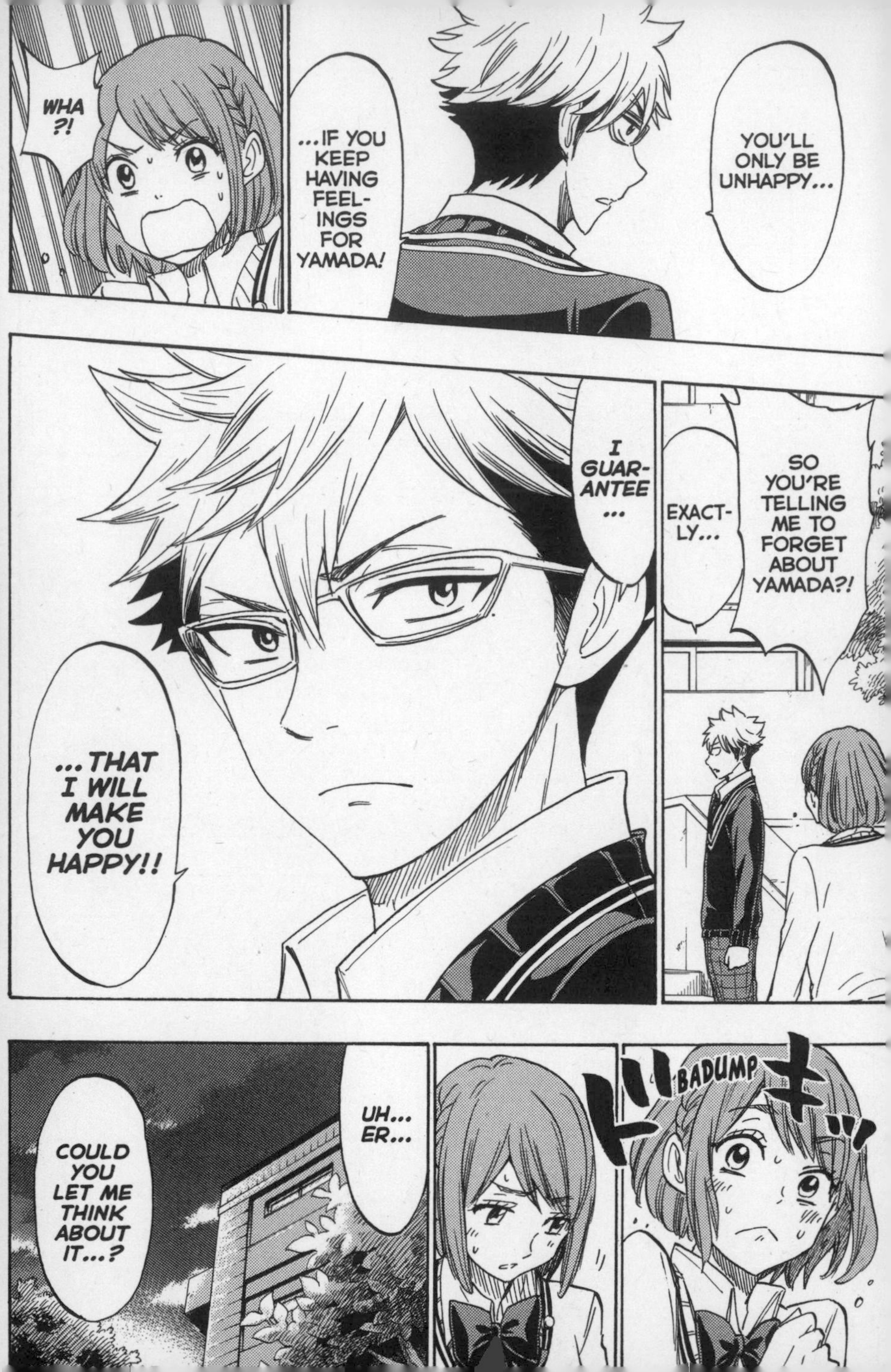
YOU'LL ONLY BE UNHAPPY...
...IF YOU KEEP HAVING FEEL-INGS FOR YAMADA!
WHA ?!
SO YOU'RE TELLING ME TO FORGET ABOUT YAMADA?!
EXACT-LY...
I GUAR-ANTEE...
...THAT I WILL MAKE YOU HAPPY!!
BADUMP
UH... ER...
COULD YOU LET ME THINK ABOUT IT...?

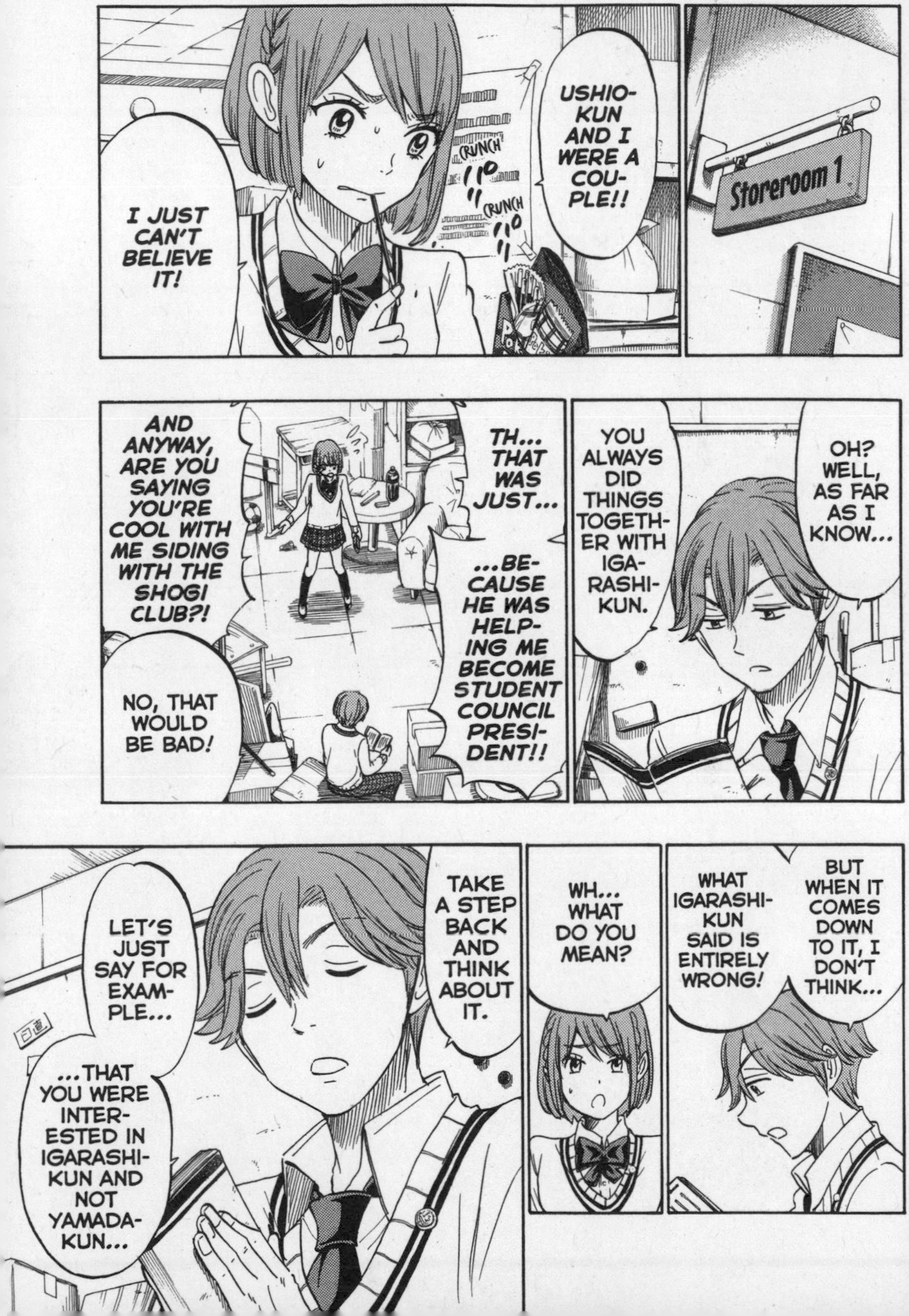
Storeroom 1
USHIO-KUN AND I WERE A COUPLE!!
CRUNCH
CRUNCH
I JUST CAN'T BELIEVE IT!
OH? WELL, AS FAR AS I KNOW...
YOU ALWAYS DID THINGS TOGETHER WITH IGARASHI-KUN.
TH... THAT WAS JUST...
...BECAUSE HE WAS HELPING ME BECOME STUDENT COUNCIL PRESIDENT!!
AND ANYWAY, ARE YOU SAYING YOU'RE COOL WITH ME SIDING WITH THE SHOGI CLUB?!
NO, THAT WOULD BE BAD!
BUT WHEN IT COMES DOWN TO IT, I DON'T THINK...
WHAT IGARASHI-KUN SAID IS ENTIRELY WRONG!
WH... WHAT DO YOU MEAN?
TAKE A STEP BACK AND THINK ABOUT IT.
LET'S JUST SAY FOR EXAMPLE...
...THAT YOU WERE INTERESTED IN IGARASHI-KUN AND NOT YAMADA-KUN...

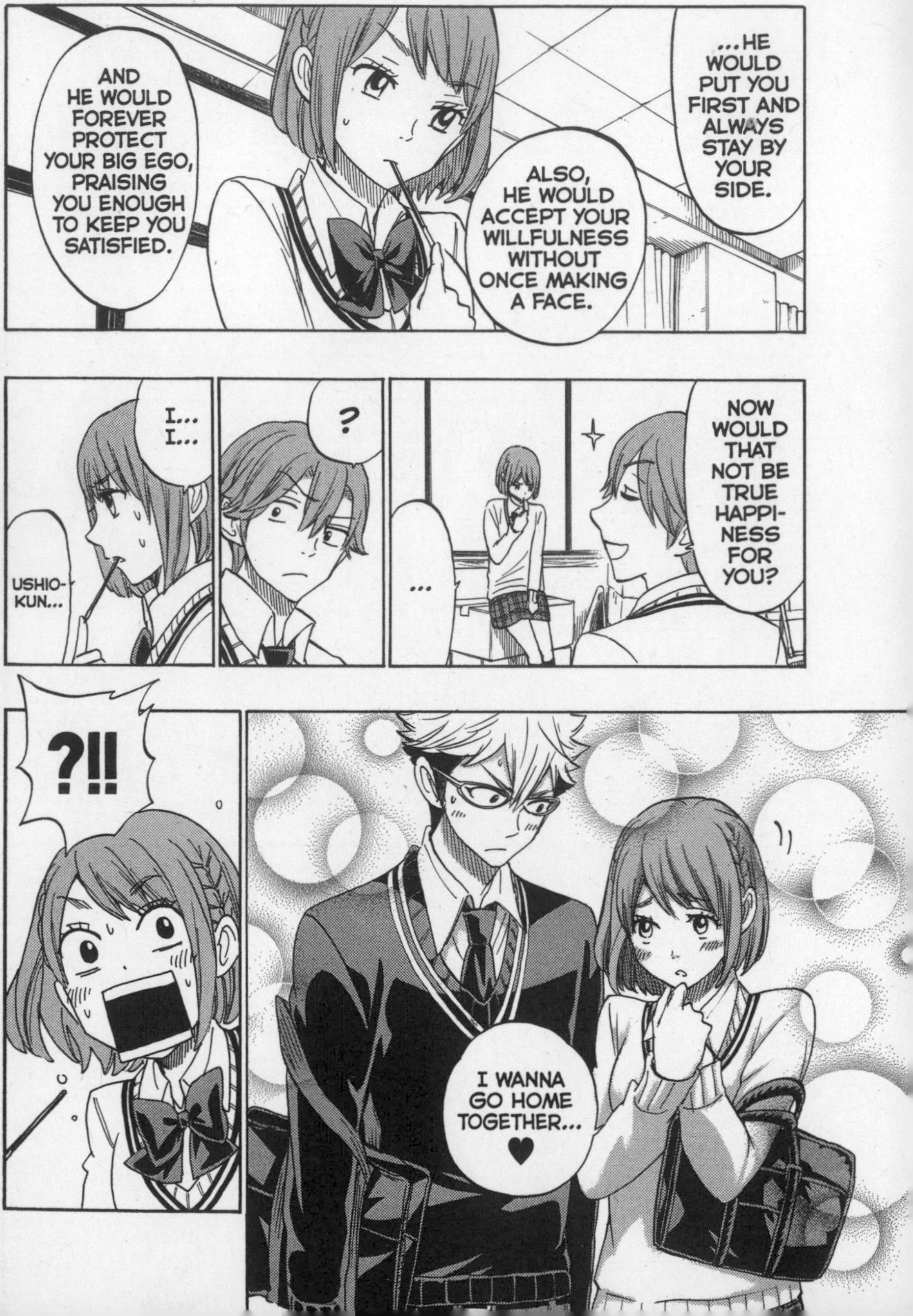
...HE WOULD PUT YOU FIRST AND ALWAYS STAY BY YOUR SIDE.
ALSO, HE WOULD ACCEPT YOUR WILLFULNESS WITHOUT ONCE MAKING A FACE.
AND HE WOULD FOREVER PROTECT YOUR BIG EGO, PRAISING YOU ENOUGH TO KEEP YOU SATISFIED.
NOW WOULD THAT NOT BE TRUE HAPPINESS FOR YOU?
...
?
I... I...
USHIO-KUN...
I WANNA GO HOME TOGETHER... ♥
?!!

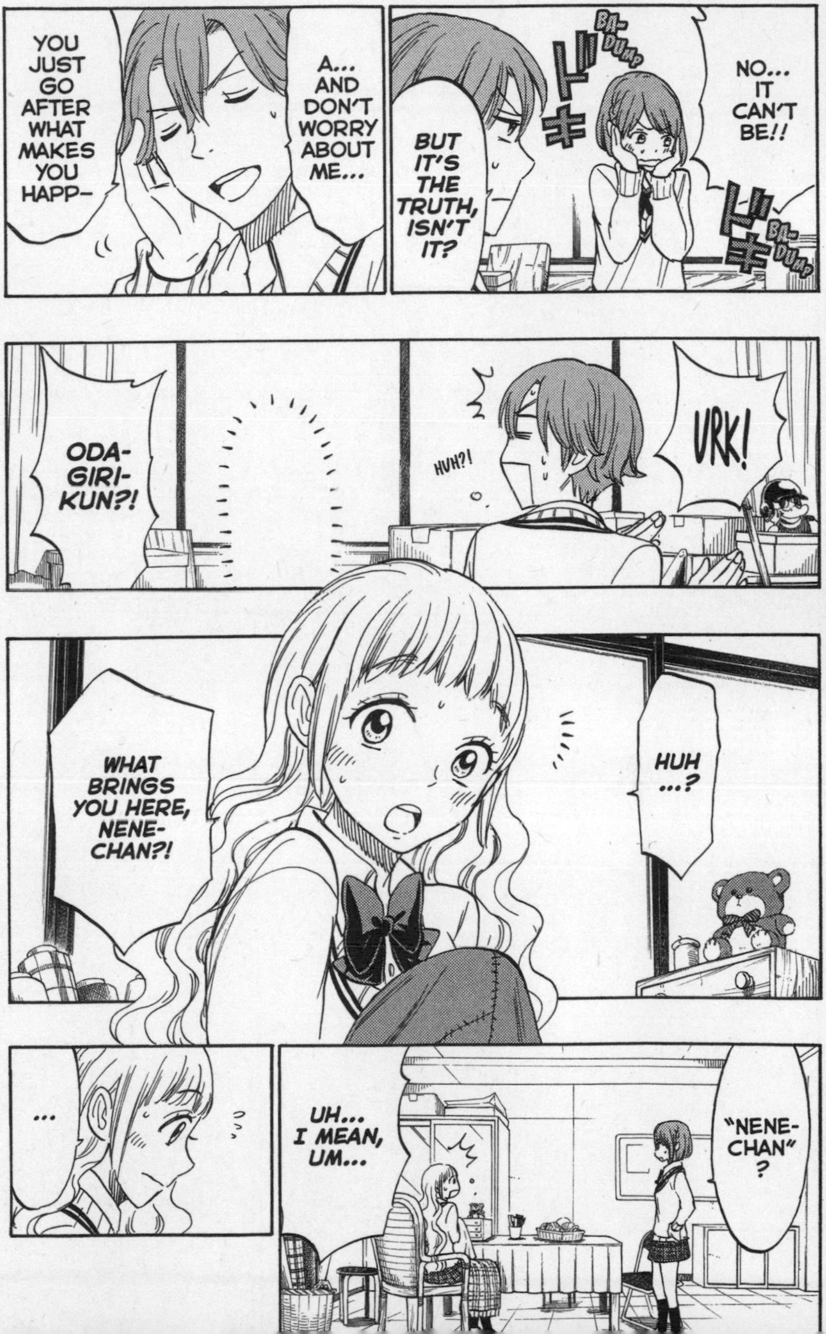
NO... IT CAN'T BE!!
BA-DUMP
BA-DUMP
BUT IT'S THE TRUTH, ISN'T IT?
A... AND DON'T WORRY ABOUT ME...
YOU JUST GO AFTER WHAT MAKES YOU HAPP-
URK!
HUH?!
ODA-GIRI-KUN?!
HUH ...?
WHAT BRINGS YOU HERE, NENE-CHAN?!
"NENE-CHAN"?
UH... I MEAN, UM...
...

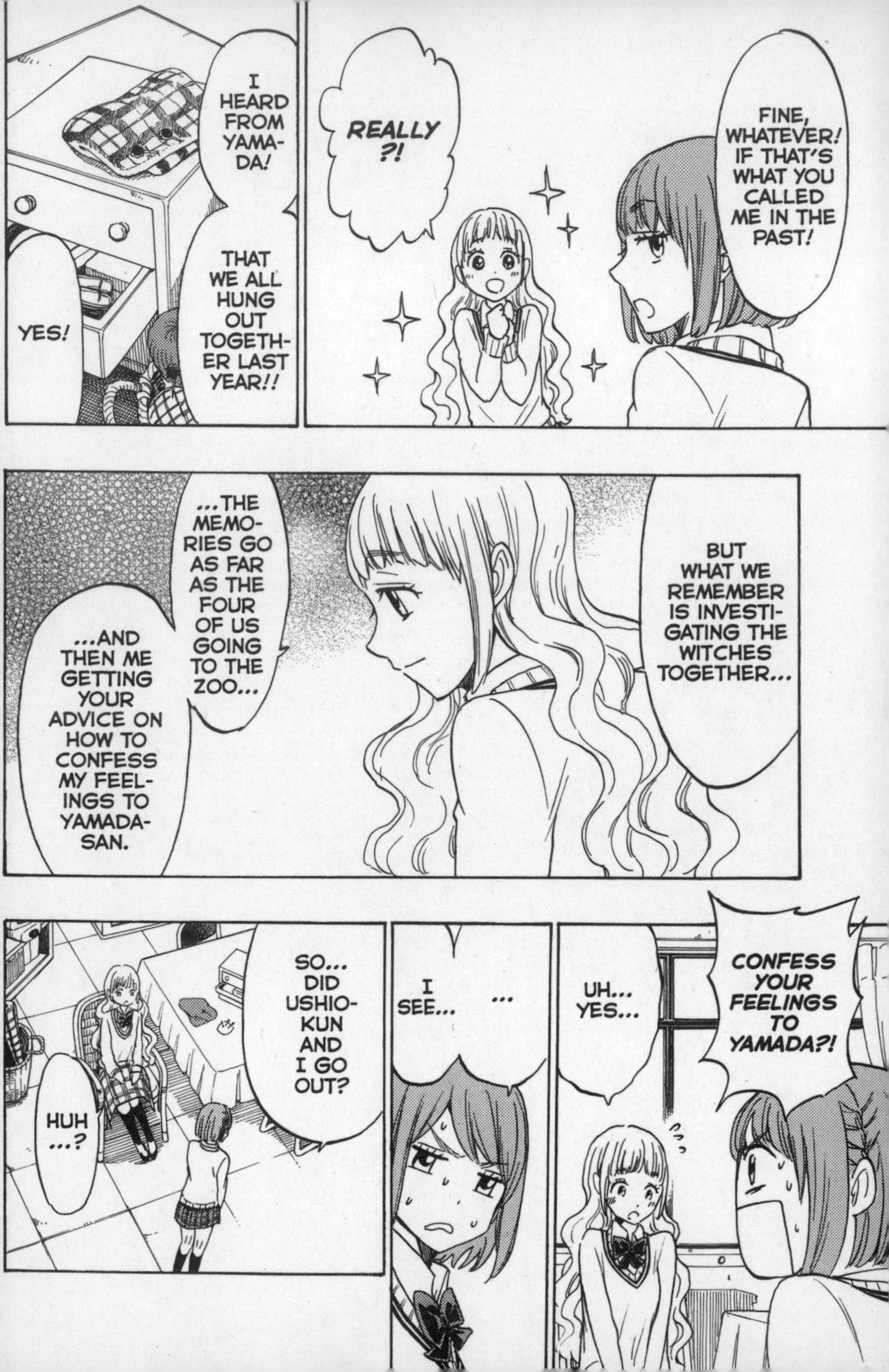
FINE, WHATEVER! IF THAT'S WHAT YOU CALLED ME IN THE PAST!
REALLY?!
I HEARD FROM YAMADA!
THAT WE ALL HUNG OUT TOGETHER LAST YEAR!!
YES!
BUT WHAT WE REMEMBER IS INVESTIGATING THE WITCHES TOGETHER...
...THE MEMORIES GO AS FAR AS THE FOUR OF US GOING TO THE ZOO...
...AND THEN ME GETTING YOUR ADVICE ON HOW TO CONFESS MY FEELINGS TO YAMADA-SAN.
CONFESS YOUR FEELINGS TO YAMADA?!
UH... YES...
...
I SEE...
SO... DID USHIO-KUN AND I GO OUT?
HUH...?

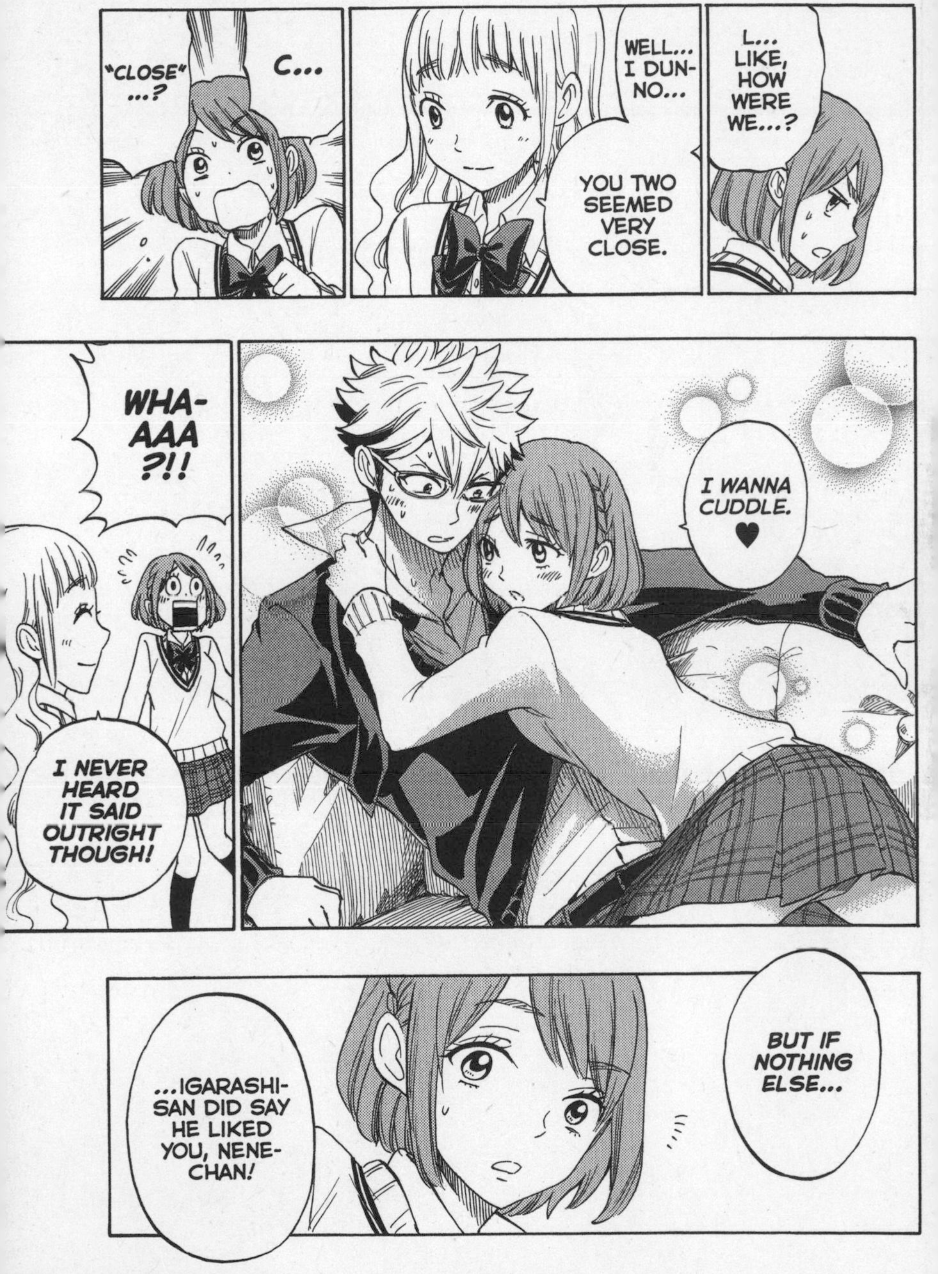
L... LIKE, HOW WERE WE...?
WELL... I DUN-NO...
YOU TWO SEEMED VERY CLOSE.
C...
"CLOSE" ...?
I WANNA CUDDLE. ♥
WHA-AAA?!!
I NEVER HEARD IT SAID OUTRIGHT THOUGH!
BUT IF NOTHING ELSE...
...IGARASHI-SAN DID SAY HE LIKED YOU, NENE-CHAN!

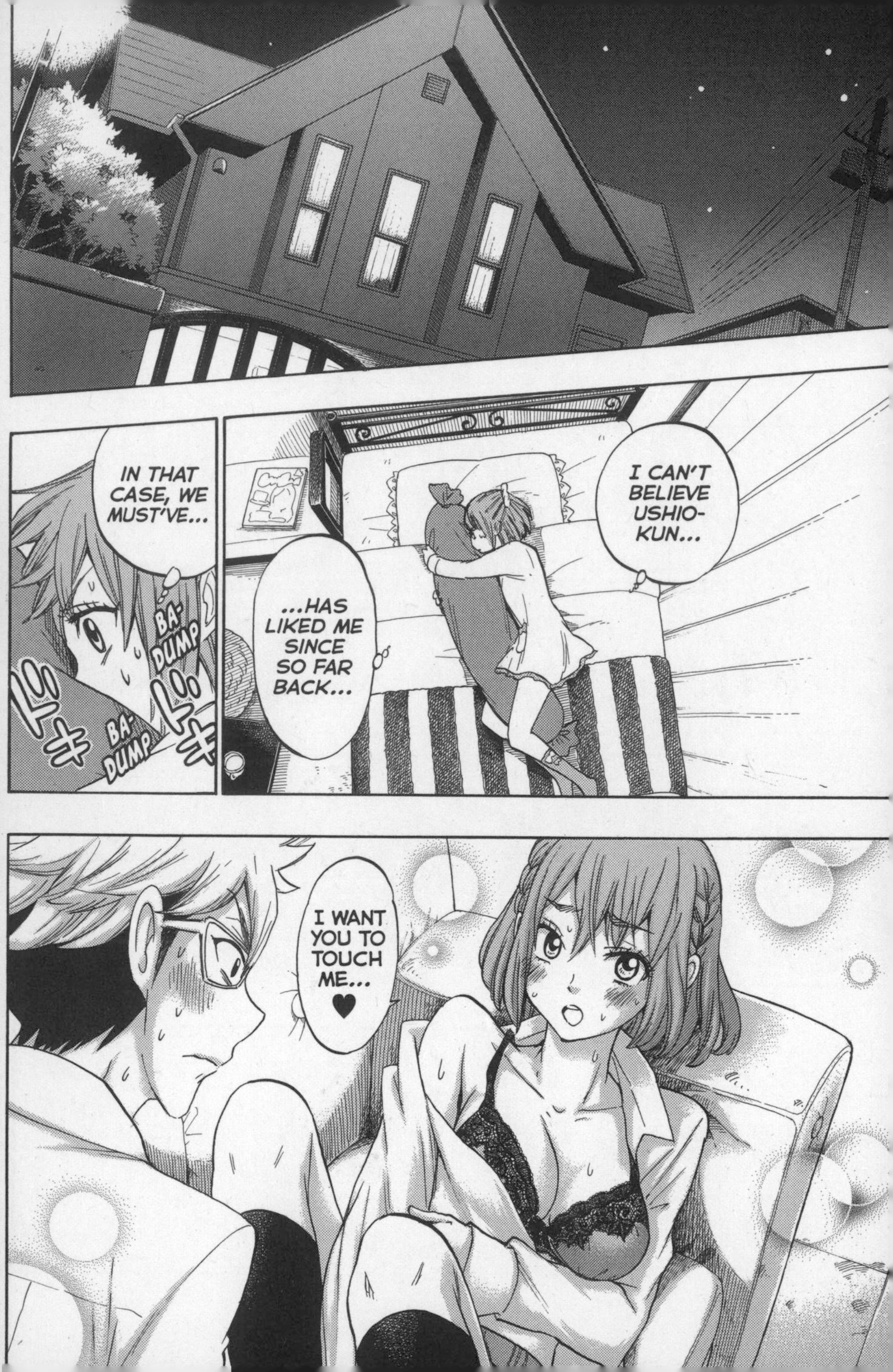
I CAN'T BELIEVE USHIO-KUN...
...HAS LIKED ME SINCE SO FAR BACK...
IN THAT CASE, WE MUST'VE...
ドキ
BA-DUMP
ドキ
BA-DUMP
I WANT YOU TO TOUCH ME... ♥

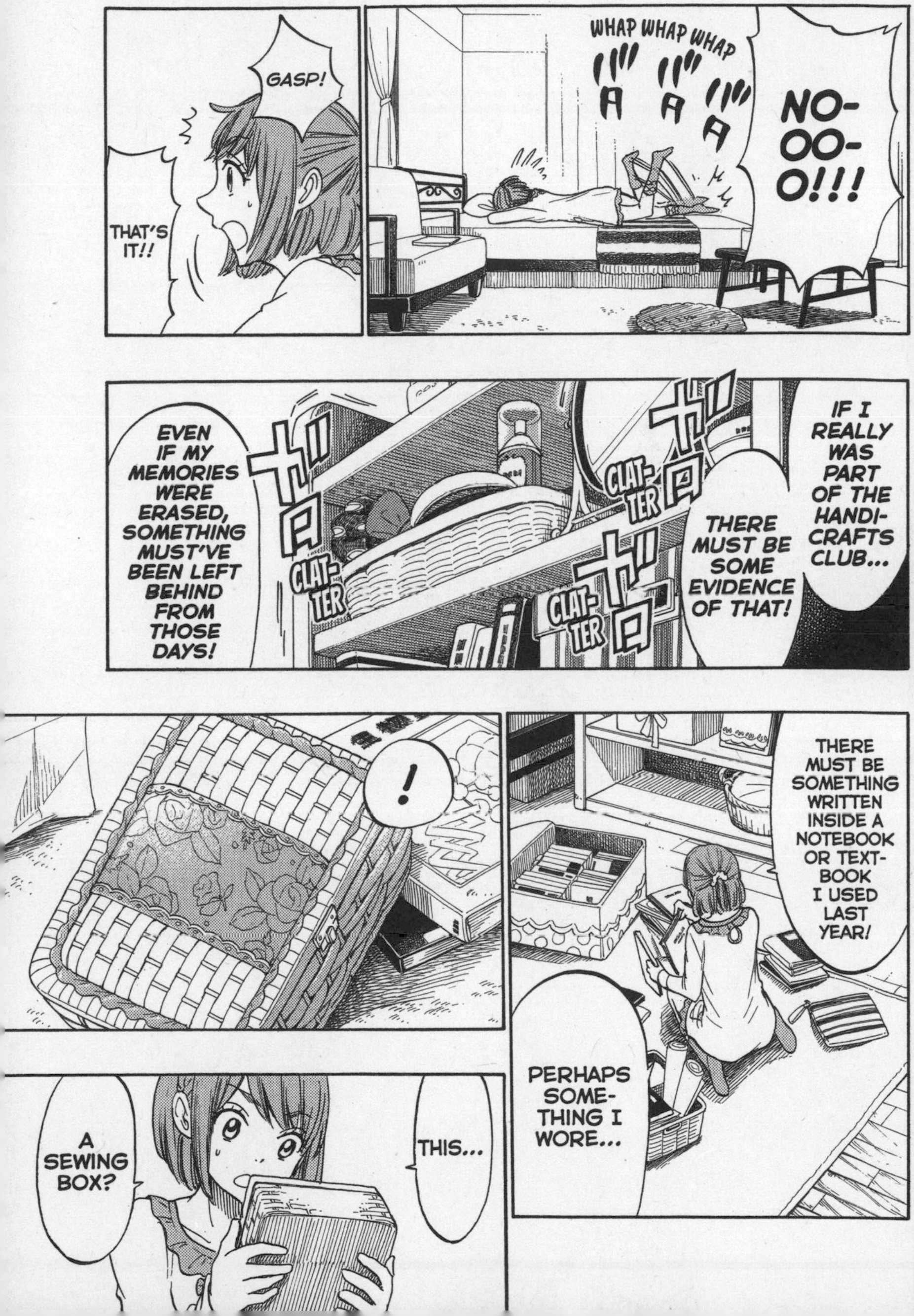
NO-OO-O!!!
WHAP WHAP WHAP
GASP!
THAT'S IT!!
IF I REALLY WAS PART OF THE HANDI-CRAFTS CLUB...
THERE MUST BE SOME EVIDENCE OF THAT!
CLAT-TER
CLAT-TER
CLAT-TER
EVEN IF MY MEMORIES WERE ERASED, SOMETHING MUST'VE BEEN LEFT BEHIND FROM THOSE DAYS!
THERE MUST BE SOMETHING WRITTEN INSIDE A NOTEBOOK OR TEXT-BOOK I USED LAST YEAR!
PERHAPS SOME-THING I WORE...
!
THIS...
A SEWING BOX?

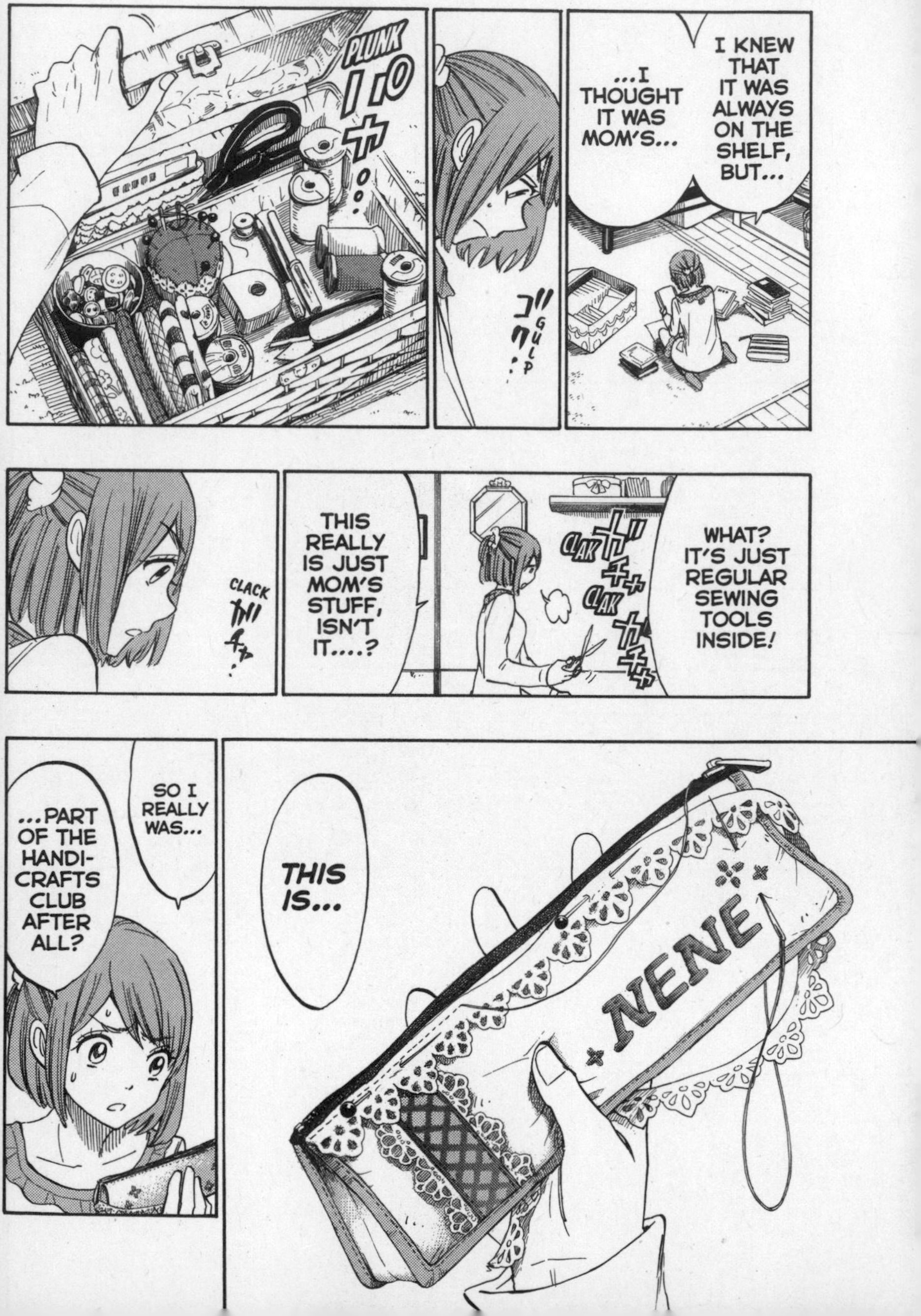
I KNEW THAT IT WAS ALWAYS ON THE SHELF, BUT...
...I THOUGHT IT WAS MOM'S...
GULP
PLUNK
WHAT? IT'S JUST REGULAR SEWING TOOLS INSIDE!
CLAK
CLAK
THIS REALLY IS JUST MOM'S STUFF, ISN'T IT....?
CLACK
THIS IS...
NENE
SO I REALLY WAS...
...PART OF THE HANDI-CRAFTS CLUB AFTER ALL?

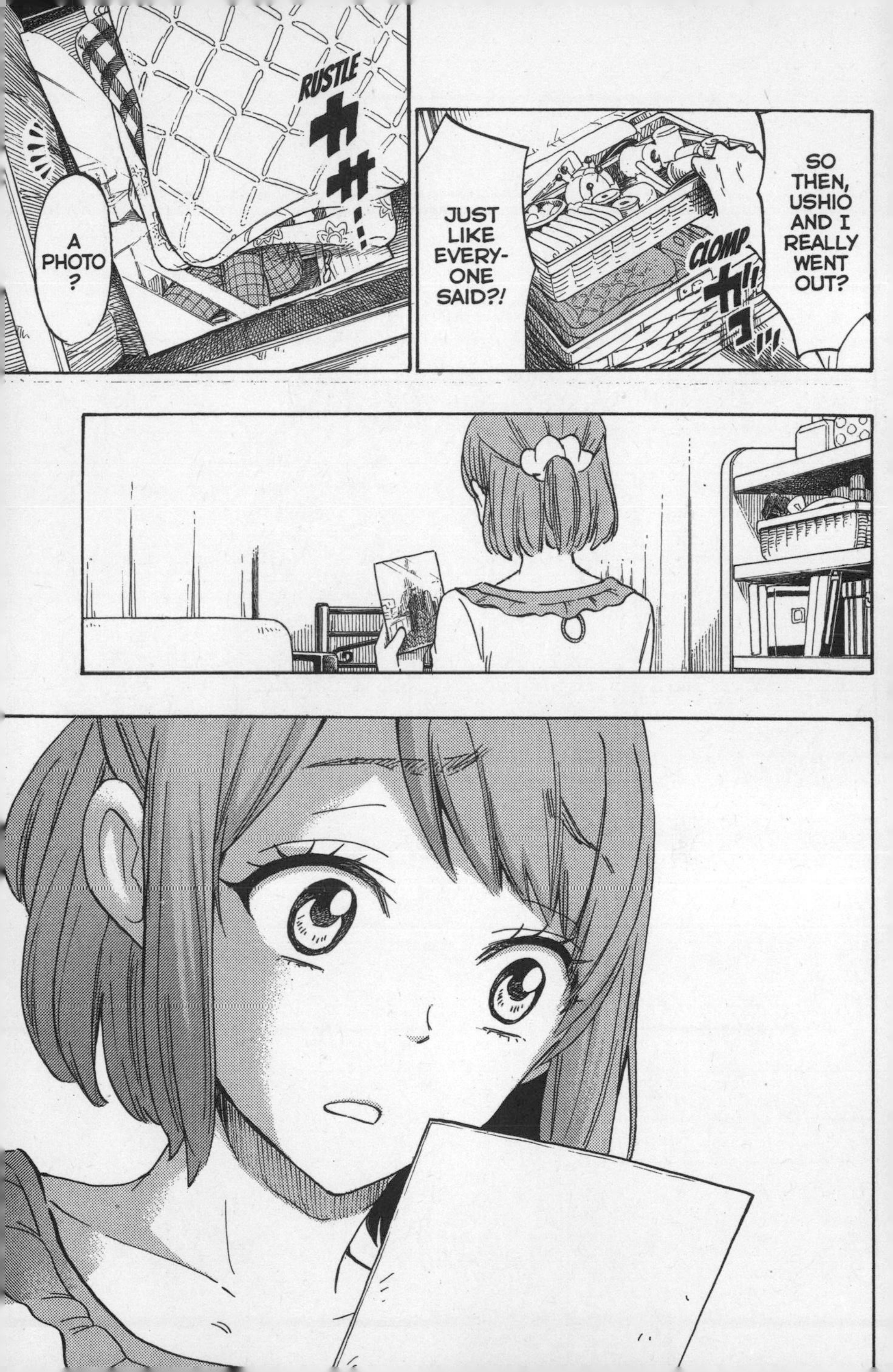
SO THEN, USHIO AND I REALLY WENT OUT?
CLOMP
JUST LIKE EVERY-ONE SAID?!
RUSTLE
A PHOTO?

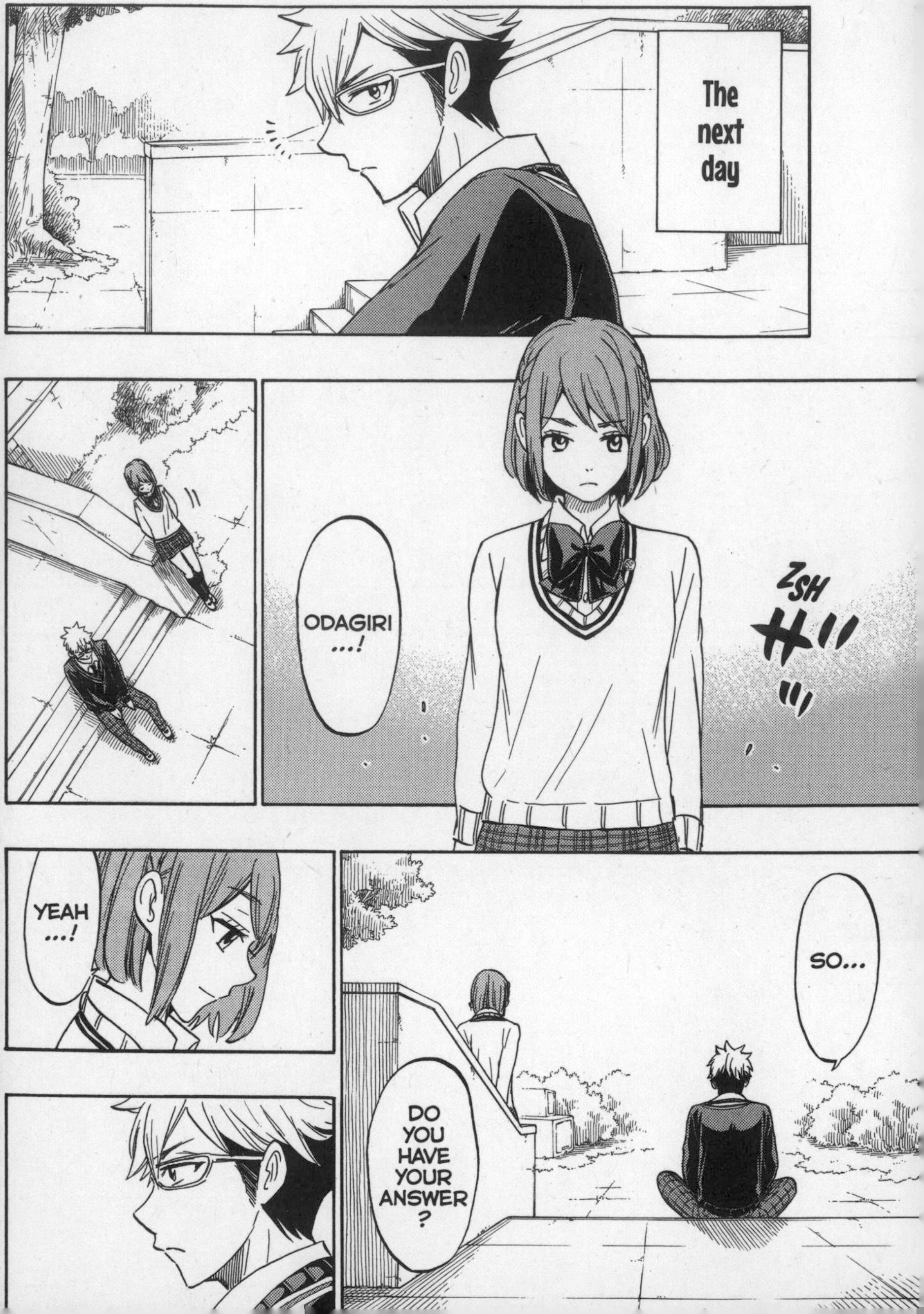
The next day
ZSH
ODAGIRI ...!
SO...
DO YOU HAVE YOUR ANSWER?
YEAH ...!

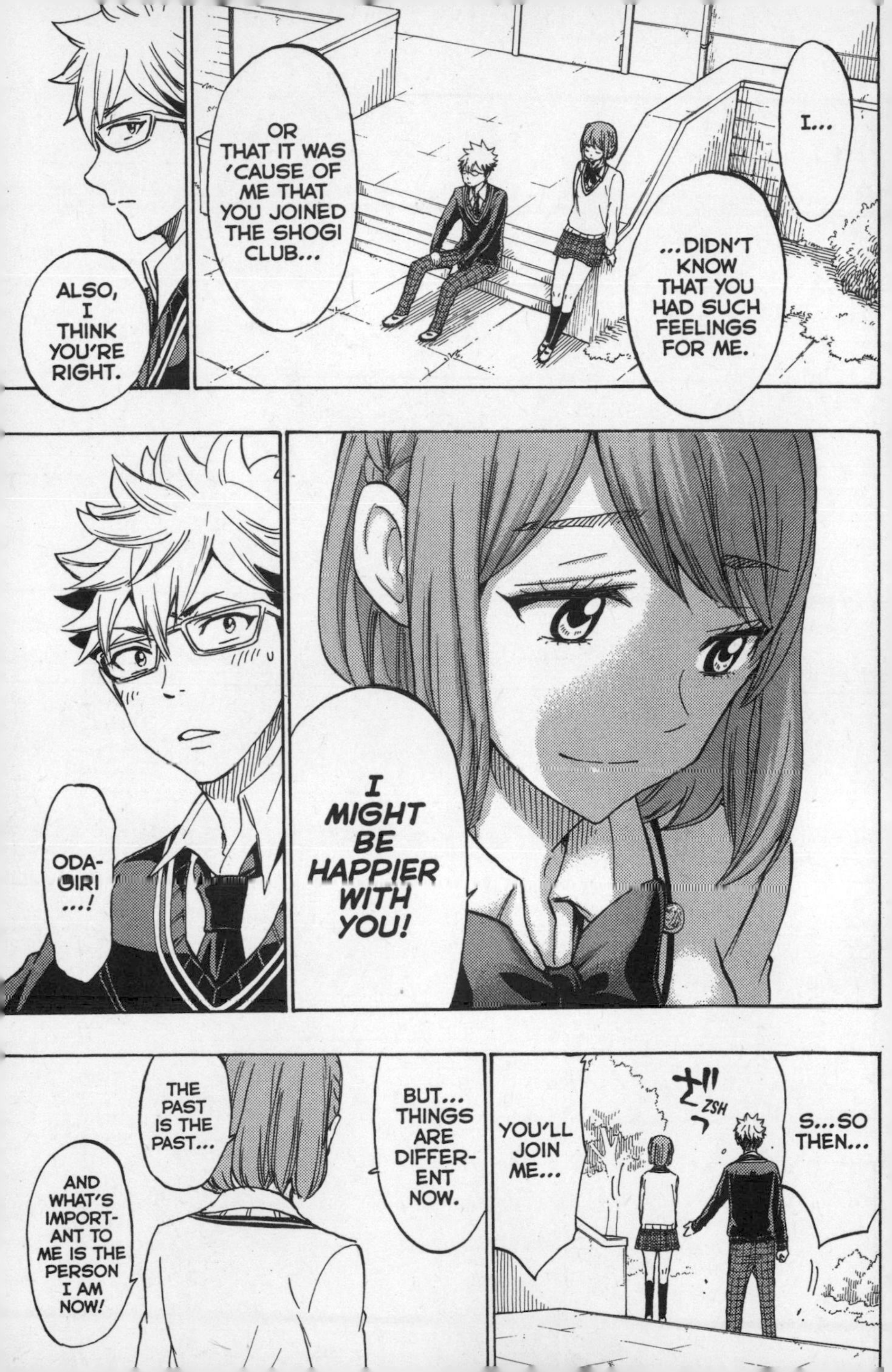
I...
...DIDN'T KNOW THAT YOU HAD SUCH FEELINGS FOR ME.
OR THAT IT WAS 'CAUSE OF ME THAT YOU JOINED THE SHOGI CLUB...
ALSO, I THINK YOU'RE RIGHT.
I MIGHT BE HAPPIER WITH YOU!
ODA-GIRI ...!
S...SO THEN...
ZSH
YOU'LL JOIN ME...
BUT... THINGS ARE DIFFER-ENT NOW.
THE PAST IS THE PAST...
AND WHAT'S IMPORT-ANT TO ME IS THE PERSON I AM NOW!

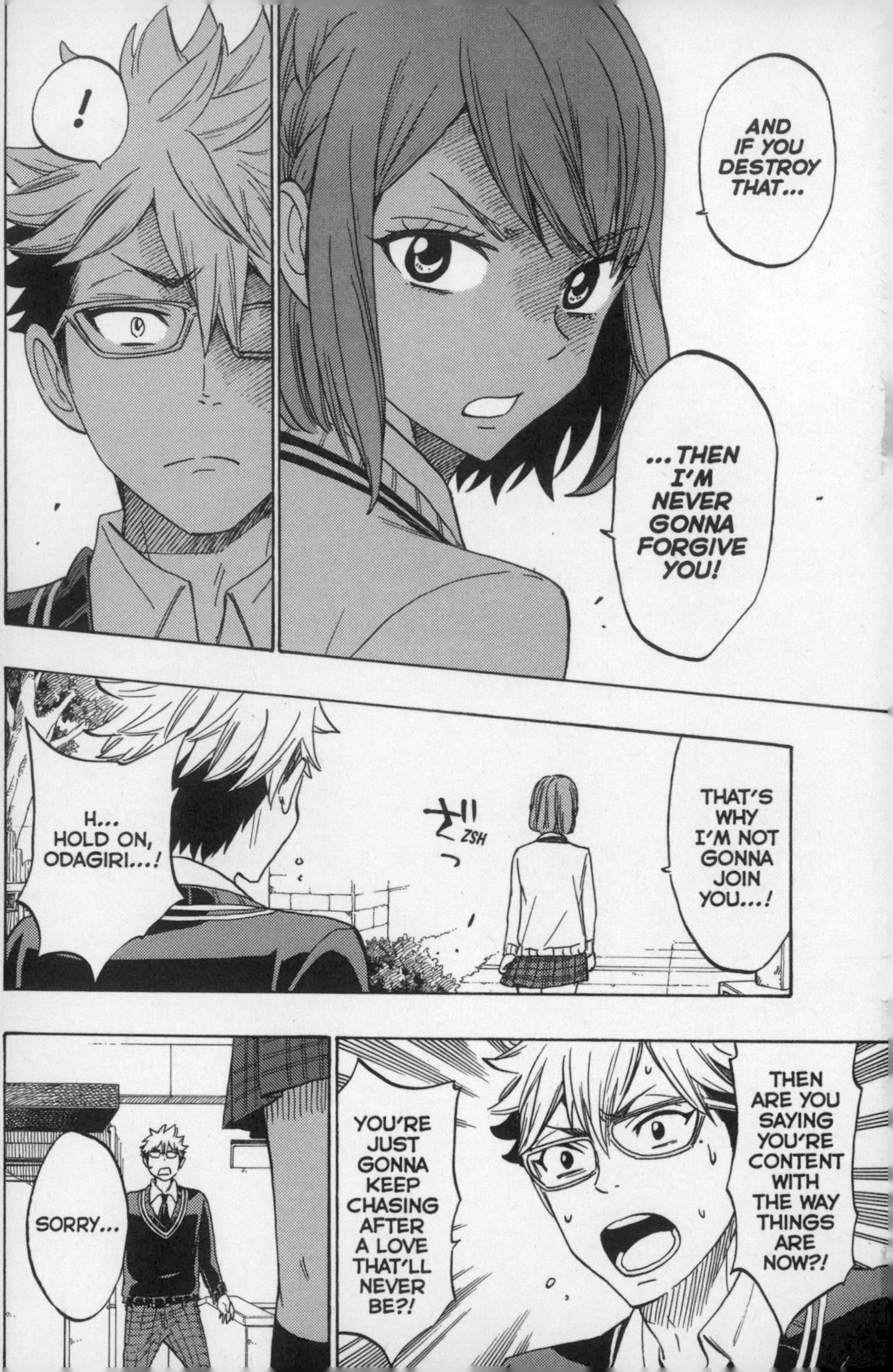
AND IF YOU DESTROY THAT...
...THEN I'M NEVER GONNA FORGIVE YOU!
!
THAT'S WHY I'M NOT GONNA JOIN YOU...!
ZSH
H... HOLD ON, ODAGIRI...!
THEN ARE YOU SAYING YOU'RE CONTENT WITH THE WAY THINGS ARE NOW?!
YOU'RE JUST GONNA KEEP CHASING AFTER A LOVE THAT'LL NEVER BE?!
SORRY...

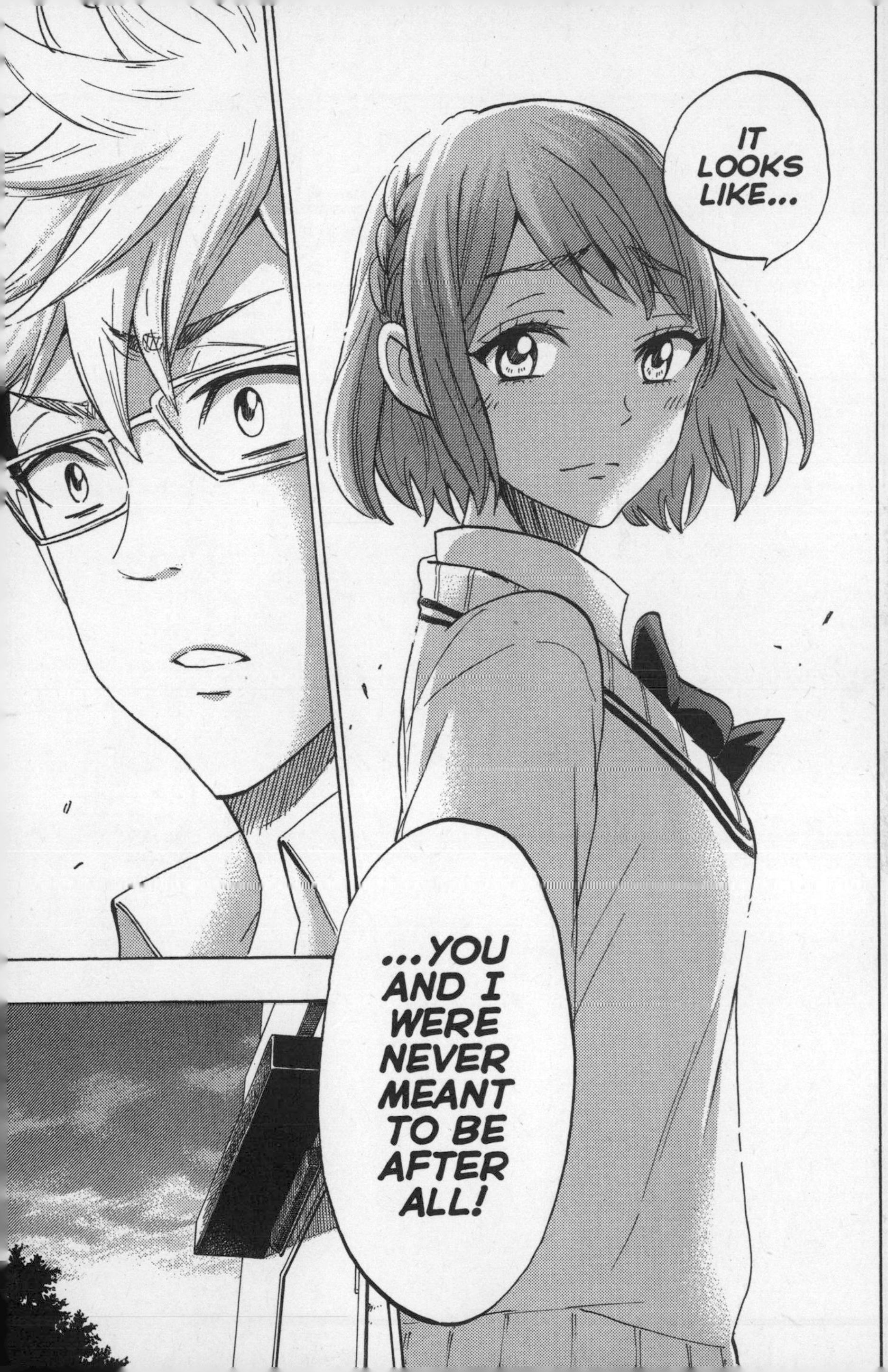
IT LOOKS LIKE...
...YOU AND I WERE NEVER MEANT TO BE AFTER ALL!

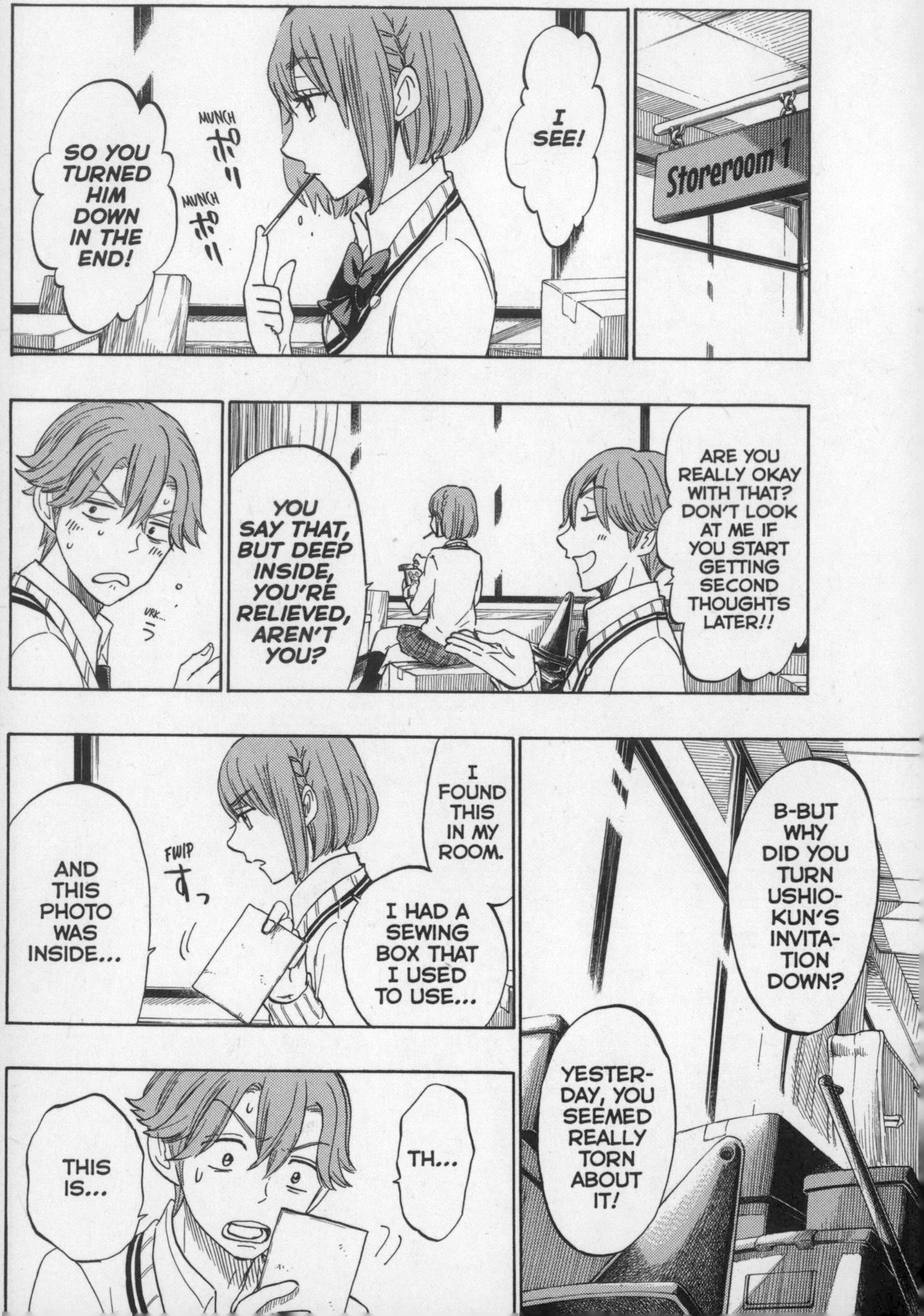
Storeroom 1
I SEE!
MUNCH ポリ
MUNCH ポリ
SO YOU TURNED HIM DOWN IN THE END!
ARE YOU REALLY OKAY WITH THAT? DON'T LOOK AT ME IF YOU START GETTING SECOND THOUGHTS LATER!!
YOU SAY THAT, BUT DEEP INSIDE, YOU'RE RELIEVED, AREN'T YOU?
URK... う
B-BUT WHY DID YOU TURN USHIO-KUN'S INVITATION DOWN?
YESTERDAY, YOU SEEMED REALLY TORN ABOUT IT!
I FOUND THIS IN MY ROOM.
I HAD A SEWING BOX THAT I USED TO USE...
FWIP すっ
AND THIS PHOTO WAS INSIDE...
TH...
THIS IS...

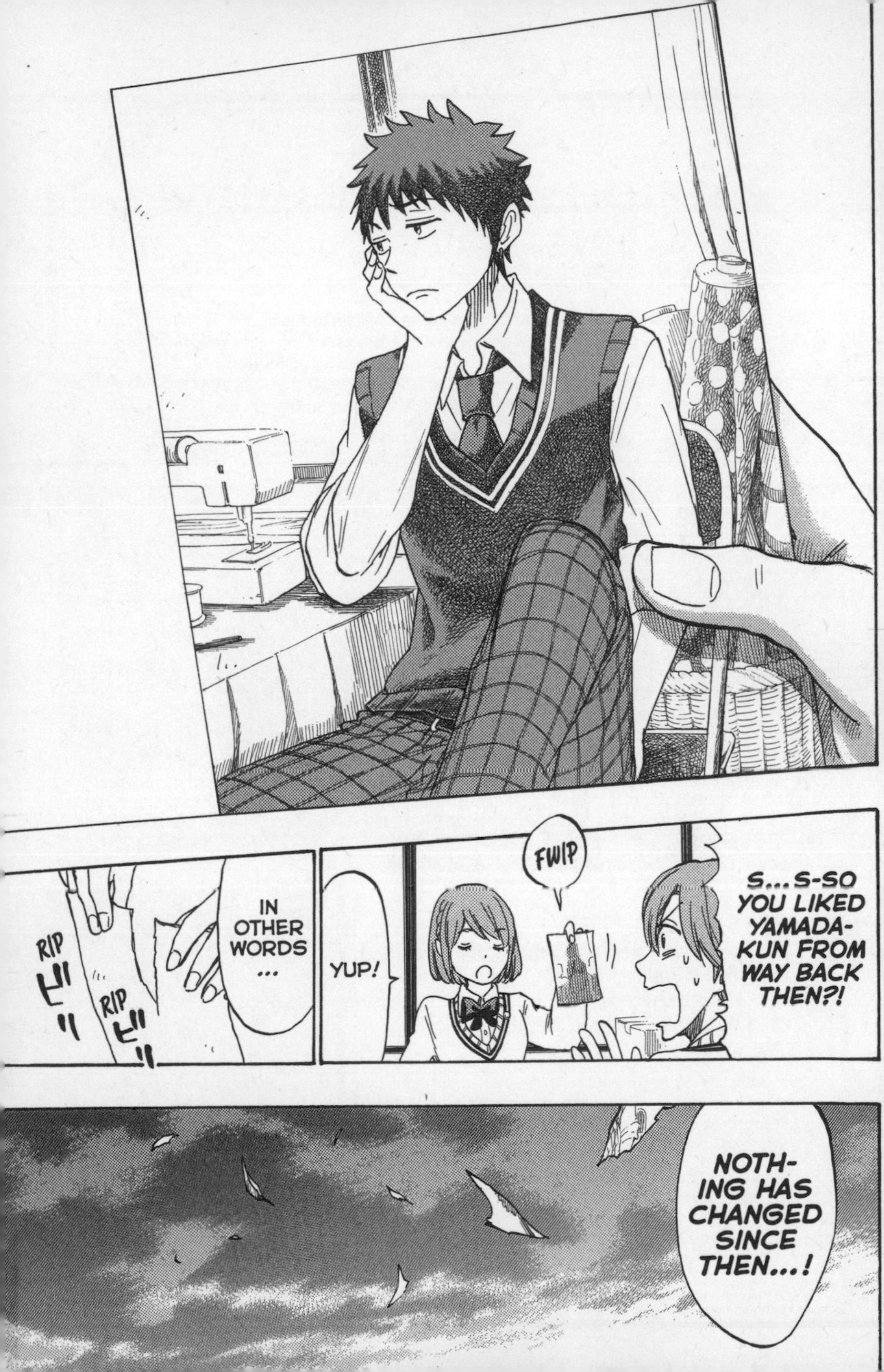

S...S-SO YOU LIKED YAMADA-KUN FROM WAY BACK THEN?!
FWIP
YUP!
IN OTHER WORDS...
RIP ビリ
RIP ビリ
NOTH-ING HAS CHANGED SINCE THEN...!

Suzaku Art Gallery

This is where we'll introduce illustrations that we've received from all of you!

Selected artists will receive **a signed shikishi from the series creator**! When you make a submission, please make sure to clearly write your address, name, and phone number! If you don't, we won't be able to send you a prize even if you're selected! Looking forward to all your submissions!

NOA.KAORI

Saitama Pref., H.N. Nouty-san

They've been talking often since that time.

宮村君…黒崎君を見てあげて…
見てない

Tokyo Pref., H.N. Mottan-san

I see you. Well, sometimes I do look his way. I mean, I do once in a blue moon.

超常現象部

Saitama Pref., H.N. Okamon-san

All 5 of our personalities really shine in this great illustration!

Shiga Pref., H.N. Ranran Marukichi-san

Takigawa-san's popularity has really taken off recently. I can't lose to her!

Please send your art here ↓

Yamada-kun and the Seven Witches: Suzaku Gallery
c/o Kodansha Comics
451 Park Ave. South, 7th Floor
New York, NY 10016

※ Please clearly write your address, name, and phone number. If your address, name, and phone number aren't included with your submission, we won't be able to send you a prize.

※ And if necessary, don't forget to include your handle name (pen name)!

Please send your letters with the understanding that your zip code, address, name, and other personal information included in your correspondence may be given to the author of this work.

Suzaku Gallery

Translation Notes

Ey-ey-ohh!!, page 48

This chant is commonly used as a cheer in Japan, but it was originally used between two armies at the start of a battle. One army would chant "ey-ey" (a call to advance) and the other army would respond "ohh" (simply meaning "response") to inspire their troops.

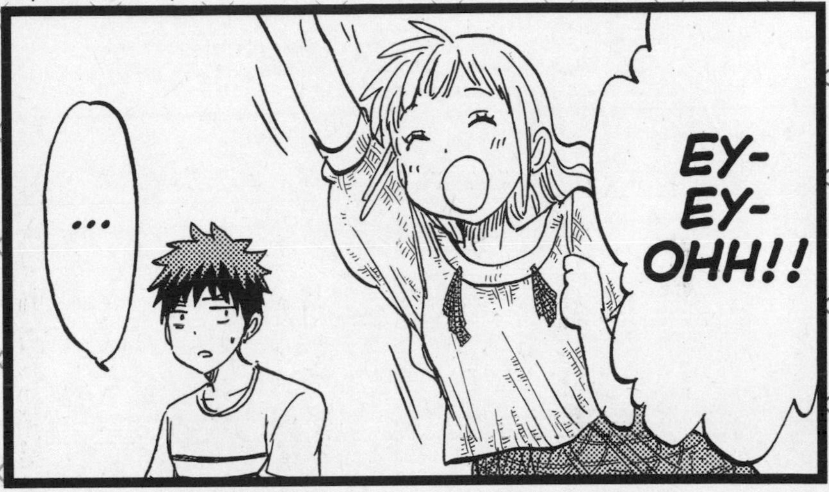
EY-EY-OHH!!
...

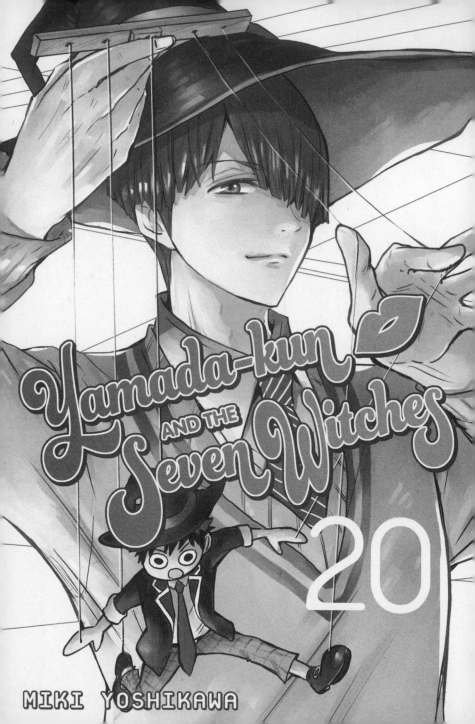

Yamada-kun
AND THE
Seven Witches

20

MIKI YOSHIKAWA

Yamada-kun and the Seven Witches

20

MIKI YOSHIKAWA

FIDGET
もじ
FIDGET
もじ

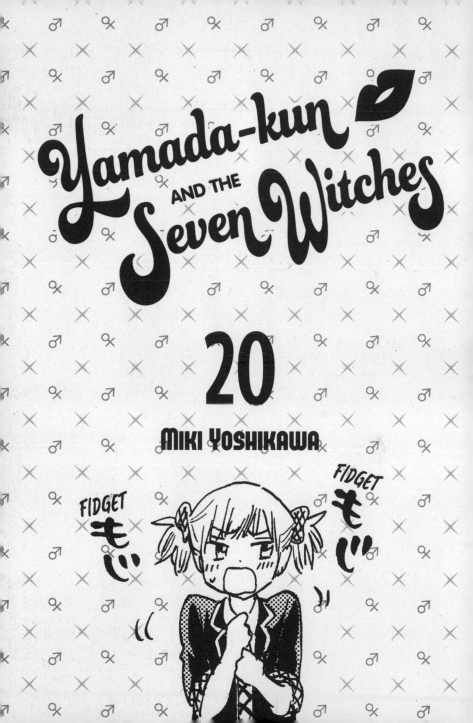

Yamada-kun and the Seven Witches

Cast of Characters

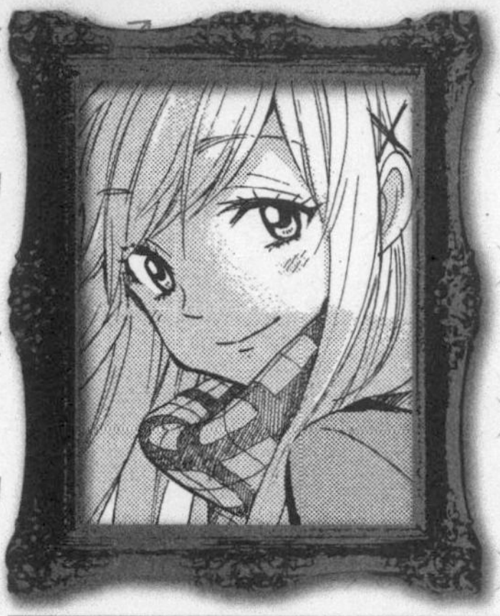

Urara Shiraishi

A second-year at Suzaku High School and president of the Supernatural Studies Club. She used to be known as the "Switch Witch" and she is Yamada's girlfriend. She's concerned about Yamada's past with Himekawa, but she trusts her boyfriend.

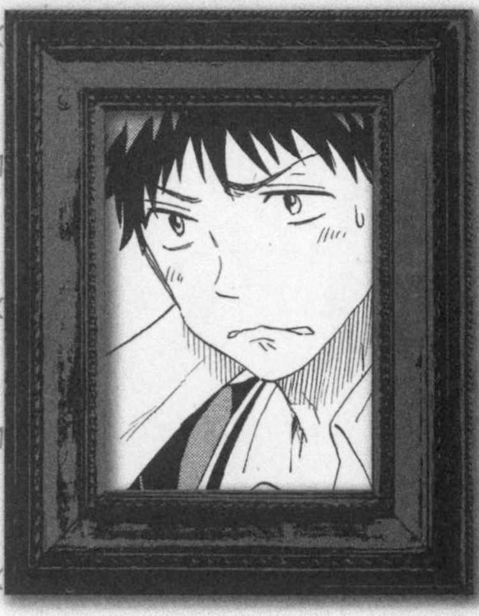

Ryu Yamada

A second-year at Suzaku High School. He's restored his erased memories by performing a ceremony, but there is still a lot that he doesn't understand, including why he has his copy ability.

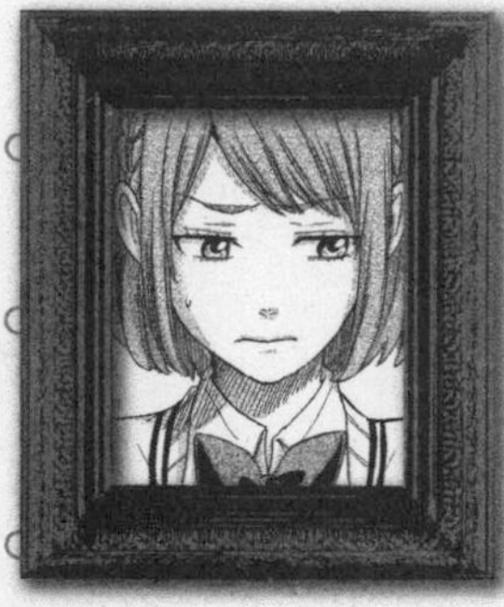

Nene Odagiri

A second-year at Suzaku High School and clerk for the Student Council. She used to be the "Charm Witch." Igarashi invited her to join the Shogi Club's mission, but she rejected his offer.

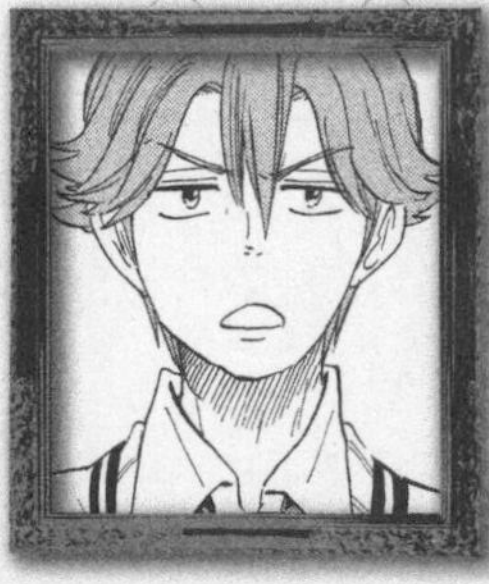

Shinichi Tamaki

A second-year at Suzaku High School and treasurer for the Student Council. He's known as the "Capture Guy" and steals the power of the witch whom he kisses. He's running to become the next Student Council president, but…

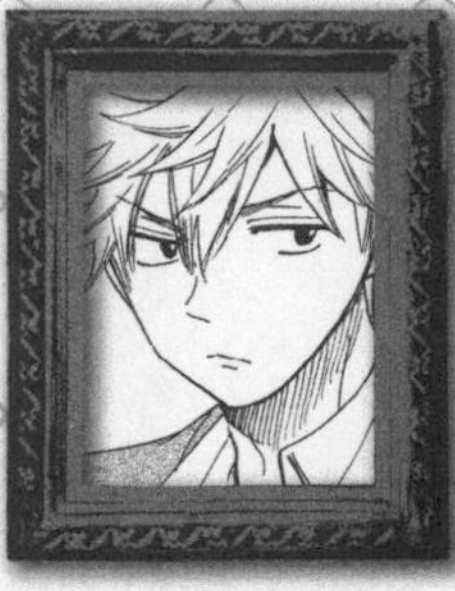

Toranosuke Miyamura

A second-year at Suzaku High School and president of the Student Council. A recall is in place, but he won't be running in the next election. He and Yamada are trying to figure out the Shogi Club's motive.

Noa Takigawa

A first-year at Suzaku High School and formerly a witch with the power to see into the past. She's a mischievous girl who's smitten with Yamada and playing along with his shenanigans. She seems to be surprisingly good at working with Miyamura and playing along with his shenanigans.

Jin Kurosaki

A first-year at Suzaku High School and one of the vice-presidents of the Student Council. He is an underclassman of few words who has an extreme reverence for Miyamura. He's a good-looking, but sort of stupid guy.

Midori Arisugawa

A first-year at Suzaku High School and one of the vice-presidents of the Student Council. She's affable and though she appears to be mild-mannered, she also displays a calculating side.

Rui Takuma

A second-year at Suzaku High School and another "Seventh Witch." He's a genius and often does things that are baffling to others.

Sora Himekawa

A second-year at Suzaku High School, member of the Handicrafts Club, and a witch who has the power of "romance." She's a klutzy and good-natured person who used to be good friends with Yamada in the past.

Nancy

A second-year at Suzaku High School and a "Seventh Witch." In the past, she was searching for witches along with Yamada, Himekawa, Odagiri, and Igarashi.

Masamune Ichijo

A second-year at Suzaku High School who belongs to the Boys' Basketball Team and is a witch with the "Power of Incitement." He's running in the election for president as a candidate aligned with the Shogi Club.

Yuri Miura

A first-year Suzaku High School student who belongs to the Shogi Club. He's a witch who has the power to manipulate others. He says he knew Himekawa before her memory got erased...

Ushio Igarashi

A second-year at Suzaku High School and vice-president of the Shogi Club. Yamada's old friend. He tried to have Odagiri join him and his colleagues, but his invite ended in failure...which is to say that he got rejected.

CONTENTS

CHAPTER 165: To be clear, I'm not gonna give it to you!

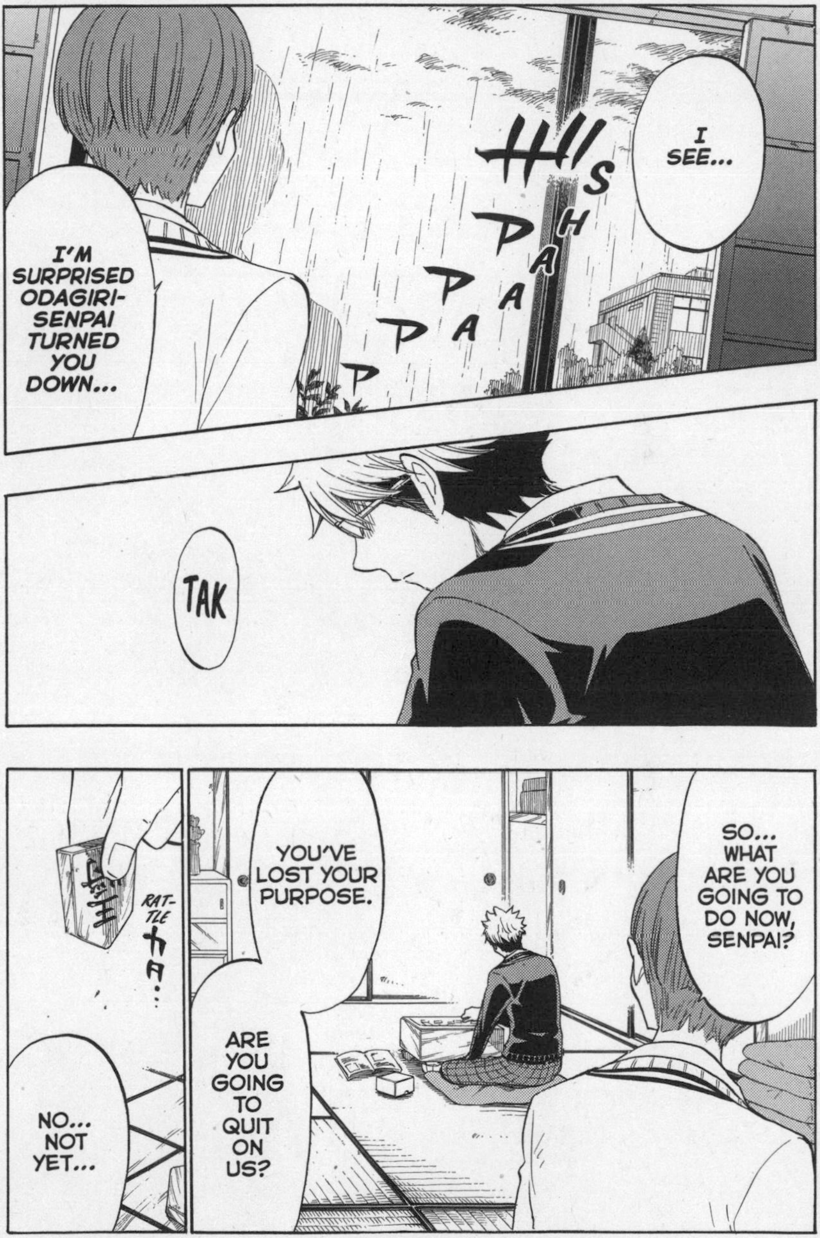

I SEE...
SHPAPAPAP
I'M SURPRISED ODAGIRI-SENPAI TURNED YOU DOWN...
TAK
SO... WHAT ARE YOU GOING TO DO NOW, SENPAI?
YOU'VE LOST YOUR PURPOSE.
ARE YOU GOING TO QUIT ON US?
RATTLE
NO... NOT YET...

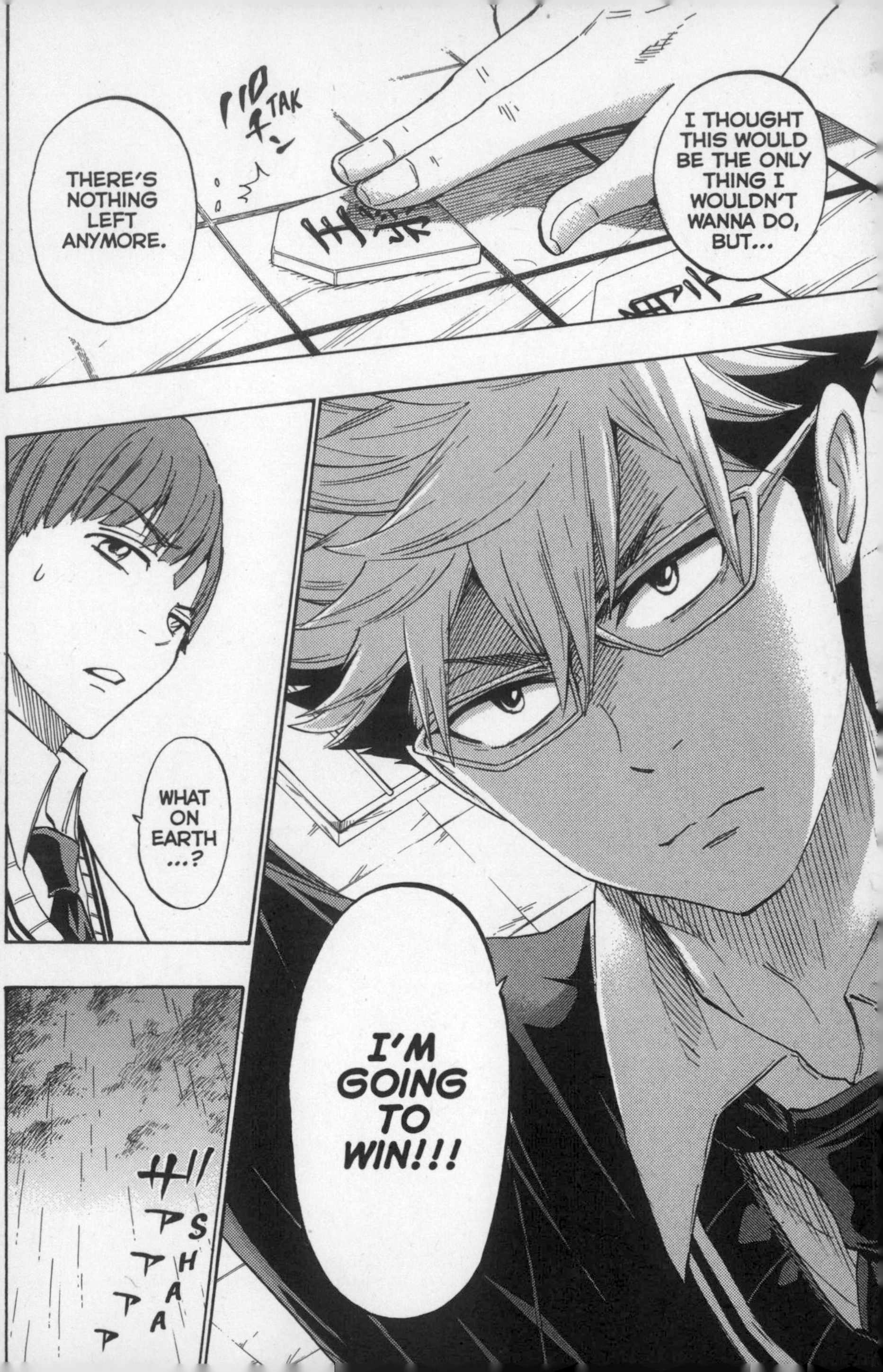
I THOUGHT THIS WOULD BE THE ONLY THING I WOULDN'T WANNA DO, BUT...
TAK
THERE'S NOTHING LEFT ANYMORE.
I'M GOING TO WIN!!!
WHAT ON EARTH ...?
SHAAA

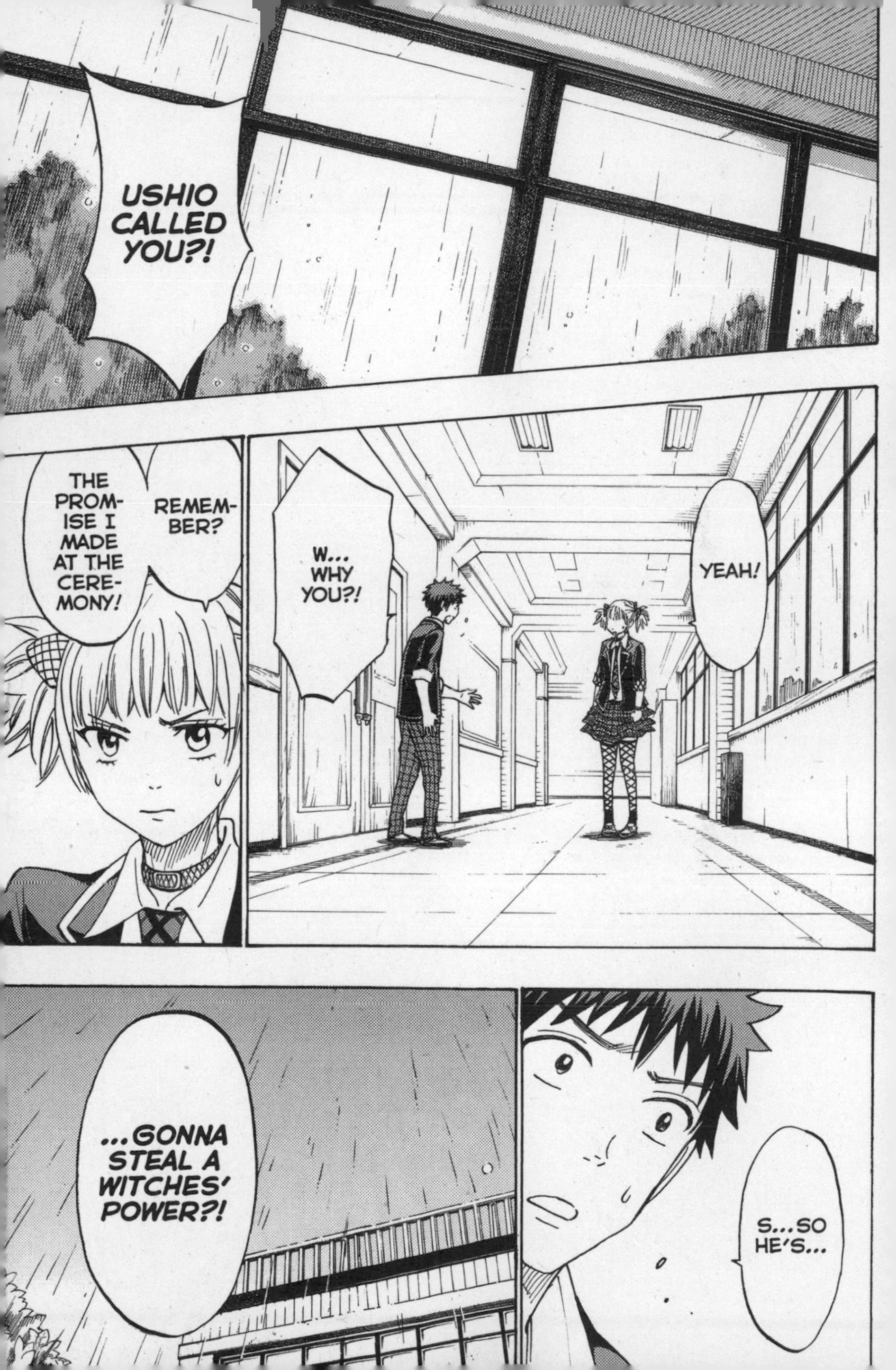
USHIO CALLED YOU?!
YEAH!
W... WHY YOU?!
REMEMBER?
THE PROMISE I MADE AT THE CEREMONY!
S...SO HE'S...
...GONNA STEAL A WITCHES' POWER?!

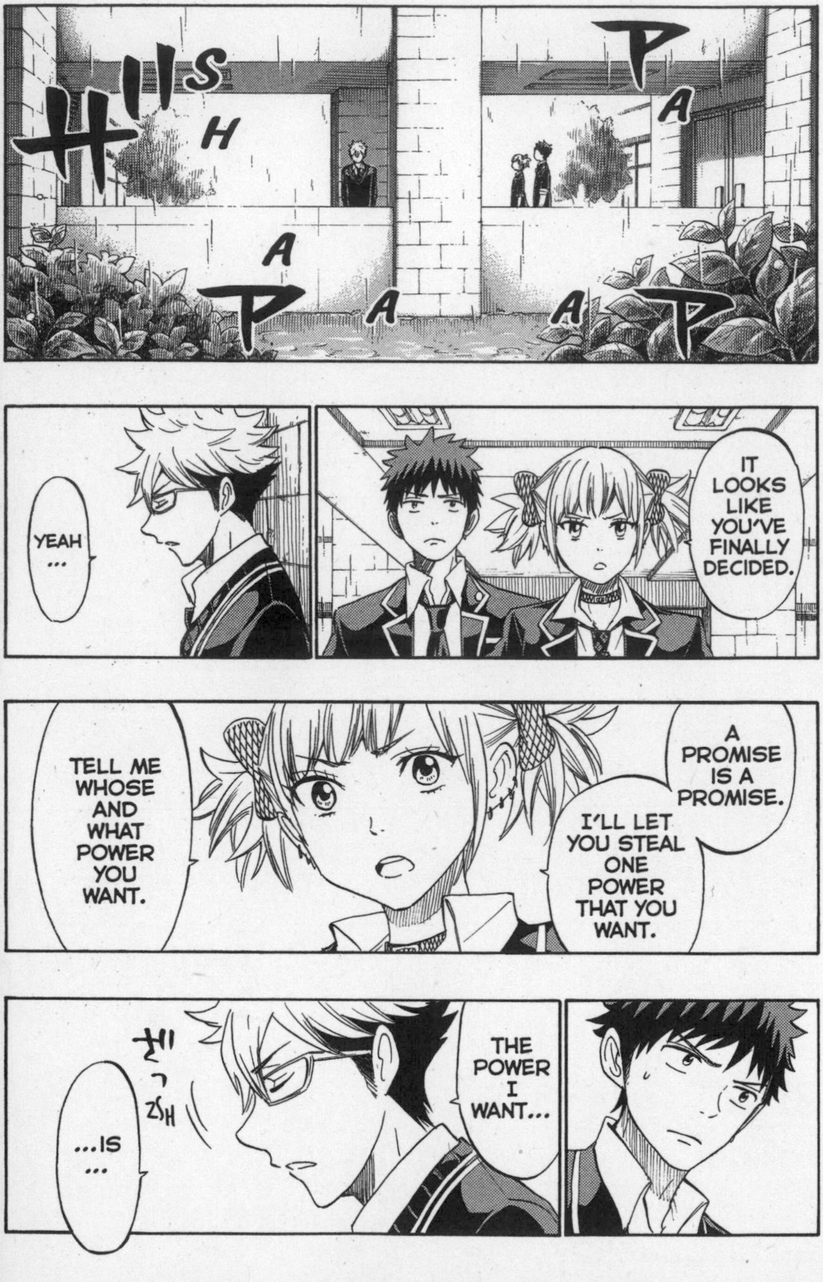
PA
A P
HISH
A
PA
IT LOOKS LIKE YOU'VE FINALLY DECIDED.
YEAH ...
A PROMISE IS A PROMISE.
I'LL LET YOU STEAL ONE POWER THAT YOU WANT.
TELL ME WHOSE AND WHAT POWER YOU WANT.
THE POWER I WANT...
ZSH
...IS ...

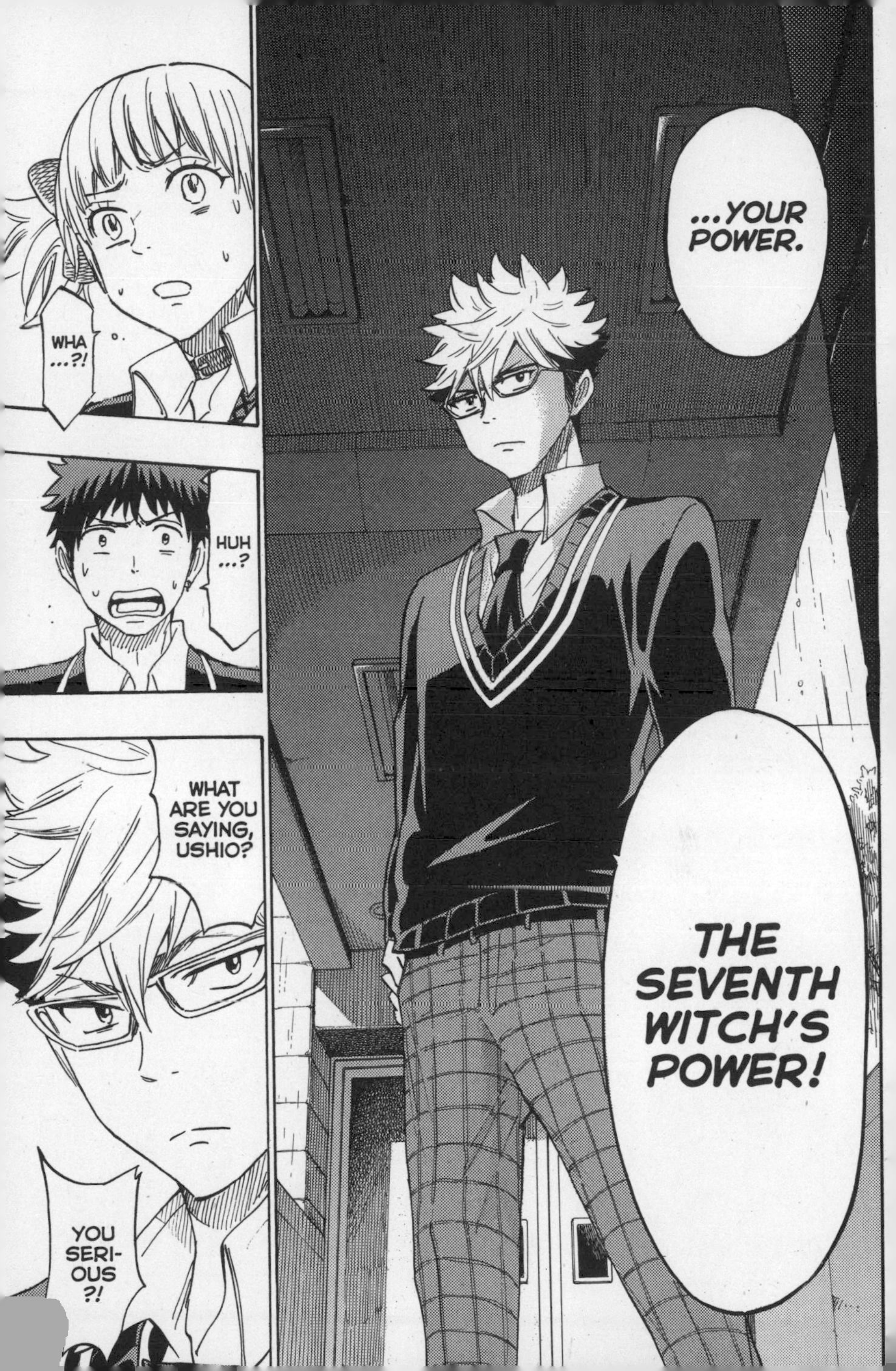
...YOUR POWER.
THE SEVENTH WITCH'S POWER!
WHA ...?!
HUH ...?
WHAT ARE YOU SAYING, USHIO?
YOU SERI-OUS ?!

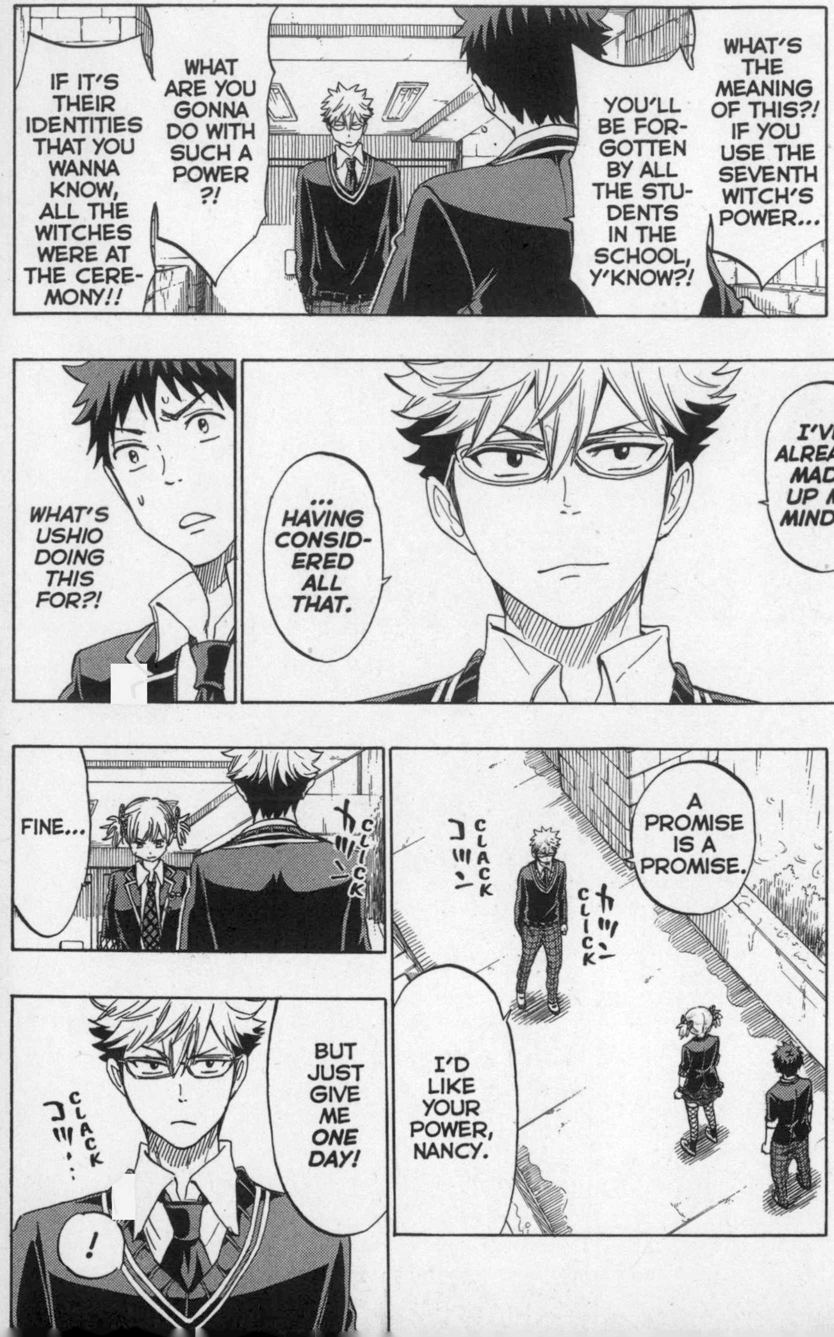
WHAT'S THE MEANING OF THIS?! IF YOU USE THE SEVENTH WITCH'S POWER...
YOU'LL BE FORGOTTEN BY ALL THE STUDENTS IN THE SCHOOL, Y'KNOW?!
WHAT ARE YOU GONNA DO WITH SUCH A POWER?!
IF IT'S THEIR IDENTITIES THAT YOU WANNA KNOW, ALL THE WITCHES WERE AT THE CEREMONY!!
I'VE ALREADY MADE UP MY MIND...
...HAVING CONSIDERED ALL THAT.
WHAT'S USHIO DOING THIS FOR?!
A PROMISE IS A PROMISE.
CLACK
CLICK
I'D LIKE YOUR POWER, NANCY.
FINE...
CLICK
BUT JUST GIVE ME ONE DAY!
CLACK
!

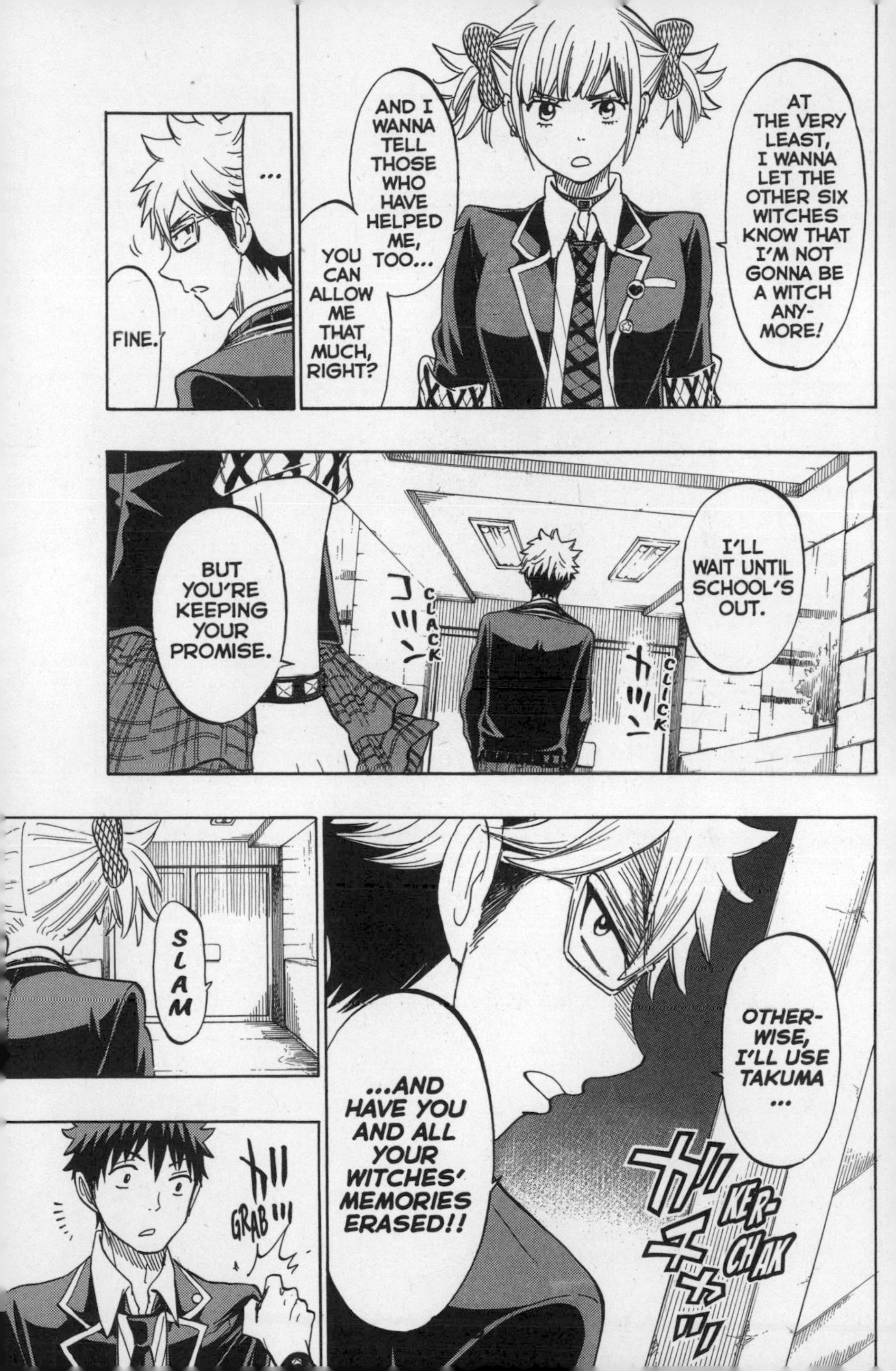

AT THE VERY LEAST, I WANNA LET THE OTHER SIX WITCHES KNOW THAT I'M NOT GONNA BE A WITCH ANY-MORE!
AND I WANNA TELL THOSE WHO HAVE HELPED ME, TOO...
YOU CAN ALLOW ME THAT MUCH, RIGHT?
...
FINE.
I'LL WAIT UNTIL SCHOOL'S OUT.
CLICK
CLACK
BUT YOU'RE KEEPING YOUR PROMISE.
OTHER-WISE, I'LL USE TAKUMA...
...AND HAVE YOU AND ALL YOUR WITCHES' MEMORIES ERASED!!
KER-CHAK
SLAM
GRAB

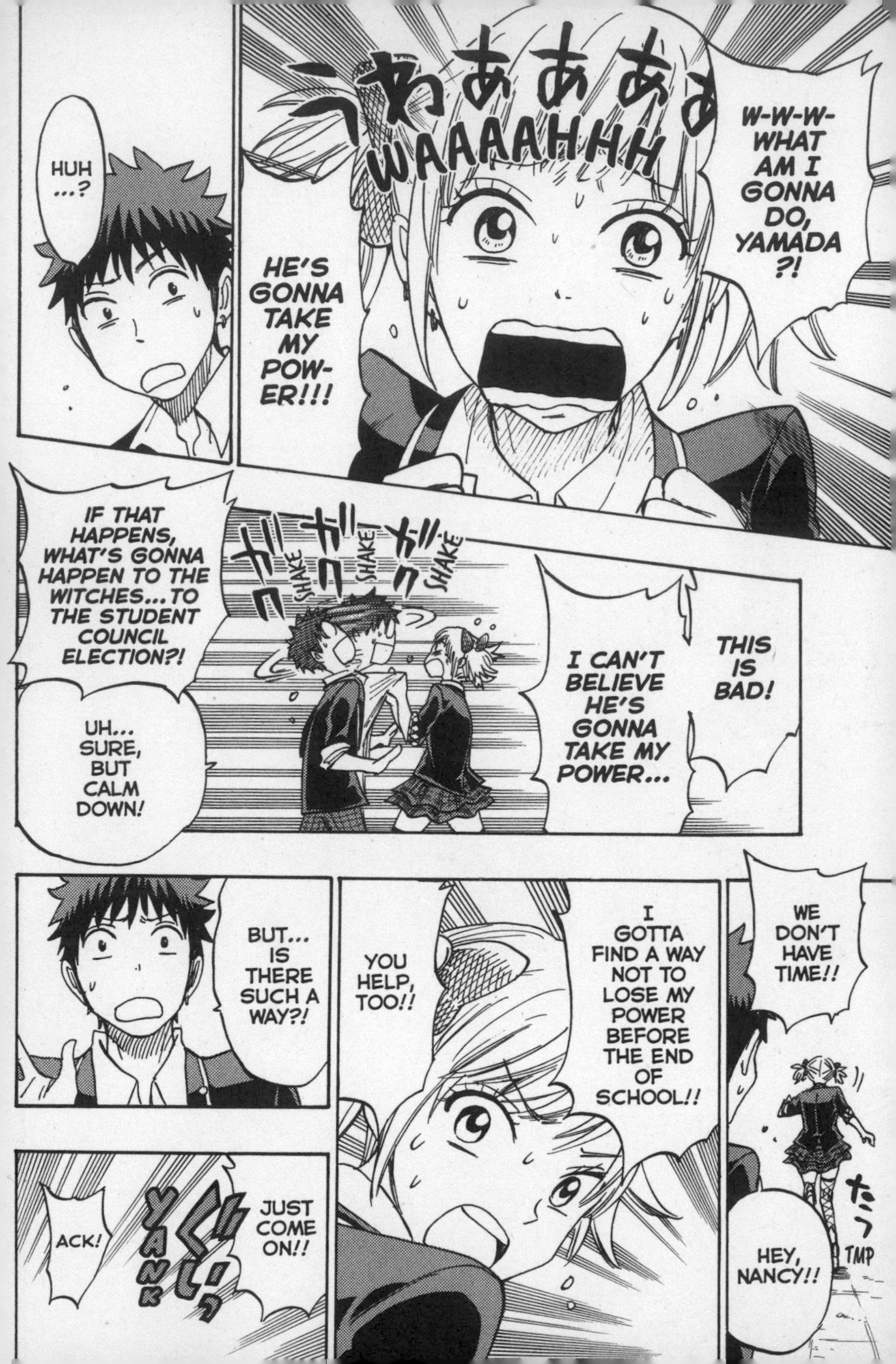

うわあああああ
WAAAAHHH
W-W-W-WHAT AM I GONNA DO, YAMADA?!
HE'S GONNA TAKE MY POW-ER!!!
HUH...?
THIS IS BAD!
I CAN'T BELIEVE HE'S GONNA TAKE MY POWER...
ガクガクガク
SHAKE SHAKE SHAKE
IF THAT HAPPENS, WHAT'S GONNA HAPPEN TO THE WITCHES...TO THE STUDENT COUNCIL ELECTION?!
UH... SURE, BUT CALM DOWN!
WE DON'T HAVE TIME!!
たっ
TMP
HEY, NANCY!!
I GOTTA FIND A WAY NOT TO LOSE MY POWER BEFORE THE END OF SCHOOL!!
YOU HELP, TOO!!
BUT... IS THERE SUCH A WAY?!
JUST COME ON!!
ぐいっ
YANK
ACK!

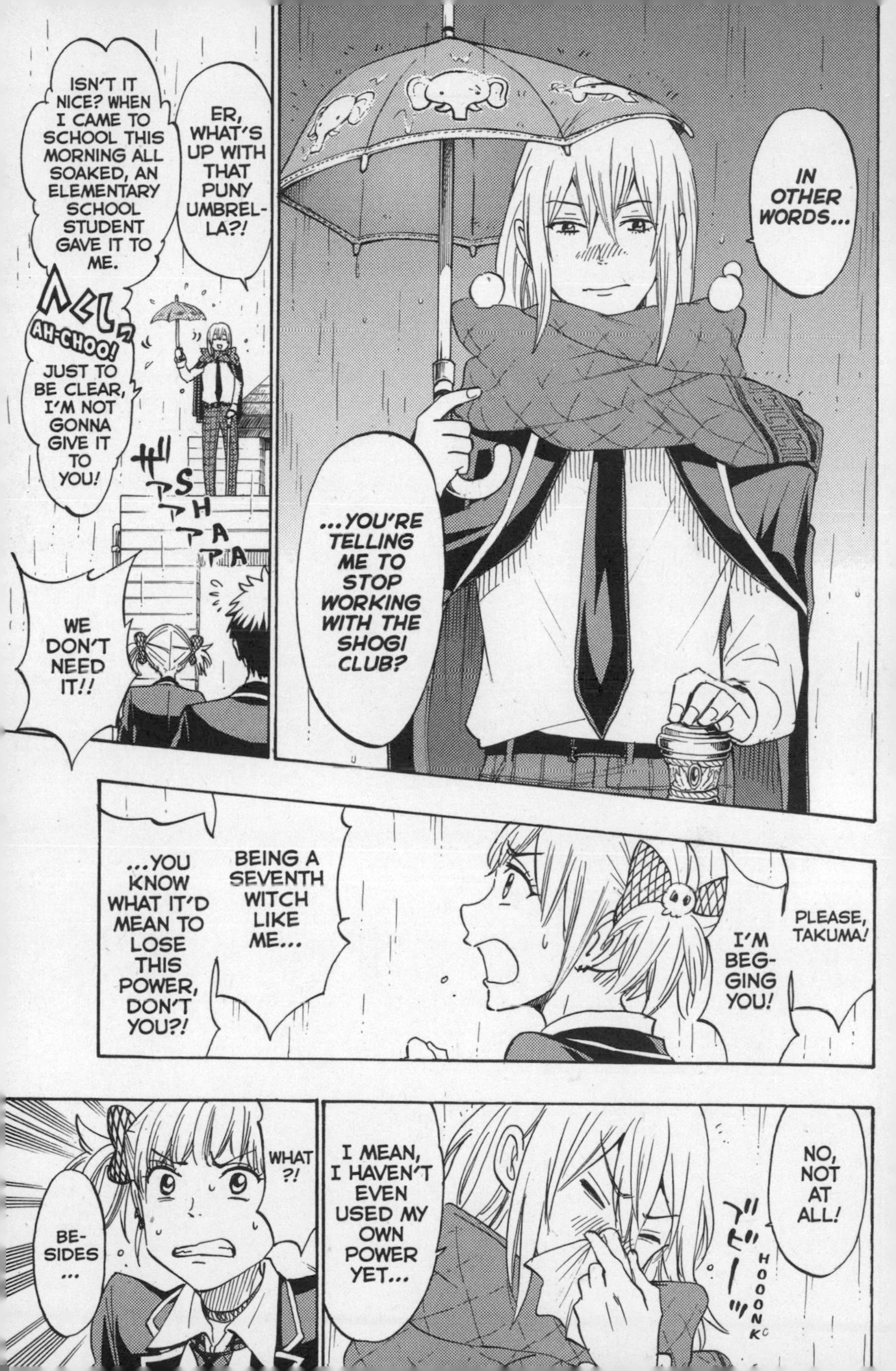
IN OTHER WORDS...
...YOU'RE TELLING ME TO STOP WORKING WITH THE SHOGI CLUB?
ER, WHAT'S UP WITH THAT PUNY UMBREL-LA?!
ISN'T IT NICE? WHEN I CAME TO SCHOOL THIS MORNING ALL SOAKED, AN ELEMENTARY SCHOOL STUDENT GAVE IT TO ME.
AH-CHOO!
JUST TO BE CLEAR, I'M NOT GONNA GIVE IT TO YOU!
SHAPA PA
WE DON'T NEED IT!!
PLEASE, TAKUMA!
I'M BEG-GING YOU!
BEING A SEVENTH WITCH LIKE ME...
...YOU KNOW WHAT IT'D MEAN TO LOSE THIS POWER, DON'T YOU?!
NO, NOT AT ALL!
HOOOONK
I MEAN, I HAVEN'T EVEN USED MY OWN POWER YET...
WHAT?!
BE-SIDES...

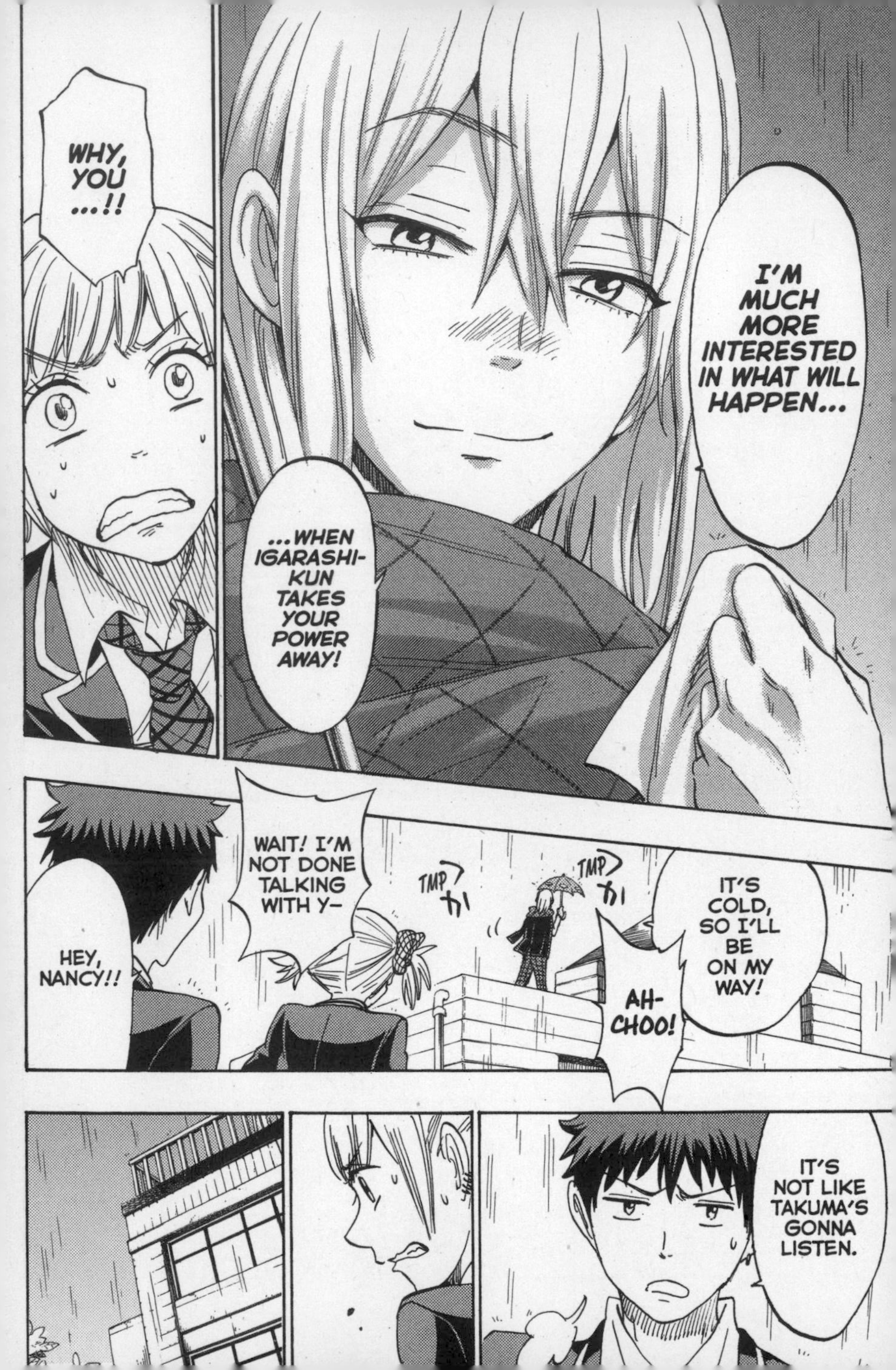
I'M MUCH MORE INTERESTED IN WHAT WILL HAPPEN...
...WHEN IGARASHI-KUN TAKES YOUR POWER AWAY!
WHY, YOU ...!!
IT'S COLD, SO I'LL BE ON MY WAY!
AH-CHOO!
TMP
TMP
WAIT! I'M NOT DONE TALKING WITH Y–
HEY, NANCY!!
IT'S NOT LIKE TAKUMA'S GONNA LISTEN.

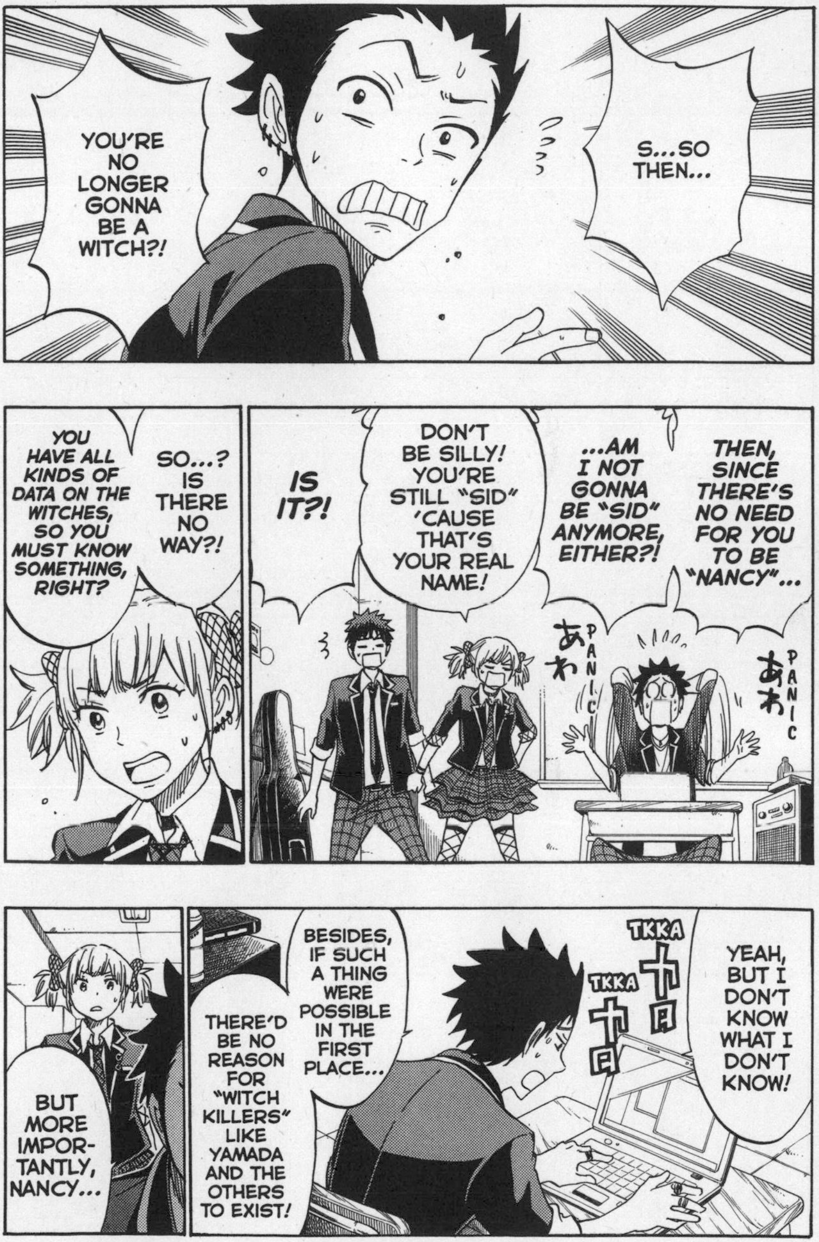
S...SO THEN...
YOU'RE NO LONGER GONNA BE A WITCH?!
THEN, SINCE THERE'S NO NEED FOR YOU TO BE "NANCY"...
...AM I NOT GONNA BE "SID" ANYMORE, EITHER?!
あわ PANIC
DON'T BE SILLY! YOU'RE STILL "SID" 'CAUSE THAT'S YOUR REAL NAME!
IS IT?!
あわ PANIC
SO...? IS THERE NO WAY?!
YOU HAVE ALL KINDS OF DATA ON THE WITCHES, SO YOU MUST KNOW SOMETHING, RIGHT?
YEAH, BUT I DON'T KNOW WHAT I DON'T KNOW!
TKKA
TKKA
BESIDES, IF SUCH A THING WERE POSSIBLE IN THE FIRST PLACE...
THERE'D BE NO REASON FOR "WITCH KILLERS" LIKE YAMADA AND THE OTHERS TO EXIST!
BUT MORE IMPORTANTLY, NANCY...

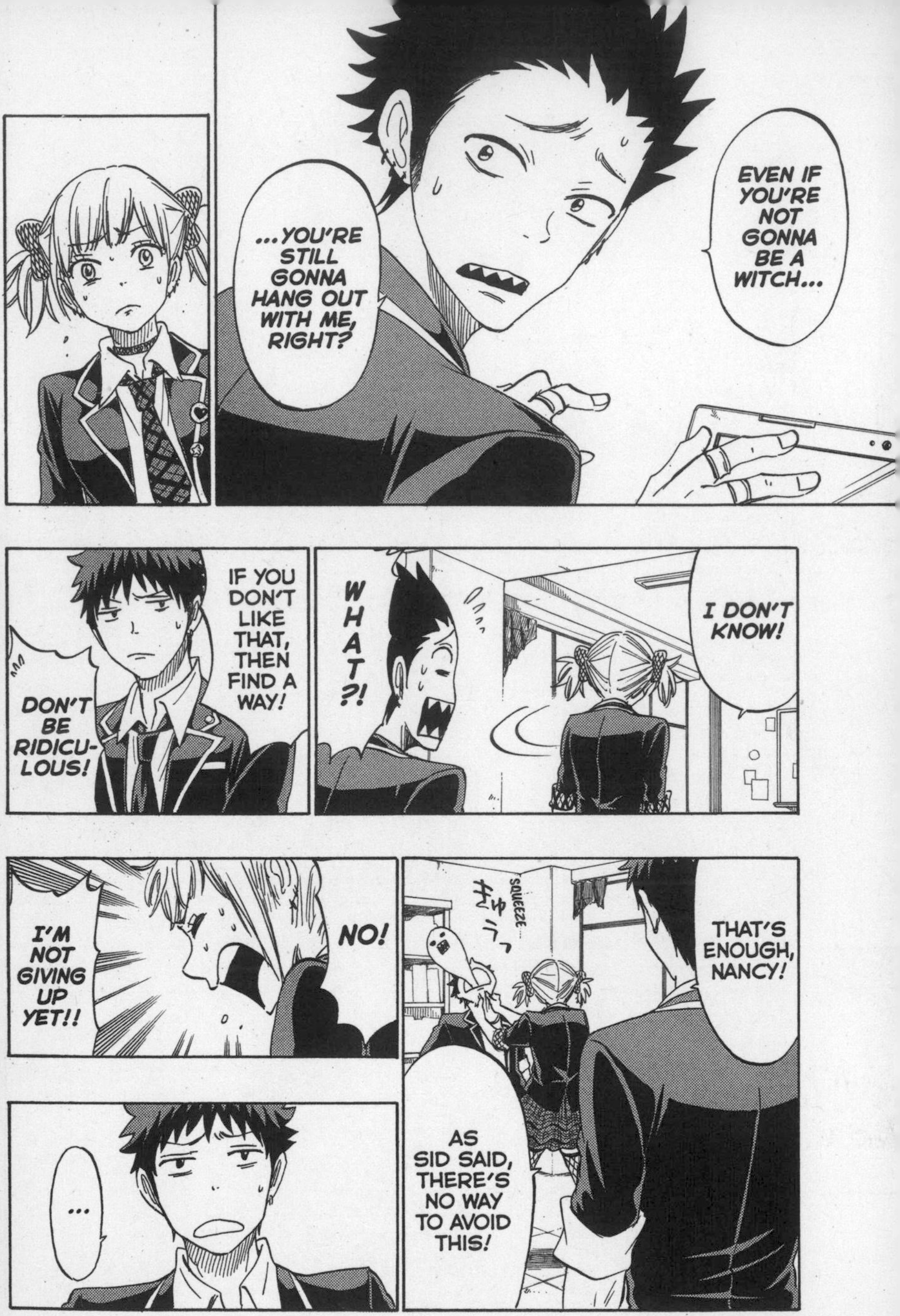
EVEN IF YOU'RE NOT GONNA BE A WITCH...
...YOU'RE STILL GONNA HANG OUT WITH ME, RIGHT?
I DON'T KNOW!
WHAT?!
IF YOU DON'T LIKE THAT, THEN FIND A WAY!
DON'T BE RIDICULOUS!
THAT'S ENOUGH, NANCY!
SQUEEZE
AS SID SAID, THERE'S NO WAY TO AVOID THIS!
NO!
I'M NOT GIVING UP YET!!
...

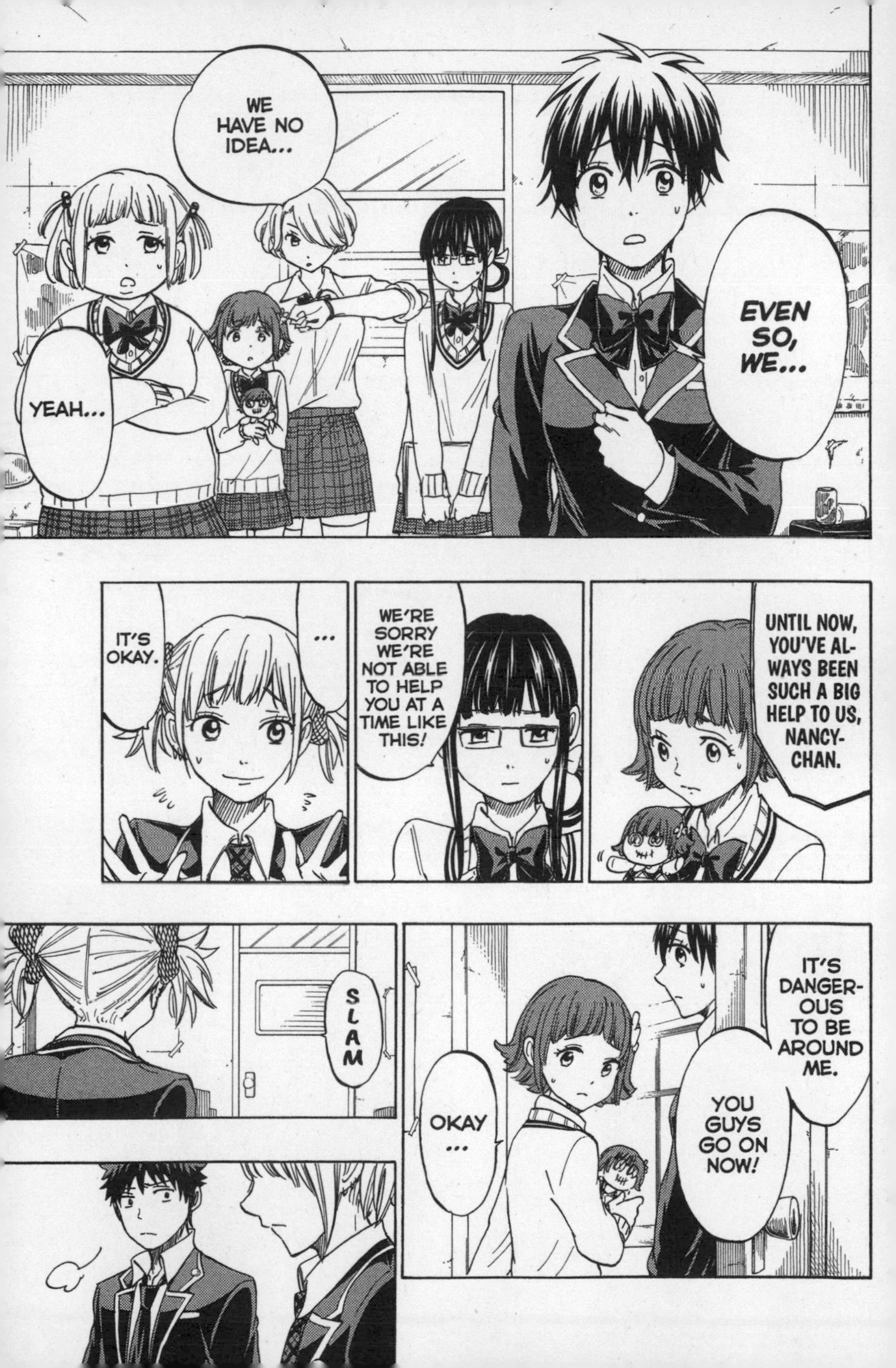
EVEN SO, WE...
WE HAVE NO IDEA...
YEAH...
UNTIL NOW, YOU'VE AL-WAYS BEEN SUCH A BIG HELP TO US, NANCY-CHAN.
WE'RE SORRY WE'RE NOT ABLE TO HELP YOU AT A TIME LIKE THIS!
...
IT'S OKAY.
IT'S DANGER-OUS TO BE AROUND ME.
YOU GUYS GO ON NOW!
OKAY...
SLAM

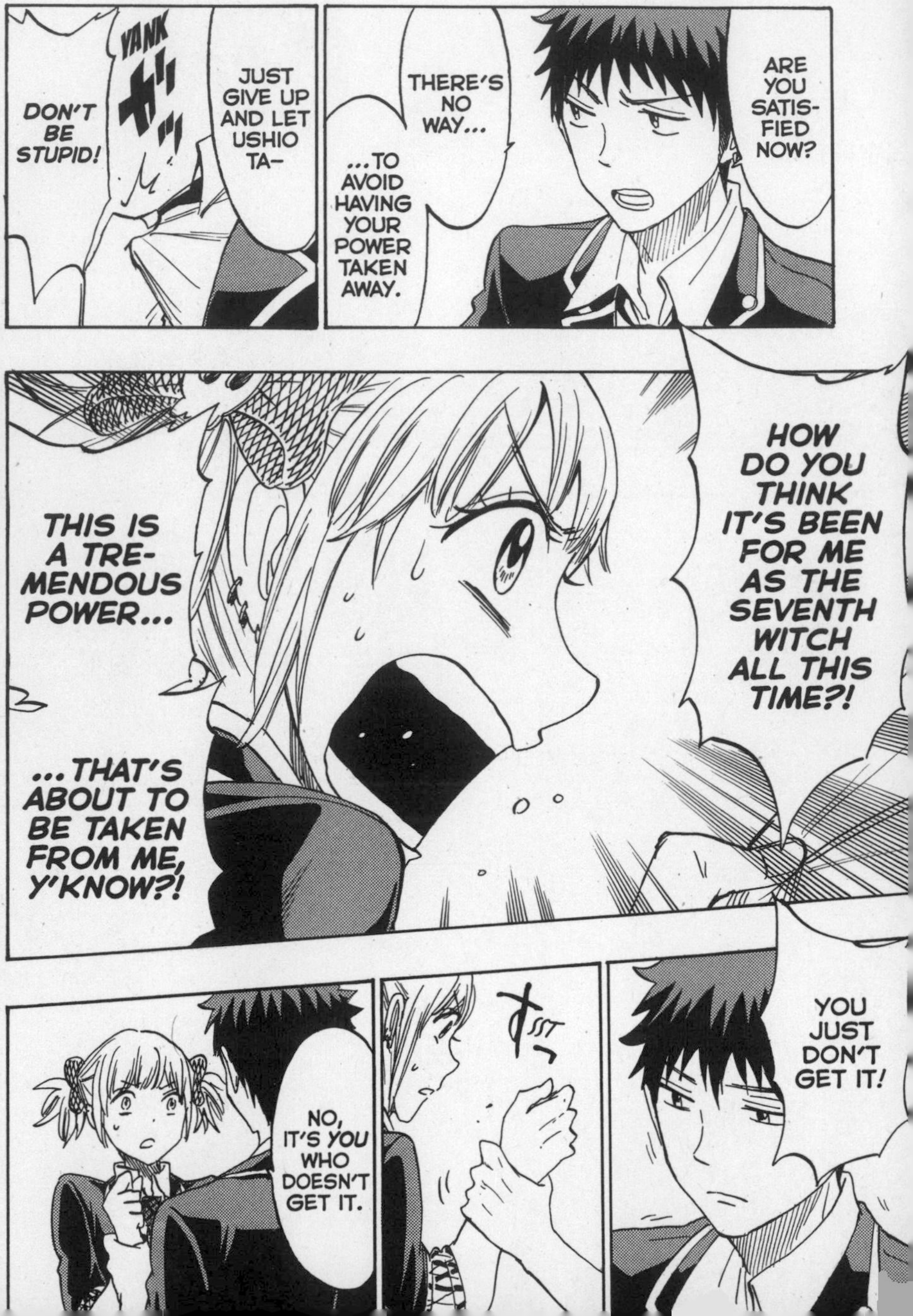
ARE YOU SATIS- FIED NOW?
THERE'S NO WAY...
...TO AVOID HAVING YOUR POWER TAKEN AWAY.
JUST GIVE UP AND LET USHIO TA-
YANK
DON'T BE STUPID!
HOW DO YOU THINK IT'S BEEN FOR ME AS THE SEVENTH WITCH ALL THIS TIME?!
THIS IS A TRE- MENDOUS POWER...
...THAT'S ABOUT TO BE TAKEN FROM ME, Y'KNOW?!
YOU JUST DON'T GET IT!
NO, IT'S YOU WHO DOESN'T GET IT.

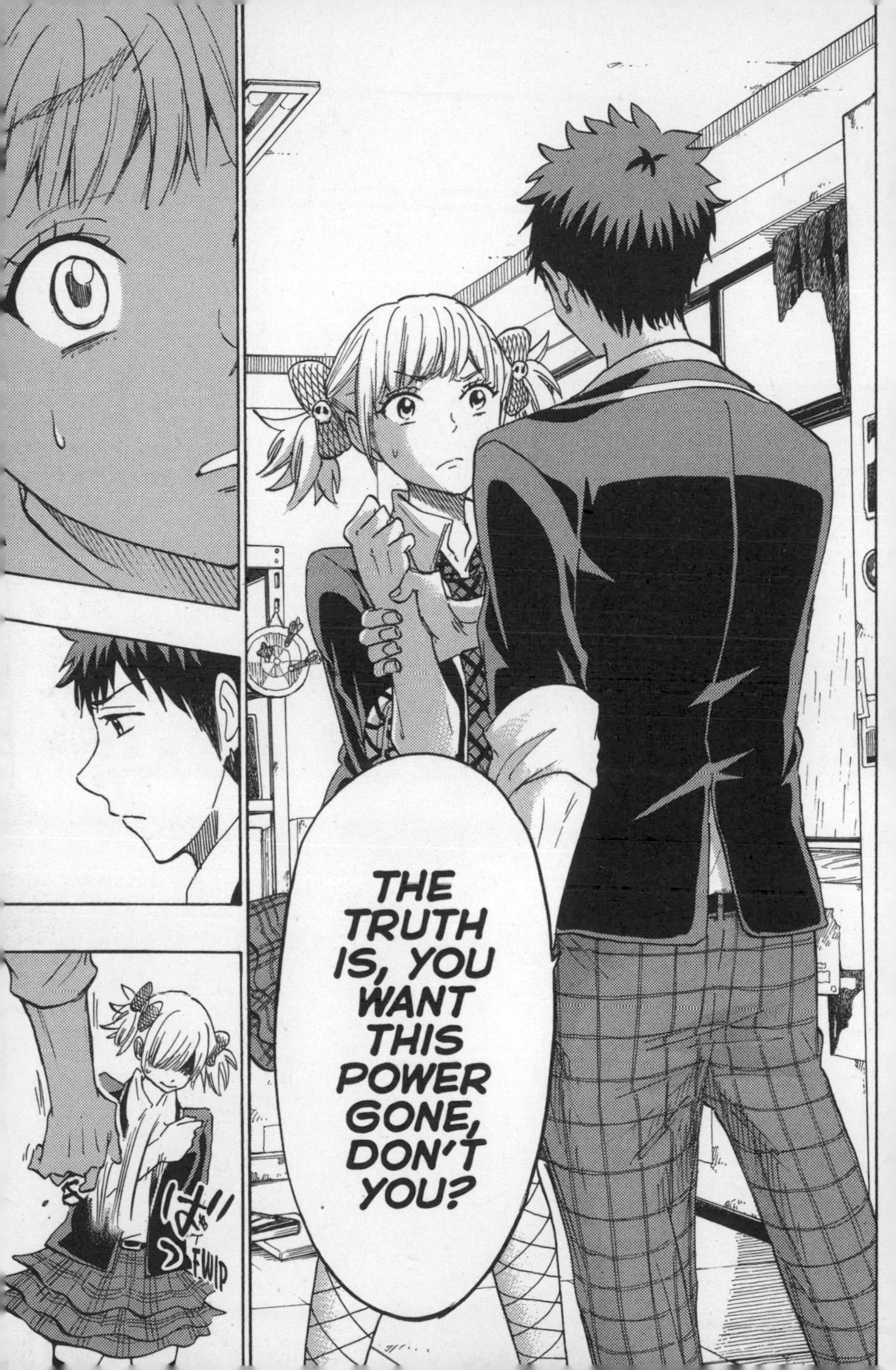
THE TRUTH IS, YOU WANT THIS POWER GONE, DON'T YOU?
FWIP

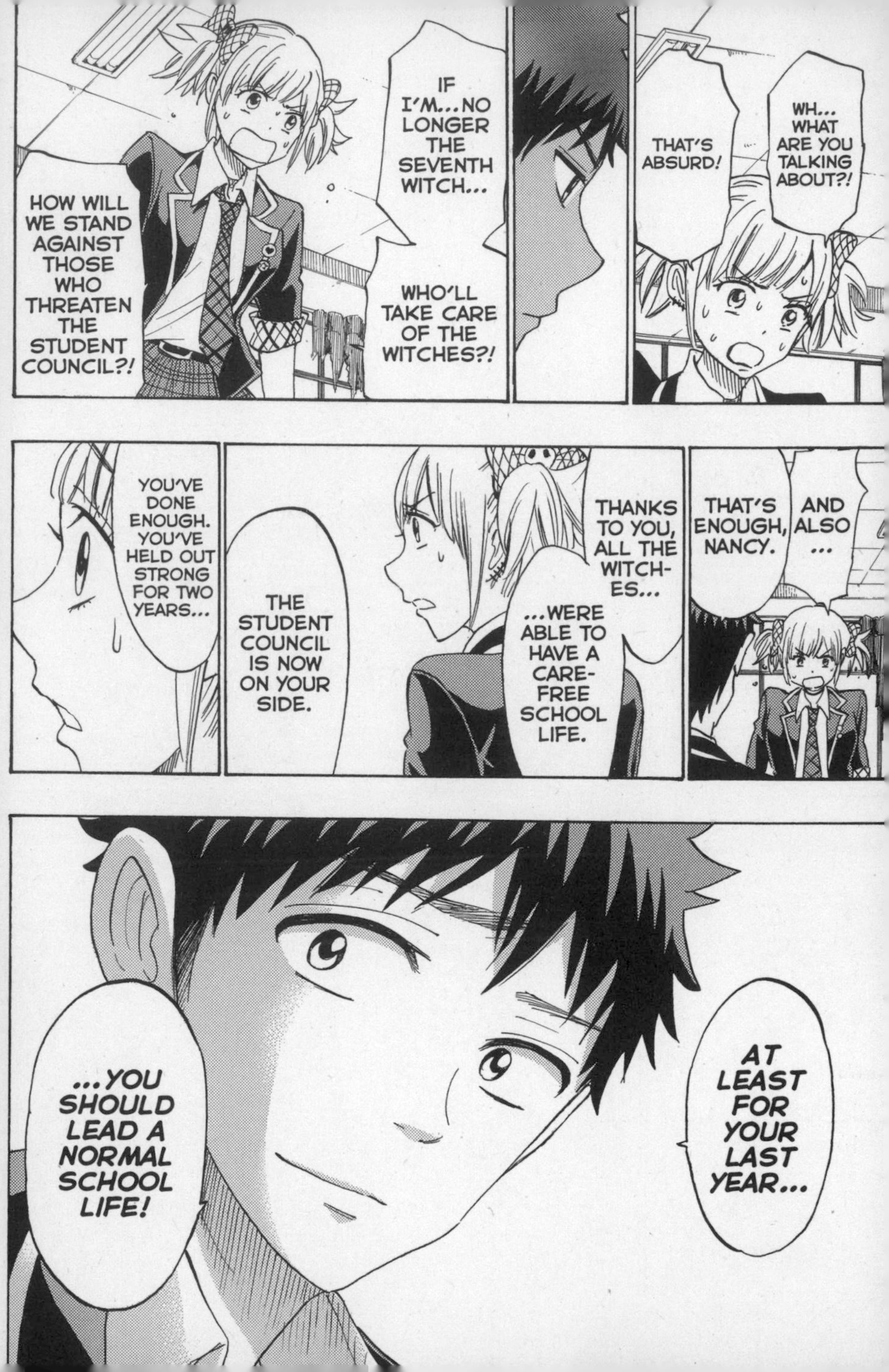
WH... WHAT ARE YOU TALKING ABOUT?!
THAT'S ABSURD!
IF I'M...NO LONGER THE SEVENTH WITCH...
WHO'LL TAKE CARE OF THE WITCHES?!
HOW WILL WE STAND AGAINST THOSE WHO THREATEN THE STUDENT COUNCIL?!
AND ALSO...
THAT'S ENOUGH, NANCY.
THANKS TO YOU, ALL THE WITCH-ES...
...WERE ABLE TO HAVE A CARE-FREE SCHOOL LIFE.
THE STUDENT COUNCIL IS NOW ON YOUR SIDE.
YOU'VE DONE ENOUGH. YOU'VE HELD OUT STRONG FOR TWO YEARS...
AT LEAST FOR YOUR LAST YEAR...
...YOU SHOULD LEAD A NORMAL SCHOOL LIFE!

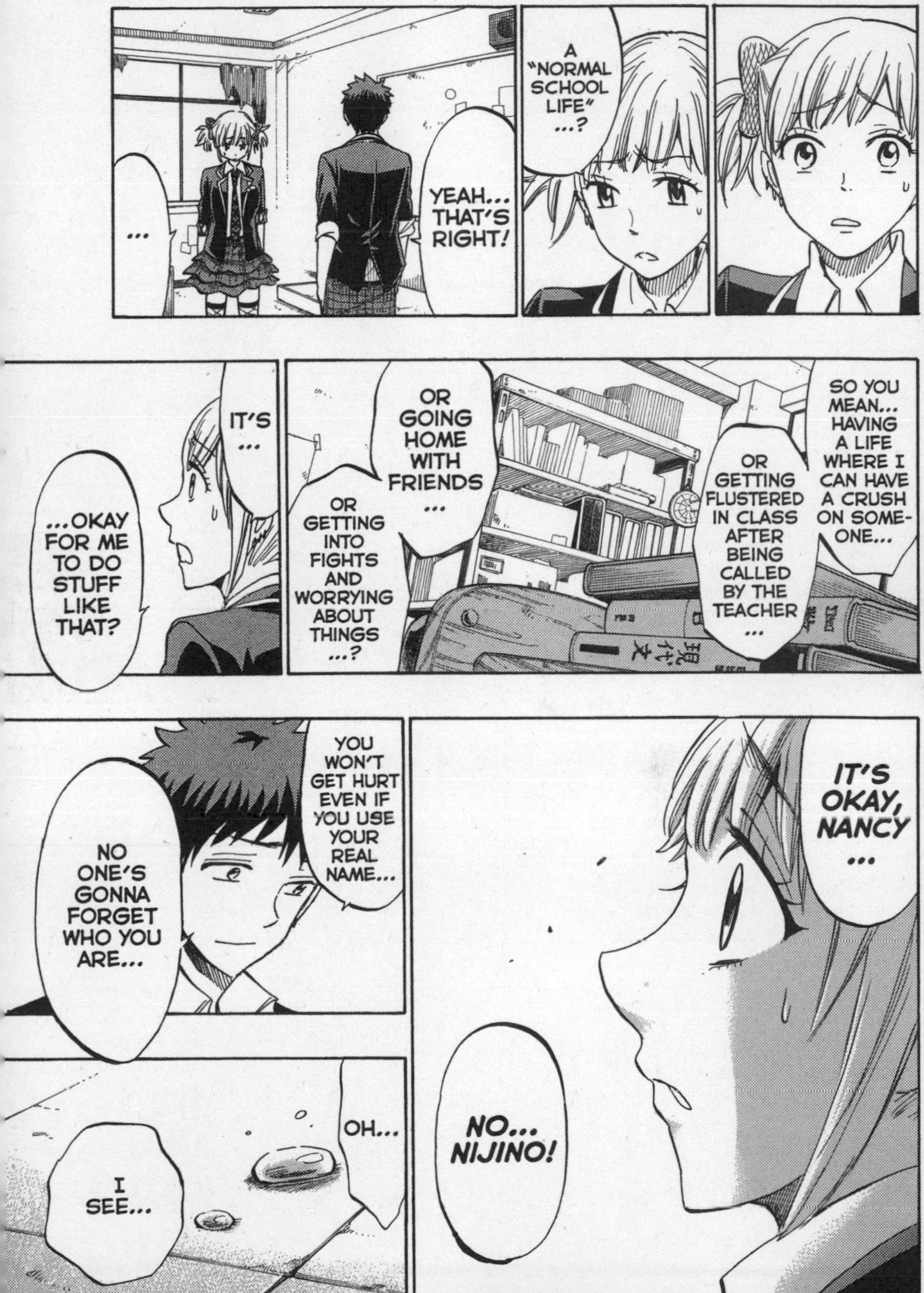
A "NORMAL SCHOOL LIFE" ...?
YEAH... THAT'S RIGHT!
...
SO YOU MEAN... HAVING A LIFE WHERE I CAN HAVE A CRUSH ON SOME-ONE...
OR GETTING FLUSTERED IN CLASS AFTER BEING CALLED BY THE TEACHER ...
現代文
OR GOING HOME WITH FRIENDS ...
OR GETTING INTO FIGHTS AND WORRYING ABOUT THINGS ...?
IT'S ...
...OKAY FOR ME TO DO STUFF LIKE THAT?
IT'S OKAY, NANCY ...
NO... NIJINO!
YOU WON'T GET HURT EVEN IF YOU USE YOUR REAL NAME...
NO ONE'S GONNA FORGET WHO YOU ARE...
OH...
I SEE...

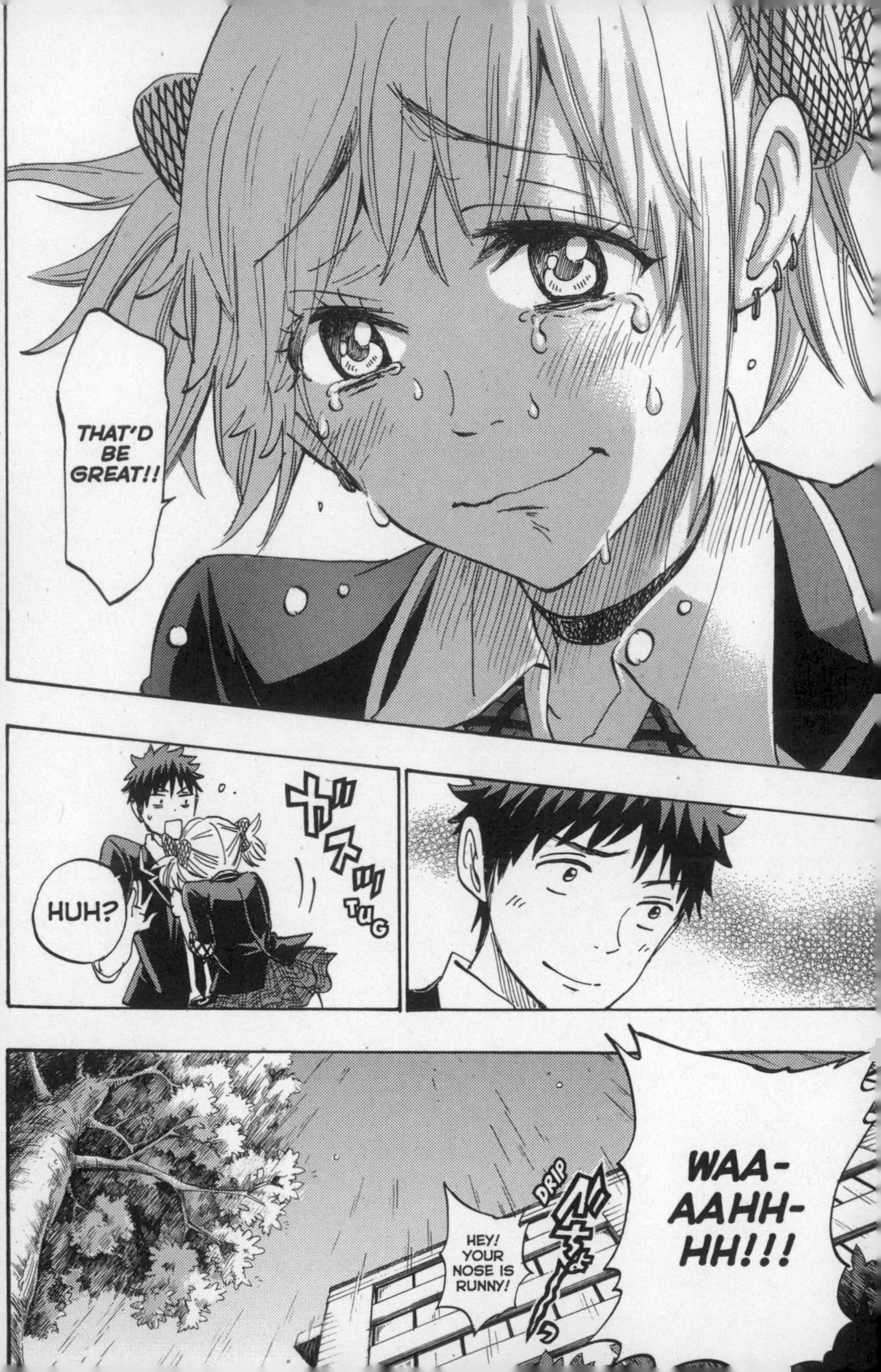
THAT'D BE GREAT!!
TUG
HUH?
WAA-AAHH-HH!!!
DRIP
HEY! YOUR NOSE IS RUNNY!

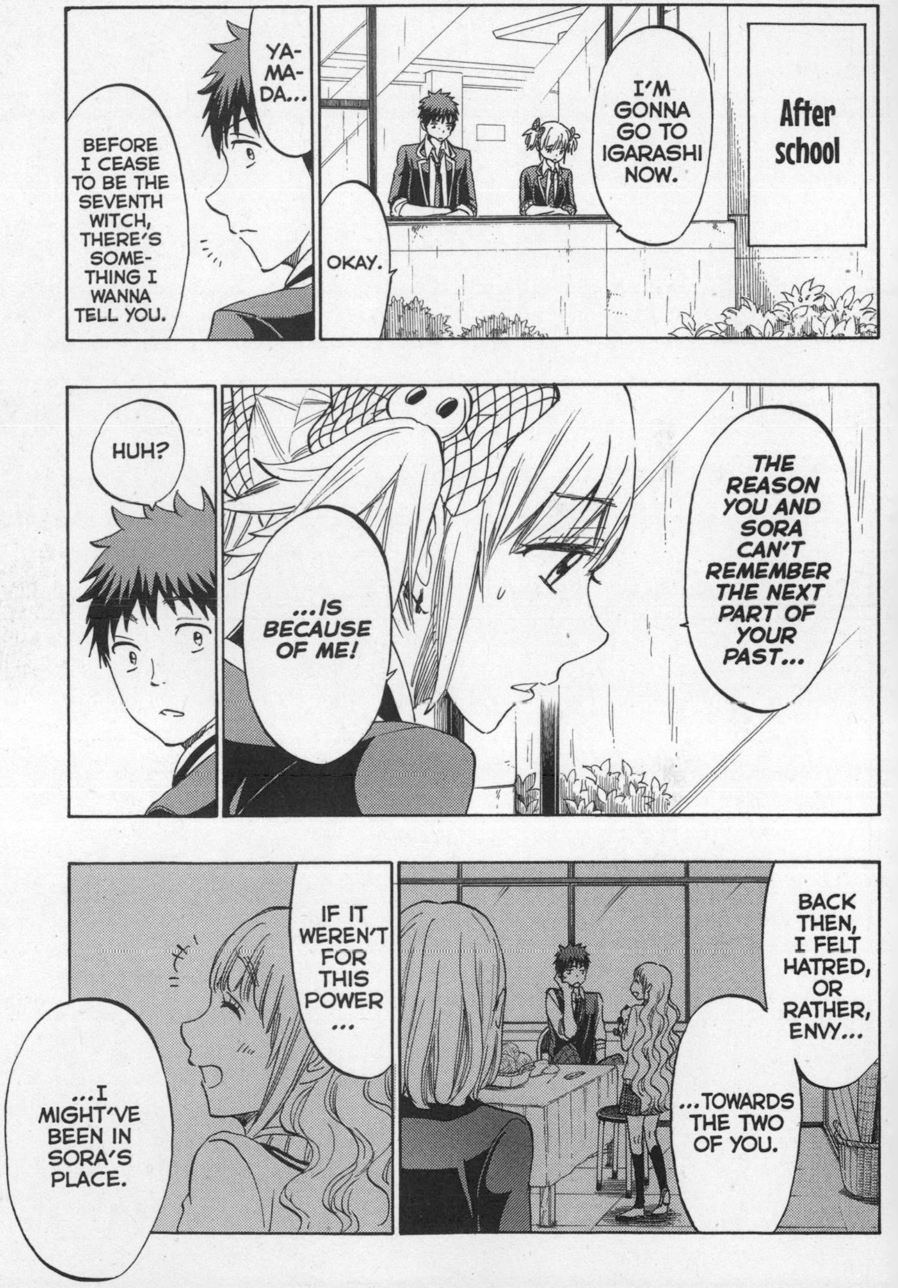
After school
I'M GONNA GO TO IGARASHI NOW.
OKAY.
YA-MA-DA...
BEFORE I CEASE TO BE THE SEVENTH WITCH, THERE'S SOME-THING I WANNA TELL YOU.
THE REASON YOU AND SORA CAN'T REMEMBER THE NEXT PART OF YOUR PAST...
...IS BECAUSE OF ME!
HUH?
BACK THEN, I FELT HATRED, OR RATHER, ENVY...
...TOWARDS THE TWO OF YOU.
IF IT WEREN'T FOR THIS POWER...
...I MIGHT'VE BEEN IN SORA'S PLACE.

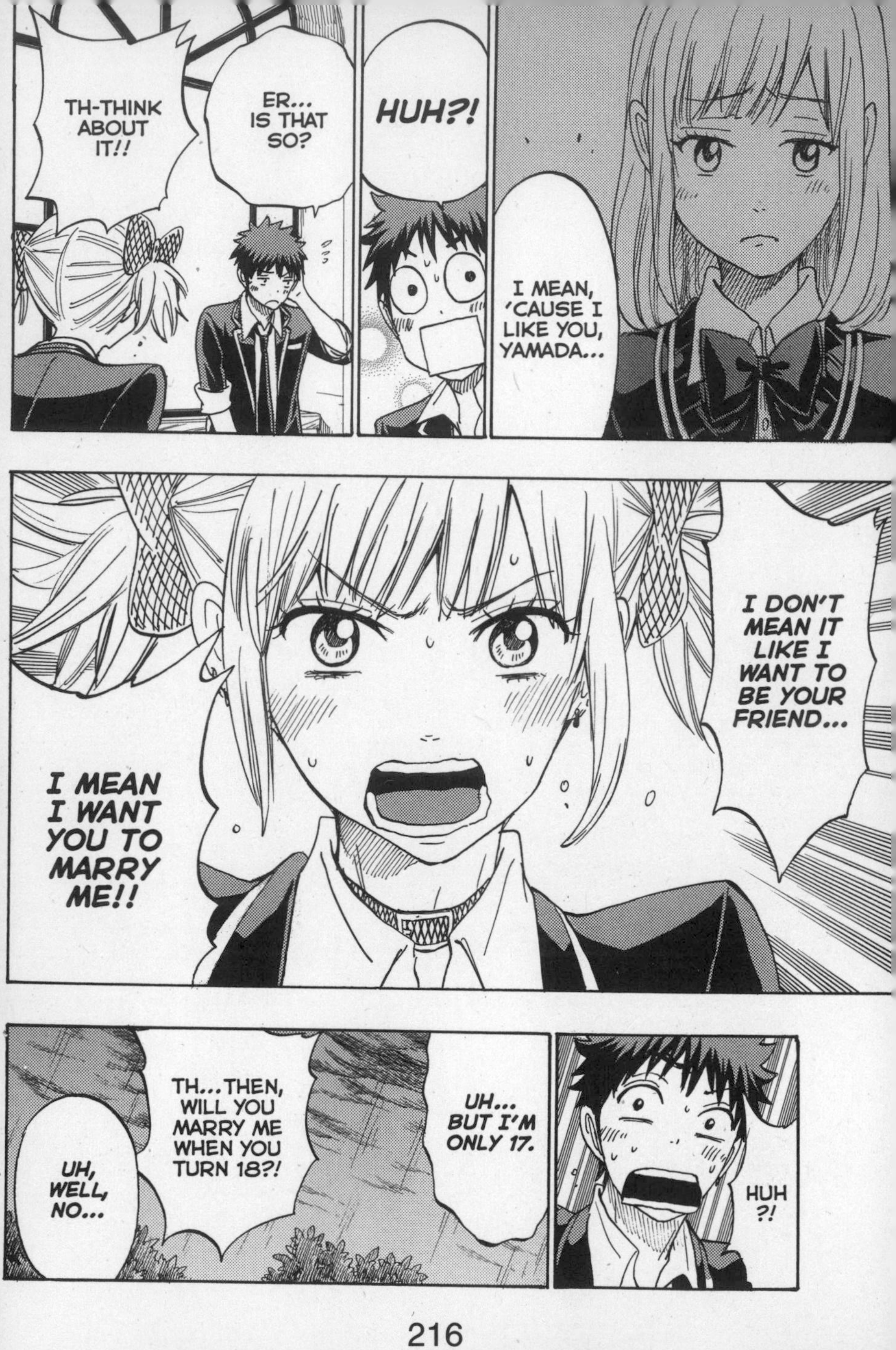
I MEAN, 'CAUSE I LIKE YOU, YAMADA...
HUH?!
ER... IS THAT SO?
TH-THINK ABOUT IT!!
I DON'T MEAN IT LIKE I WANT TO BE YOUR FRIEND...
I MEAN I WANT YOU TO MARRY ME!!
HUH ?!
UH... BUT I'M ONLY 17.
TH...THEN, WILL YOU MARRY ME WHEN YOU TURN 18?!
UH, WELL, NO...

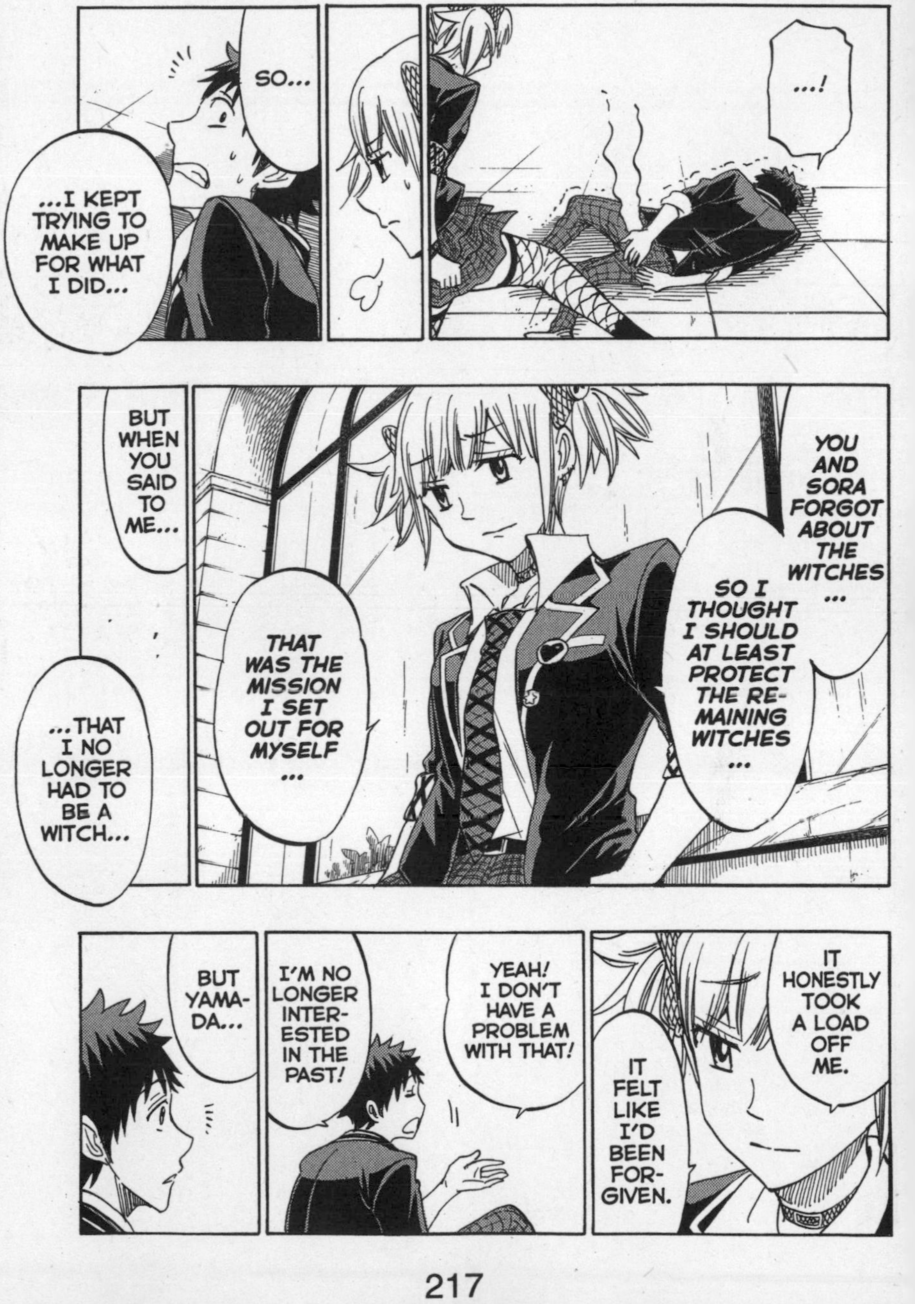

...!
SO...
...I KEPT TRYING TO MAKE UP FOR WHAT I DID...
YOU AND SORA FORGOT ABOUT THE WITCHES ...
SO I THOUGHT I SHOULD AT LEAST PROTECT THE RE-MAINING WITCHES ...
THAT WAS THE MISSION I SET OUT FOR MYSELF ...
BUT WHEN YOU SAID TO ME...
...THAT I NO LONGER HAD TO BE A WITCH...
IT HONESTLY TOOK A LOAD OFF ME.
IT FELT LIKE I'D BEEN FOR-GIVEN.
YEAH! I DON'T HAVE A PROBLEM WITH THAT!
I'M NO LONGER INTER-ESTED IN THE PAST!
BUT YAMA-DA...

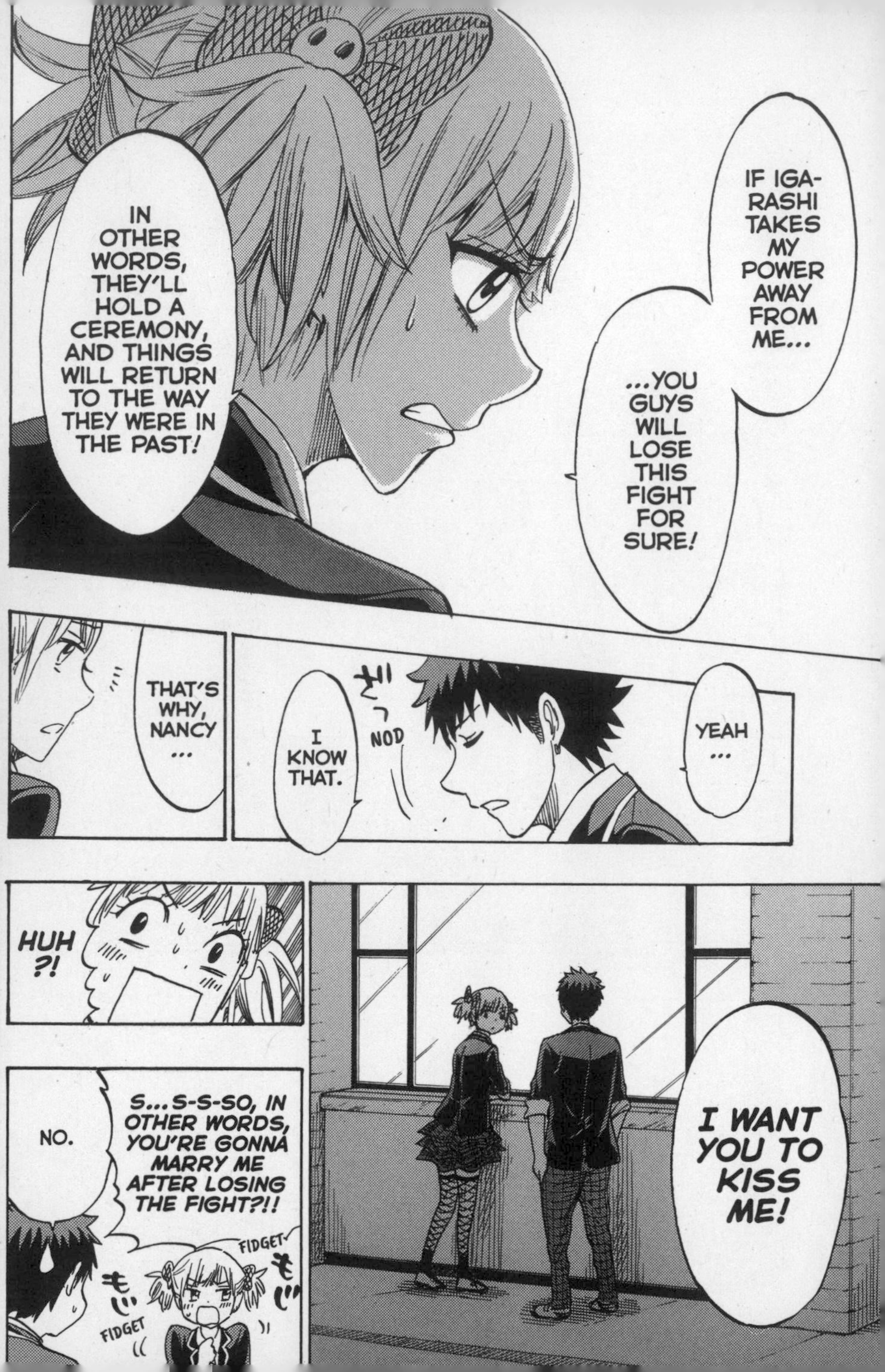
IF IGA-RASHI TAKES MY POWER AWAY FROM ME...
...YOU GUYS WILL LOSE THIS FIGHT FOR SURE!
IN OTHER WORDS, THEY'LL HOLD A CEREMONY, AND THINGS WILL RETURN TO THE WAY THEY WERE IN THE PAST!
YEAH...
NOD
I KNOW THAT.
THAT'S WHY, NANCY...
I WANT YOU TO KISS ME!
HUH?!
S...S-S-SO, IN OTHER WORDS, YOU'RE GONNA MARRY ME AFTER LOSING THE FIGHT?!!
NO.
FIDGET
FIDGET

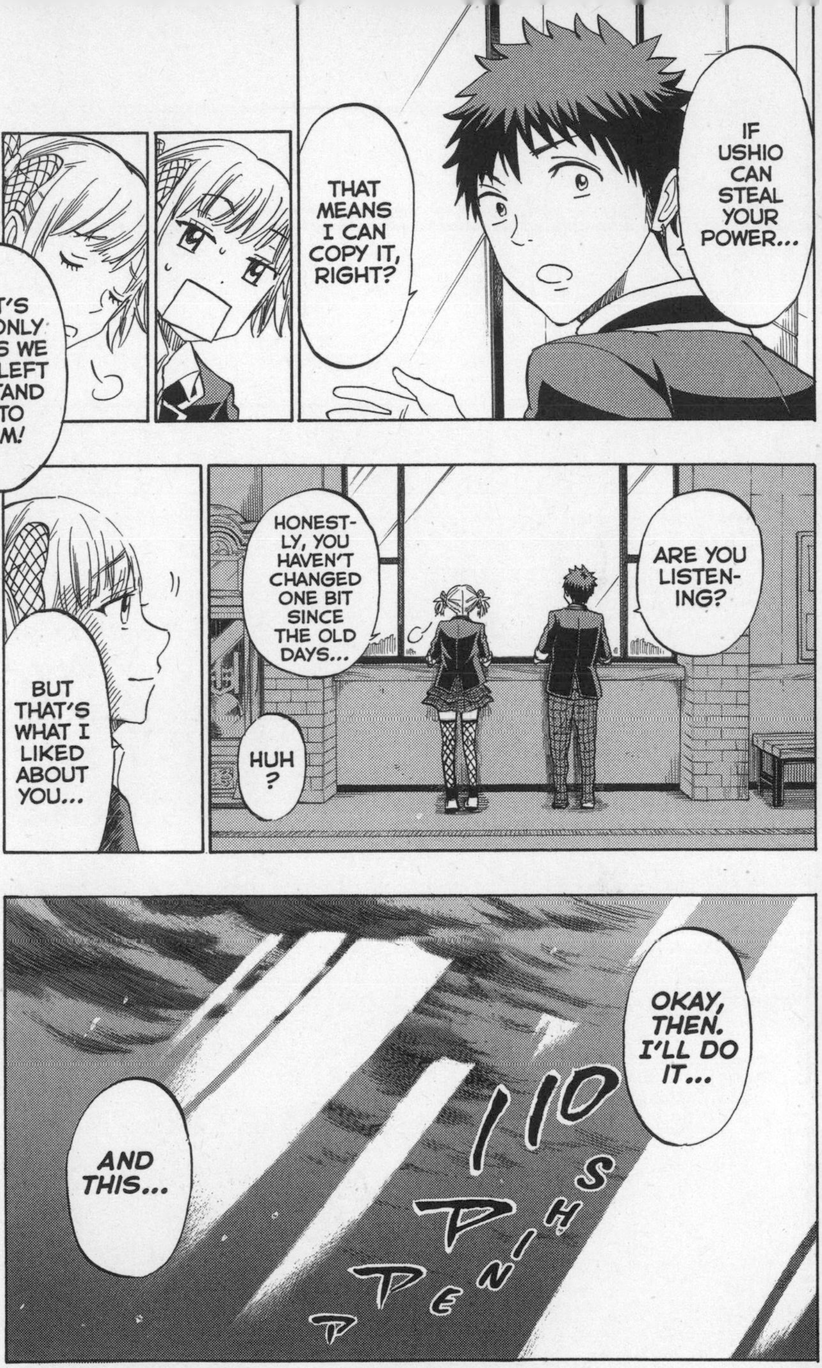
IF USHIO CAN STEAL YOUR POWER...
THAT MEANS I CAN COPY IT, RIGHT?
THAT'S THE ONLY MEANS WE HAVE LEFT TO STAND UP TO THEM!
ARE YOU LISTENING?
HONEST-LY, YOU HAVEN'T CHANGED ONE BIT SINCE THE OLD DAYS...
HUH?
BUT THAT'S WHAT I LIKED ABOUT YOU...
OKAY, THEN. I'LL DO IT...
AND THIS...

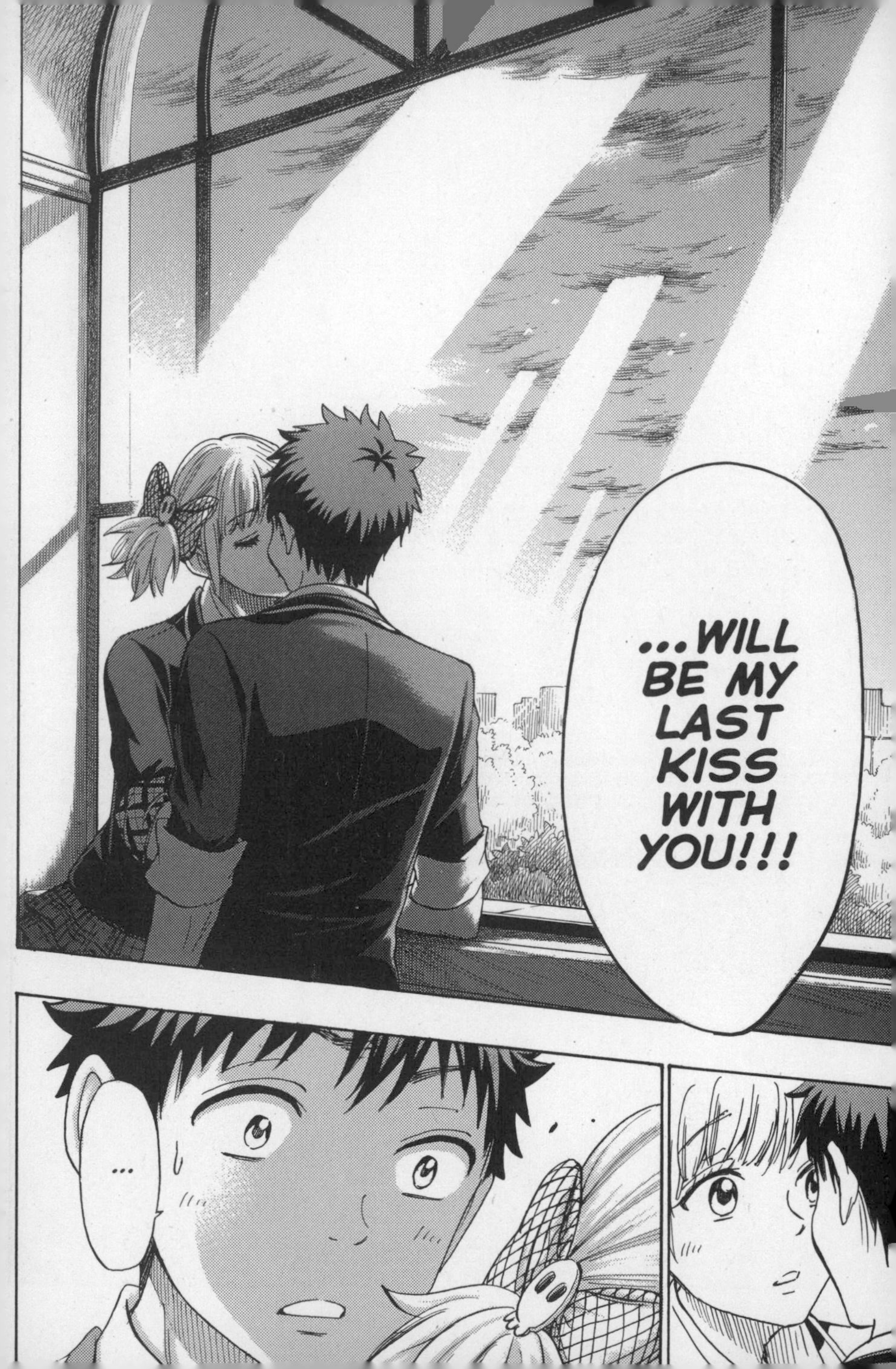
...WILL BE MY LAST KISS WITH YOU!!!
...

CHAPTER 166: Kiss as much as we want!

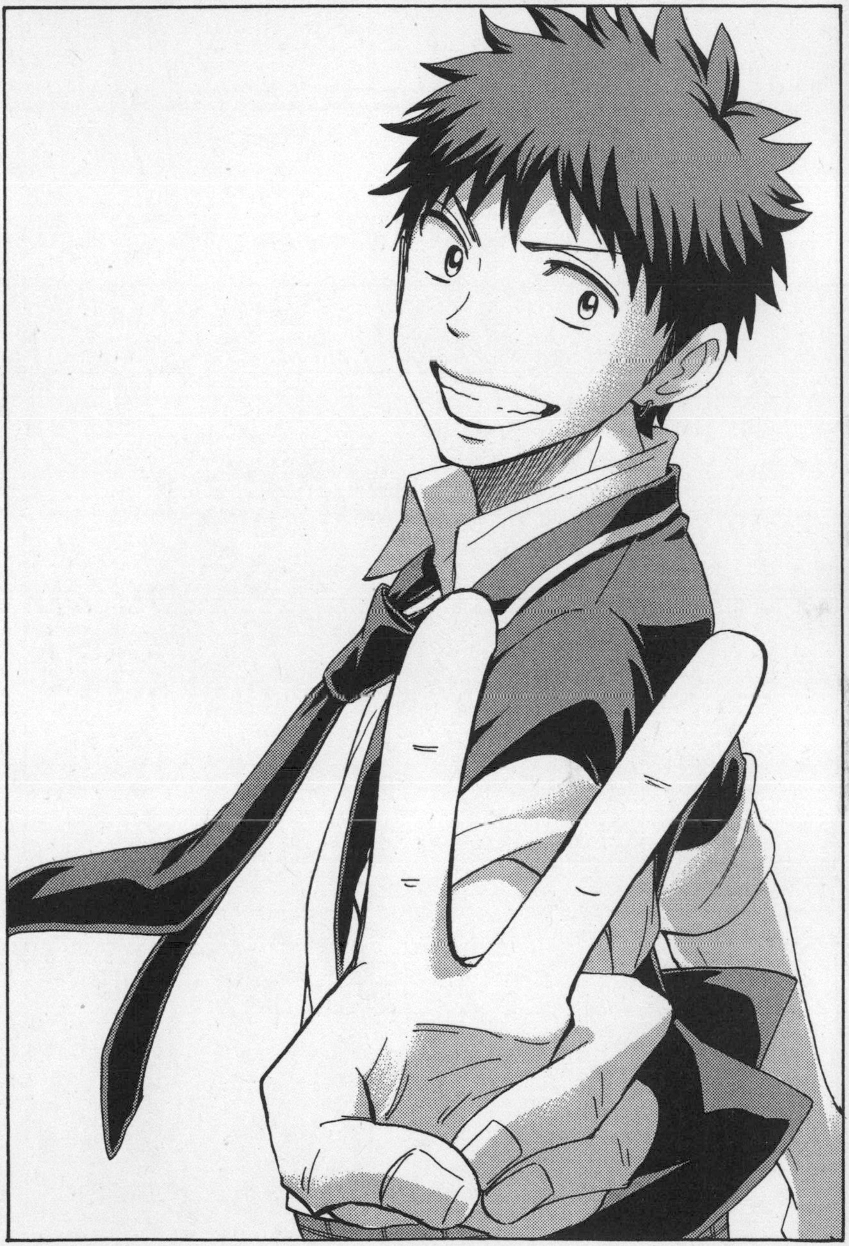

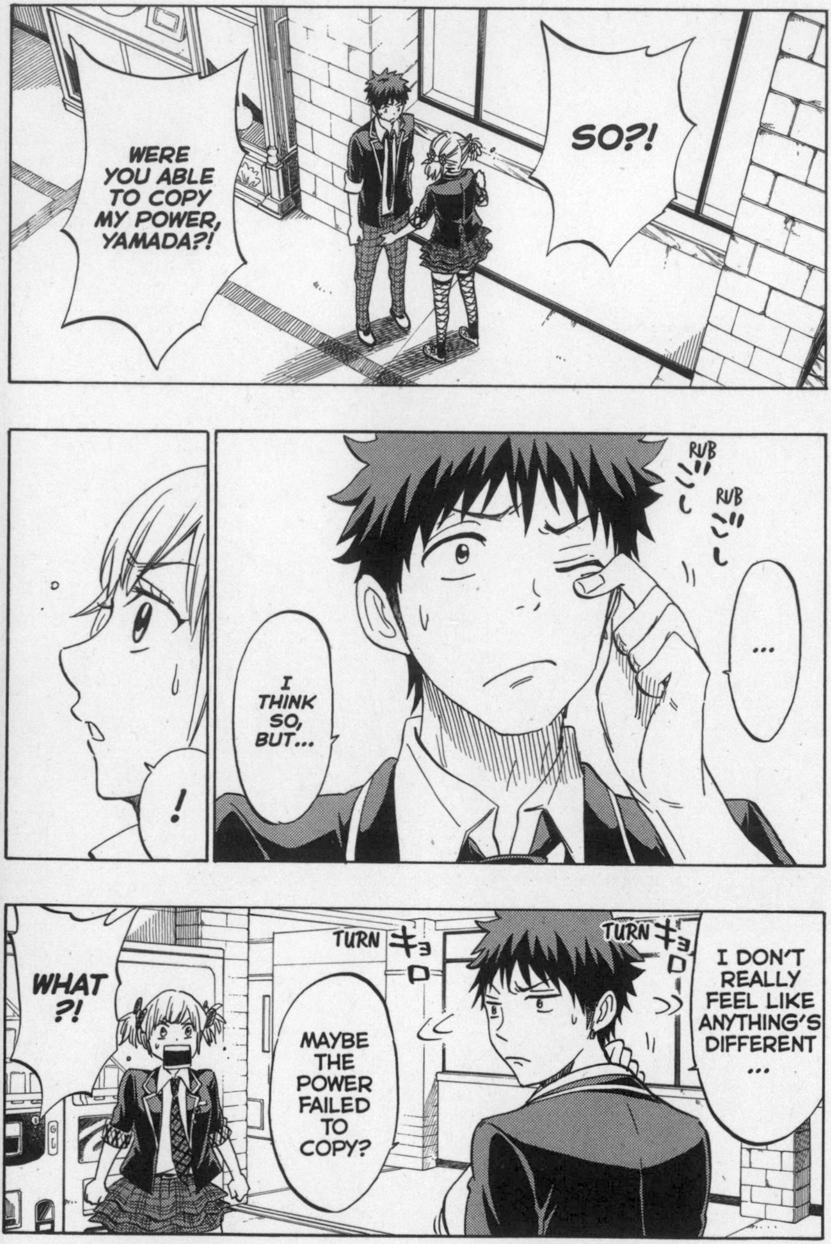
SO?!
WERE YOU ABLE TO COPY MY POWER, YAMADA?!
RUB ゴシ
RUB ゴシ
...
I THINK SO, BUT...
!
I DON'T REALLY FEEL LIKE ANYTHING'S DIFFERENT ...
TURN キョロ
MAYBE THE POWER FAILED TO COPY?
TURN キョロ
WHAT ?!

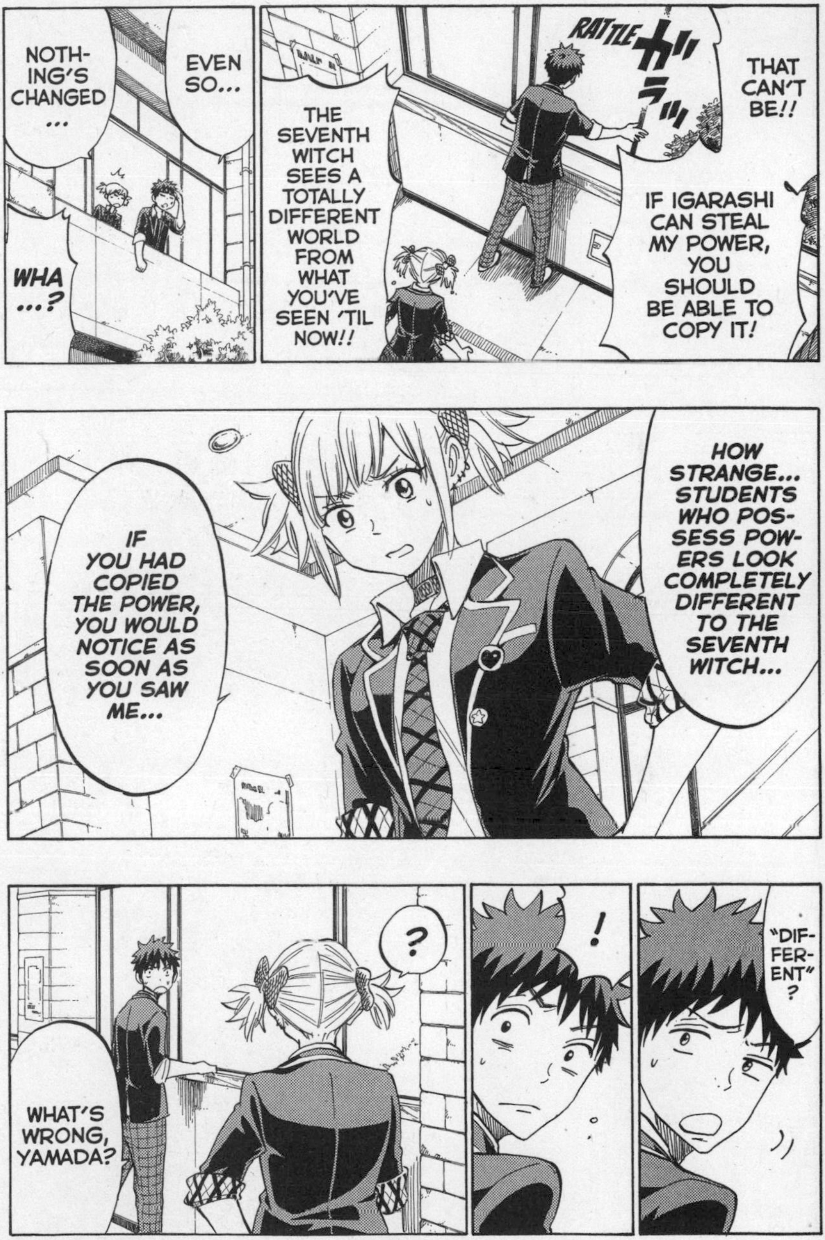
THAT CAN'T BE!!
RATTLE
IF IGARASHI CAN STEAL MY POWER, YOU SHOULD BE ABLE TO COPY IT!
THE SEVENTH WITCH SEES A TOTALLY DIFFERENT WORLD FROM WHAT YOU'VE SEEN 'TIL NOW!!
EVEN SO...
NOTHING'S CHANGED...
WHA...?
HOW STRANGE... STUDENTS WHO POSSESS POWERS LOOK COMPLETELY DIFFERENT TO THE SEVENTH WITCH...
IF YOU HAD COPIED THE POWER, YOU WOULD NOTICE AS SOON AS YOU SAW ME...
"DIFFERENT"?
!
?
WHAT'S WRONG, YAMADA?

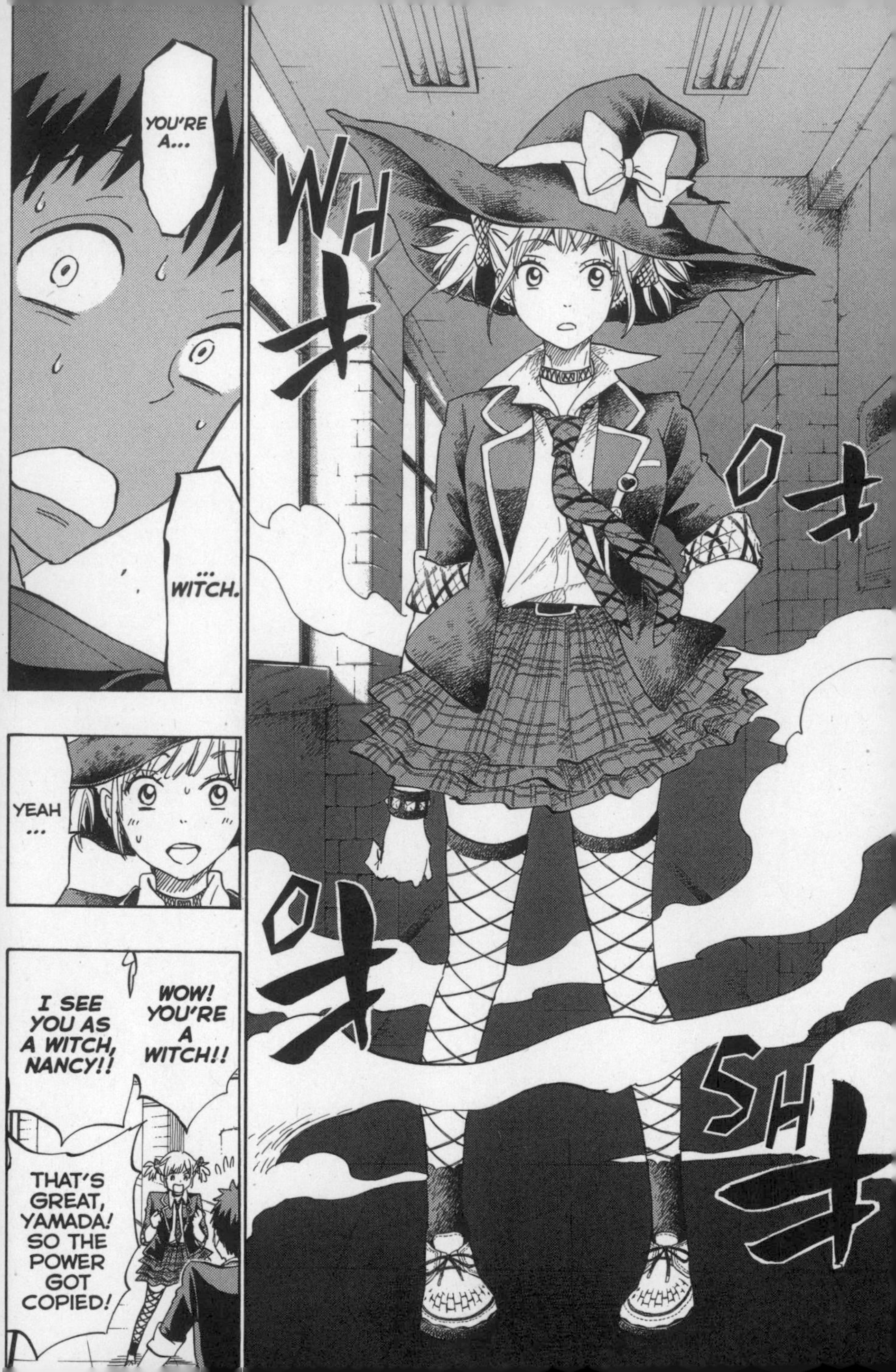
WH
O
O
SH
YOU'RE A...
...WITCH.
YEAH...
WOW! YOU'RE A WITCH!!
I SEE YOU AS A WITCH, NANCY!!
THAT'S GREAT, YAMADA! SO THE POWER GOT COPIED!

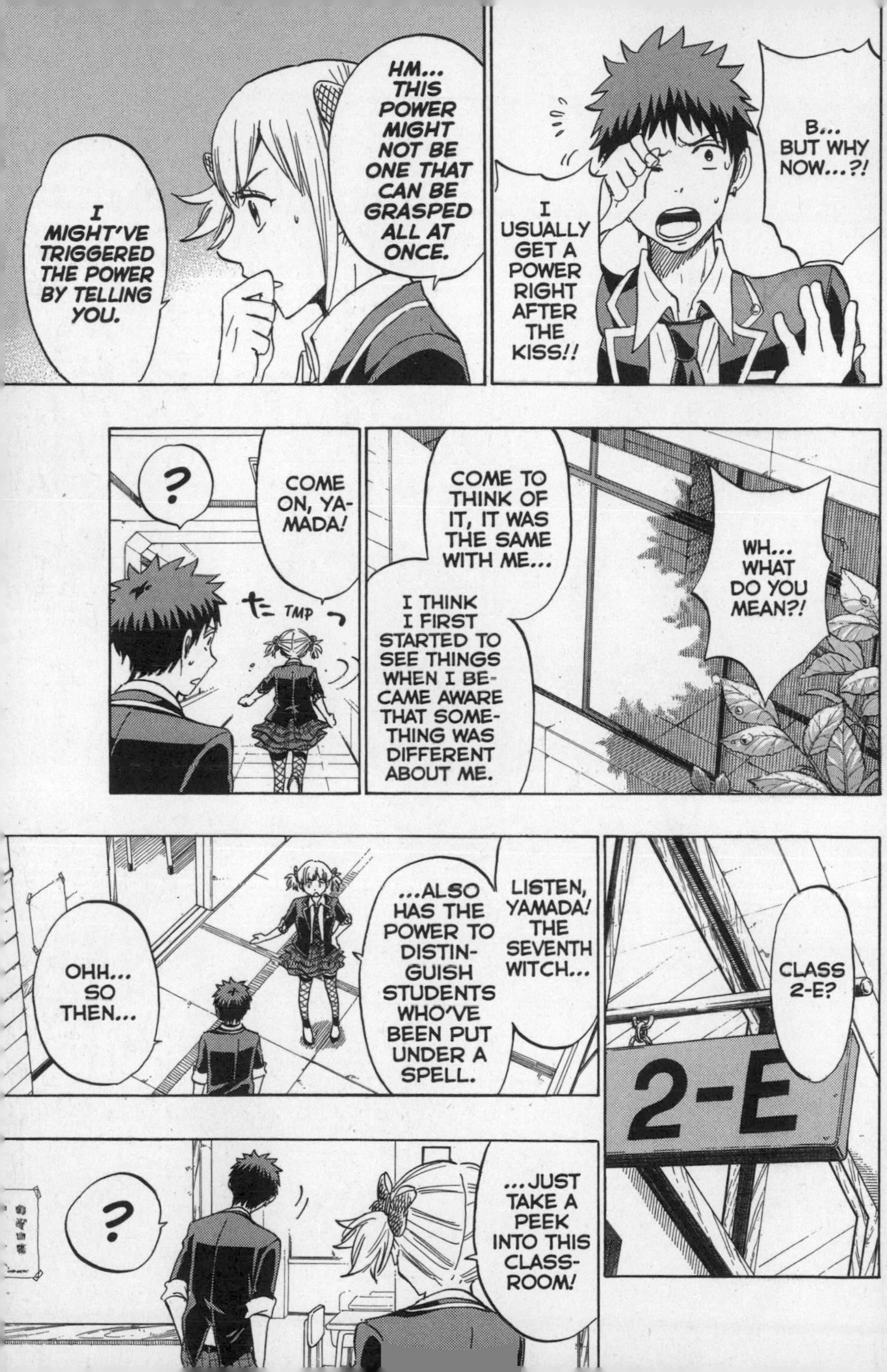

B... BUT WHY NOW...?!
I USUALLY GET A POWER RIGHT AFTER THE KISS!!
HM... THIS POWER MIGHT NOT BE ONE THAT CAN BE GRASPED ALL AT ONCE.
I MIGHT'VE TRIGGERED THE POWER BY TELLING YOU.
WH... WHAT DO YOU MEAN?!
COME TO THINK OF IT, IT WAS THE SAME WITH ME...
I THINK I FIRST STARTED TO SEE THINGS WHEN I BECAME AWARE THAT SOMETHING WAS DIFFERENT ABOUT ME.
COME ON, YAMADA!
TMP
?
CLASS 2-E?
2-E
LISTEN, YAMADA! THE SEVENTH WITCH...
...ALSO HAS THE POWER TO DISTINGUISH STUDENTS WHO'VE BEEN PUT UNDER A SPELL.
OHH... SO THEN...
...JUST TAKE A PEEK INTO THIS CLASSROOM!
?

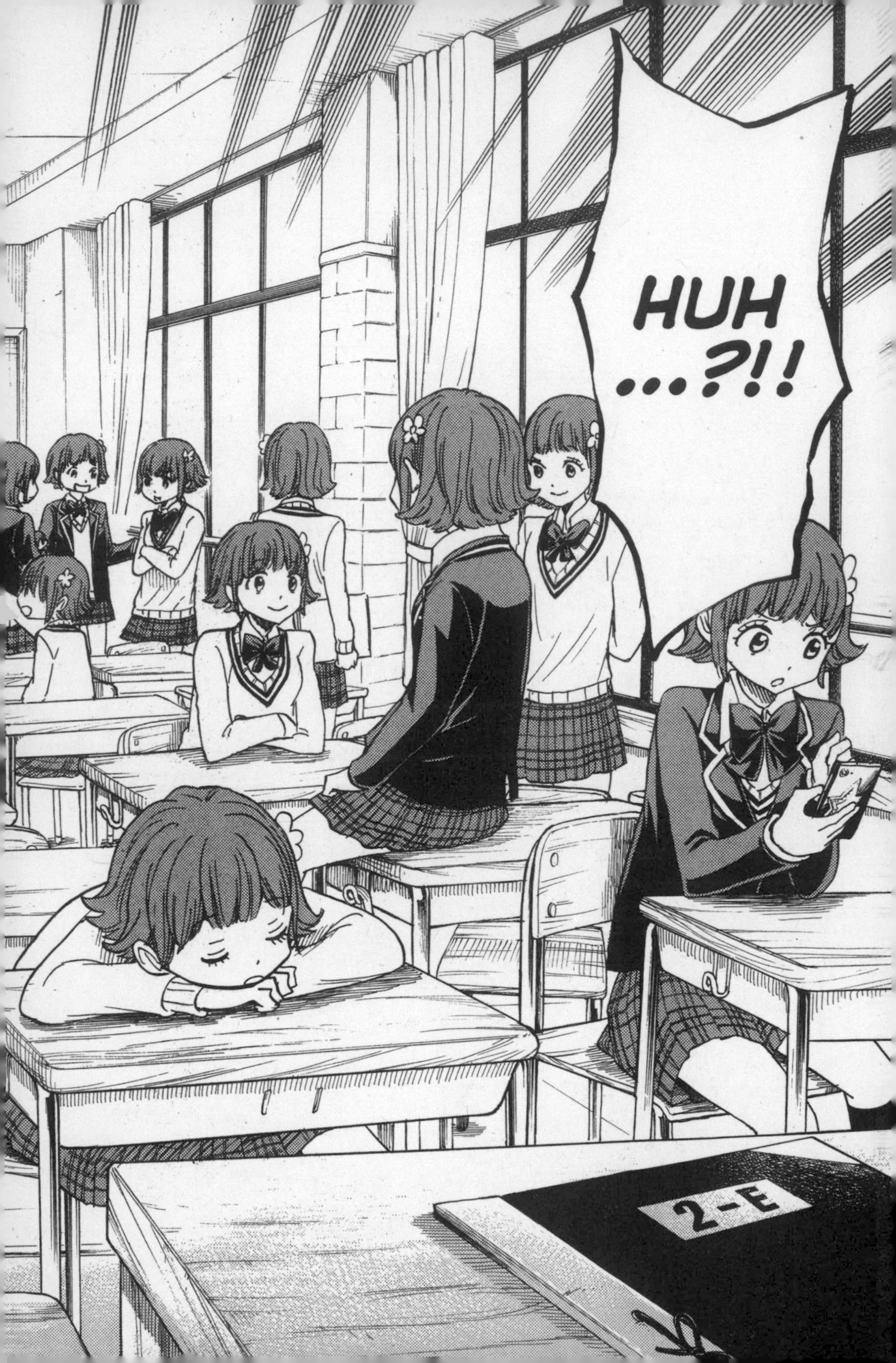
HUH ...?!!
2-E

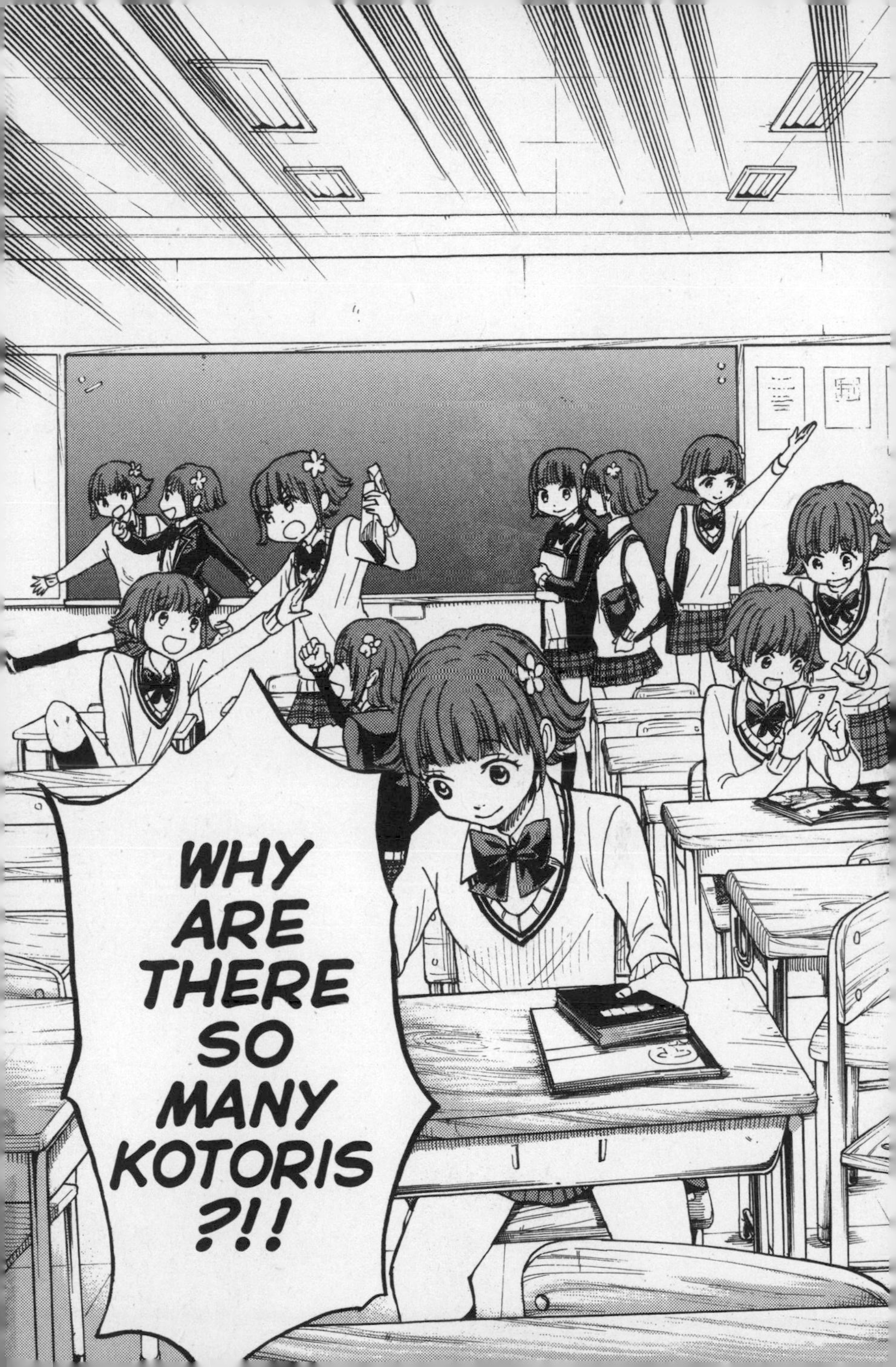
WHY ARE THERE SO MANY KOTORIS ?!!

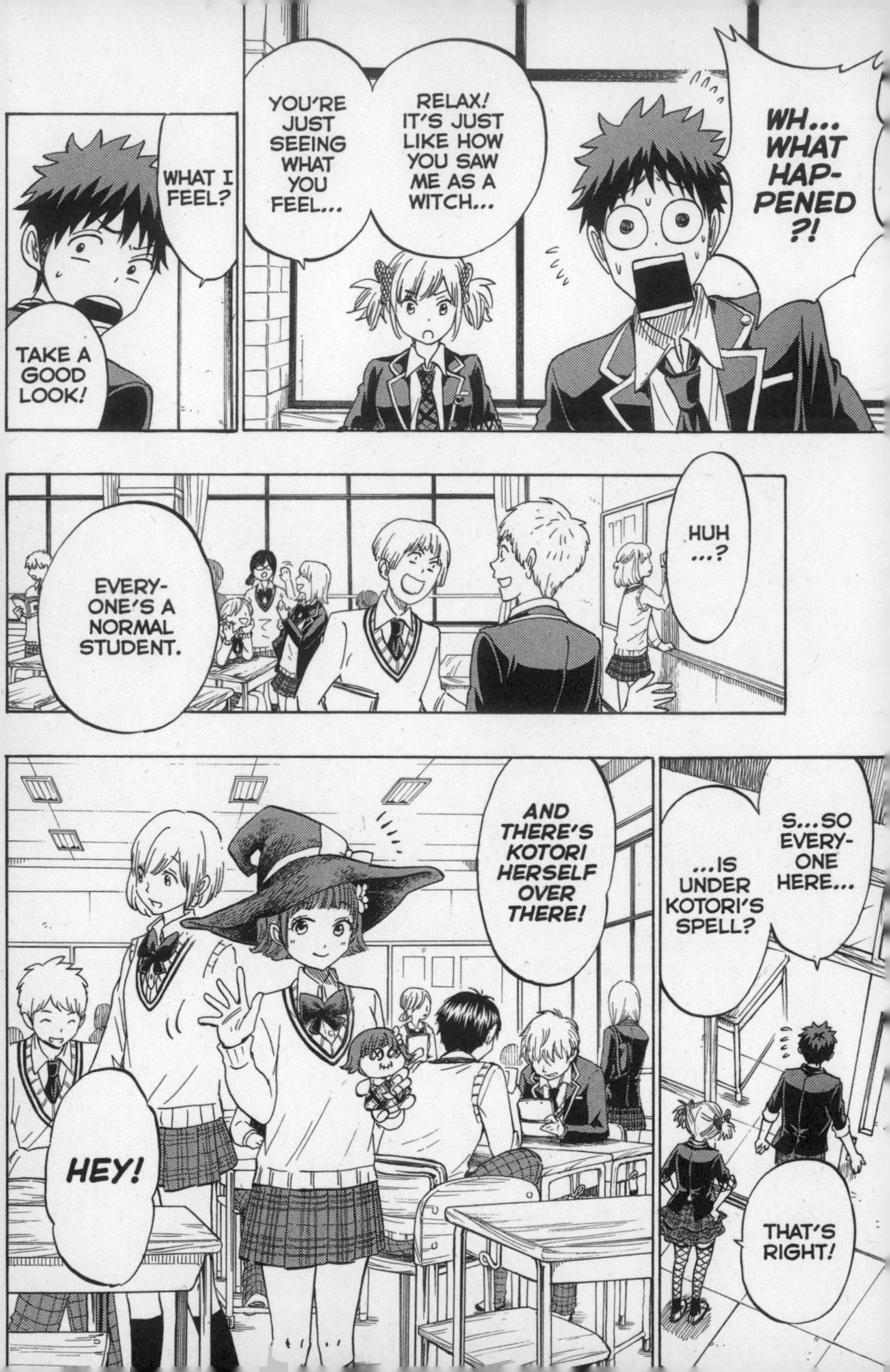
WH... WHAT HAPPENED?!
RELAX! IT'S JUST LIKE HOW YOU SAW ME AS A WITCH...
YOU'RE JUST SEEING WHAT YOU FEEL...
WHAT I FEEL?
TAKE A GOOD LOOK!
HUH ...?
EVERYONE'S A NORMAL STUDENT.
S...SO EVERYONE HERE...
...IS UNDER KOTORI'S SPELL?
THAT'S RIGHT!
AND THERE'S KOTORI HERSELF OVER THERE!
HEY!

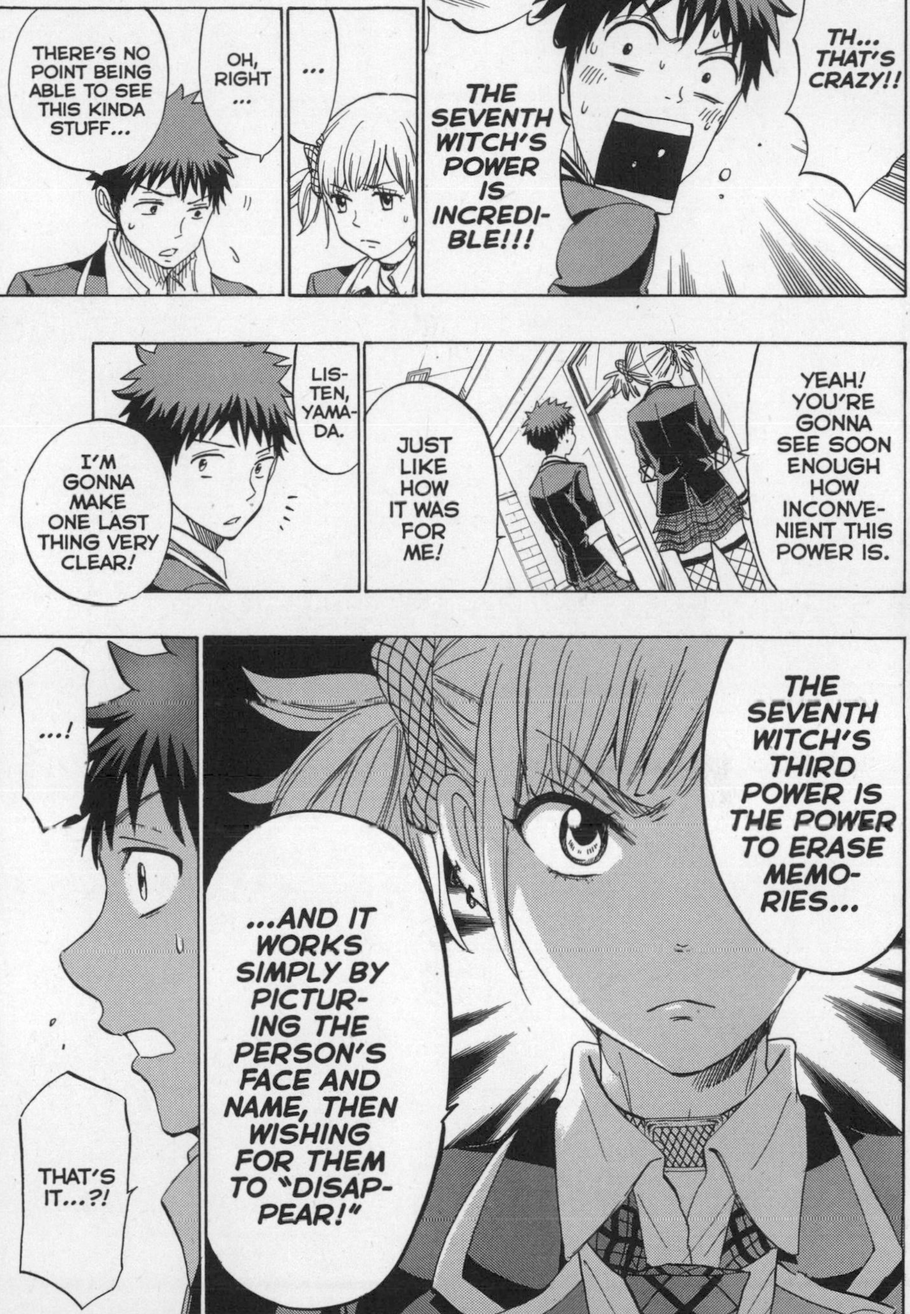
TH... THAT'S CRAZY!!
THE SEVENTH WITCH'S POWER IS INCREDI-BLE!!!
...
OH, RIGHT ...
THERE'S NO POINT BEING ABLE TO SEE THIS KINDA STUFF...
YEAH! YOU'RE GONNA SEE SOON ENOUGH HOW INCONVE-NIENT THIS POWER IS.
JUST LIKE HOW IT WAS FOR ME!
LIS-TEN, YAMA-DA.
I'M GONNA MAKE ONE LAST THING VERY CLEAR!
THE SEVENTH WITCH'S THIRD POWER IS THE POWER TO ERASE MEMO-RIES...
...AND IT WORKS SIMPLY BY PICTUR-ING THE PERSON'S FACE AND NAME, THEN WISHING FOR THEM TO "DISAP-PEAR!"
...!
THAT'S IT...?!

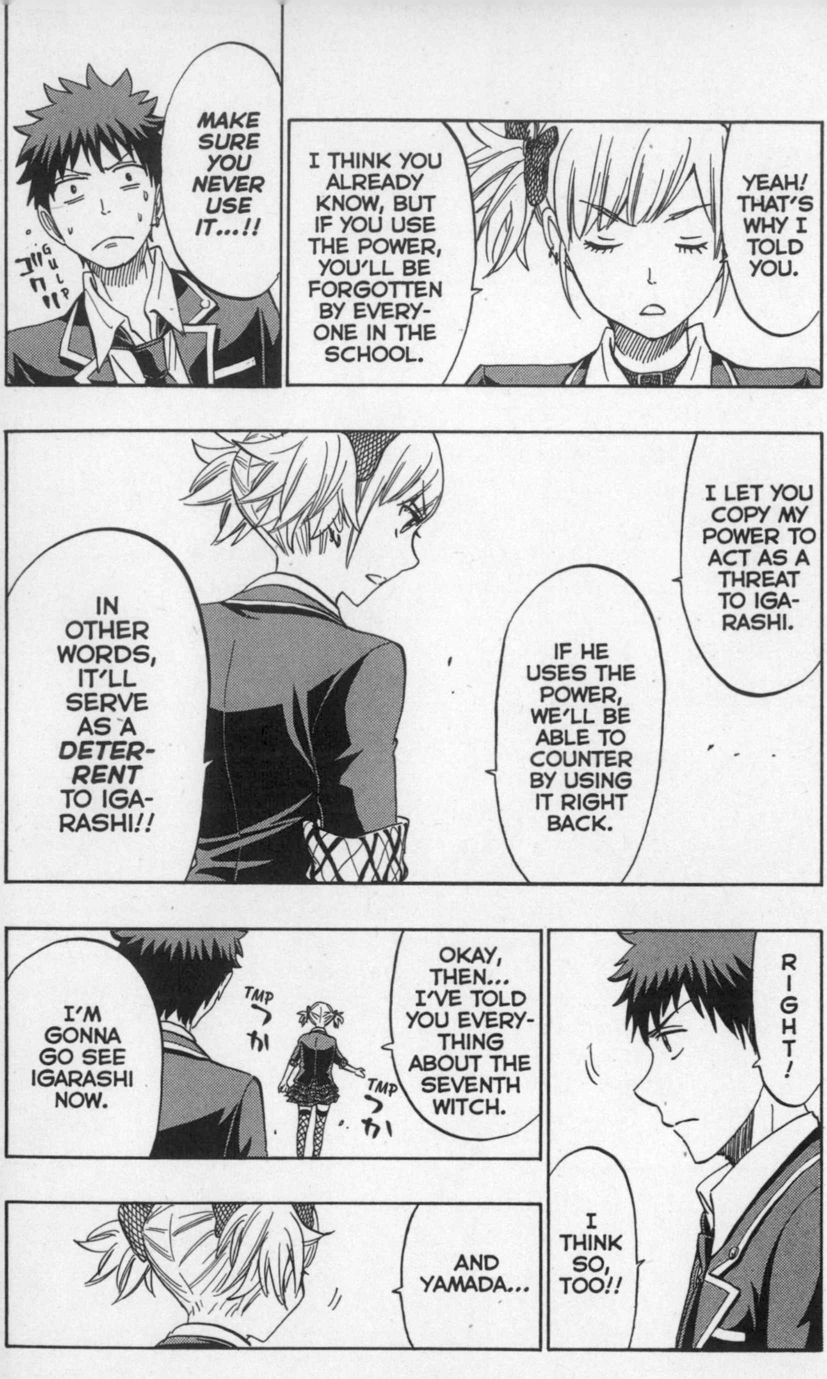
YEAH! THAT'S WHY I TOLD YOU.
I THINK YOU ALREADY KNOW, BUT IF YOU USE THE POWER, YOU'LL BE FORGOTTEN BY EVERYONE IN THE SCHOOL.
MAKE SURE YOU NEVER USE IT...!!
GULP
I LET YOU COPY MY POWER TO ACT AS A THREAT TO IGARASHI.
IF HE USES THE POWER, WE'LL BE ABLE TO COUNTER BY USING IT RIGHT BACK.
IN OTHER WORDS, IT'LL SERVE AS A *DETERRENT* TO IGARASHI!!
RIGHT!
I THINK SO, TOO!!
OKAY, THEN... I'VE TOLD YOU EVERYTHING ABOUT THE SEVENTH WITCH.
TMP
TMP
I'M GONNA GO SEE IGARASHI NOW.
AND YAMADA...

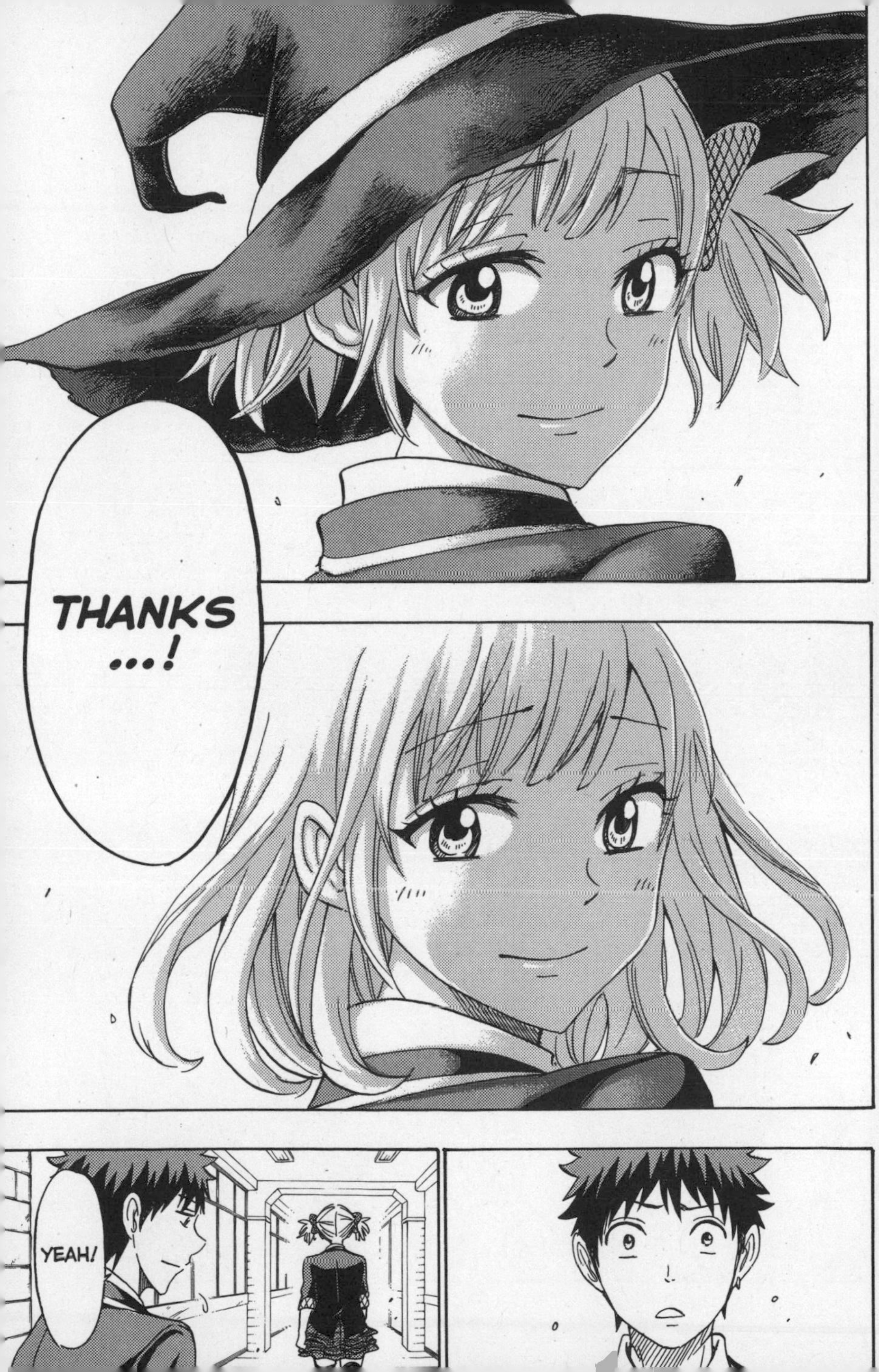
THANKS ...!
YEAH!

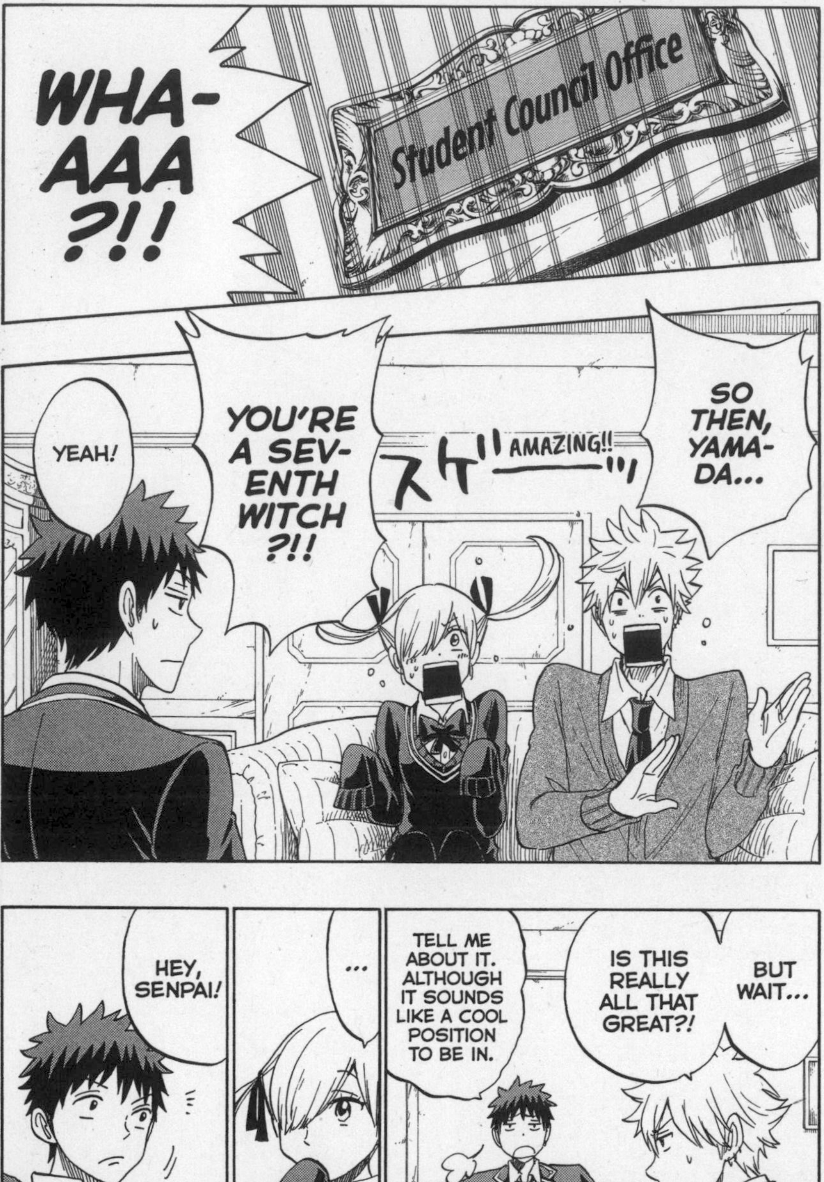

Student Council Office
WHA-AAA?!!
SO THEN, YAMA-DA...
スゲーッ AMAZING!!
YOU'RE A SEV-ENTH WITCH?!!
YEAH!
BUT WAIT...
IS THIS REALLY ALL THAT GREAT?!
TELL ME ABOUT IT. ALTHOUGH IT SOUNDS LIKE A COOL POSITION TO BE IN.
...
HEY, SENPAI!

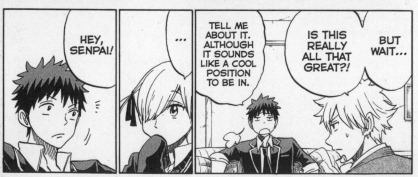

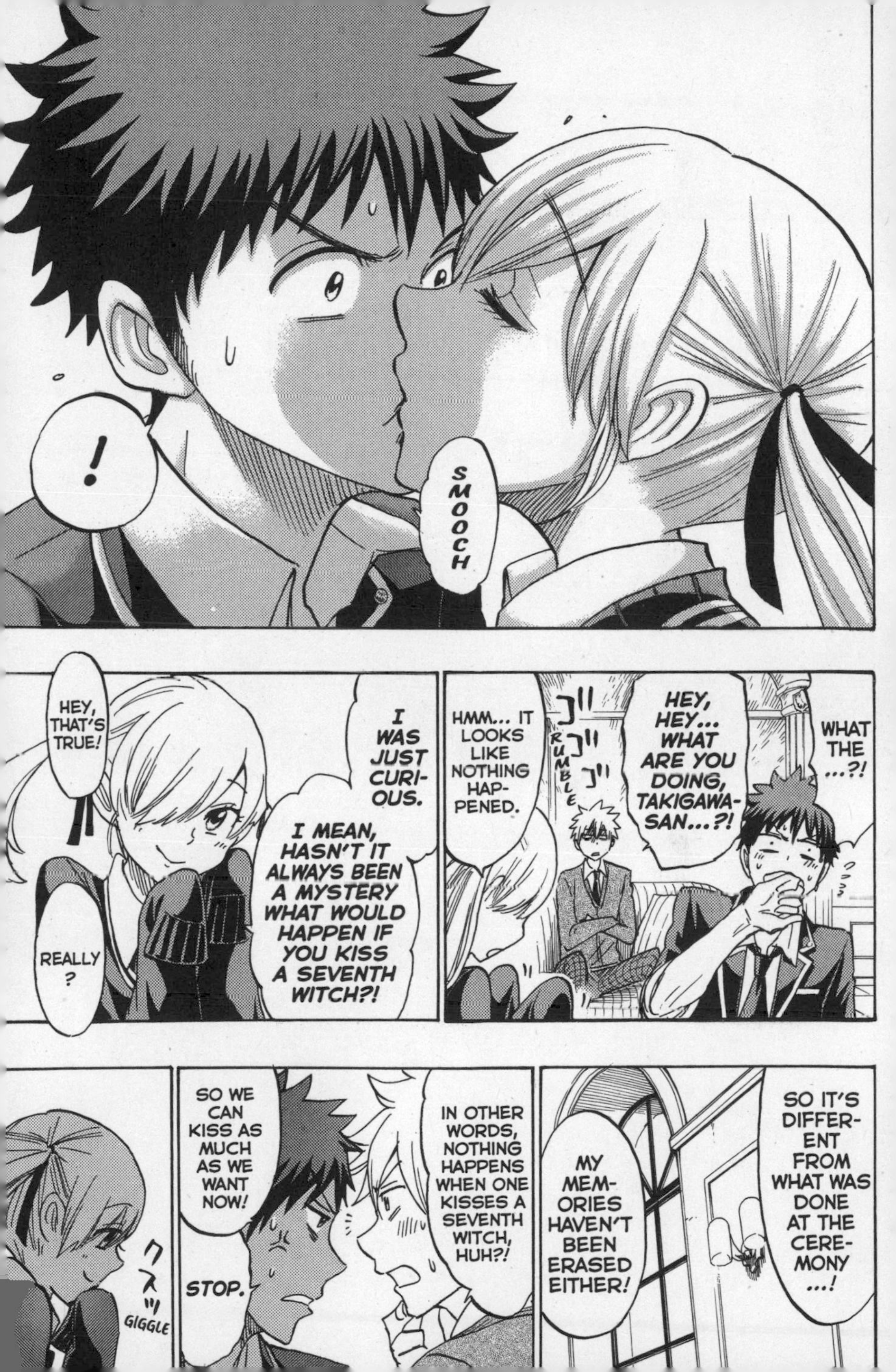
SMOOCH
!
WHAT THE ...?!
HEY, HEY... WHAT ARE YOU DOING, TAKIGAWA-SAN...?!
RUMBLE
HMM... IT LOOKS LIKE NOTHING HAPPENED.
I WAS JUST CURIOUS.
I MEAN, HASN'T IT ALWAYS BEEN A MYSTERY WHAT WOULD HAPPEN IF YOU KISS A SEVENTH WITCH?!
HEY, THAT'S TRUE!
REALLY?
SO IT'S DIFFERENT FROM WHAT WAS DONE AT THE CEREMONY...!
MY MEMORIES HAVEN'T BEEN ERASED EITHER!
IN OTHER WORDS, NOTHING HAPPENS WHEN ONE KISSES A SEVENTH WITCH, HUH?!
SO WE CAN KISS AS MUCH AS WE WANT NOW!
STOP.
クスッ
GIGGLE

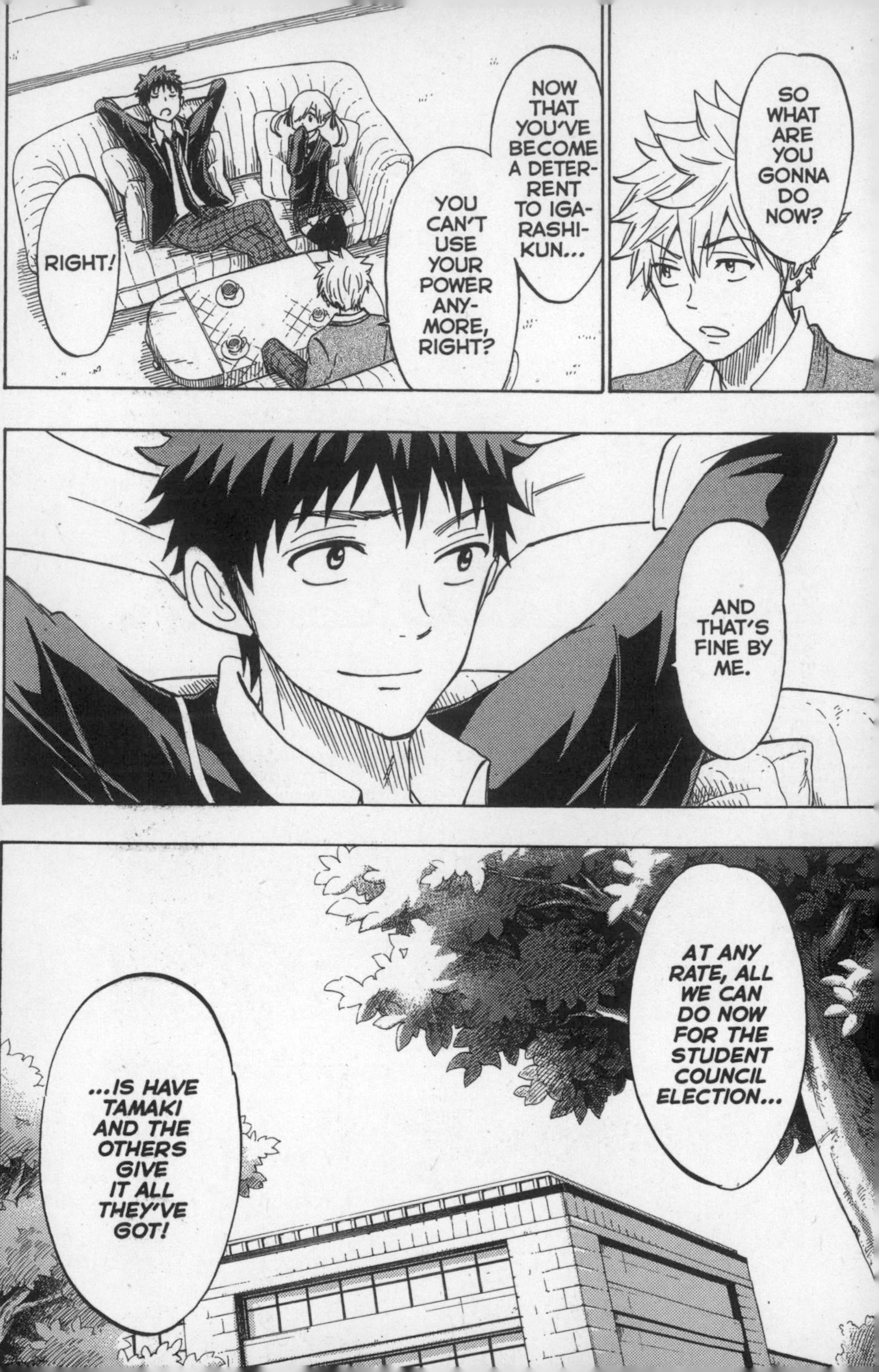
SO WHAT ARE YOU GONNA DO NOW?
NOW THAT YOU'VE BECOME A DETERRENT TO IGARASHI-KUN...
YOU CAN'T USE YOUR POWER ANYMORE, RIGHT?
RIGHT!
AND THAT'S FINE BY ME.
AT ANY RATE, ALL WE CAN DO NOW FOR THE STUDENT COUNCIL ELECTION...
...IS HAVE TAMAKI AND THE OTHERS GIVE IT ALL THEY'VE GOT!

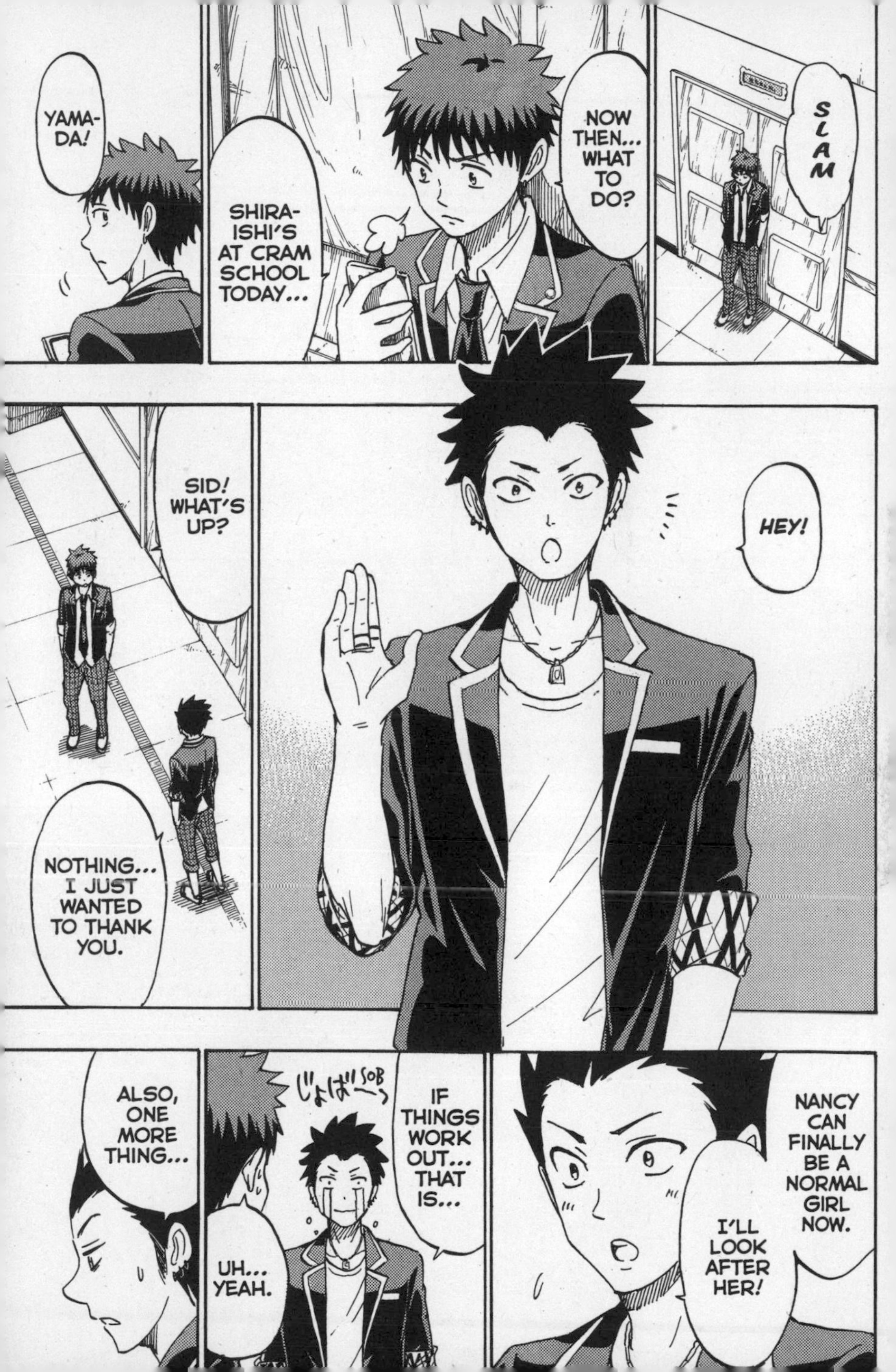
SLAM
NOW THEN... WHAT TO DO?
SHIRAISHI'S AT CRAM SCHOOL TODAY...
YAMADA!
HEY!
SID! WHAT'S UP?
NOTHING... I JUST WANTED TO THANK YOU.
NANCY CAN FINALLY BE A NORMAL GIRL NOW.
I'LL LOOK AFTER HER!
IF THINGS WORK OUT... THAT IS...
じょば〜 SOB
UH... YEAH.
ALSO, ONE MORE THING...

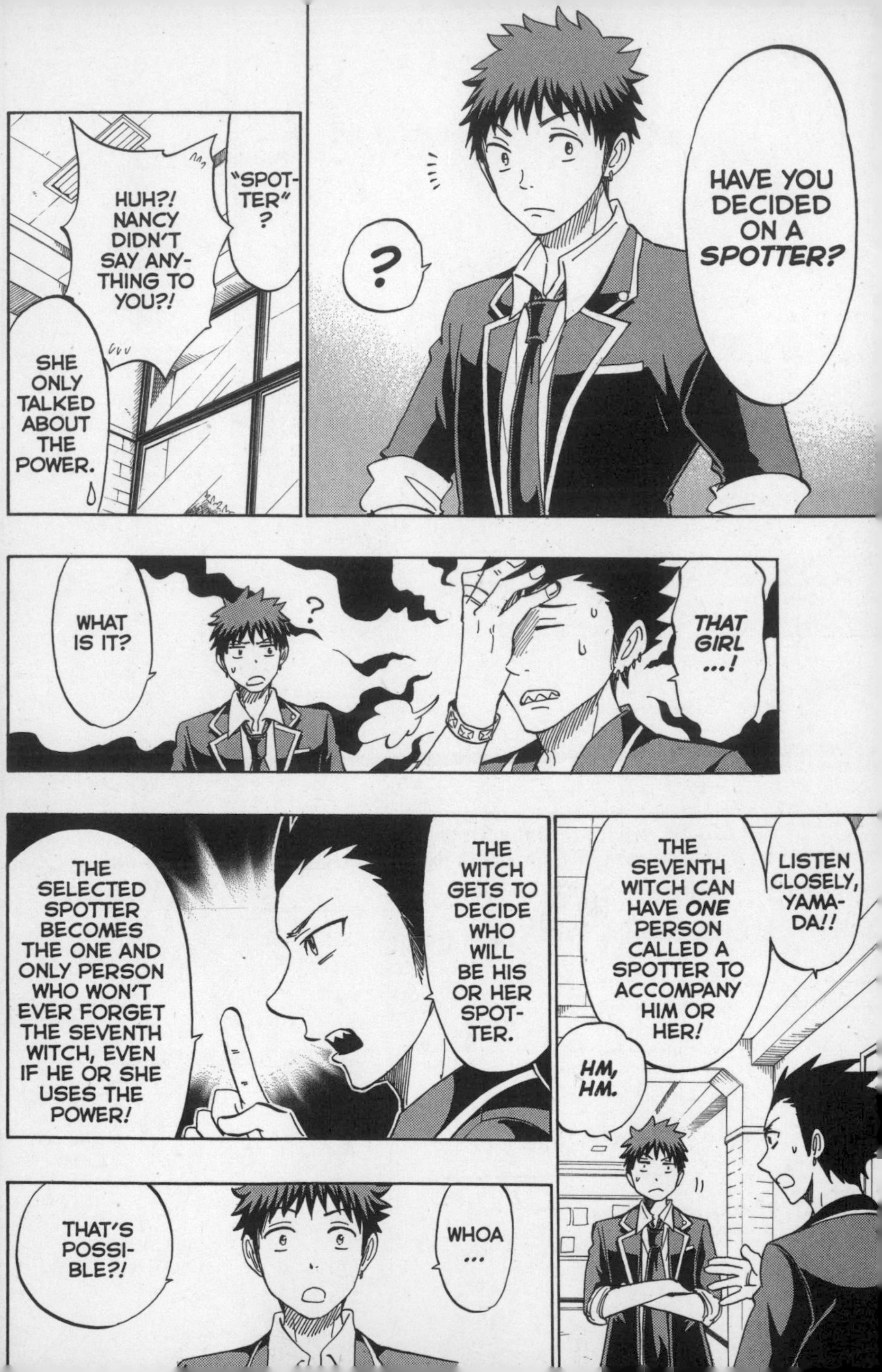
HAVE YOU DECIDED ON A SPOTTER?
?
"SPOTTER"?
HUH?! NANCY DIDN'T SAY ANYTHING TO YOU?!
SHE ONLY TALKED ABOUT THE POWER.
THAT GIRL ...!
WHAT IS IT?
LISTEN CLOSELY, YAMADA!!
THE SEVENTH WITCH CAN HAVE ONE PERSON CALLED A SPOTTER TO ACCOMPANY HIM OR HER!
HM, HM.
THE WITCH GETS TO DECIDE WHO WILL BE HIS OR HER SPOTTER.
THE SELECTED SPOTTER BECOMES THE ONE AND ONLY PERSON WHO WON'T EVER FORGET THE SEVENTH WITCH, EVEN IF HE OR SHE USES THE POWER!
WHOA ...
THAT'S POSSIBLE?!

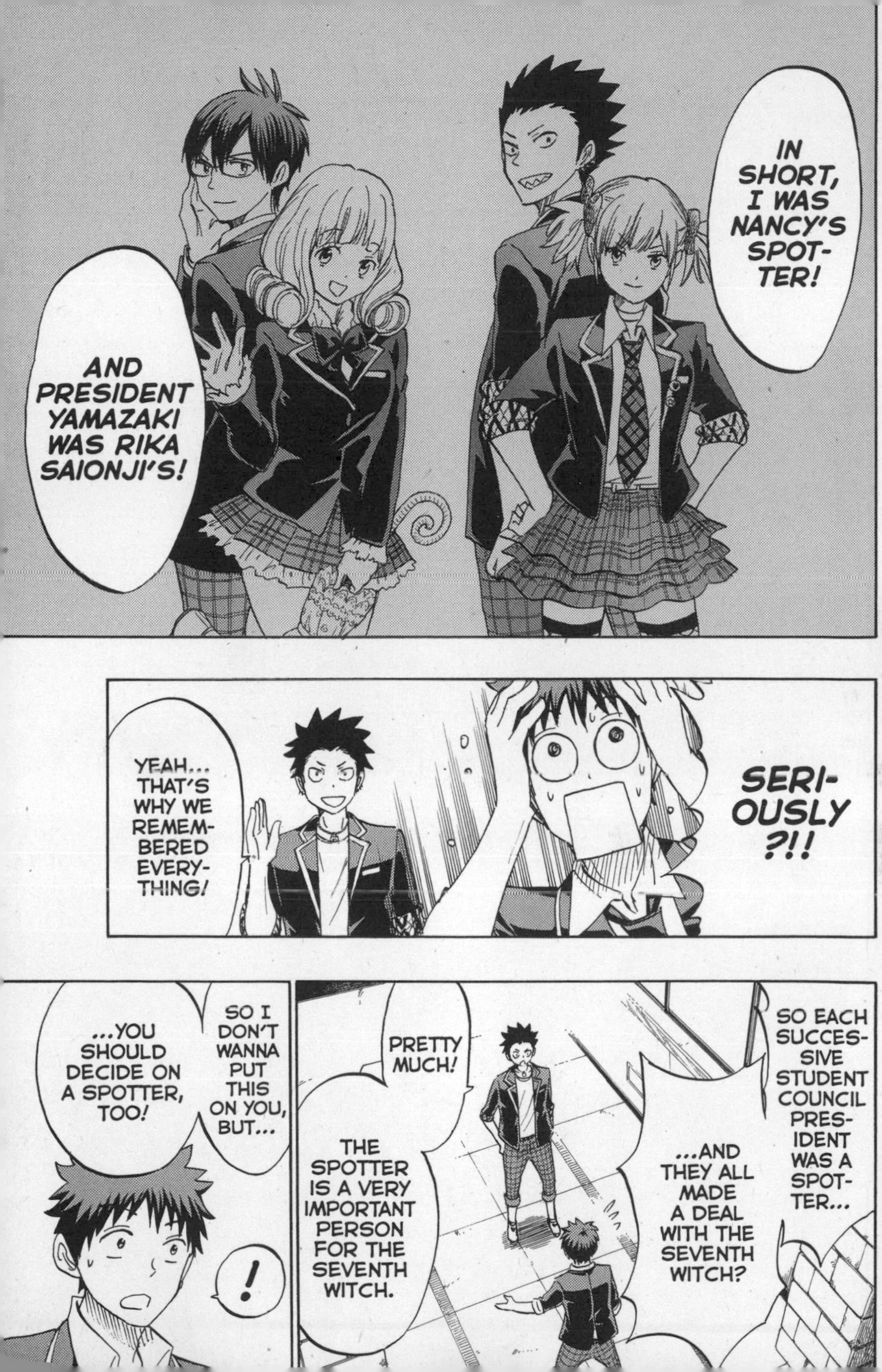
IN SHORT, I WAS NANCY'S SPOTTER!
AND PRESIDENT YAMAZAKI WAS RIKA SAIONJI'S!
SERIOUSLY?!!
YEAH... THAT'S WHY WE REMEMBERED EVERYTHING!
SO EACH SUCCESSIVE STUDENT COUNCIL PRESIDENT WAS A SPOTTER...
...AND THEY ALL MADE A DEAL WITH THE SEVENTH WITCH?
PRETTY MUCH!
THE SPOTTER IS A VERY IMPORTANT PERSON FOR THE SEVENTH WITCH.
SO I DON'T WANNA PUT THIS ON YOU, BUT...
...YOU SHOULD DECIDE ON A SPOTTER, TOO!
!

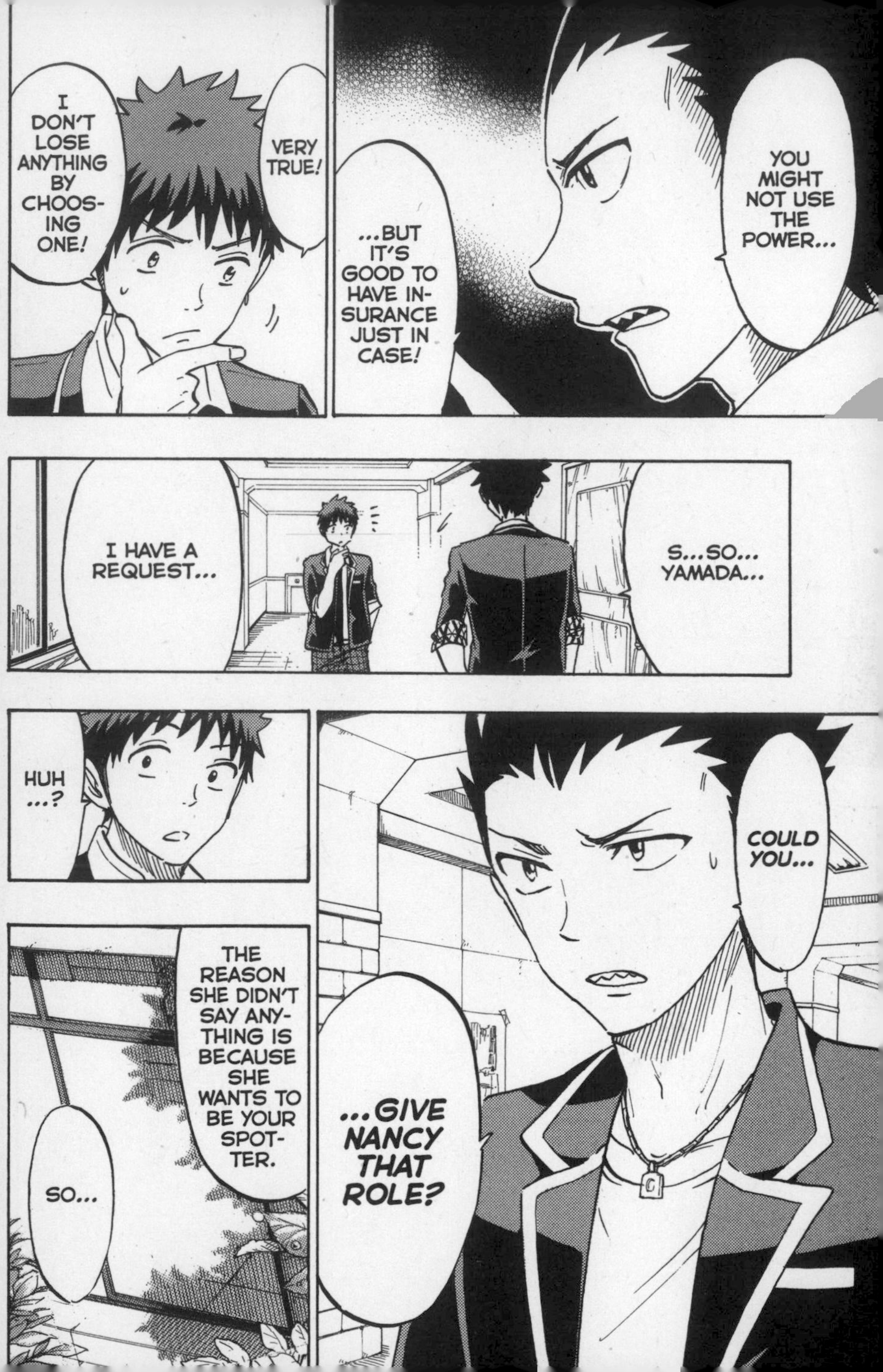
YOU MIGHT NOT USE THE POWER...
...BUT IT'S GOOD TO HAVE INSURANCE JUST IN CASE!
VERY TRUE!
I DON'T LOSE ANYTHING BY CHOOSING ONE!
S...SO... YAMADA...
I HAVE A REQUEST...
COULD YOU...
...GIVE NANCY THAT ROLE?
HUH ...?
THE REASON SHE DIDN'T SAY ANYTHING IS BECAUSE SHE WANTS TO BE YOUR SPOTTER.
SO...

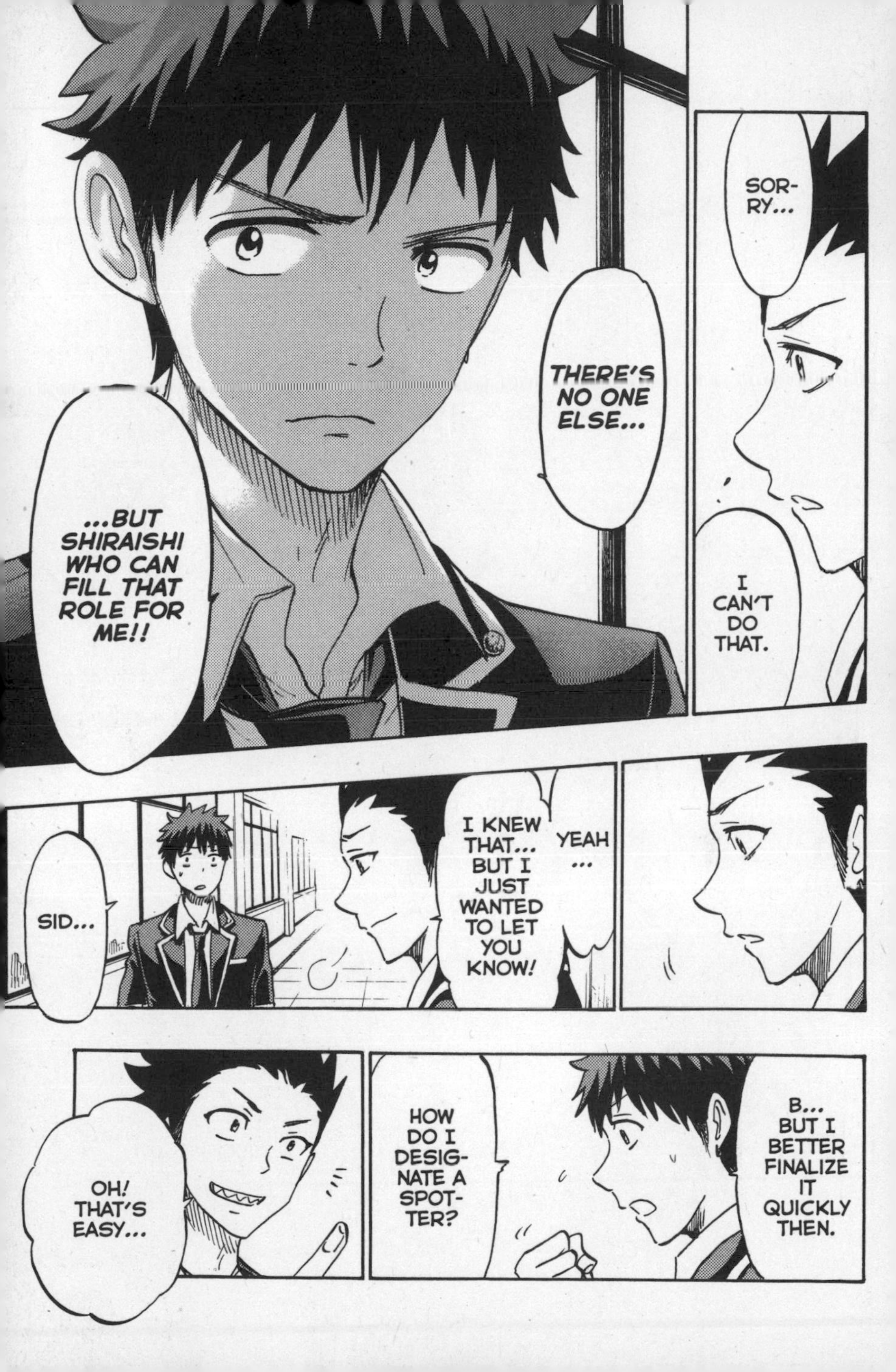
THERE'S NO ONE ELSE...
...BUT SHIRAISHI WHO CAN FILL THAT ROLE FOR ME!!
SOR-RY...
I CAN'T DO THAT.
YEAH...
I KNEW THAT... BUT I JUST WANTED TO LET YOU KNOW!
SID...
B... BUT I BETTER FINALIZE IT QUICKLY THEN.
HOW DO I DESIGNATE A SPOTTER?
OH! THAT'S EASY...

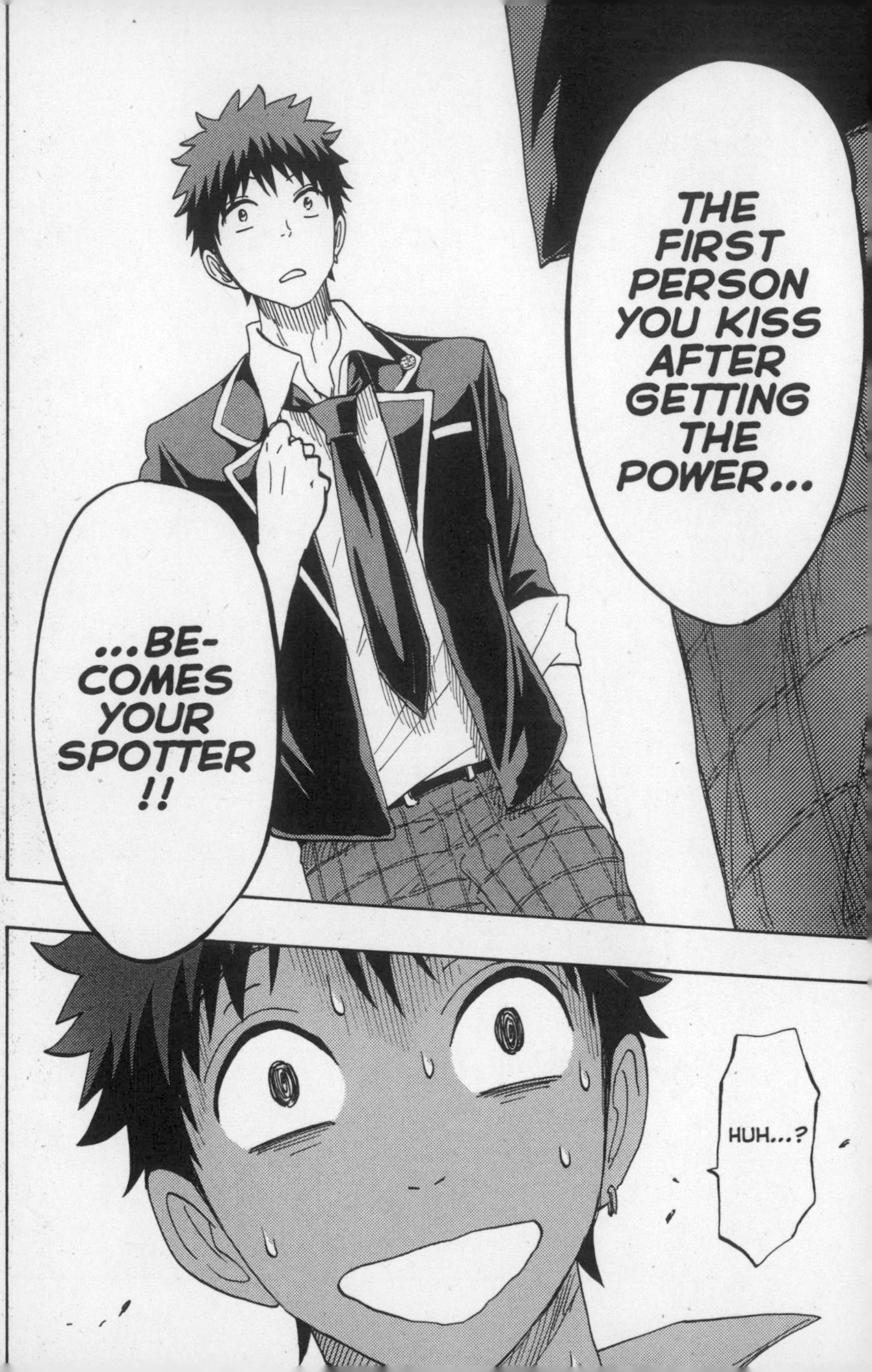
THE FIRST PERSON YOU KISS AFTER GETTING THE POWER...
...BE-COMES YOUR SPOTTER!!
HUH...?

CHAPTER 167: It's like I became Senpai's wife!

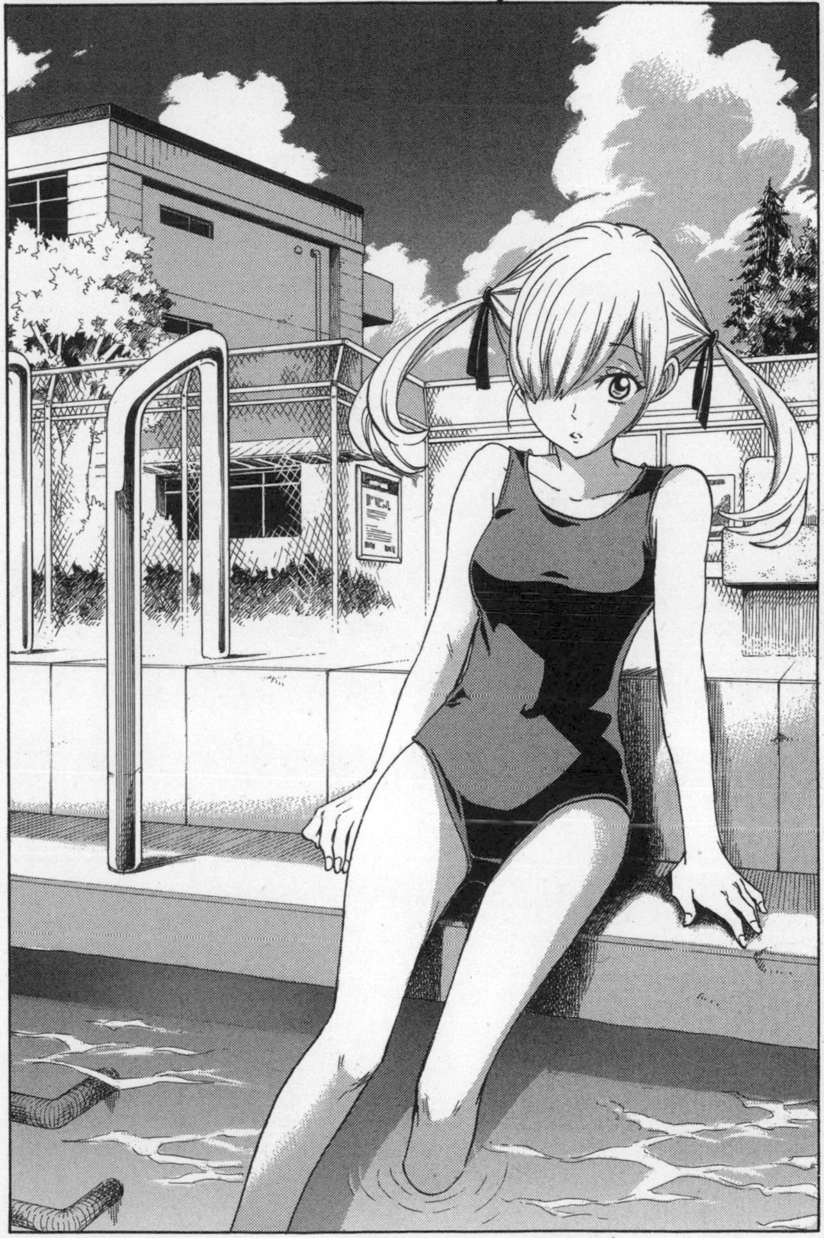

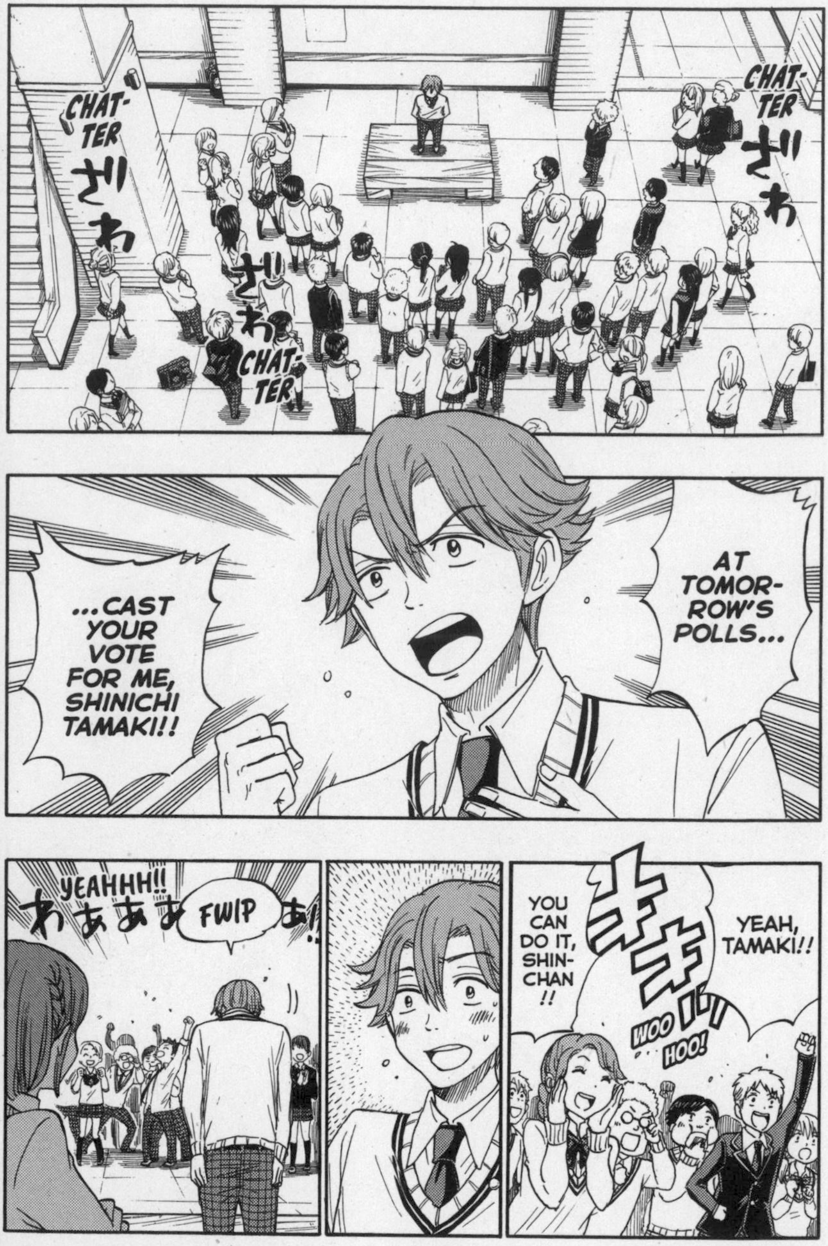
CHAT-TER
ざわ
CHAT-TER
ざわ
ざわ
CHAT-TER
AT TOMORROW'S POLLS...
...CAST YOUR VOTE FOR ME, SHINICHI TAMAKI!!
YEAH, TAMAKI!!
キキ!!
WOO HOO!
YOU CAN DO IT, SHIN-CHAN!!
YEAHHH!!
わあああ
あ!!
FWIP

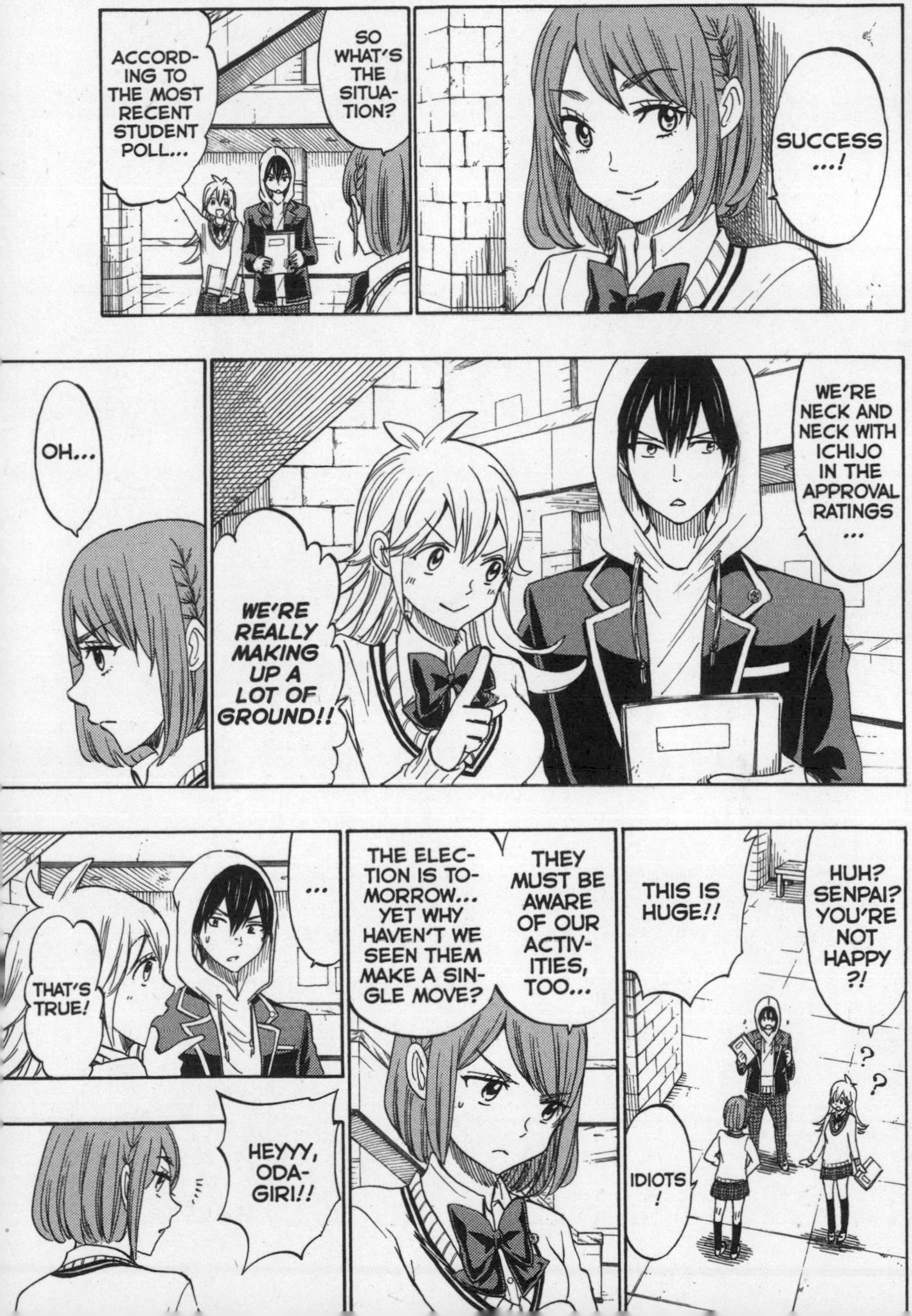
SUCCESS...!
SO WHAT'S THE SITUATION?
ACCORDING TO THE MOST RECENT STUDENT POLL...
WE'RE NECK AND NECK WITH ICHIJO IN THE APPROVAL RATINGS...
WE'RE REALLY MAKING UP A LOT OF GROUND!!
OH...
HUH? SENPAI? YOU'RE NOT HAPPY?!
THIS IS HUGE!!
IDIOTS!
THEY MUST BE AWARE OF OUR ACTIVITIES, TOO...
THE ELECTION IS TOMORROW... YET WHY HAVEN'T WE SEEN THEM MAKE A SINGLE MOVE?
...
THAT'S TRUE!
HEYYY, ODAGIRI!!

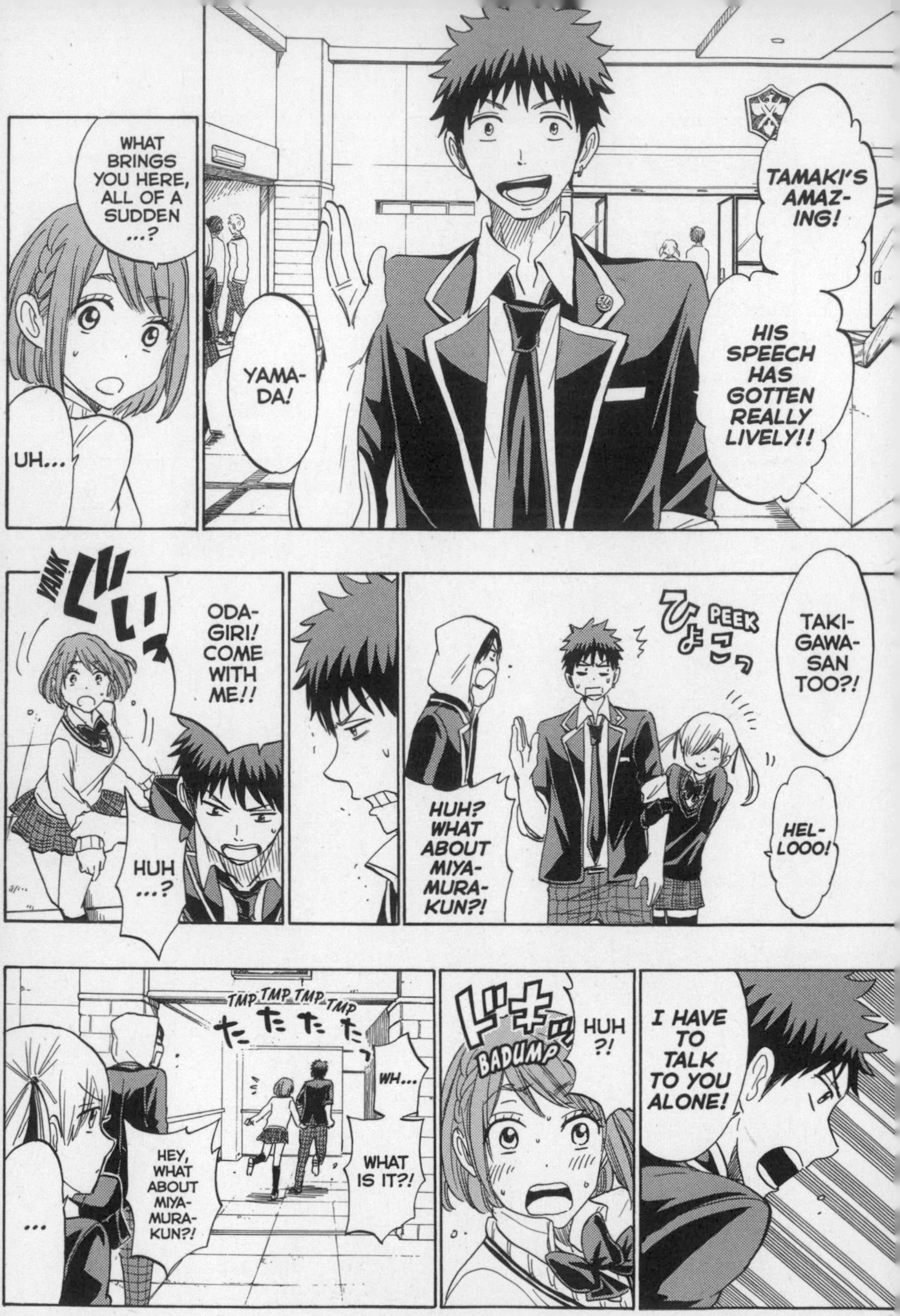
TAMAKI'S AMAZ-ING!
HIS SPEECH HAS GOTTEN REALLY LIVELY!!
YAMA-DA!
WHAT BRINGS YOU HERE, ALL OF A SUDDEN ...?
UH...
TAKI-GAWA-SAN TOO?!
ひょこっ
PEEK
HEL-LOOO!
HUH? WHAT ABOUT MIYA-MURA-KUN?!
ODA-GIRI! COME WITH ME!!
じいっ
YANK
HUH ...?
I HAVE TO TALK TO YOU ALONE!
HUH ?!
ドキッ
BADUMP
たたたたっ
TMP TMP TMP TMP
WH...
WHAT IS IT?!
HEY, WHAT ABOUT MIYA-MURA-KUN?!
...

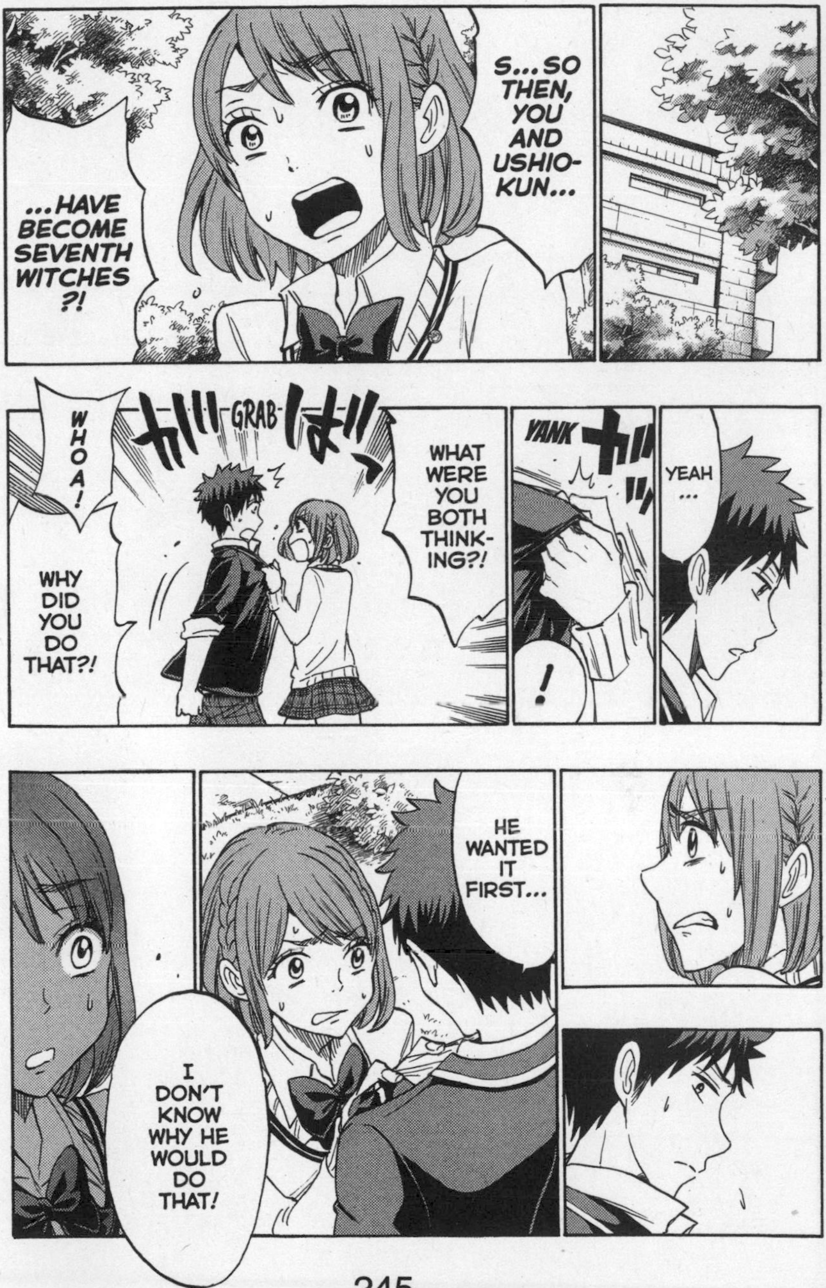
S...SO THEN, YOU AND USHIO-KUN...
...HAVE BECOME SEVENTH WITCHES?!
YEAH...
YANK
!
WHAT WERE YOU BOTH THINKING?!
GRAB
WHOA!
WHY DID YOU DO THAT?!
HE WANTED IT FIRST...
I DON'T KNOW WHY HE WOULD DO THAT!

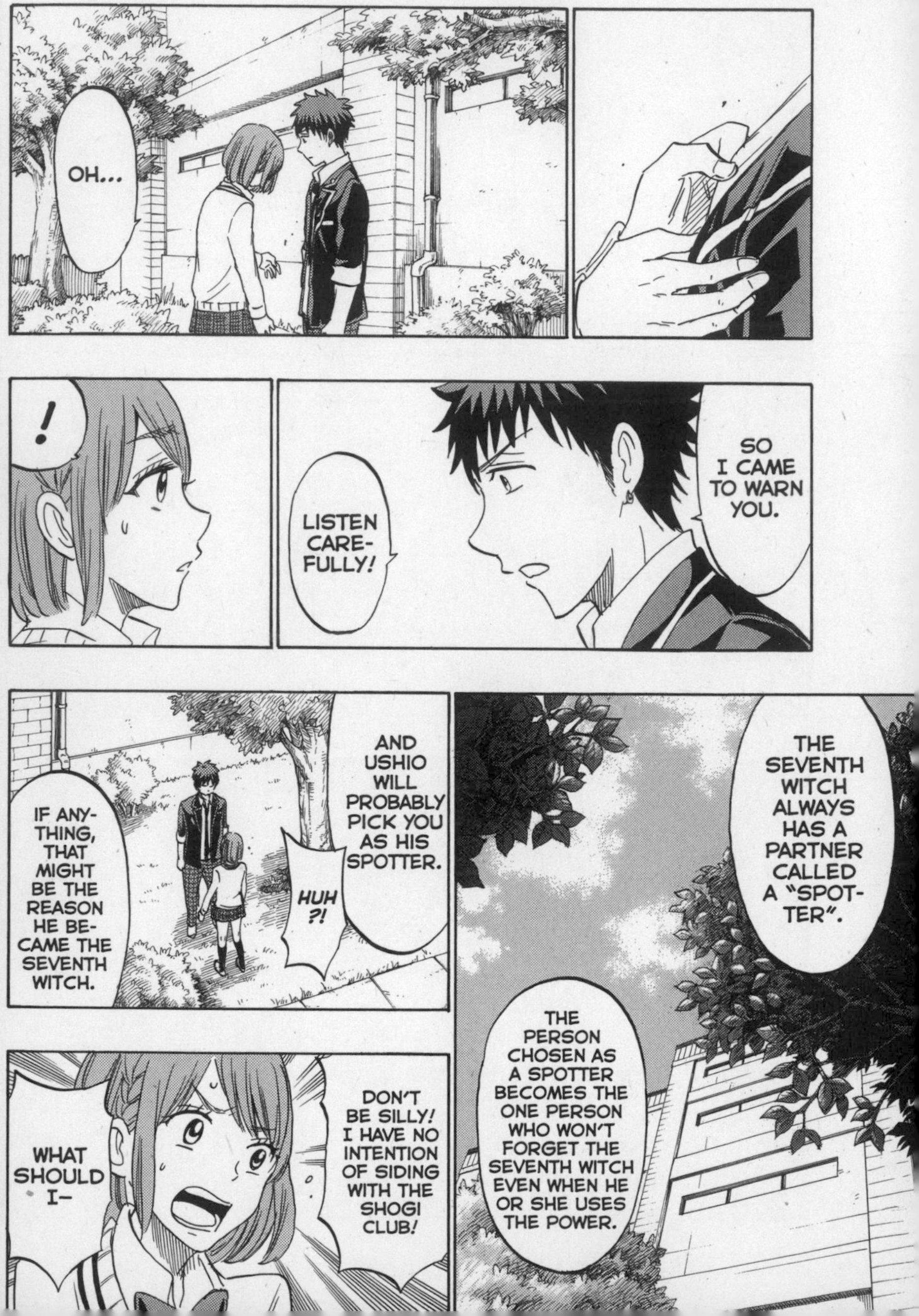
OH...
SO I CAME TO WARN YOU.
LISTEN CAREFULLY!
!
THE SEVENTH WITCH ALWAYS HAS A PARTNER CALLED A "SPOTTER".
THE PERSON CHOSEN AS A SPOTTER BECOMES THE ONE PERSON WHO WON'T FORGET THE SEVENTH WITCH EVEN WHEN HE OR SHE USES THE POWER.
AND USHIO WILL PROBABLY PICK YOU AS HIS SPOTTER.
HUH?!
IF ANYTHING, THAT MIGHT BE THE REASON HE BECAME THE SEVENTH WITCH.
DON'T BE SILLY! I HAVE NO INTENTION OF SIDING WITH THE SHOGI CLUB!
WHAT SHOULD I–

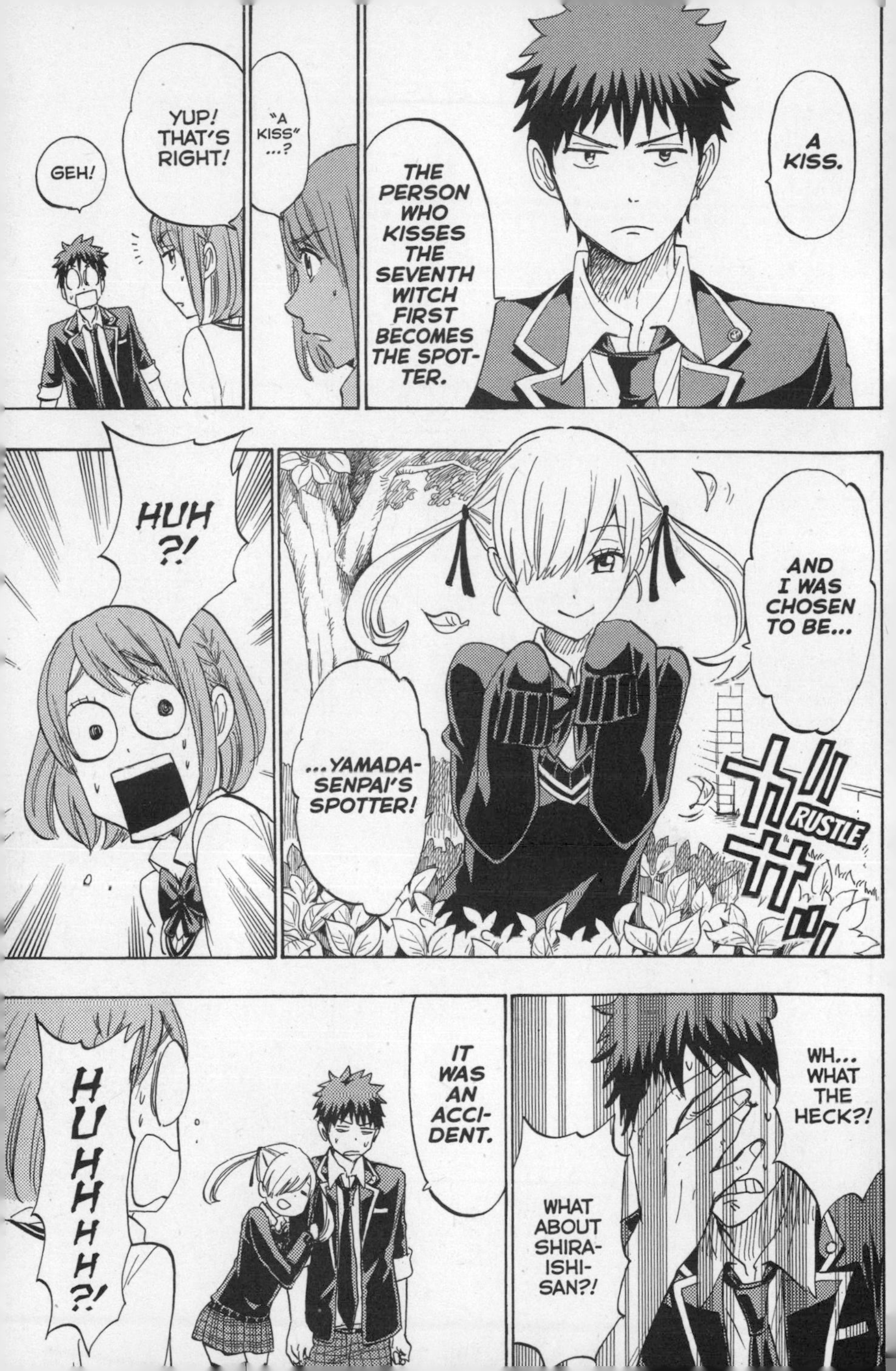
A KISS.
THE PERSON WHO KISSES THE SEVENTH WITCH FIRST BECOMES THE SPOTTER.
"A KISS" ...?
YUP! THAT'S RIGHT!
GEH!
AND I WAS CHOSEN TO BE...
...YAMADA-SENPAI'S SPOTTER!
RUSTLE
HUH?!
WH... WHAT THE HECK?!
WHAT ABOUT SHIRAISHI-SAN?!
IT WAS AN ACCIDENT.
HUHHHHH?!

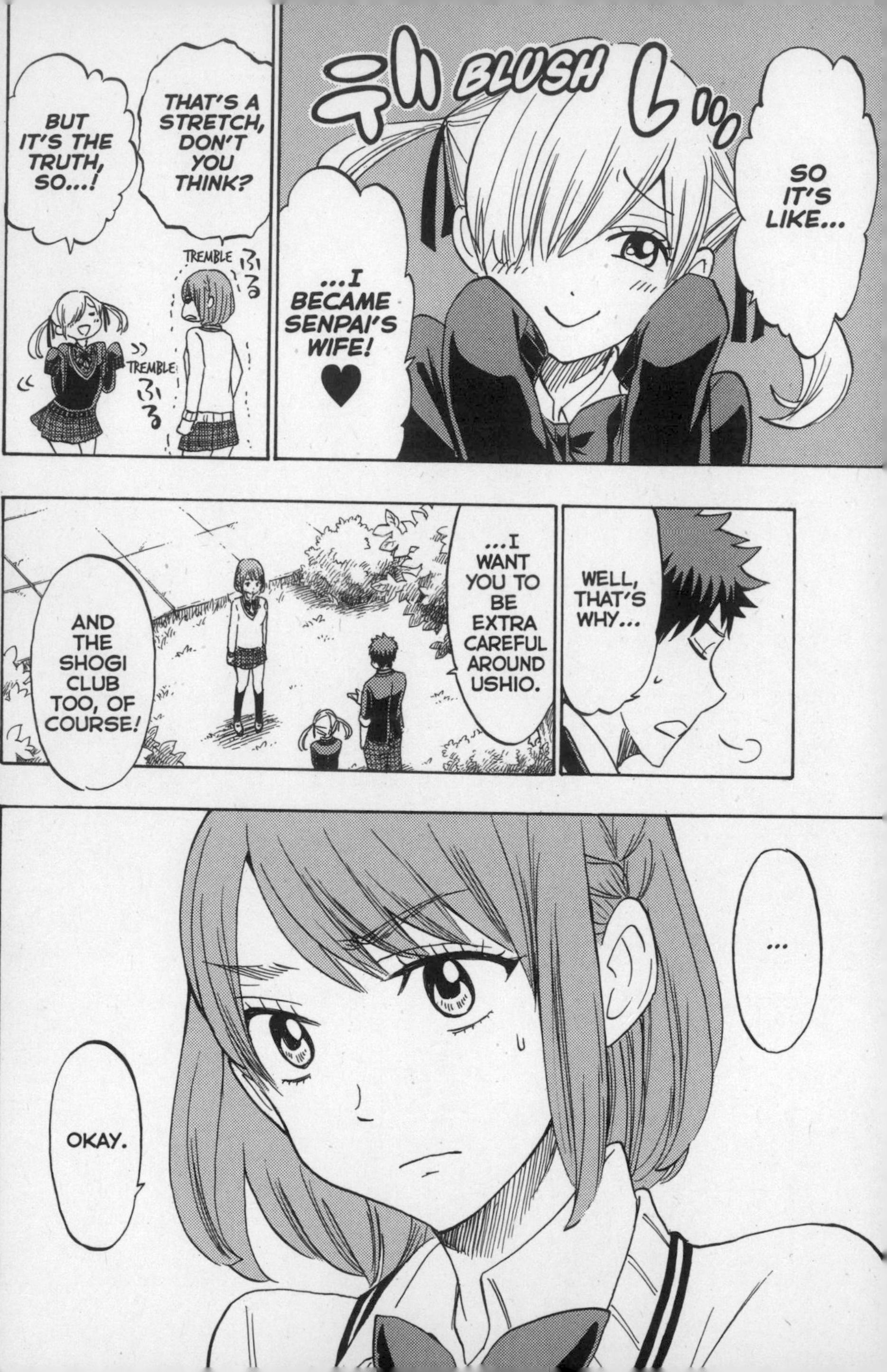
BLUSH
SO IT'S LIKE...
...I BECAME SENPAI'S WIFE! ♥
THAT'S A STRETCH, DON'T YOU THINK?
BUT IT'S THE TRUTH, SO...!
TREMBLE ふる
TREMBLE ふる
WELL, THAT'S WHY...
...I WANT YOU TO BE EXTRA CAREFUL AROUND USHIO.
AND THE SHOGI CLUB TOO, OF COURSE!
...
OKAY.

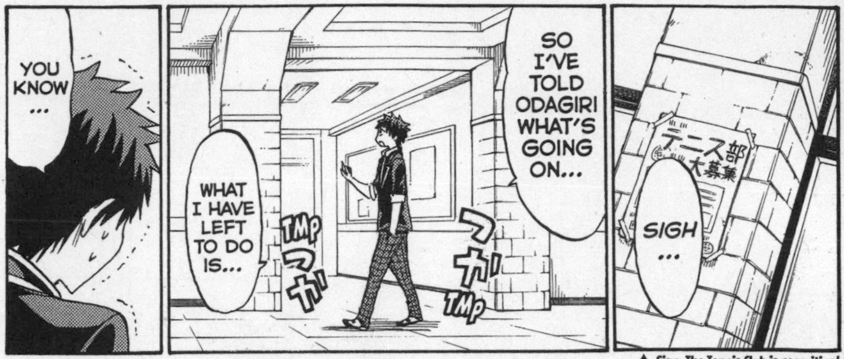
テニス部
大募集
SIGH ...
SO I'VE TOLD ODAGIRI WHAT'S GOING ON...
TMp
TMp
WHAT I HAVE LEFT TO DO IS...
YOU KNOW ...

▲ Sign: The Tennis Club is recruiting!

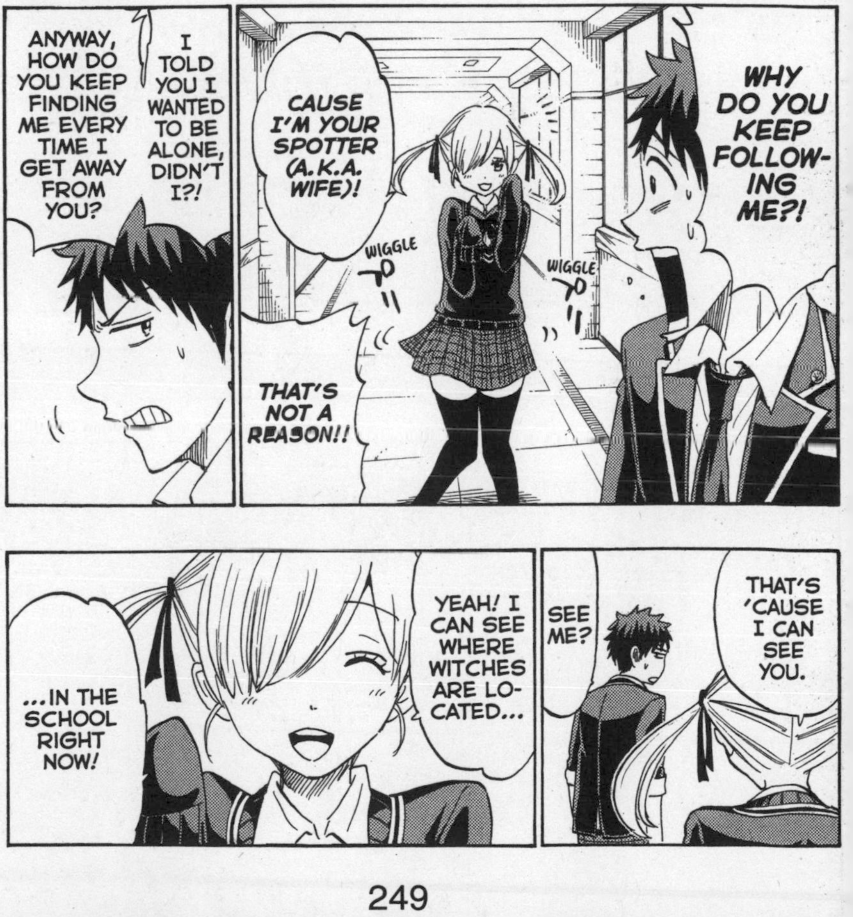
WHY DO YOU KEEP FOLLOW-ING ME?!
CAUSE I'M YOUR SPOTTER (A.K.A. WIFE)!
WIGGLE
WIGGLE
THAT'S NOT A REASON!!
I TOLD YOU I WANTED TO BE ALONE, DIDN'T I?!
ANYWAY, HOW DO YOU KEEP FINDING ME EVERY TIME I GET AWAY FROM YOU?
THAT'S 'CAUSE I CAN SEE YOU.
SEE ME?
YEAH! I CAN SEE WHERE WITCHES ARE LO-CATED...
...IN THE SCHOOL RIGHT NOW!

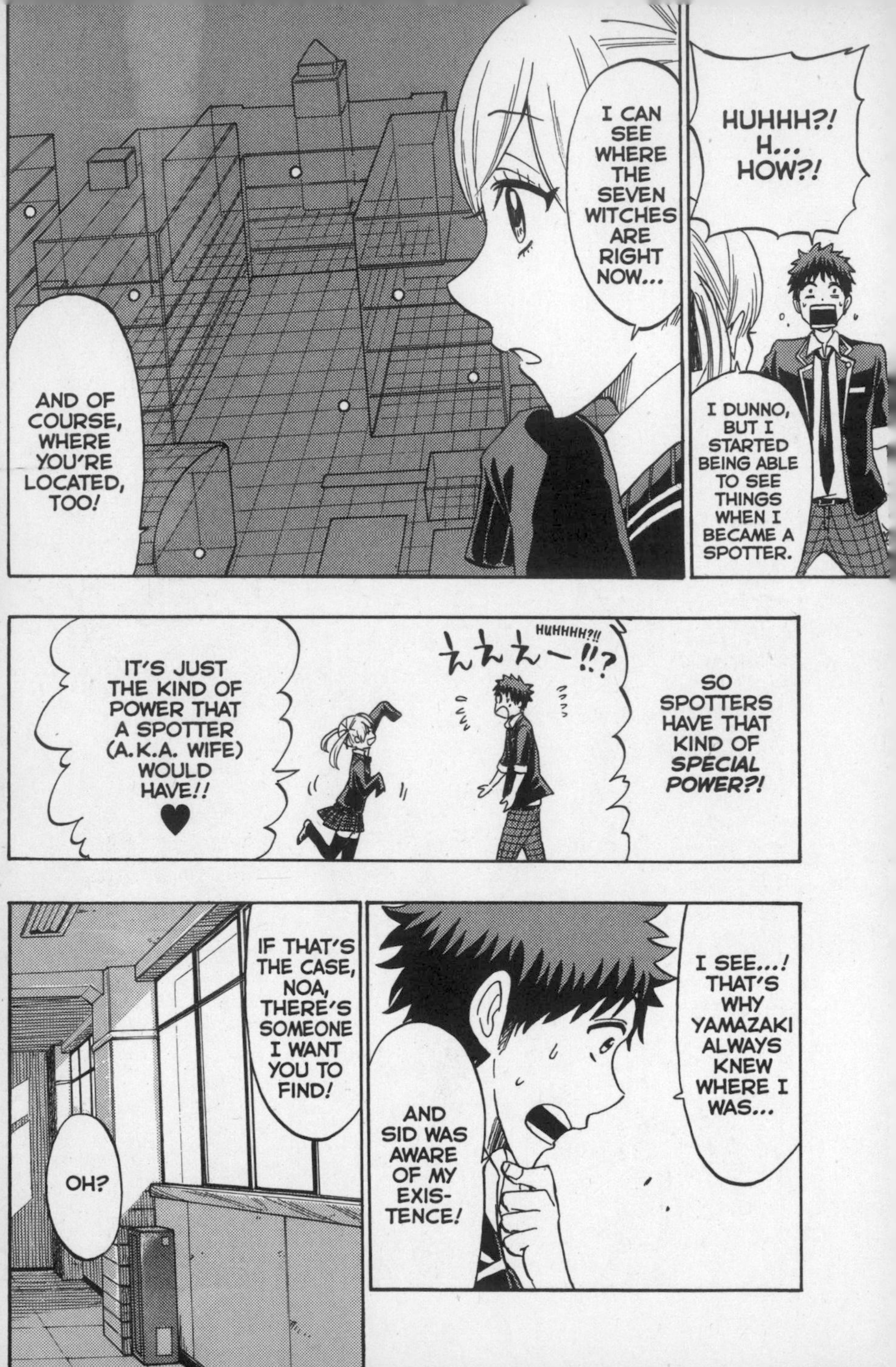
HUHHH?! H... HOW?!
I DUNNO, BUT I STARTED BEING ABLE TO SEE THINGS WHEN I BECAME A SPOTTER.
I CAN SEE WHERE THE SEVEN WITCHES ARE RIGHT NOW...
AND OF COURSE, WHERE YOU'RE LOCATED, TOO!
SO SPOTTERS HAVE THAT KIND OF *SPECIAL POWER?!*
HUHHHH?!!
えええー!!?
IT'S JUST THE KIND OF POWER THAT A SPOTTER (A.K.A. WIFE) WOULD HAVE!! ♥
I SEE...! THAT'S WHY YAMAZAKI ALWAYS KNEW WHERE I WAS...
AND SID WAS AWARE OF MY EXIS-TENCE!
IF THAT'S THE CASE, NOA, THERE'S SOMEONE I WANT YOU TO FIND!
OH?

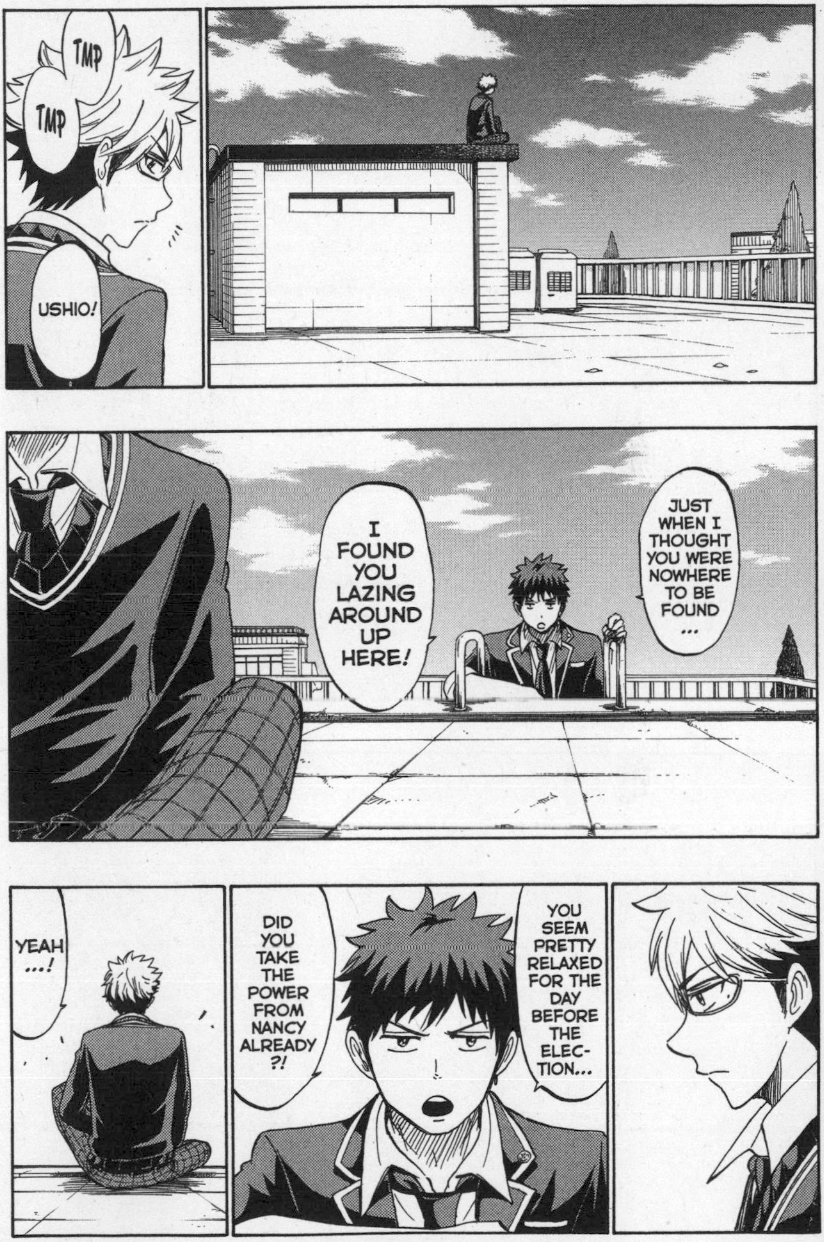
TMP
TMP
USHIO!
JUST WHEN I THOUGHT YOU WERE NOWHERE TO BE FOUND...
I FOUND YOU LAZING AROUND UP HERE!
YOU SEEM PRETTY RELAXED FOR THE DAY BEFORE THE ELECTION...
DID YOU TAKE THE POWER FROM NANCY ALREADY?!
YEAH...!

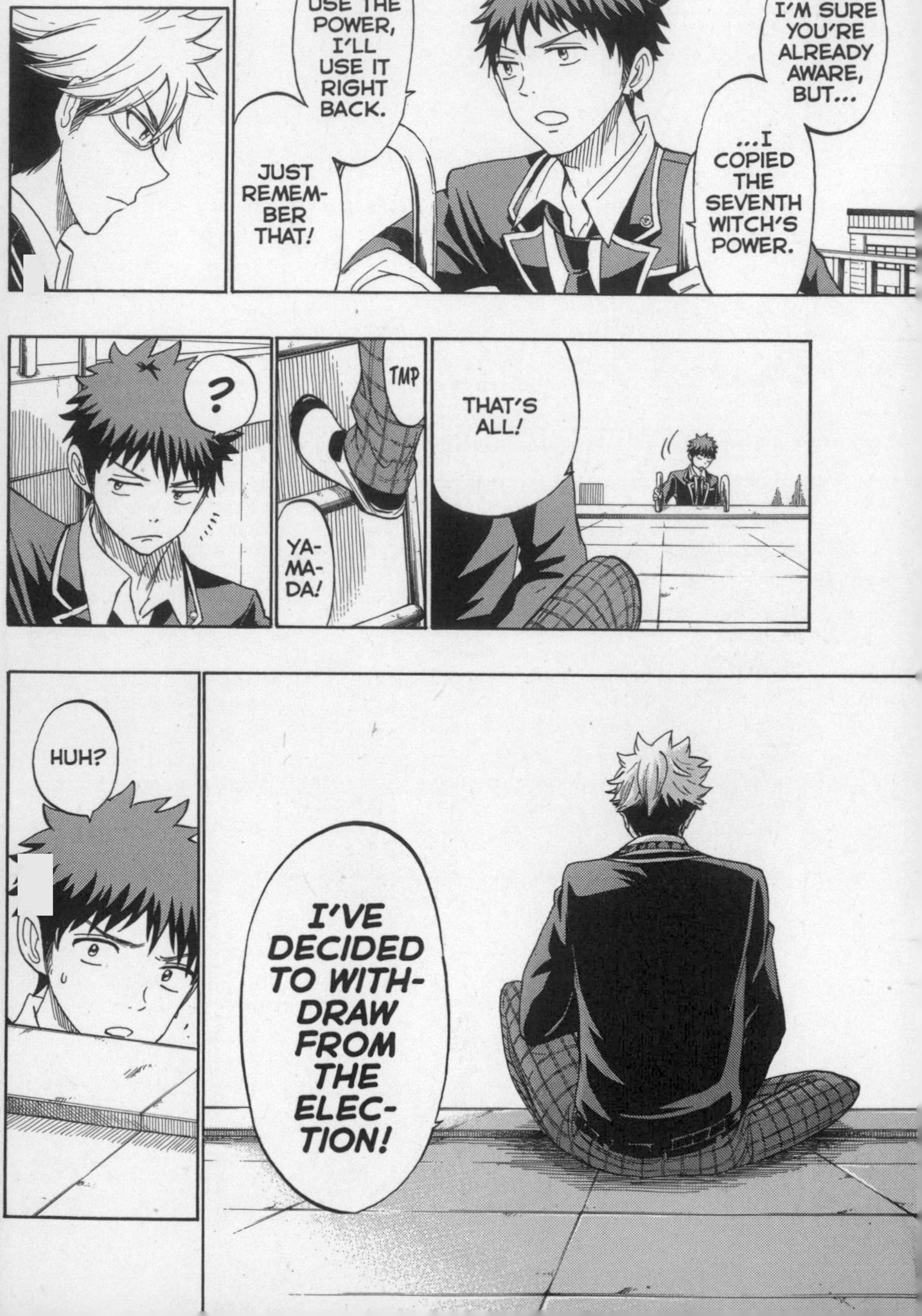
THEN I'M SURE YOU'RE ALREADY AWARE, BUT...
...I COPIED THE SEVENTH WITCH'S POWER.
IF YOU USE THE POWER, I'LL USE IT RIGHT BACK.
JUST REMEMBER THAT!
THAT'S ALL!
TMP
YAMADA!
?
I'VE DECIDED TO WITHDRAW FROM THE ELECTION!
HUH?

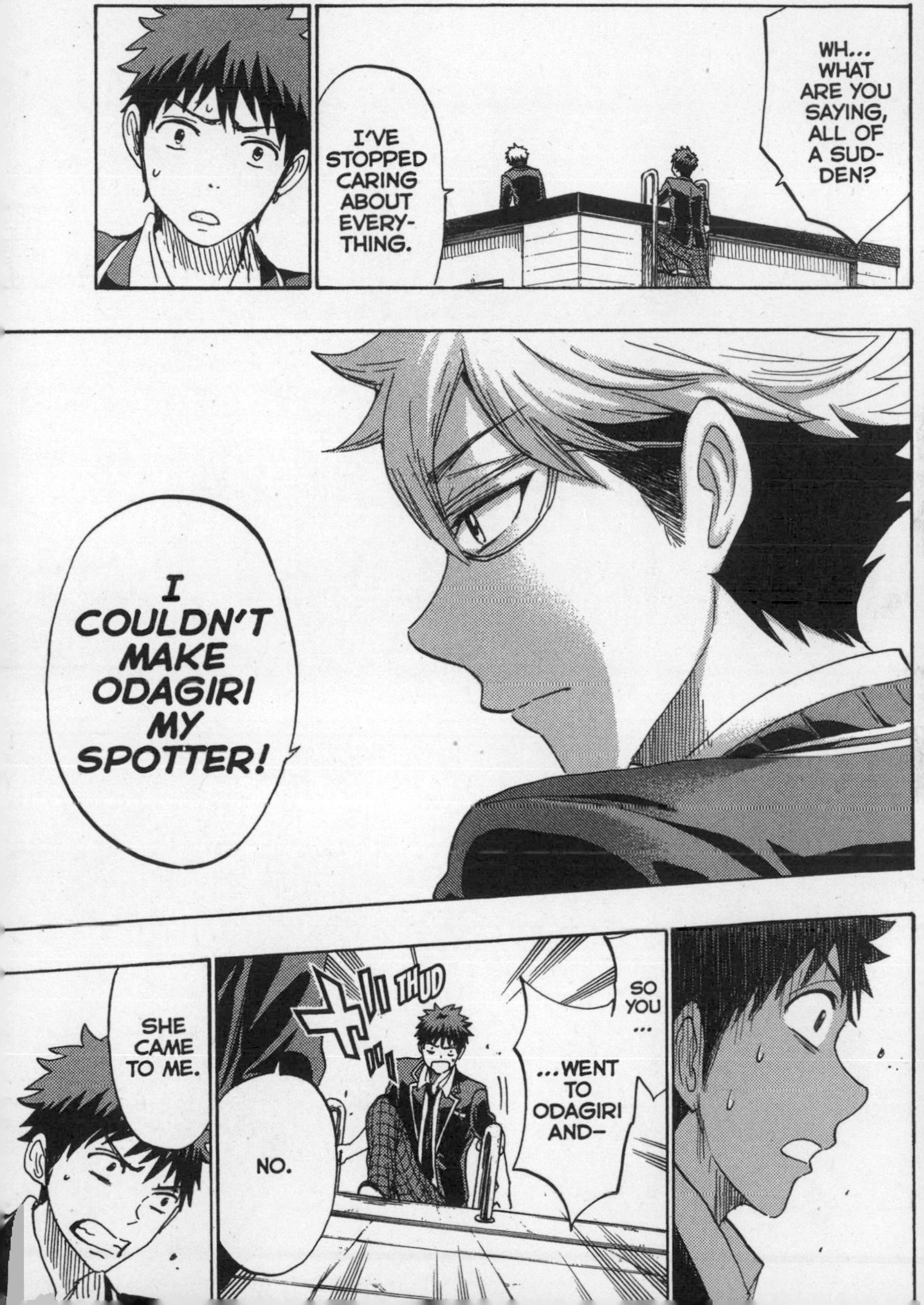
WH... WHAT ARE YOU SAYING, ALL OF A SUD-DEN?
I'VE STOPPED CARING ABOUT EVERY-THING.
I COULDN'T MAKE ODAGIRI MY SPOTTER!
SO YOU ...
...WENT TO ODAGIRI AND–
THUD
NO.
SHE CAME TO ME.

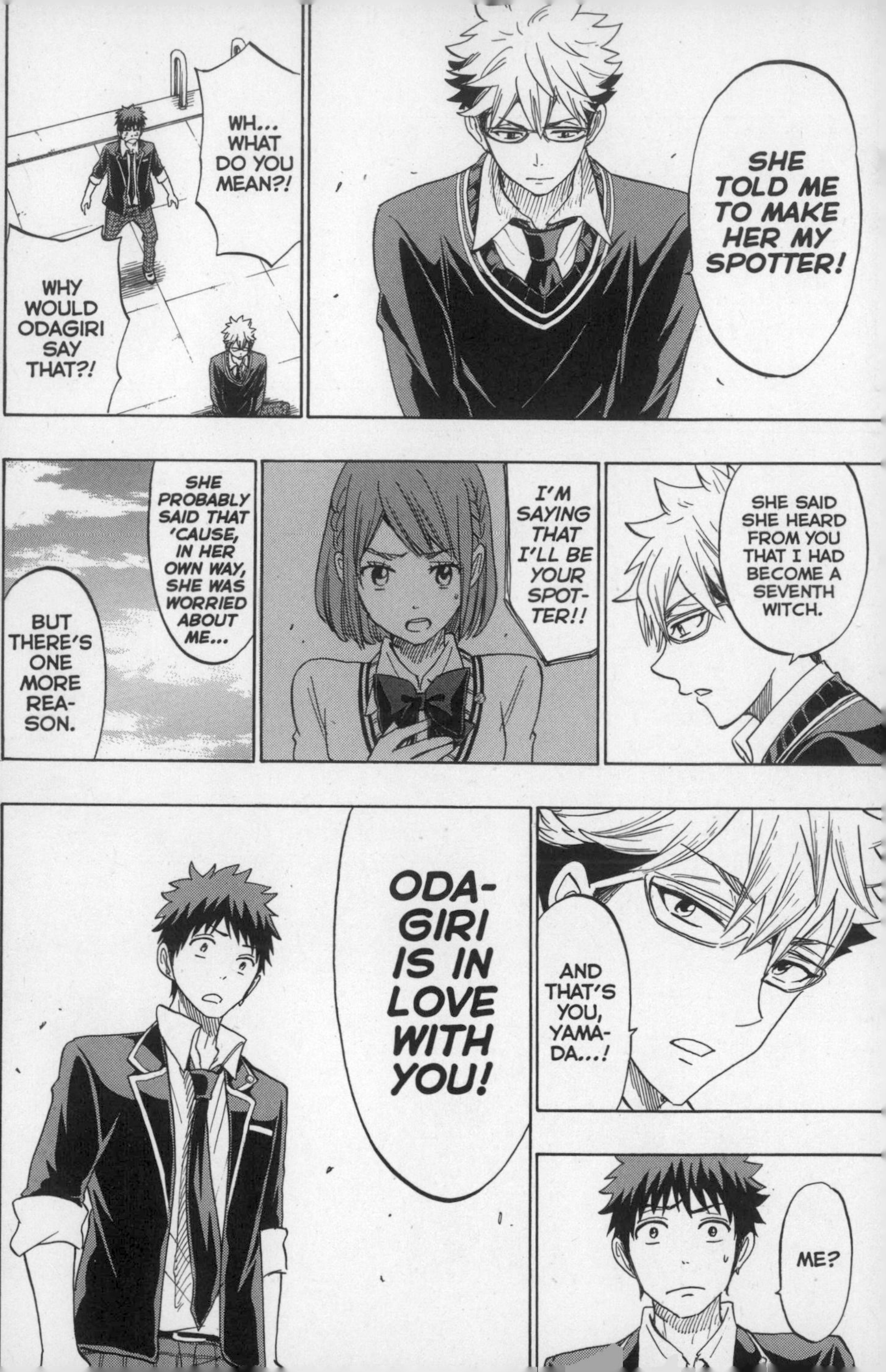
SHE TOLD ME TO MAKE HER MY SPOTTER!
WH... WHAT DO YOU MEAN?!
WHY WOULD ODAGIRI SAY THAT?!
SHE SAID SHE HEARD FROM YOU THAT I HAD BECOME A SEVENTH WITCH.
I'M SAYING THAT I'LL BE YOUR SPOT-TER!!
SHE PROBABLY SAID THAT 'CAUSE, IN HER OWN WAY, SHE WAS WORRIED ABOUT ME...
BUT THERE'S ONE MORE REA-SON.
AND THAT'S YOU, YAMA-DA...!
ME?
ODA-GIRI IS IN LOVE WITH YOU!

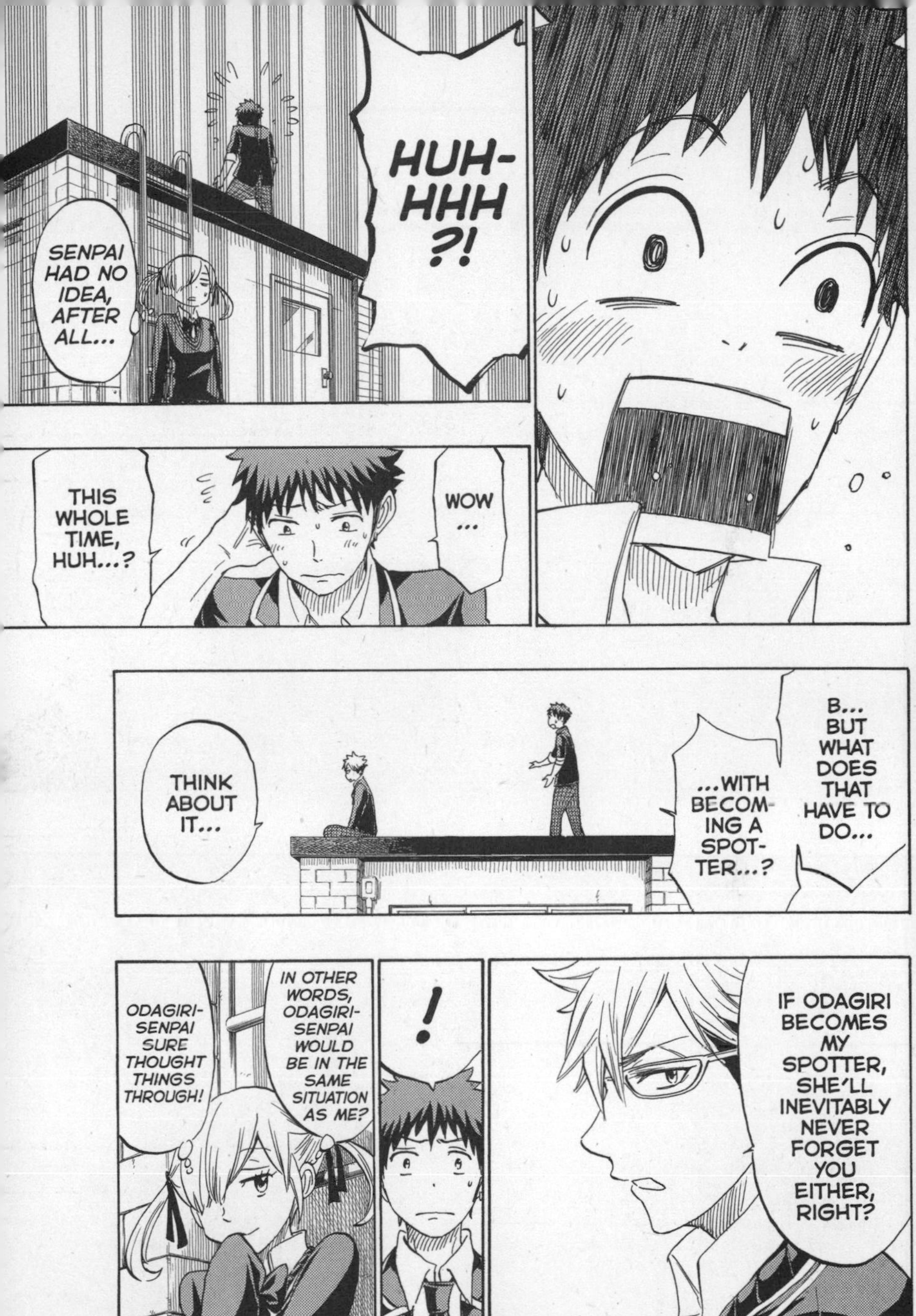
HUH-HHH?!
SENPAI HAD NO IDEA, AFTER ALL...
WOW...
THIS WHOLE TIME, HUH...?
B... BUT WHAT DOES THAT HAVE TO DO...
...WITH BECOMING A SPOTTER...?
THINK ABOUT IT...
IF ODAGIRI BECOMES MY SPOTTER, SHE'LL INEVITABLY NEVER FORGET YOU EITHER, RIGHT?
!
IN OTHER WORDS, ODAGIRI-SENPAI WOULD BE IN THE SAME SITUATION AS ME?
ODAGIRI-SENPAI SURE THOUGHT THINGS THROUGH!

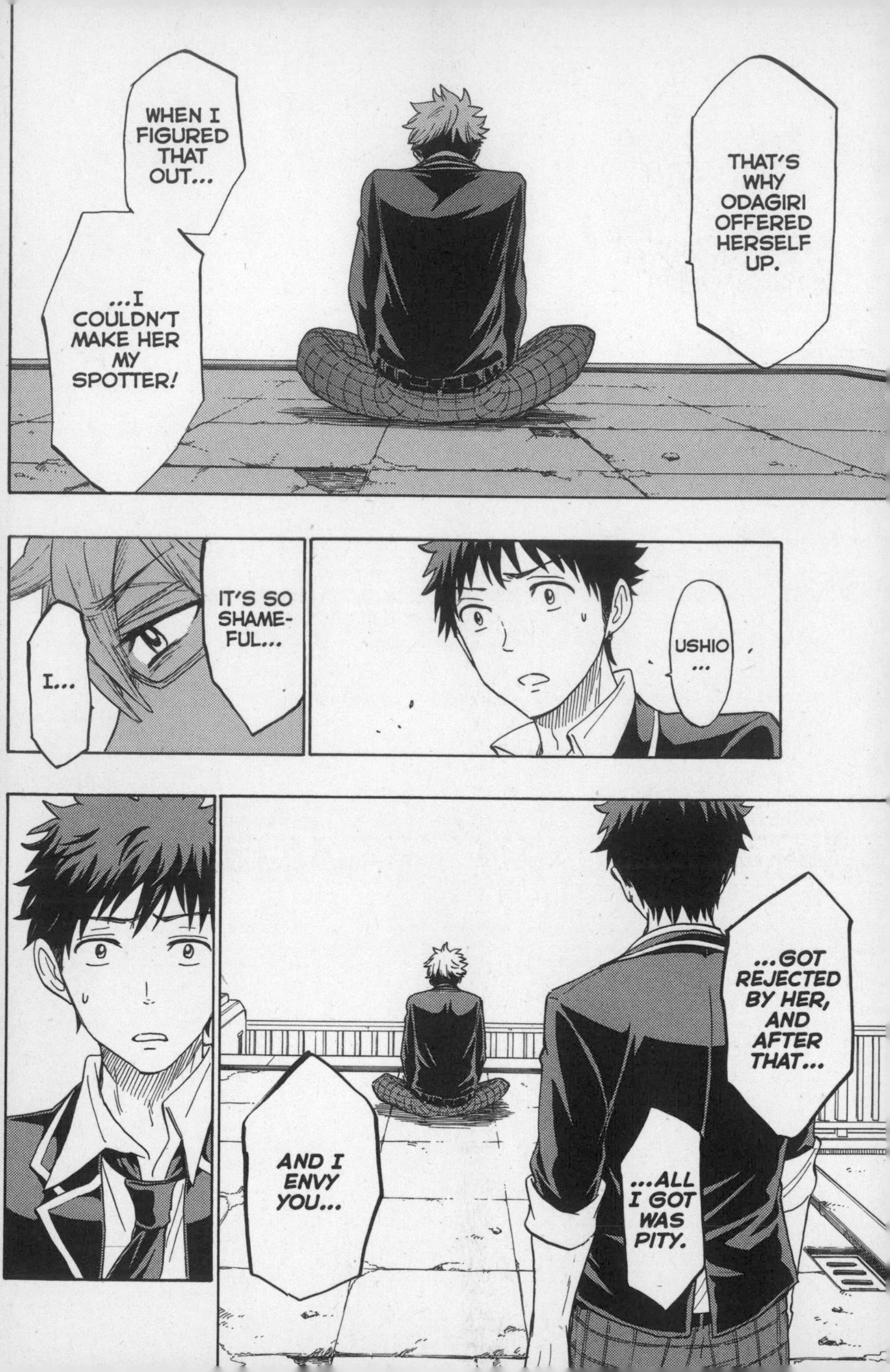
THAT'S WHY ODAGIRI OFFERED HERSELF UP.
WHEN I FIGURED THAT OUT...
...I COULDN'T MAKE HER MY SPOTTER!
USHIO...
IT'S SO SHAME-FUL...
I...
...GOT REJECTED BY HER, AND AFTER THAT...
...ALL I GOT WAS PITY.
AND I ENVY YOU...

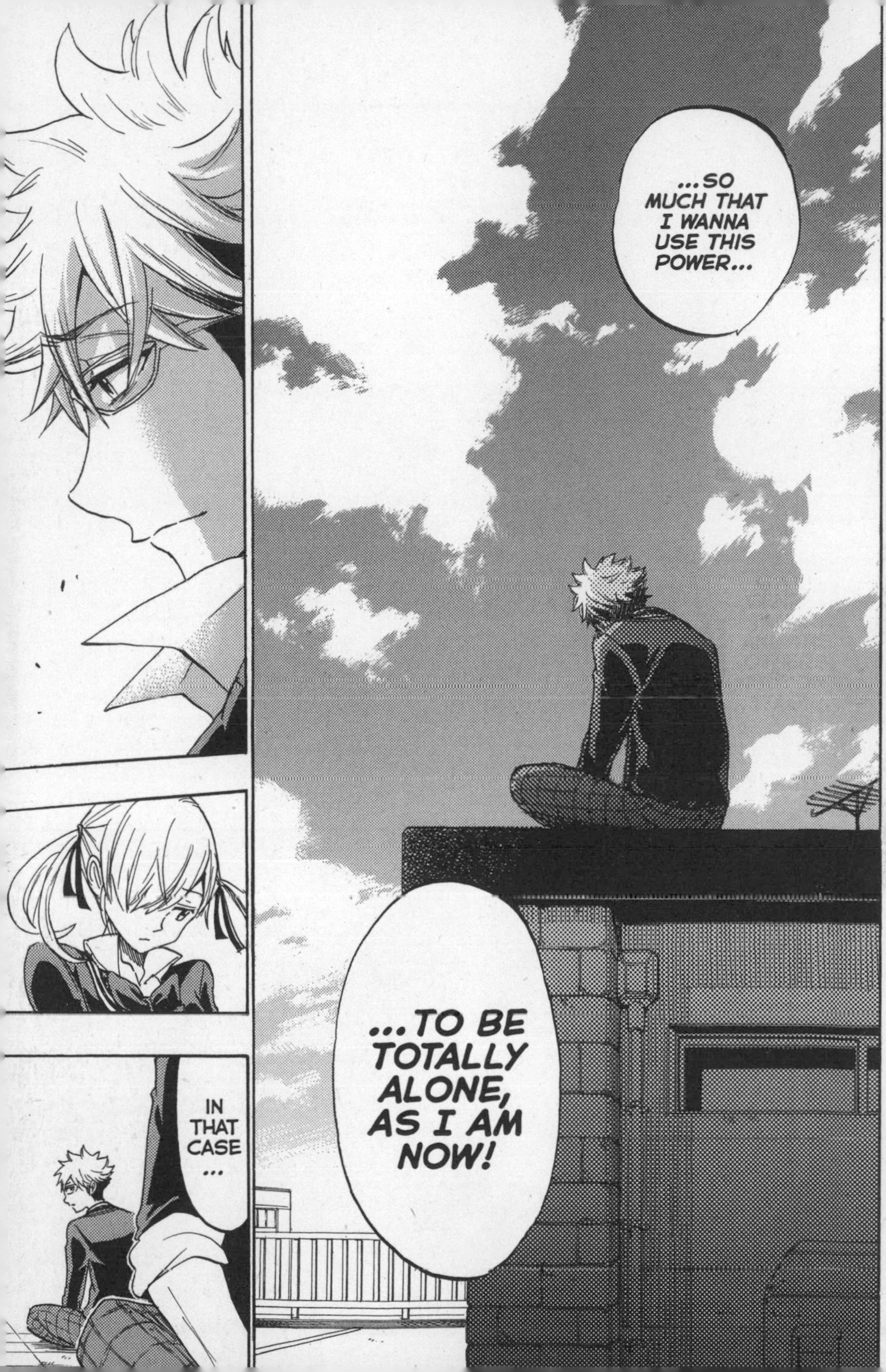
...SO MUCH THAT I WANNA USE THIS POWER...
...TO BE TOTALLY ALONE, AS I AM NOW!
IN THAT CASE ...

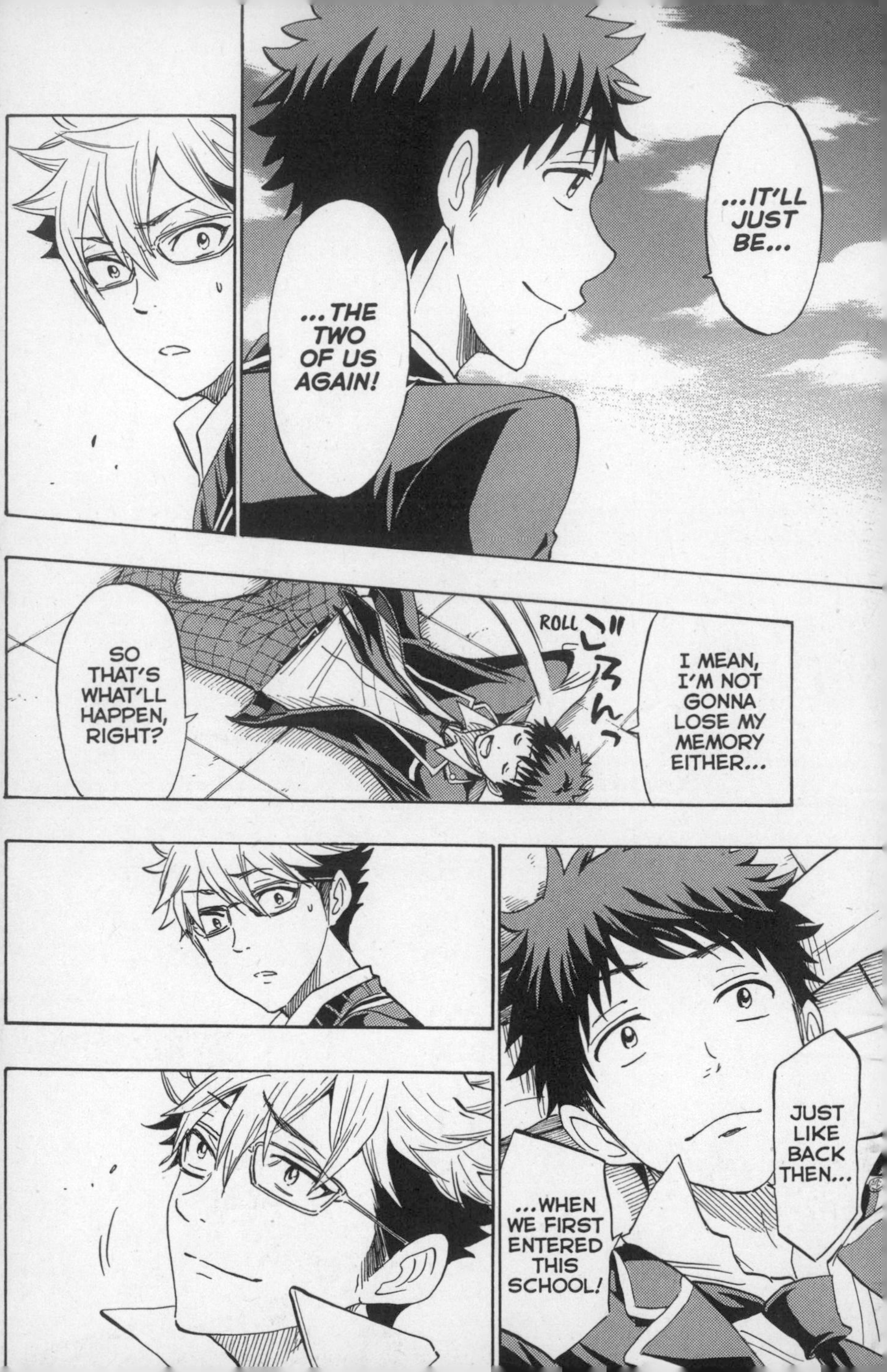
...IT'LL JUST BE...
...THE TWO OF US AGAIN!
I MEAN, I'M NOT GONNA LOSE MY MEMORY EITHER...
ROLL ごろん
SO THAT'S WHAT'LL HAPPEN, RIGHT?
JUST LIKE BACK THEN...
...WHEN WE FIRST ENTERED THIS SCHOOL!

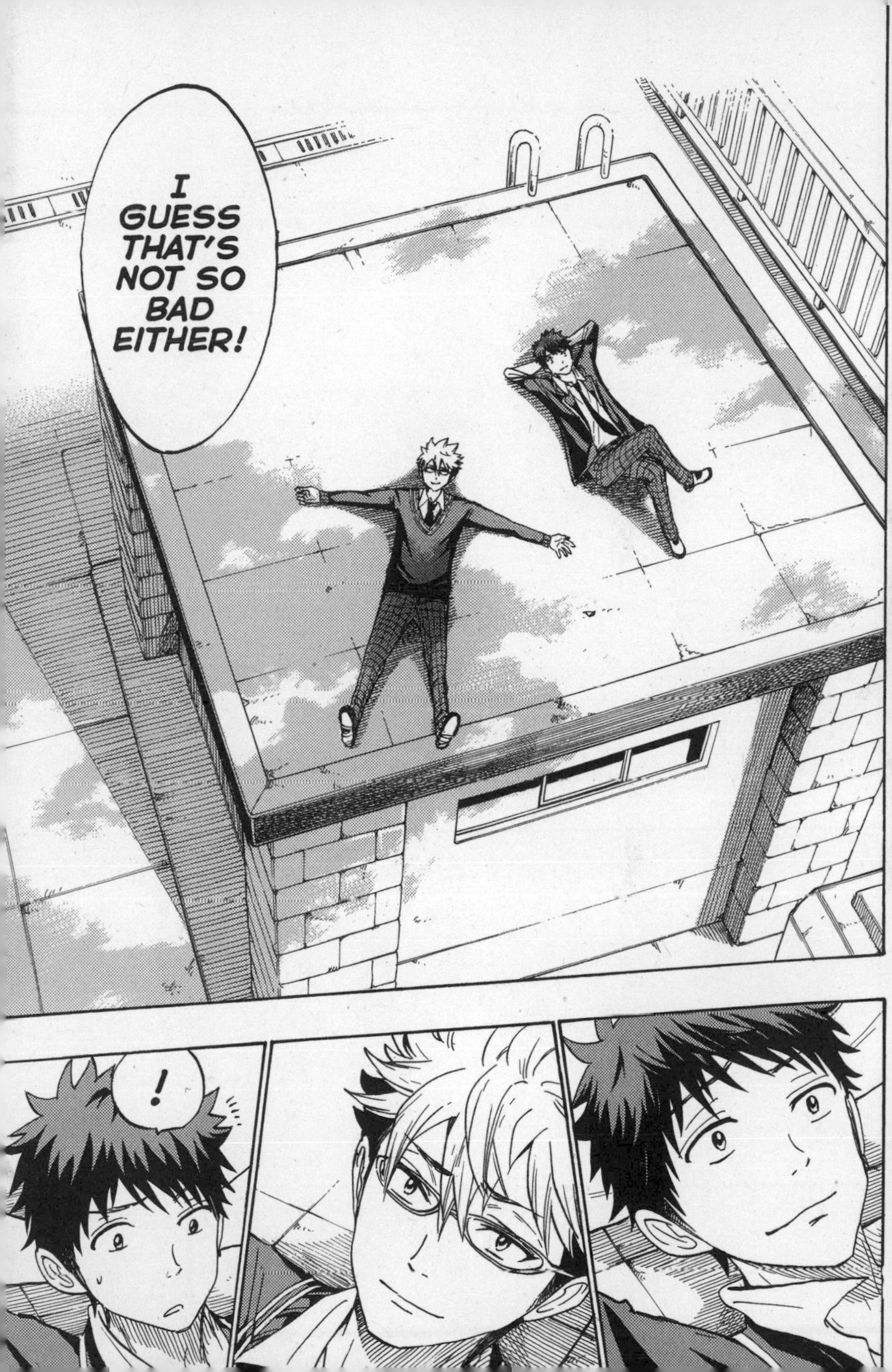

I GUESS THAT'S NOT SO BAD EITHER!
!

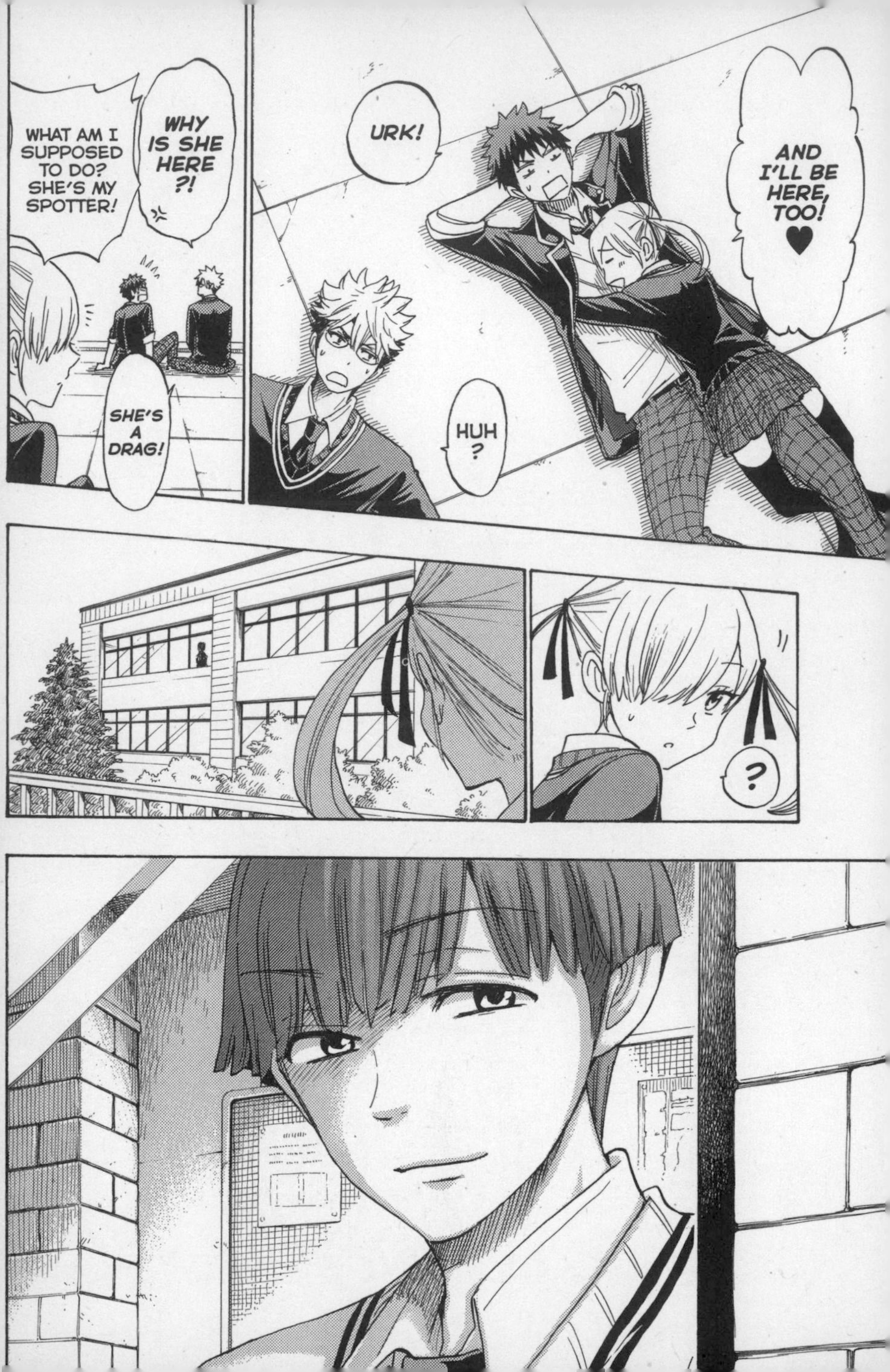

AND I'LL BE HERE, TOO! ♥
URK!
HUH?
WHY IS SHE HERE?!
WHAT AM I SUPPOSED TO DO? SHE'S MY SPOTTER!
SHE'S A DRAG!
?

CHAPTER 168: You're not a cute kohai at all.

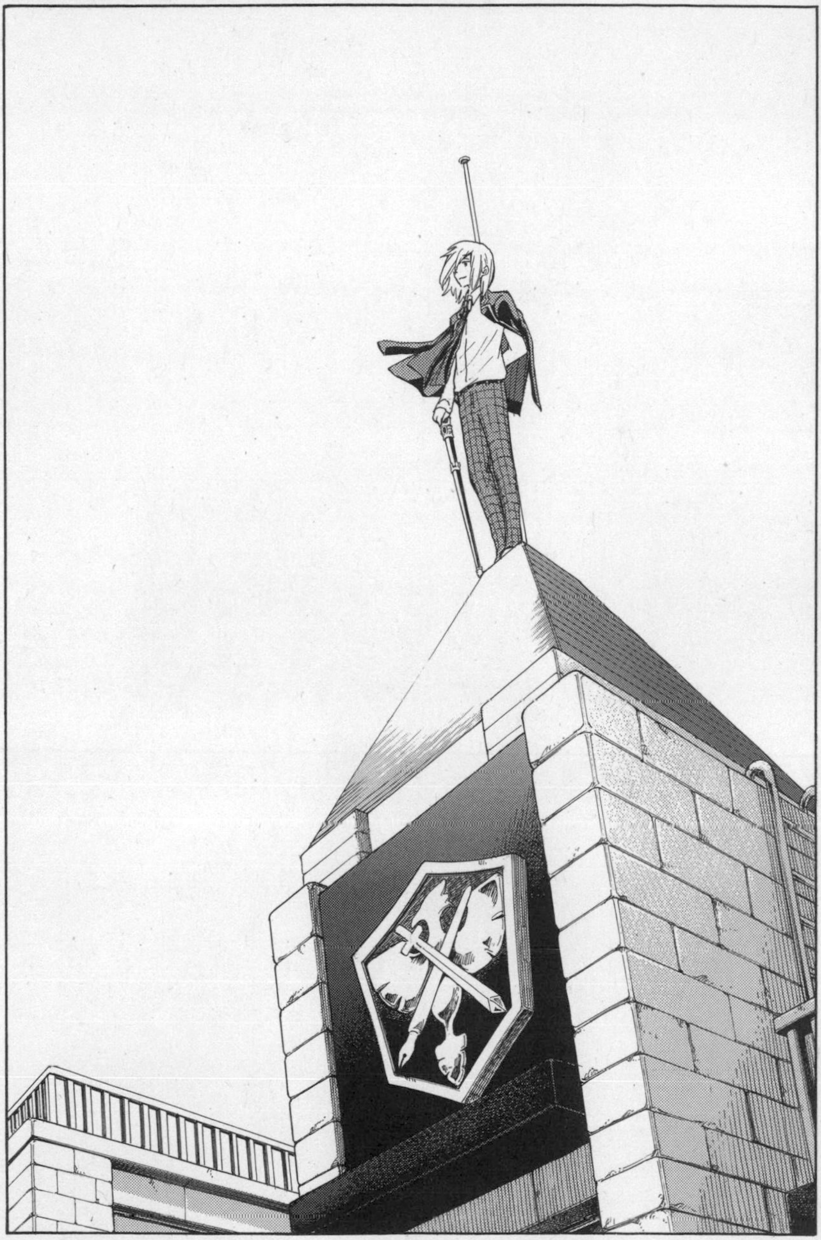

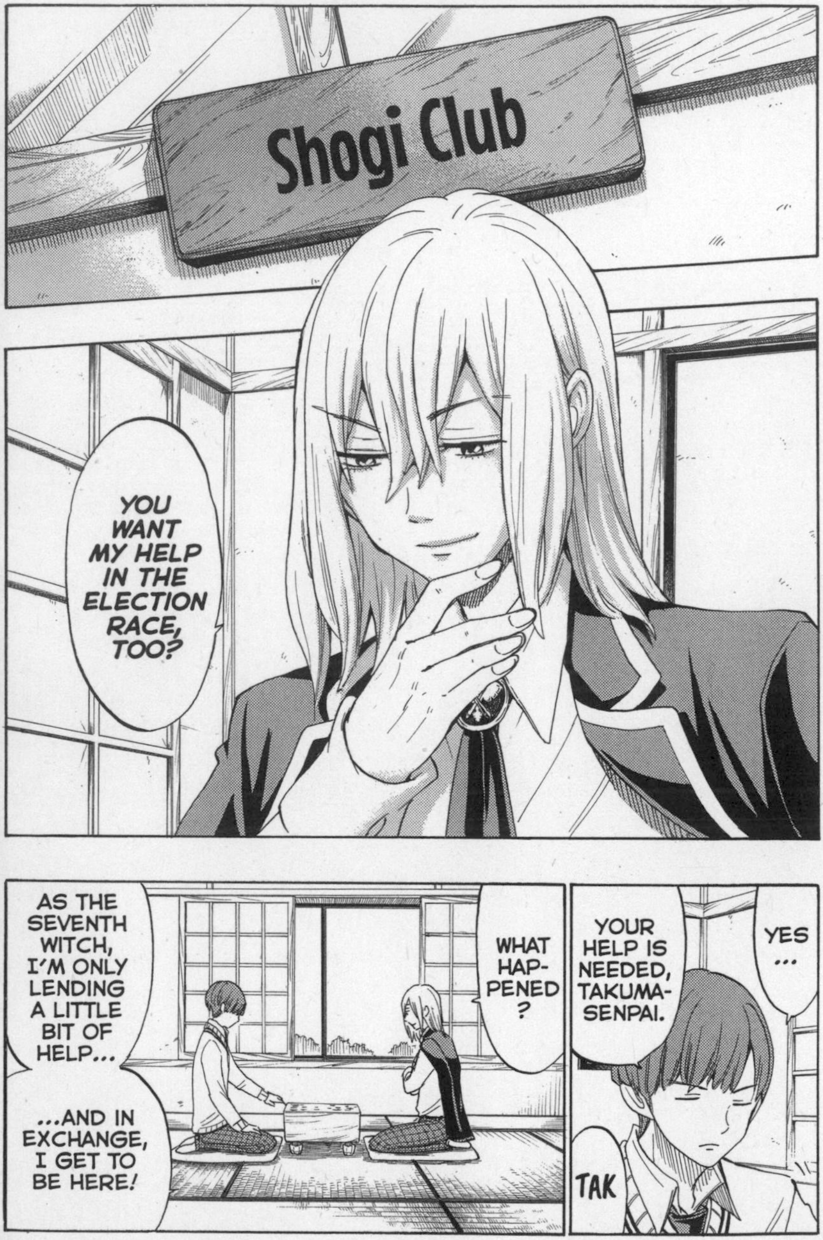
Shogi Club
YOU WANT MY HELP IN THE ELECTION RACE, TOO?
YES ...
YOUR HELP IS NEEDED, TAKUMA-SENPAI.
TAK
WHAT HAP-PENED ?
AS THE SEVENTH WITCH, I'M ONLY LENDING A LITTLE BIT OF HELP...
...AND IN EXCHANGE, I GET TO BE HERE!

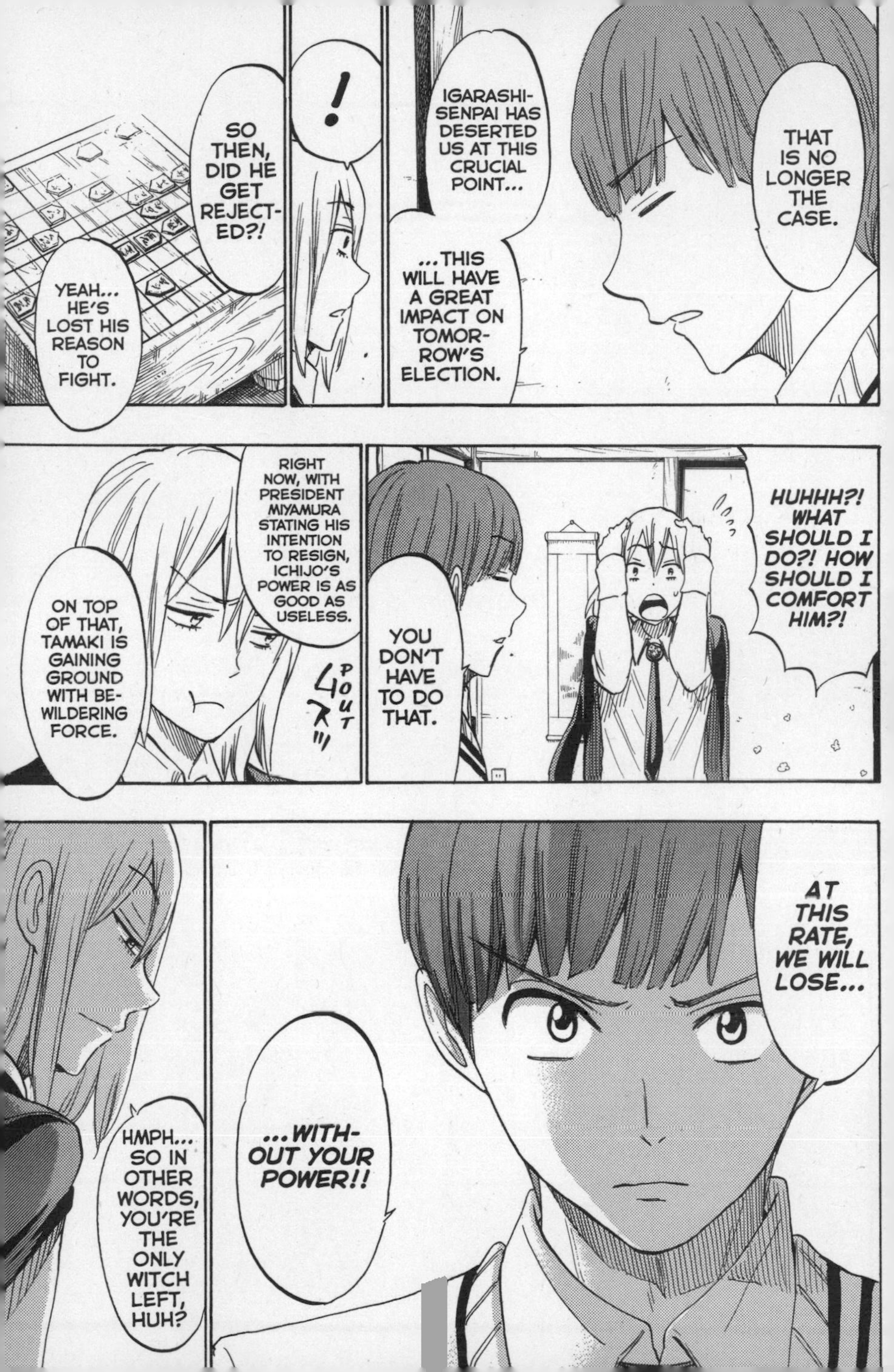
THAT IS NO LONGER THE CASE.
IGARASHI-SENPAI HAS DESERTED US AT THIS CRUCIAL POINT...
...THIS WILL HAVE A GREAT IMPACT ON TOMORROW'S ELECTION.
!
SO THEN, DID HE GET REJECTED?!
YEAH... HE'S LOST HIS REASON TO FIGHT.
HUHHH?! WHAT SHOULD I DO?! HOW SHOULD I COMFORT HIM?!
YOU DON'T HAVE TO DO THAT.
RIGHT NOW, WITH PRESIDENT MIYAMURA STATING HIS INTENTION TO RESIGN, ICHIJO'S POWER IS AS GOOD AS USELESS.
POUT
ON TOP OF THAT, TAMAKI IS GAINING GROUND WITH BEWILDERING FORCE.
AT THIS RATE, WE WILL LOSE...
...WITHOUT YOUR POWER!!
HMPH... SO IN OTHER WORDS, YOU'RE THE ONLY WITCH LEFT, HUH?

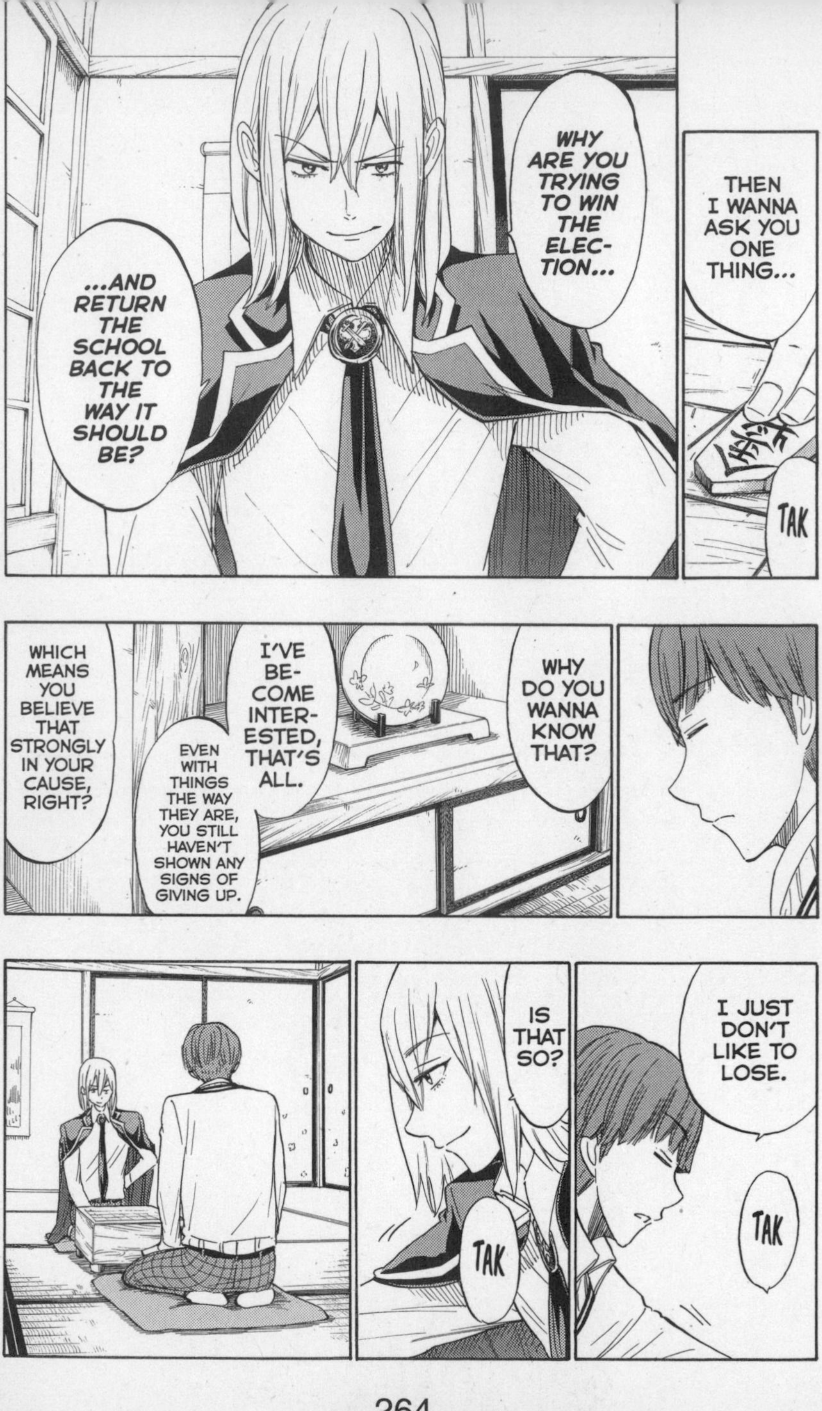
THEN I WANNA ASK YOU ONE THING...
TAK
WHY ARE YOU TRYING TO WIN THE ELEC- TION...
...AND RETURN THE SCHOOL BACK TO THE WAY IT SHOULD BE?
WHY DO YOU WANNA KNOW THAT?
I'VE BE- COME INTER- ESTED, THAT'S ALL.
EVEN WITH THINGS THE WAY THEY ARE, YOU STILL HAVEN'T SHOWN ANY SIGNS OF GIVING UP.
WHICH MEANS YOU BELIEVE THAT STRONGLY IN YOUR CAUSE, RIGHT?
I JUST DON'T LIKE TO LOSE.
TAK
IS THAT SO?
TAK

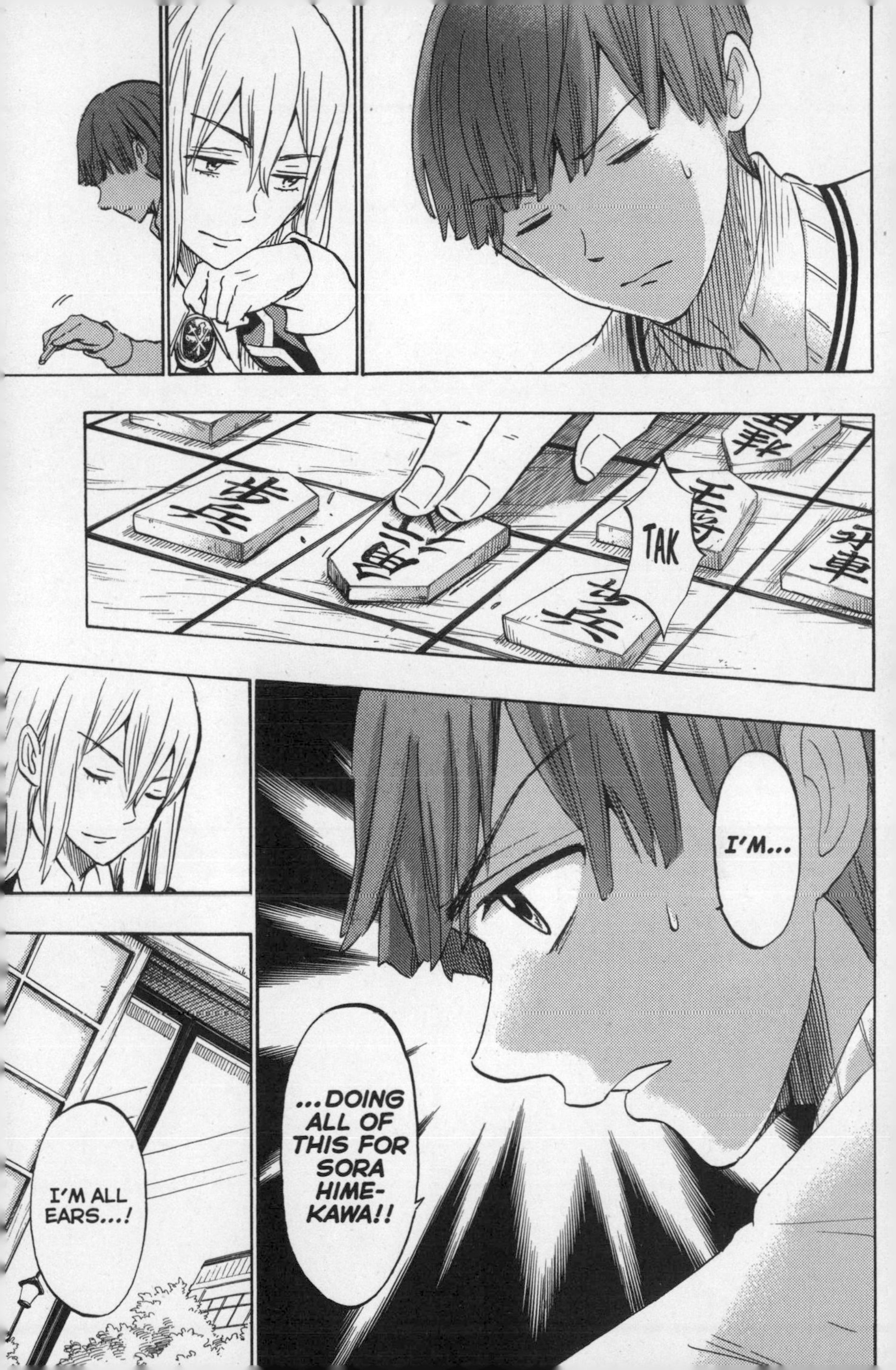
TAK
I'M...
...DOING ALL OF THIS FOR SORA HIME-KAWA!!
I'M ALL EARS...!

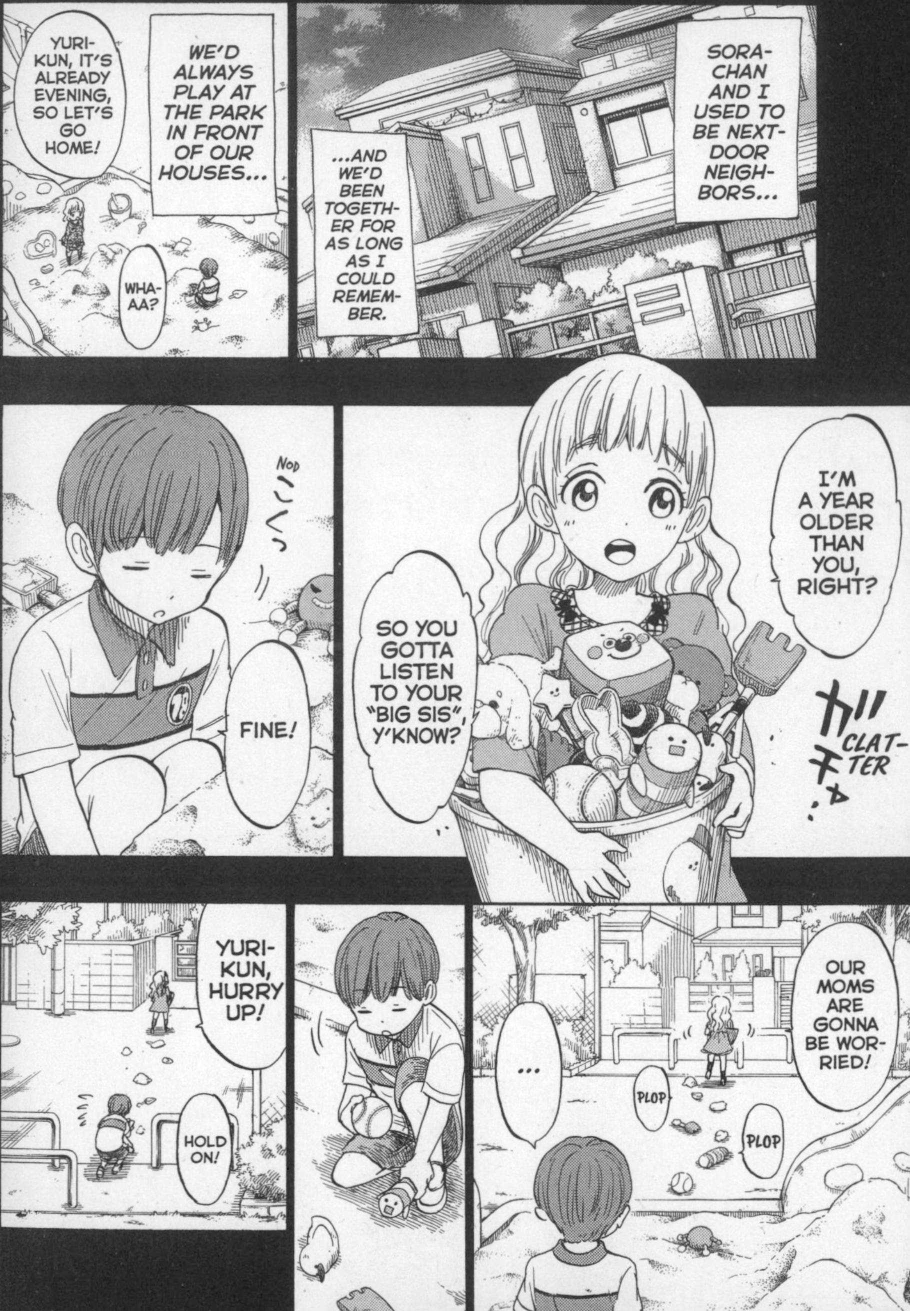
SORA-CHAN AND I USED TO BE NEXT-DOOR NEIGHBORS...
...AND WE'D BEEN TOGETHER FOR AS LONG AS I COULD REMEMBER.
WE'D ALWAYS PLAY AT THE PARK IN FRONT OF OUR HOUSES...
YURI-KUN, IT'S ALREADY EVENING, SO LET'S GO HOME!
WHAA-AA?
I'M A YEAR OLDER THAN YOU, RIGHT?
SO YOU GOTTA LISTEN TO YOUR "BIG SIS", Y'KNOW?
ガチャ CLAT-TER
こくっ NOD
FINE!
OUR MOMS ARE GONNA BE WOR-RIED!
...
PLOP
PLOP
YURI-KUN, HURRY UP!
HOLD ON!

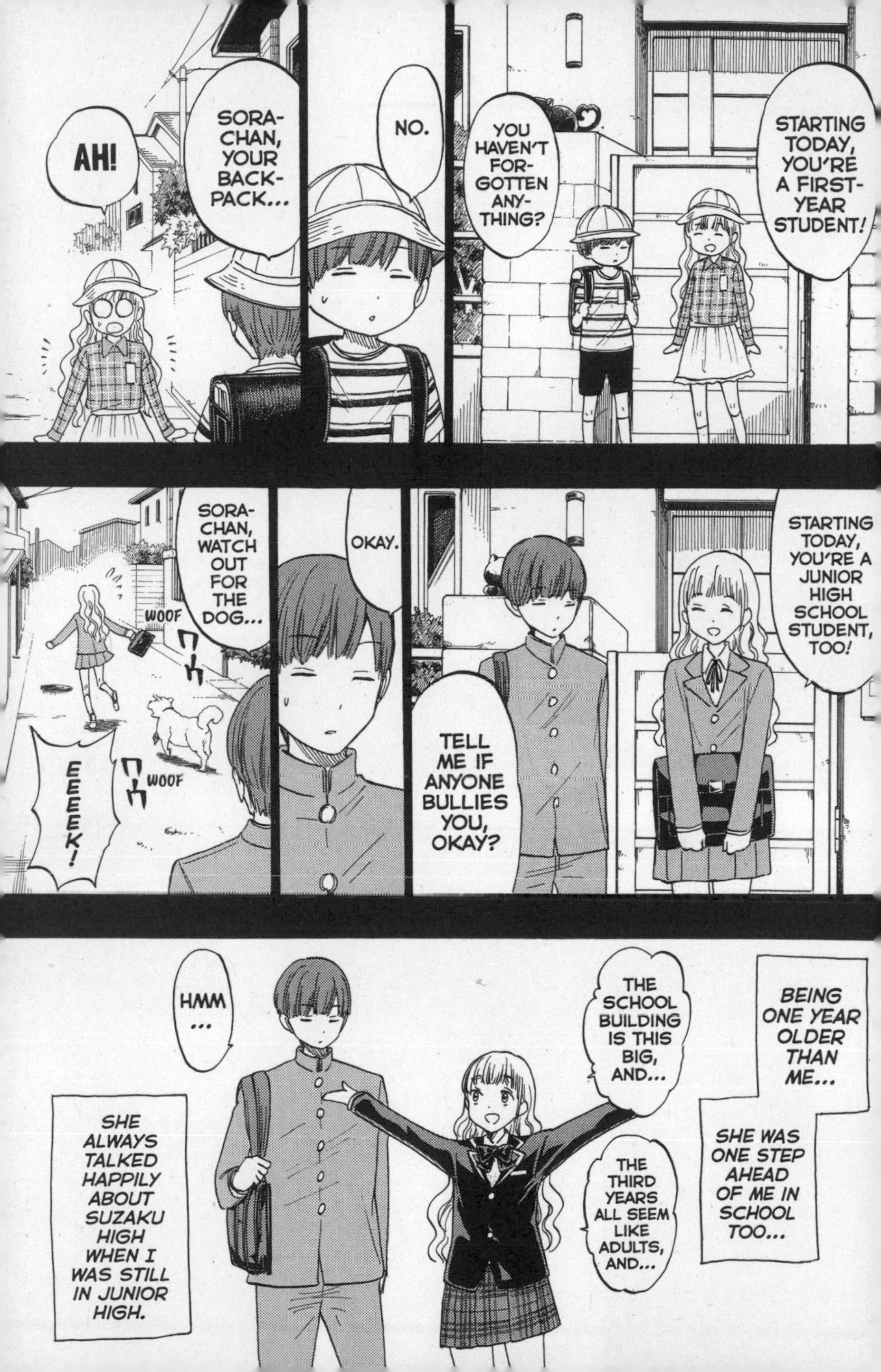
STARTING TODAY, YOU'RE A FIRST-YEAR STUDENT!
YOU HAVEN'T FORGOTTEN ANYTHING?
NO.
SORA-CHAN, YOUR BACKPACK...
AH!
STARTING TODAY, YOU'RE A JUNIOR HIGH SCHOOL STUDENT, TOO!
TELL ME IF ANYONE BULLIES YOU, OKAY?
OKAY.
SORA-CHAN, WATCH OUT FOR THE DOG...
WOOF
WOOF
EEEEK!
BEING ONE YEAR OLDER THAN ME...
SHE WAS ONE STEP AHEAD OF ME IN SCHOOL TOO...
THE SCHOOL BUILDING IS THIS BIG, AND...
THE THIRD YEARS ALL SEEM LIKE ADULTS, AND...
HMM...
SHE ALWAYS TALKED HAPPILY ABOUT SUZAKU HIGH WHEN I WAS STILL IN JUNIOR HIGH.

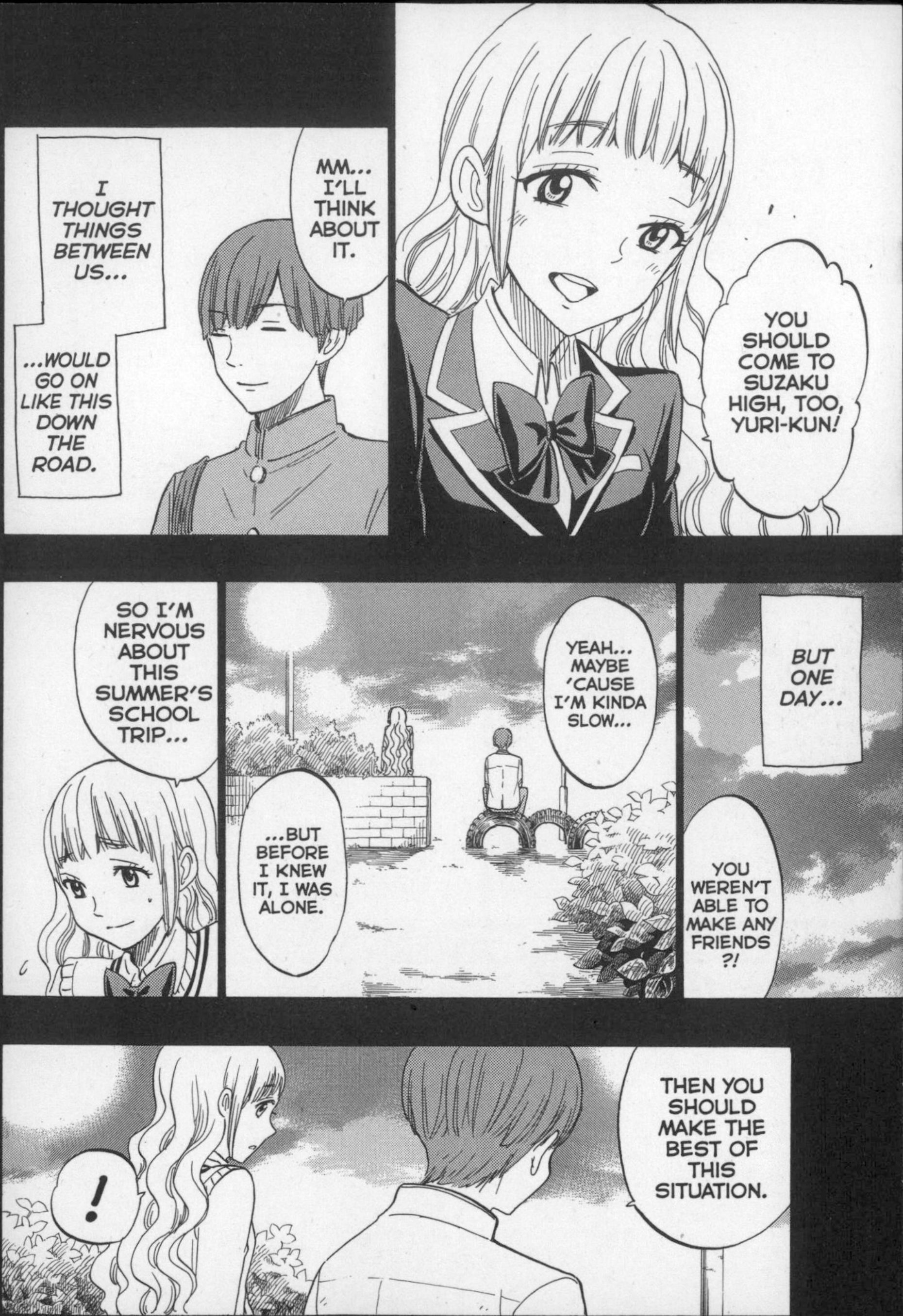
YOU SHOULD COME TO SUZAKU HIGH, TOO, YURI-KUN!
MM... I'LL THINK ABOUT IT.
I THOUGHT THINGS BETWEEN US...
...WOULD GO ON LIKE THIS DOWN THE ROAD.
BUT ONE DAY...
YOU WEREN'T ABLE TO MAKE ANY FRIENDS ?!
YEAH... MAYBE 'CAUSE I'M KINDA SLOW...
...BUT BEFORE I KNEW IT, I WAS ALONE.
SO I'M NERVOUS ABOUT THIS SUMMER'S SCHOOL TRIP...
THEN YOU SHOULD MAKE THE BEST OF THIS SITUATION.
!

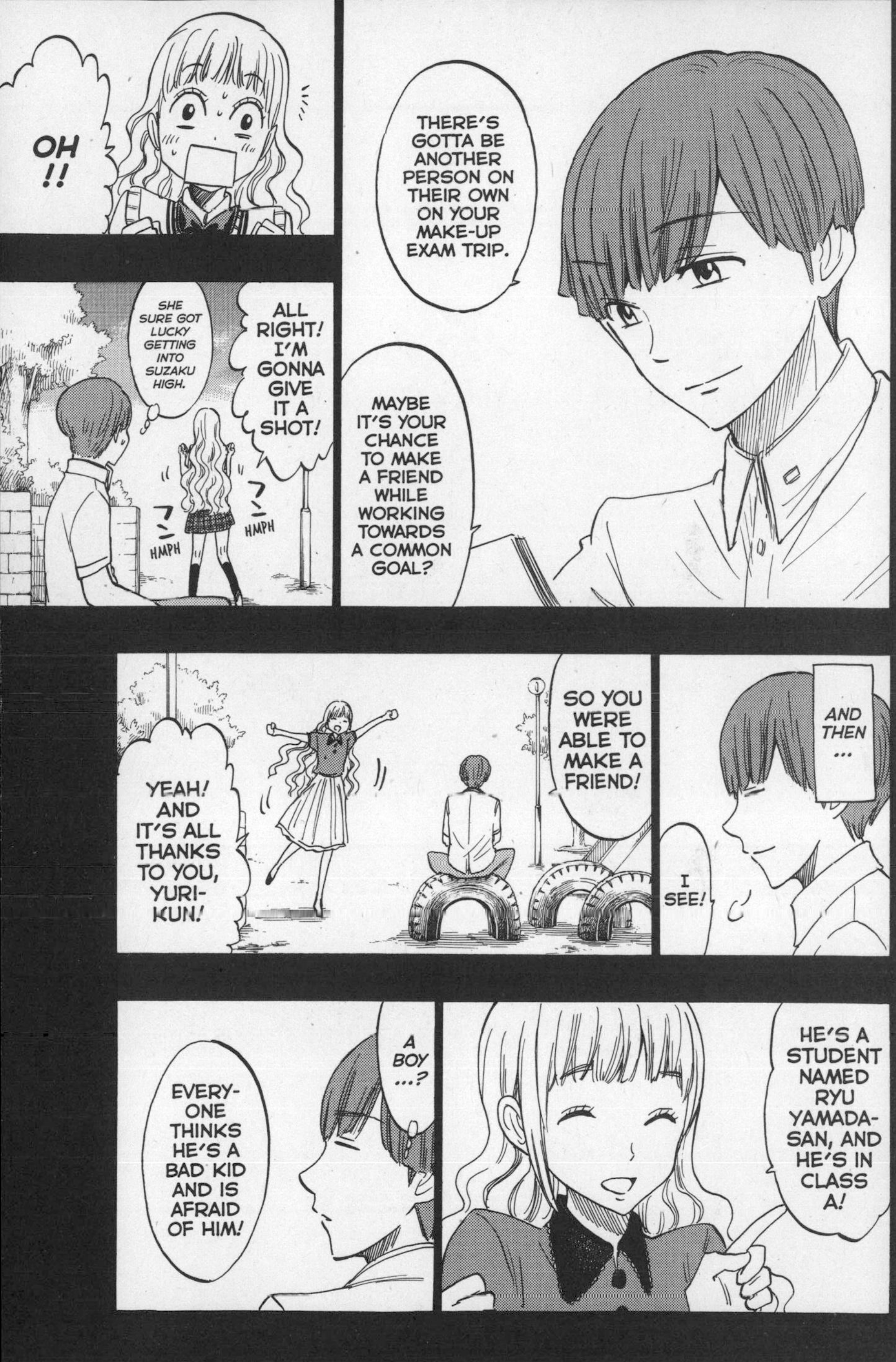
THERE'S GOTTA BE ANOTHER PERSON ON THEIR OWN ON YOUR MAKE-UP EXAM TRIP.
MAYBE IT'S YOUR CHANCE TO MAKE A FRIEND WHILE WORKING TOWARDS A COMMON GOAL?
OH !!
ALL RIGHT! I'M GONNA GIVE IT A SHOT!
SHE SURE GOT LUCKY GETTING INTO SUZAKU HIGH.
HMPH
HMPH
AND THEN ...
I SEE!
SO YOU WERE ABLE TO MAKE A FRIEND!
YEAH! AND IT'S ALL THANKS TO YOU, YURI-KUN!
HE'S A STUDENT NAMED RYU YAMADA-SAN, AND HE'S IN CLASS A!
A BOY ...?
EVERY-ONE THINKS HE'S A BAD KID AND IS AFRAID OF HIM!

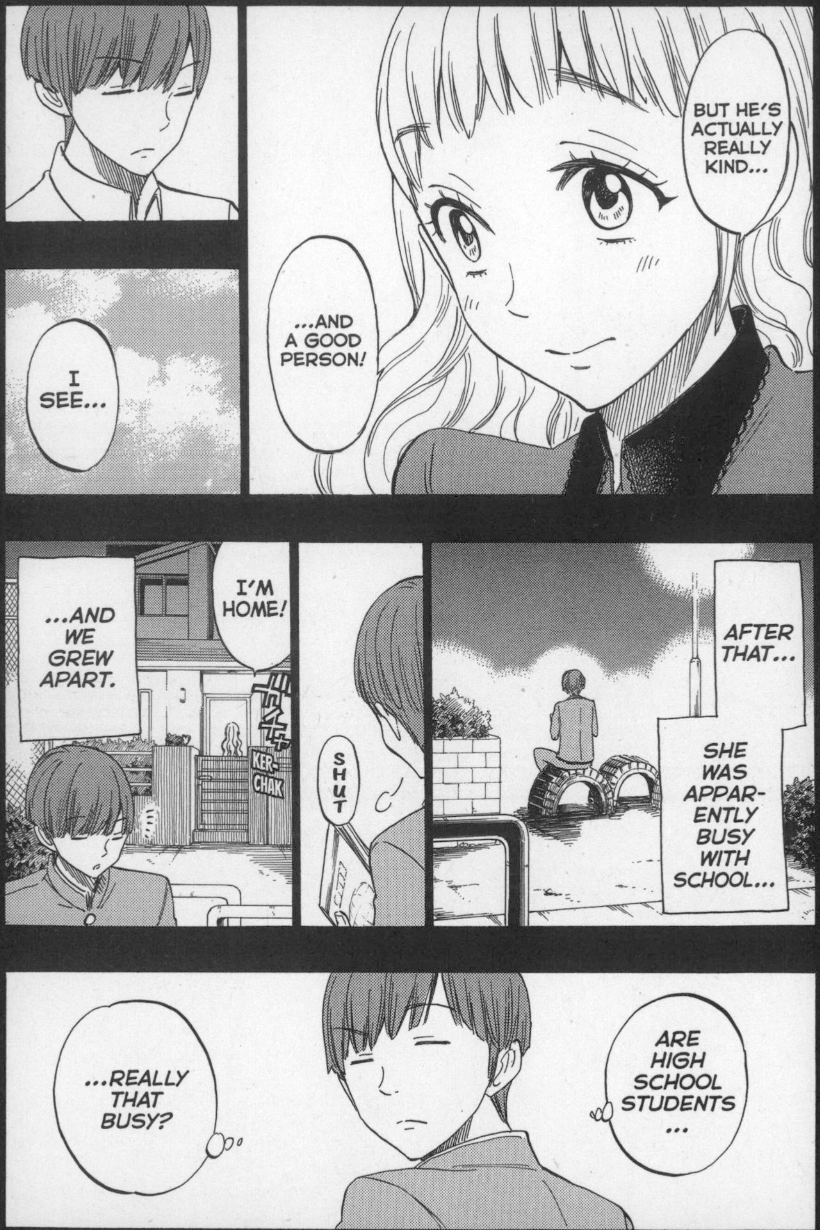
BUT HE'S ACTUALLY REALLY KIND...
...AND A GOOD PERSON!
I SEE...
AFTER THAT...
SHE WAS APPARENTLY BUSY WITH SCHOOL...
SHUT
I'M HOME!
...AND WE GREW APART.
KER-CHAK
ARE HIGH SCHOOL STUDENTS ...
...REALLY THAT BUSY?

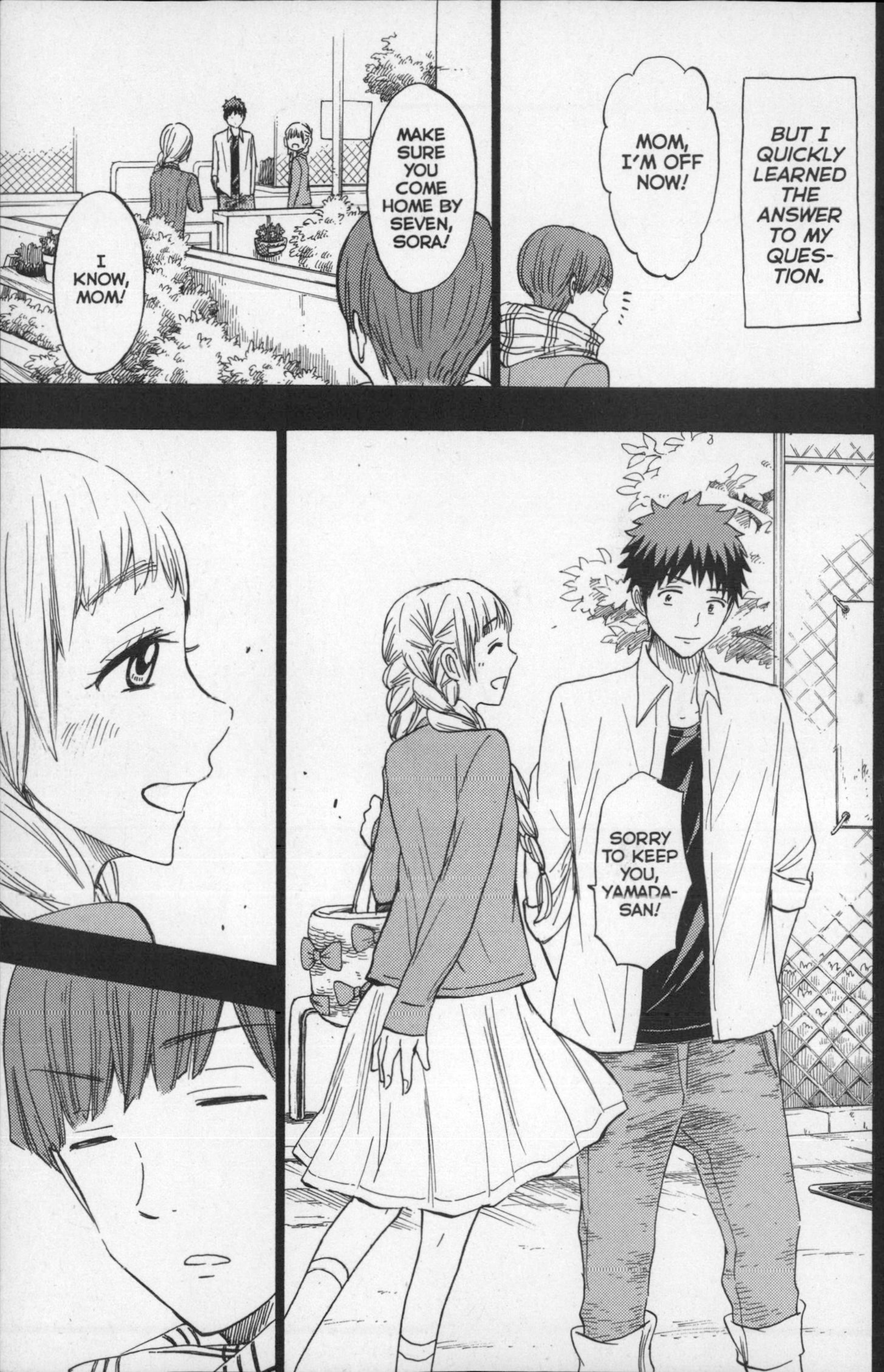
BUT I QUICKLY LEARNED THE ANSWER TO MY QUES-TION.
MOM, I'M OFF NOW!
MAKE SURE YOU COME HOME BY SEVEN, SORA!
I KNOW, MOM!
SORRY TO KEEP YOU, YAMADA-SAN!

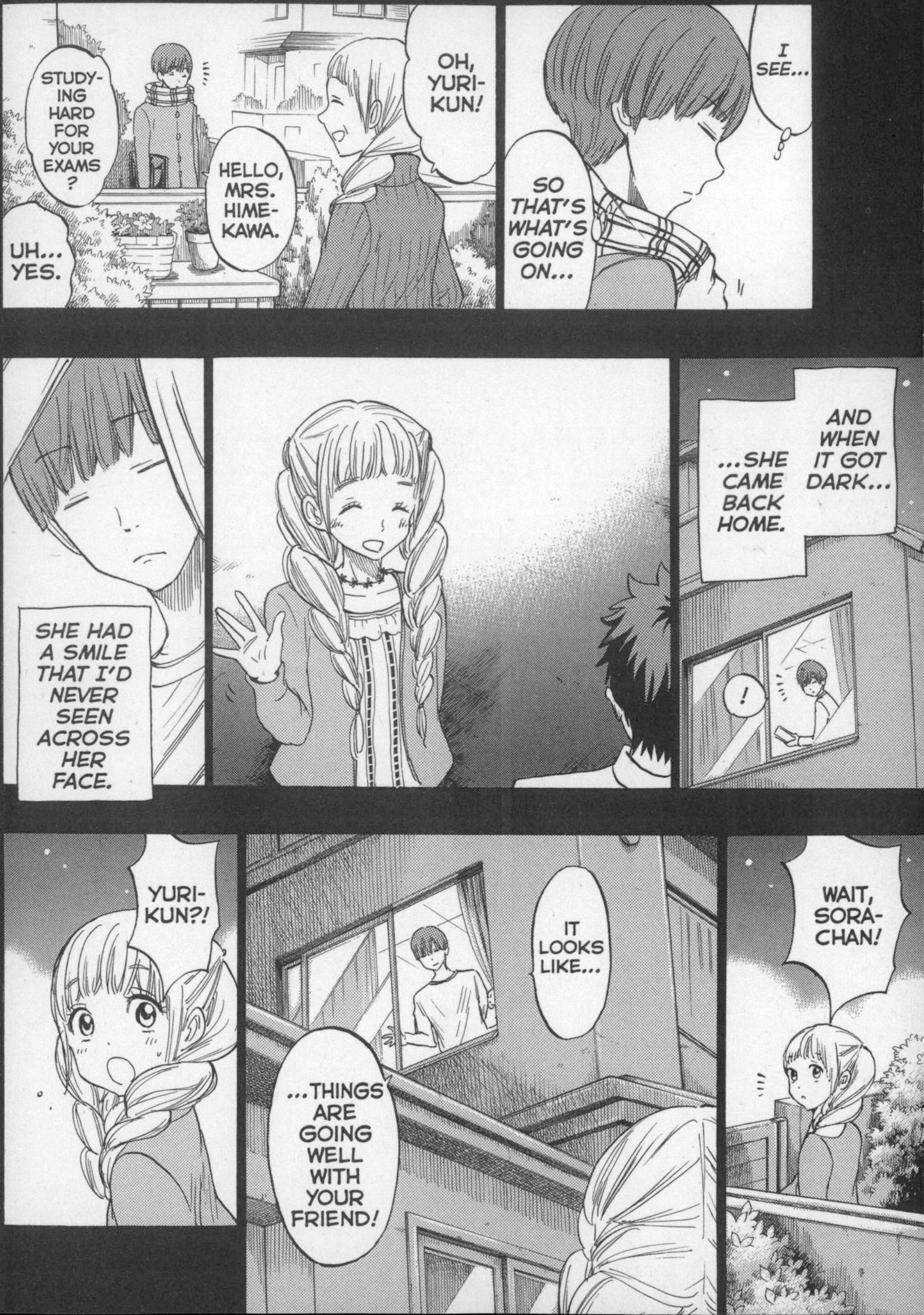
I SEE...
SO THAT'S WHAT'S GOING ON...
OH, YURI-KUN!
HELLO, MRS. HIME-KAWA.
STUDY-ING HARD FOR YOUR EXAMS?
UH... YES.
AND WHEN IT GOT DARK...
...SHE CAME BACK HOME.
!
SHE HAD A SMILE THAT I'D NEVER SEEN ACROSS HER FACE.
WAIT, SORA-CHAN!
IT LOOKS LIKE...
...THINGS ARE GOING WELL WITH YOUR FRIEND!
YURI-KUN?!

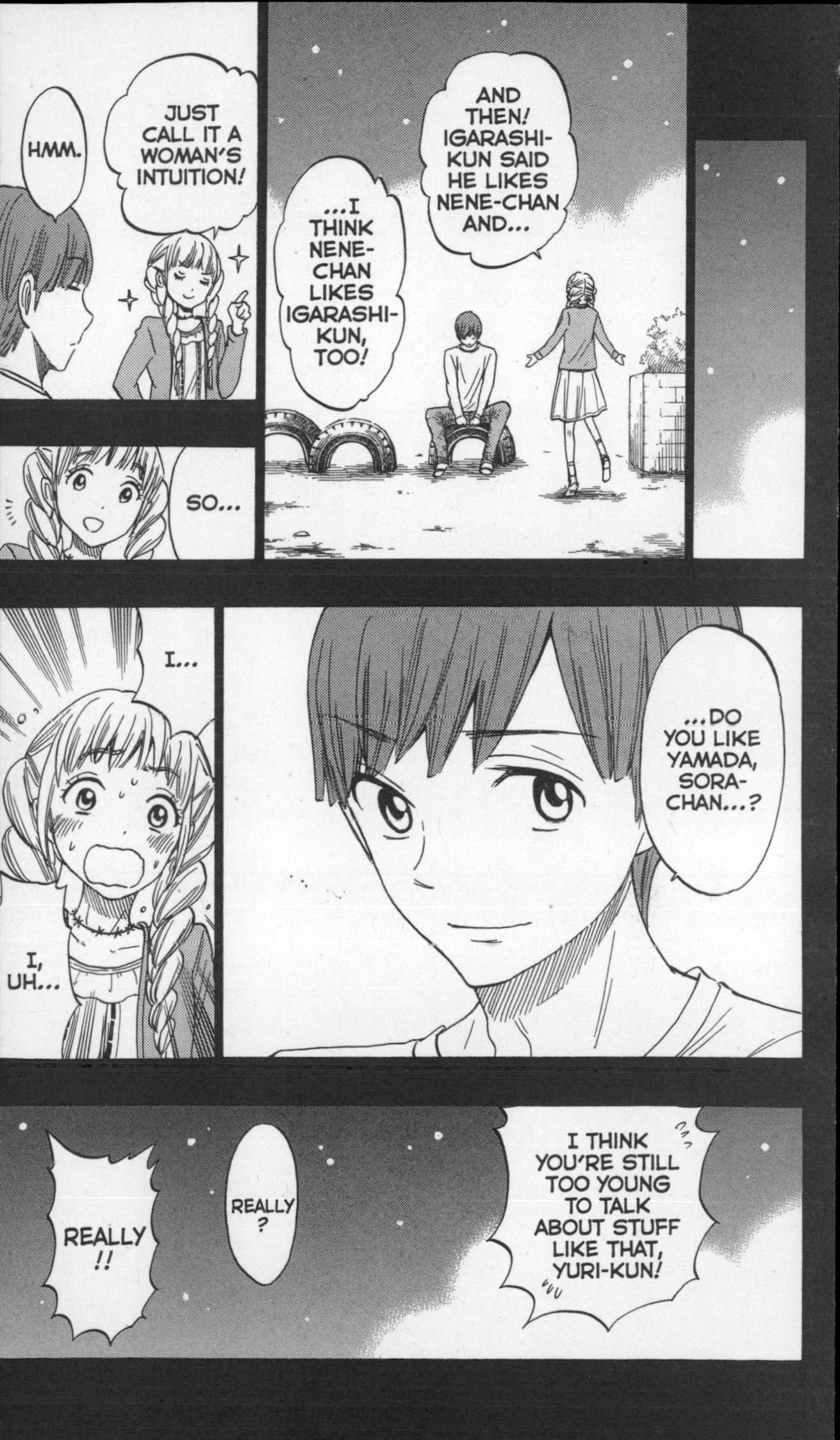
AND THEN! IGARASHI-KUN SAID HE LIKES NENE-CHAN AND...
...I THINK NENE-CHAN LIKES IGARASHI-KUN, TOO!
JUST CALL IT A WOMAN'S INTUITION!
HMM.
SO...
...DO YOU LIKE YAMADA, SORA-CHAN...?
I...
I, UH...
I THINK YOU'RE STILL TOO YOUNG TO TALK ABOUT STUFF LIKE THAT, YURI-KUN!
REALLY?
REALLY!!

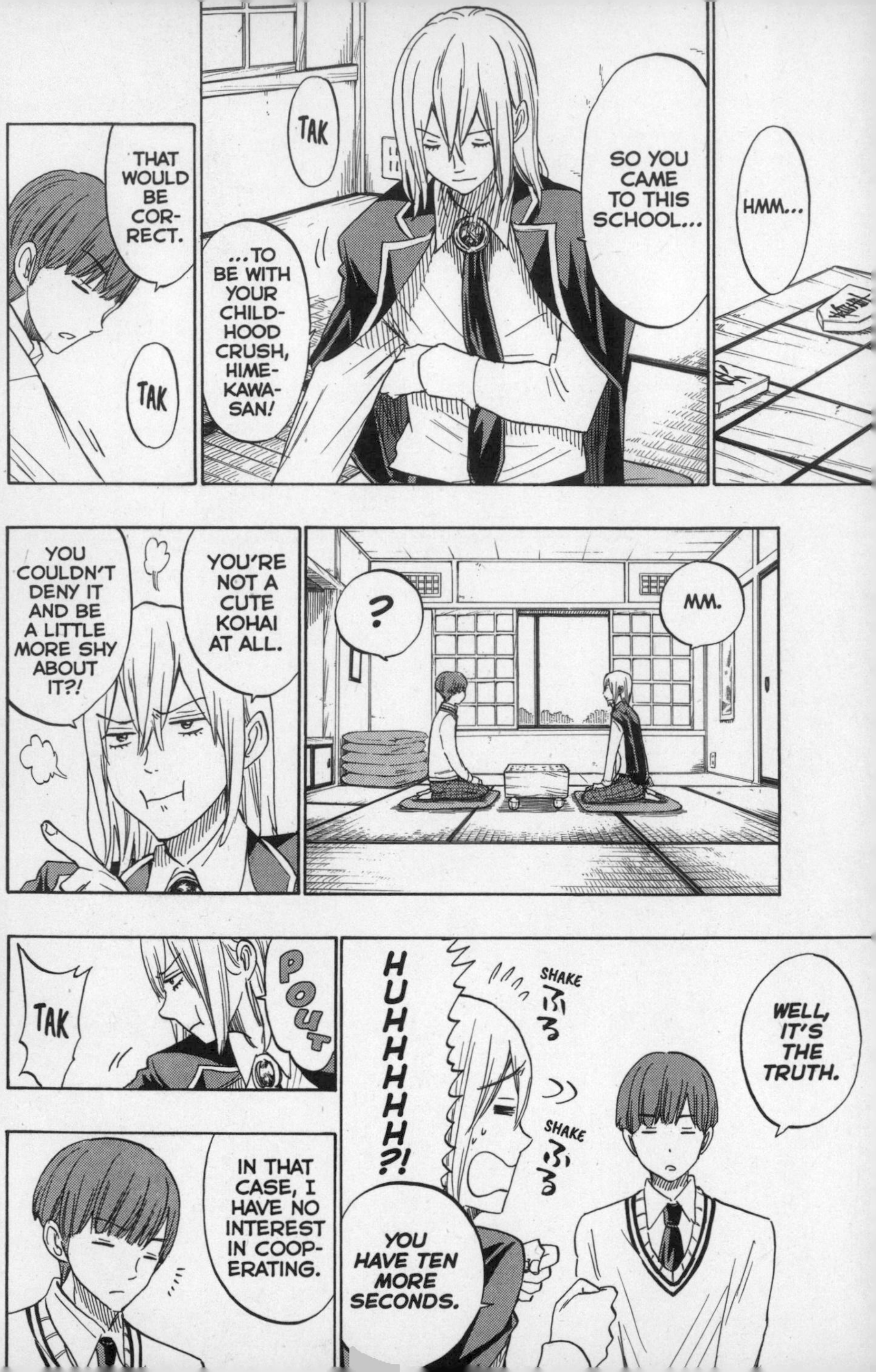
HMM...
SO YOU CAME TO THIS SCHOOL...
TAK
...TO BE WITH YOUR CHILD-HOOD CRUSH, HIME-KAWA-SAN!
THAT WOULD BE COR-RECT.
TAK
MM.
?
YOU'RE NOT A CUTE KOHAI AT ALL.
YOU COULDN'T DENY IT AND BE A LITTLE MORE SHY ABOUT IT?!
WELL, IT'S THE TRUTH.
SHAKE
ふる
HUHHHHHH?!
SHAKE
ふる
YOU HAVE TEN MORE SECONDS.
POUT
TAK
IN THAT CASE, I HAVE NO INTEREST IN COOP-ERATING.

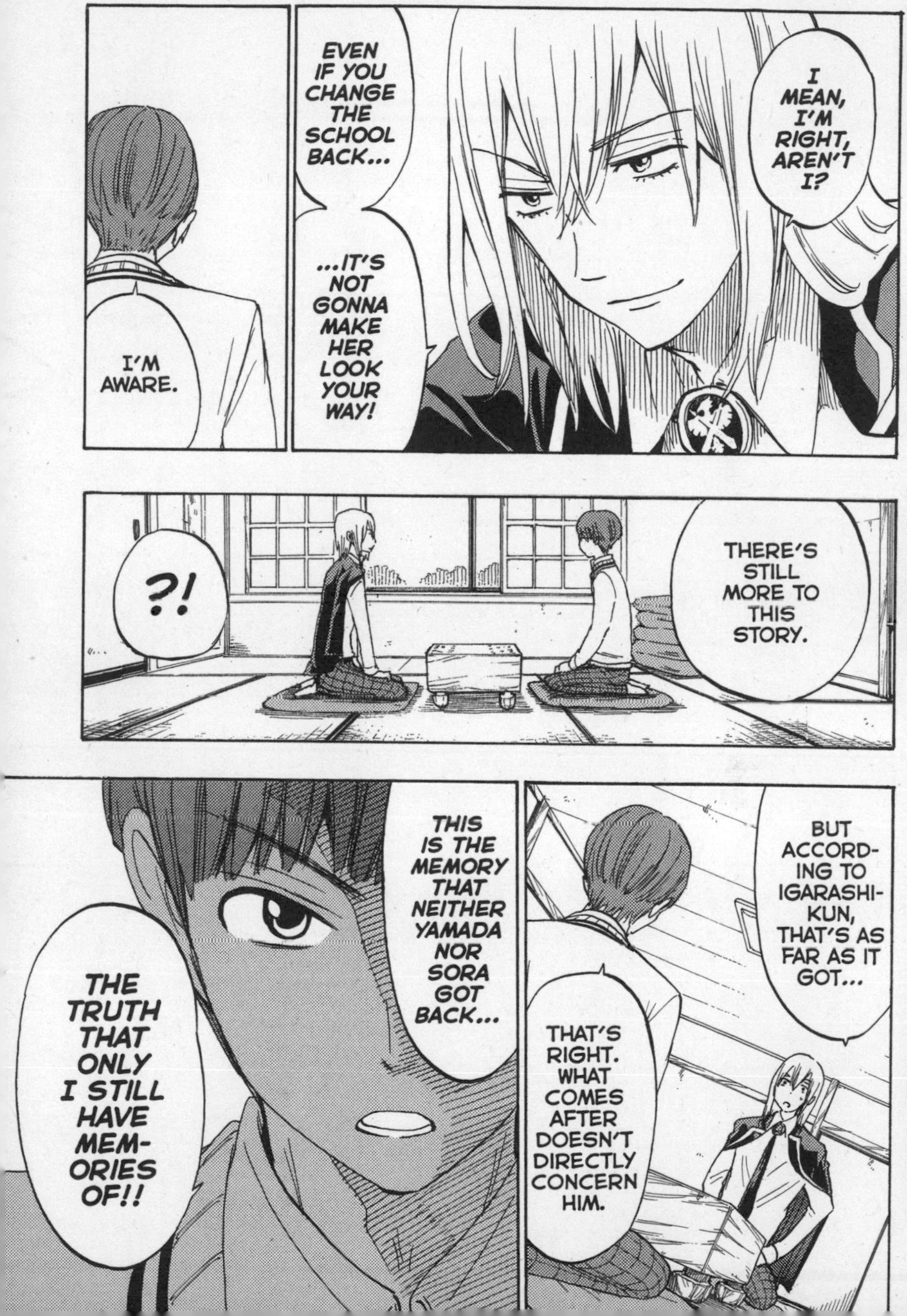
I MEAN, I'M RIGHT, AREN'T I?
EVEN IF YOU CHANGE THE SCHOOL BACK...
...IT'S NOT GONNA MAKE HER LOOK YOUR WAY!
I'M AWARE.
THERE'S STILL MORE TO THIS STORY.
?!
BUT ACCORDING TO IGARASHI-KUN, THAT'S AS FAR AS IT GOT...
THAT'S RIGHT. WHAT COMES AFTER DOESN'T DIRECTLY CONCERN HIM.
THIS IS THE MEMORY THAT NEITHER YAMADA NOR SORA GOT BACK...
THE TRUTH THAT ONLY I STILL HAVE MEMORIES OF!!

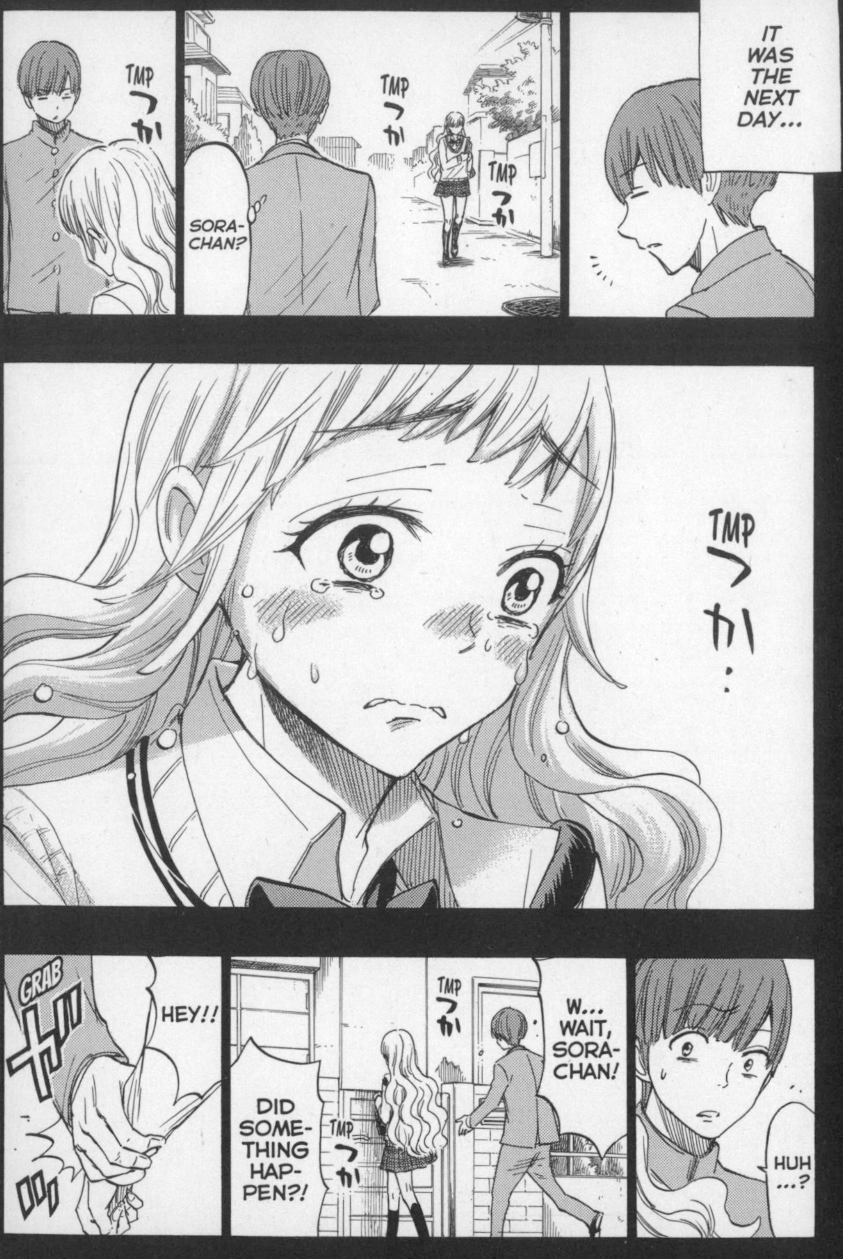
IT WAS THE NEXT DAY...
TMP つか
TMP つか
SORA-CHAN?
TMP つか
TMP つか...
HUH ...?
W... WAIT, SORA-CHAN!
TMP つか
DID SOME-THING HAP-PEN?!
TMP つか
HEY!!
GRAB

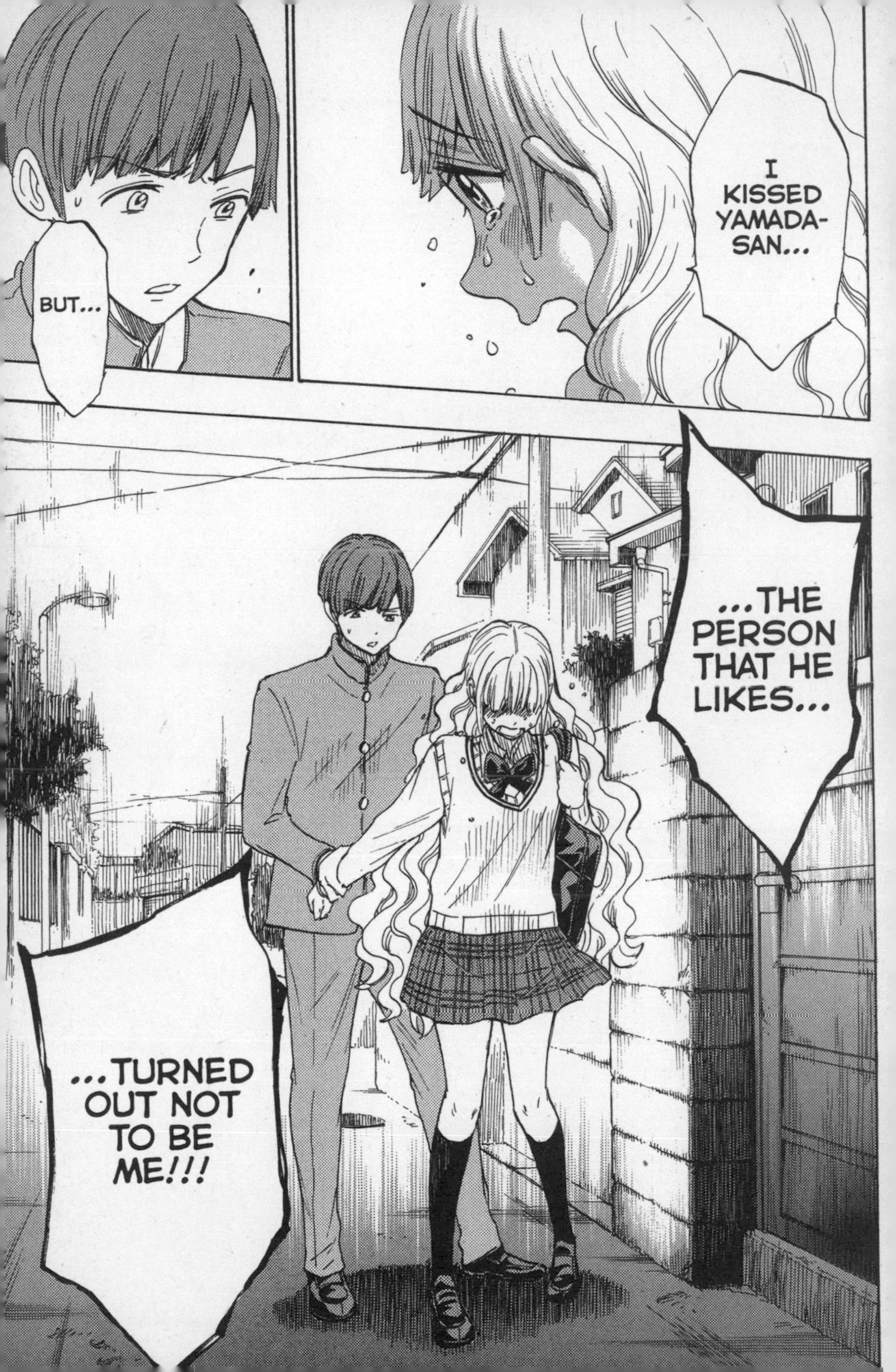
I KISSED YAMADA-SAN...
BUT...
...THE PERSON THAT HE LIKES...
...TURNED OUT NOT TO BE ME!!!

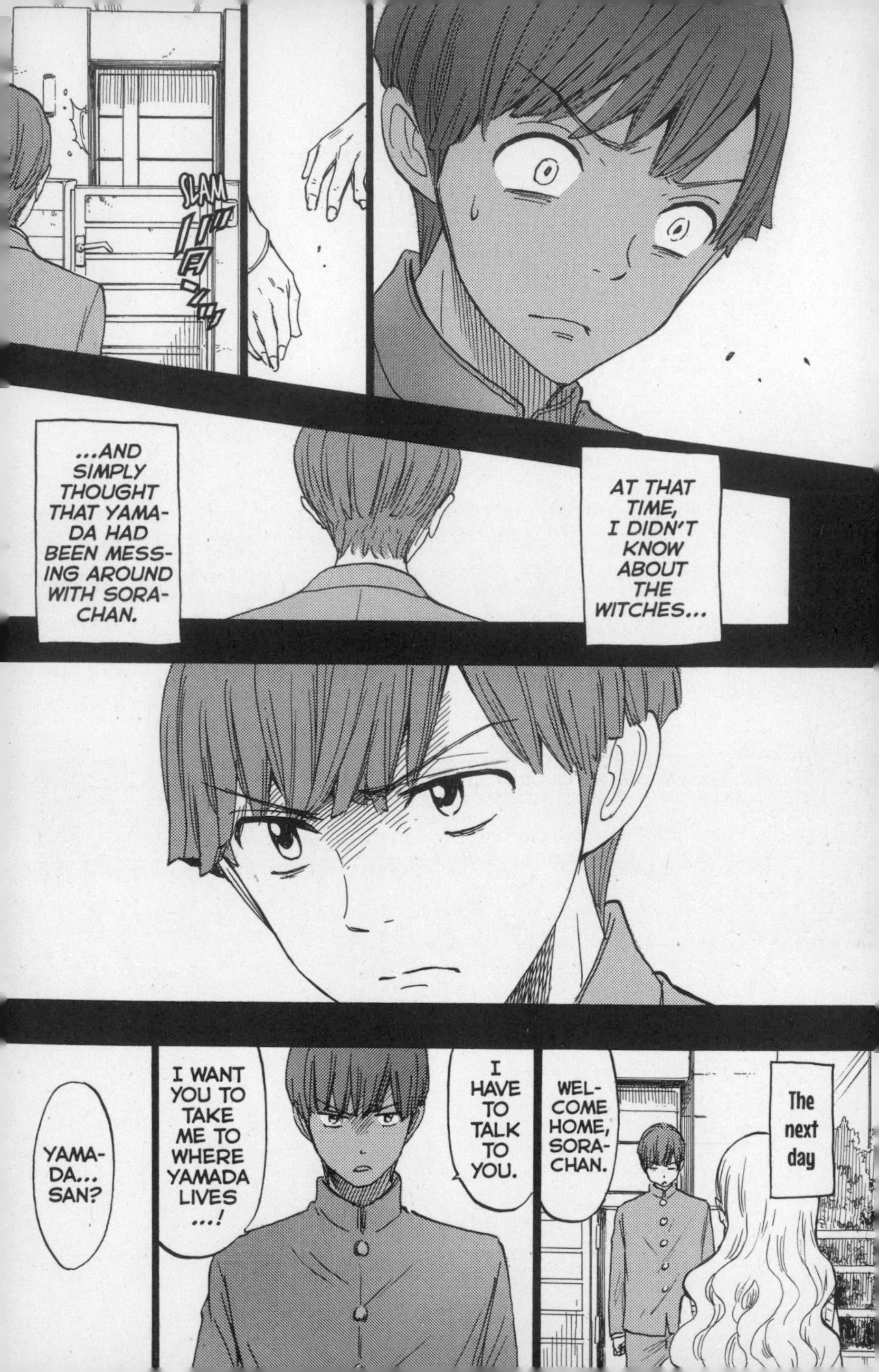
SLAM
AT THAT TIME, I DIDN'T KNOW ABOUT THE WITCHES...
...AND SIMPLY THOUGHT THAT YAMADA HAD BEEN MESSING AROUND WITH SORA-CHAN.
The next day
WELCOME HOME, SORA-CHAN.
I HAVE TO TALK TO YOU.
I WANT YOU TO TAKE ME TO WHERE YAMADA LIVES...!
YAMADA... SAN?

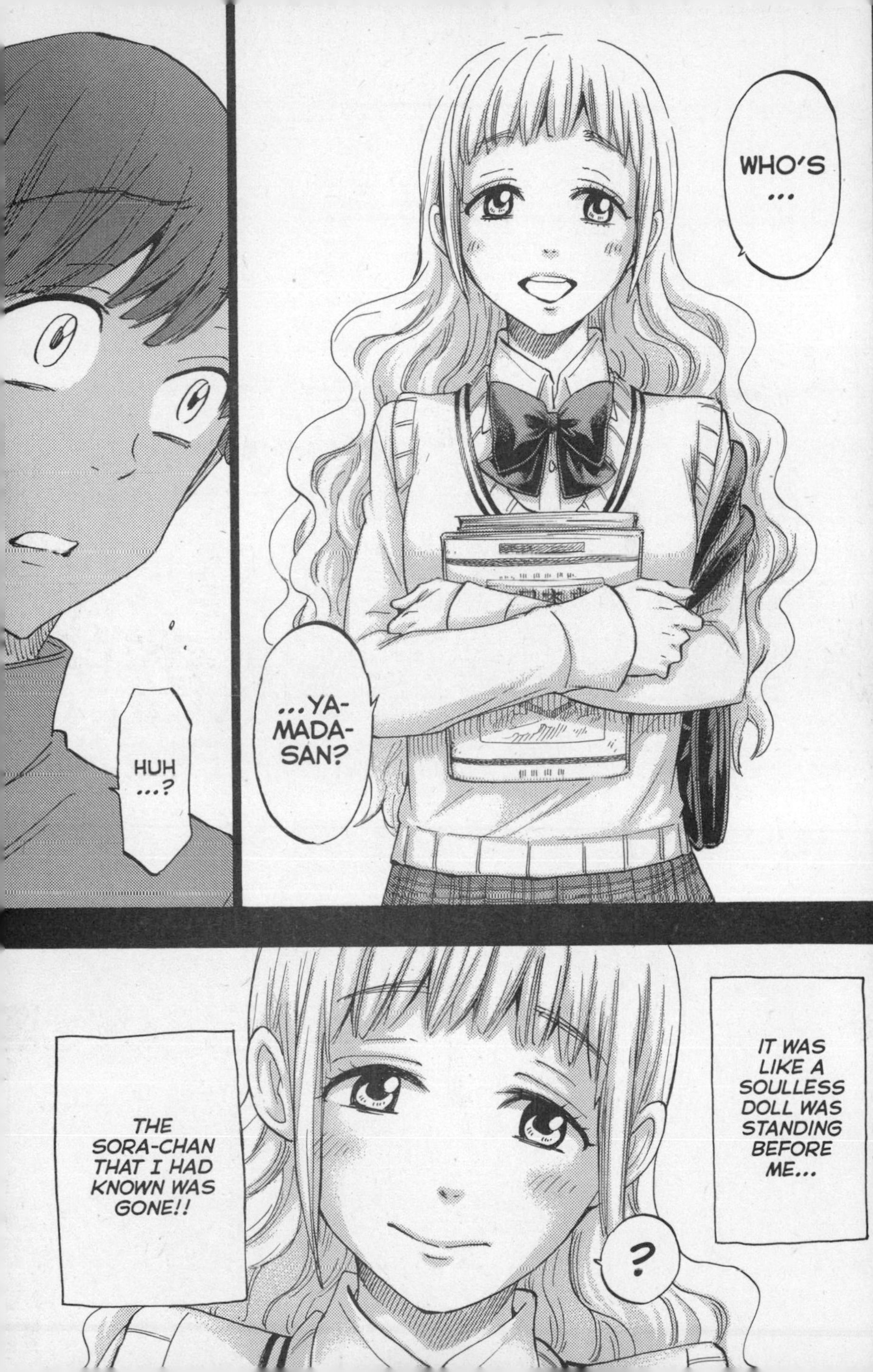
WHO'S ...
...YA-MADA-SAN?
HUH ...?
IT WAS LIKE A SOULLESS DOLL WAS STANDING BEFORE ME...
?
THE SORA-CHAN THAT I HAD KNOWN WAS GONE!!

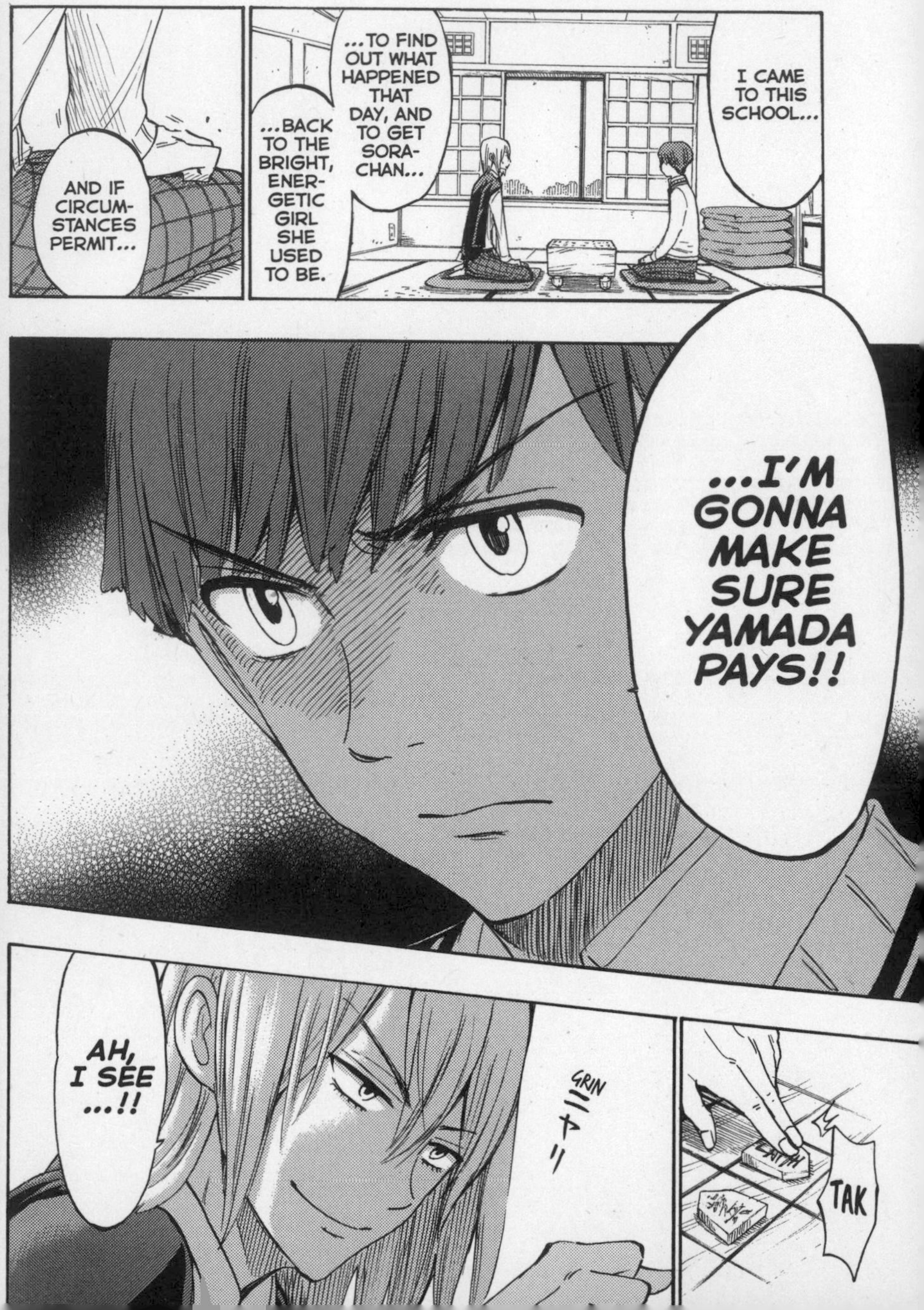
I CAME TO THIS SCHOOL...
...TO FIND OUT WHAT HAPPENED THAT DAY, AND TO GET SORA-CHAN...
...BACK TO THE BRIGHT, ENERGETIC GIRL SHE USED TO BE.
AND IF CIRCUMSTANCES PERMIT...
...I'M GONNA MAKE SURE YAMADA PAYS!!
TAK
AH, I SEE ...!!
GRIN

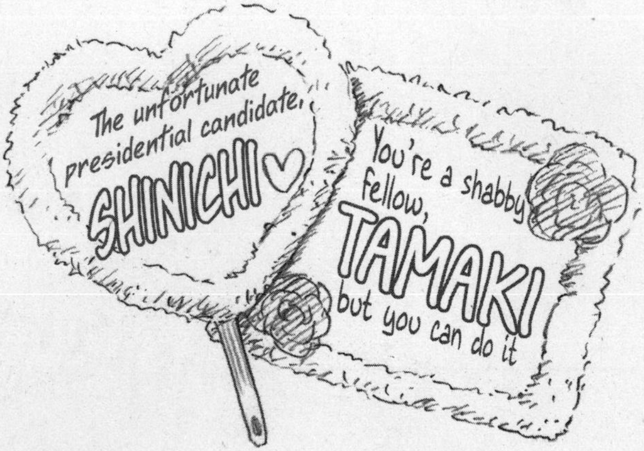
The unfortunate presidential candidate,
SHINICHI♡
You're a shabby fellow,
TAMAKI
but you can do it

Yamada-kun
AND THE
Seven Witches

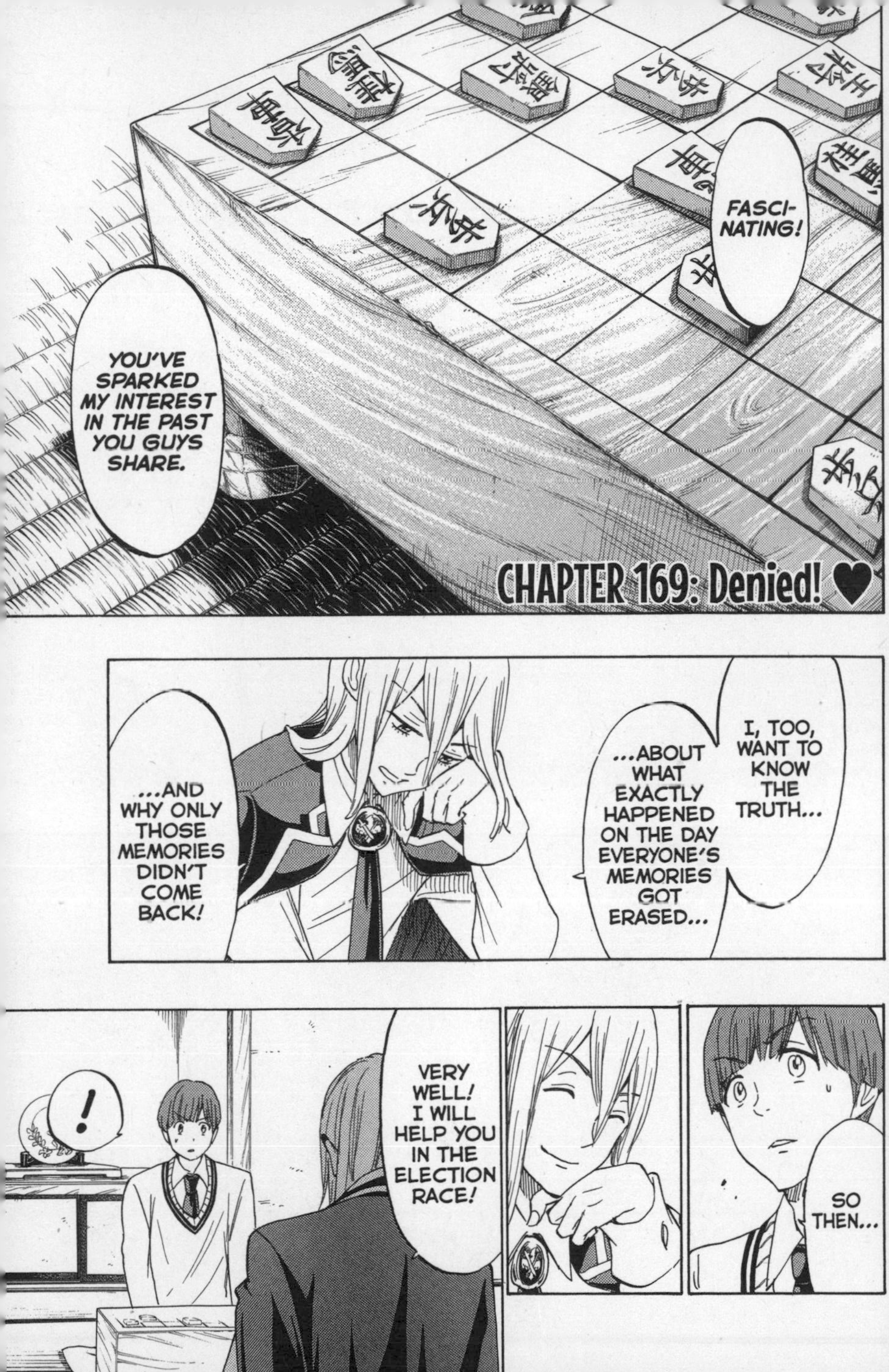
FASCINATING!
YOU'VE SPARKED MY INTEREST IN THE PAST YOU GUYS SHARE.
CHAPTER 169: Denied! ♥
I, TOO, WANT TO KNOW THE TRUTH...
...ABOUT WHAT EXACTLY HAPPENED ON THE DAY EVERYONE'S MEMORIES GOT ERASED...
...AND WHY ONLY THOSE MEMORIES DIDN'T COME BACK!
SO THEN...
VERY WELL! I WILL HELP YOU IN THE ELECTION RACE!
!

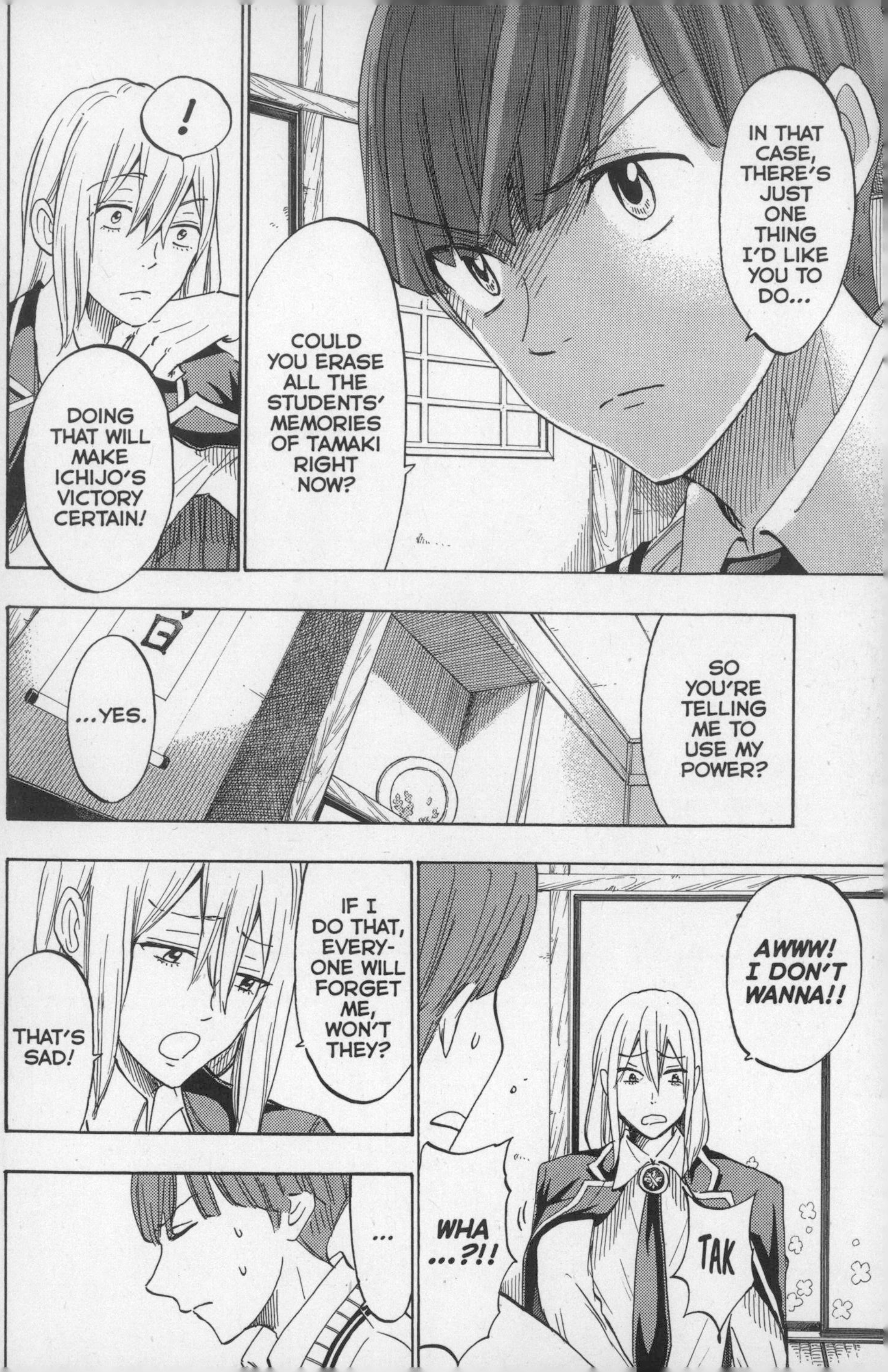
IN THAT CASE, THERE'S JUST ONE THING I'D LIKE YOU TO DO...
COULD YOU ERASE ALL THE STUDENTS' MEMORIES OF TAMAKI RIGHT NOW?
!
DOING THAT WILL MAKE ICHIJO'S VICTORY CERTAIN!
SO YOU'RE TELLING ME TO USE MY POWER?
...YES.
AWWW! I DON'T WANNA!!
TAK
WHA ...?!!
IF I DO THAT, EVERY-ONE WILL FORGET ME, WON'T THEY?
THAT'S SAD!
...

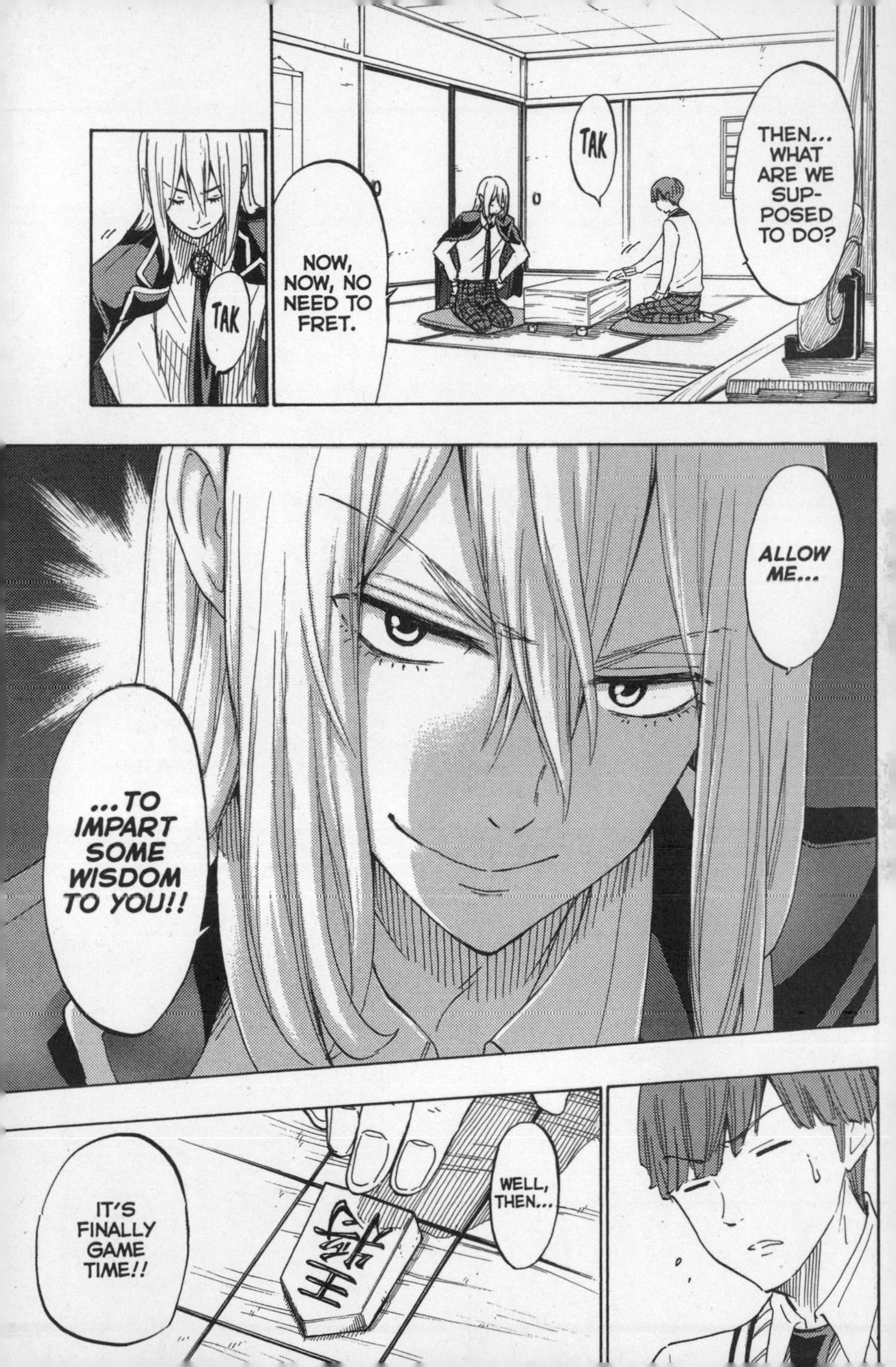
THEN... WHAT ARE WE SUP-POSED TO DO?
TAK
NOW, NOW, NO NEED TO FRET.
TAK
ALLOW ME...
...TO IMPART SOME WISDOM TO YOU!!
WELL, THEN...
IT'S FINALLY GAME TIME!!

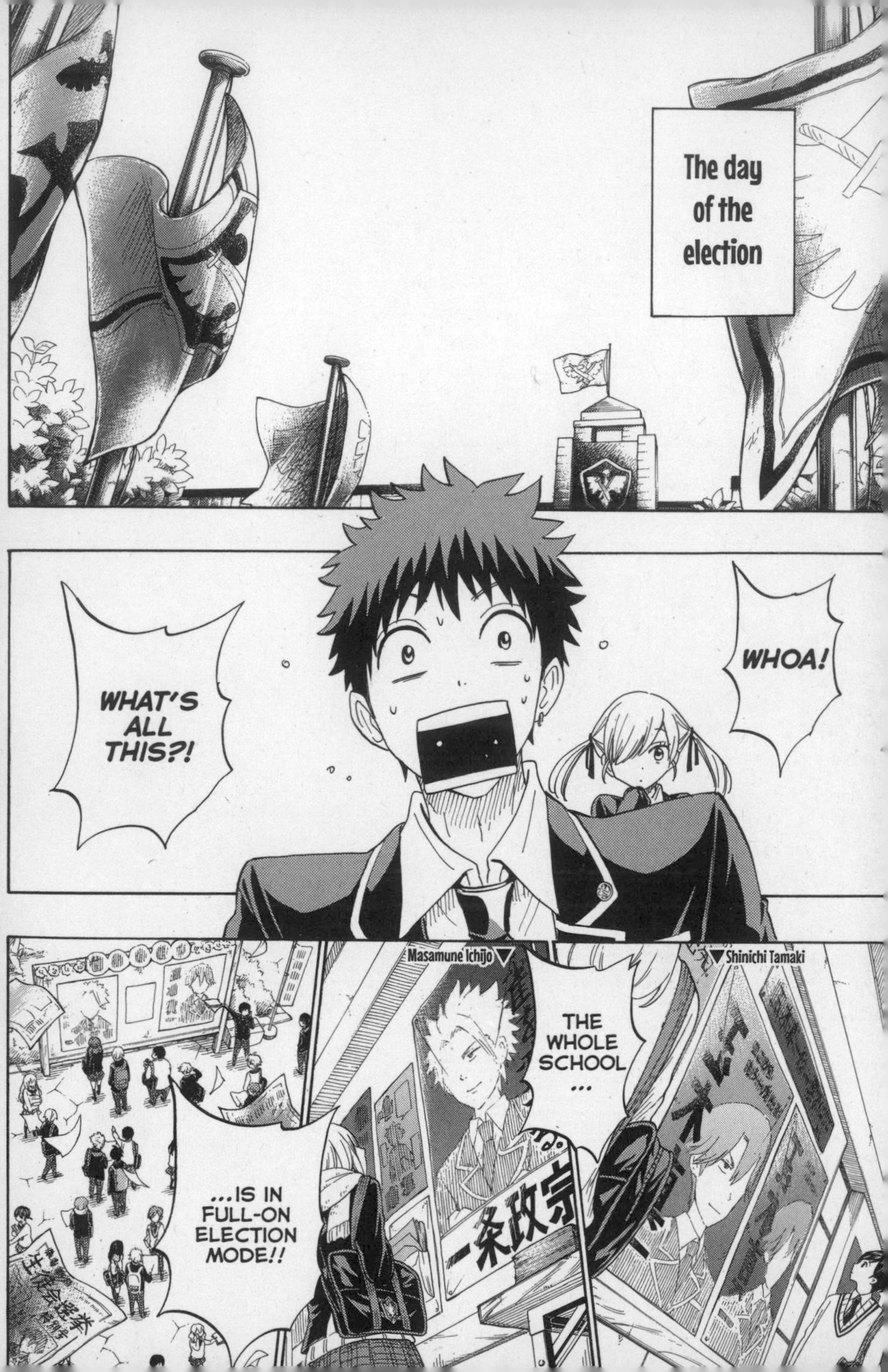
The day of the election
WHOA!
WHAT'S ALL THIS?!
Shinichi Tamaki
Masamune Ichijo
THE WHOLE SCHOOL ...
一条政宗
...IS IN FULL-ON ELECTION MODE!!

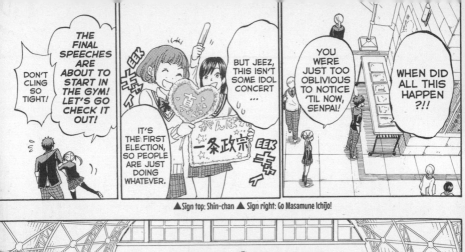

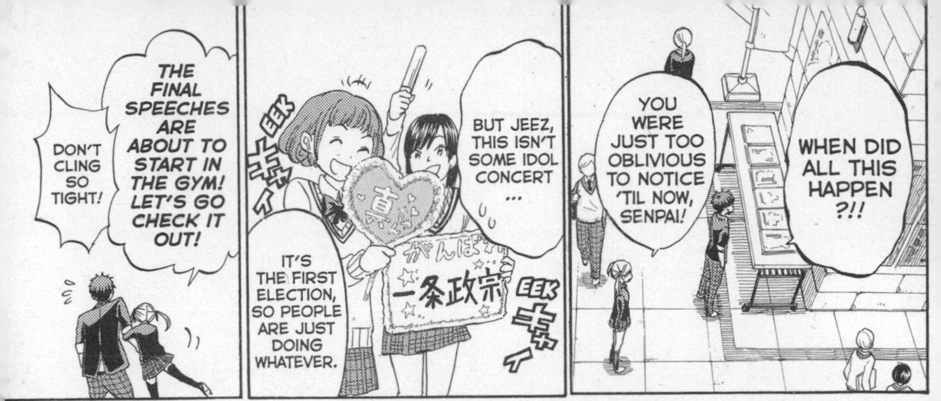
WHEN DID ALL THIS HAPPEN?!!
YOU WERE JUST TOO OBLIVIOUS TO NOTICE 'TIL NOW, SENPAI!
BUT JEEZ, THIS ISN'T SOME IDOL CONCERT ...
EEK
EEK
IT'S THE FIRST ELECTION, SO PEOPLE ARE JUST DOING WHATEVER.
一条政宗
THE FINAL SPEECHES ARE ABOUT TO START IN THE GYM! LET'S GO CHECK IT OUT!
DON'T CLING SO TIGHT!

▲Sign top: Shin-chan ▲ Sign right: Go Masamune Ichijo!

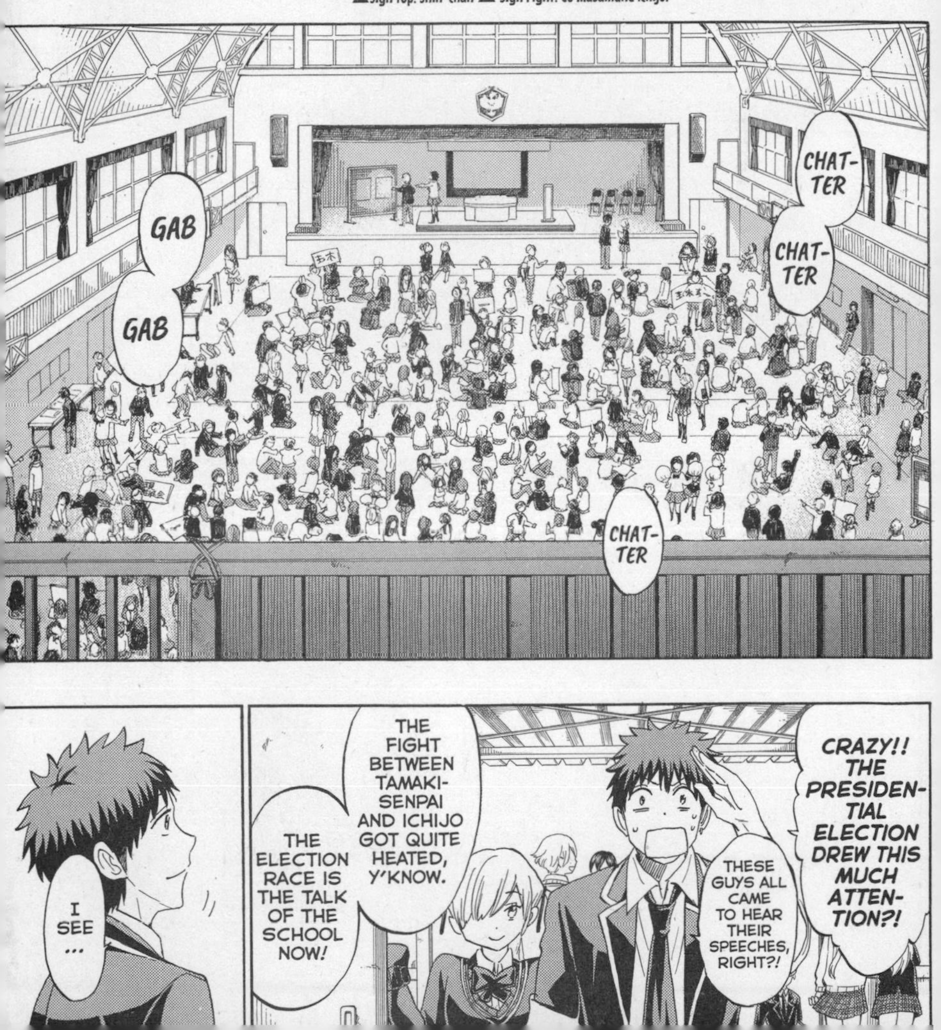
CHAT-TER
CHAT-TER
GAB
GAB
CHAT-TER
CRAZY!! THE PRESIDEN-TIAL ELECTION DREW THIS MUCH ATTEN-TION?!
THESE GUYS ALL CAME TO HEAR THEIR SPEECHES, RIGHT?!
THE FIGHT BETWEEN TAMAKI-SENPAI AND ICHIJO GOT QUITE HEATED, Y'KNOW.
THE ELECTION RACE IS THE TALK OF THE SCHOOL NOW!
I SEE ...

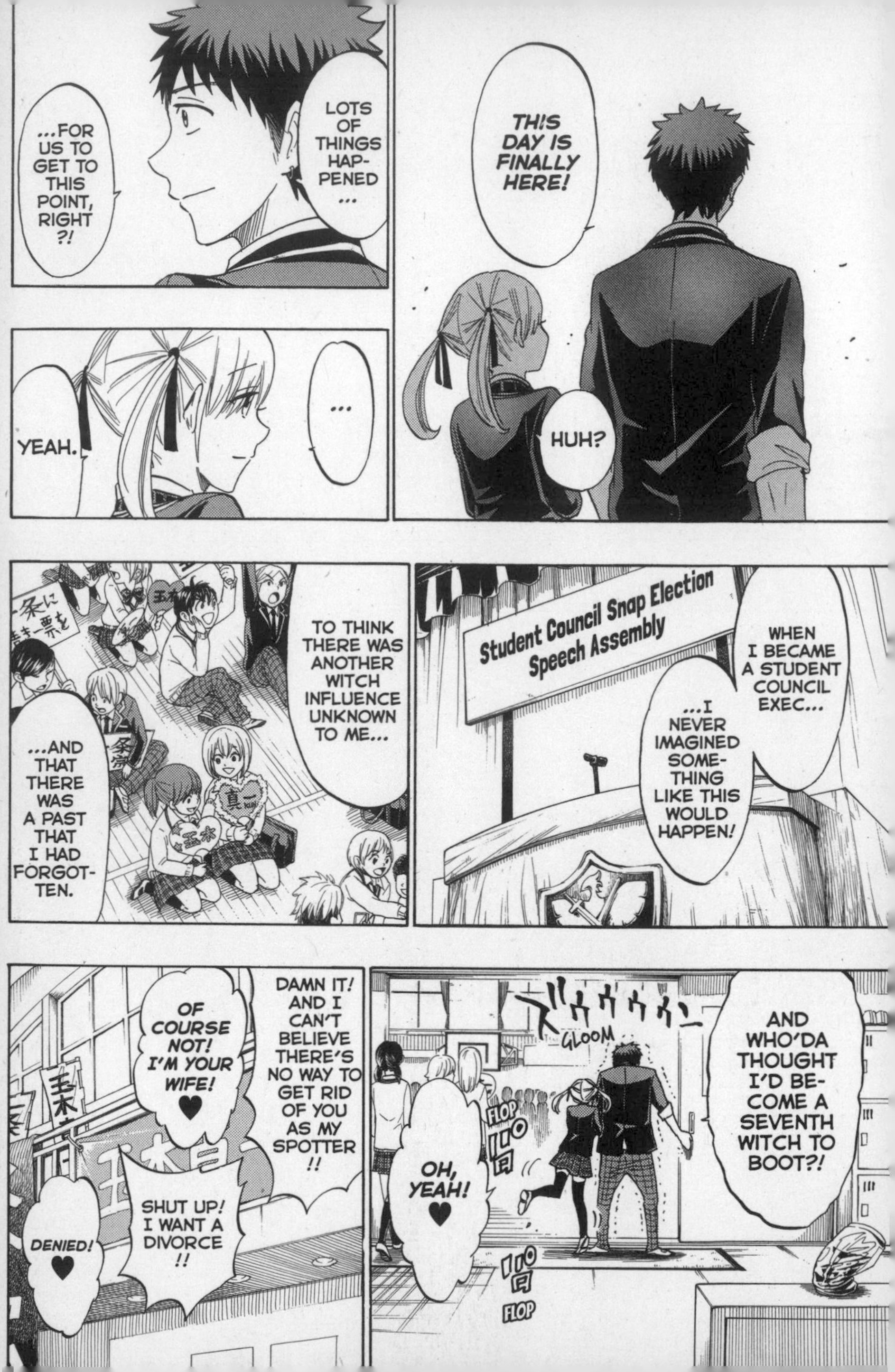
THIS DAY IS FINALLY HERE!
HUH?
LOTS OF THINGS HAPPENED...
...FOR US TO GET TO THIS POINT, RIGHT?!
...
YEAH.
Student Council Snap Election Speech Assembly
WHEN I BECAME A STUDENT COUNCIL EXEC...
...I NEVER IMAGINED SOMETHING LIKE THIS WOULD HAPPEN!
TO THINK THERE WAS ANOTHER WITCH INFLUENCE UNKNOWN TO ME...
...AND THAT THERE WAS A PAST THAT I HAD FORGOTTEN.
AND WHO'DA THOUGHT I'D BECOME A SEVENTH WITCH TO BOOT?!
GLOOM
FLOP
OH, YEAH! ♥
FLOP
DAMN IT! AND I CAN'T BELIEVE THERE'S NO WAY TO GET RID OF YOU AS MY SPOTTER!!
OF COURSE NOT! I'M YOUR WIFE! ♥
SHUT UP! I WANT A DIVORCE!!
DENIED! ♥

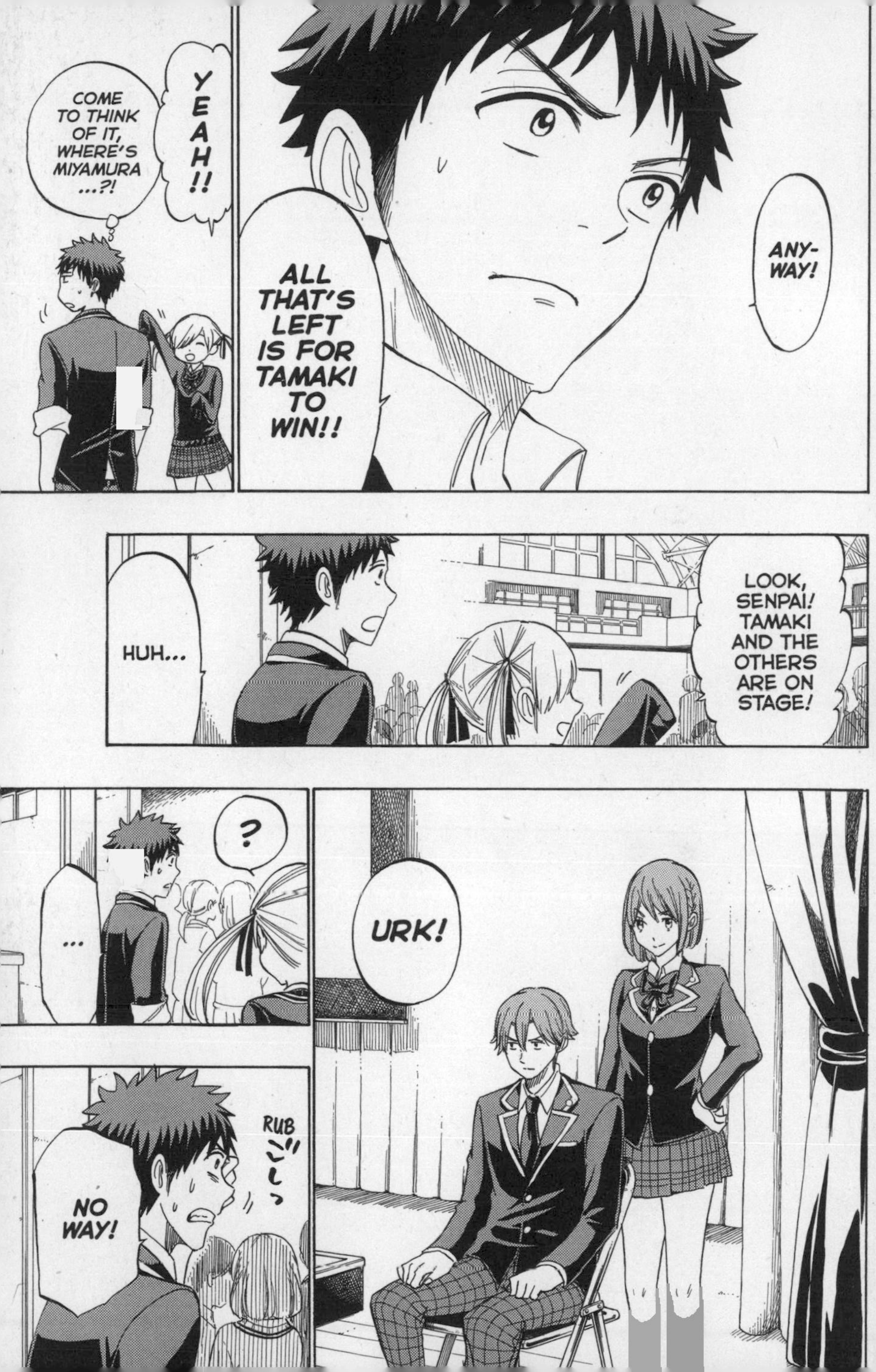
ANY-WAY!
ALL THAT'S LEFT IS FOR TAMAKI TO WIN!!
YEAH!!
COME TO THINK OF IT, WHERE'S MIYAMURA ...?!
LOOK, SENPAI! TAMAKI AND THE OTHERS ARE ON STAGE!
HUH...
URK!
?
...
RUB ごしっ
NO WAY!

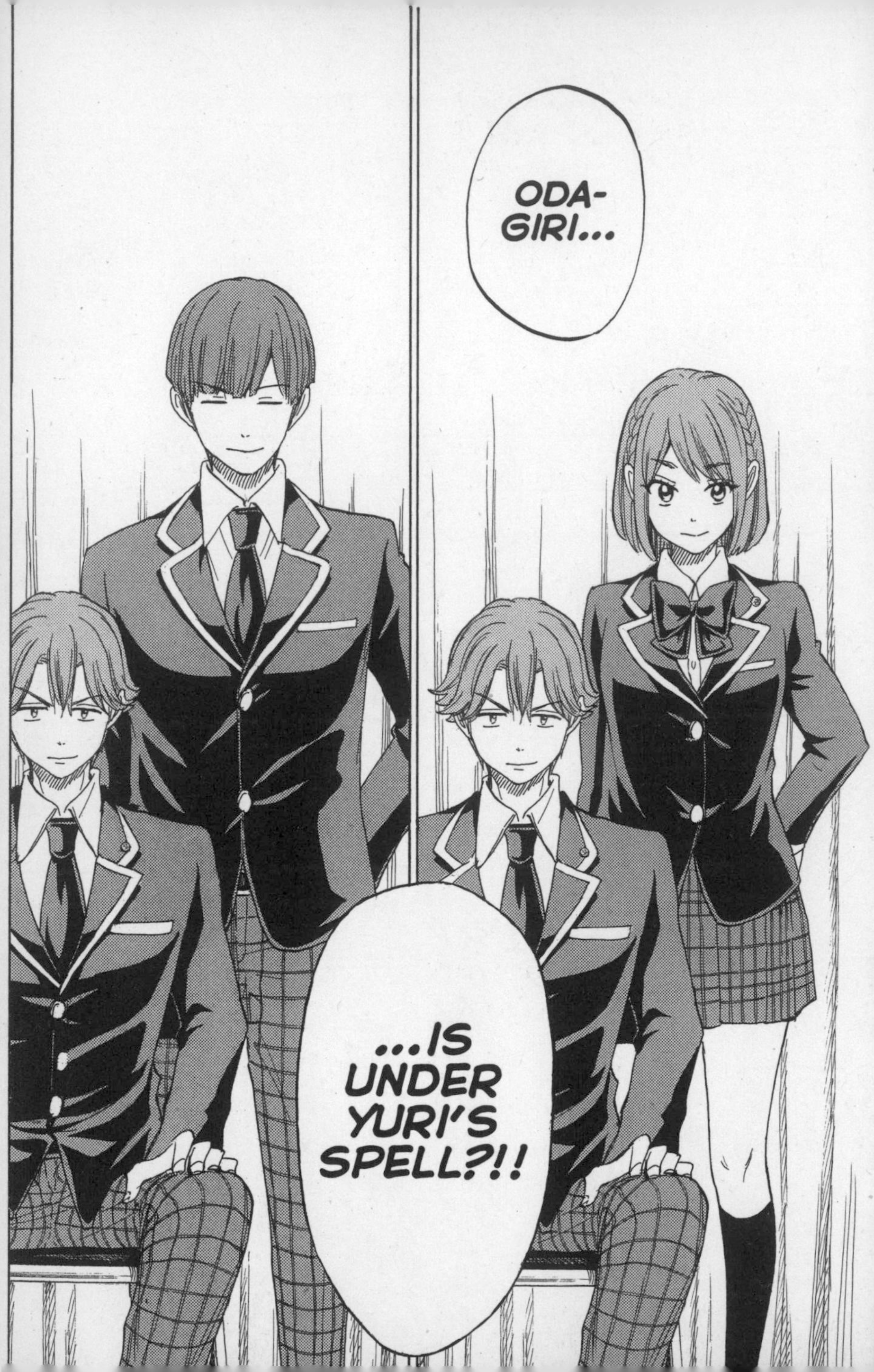
ODA-GIRI...
...IS UNDER YURI'S SPELL?!!

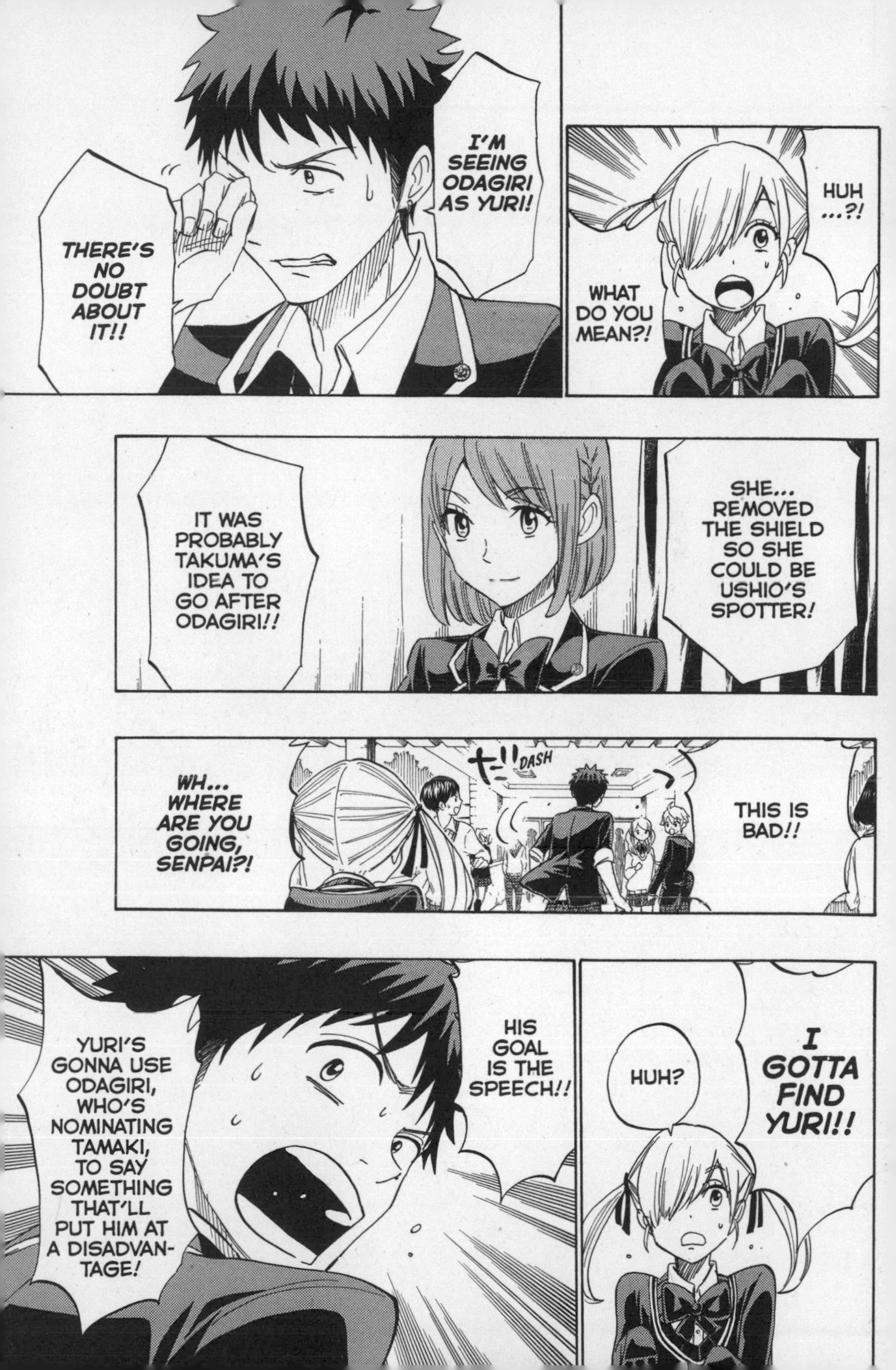
HUH ...?!
WHAT DO YOU MEAN?!
I'M SEEING ODAGIRI AS YURI!
THERE'S NO DOUBT ABOUT IT!!
SHE... REMOVED THE SHIELD SO SHE COULD BE USHIO'S SPOTTER!
IT WAS PROBABLY TAKUMA'S IDEA TO GO AFTER ODAGIRI!!
THIS IS BAD!!
DASH
WH... WHERE ARE YOU GOING, SENPAI?!
I GOTTA FIND YURI!!
HUH?
HIS GOAL IS THE SPEECH!!
YURI'S GONNA USE ODAGIRI, WHO'S NOMINATING TAMAKI, TO SAY SOMETHING THAT'LL PUT HIM AT A DISADVANTAGE!

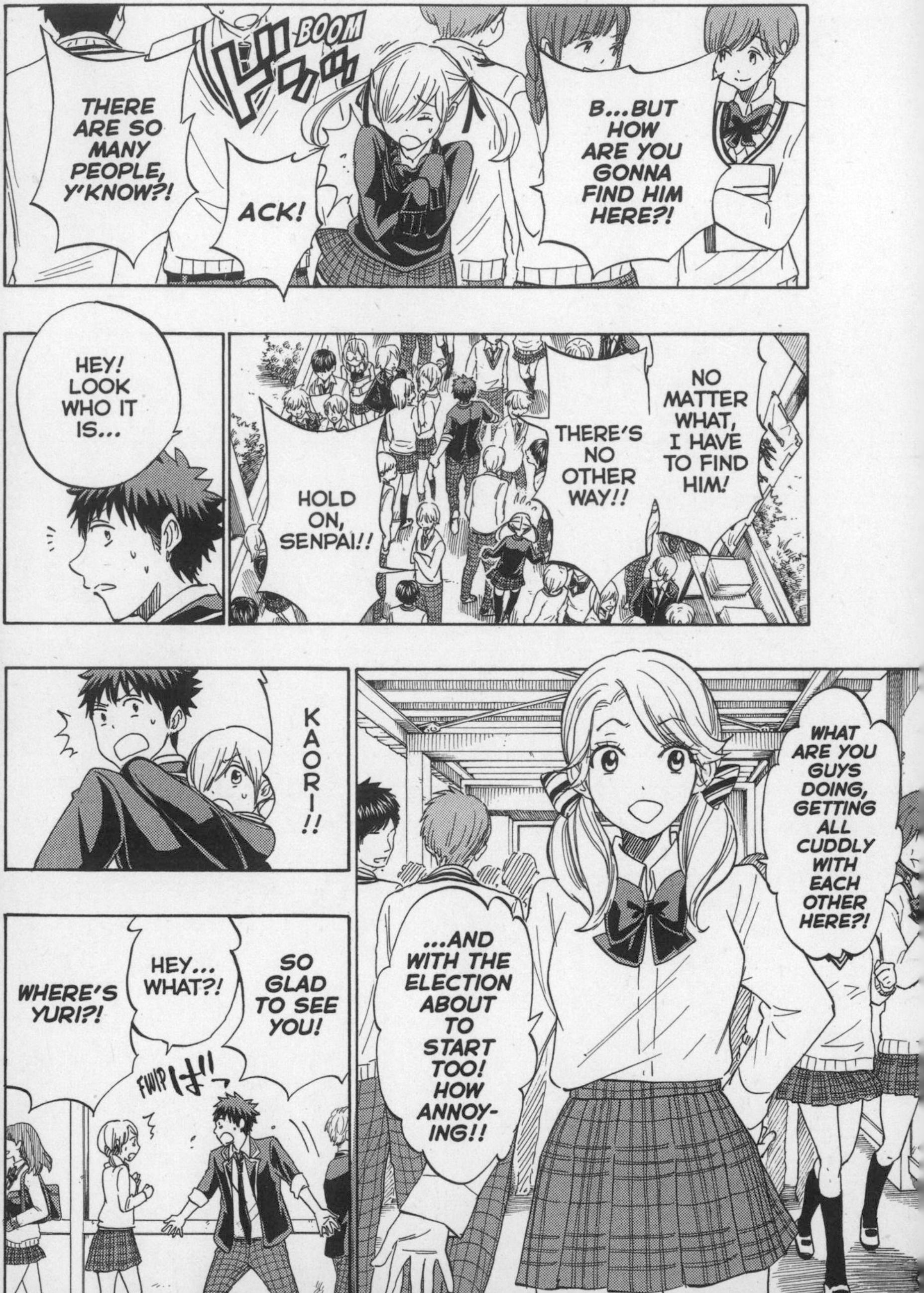

B...BUT HOW ARE YOU GONNA FIND HIM HERE?!
BOOM
THERE ARE SO MANY PEOPLE, Y'KNOW?!
ACK!
NO MATTER WHAT, I HAVE TO FIND HIM!
THERE'S NO OTHER WAY!!
HOLD ON, SENPAI!!
HEY! LOOK WHO IT IS...
WHAT ARE YOU GUYS DOING, GETTING ALL CUDDLY WITH EACH OTHER HERE?!
...AND WITH THE ELECTION ABOUT TO START TOO! HOW ANNOY-ING!!
KAORI!!
SO GLAD TO SEE YOU!
HEY... WHAT?!
WHERE'S YURI?!
FWIP ぱっ

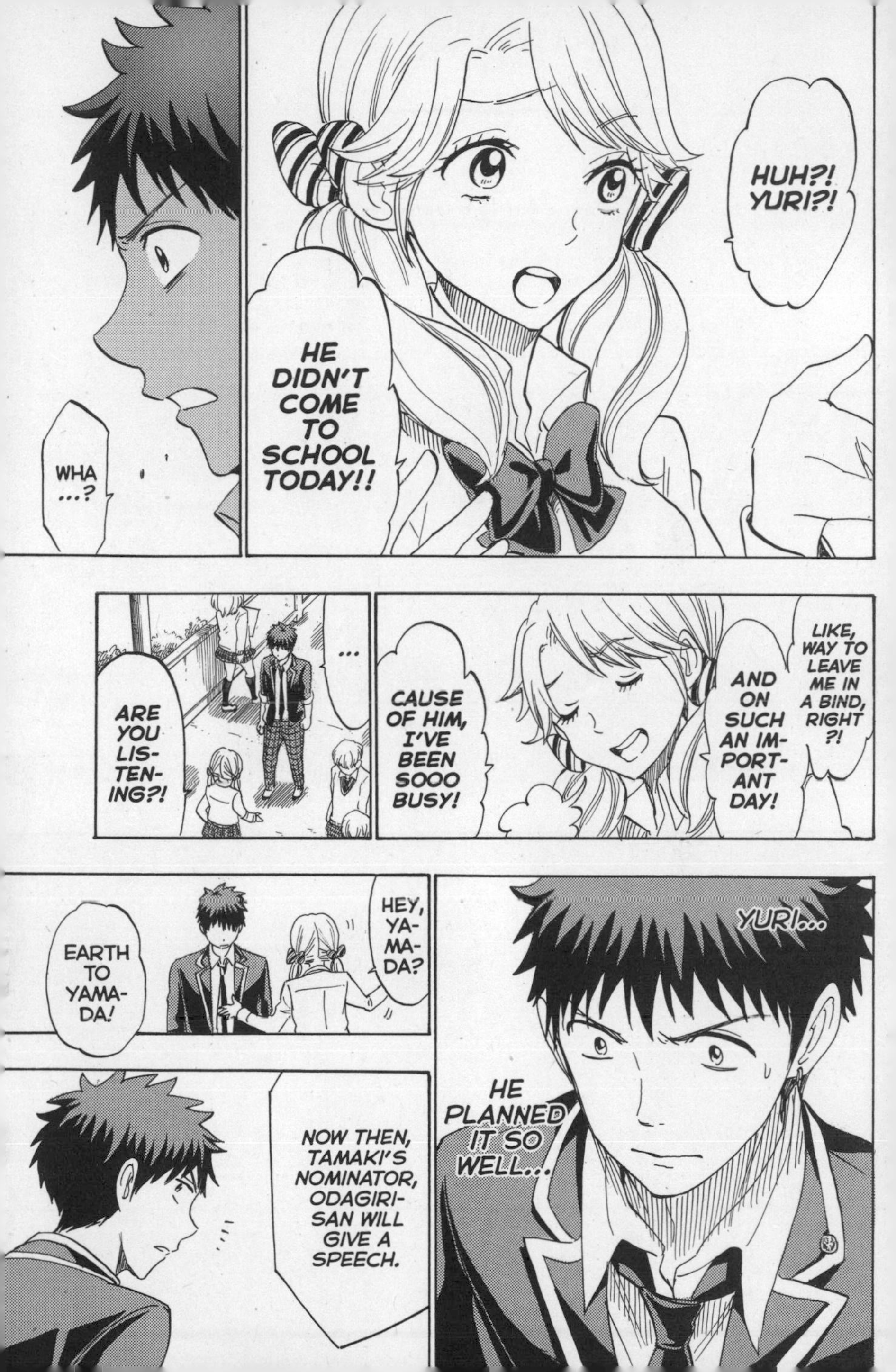

HUH?! YURI?!
HE DIDN'T COME TO SCHOOL TODAY!!
WHA...?
LIKE, WAY TO LEAVE ME IN A BIND, RIGHT?!
AND ON SUCH AN IMPORTANT DAY!
CAUSE OF HIM, I'VE BEEN SOOO BUSY!
...
ARE YOU LISTENING?!
YURI...
HE PLANNED IT SO WELL...
HEY, YAMADA?
EARTH TO YAMADA!
NOW THEN, TAMAKI'S NOMINATOR, ODAGIRI-SAN WILL GIVE A SPEECH.

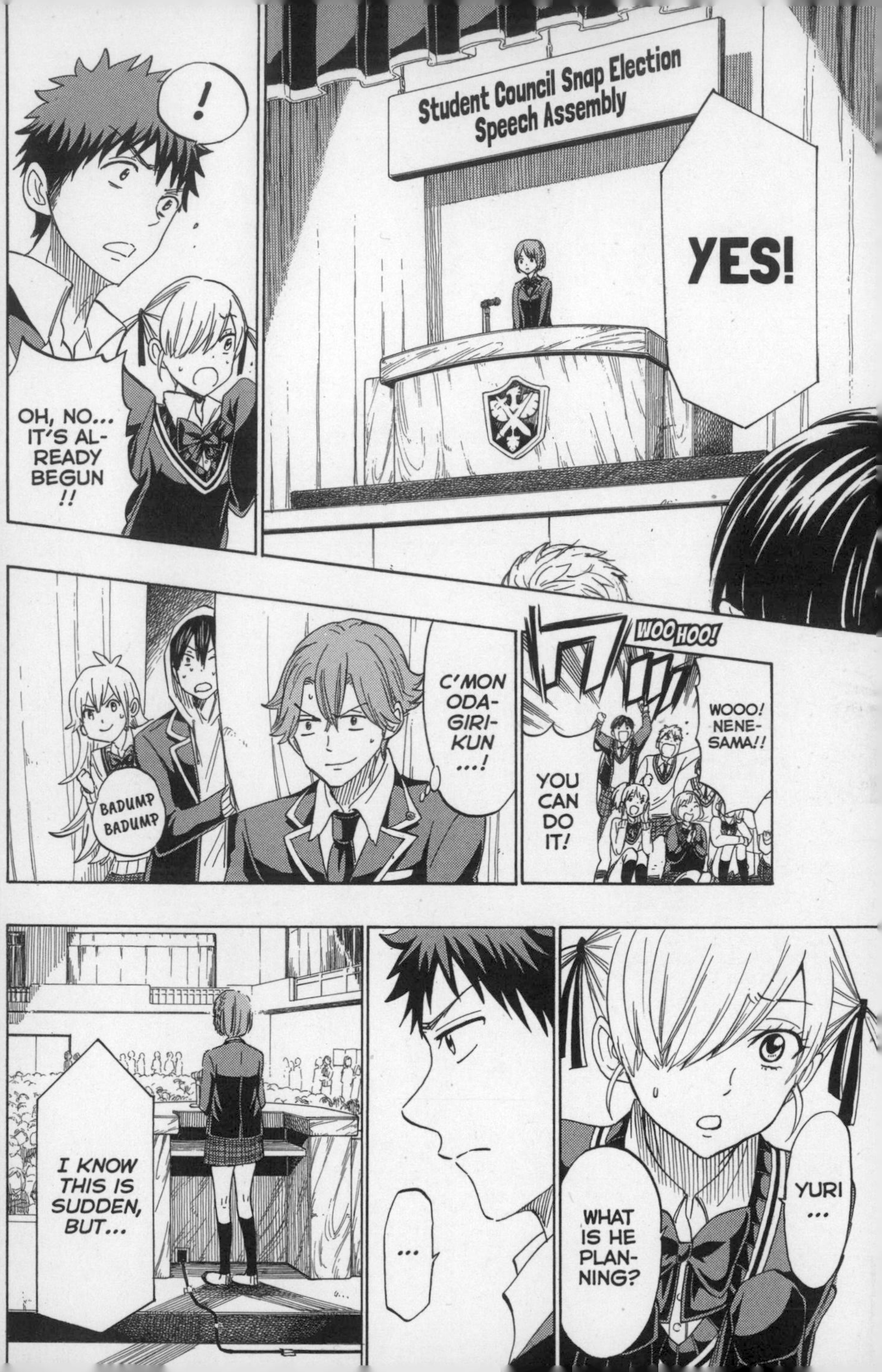
Student Council Snap Election Speech Assembly
YES!
!
OH, NO... IT'S AL-READY BEGUN !!
WOO HOO!
WOOO! NENE-SAMA!!
YOU CAN DO IT!
C'MON ODA-GIRI-KUN ...!
BADUMP BADUMP
YURI ...
WHAT IS HE PLAN-NING?
...
I KNOW THIS IS SUDDEN, BUT...

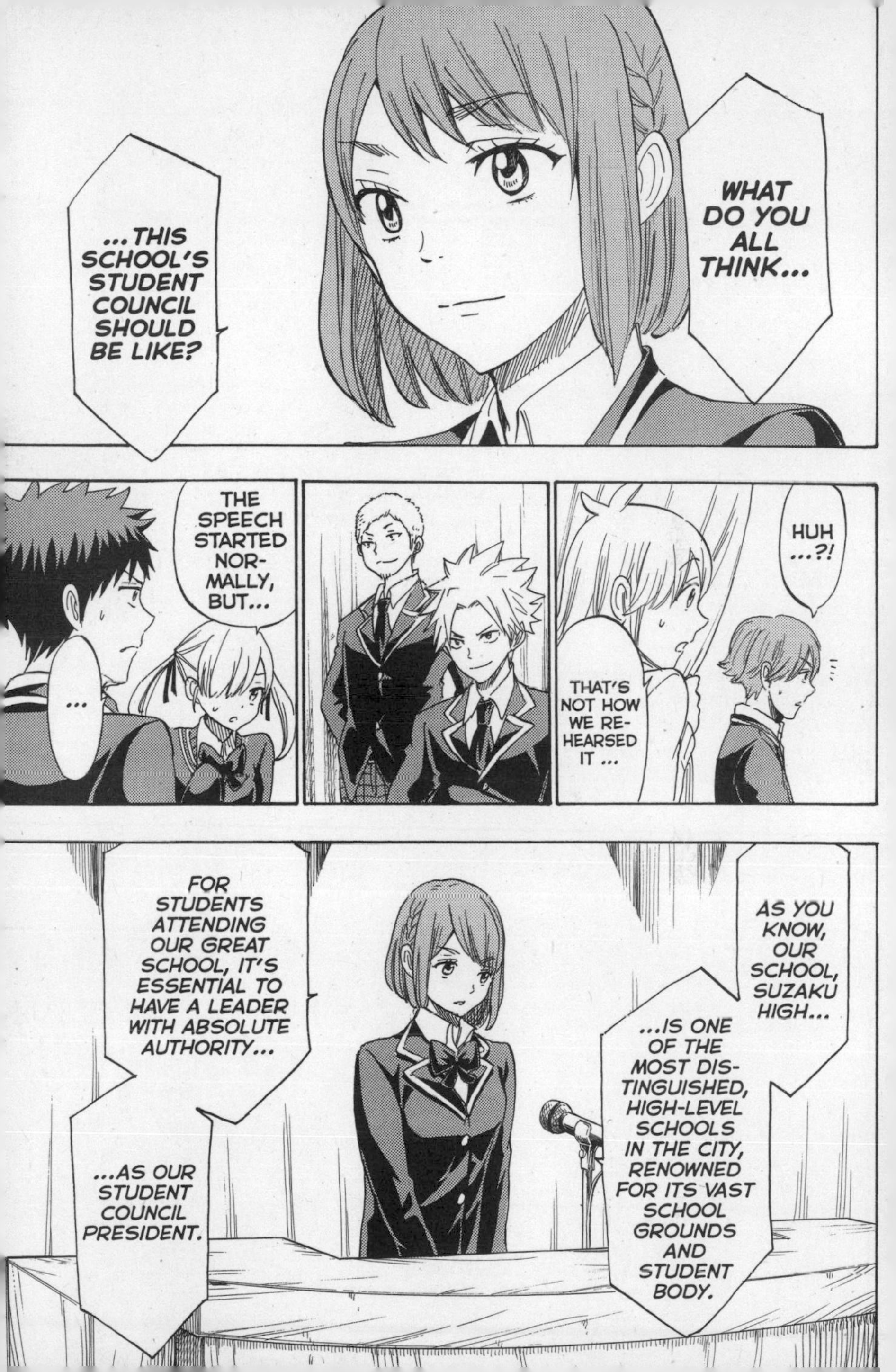
WHAT DO YOU ALL THINK...
...THIS SCHOOL'S STUDENT COUNCIL SHOULD BE LIKE?
HUH ...?!
THAT'S NOT HOW WE REHEARSED IT ...
THE SPEECH STARTED NORMALLY, BUT...
...
AS YOU KNOW, OUR SCHOOL, SUZAKU HIGH...
...IS ONE OF THE MOST DISTINGUISHED, HIGH-LEVEL SCHOOLS IN THE CITY, RENOWNED FOR ITS VAST SCHOOL GROUNDS AND STUDENT BODY.
FOR STUDENTS ATTENDING OUR GREAT SCHOOL, IT'S ESSENTIAL TO HAVE A LEADER WITH ABSOLUTE AUTHORITY...
...AS OUR STUDENT COUNCIL PRESIDENT.

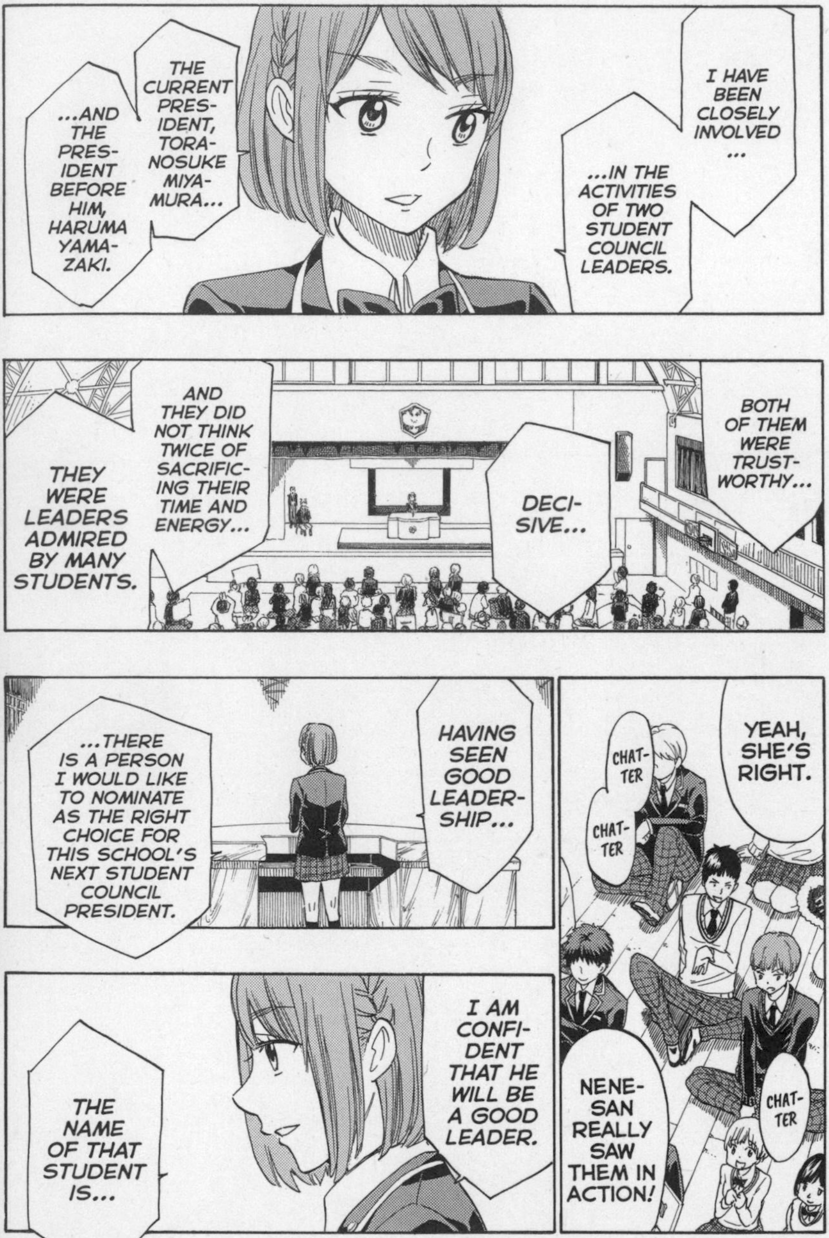
I HAVE BEEN CLOSELY INVOLVED...
...IN THE ACTIVITIES OF TWO STUDENT COUNCIL LEADERS.
THE CURRENT PRESIDENT, TORANOSUKE MIYAMURA...
...AND THE PRESIDENT BEFORE HIM, HARUMA YAMAZAKI.
BOTH OF THEM WERE TRUSTWORTHY...
DECISIVE...
AND THEY DID NOT THINK TWICE OF SACRIFICING THEIR TIME AND ENERGY...
THEY WERE LEADERS ADMIRED BY MANY STUDENTS.
YEAH, SHE'S RIGHT.
CHATTER
CHATTER
CHATTER
NENE-SAN REALLY SAW THEM IN ACTION!
HAVING SEEN GOOD LEADERSHIP...
...THERE IS A PERSON I WOULD LIKE TO NOMINATE AS THE RIGHT CHOICE FOR THIS SCHOOL'S NEXT STUDENT COUNCIL PRESIDENT.
I AM CONFIDENT THAT HE WILL BE A GOOD LEADER.
THE NAME OF THAT STUDENT IS...

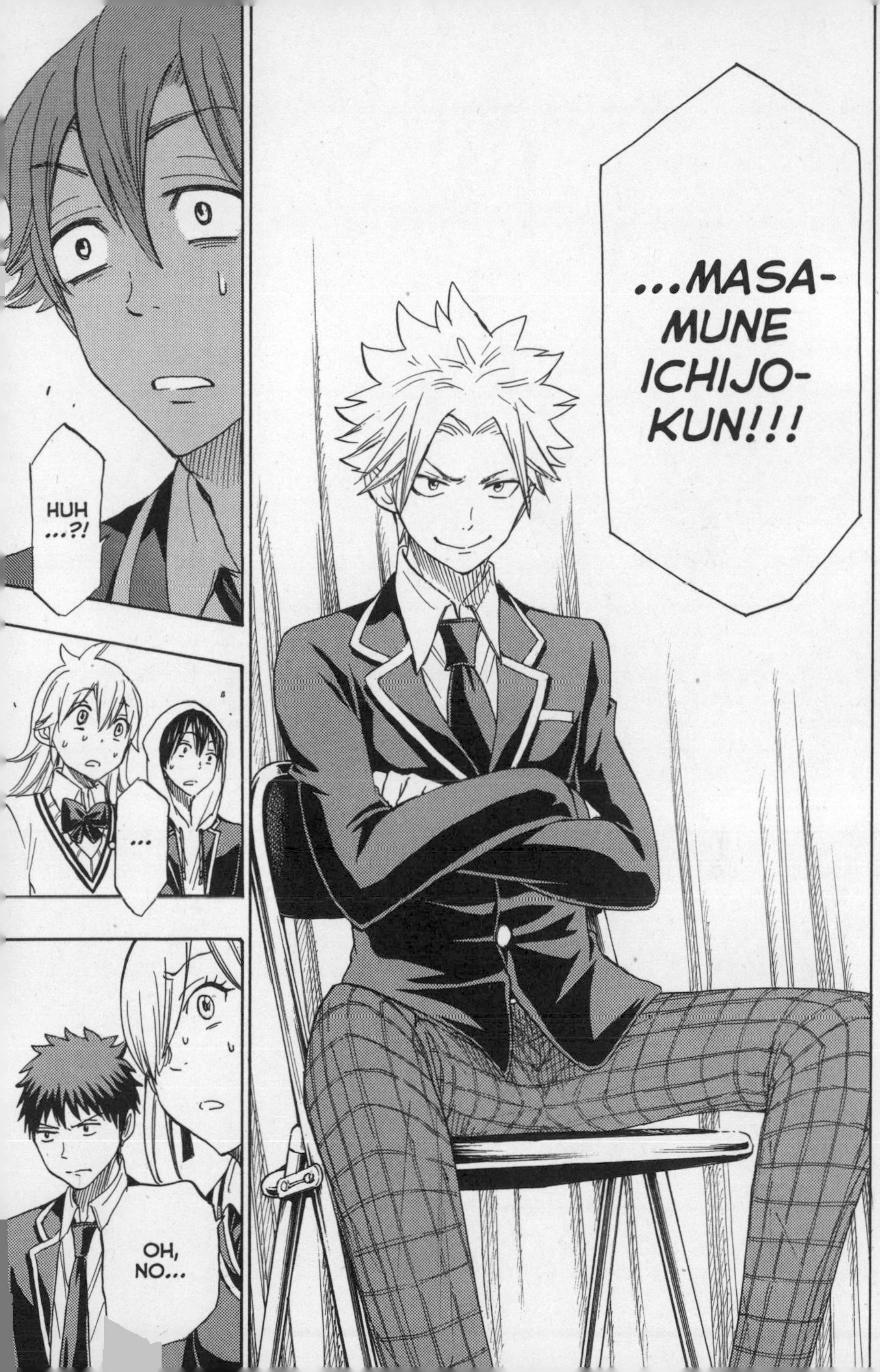
...MASA-MUNE ICHIJO-KUN!!!
HUH ...?!
...
OH, NO...

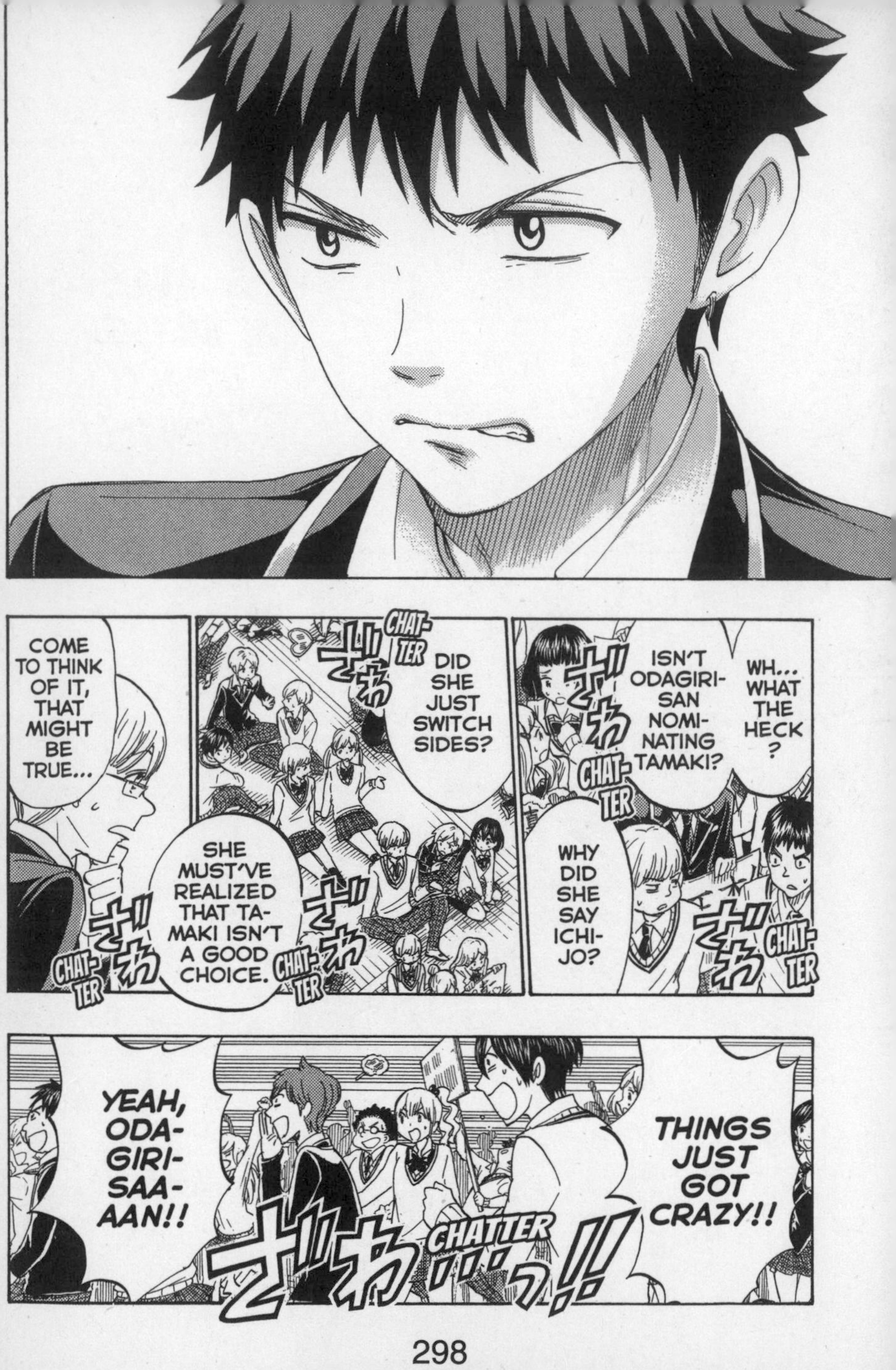
WH... WHAT THE HECK?
CHAT-TER
ISN'T ODAGIRI-SAN NOMINATING TAMAKI?
CHAT-TER
WHY DID SHE SAY ICHIJO?
CHAT-TER
DID SHE JUST SWITCH SIDES?
CHAT-TER
SHE MUST'VE REALIZED THAT TA-MAKI ISN'T A GOOD CHOICE.
COME TO THINK OF IT, THAT MIGHT BE TRUE...
CHAT-TER
THINGS JUST GOT CRAZY!!
YEAH, ODA-GIRI-SAAA-AAN!!
CHATTER

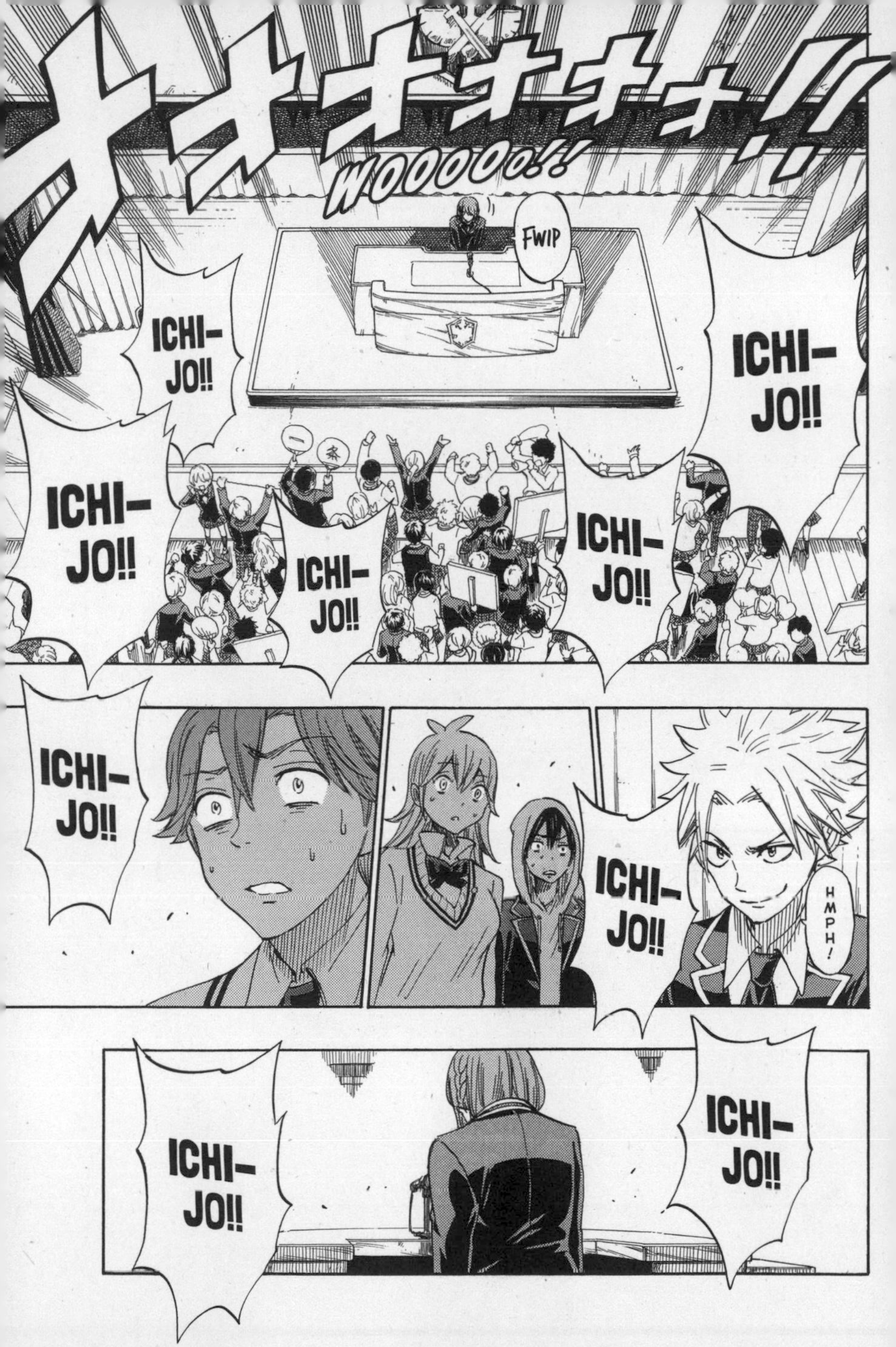

オオオオオォ!!
WOOOOOo!!
FWIP
ICHI-JO!!
ICHI-JO!!
ICHI-JO!!
ICHI-JO!!
ICHI-JO!!
ICHI-JO!!
HMPH!
ICHI-JO!!
ICHI-JO!!
ICHI-JO!!

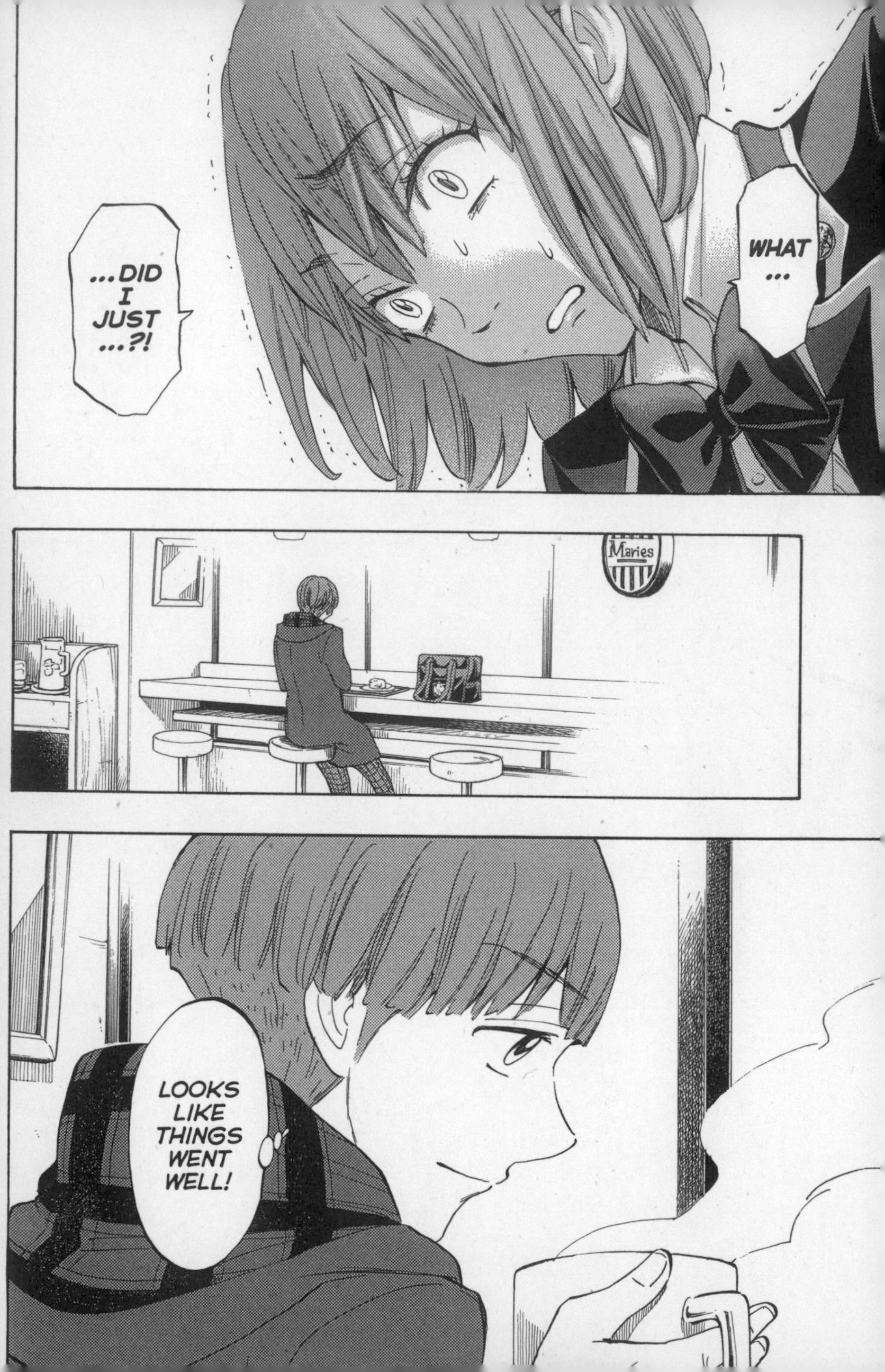
WHAT ...
...DID I JUST ...?!
Maries
LOOKS LIKE THINGS WENT WELL!

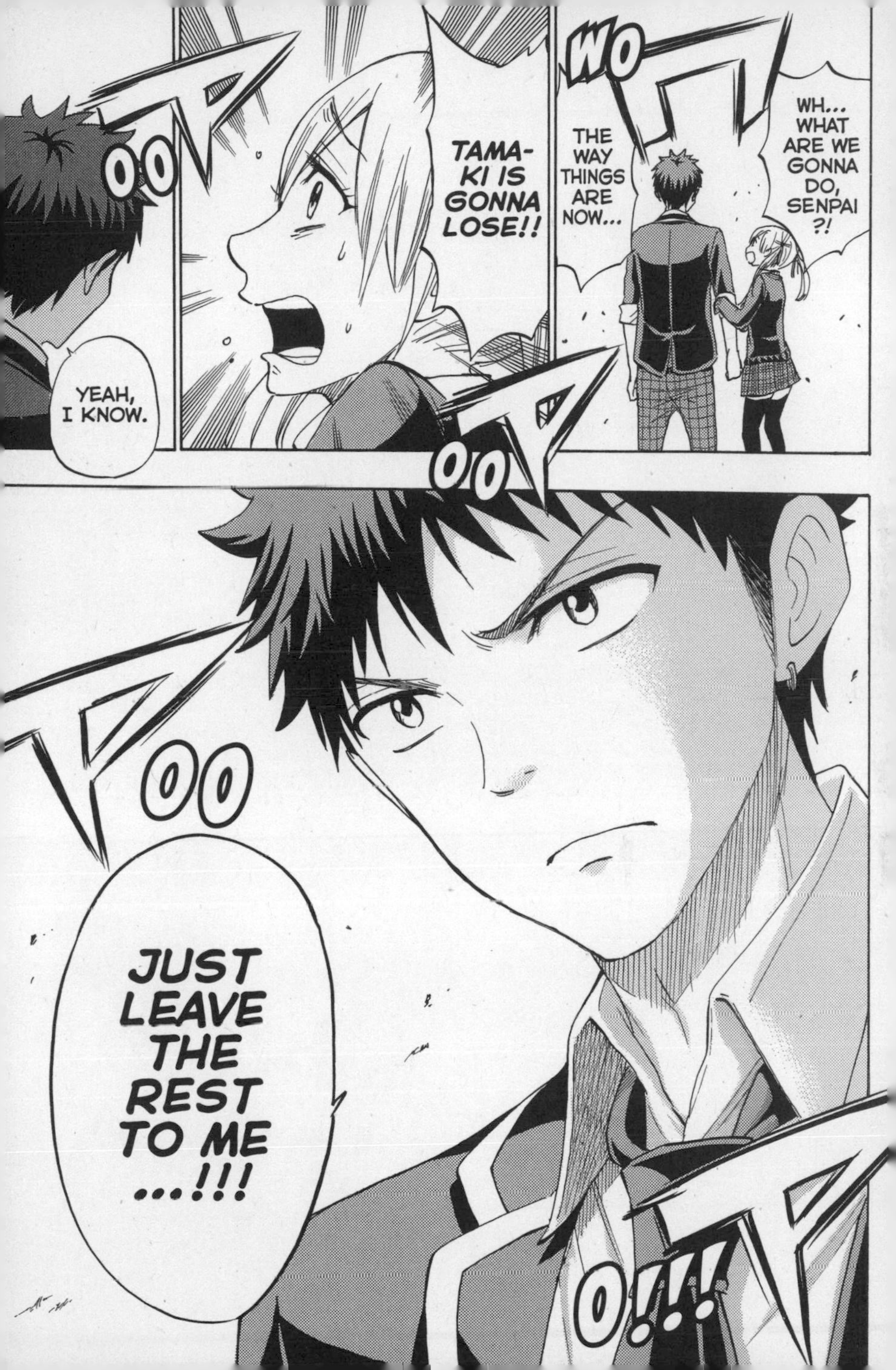
WO
WH... WHAT ARE WE GONNA DO, SENPAI?!
THE WAY THINGS ARE NOW...
OO
TAMAKI IS GONNA LOSE!!
OO
YEAH, I KNOW.
OO
JUST LEAVE THE REST TO ME ...!!!
O!!!

Yamada-kun
AND THE
Seven Witches

CHAPTER 170: I'll definitely come back...!

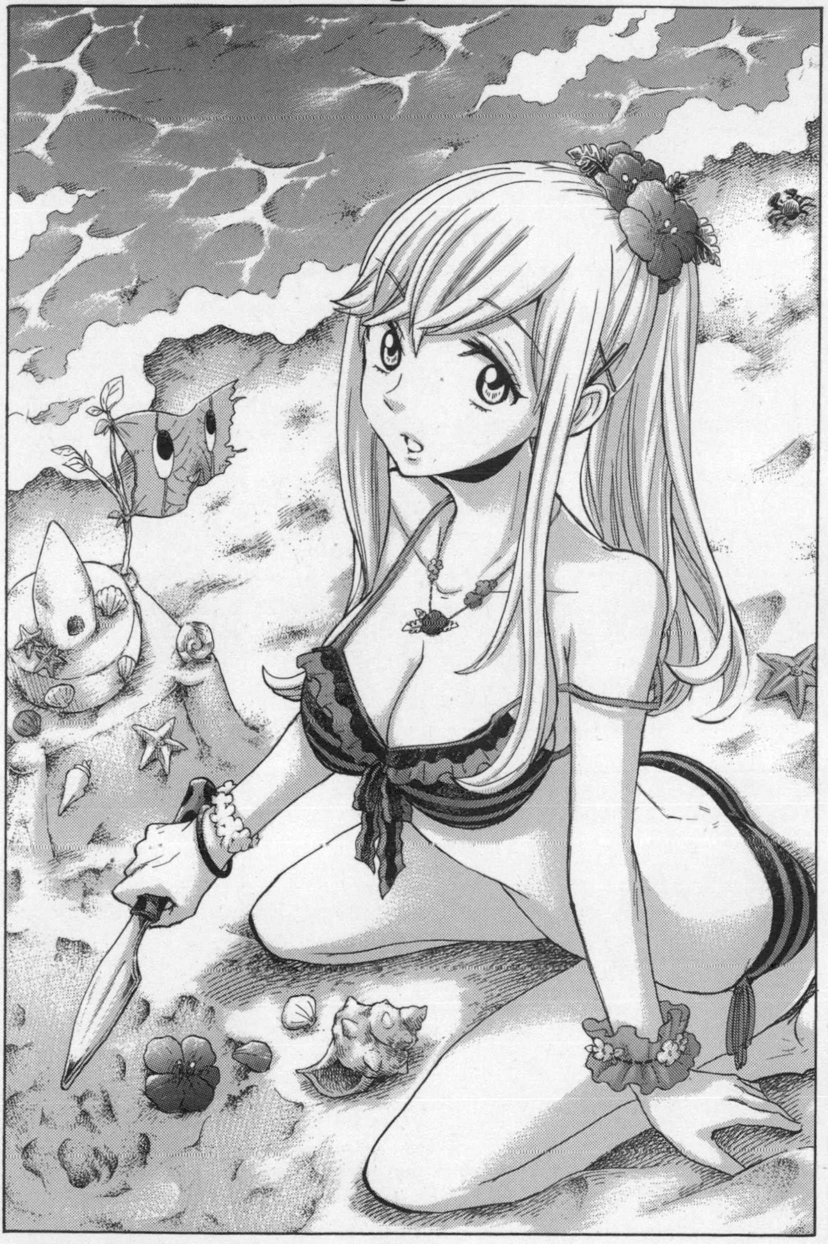

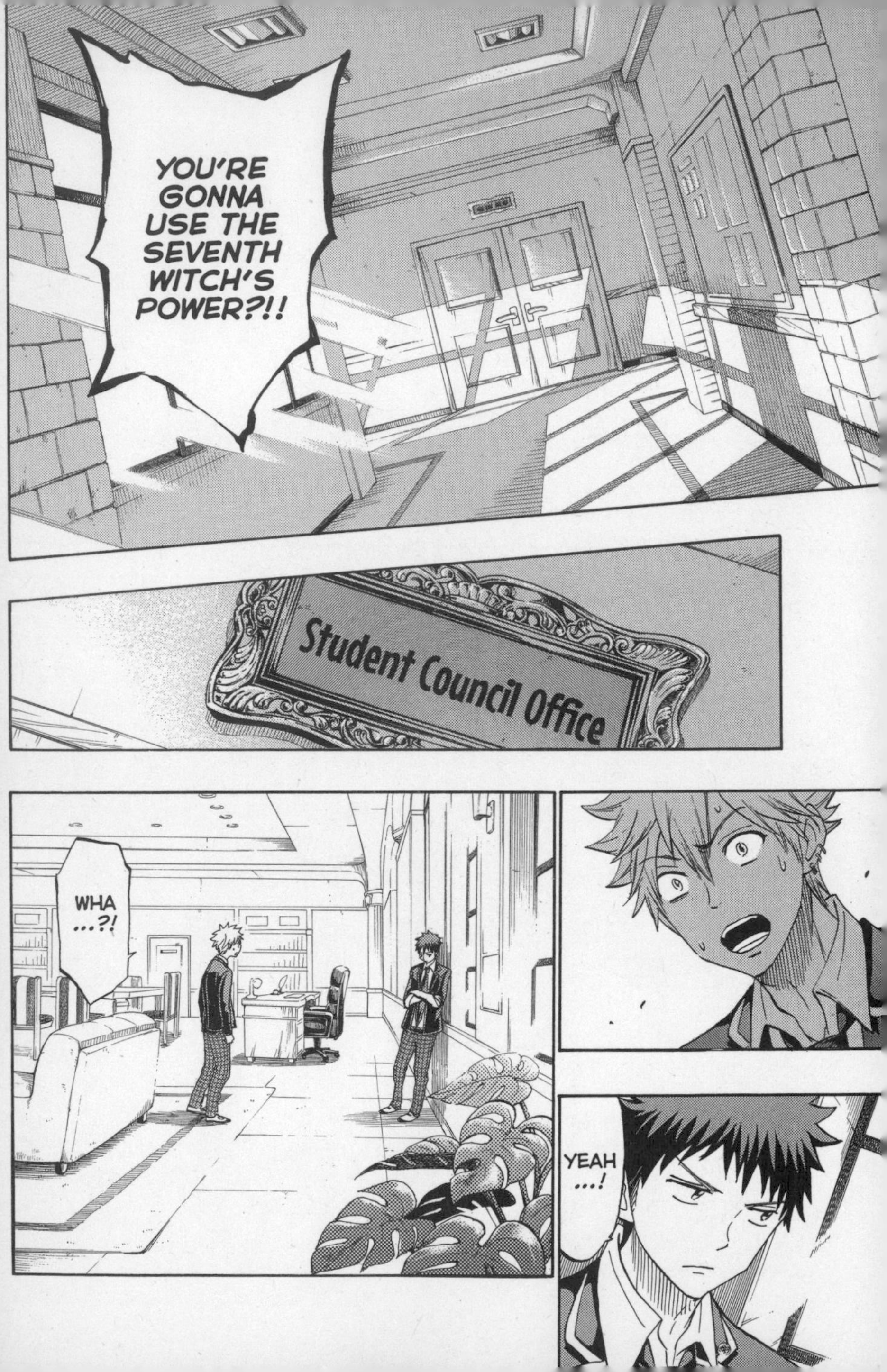
YOU'RE GONNA USE THE SEVENTH WITCH'S POWER?!!
Student Council Office
YEAH ...!
WHA ...?!

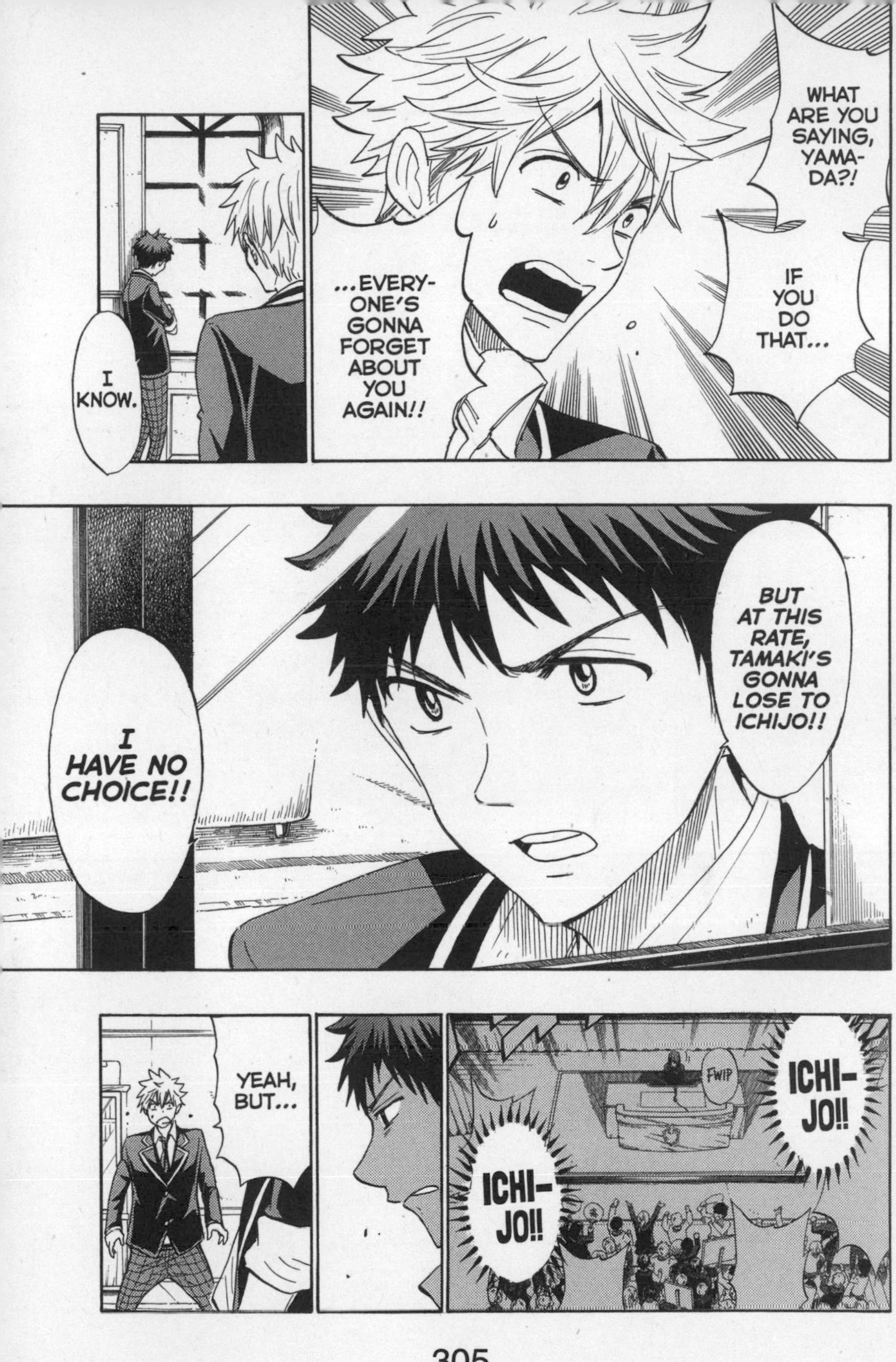
WHAT ARE YOU SAYING, YAMADA?!
IF YOU DO THAT...
...EVERYONE'S GONNA FORGET ABOUT YOU AGAIN!!
I KNOW.
BUT AT THIS RATE, TAMAKI'S GONNA LOSE TO ICHIJO!!
I HAVE NO CHOICE!!
FWIP
ICHI-JO!!
ICHI-JO!!
YEAH, BUT...

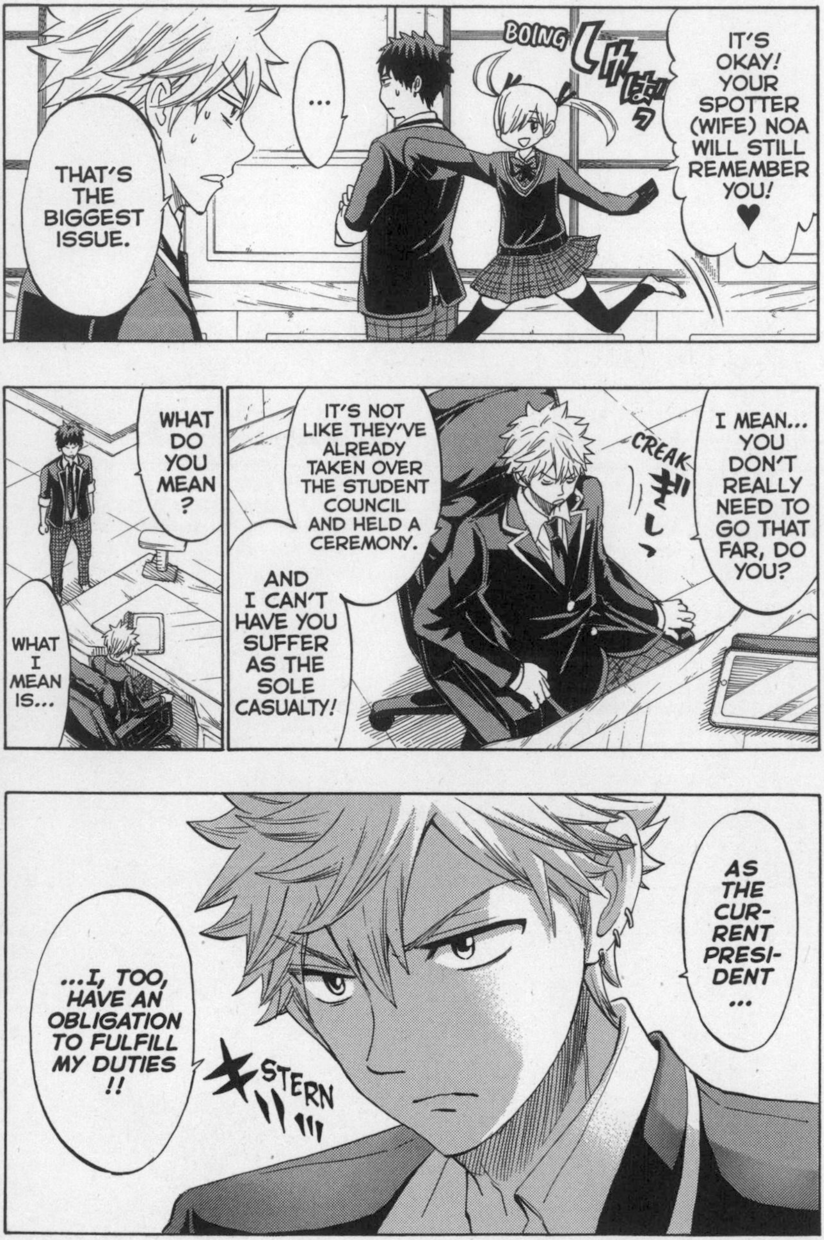
IT'S OKAY! YOUR SPOTTER (WIFE) NOA WILL STILL REMEMBER YOU! ♥
BOING
...
THAT'S THE BIGGEST ISSUE.
I MEAN... YOU DON'T REALLY NEED TO GO THAT FAR, DO YOU?
CREAK
IT'S NOT LIKE THEY'VE ALREADY TAKEN OVER THE STUDENT COUNCIL AND HELD A CEREMONY.
AND I CAN'T HAVE YOU SUFFER AS THE SOLE CASUALTY!
WHAT DO YOU MEAN?
WHAT I MEAN IS...
AS THE CUR-RENT PRESI-DENT...
STERN
...I, TOO, HAVE AN OBLIGATION TO FULFILL MY DUTIES!!

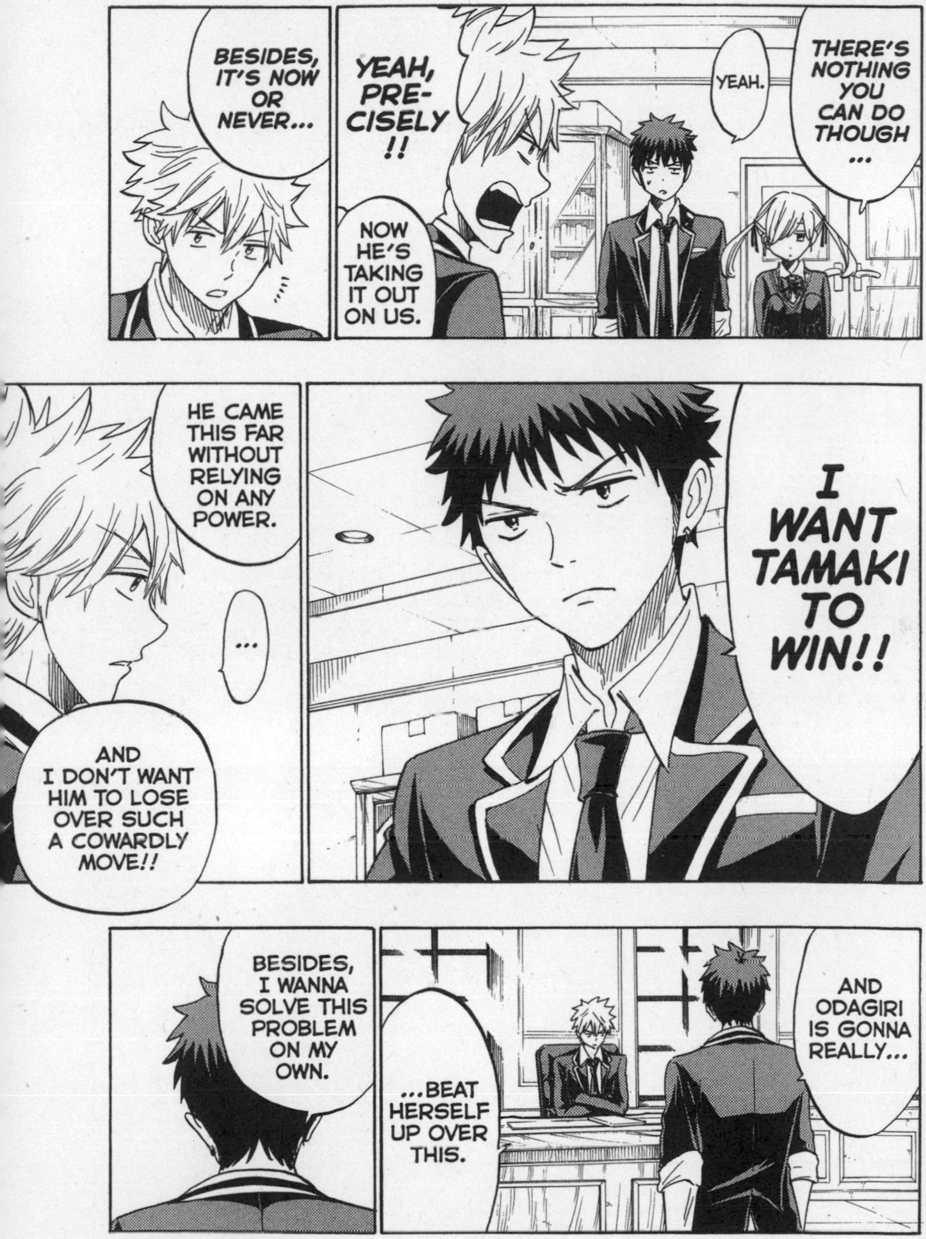
THERE'S NOTHING YOU CAN DO THOUGH ...
YEAH.
YEAH, PRE-CISELY!!
NOW HE'S TAKING IT OUT ON US.
BESIDES, IT'S NOW OR NEVER...
I WANT TAMAKI TO WIN!!
HE CAME THIS FAR WITHOUT RELYING ON ANY POWER.
...
AND I DON'T WANT HIM TO LOSE OVER SUCH A COWARDLY MOVE!!
AND ODAGIRI IS GONNA REALLY...
...BEAT HERSELF UP OVER THIS.
BESIDES, I WANNA SOLVE THIS PROBLEM ON MY OWN.

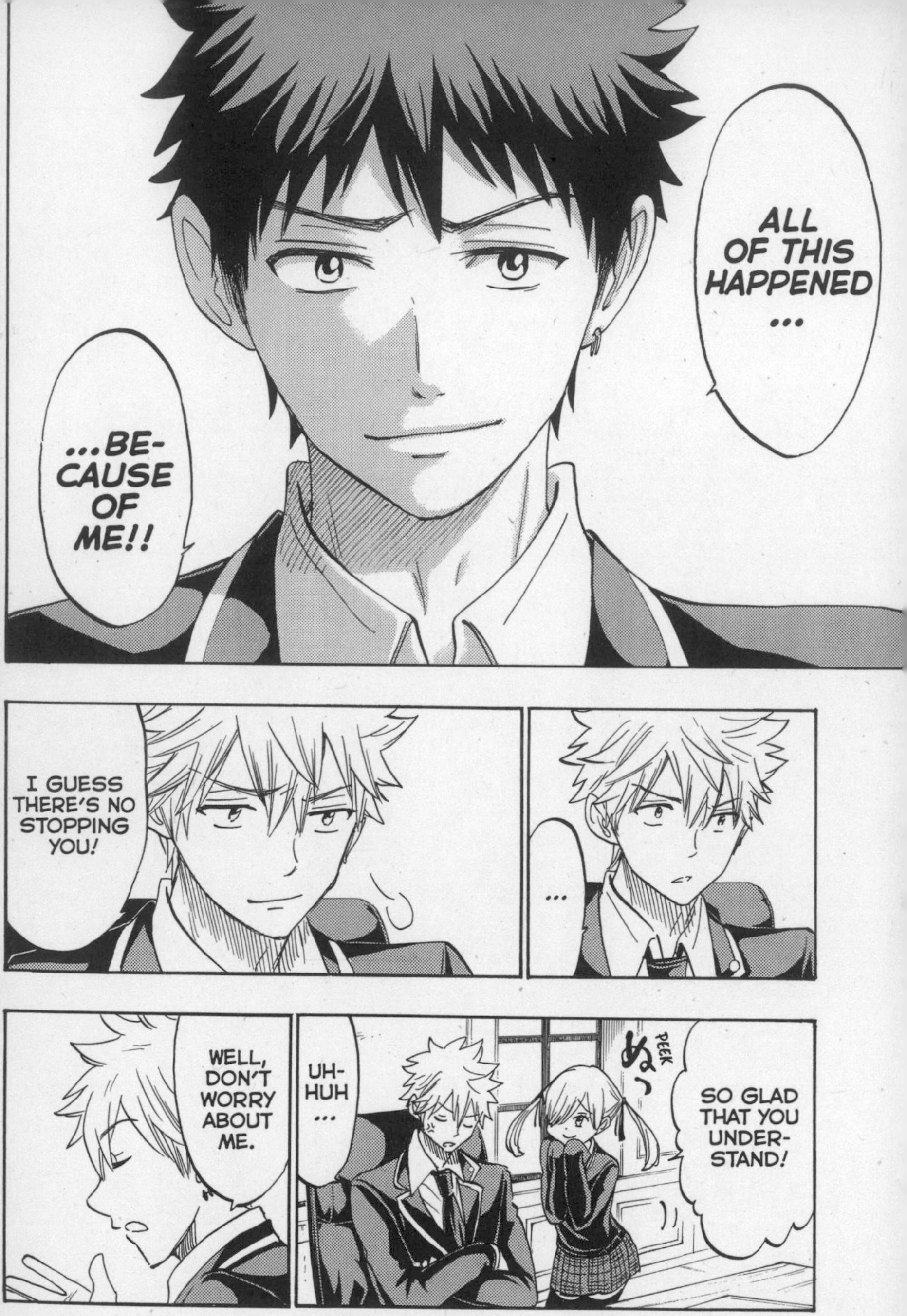
ALL OF THIS HAPPENED ...
...BE-CAUSE OF ME!!
...
I GUESS THERE'S NO STOPPING YOU!
SO GLAD THAT YOU UNDER-STAND!
ぬっ PEEK
UH-HUH ...
WELL, DON'T WORRY ABOUT ME.

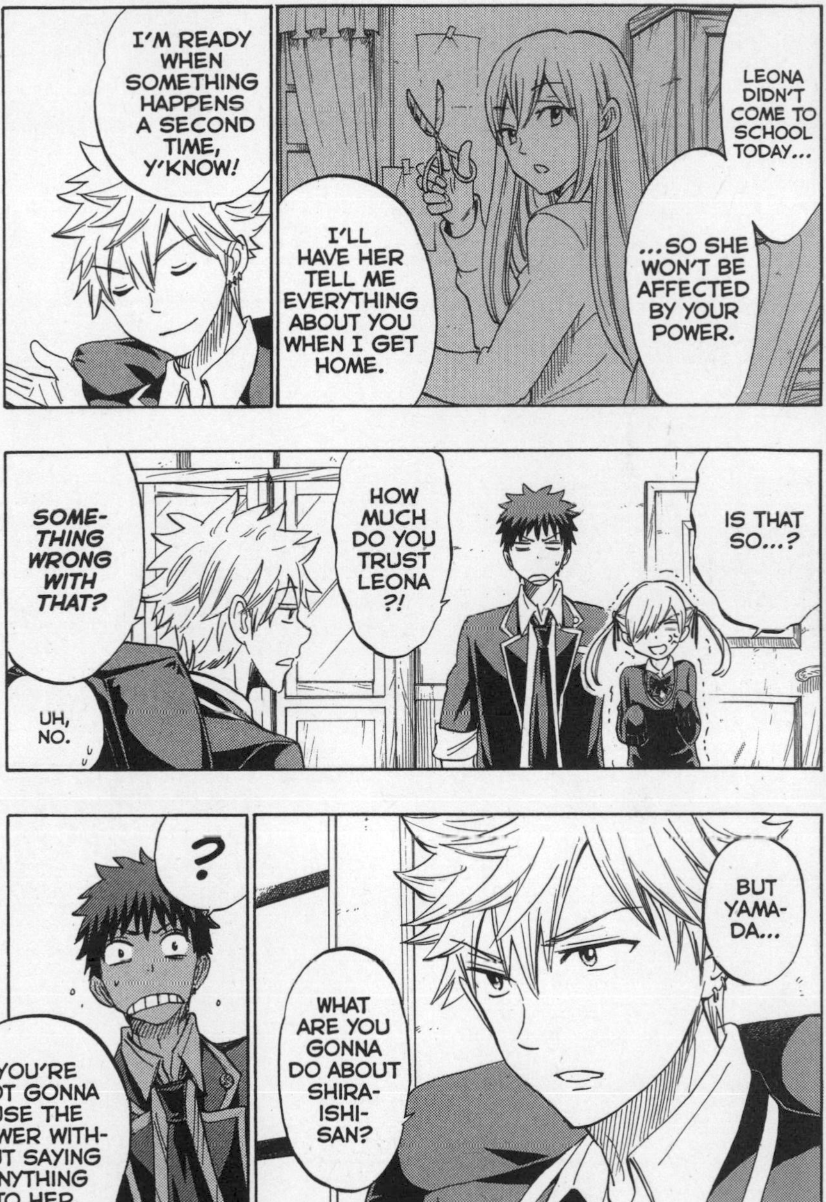
LEONA DIDN'T COME TO SCHOOL TODAY...
...SO SHE WON'T BE AFFECTED BY YOUR POWER.
I'LL HAVE HER TELL ME EVERYTHING ABOUT YOU WHEN I GET HOME.
I'M READY WHEN SOMETHING HAPPENS A SECOND TIME, Y'KNOW!
IS THAT SO...?
HOW MUCH DO YOU TRUST LEONA?!
SOME-THING WRONG WITH THAT?
UH, NO.
BUT YAMA-DA...
WHAT ARE YOU GONNA DO ABOUT SHIRA-ISHI-SAN?
?
YOU'RE NOT GONNA USE THE POWER WITH-OUT SAYING ANYTHING TO HER, ARE YOU?

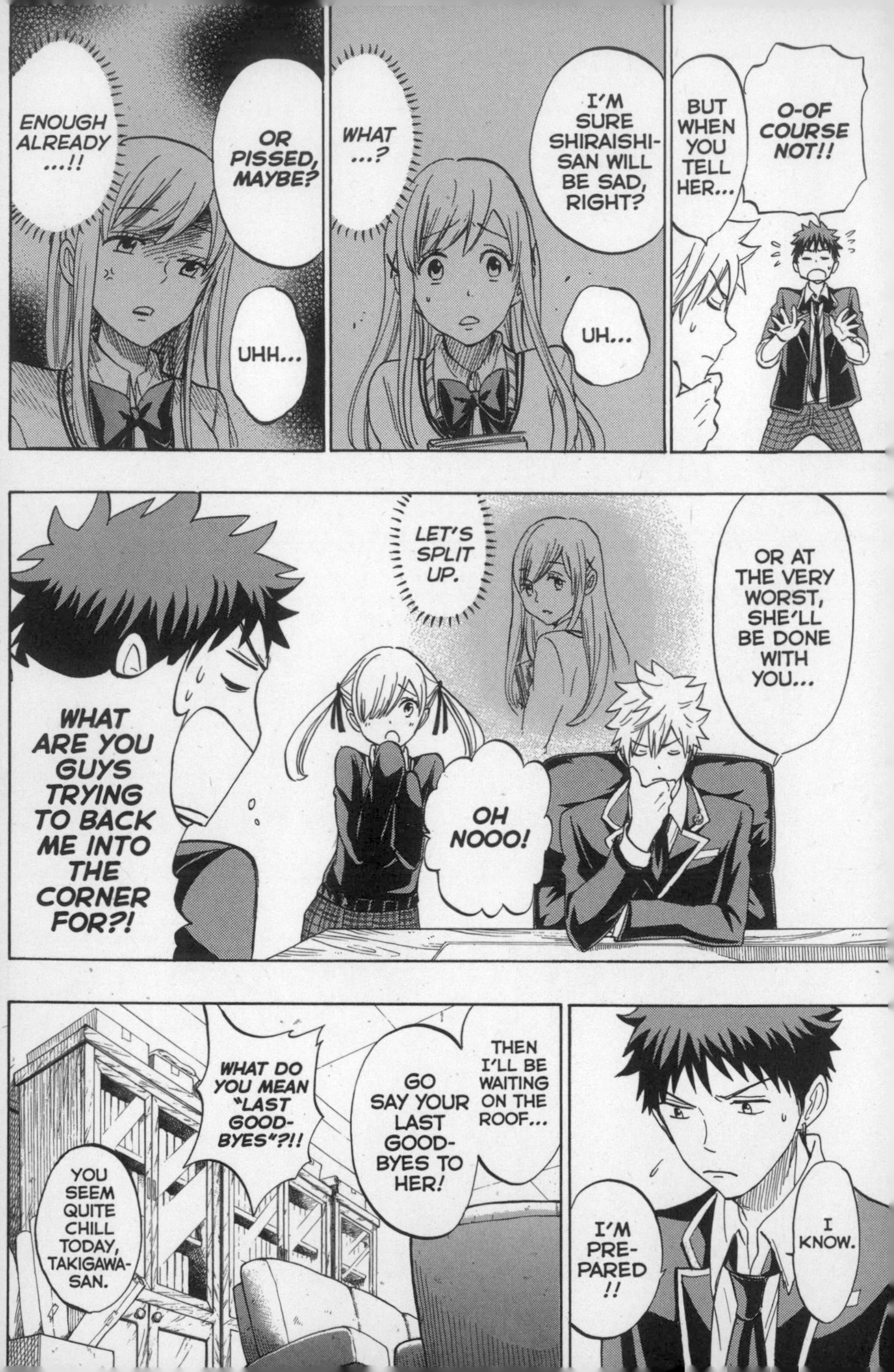
O-OF COURSE NOT!!
BUT WHEN YOU TELL HER...
I'M SURE SHIRAISHI-SAN WILL BE SAD, RIGHT?
WHAT ...?
UH...
OR PISSED, MAYBE?
ENOUGH ALREADY ...!!
UHH...
OR AT THE VERY WORST, SHE'LL BE DONE WITH YOU...
LET'S SPLIT UP.
OH NOOO!
WHAT ARE YOU GUYS TRYING TO BACK ME INTO THE CORNER FOR?!
I KNOW.
I'M PRE-PARED!!
THEN I'LL BE WAITING ON THE ROOF...
GO SAY YOUR LAST GOOD-BYES TO HER!
WHAT DO YOU MEAN "LAST GOOD-BYES"?!!
YOU SEEM QUITE CHILL TODAY, TAKIGAWA-SAN.

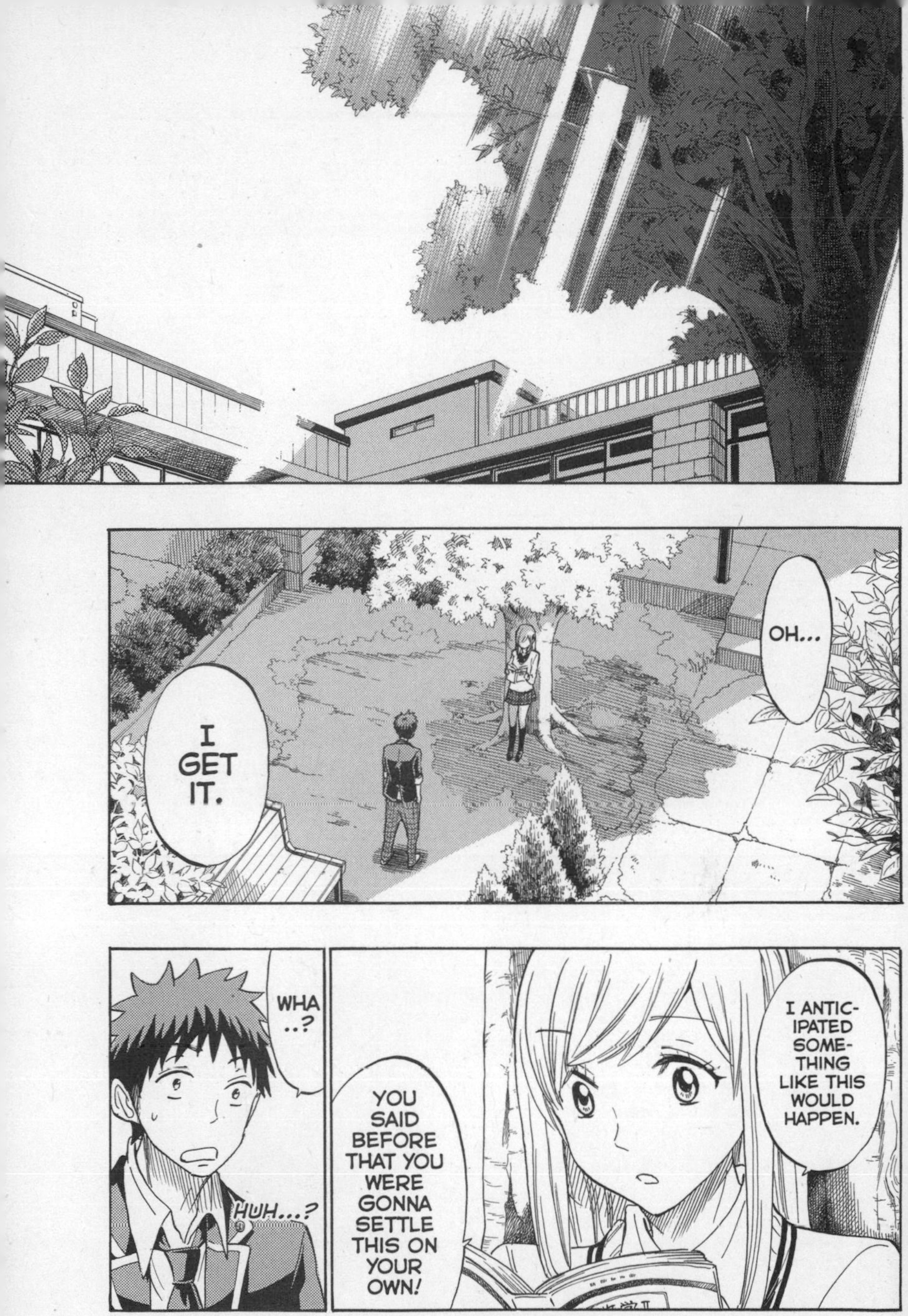
OH...
I GET IT.
I ANTICIPATED SOMETHING LIKE THIS WOULD HAPPEN.
YOU SAID BEFORE THAT YOU WERE GONNA SETTLE THIS ON YOUR OWN!
WHA..?
HUH...?

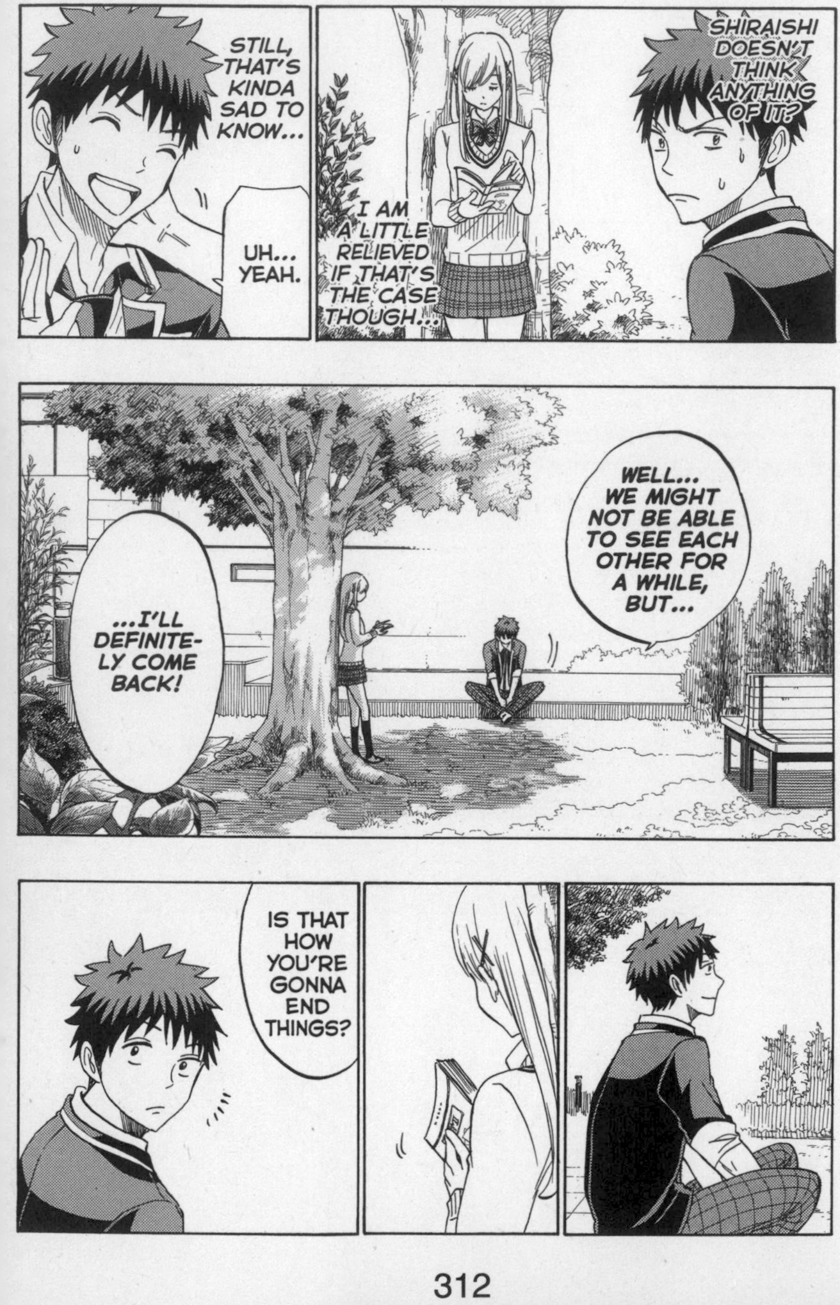
SHIRAISHI DOESN'T THINK ANYTHING OF IT?
I AM A LITTLE RELIEVED IF THAT'S THE CASE THOUGH...
STILL, THAT'S KINDA SAD TO KNOW...
UH... YEAH.
WELL... WE MIGHT NOT BE ABLE TO SEE EACH OTHER FOR A WHILE, BUT...
...I'LL DEFINITE-LY COME BACK!
IS THAT HOW YOU'RE GONNA END THINGS?

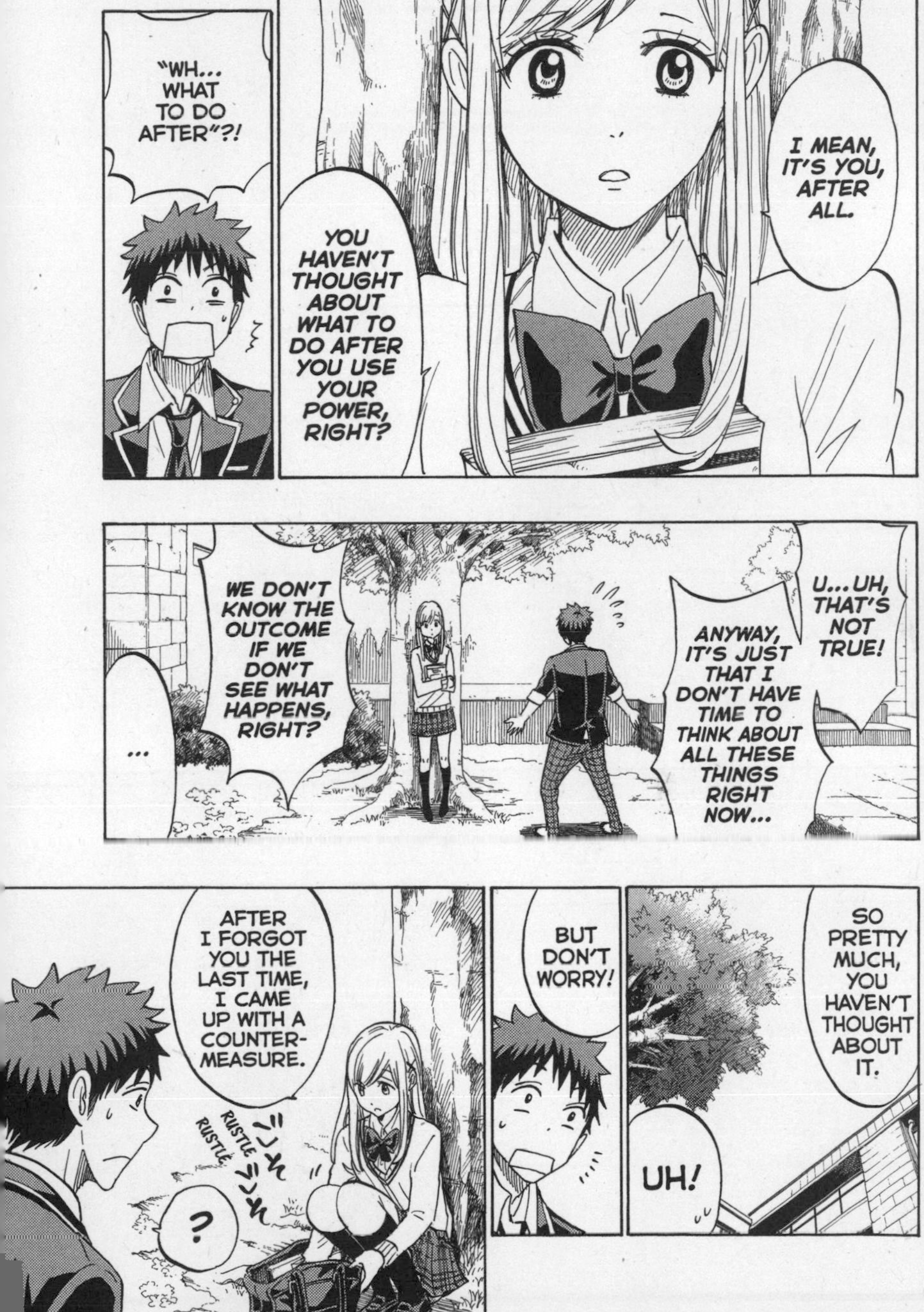
I MEAN, IT'S YOU, AFTER ALL.
YOU HAVEN'T THOUGHT ABOUT WHAT TO DO AFTER YOU USE YOUR POWER, RIGHT?
"WH... WHAT TO DO AFTER"?!
U...UH, THAT'S NOT TRUE!
ANYWAY, IT'S JUST THAT I DON'T HAVE TIME TO THINK ABOUT ALL THESE THINGS RIGHT NOW...
WE DON'T KNOW THE OUTCOME IF WE DON'T SEE WHAT HAPPENS, RIGHT?
...
SO PRETTY MUCH, YOU HAVEN'T THOUGHT ABOUT IT.
UH!
BUT DON'T WORRY!
AFTER I FORGOT YOU THE LAST TIME, I CAME UP WITH A COUNTER-MEASURE.
RUSTLE
RUSTLE
?

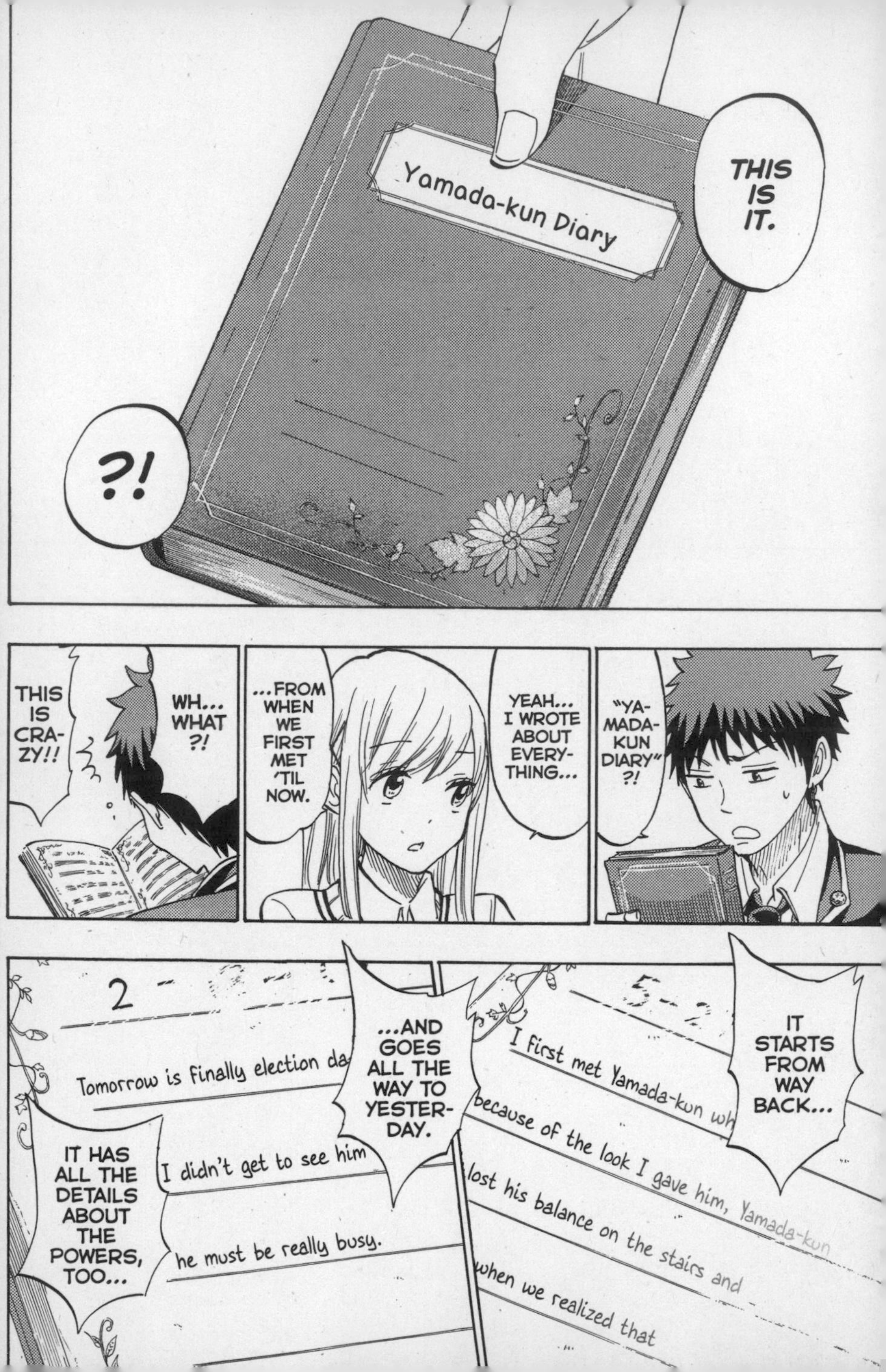
Yamada-kun Diary
THIS IS IT.
?!
"YA-MADA-KUN DIARY"?!
YEAH... I WROTE ABOUT EVERY-THING...
...FROM WHEN WE FIRST MET 'TIL NOW.
WH... WHAT?!
THIS IS CRA-ZY!!
IT STARTS FROM WAY BACK...
I first met Yamada-kun
because of the look I gave him, Yamada-kun
lost his balance on the stairs and
when we realized that
...AND GOES ALL THE WAY TO YESTER-DAY.
2
Tomorrow is finally election
I didn't get to see him
he must be really busy.
IT HAS ALL THE DETAILS ABOUT THE POWERS, TOO...

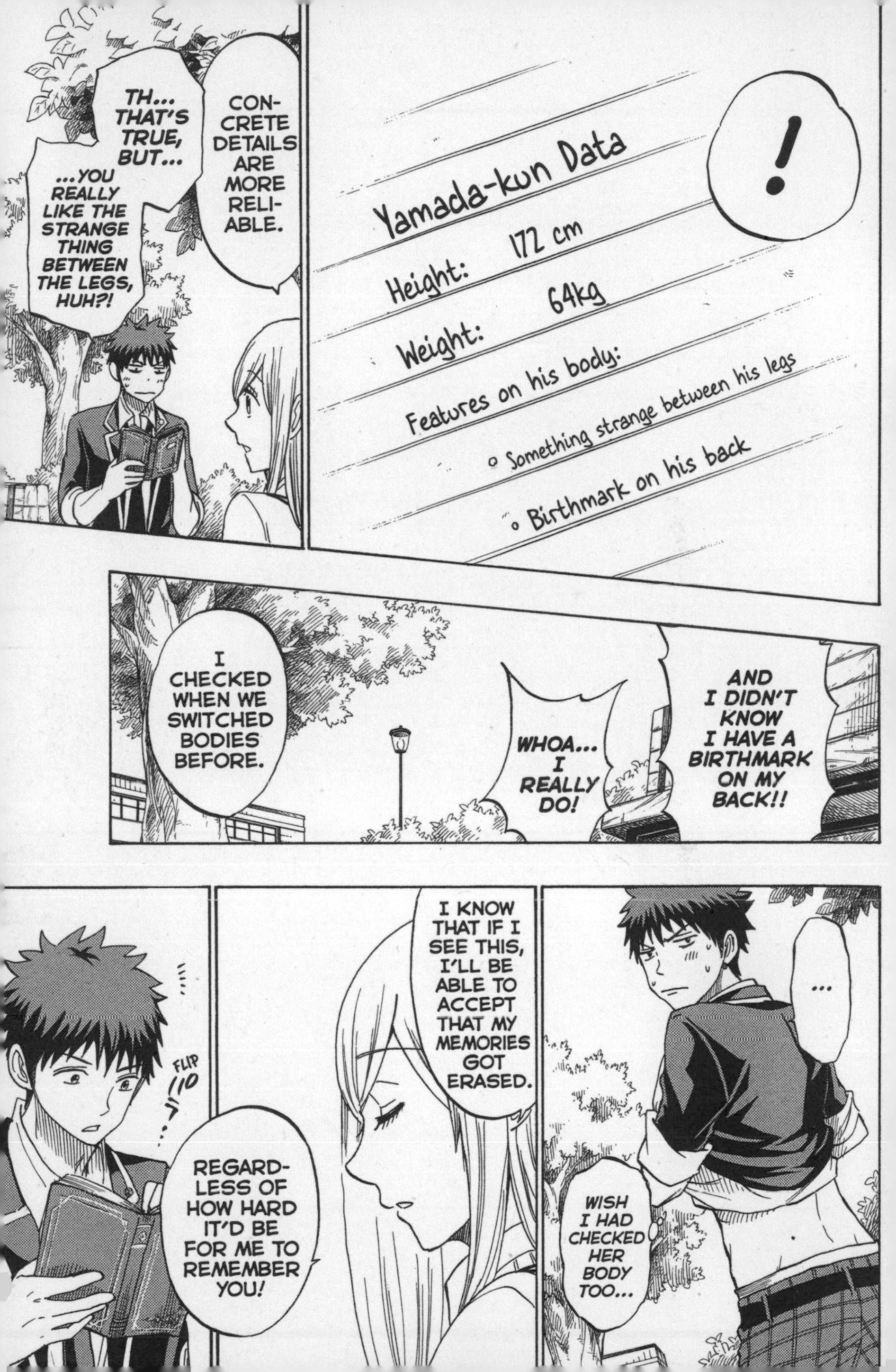
!
Yamada-kun Data
Height: 172 cm
Weight: 64kg
Features on his body:
∘ Something strange between his legs
∘ Birthmark on his back
CON-CRETE DETAILS ARE MORE RELI-ABLE.
TH... THAT'S TRUE, BUT...
...YOU REALLY LIKE THE STRANGE THING BETWEEN THE LEGS, HUH?!
AND I DIDN'T KNOW I HAVE A BIRTHMARK ON MY BACK!!
WHOA... I REALLY DO!
I CHECKED WHEN WE SWITCHED BODIES BEFORE.
...
WISH I HAD CHECKED HER BODY TOO...
I KNOW THAT IF I SEE THIS, I'LL BE ABLE TO ACCEPT THAT MY MEMORIES GOT ERASED.
FLIP
REGARD-LESS OF HOW HARD IT'D BE FOR ME TO REMEMBER YOU!

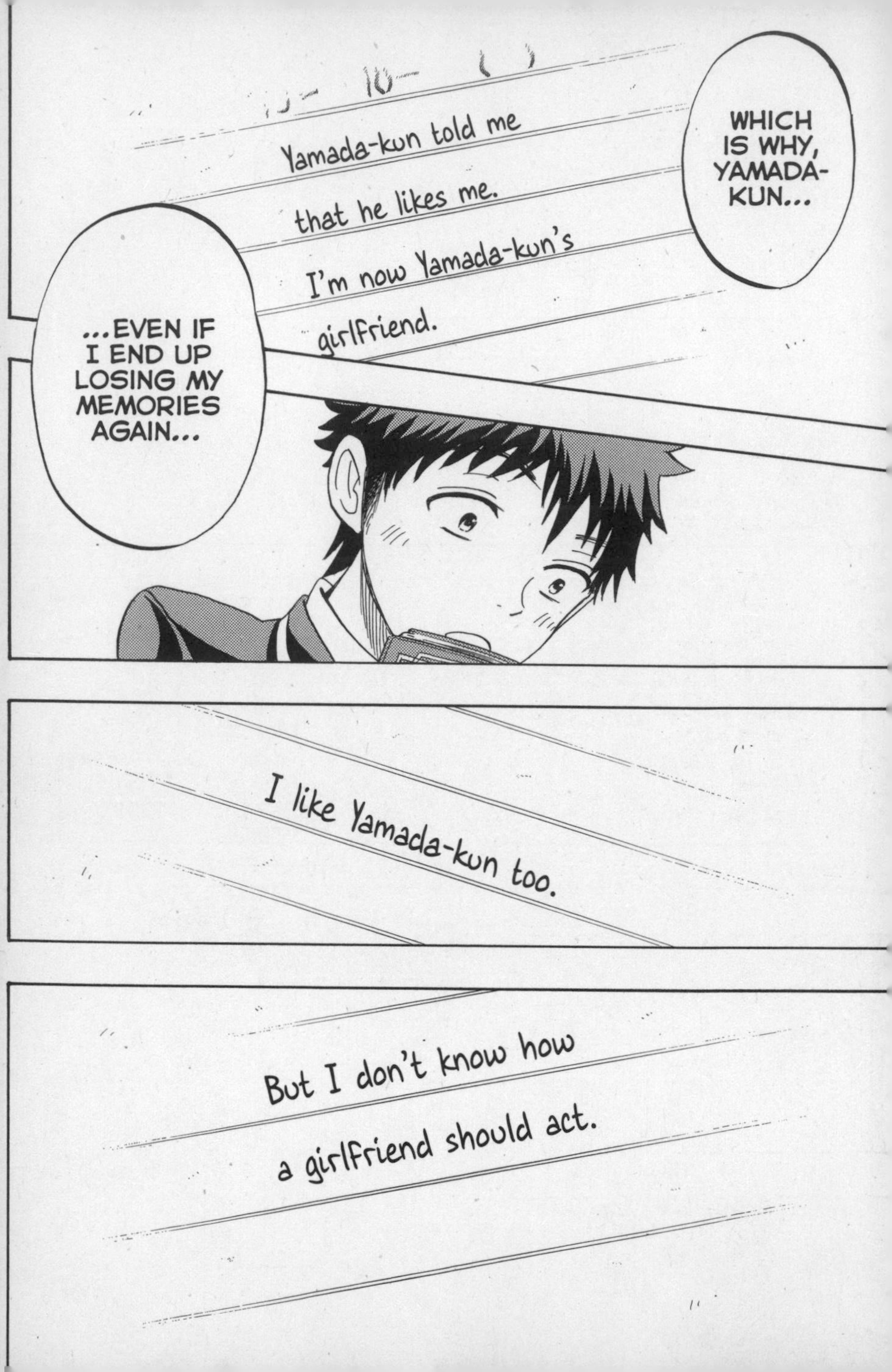
WHICH IS WHY, YAMADA-KUN...
Yamada-kun told me that he likes me.
I'm now Yamada-kun's girlfriend.
...EVEN IF I END UP LOSING MY MEMORIES AGAIN...
I like Yamada-kun too.
But I don't know how a girlfriend should act.

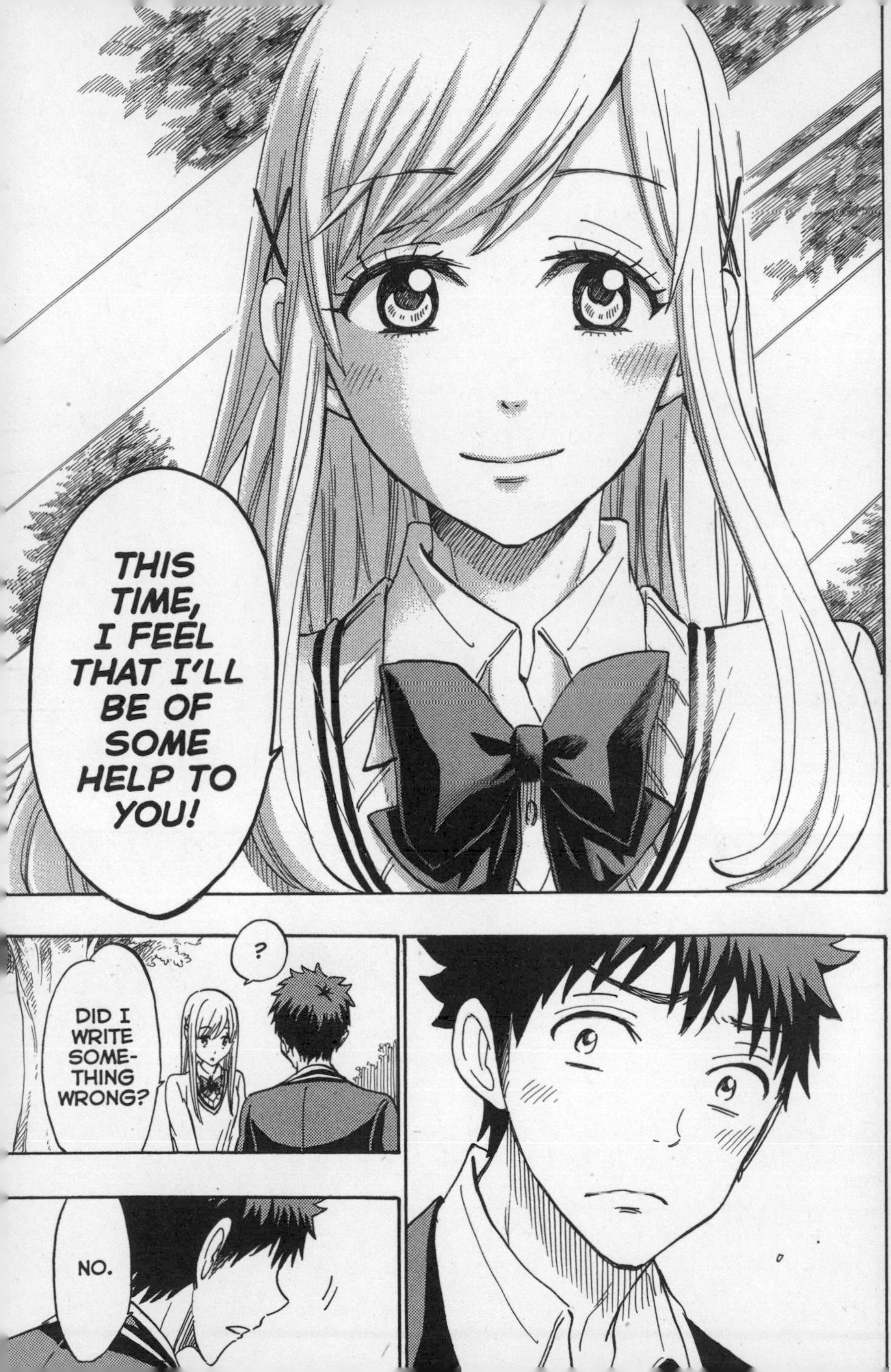
THIS TIME, I FEEL THAT I'LL BE OF SOME HELP TO YOU!
?
DID I WRITE SOME-THING WRONG?
NO.

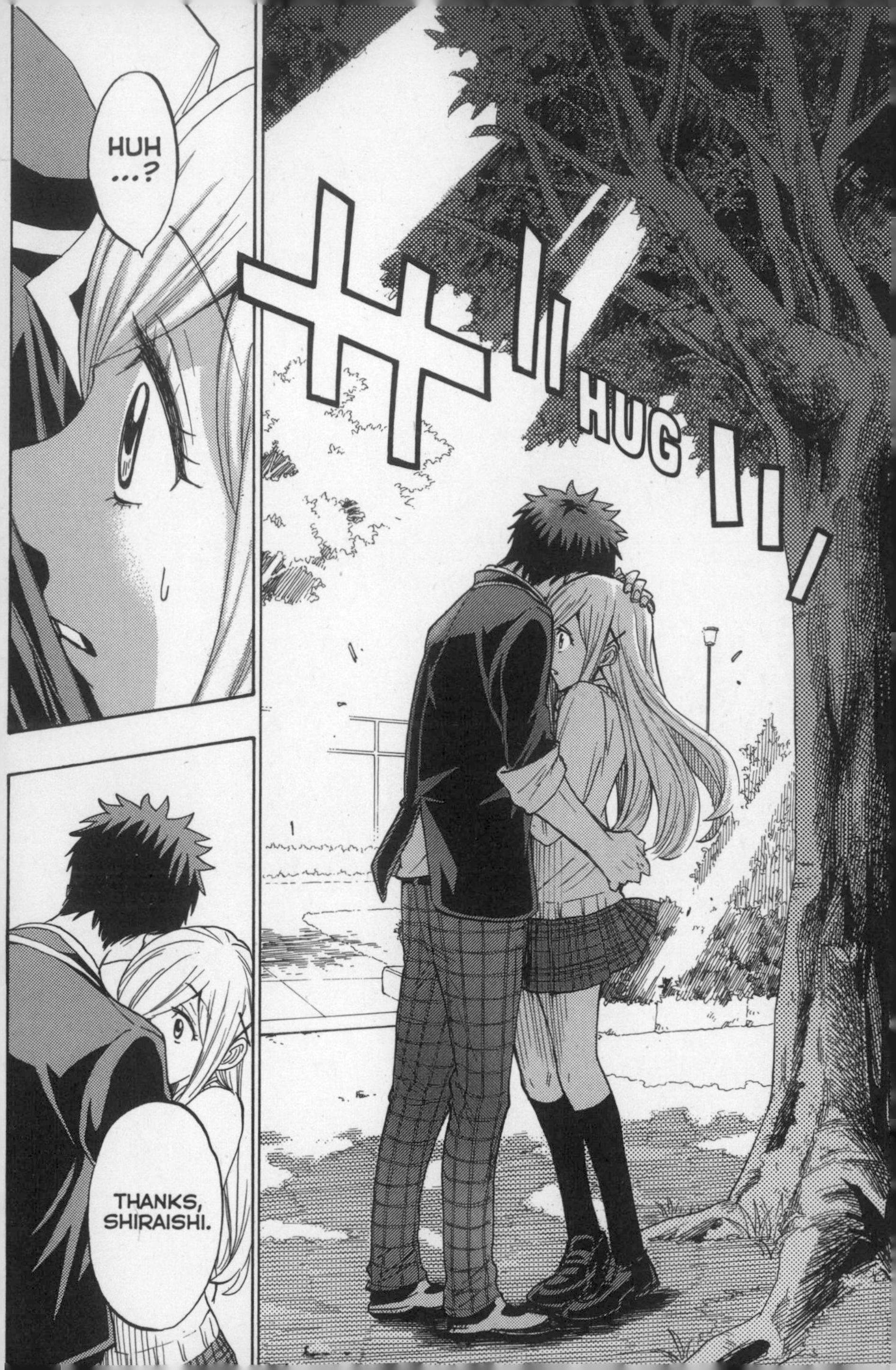
HUG
HUH ...?
THANKS, SHIRAISHI.

...I'M SORRY TO DO THIS TO YOU!!

AND...

YEAH... I'LL BE BACK!!

COME BACK AS SOON AS YOU CAN!

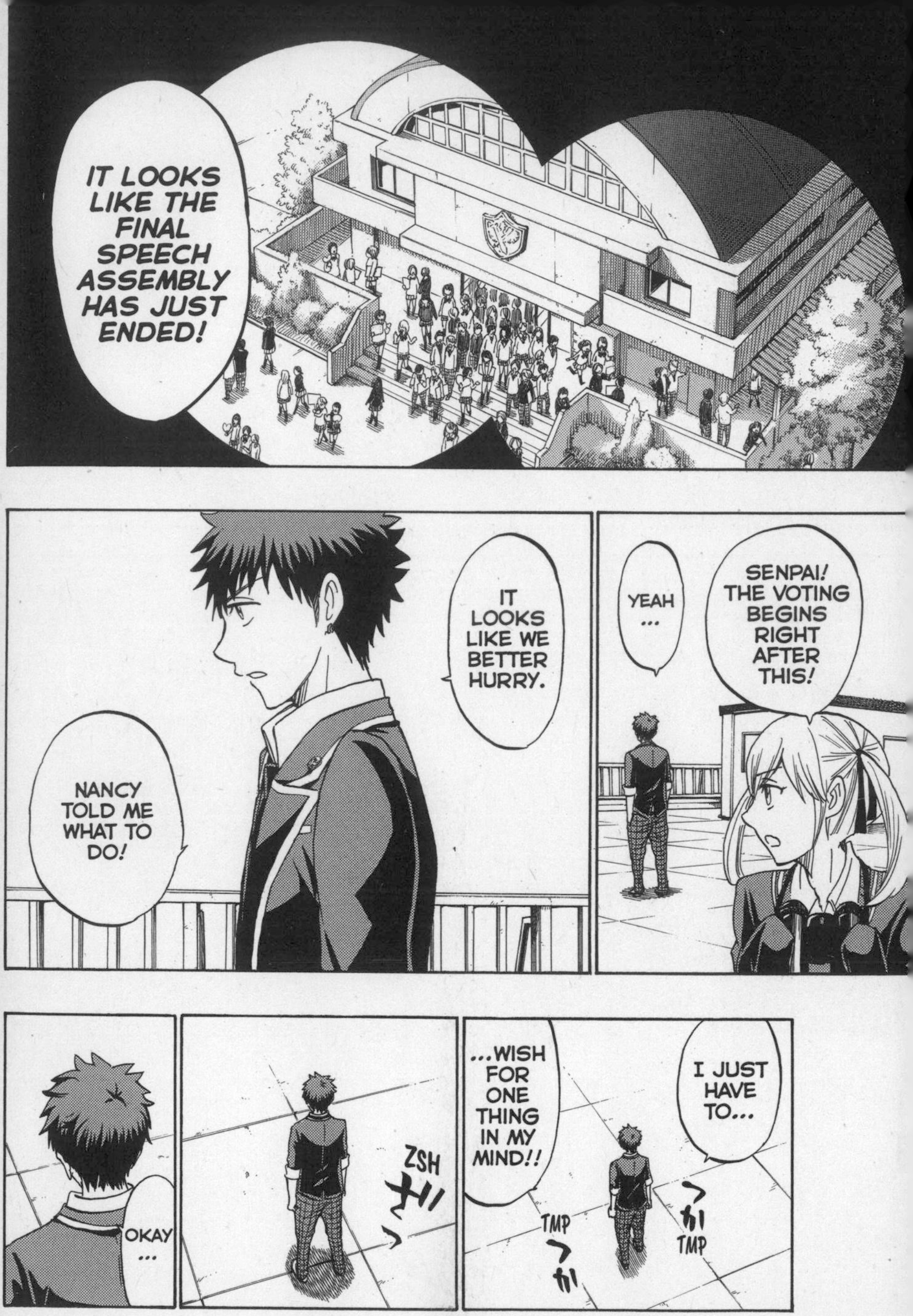
IT LOOKS LIKE THE FINAL SPEECH ASSEMBLY HAS JUST ENDED!
SENPAI! THE VOTING BEGINS RIGHT AFTER THIS!
YEAH...
IT LOOKS LIKE WE BETTER HURRY.
NANCY TOLD ME WHAT TO DO!
I JUST HAVE TO...
TMP
TMP
...WISH FOR ONE THING IN MY MIND!!
ZSH
OKAY...

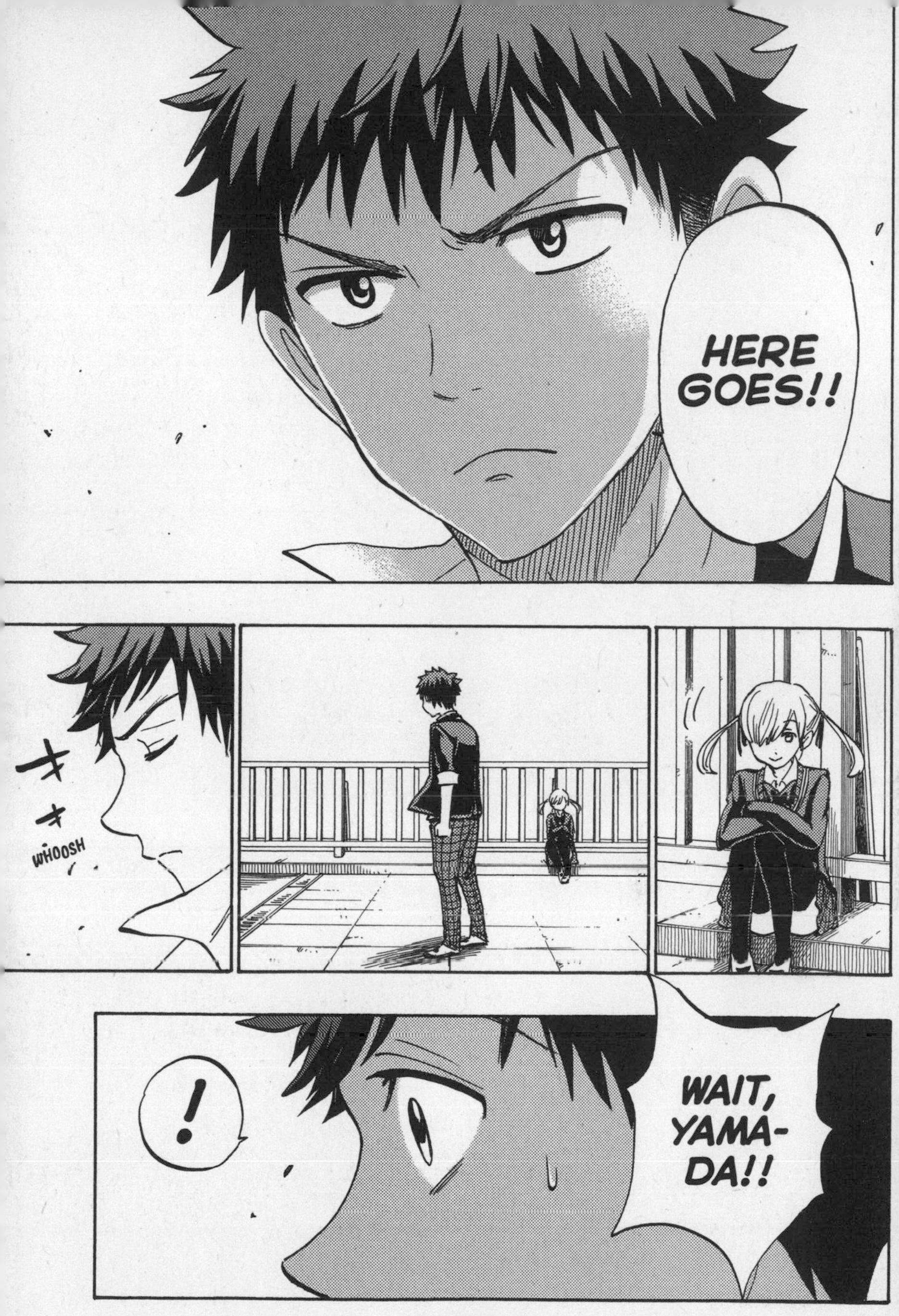
HERE GOES!!
WHOOSH
WAIT, YAMA-DA!!
!

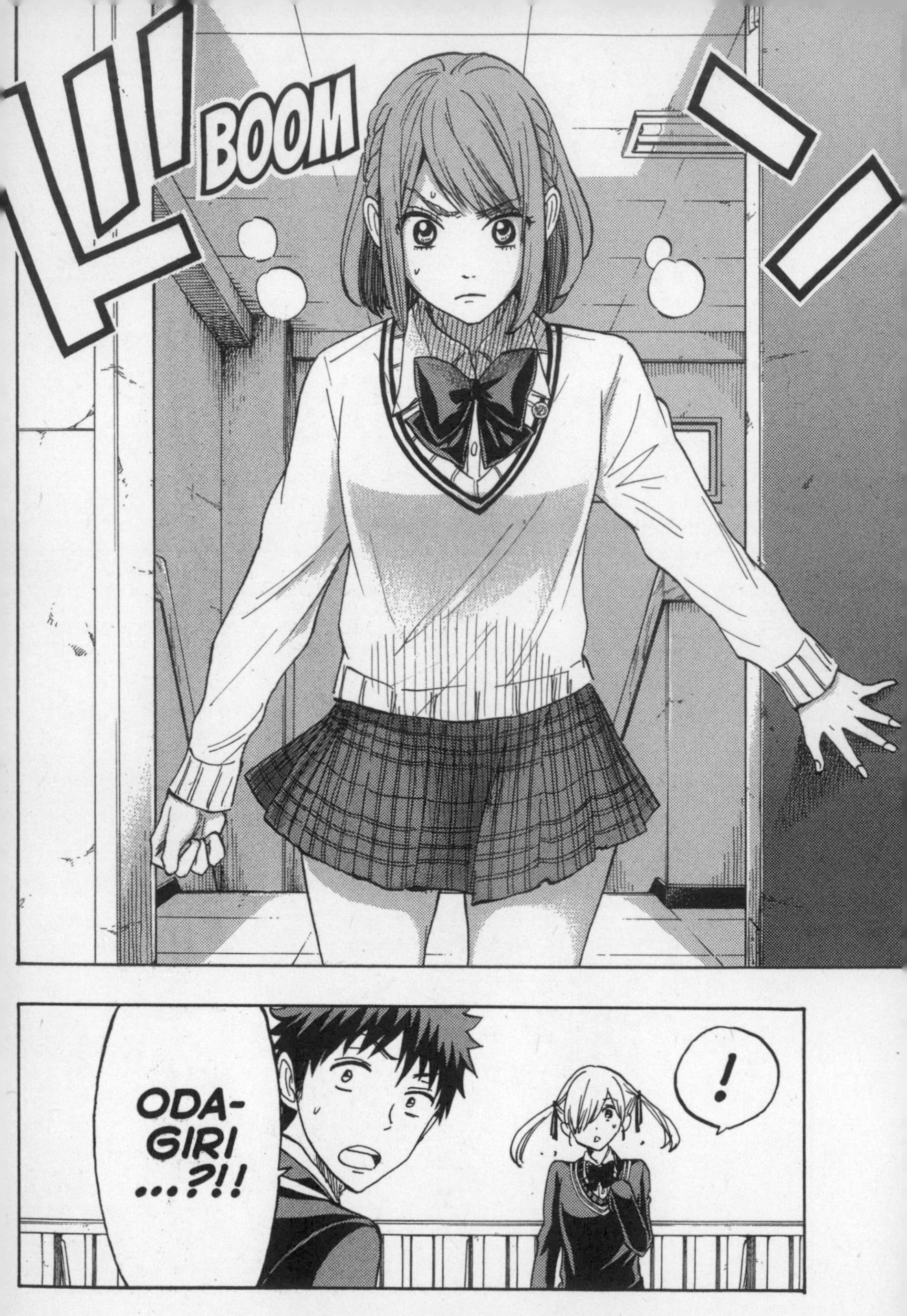
BOOM
!
ODA-GIRI ...?!!

CHAPTER 171: It's a bloodbath!

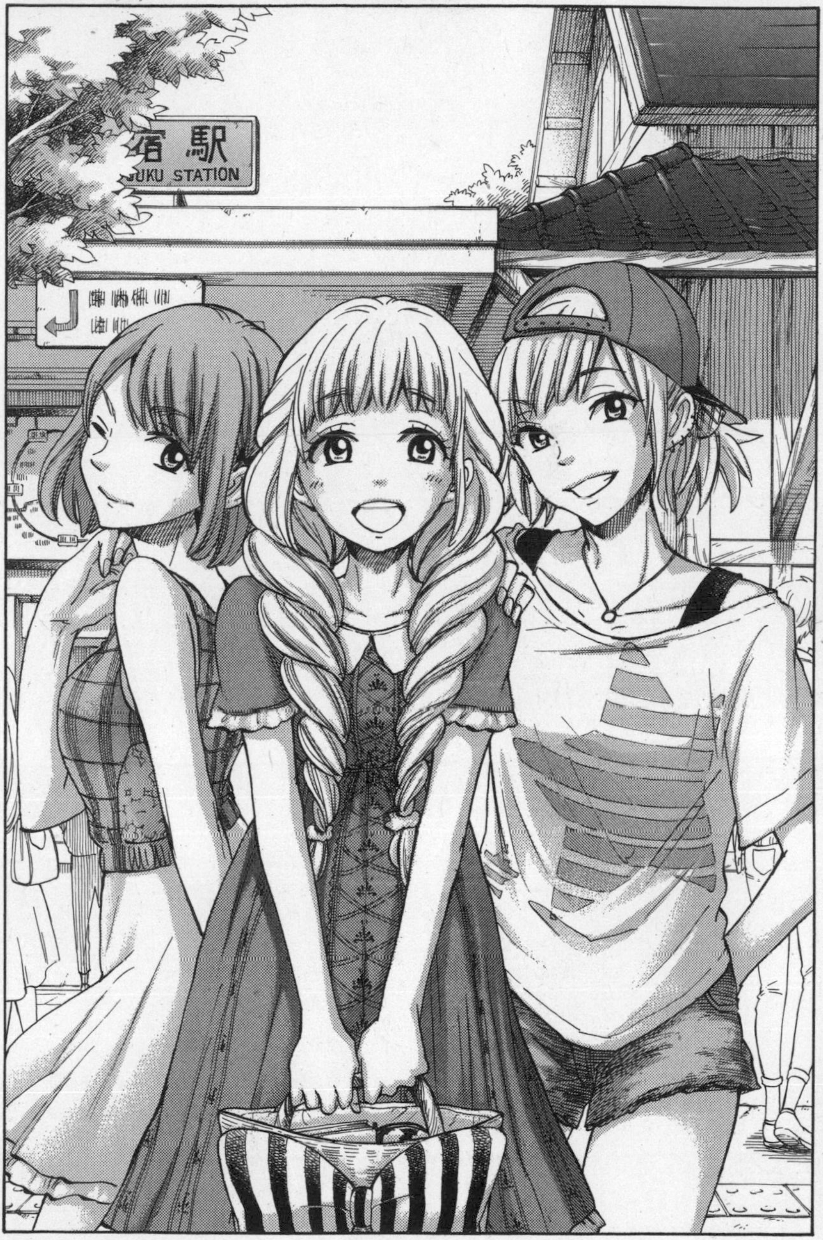
宿駅
UKU STATION

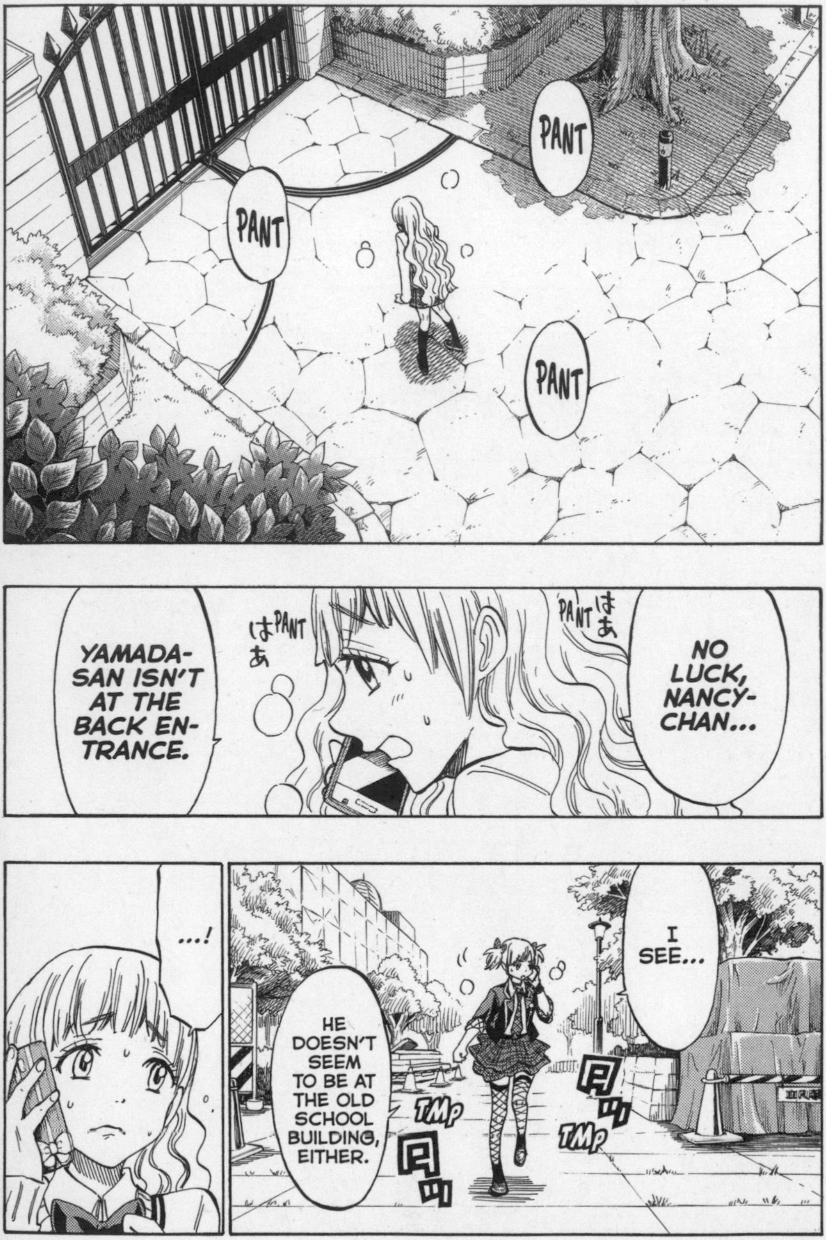
PANT
PANT
PANT
NO LUCK, NANCY-CHAN...
PANT はあ
はあ PANT
YAMADA-SAN ISN'T AT THE BACK EN-TRANCE.
I SEE...
TMP
TMP
HE DOESN'T SEEM TO BE AT THE OLD SCHOOL BUILDING, EITHER.
...!

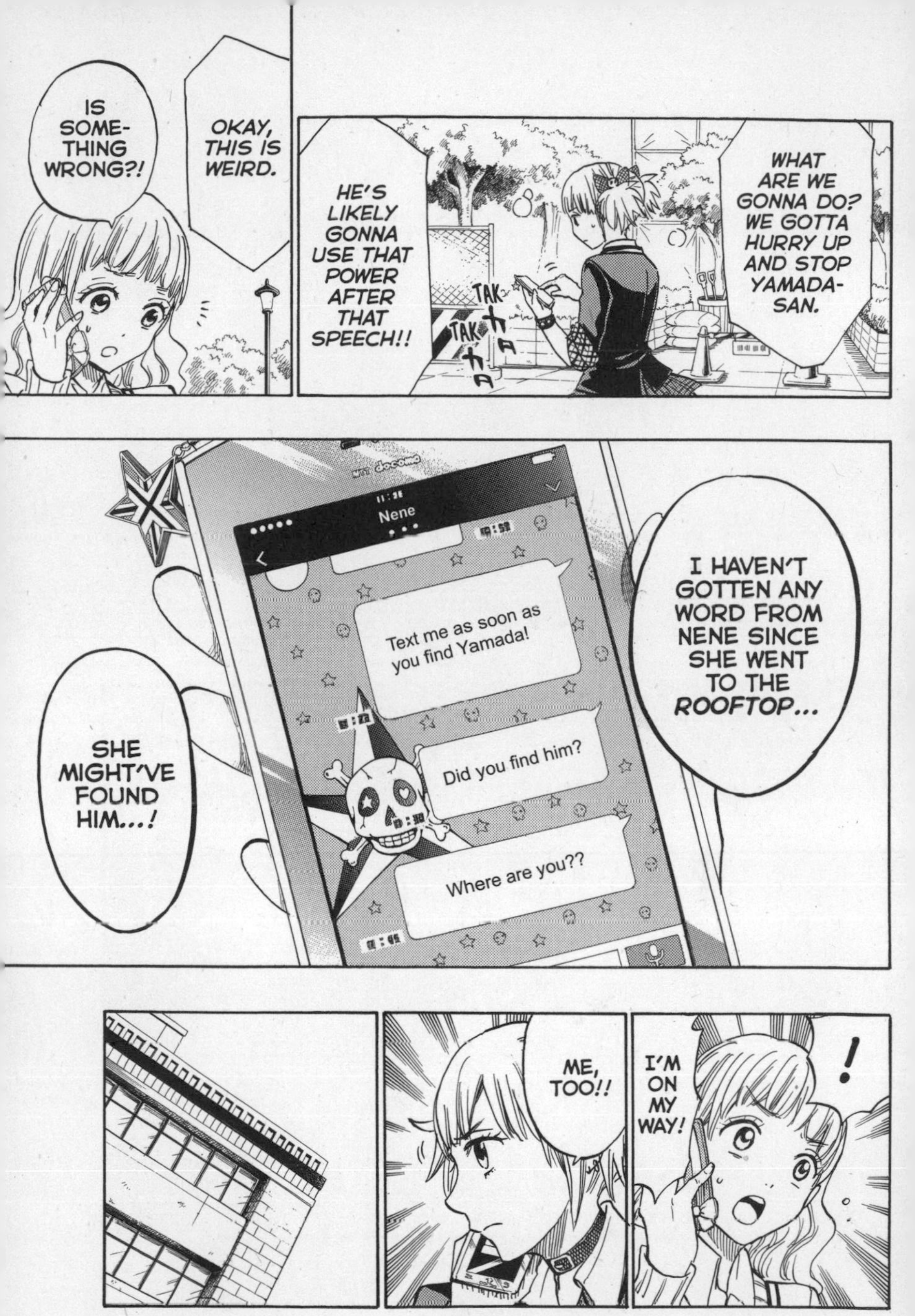
WHAT ARE WE GONNA DO? WE GOTTA HURRY UP AND STOP YAMADA-SAN.
HE'S LIKELY GONNA USE THAT POWER AFTER THAT SPEECH!!
TAK TAK
OKAY, THIS IS WEIRD.
IS SOME-THING WRONG?!
I HAVEN'T GOTTEN ANY WORD FROM NENE SINCE SHE WENT TO THE *ROOFTOP*...
docomo
Nene
Text me as soon as you find Yamada!
Did you find him?
Where are you??
SHE MIGHT'VE FOUND HIM...!
!
I'M ON MY WAY!
ME, TOO!!

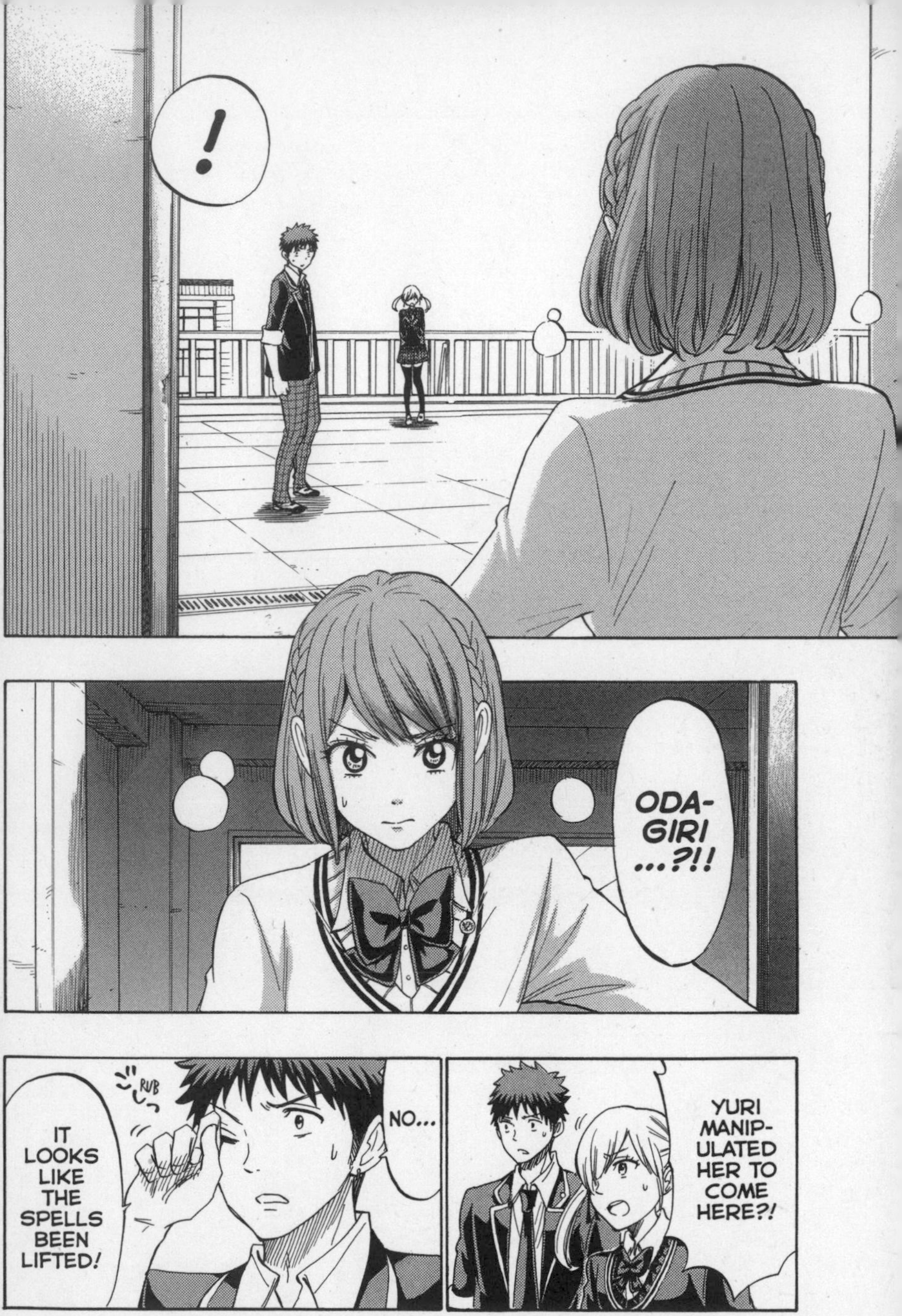
!
ODA-GIRI...?!!
YURI MANIP-ULATED HER TO COME HERE?!
NO...
RUB
IT LOOKS LIKE THE SPELLS BEEN LIFTED!

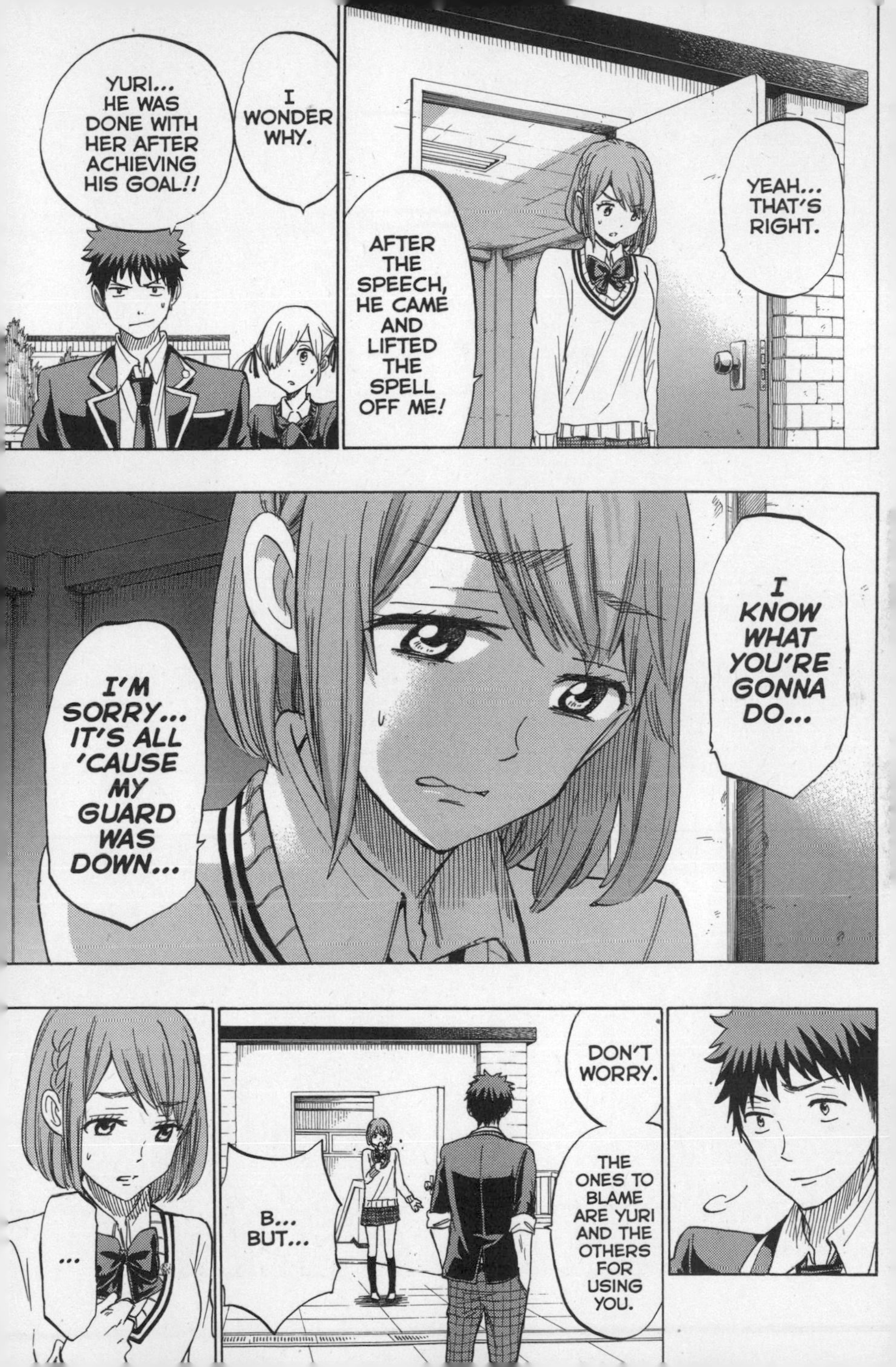
YEAH... THAT'S RIGHT.
AFTER THE SPEECH, HE CAME AND LIFTED THE SPELL OFF ME!
I WONDER WHY.
YURI... HE WAS DONE WITH HER AFTER ACHIEVING HIS GOAL!!
I KNOW WHAT YOU'RE GONNA DO...
I'M SORRY... IT'S ALL 'CAUSE MY GUARD WAS DOWN...
DON'T WORRY.
THE ONES TO BLAME ARE YURI AND THE OTHERS FOR USING YOU.
B... BUT...
...

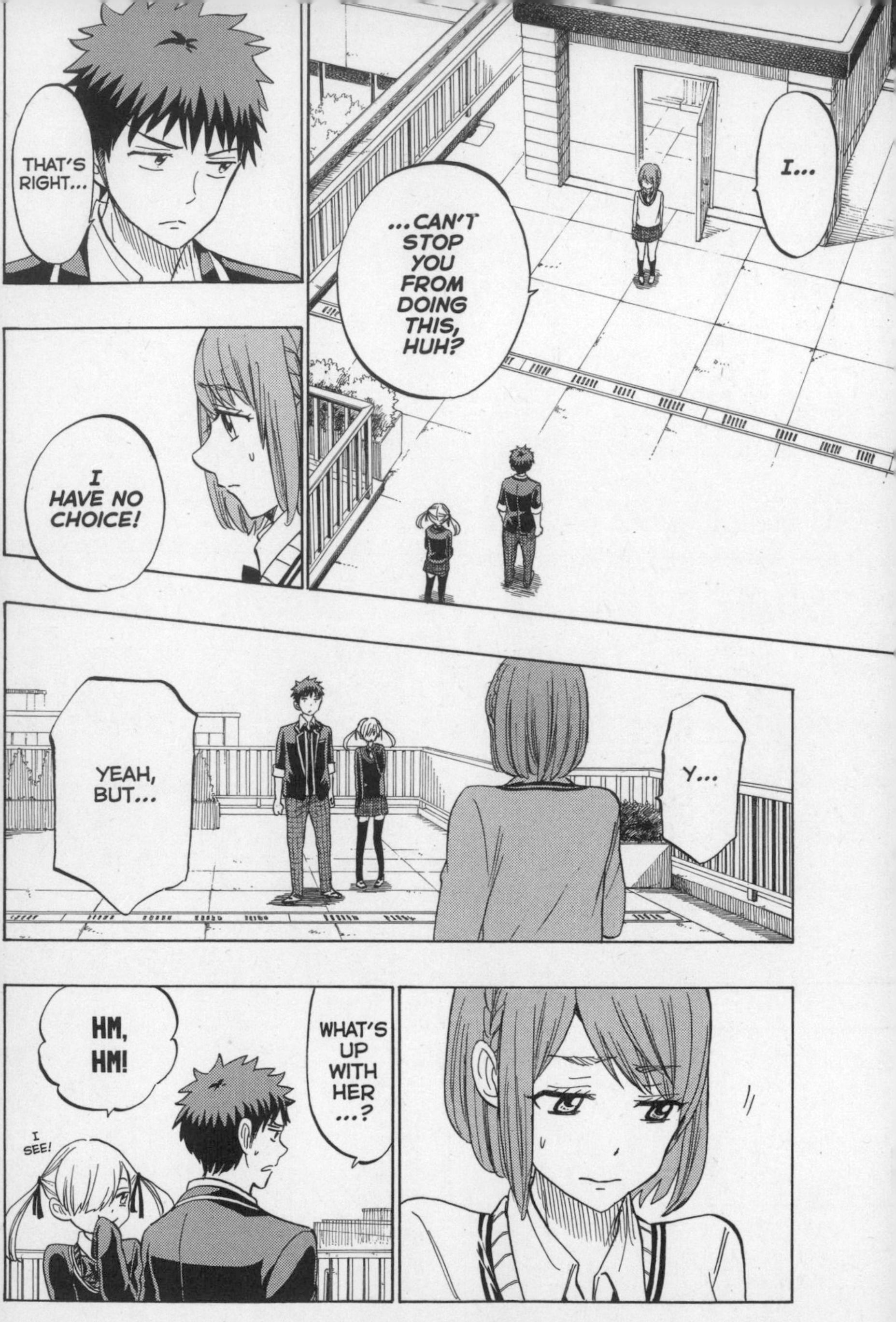
I...
...CAN'T STOP YOU FROM DOING THIS, HUH?
THAT'S RIGHT...
I HAVE NO CHOICE!
Y...
YEAH, BUT...
WHAT'S UP WITH HER ...?
HM, HM!
I SEE!

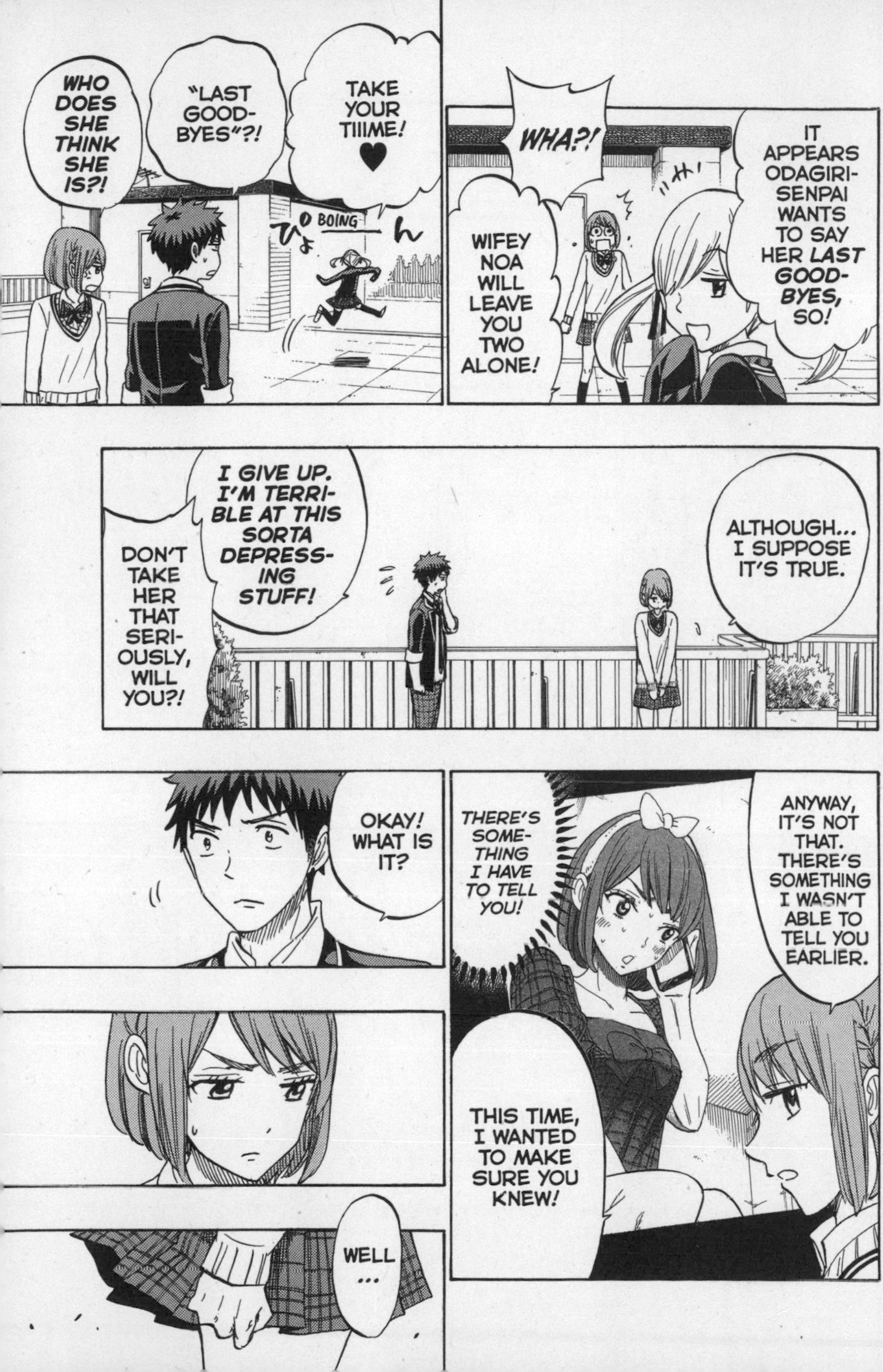
IT APPEARS ODAGIRI-SENPAI WANTS TO SAY HER LAST GOODBYES, SO!
WIFEY NOA WILL LEAVE YOU TWO ALONE!
WHA?!
TAKE YOUR TIIIME! ♥
BOING
"LAST GOODBYES"?!
WHO DOES SHE THINK SHE IS?!
ALTHOUGH... I SUPPOSE IT'S TRUE.
I GIVE UP. I'M TERRIBLE AT THIS SORTA DEPRESSING STUFF!
DON'T TAKE HER THAT SERIOUSLY, WILL YOU?!
ANYWAY, IT'S NOT THAT. THERE'S SOMETHING I WASN'T ABLE TO TELL YOU EARLIER.
THERE'S SOMETHING I HAVE TO TELL YOU!
THIS TIME, I WANTED TO MAKE SURE YOU KNEW!
OKAY! WHAT IS IT?
WELL ...

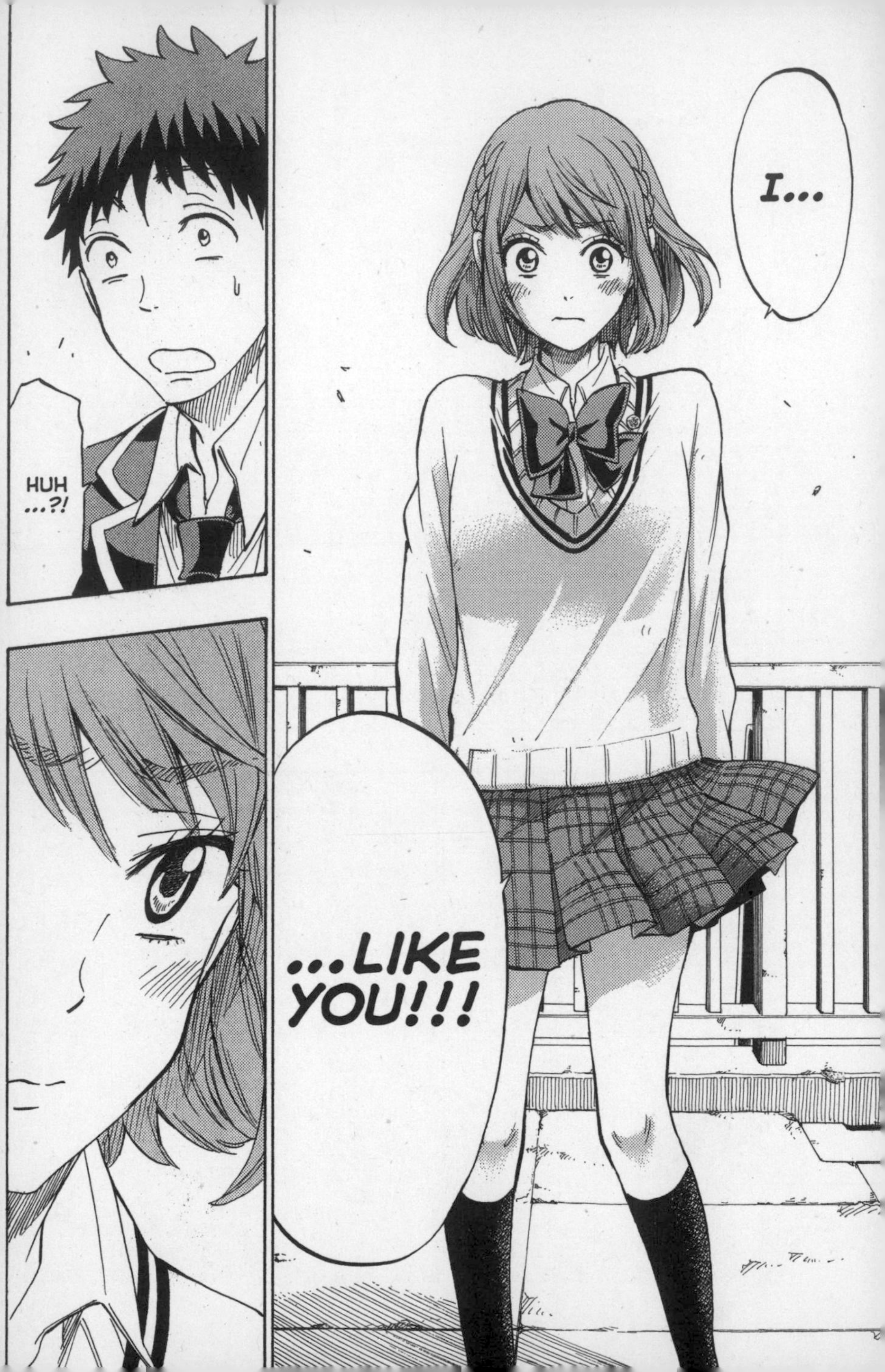
I...
...LIKE YOU!!!
HUH ...?!

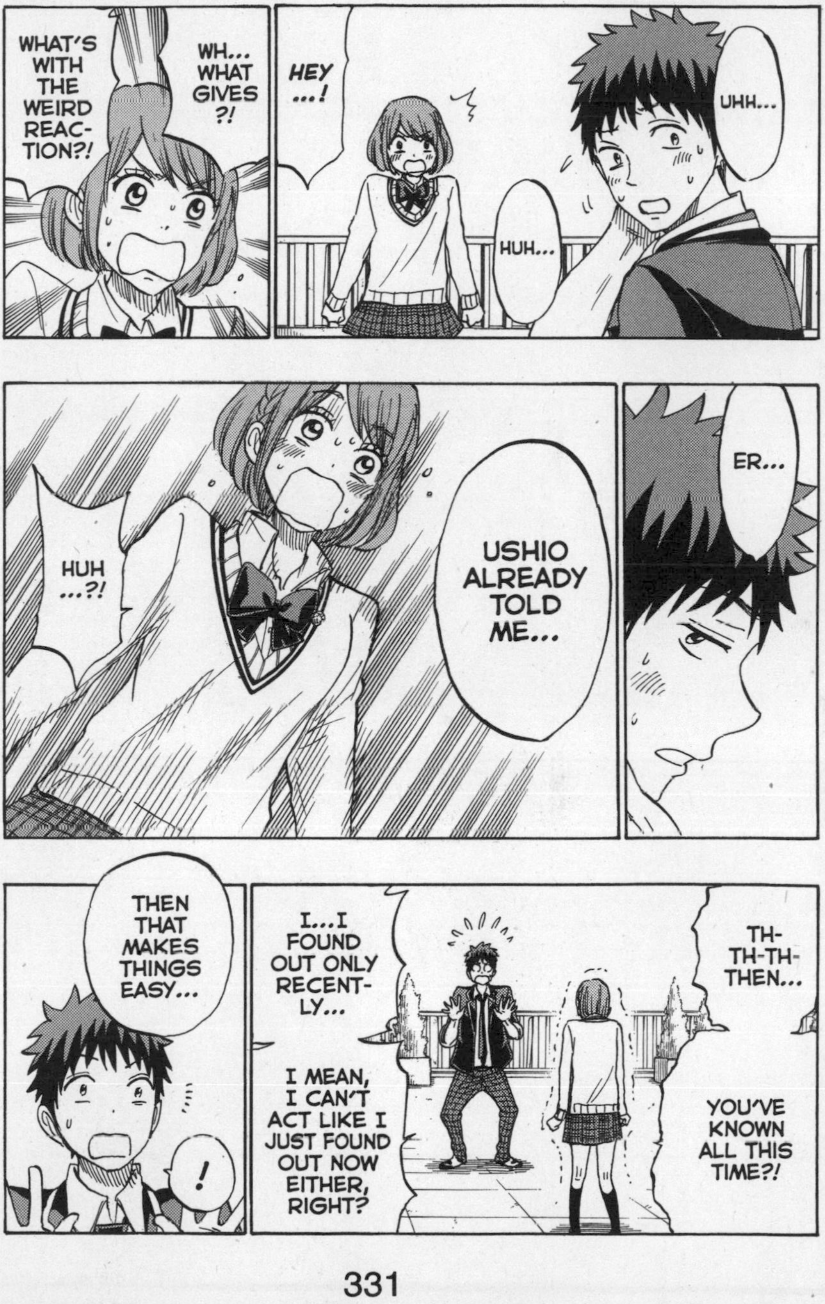
UHH...
HEY ...!
HUH...
WH... WHAT GIVES?!
WHAT'S WITH THE WEIRD REAC-TION?!
ER...
USHIO ALREADY TOLD ME...
HUH ...?!
TH-TH-TH-THEN...
YOU'VE KNOWN ALL THIS TIME?!
I...I FOUND OUT ONLY RECENT-LY...
I MEAN, I CAN'T ACT LIKE I JUST FOUND OUT NOW EITHER, RIGHT?
THEN THAT MAKES THINGS EASY...
!

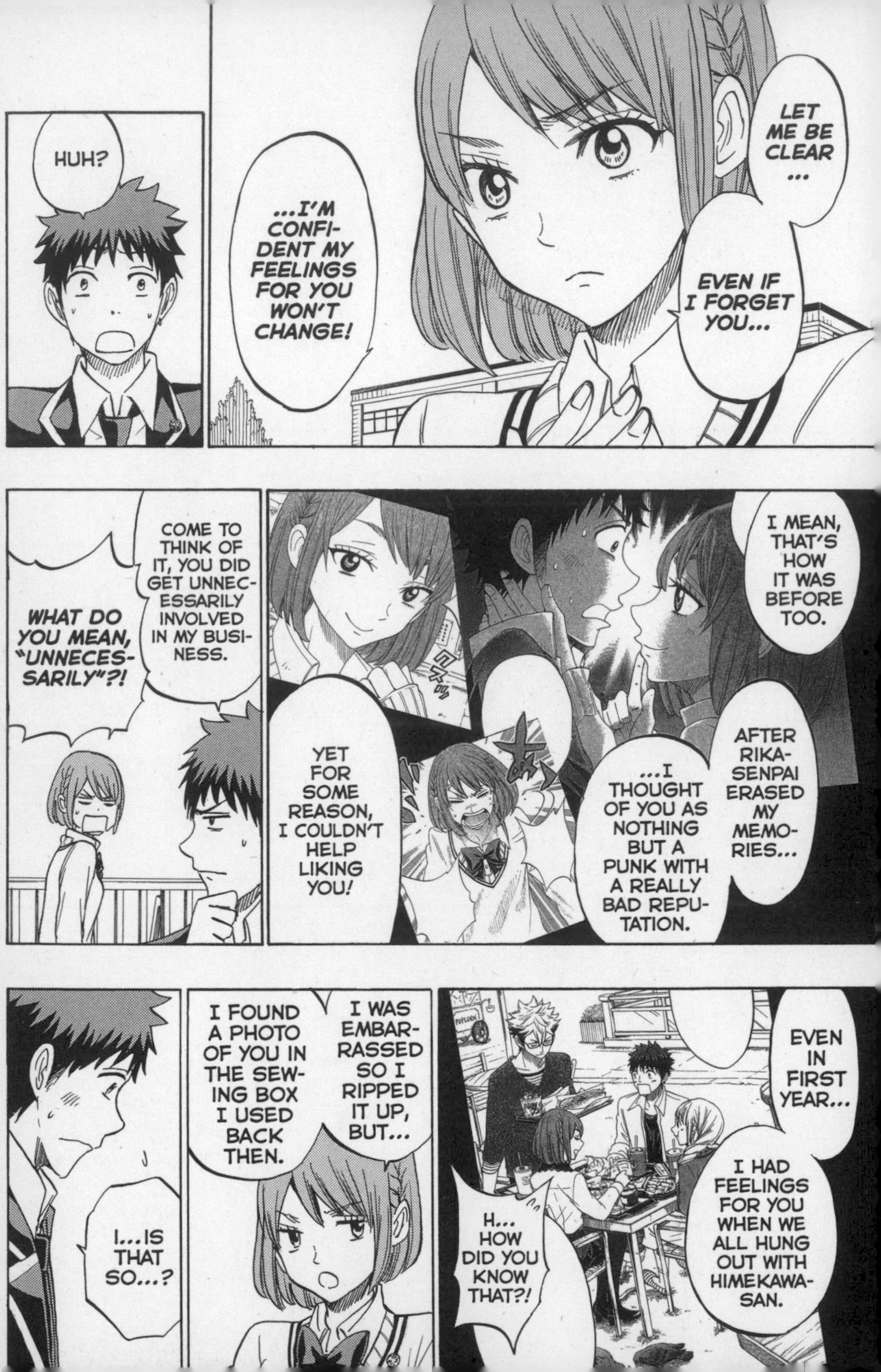

LET ME BE CLEAR ...
EVEN IF I FORGET YOU...
...I'M CONFIDENT MY FEELINGS FOR YOU WON'T CHANGE!
HUH?
I MEAN, THAT'S HOW IT WAS BEFORE TOO.
AFTER RIKA-SENPAI ERASED MY MEMORIES...
...I THOUGHT OF YOU AS NOTHING BUT A PUNK WITH A REALLY BAD REPUTATION.
YET FOR SOME REASON, I COULDN'T HELP LIKING YOU!
COME TO THINK OF IT, YOU DID GET UNNECESSARILY INVOLVED IN MY BUSINESS.
WHAT DO YOU MEAN, "UNNECESSARILY"?!
EVEN IN FIRST YEAR...
I HAD FEELINGS FOR YOU WHEN WE ALL HUNG OUT WITH HIMEKAWA-SAN.
POPCORN
H... HOW DID YOU KNOW THAT?!
I WAS EMBARRASSED SO I RIPPED IT UP, BUT...
I FOUND A PHOTO OF YOU IN THE SEWING BOX I USED BACK THEN.
I...IS THAT SO...?

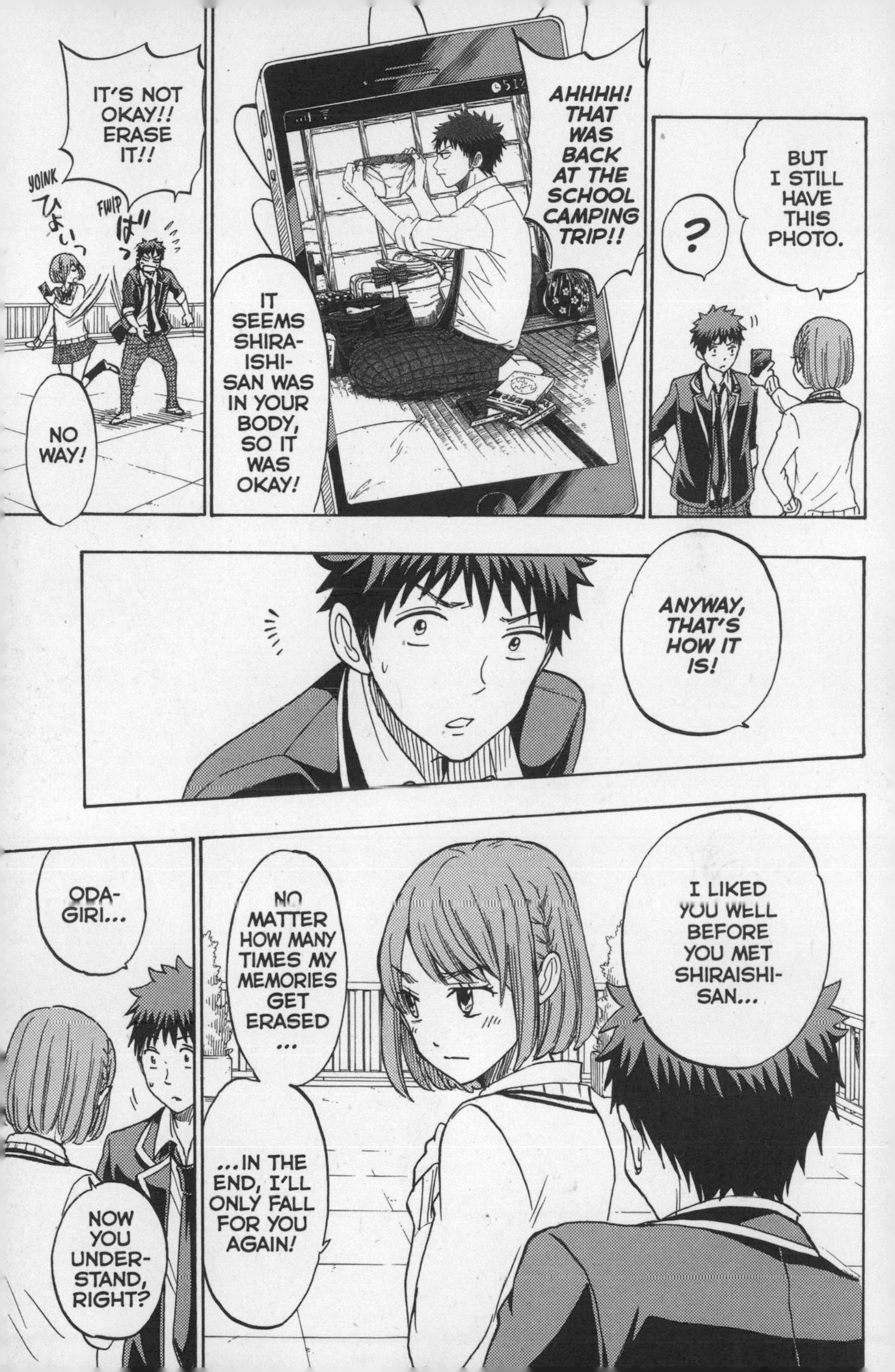
BUT I STILL HAVE THIS PHOTO.
?
AHHHH! THAT WAS BACK AT THE SCHOOL CAMPING TRIP!!
IT SEEMS SHIRAISHI-SAN WAS IN YOUR BODY, SO IT WAS OKAY!
IT'S NOT OKAY!! ERASE IT!!
YOINK ひょいっ
FWIP ばっ
NO WAY!
ANYWAY, THAT'S HOW IT IS!
I LIKED YOU WELL BEFORE YOU MET SHIRAISHI-SAN...
NO MATTER HOW MANY TIMES MY MEMORIES GET ERASED...
...IN THE END, I'LL ONLY FALL FOR YOU AGAIN!
ODAGIRI...
NOW YOU UNDERSTAND, RIGHT?

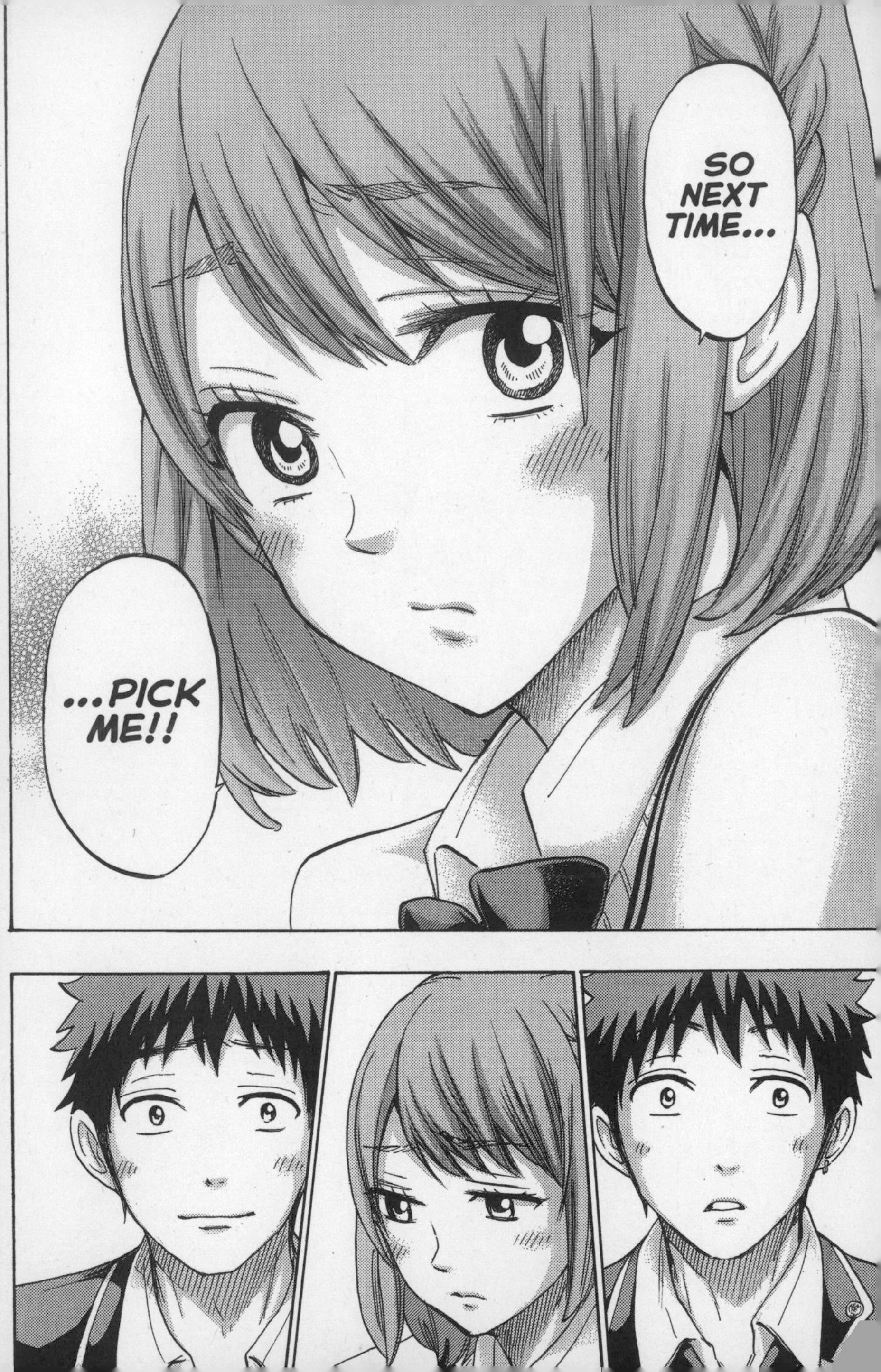
SO NEXT TIME...
...PICK ME!!

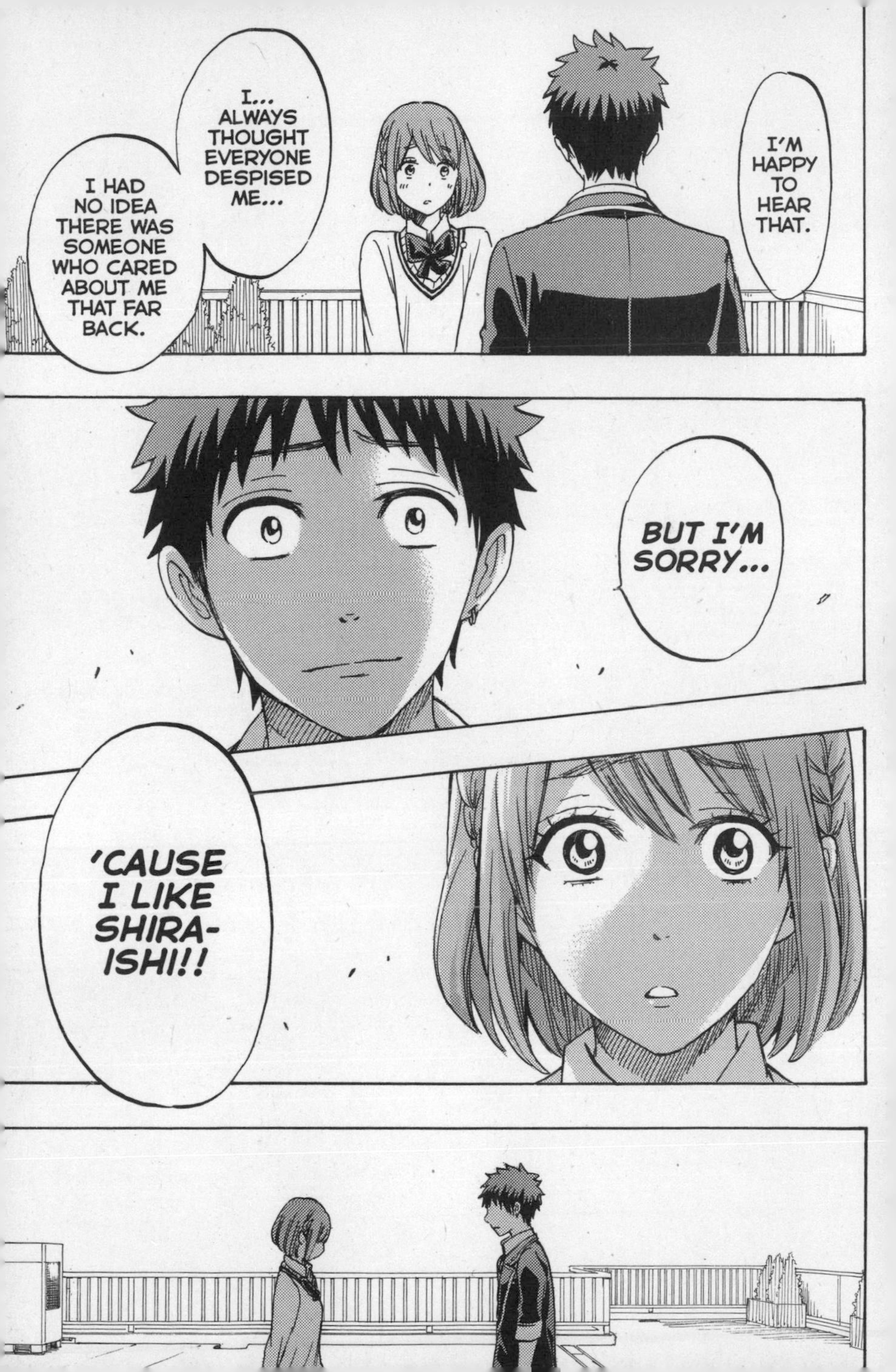
I'M HAPPY TO HEAR THAT.
I... ALWAYS THOUGHT EVERYONE DESPISED ME...
I HAD NO IDEA THERE WAS SOMEONE WHO CARED ABOUT ME THAT FAR BACK.
BUT I'M SORRY...
'CAUSE I LIKE SHIRA-ISHI!!

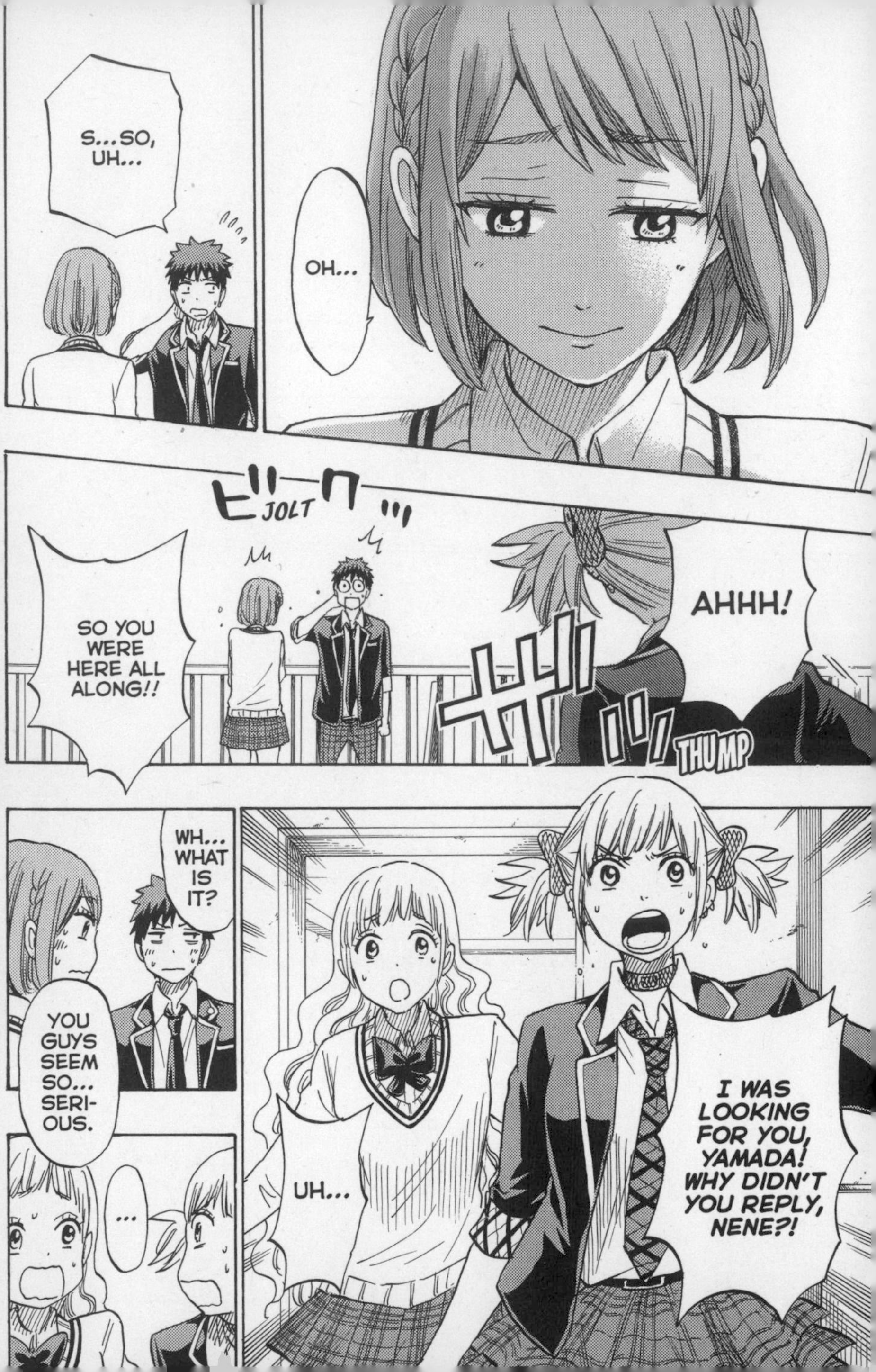
OH...
S...SO, UH...
AHHH!
ビクッ JOLT
SO YOU WERE HERE ALL ALONG!!
ザッ THUMP
I WAS LOOKING FOR YOU, YAMADA! WHY DIDN'T YOU REPLY, NENE?!
UH...
WH... WHAT IS IT?
YOU GUYS SEEM SO... SERI-OUS.
...

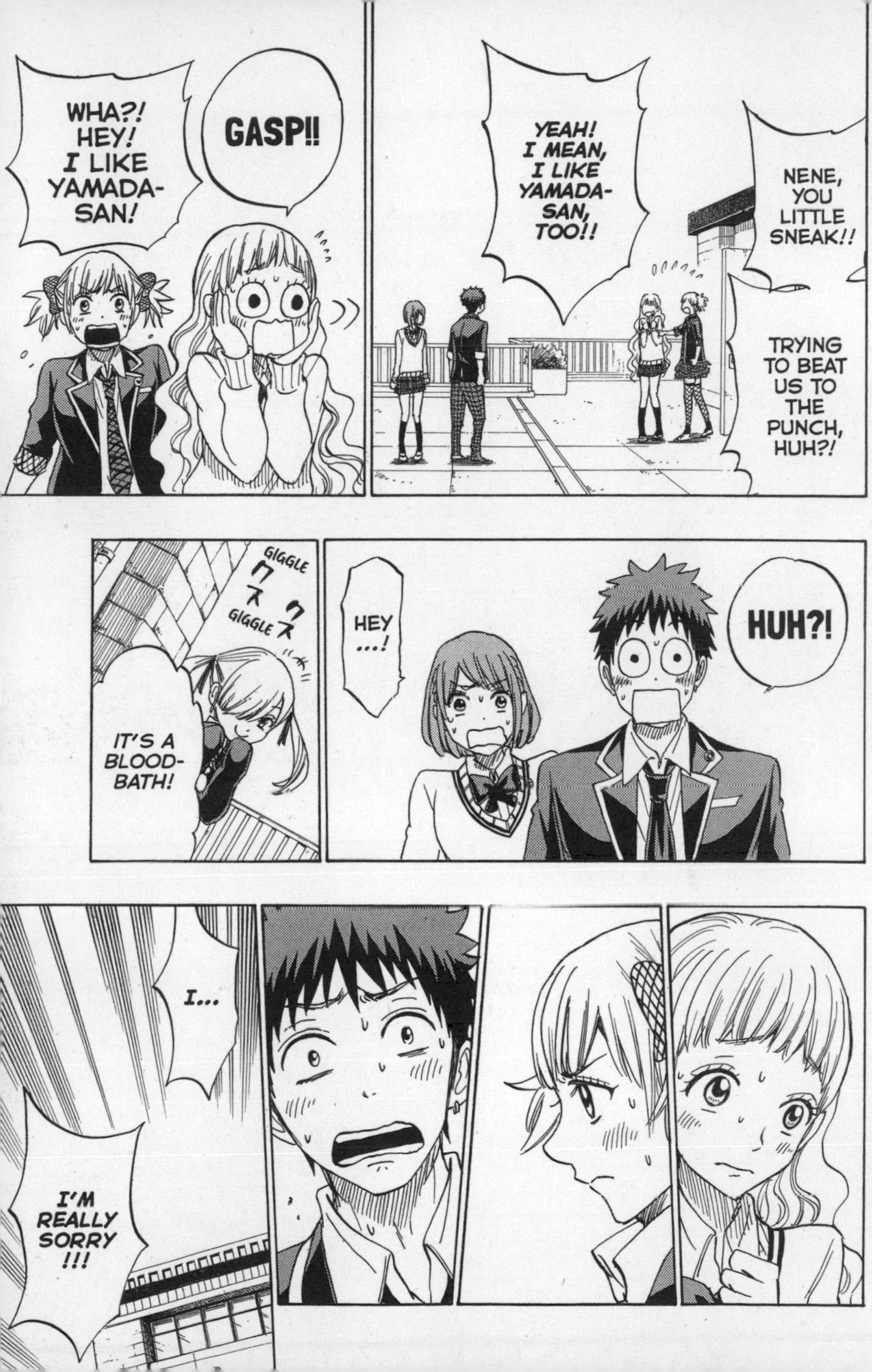
NENE, YOU LITTLE SNEAK!!
TRYING TO BEAT US TO THE PUNCH, HUH?!
YEAH! I MEAN, I LIKE YAMADA-SAN, TOO!!
GASP!!
WHA?! HEY! I LIKE YAMADA-SAN!
HUH?!
HEY ...!
GIGGLE クス
GIGGLE クス
IT'S A BLOOD-BATH!
I...
I'M REALLY SORRY!!!

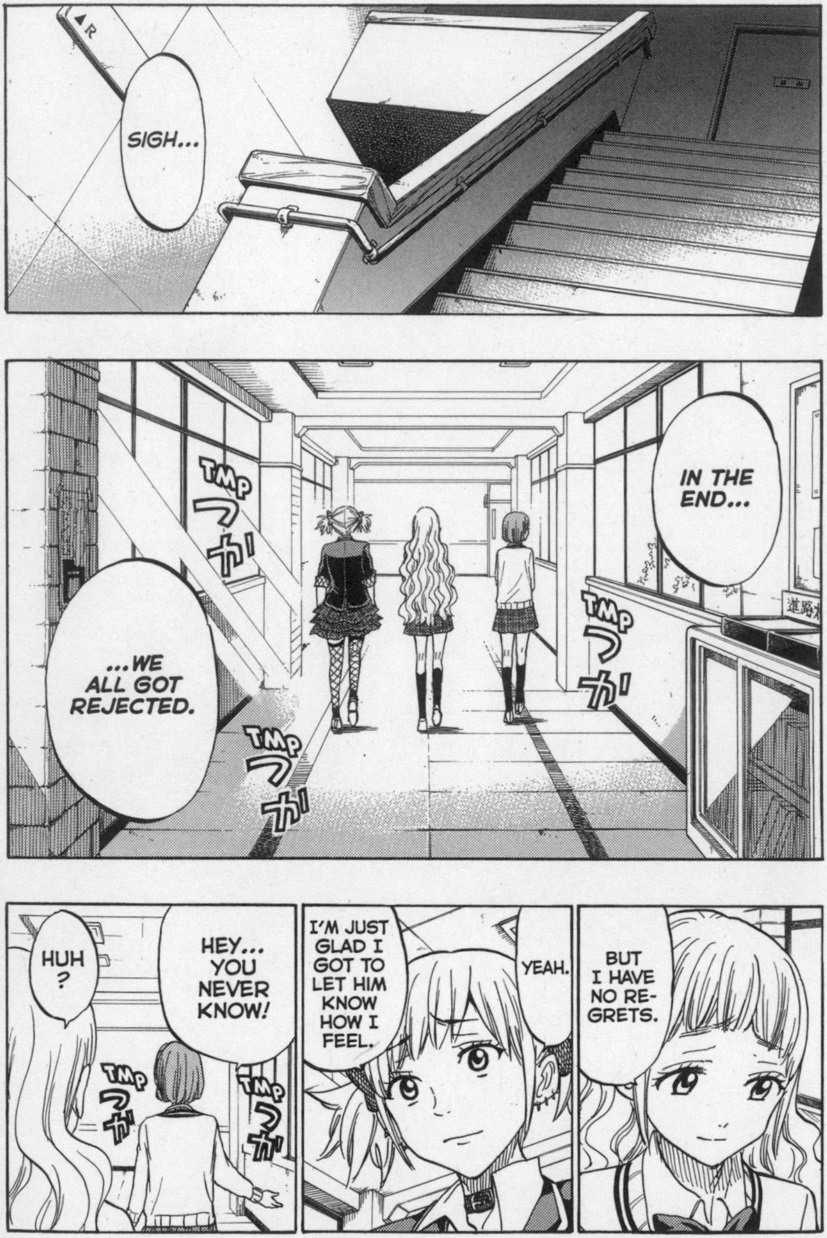
SIGH...
IN THE END...
TMP
...WE ALL GOT REJECTED.
TMP
TMP
BUT I HAVE NO RE-GRETS.
YEAH.
I'M JUST GLAD I GOT TO LET HIM KNOW HOW I FEEL.
TMP
HEY... YOU NEVER KNOW!
TMP
HUH?

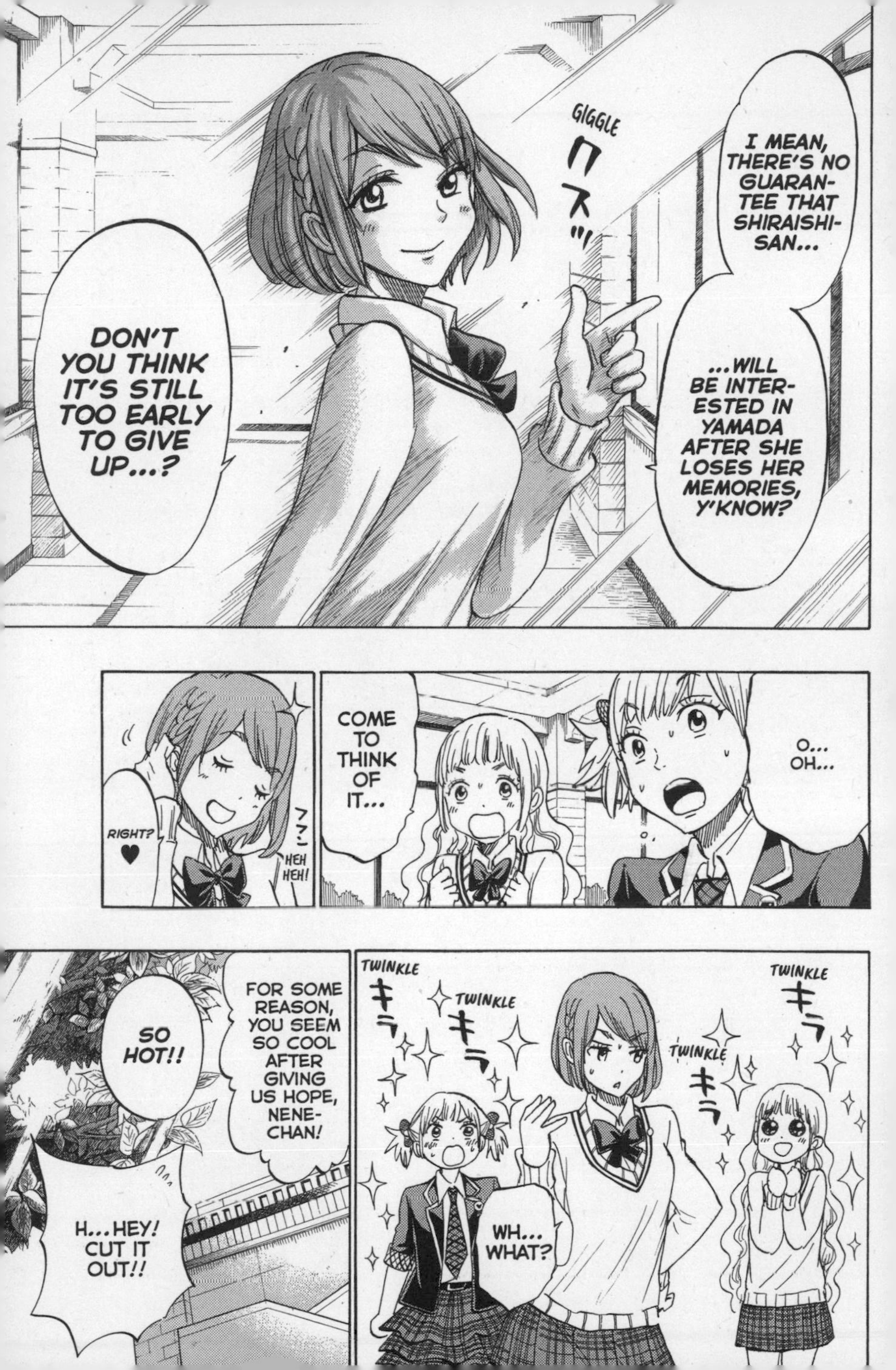
I MEAN, THERE'S NO GUARANTEE THAT SHIRAISHI-SAN...
GIGGLE
クスッ
...WILL BE INTERESTED IN YAMADA AFTER SHE LOSES HER MEMORIES, Y'KNOW?
DON'T YOU THINK IT'S STILL TOO EARLY TO GIVE UP...?
O... OH...
COME TO THINK OF IT...
HEH HEH!
RIGHT? ♥
TWINKLE
キラ
TWINKLE
キラ
WH... WHAT?
TWINKLE
キラ
TWINKLE
キラ
FOR SOME REASON, YOU SEEM SO COOL AFTER GIVING US HOPE, NENE-CHAN!
SO HOT!!
H...HEY! CUT IT OUT!!

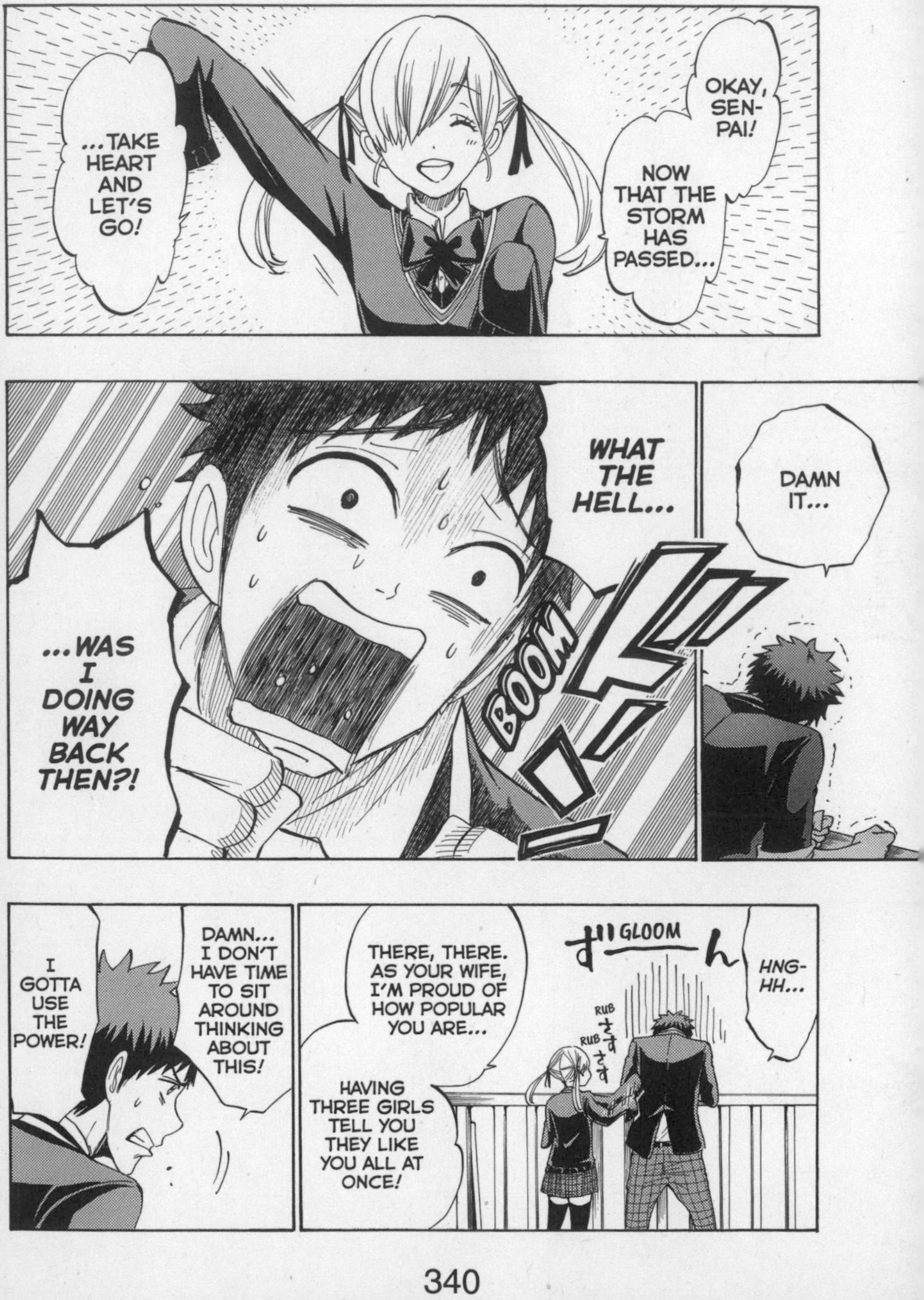
OKAY, SEN-PAI!
NOW THAT THE STORM HAS PASSED...
...TAKE HEART AND LET'S GO!
DAMN IT...
WHAT THE HELL...
BOOM
...WAS I DOING WAY BACK THEN?!
HNG-HH...
ずーん GLOOM
THERE, THERE. AS YOUR WIFE, I'M PROUD OF HOW POPULAR YOU ARE...
RUB さす RUB さす
HAVING THREE GIRLS TELL YOU THEY LIKE YOU ALL AT ONCE!
DAMN... I DON'T HAVE TIME TO SIT AROUND THINKING ABOUT THIS!
I GOTTA USE THE POWER!

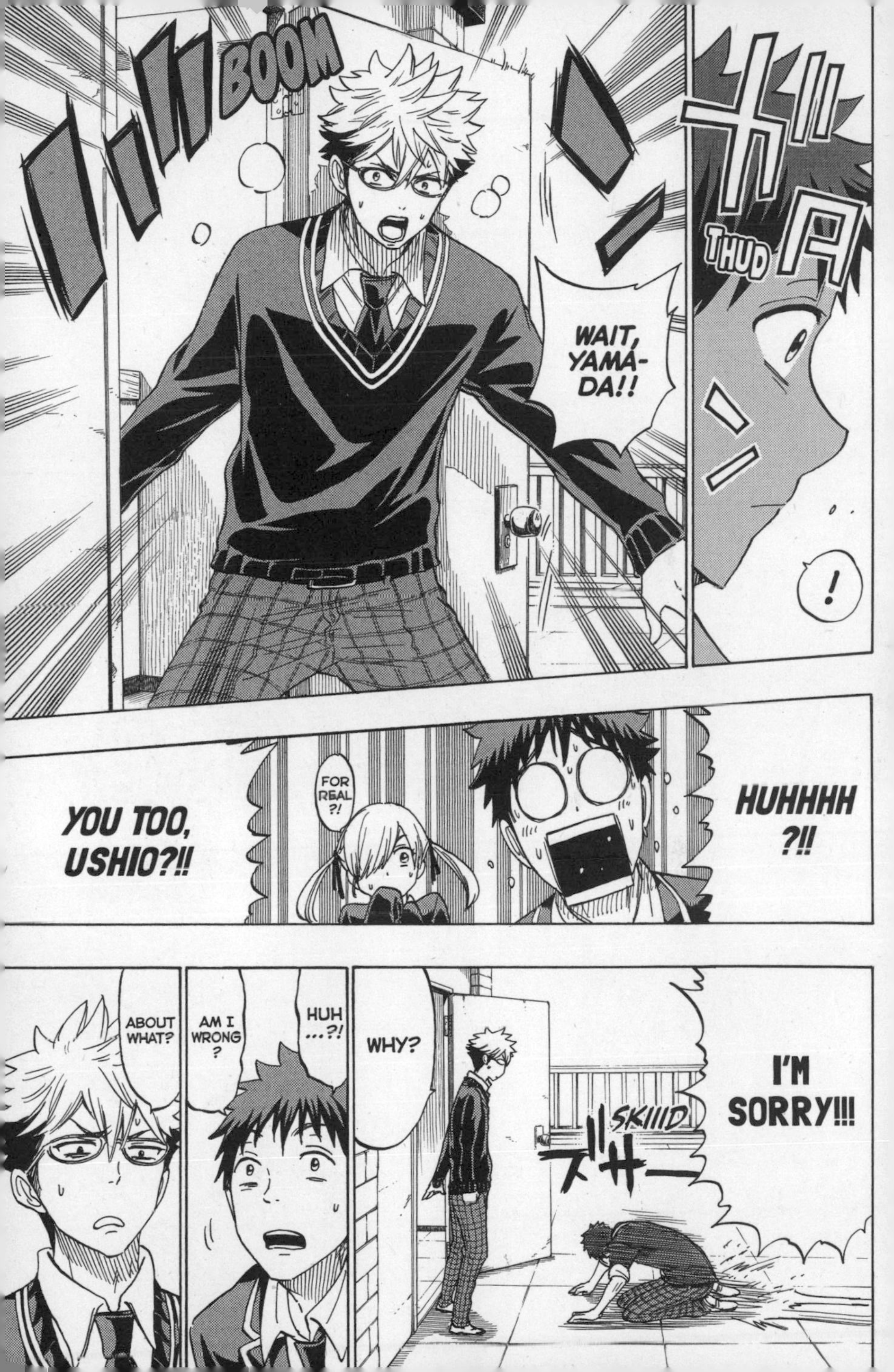
THUD
!
BOOM
WAIT, YAMA-DA!!
HUHHHH ?!!
FOR REAL ?!
YOU TOO, USHIO?!!
I'M SORRY!!!
SKIIID
WHY?
HUH ...?!
AM I WRONG ?
ABOUT WHAT?

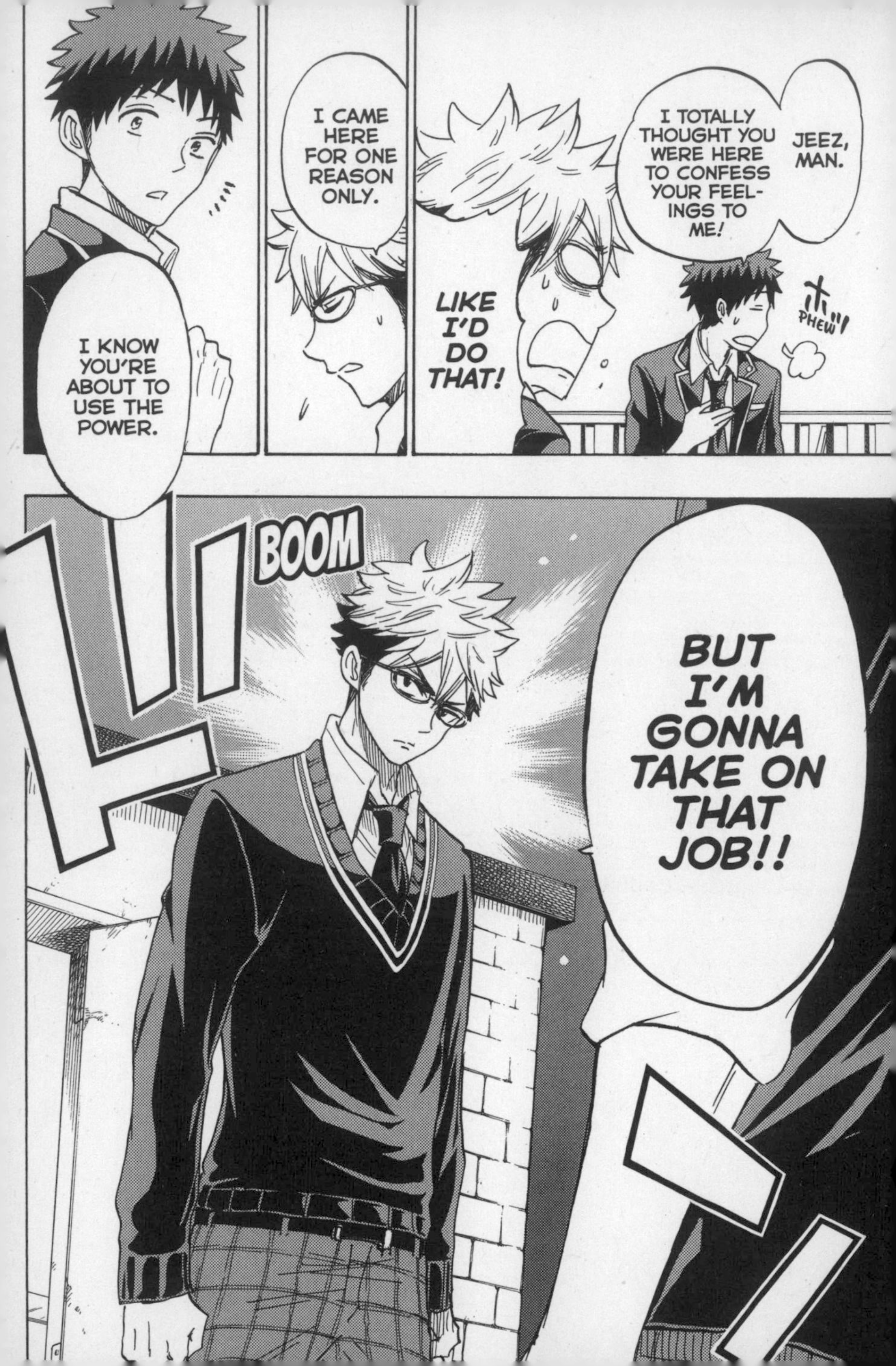
JEEZ, MAN.
I TOTALLY THOUGHT YOU WERE HERE TO CONFESS YOUR FEEL-INGS TO ME!
PHEW
LIKE I'D DO THAT!
I CAME HERE FOR ONE REASON ONLY.
I KNOW YOU'RE ABOUT TO USE THE POWER.
BUT I'M GONNA TAKE ON THAT JOB!!
BOOM

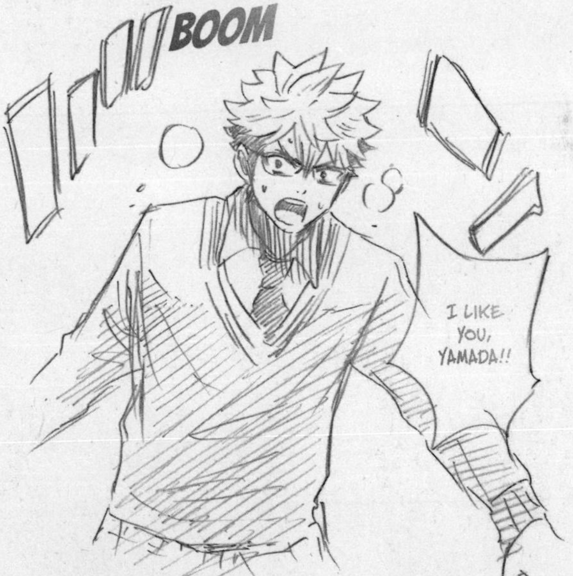
BOOM
I LIKE YOU, YAMADA!!

Yamada-kun
AND THE
Seven Witches

CHAPTER 172: Stop fighting over meee. ♥

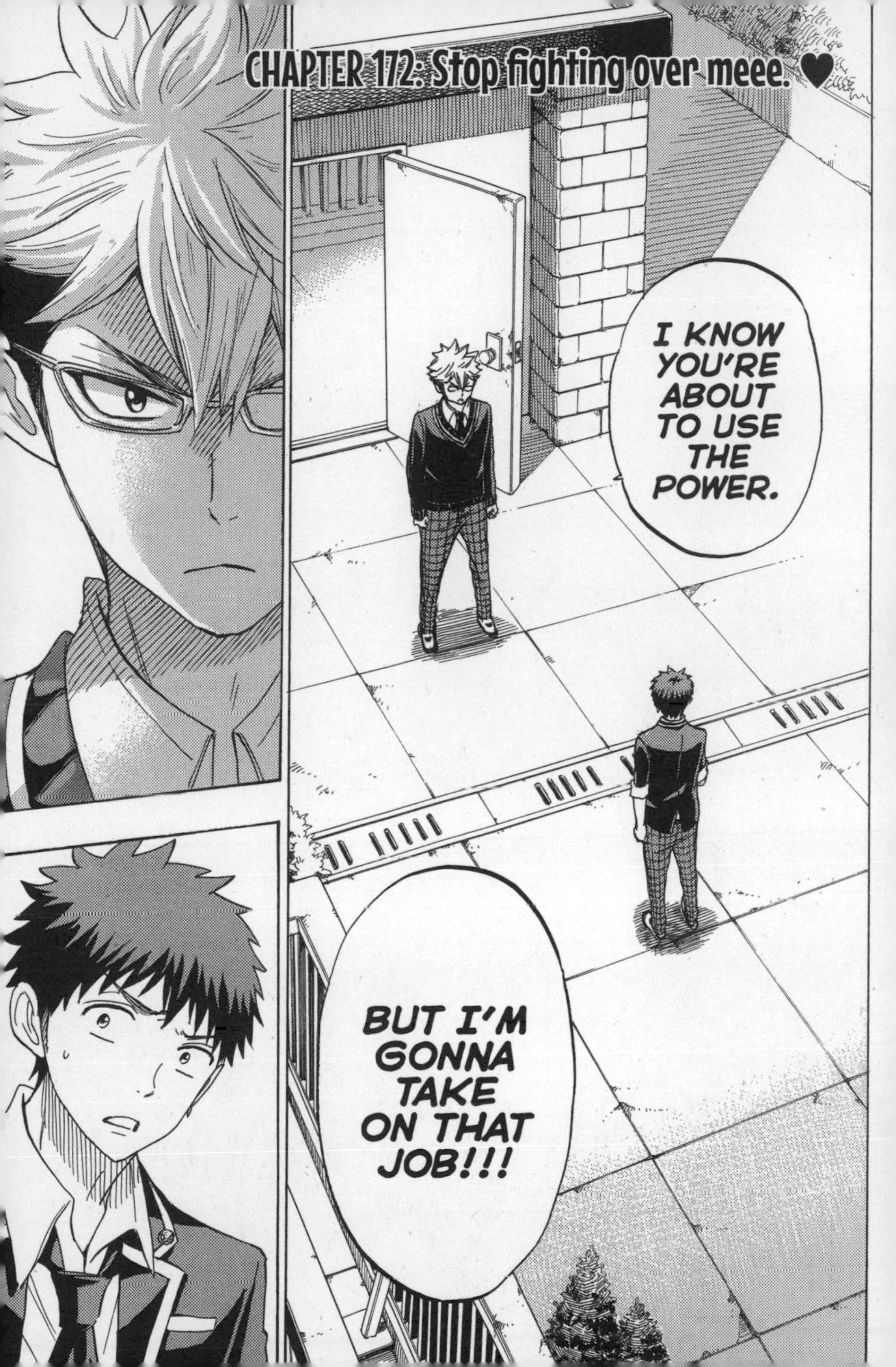
I KNOW YOU'RE ABOUT TO USE THE POWER.
BUT I'M GONNA TAKE ON THAT JOB!!!

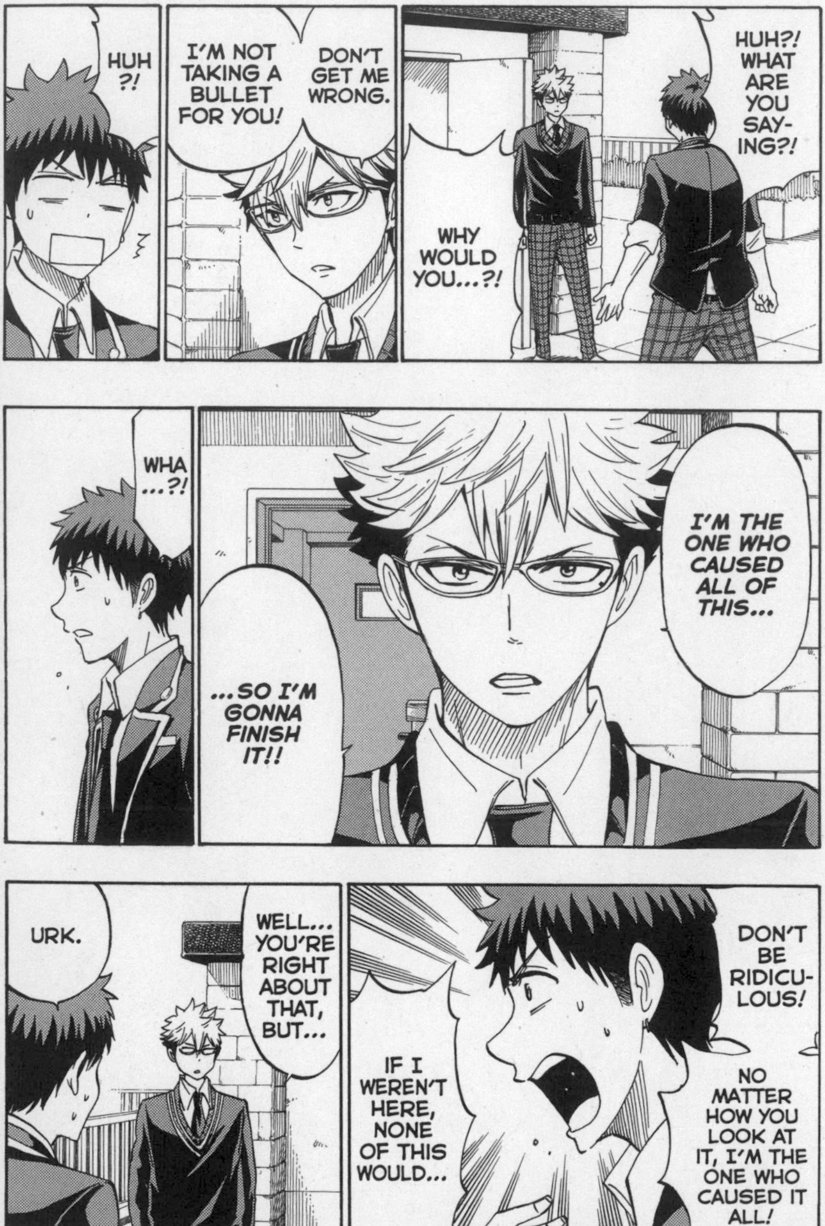
HUH?! WHAT ARE YOU SAYING?!
WHY WOULD YOU...?!
DON'T GET ME WRONG.
I'M NOT TAKING A BULLET FOR YOU!
HUH ?!
I'M THE ONE WHO CAUSED ALL OF THIS...
...SO I'M GONNA FINISH IT!!
WHA ...?!
DON'T BE RIDICULOUS!
NO MATTER HOW YOU LOOK AT IT, I'M THE ONE WHO CAUSED IT ALL!
IF I WEREN'T HERE, NONE OF THIS WOULD...
WELL... YOU'RE RIGHT ABOUT THAT, BUT...
URK.

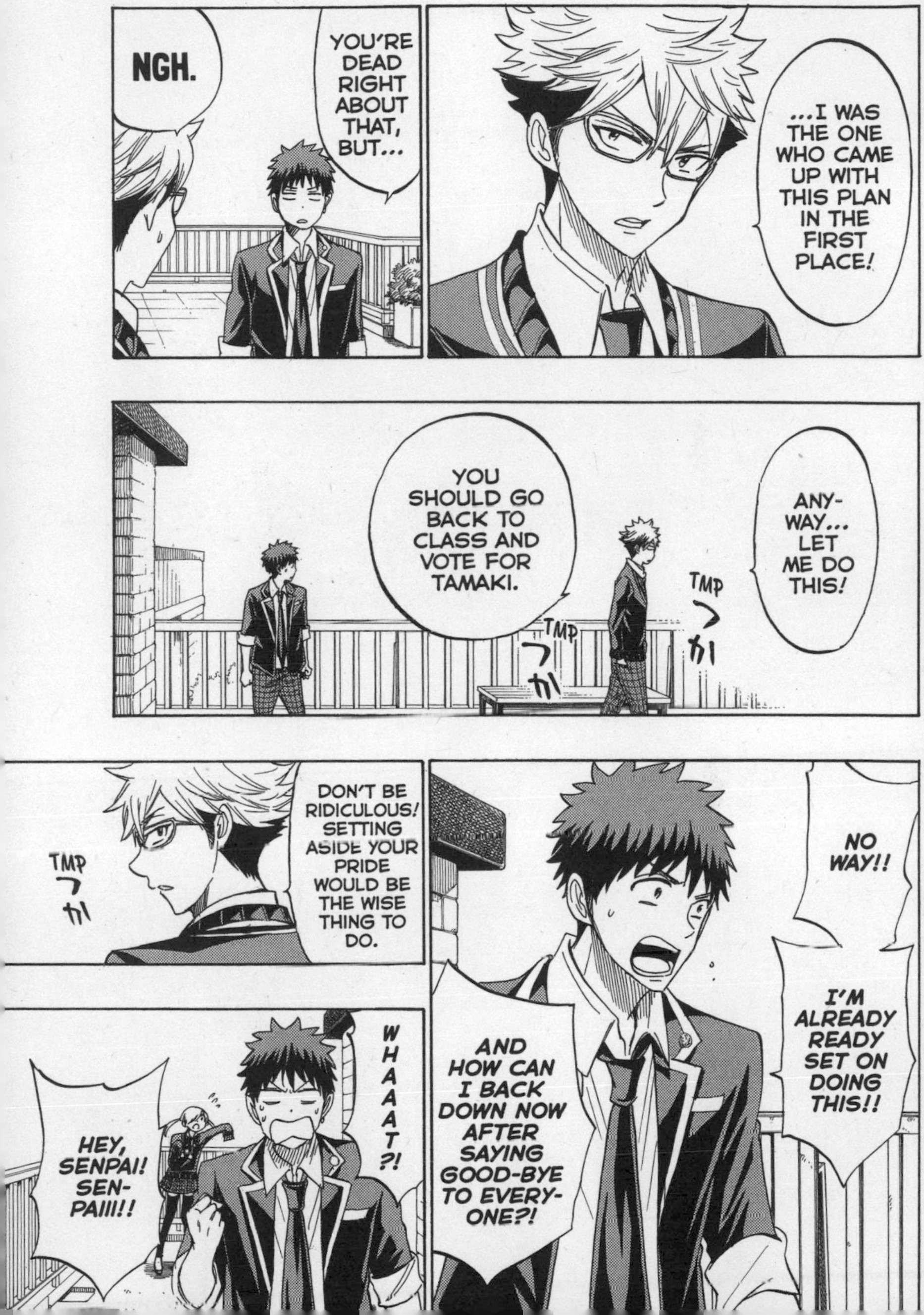
...I WAS THE ONE WHO CAME UP WITH THIS PLAN IN THE FIRST PLACE!
YOU'RE DEAD RIGHT ABOUT THAT, BUT...
NGH.
ANY-WAY... LET ME DO THIS!
TMP つ カ
YOU SHOULD GO BACK TO CLASS AND VOTE FOR TAMAKI.
TMP つ カ
NO WAY!!
I'M ALREADY READY SET ON DOING THIS!!
AND HOW CAN I BACK DOWN NOW AFTER SAYING GOOD-BYE TO EVERY-ONE?!
DON'T BE RIDICULOUS! SETTING ASIDE YOUR PRIDE WOULD BE THE WISE THING TO DO.
TMP つ カ
WHAAAAT?!
HEY, SENPAI! SEN-PAIII!!

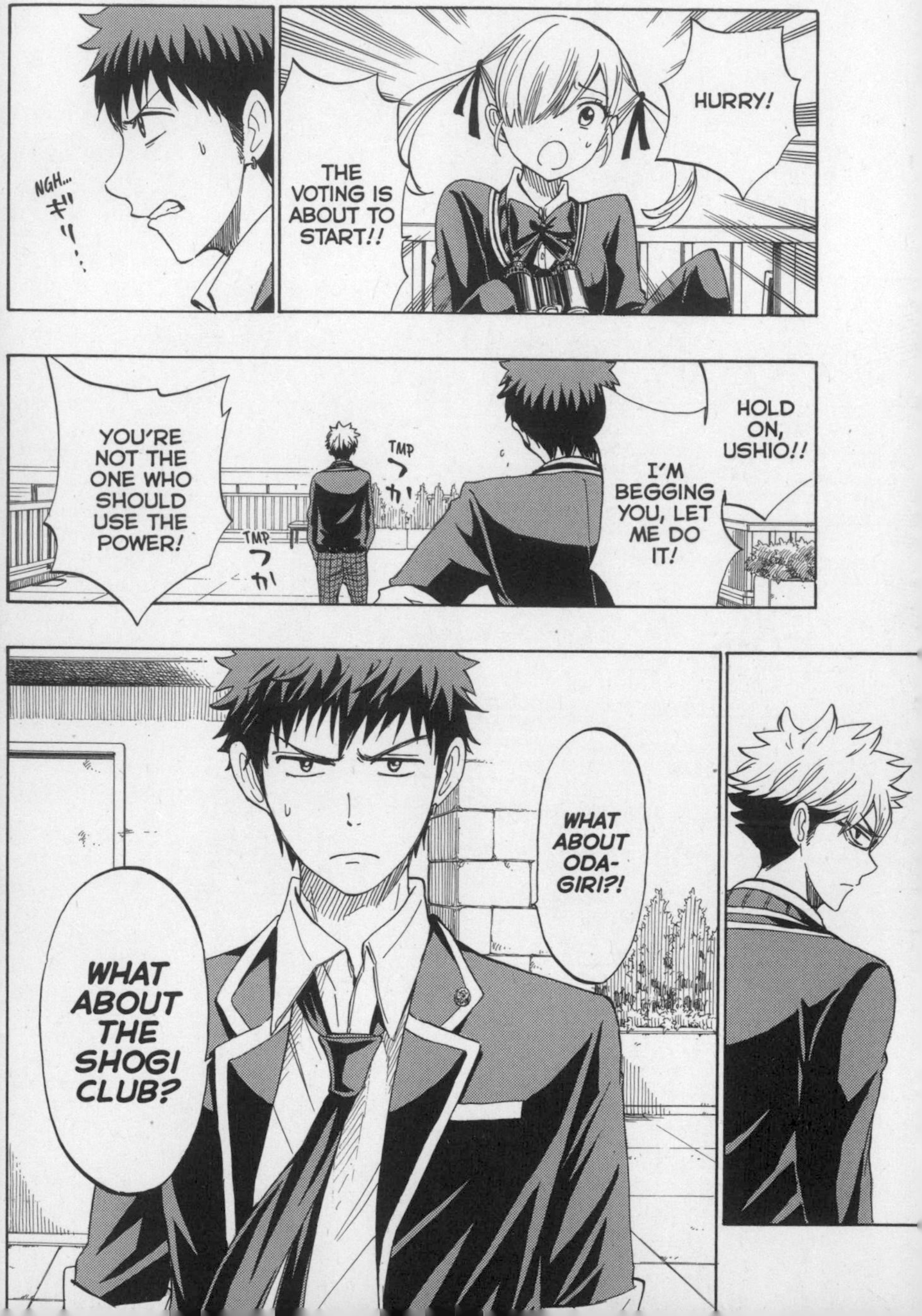
HURRY!
THE VOTING IS ABOUT TO START!!
NGH... ギリ…
HOLD ON, USHIO!!
I'M BEGGING YOU, LET ME DO IT!
TMP つか
TMP つか
YOU'RE NOT THE ONE WHO SHOULD USE THE POWER!
WHAT ABOUT ODA-GIRI?!
WHAT ABOUT THE SHOGI CLUB?

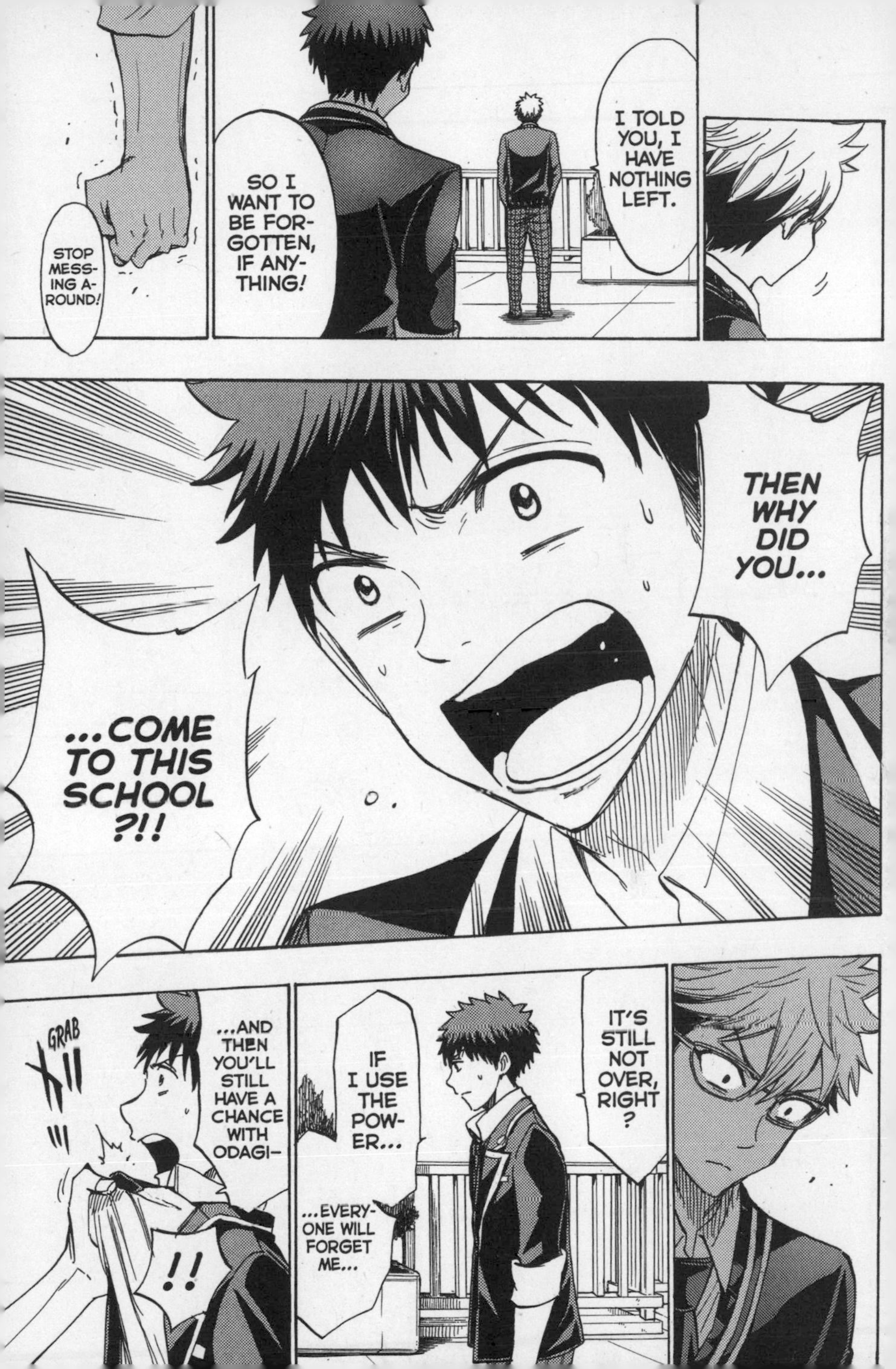
I TOLD YOU, I HAVE NOTHING LEFT.
SO I WANT TO BE FORGOTTEN, IF ANYTHING!
STOP MESSING AROUND!
THEN WHY DID YOU...
...COME TO THIS SCHOOL ?!!
IT'S STILL NOT OVER, RIGHT ?
IF I USE THE POWER...
...EVERYONE WILL FORGET ME...
...AND THEN YOU'LL STILL HAVE A CHANCE WITH ODAGI-
GRAB
!!

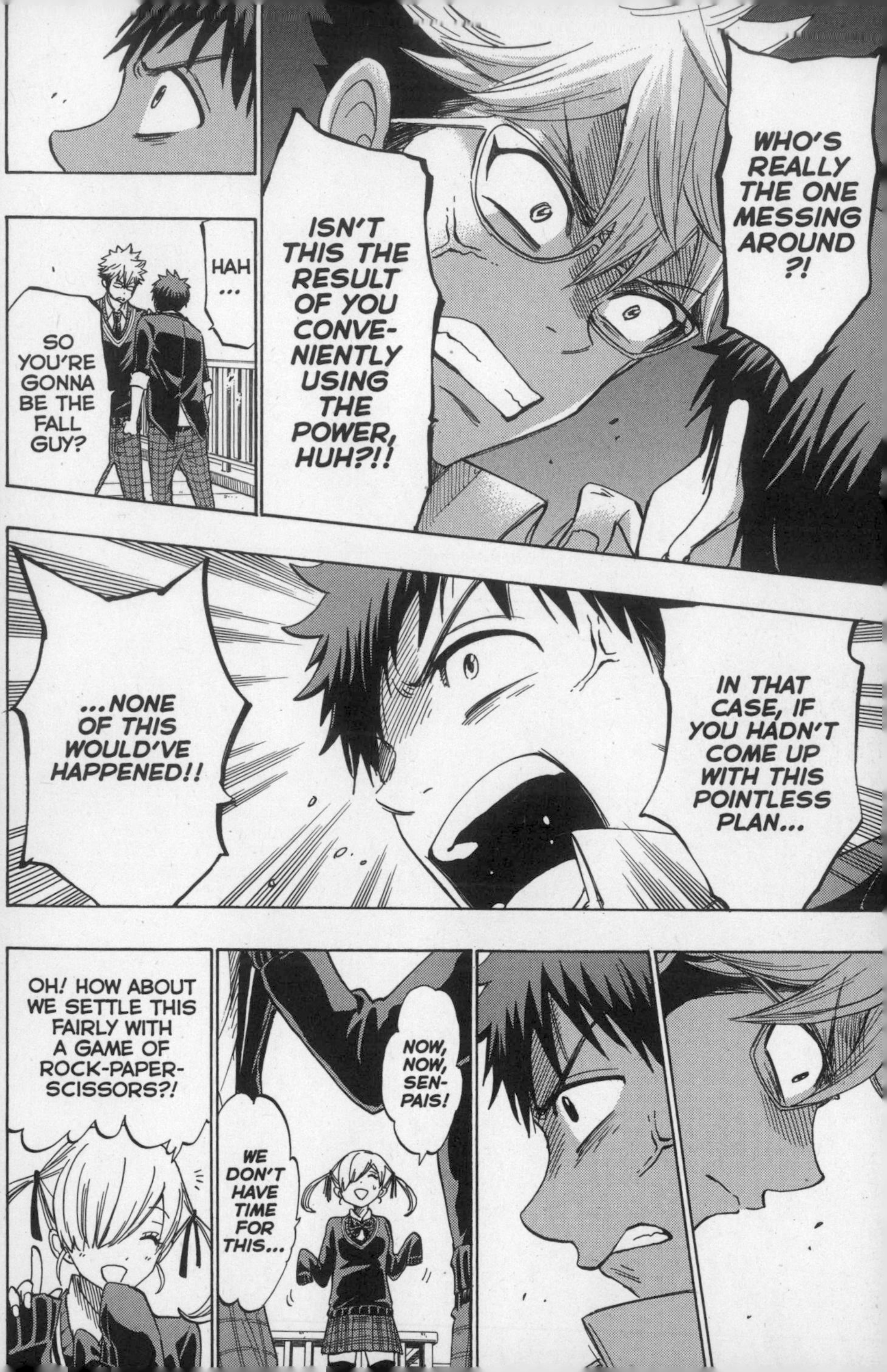
WHO'S REALLY THE ONE MESSING AROUND?!
ISN'T THIS THE RESULT OF YOU CONVENIENTLY USING THE POWER, HUH?!!
HAH...
SO YOU'RE GONNA BE THE FALL GUY?
IN THAT CASE, IF YOU HADN'T COME UP WITH THIS POINTLESS PLAN...
...NONE OF THIS WOULD'VE HAPPENED!!
NOW, NOW, SEN-PAIS!
WE DON'T HAVE TIME FOR THIS...
OH! HOW ABOUT WE SETTLE THIS FAIRLY WITH A GAME OF ROCK-PAPER-SCISSORS?!

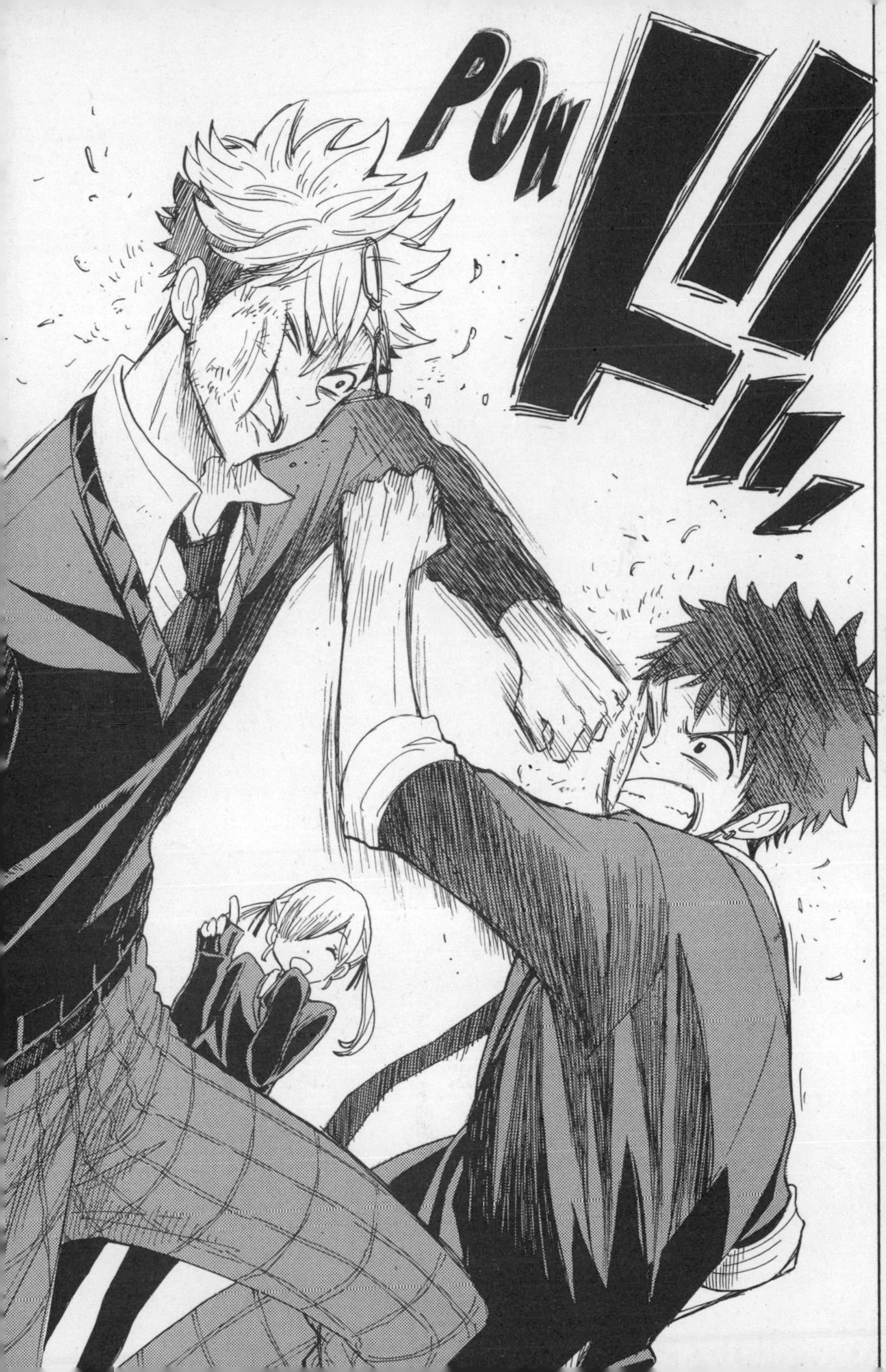
POW!!!

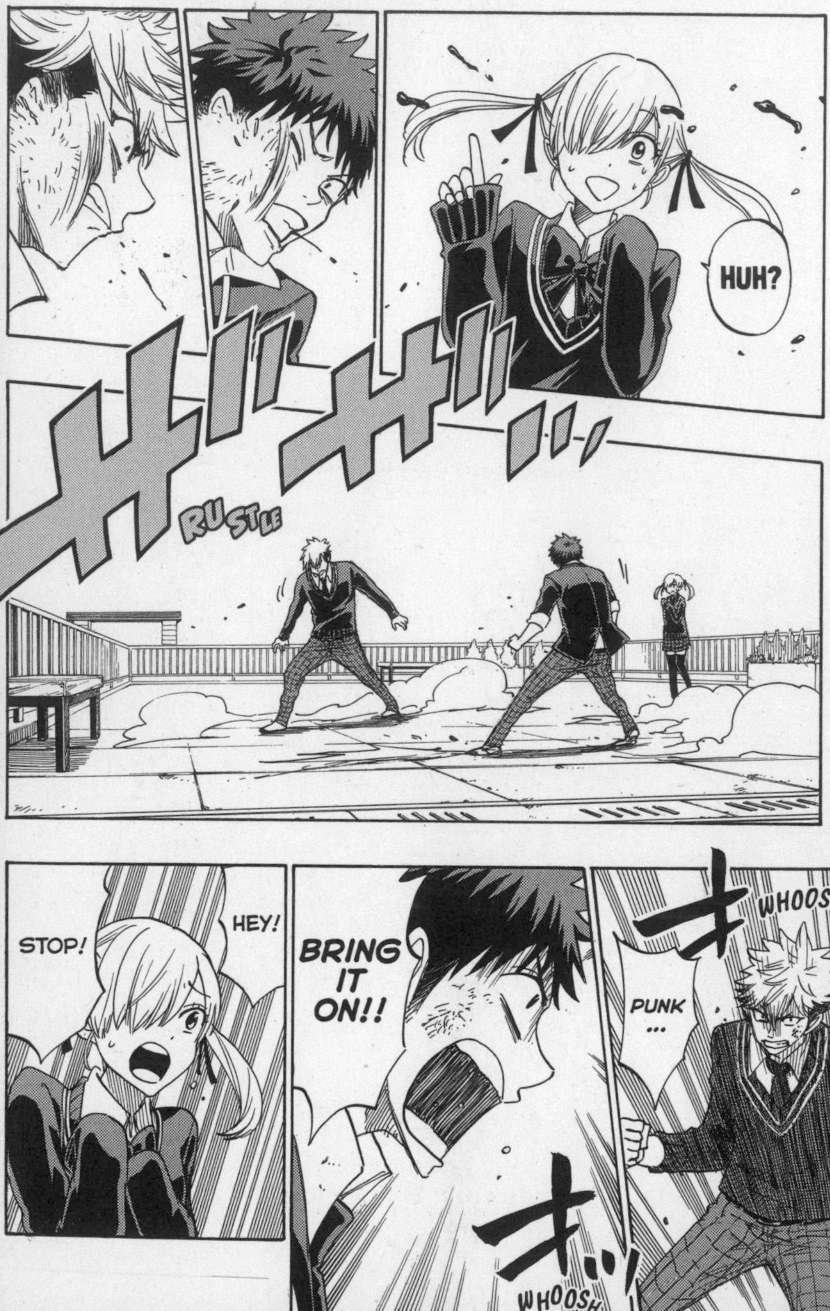
HUH?
RUSTLE
WHOOSH
PUNK ...
WHOOSH
BRING IT ON!!
HEY!
STOP!

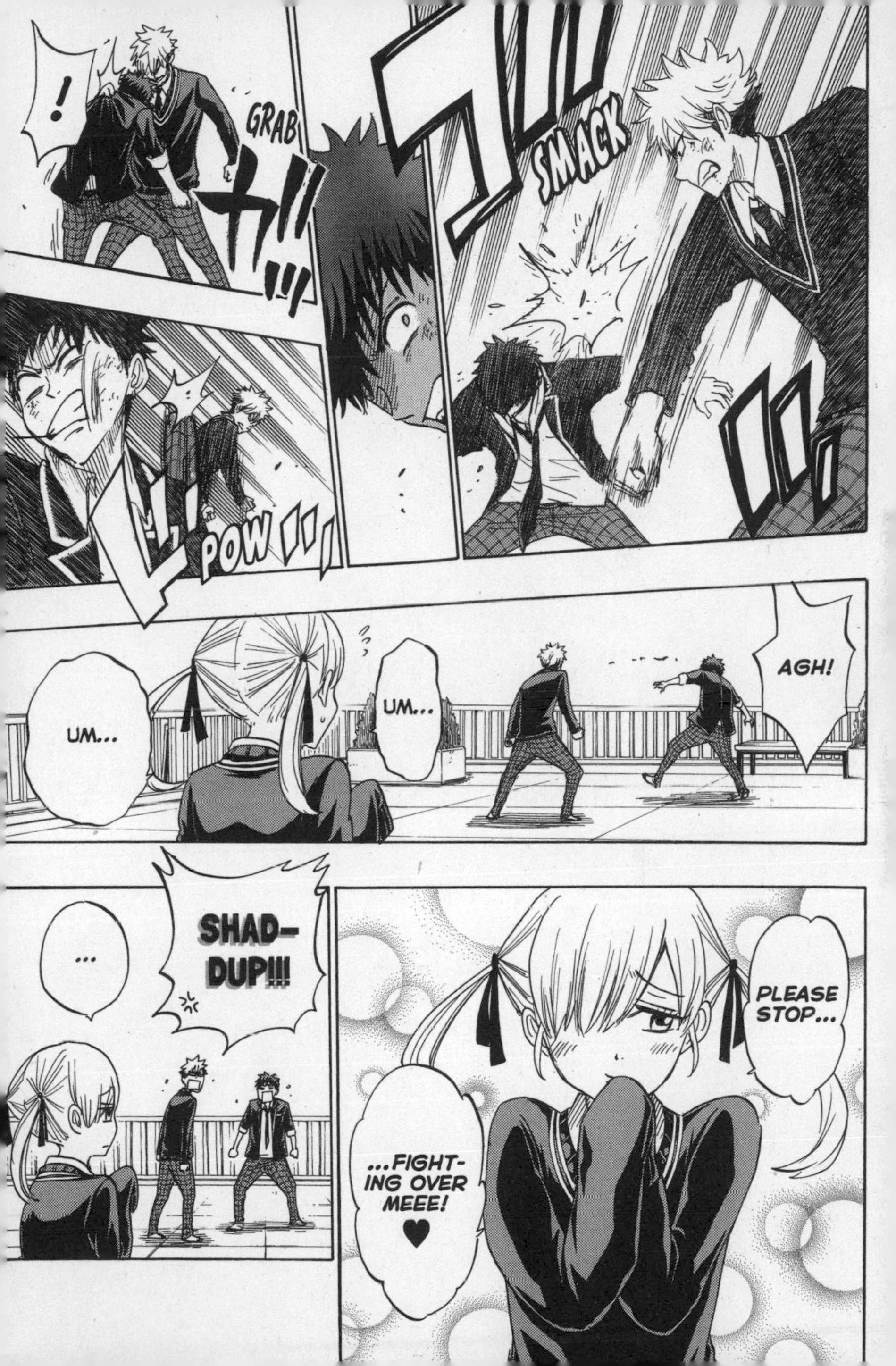
SMACK
!
GRAB
POW
AGH!
UM...
UM...
PLEASE STOP...
...FIGHT-ING OVER MEEE! ♥
SHAD-DUP!!!
...

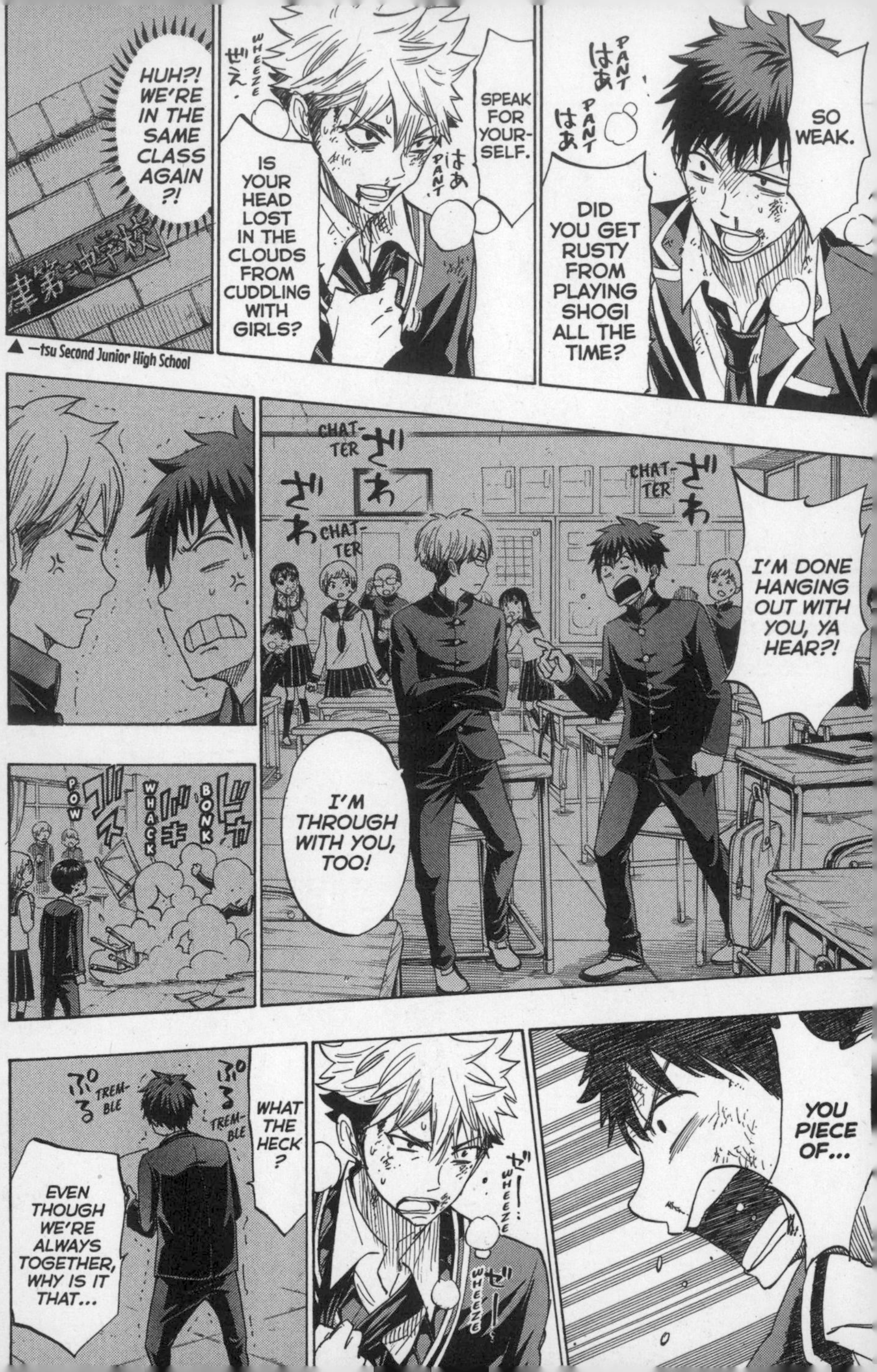

SO WEAK.
PANT はあ
PANT はあ
DID YOU GET RUSTY FROM PLAYING SHOGI ALL THE TIME?
SPEAK FOR YOURSELF.
WHEEZE ぜえ
PANT はあ
IS YOUR HEAD LOST IN THE CLOUDS FROM CUDDLING WITH GIRLS?
HUH?! WE'RE IN THE SAME CLASS AGAIN?!
津第二中学校
▲ —tsu Second Junior High School
CHATTER ざわ
CHATTER ざわ
CHATTER ざわ
I'M DONE HANGING OUT WITH YOU, YA HEAR?!
I'M THROUGH WITH YOU, TOO!
BONK ドカ
WHACK バキ
POW ゴス
YOU PIECE OF...
WHAT THE HECK?
WHEEZE ぜー
WHEEZE ぜー
TREMBLE ぷる
TREMBLE ぷる
EVEN THOUGH WE'RE ALWAYS TOGETHER, WHY IS IT THAT...

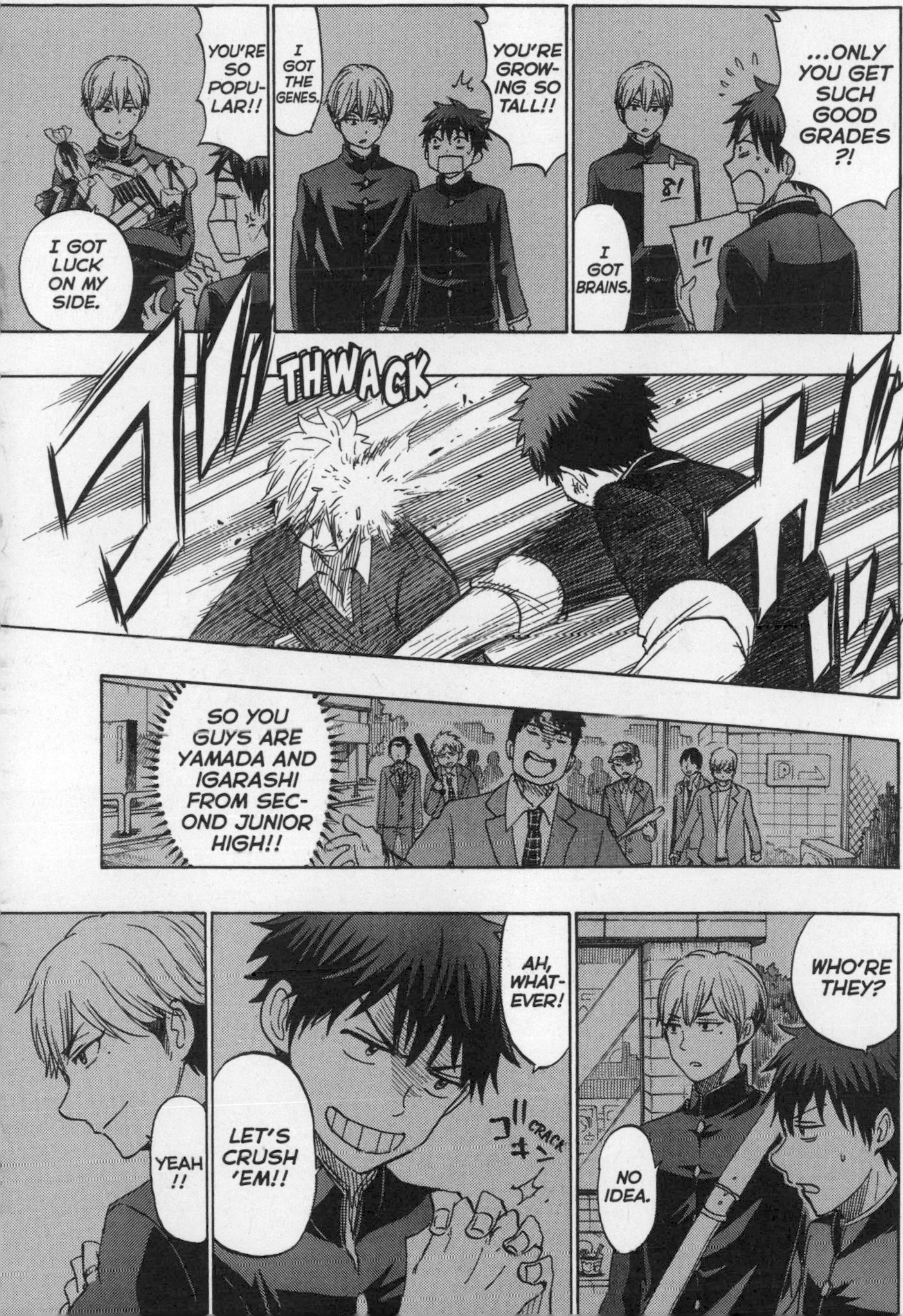
...ONLY YOU GET SUCH GOOD GRADES ?!
I GOT BRAINS.
YOU'RE GROWING SO TALL!!
I GOT THE GENES.
YOU'RE SO POPULAR!!
I GOT LUCK ON MY SIDE.
THWACK
SO YOU GUYS ARE YAMADA AND IGARASHI FROM SECOND JUNIOR HIGH!!
WHO'RE THEY?
NO IDEA.
AH, WHATEVER!
LET'S CRUSH 'EM!!
CRACK
YEAH!!

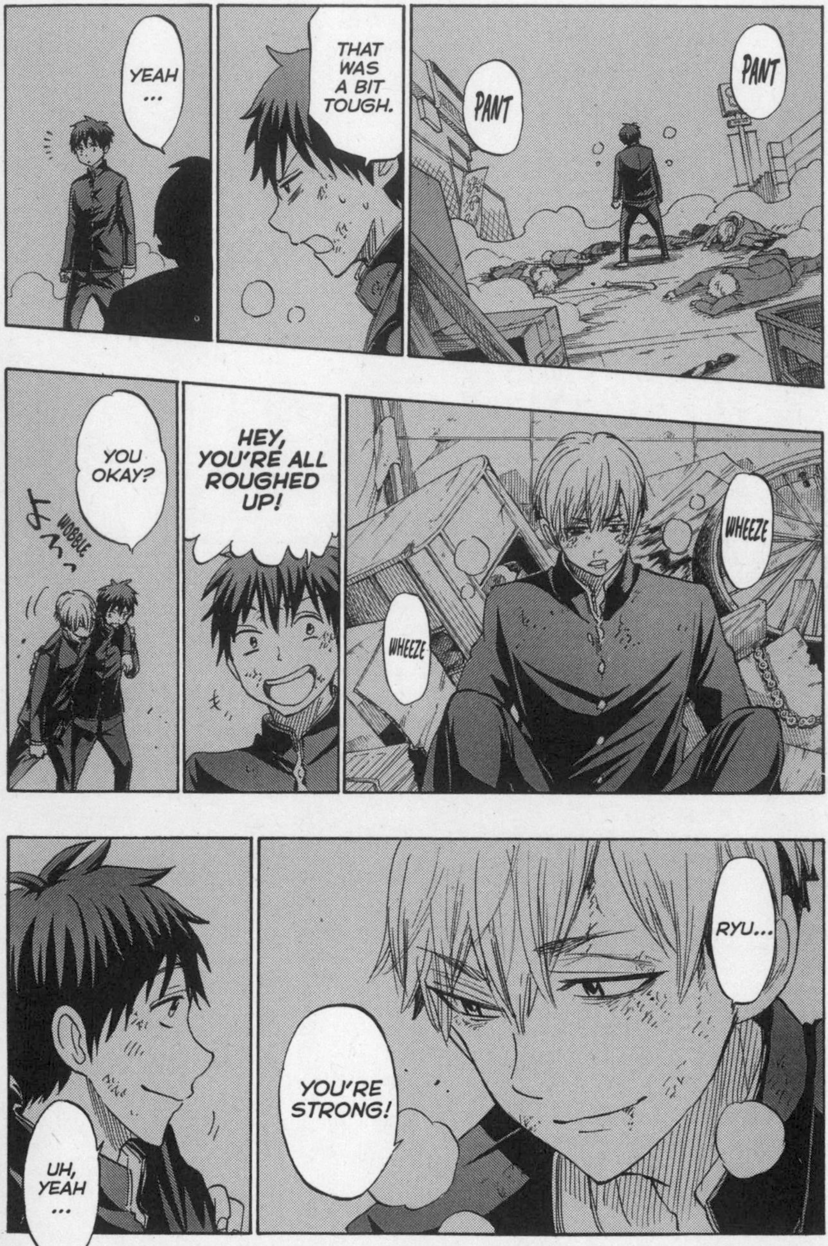
PANT
PANT
THAT WAS A BIT TOUGH.
YEAH ...
WHEEZE
WHEEZE
HEY, YOU'RE ALL ROUGHED UP!
YOU OKAY?
WOBBLE
RYU...
YOU'RE STRONG!
UH, YEAH ...

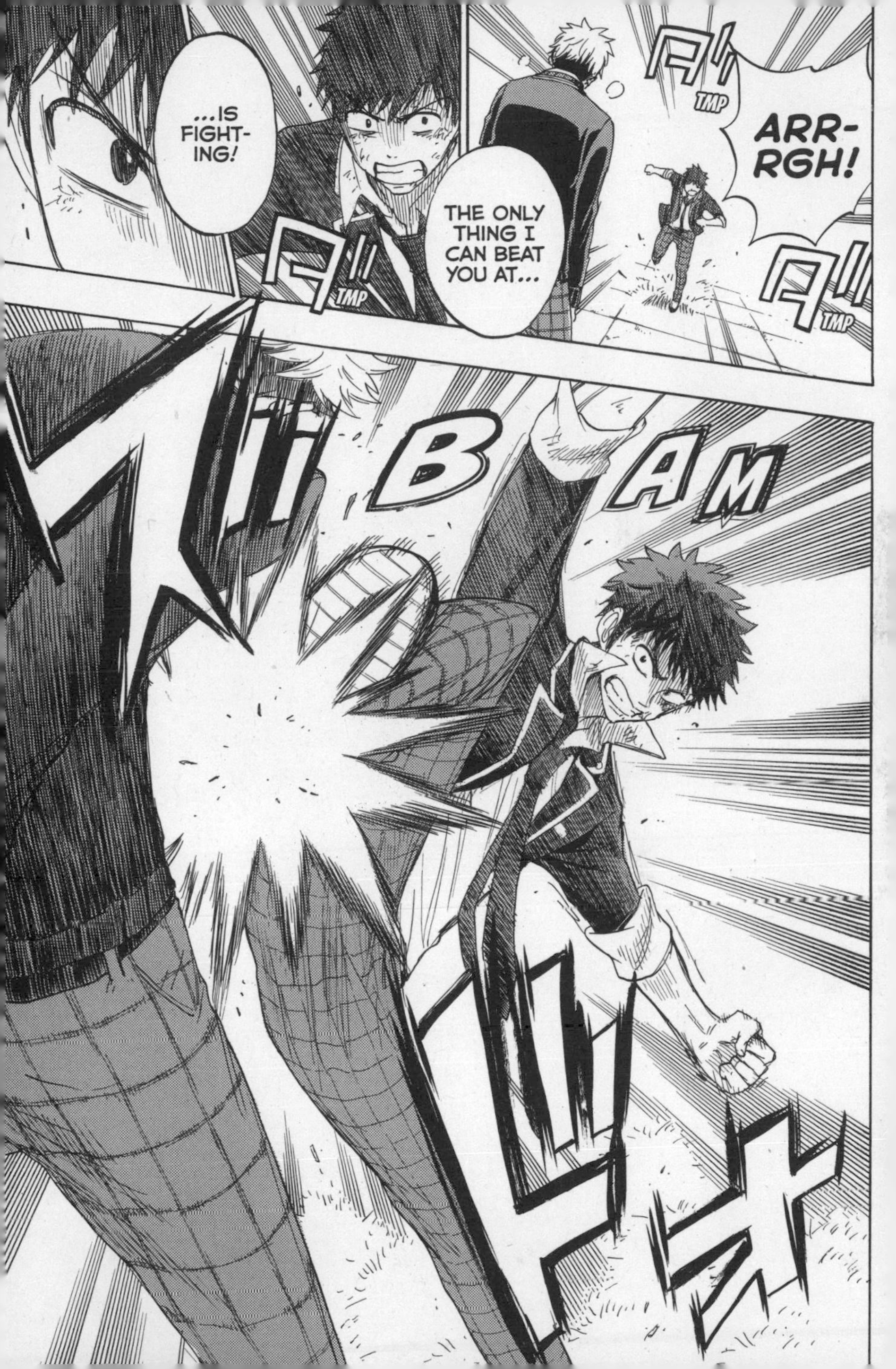
TMP
ARR-
RGH!
TMP
THE ONLY THING I CAN BEAT YOU AT...
...IS FIGHT-
ING!
TMP
BAM

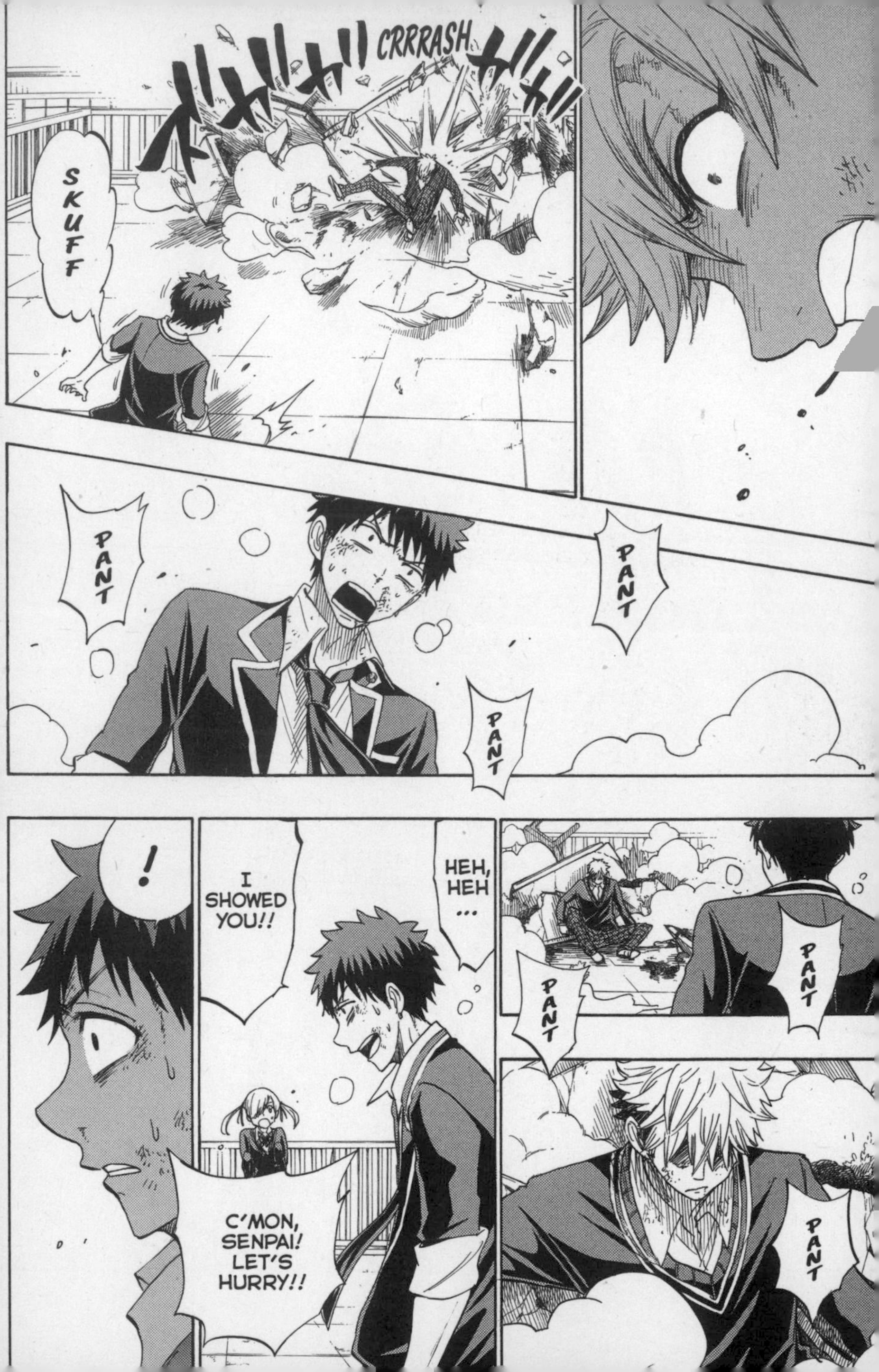
CRRRASH
SKUFF
PANT
PANT
PANT
PANT
PANT
PANT
HEH, HEH ...
I SHOWED YOU!!
C'MON, SENPAI! LET'S HURRY!!
!

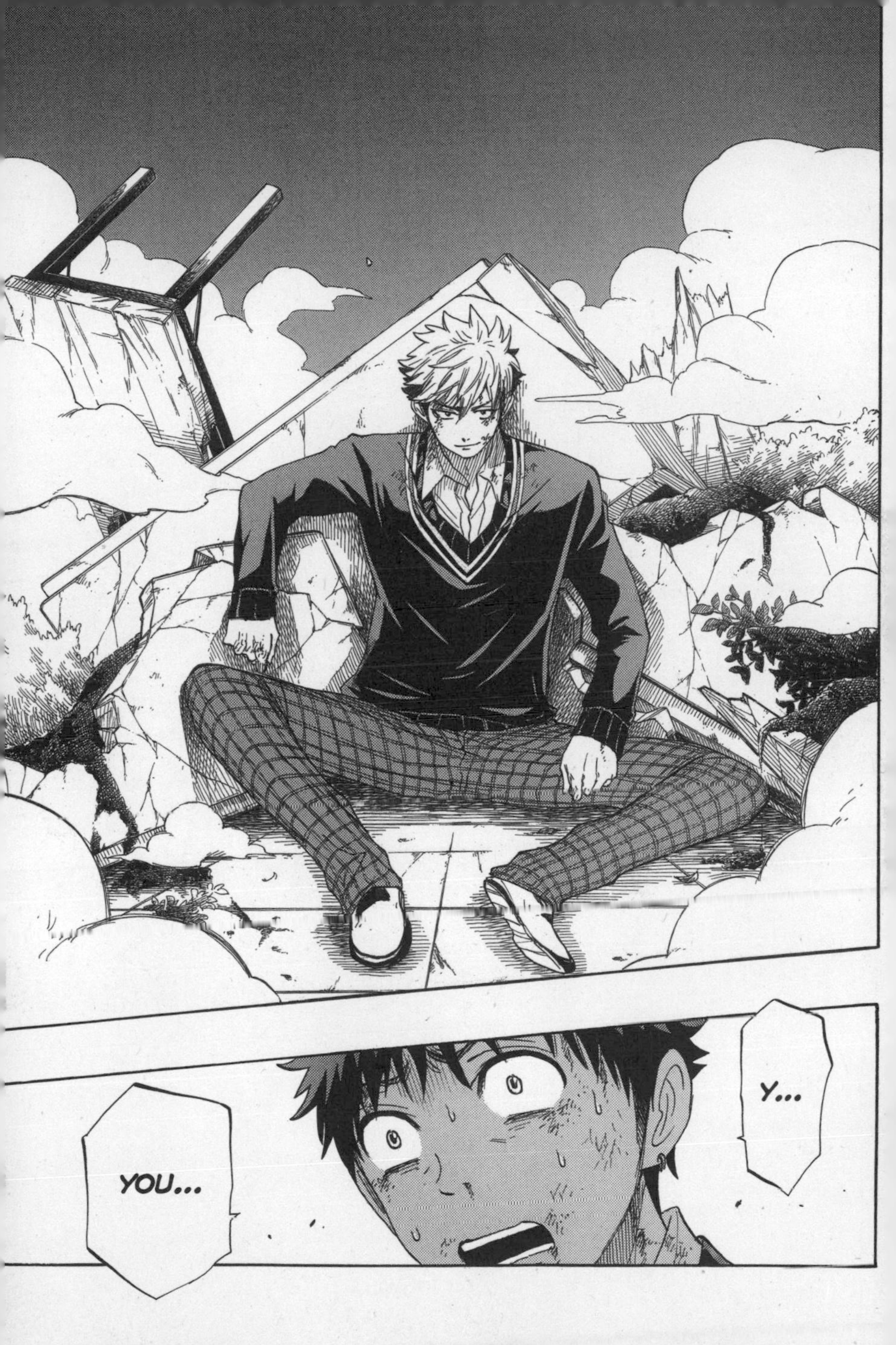
Y...
YOU...

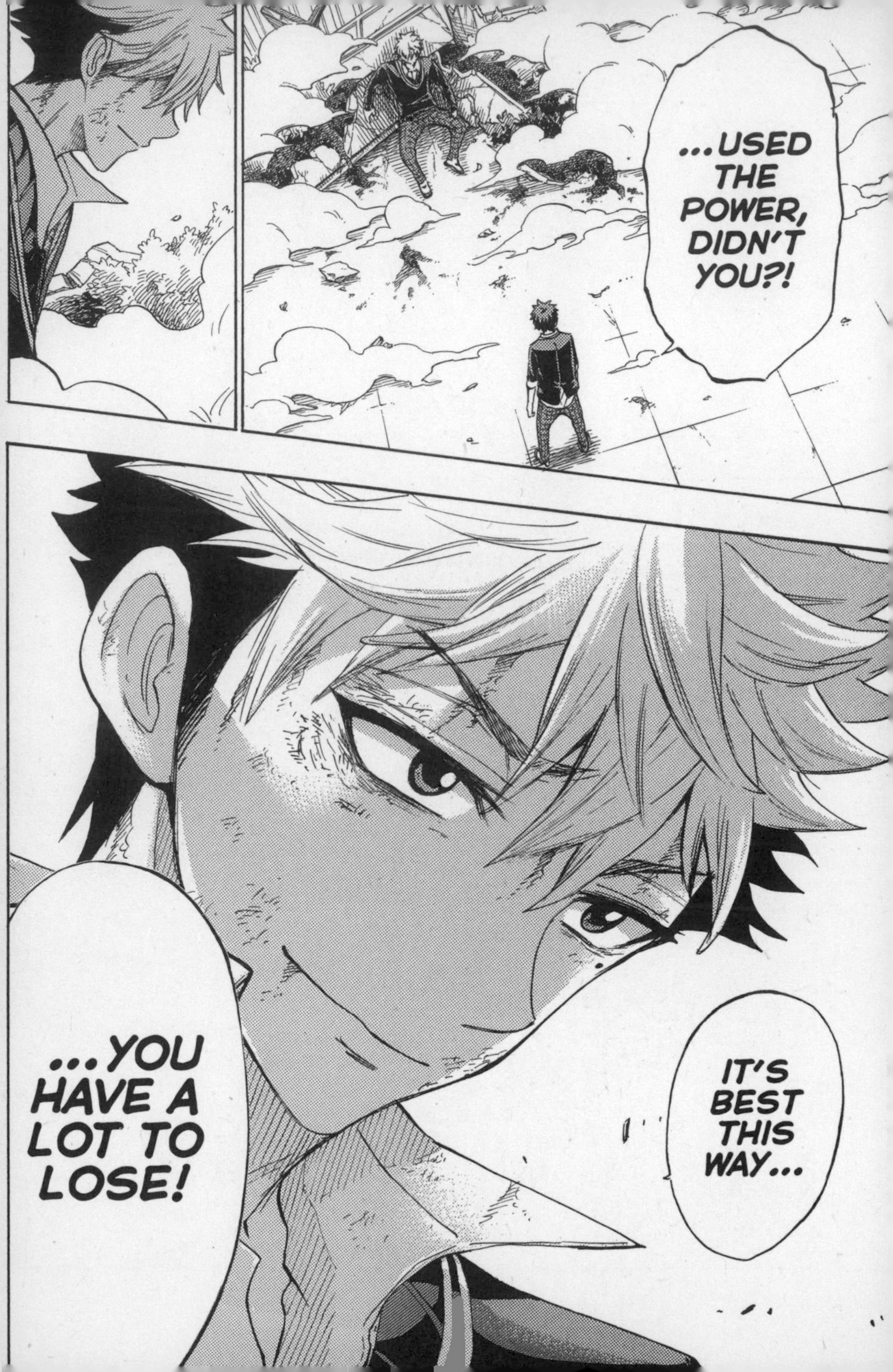
...USED THE POWER, DIDN'T YOU?!
IT'S BEST THIS WAY...
...YOU HAVE A LOT TO LOSE!

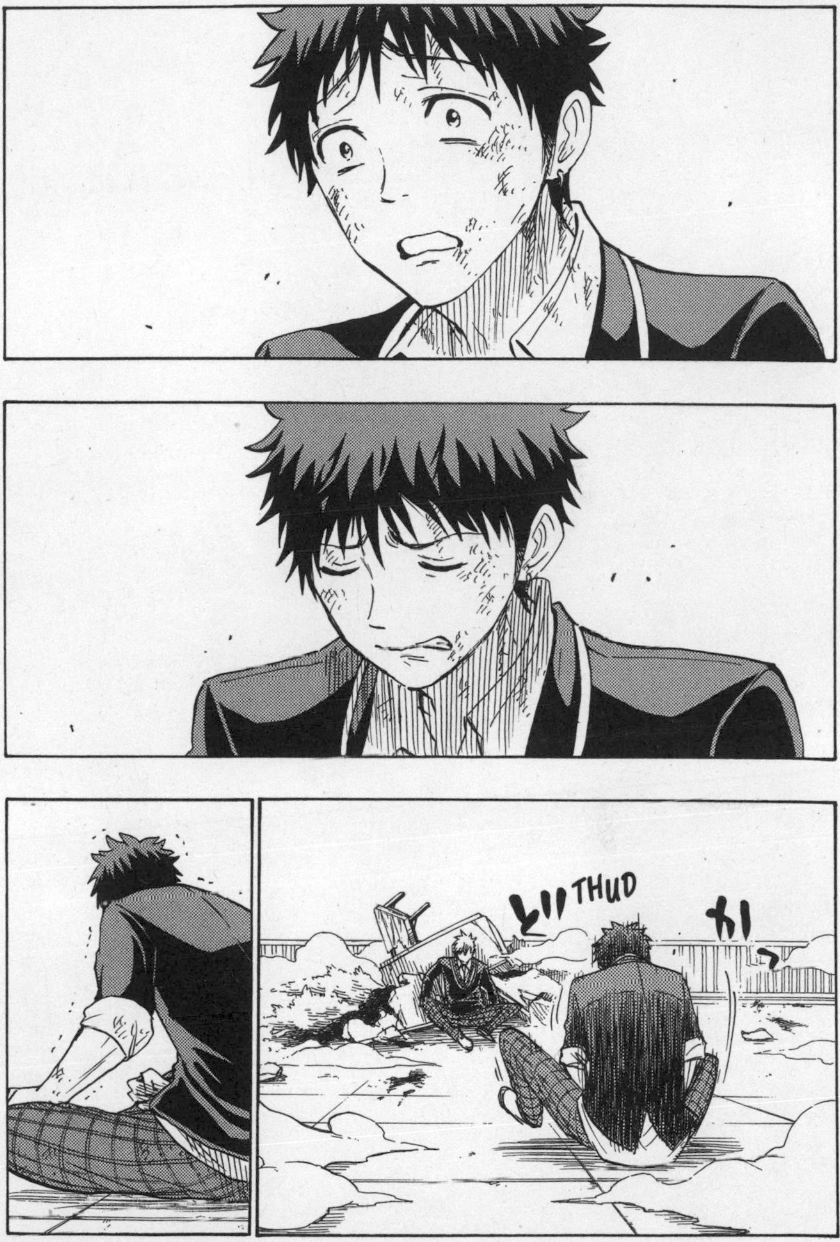
THUD

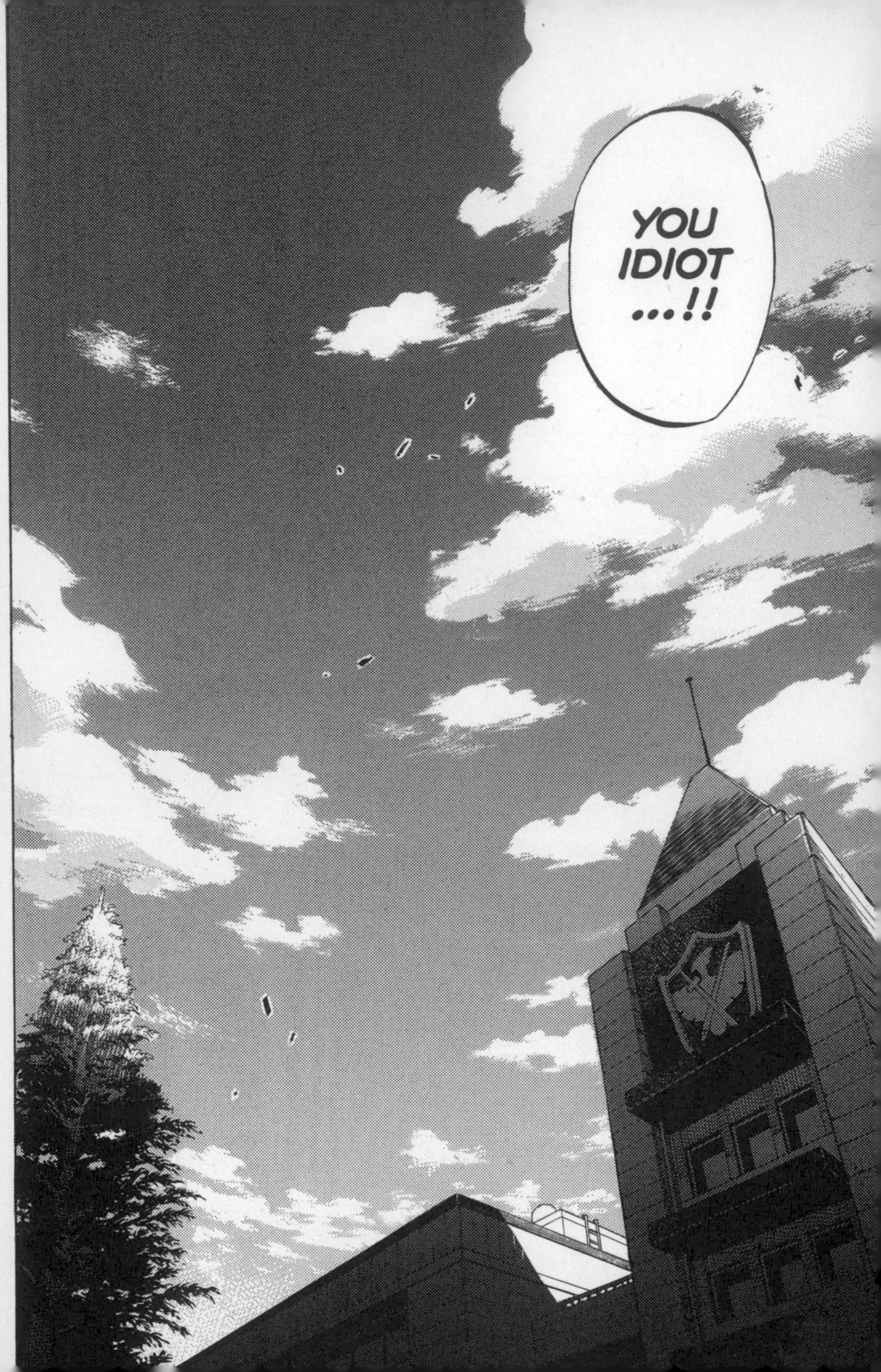
YOU IDIOT ...!!

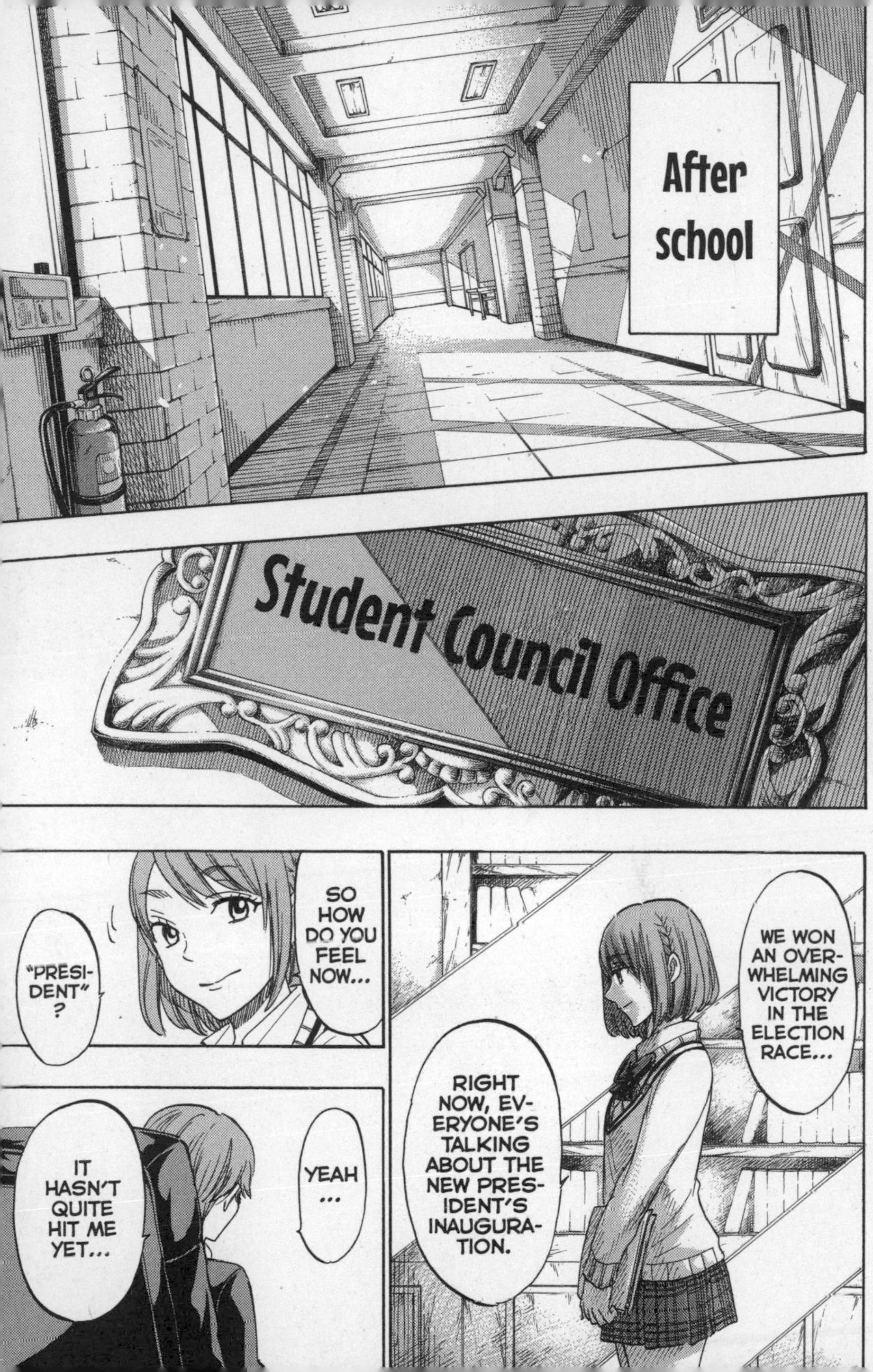
After school
Student Council Office
WE WON AN OVERWHELMING VICTORY IN THE ELECTION RACE...
RIGHT NOW, EVERYONE'S TALKING ABOUT THE NEW PRESIDENT'S INAUGURATION.
SO HOW DO YOU FEEL NOW...
"PRESIDENT"?
YEAH...
IT HASN'T QUITE HIT ME YET...

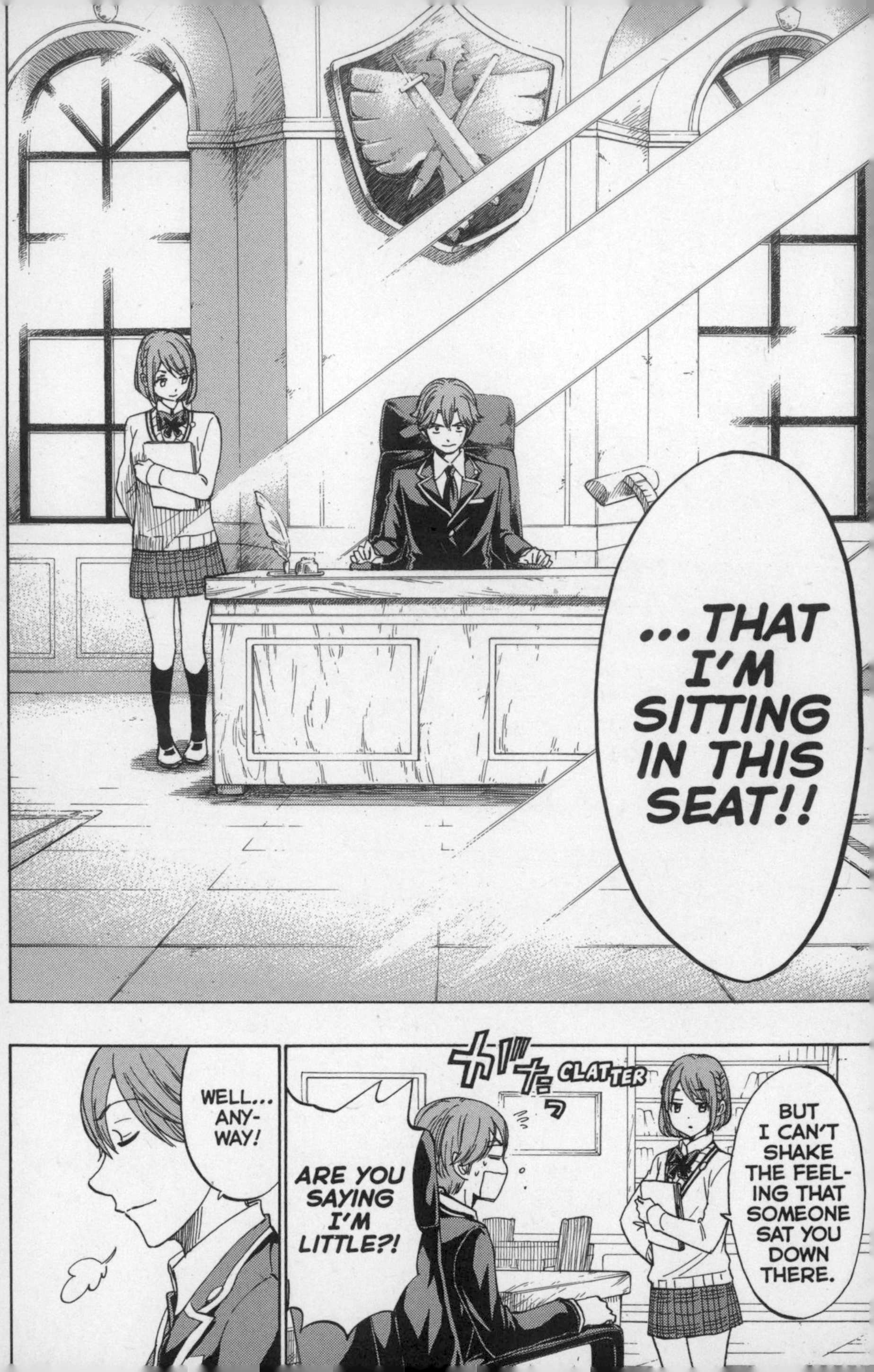
...THAT I'M SITTING IN THIS SEAT!!
BUT I CAN'T SHAKE THE FEEL-ING THAT SOMEONE SAT YOU DOWN THERE.
CLATTER
ARE YOU SAYING I'M LITTLE?!
WELL... ANY-WAY!

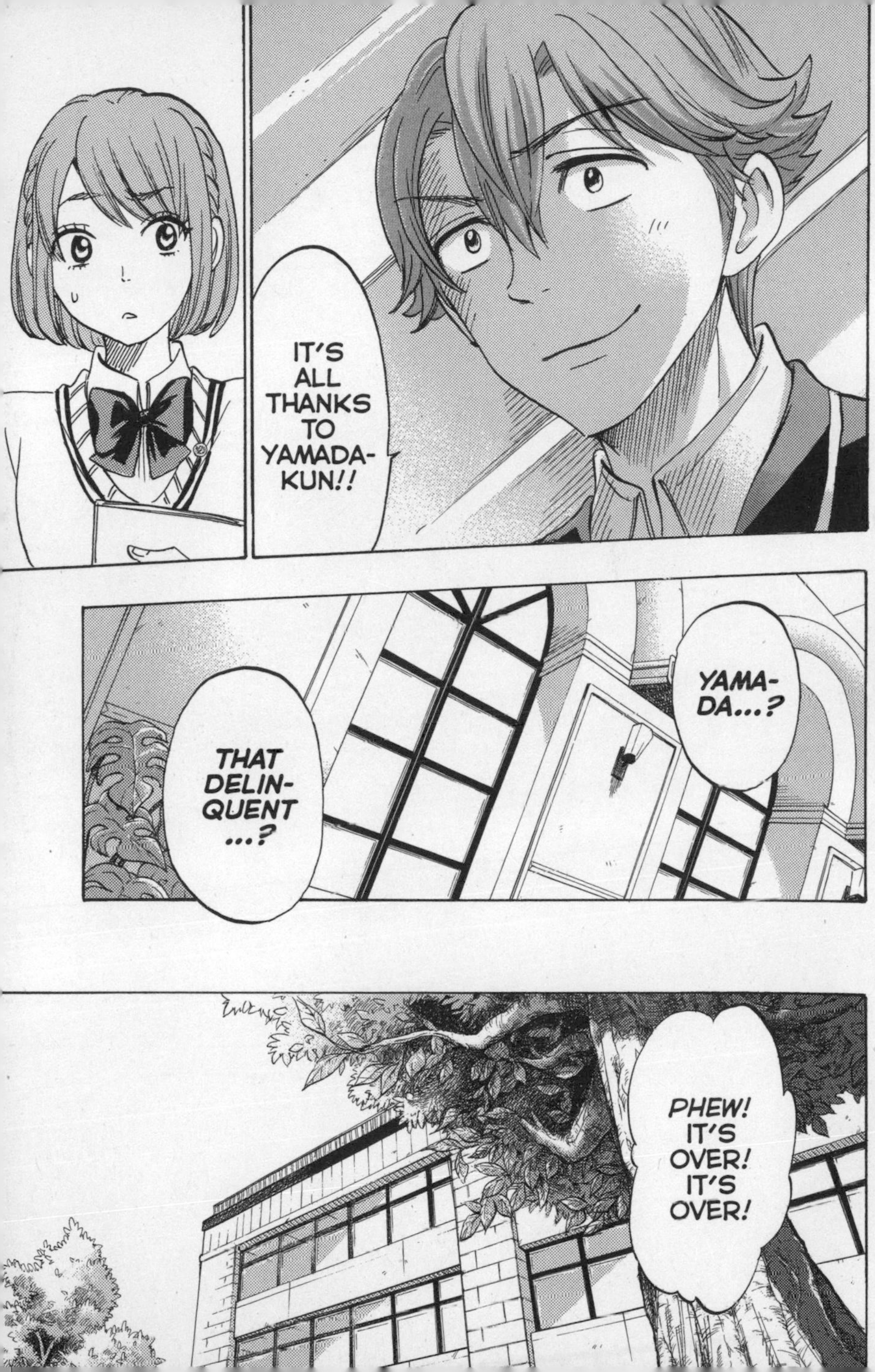
IT'S ALL THANKS TO YAMADA-KUN!!
YAMA-DA...?
THAT DELIN-QUENT ...?
PHEW! IT'S OVER! IT'S OVER!

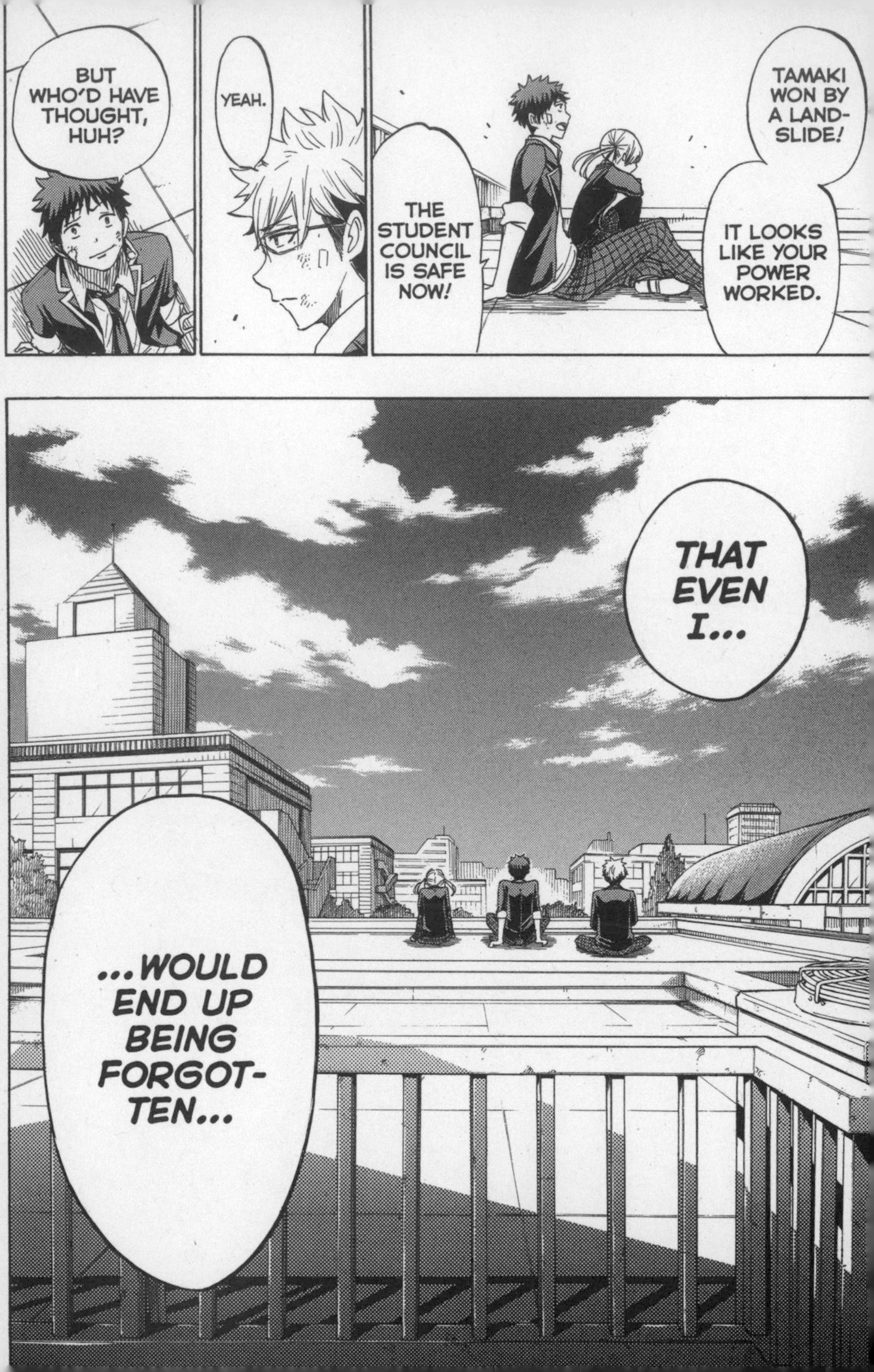
TAMAKI WON BY A LAND-SLIDE!
IT LOOKS LIKE YOUR POWER WORKED.
THE STUDENT COUNCIL IS SAFE NOW!
YEAH.
BUT WHO'D HAVE THOUGHT, HUH?
THAT EVEN I...
...WOULD END UP BEING FORGOT-TEN...

SUZAKU HIGH SCHOOL UNDERGROUND WEBSITE

 It's Q&A Corner #13! Let's start, start, start!

 We haven't had a Q&A session since Volume 17. Don't say you forgot about it!

 Now then, let's bring out our guest for today, **Nene Odagiri-chan!** Come on in!!

 # Hey! Honestly, I'm fed up with waiting!!!

 Uh, calm down, Odagiri!! (SHAKE SHAKE SHAKE) Nothing's gonna get solved by you shaking me by the collar!

 Ahh... I feel better now. Bring on the questions.

 What the heck?! All you did was let it out on me!

 It seems like the rivalry from your Student Council vice-president days hasn't gone anywhere...

Q1. Nene-san, you seem like an older sister given how well put-together you are. Do you have any siblings?

Tokyo Prefecture, H.N Kawa-chan-san

I have two younger brothers! One's a third-year student in junior high, and the other is a sixth-year student in elementary school. We normally get along, although it can get noisy. We hardly fight, and the both of them are well-behaved kids who listen to what I say.

You've totally won over your two brothers, huh... Did you make them suffer when they were kids, or...?

Hey, can you not? The two of them respect me as their older sister, okay?

Younger brothers! How great! I wish I had one!!!

You weren't really listening...

Q2. Please tell us what you do on your days off!

Saitama Prefecture, H.N Misato-san

I usually make sweets or go shopping.

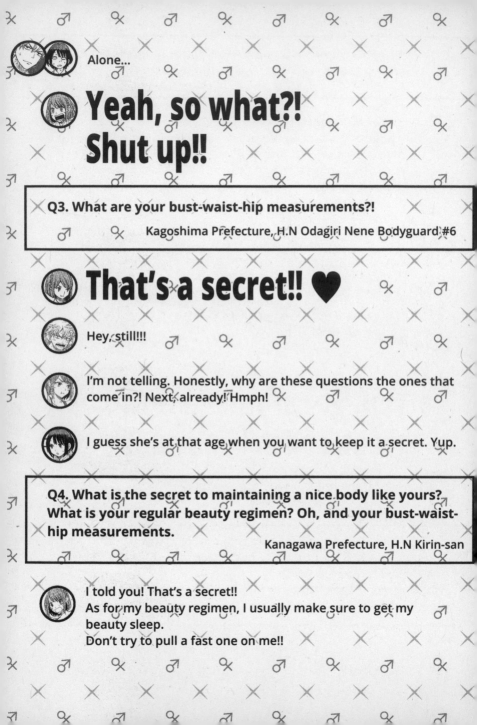

Alone...

Yeah, so what?! Shut up!!

Q3. What are your bust-waist-hip measurements?!

Kagoshima Prefecture, H.N Odagiri Nene Bodyguard #6

That's a secret!! ♥

Hey, still!!!

I'm not telling. Honestly, why are these questions the ones that come in?! Next, already! Hmph!

I guess she's at that age when you want to keep it a secret. Yup.

Q4. What is the secret to maintaining a nice body like yours? What is your regular beauty regimen? Oh, and your bust-waist-hip measurements.

Kanagawa Prefecture, H.N Kirin-san

I told you! That's a secret!!
As for my beauty regimen, I usually make sure to get my beauty sleep.
Don't try to pull a fast one on me!!

Q5. What subject are you good at, and what subject are you bad at? Also, what are your bust-waist-hip measurements!
Akita Prefecture, H.N Beshi-san

Me? Have a bad subject? Seriously?
I'm good at all subjects!! And my bust-waist-hip measurements are a secret!!

But Odagiri-san, the other day, you got a 62 in Modern Literature. That's not so great, wouldn't you say?

H...How do you know that?!

B: 88, W: 58, H: 86

H...How do you know THAT?!!
What?! What the heck is your problem?! Ahhh!

Anyway, shall we end it here for Nene-chan's issue?
Our next guest will be **Tamaki!!**

We'll be waiting for your questions to Tamaki. If we don't get any, he's gonna be seriously disappointed...

Please send your correspondence here ↓

Yamada-kun and the Seven Witches: Underground Website
c/o Kodansha Comics
451 Park Ave. South, 7th Floor
New York, NY 10016

Don't' forget to include your handle name (pen name)!

Have these two been spying on me...?

Suzaku Gallery

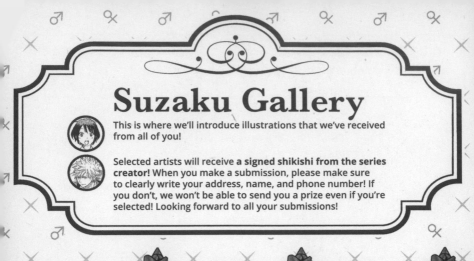

This is where we'll introduce illustrations that we've received from all of you!

Selected artists will receive **a signed shikishi from the series creator!** When you make a submission, please make sure to clearly write your address, name, and phone number! If you don't, we won't be able to send you a prize even if you're selected! Looking forward to all your submissions!

山田くんと7人の魔女 姫川そら

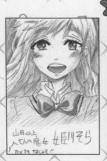

Nagasaki Pref., H.N. Terachan-san

The person in front of Himekawa-san's smile... could it be me?!

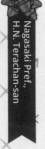

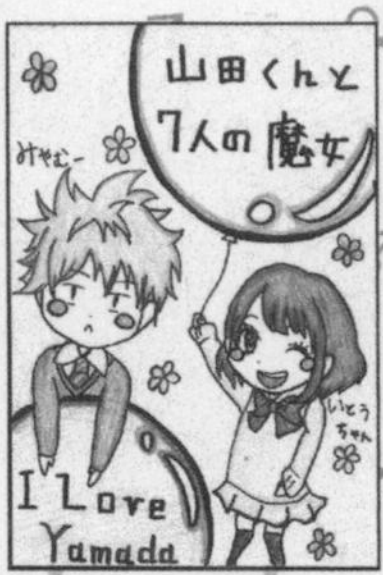

山田くんと 7人の魔女
I Love Yamada

Aomori Pref., H.N. SS-san

Hey, Miyamura! You should look a little happier!

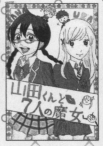

山田くんと 7人の魔女

Niigata Pref., H.N. Kome Student Council Pres-san

I've seen that girl with the glasses before... Was she a student at Mon Shiro High School?

やきそばパン
by 山田

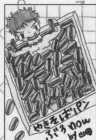

Saitama Pref., H.N. happy-san

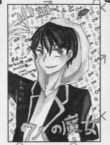

This is something I hoped Yamada would do someday! It's scary that he's doing that with such glee, though.

7人の魔女

Kumamoto Pref., H.N. Shioame-san

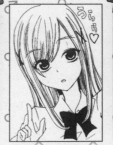

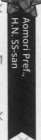

Wearing hoodies in school is forbidden, y'know. Don't get carried away just because you're a school exec.

うらら

Ibaraki Pref., H.N. Kayutabashi-san

When Urara-chan stares at you, you can't help but get lost in her eyes! ♥

山田くんと七人の魔女
いつも応援しています!

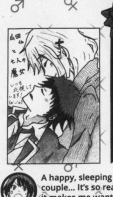

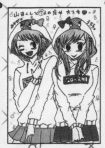

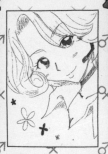

Tokyo Pref.,
H.N. Yuria-san

A happy, sleeping couple... It's so real it makes me want to explode!!

SOBAMI

Osaka Pref.,
H.N, Ririka Miyasu-san

The two of them are wearing...Sobami hoodies! Maybe Yamada and I will do that next time.

Aichi Pref.,
H.N, Naura-san

What hides behind Kikuchi-san's beautiful smile is a mystery...

アニメ化!

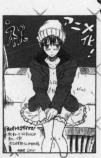

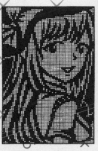

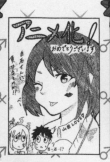

Tokyo Pref.,
H.N, Editor Garashi-san

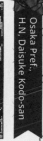

Is this an entry from the editorial department at Magazine?! They really like Konno-san, huh.

Osaka Pref.,
H.N, Daisuke Kodo-san

So this is mosaic art, huh? It's a masterpiece!!

アニメ化!
おめでとうございます
山田LOVE

Osaka Pref.,
H.N, Suzuka Koshi-san

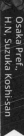

Her jealousy for Urara-chan is even too much for Yamada.

Please send your art here ↓

Yamada-kun and the Seven Witches: Suzaku Gallery
c/o Kodansha Comics
451 Park Ave. South, 7th Floor
New York, NY 10016

※ Please clearly write your address, name, and phone number. If your address, name, and phone number aren't included with your submission, we won't be able to send you a prize.

※ And if necessary, don't forget to include your handle name (pen name)!

Please send your letters with the understanding that your zip code, address, name, and other personal information included in your correspondence may be given to the author of this work.

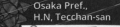

Osaka Pref.,
H.N, Tecchan-san

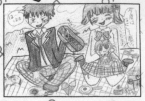

Yamada seems to be having fun despite looking like he's not really into it.

Suzaku Gallery

Haruma Yamazaki's School Tour

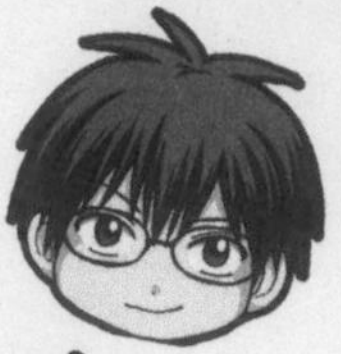

As Suzaku High's Student Council President, I'd like to introduce you to the various areas of the school. Our school takes pride in its large campus, and with so many famous spots, we won't be able to cover them all here. This time, I'll just show you one section!

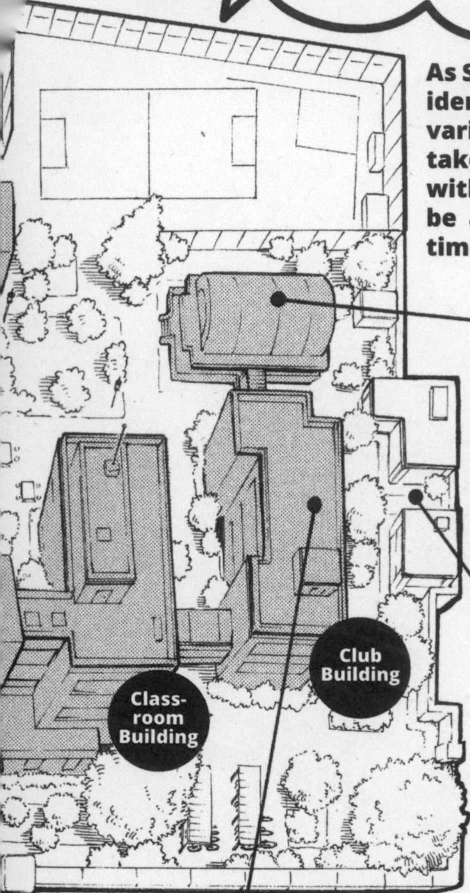
Club Building
Classroom Building

The Gym

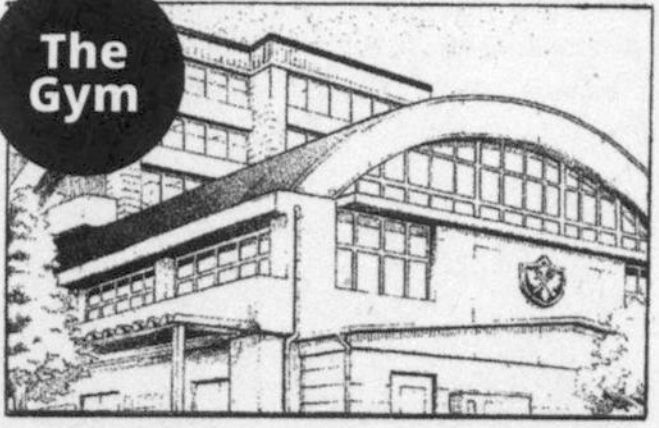

I'm proud to say that our gymnasium is large enough to hold the entire student body. It doesn't get any better than playing badminton here!!

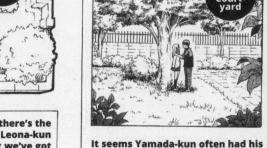

The Rear Courtyard

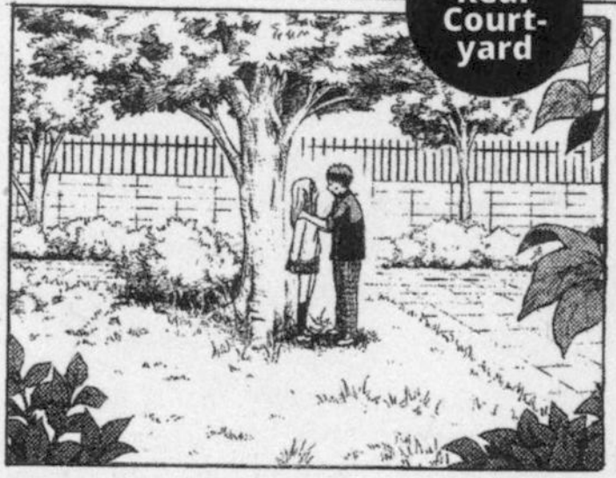

It seems Yamada-kun often had his kisses here. There's a lot of nature on our campus, so there are plenty of places like this. However, fooling around on campus is strictly prohibited...

In the corner of the club building, there's the Supernatural Studies Club, where Leona-kun and I used to go to. I'm happy that we've got some good kohai continuing the club. What? They aren't actually doing stuff related to the Supernatural Studies Club? Well, then, I should pay them a visit after my exams are over. Give them a piece of my mind, while I'm at it.

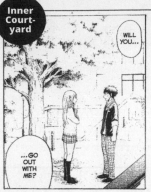

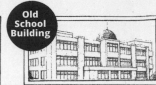

Old School Building

Now, they're working on the new school building. The fruits of my labor! ★

Inner Courtyard

WILL YOU...
...GO OUT WITH ME?

This was the place where Yamada-kun asked Shiraishi-kun out, right? Hmm... He picked a nice spot, didn't he? I could see everything from the student council office, though.

Special Classroom Building
Classroom Building

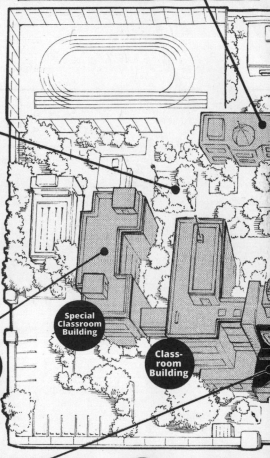

Ah, my old nest.
You can go to the ceremony space from here, and it's also connected to the principal's office. Come to think of it, I think the book I hid inside the desk is still there...
Ah, well.

Student Council Office

Student Council Office

Supernatural Studies Clubroom

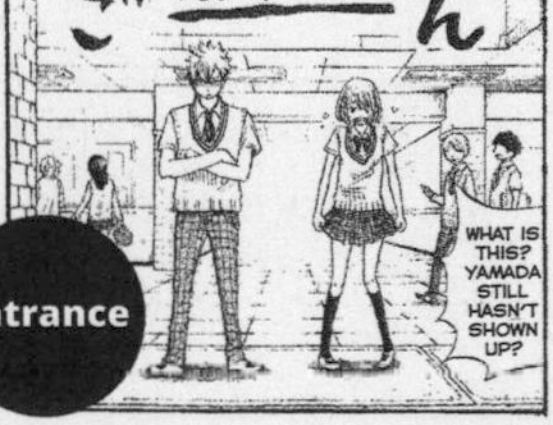

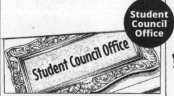

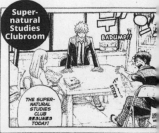

BADUMP!!
STICK!
THE SUPERNATURAL STUDIES CLUB RESUMES TODAY!

Entrance

DOONG
WHAT IS THIS? YAMADA STILL HASN'T SHOWN UP?

Lots of students pass through here every day. Although they stand in awe when I come, like Moses and the Ten Commandments. Ha ha ha ha ha!!

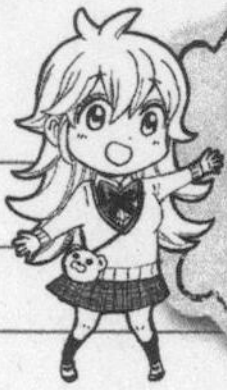

KUROSAKI AND MIDORI'S OUTFIT WALKTHROUGH

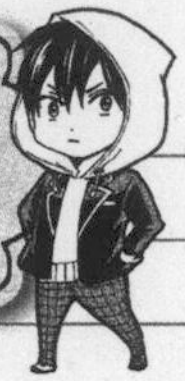

GIRLS

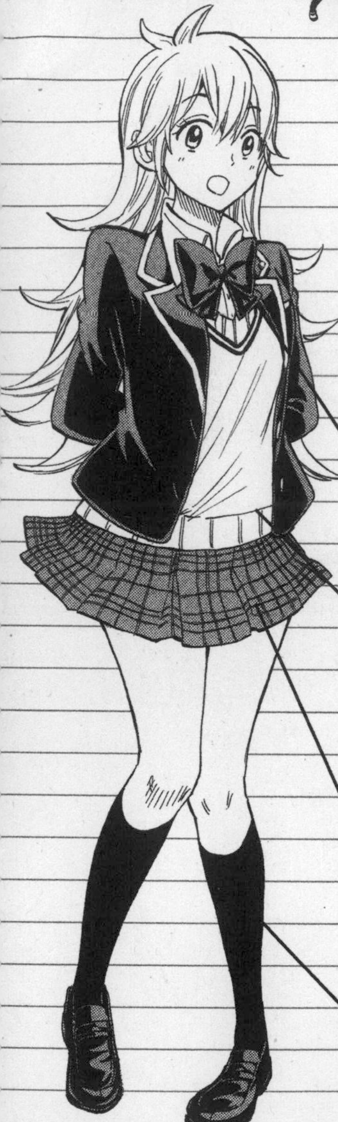

For everyone who wants to know more about Suzaku High, we'd like to introduce the school outfits!

Since I'm an exec on the Student Council, I guess I have no choice but to help. It doesn't mean I have nothing better to do!!

Considering that, you sure struck a confident pose...

President Miyamura might check this page out!!

I doubt it...

RIBBON

It's deep red with thin white stripes!

SWEATER VEST (UNISEX)

There are two colors you can choose from, white and navy, although white is more popular in the school! (optional purchase)

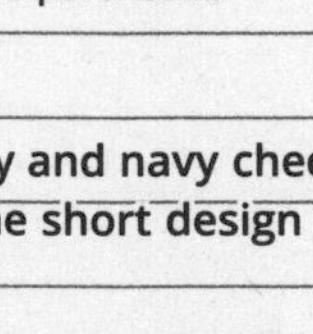
Boys: Blue
Girls: Red

On the white sweater vest, the color of the stripe is different depending on the gender. The navy one has a white stripe for both.

SKIRT

The girls have a gray and navy checkered skirt. These days, the short design is also popular!

SOCKS

The socks are dark gray, like the blazer. The Suzaku High emblem is faintly displayed on the sides!

BOYS

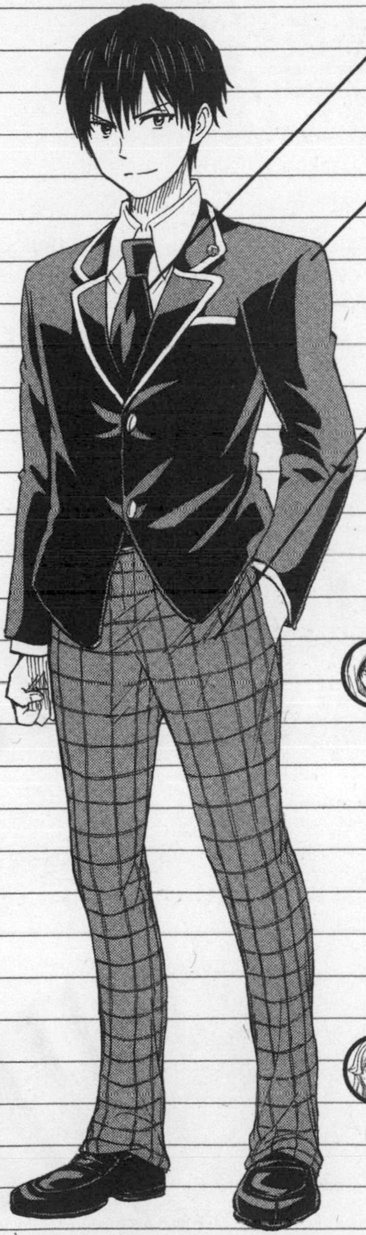

NECKTIE

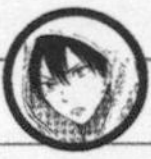

It's an ultramarine necktie with thin white stripes.

BLAZER (UNISEX)

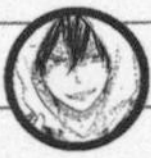

The blazer's a dark gray color, almost black. Around the collar is a modern white line.

SLACKS

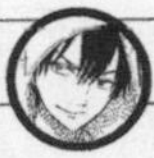

The boys have gray pants that are checkered with blue.

OTHER (UNISEX) DUFFEL COAT

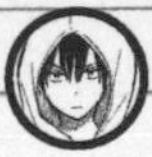

Dark gray, with a checkered pattern on the inside of the hood that is the same as the slacks and skirt. It's an optional purchase, but not many people have it since it's expensive. (Miyamura-kun has one)

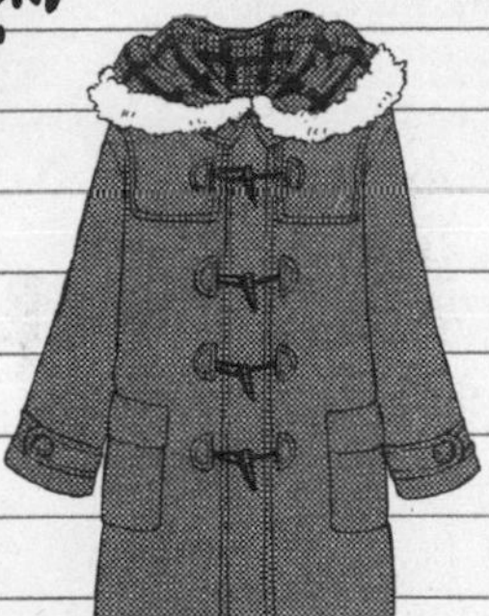

SCHOOL BAG

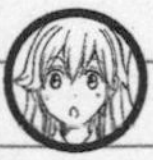

Comes in cotton and leather. The cotton one is popular with the boys, and the leather one with the girls.

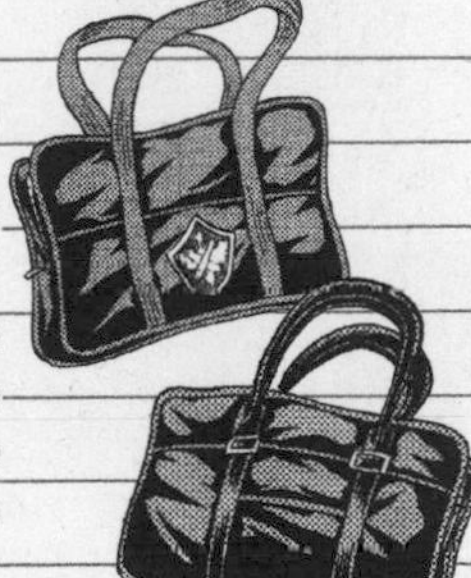

Teach me, Yamada-kun!

THE PLACE WHERE RIDDLES ARE SOLVED

LONG TIME NO SEE!

HABIT

YAMA-DA-KUN, YOU MAKE A STRANGE FACE WHEN YOU'RE DEEP IN THOUGHT.
HUH?!
YOU HAVEN'T NOTICED?
LIKE WHEN YOU'RE TAKING A TEST...
YOU ALWAYS MAKE THAT FACE.
WHAT KIND OF FACE ARE YOU TALKING ABOUT...?
THAT ONE.

THE CURRENT STATE OF CLUB ACTIVITIES

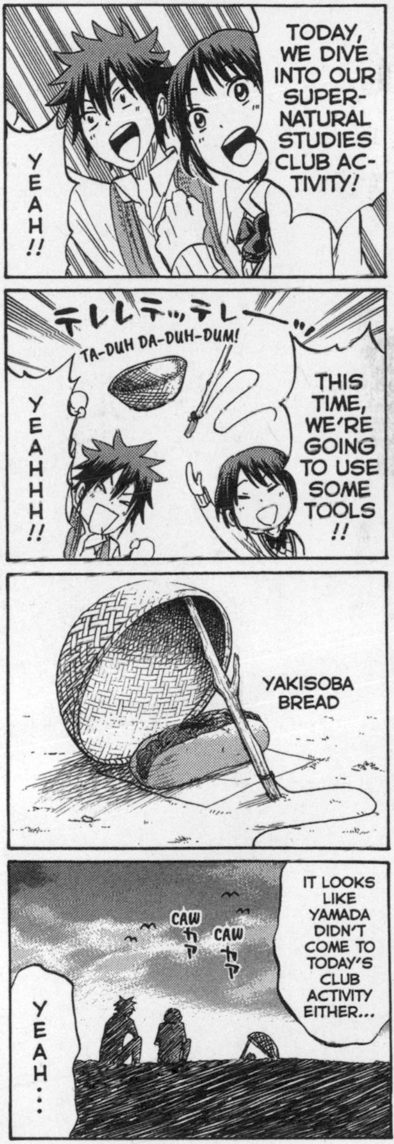
TODAY, WE DIVE INTO OUR SUPER-NATURAL STUDIES CLUB ACTIVITY!
YEAH!!
テレレテッテレー
TA-DUH DA-DUH-DUM!
THIS TIME, WE'RE GOING TO USE SOME TOOLS!!
YEAHHH!!
YAKISOBA BREAD
IT LOOKS LIKE YAMADA DIDN'T COME TO TODAY'S CLUB ACTIVITY EITHER...
CAW
カァ
CAW
カァ
YEAH...

FATED ENCOUNTER

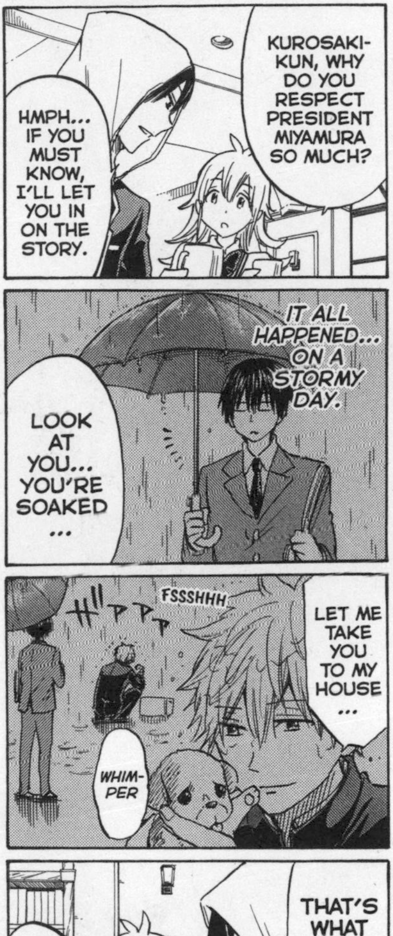
KUROSAKI-KUN, WHY DO YOU RESPECT PRESIDENT MIYAMURA SO MUCH?
HMPH... IF YOU MUST KNOW, I'LL LET YOU IN ON THE STORY.
IT ALL HAPPENED... ON A STORMY DAY.
LOOK AT YOU... YOU'RE SOAKED...
LET ME TAKE YOU TO MY HOUSE...
FSSSHHH
WHIMPER
THAT'S WHAT STARTED IT ALL.
LIAR.

KOTORI'S SECRET

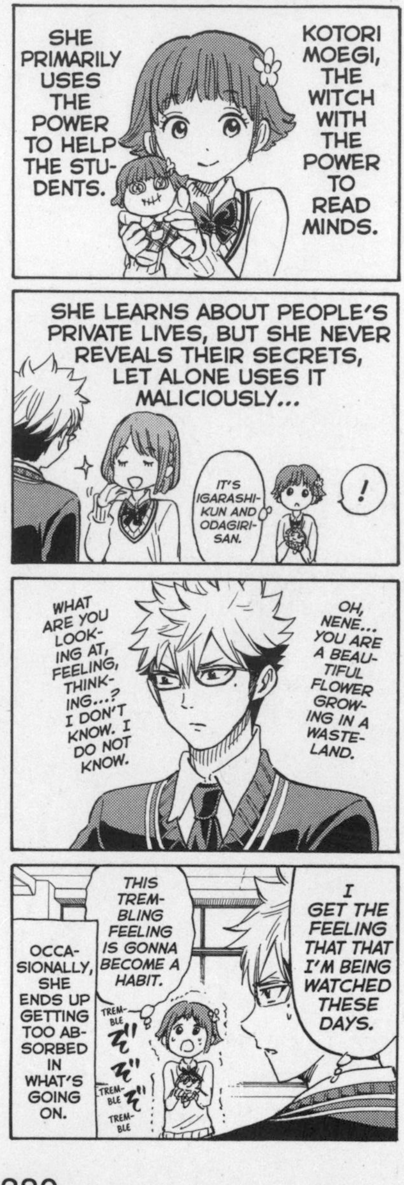
KOTORI MOEGI, THE WITCH WITH THE POWER TO READ MINDS.
SHE PRIMARILY USES THE POWER TO HELP THE STUDENTS.
SHE LEARNS ABOUT PEOPLE'S PRIVATE LIVES, BUT SHE NEVER REVEALS THEIR SECRETS, LET ALONE USES IT MALICIOUSLY...
!
IT'S IGARASHI-KUN AND ODAGIRI-SAN.
OH, NENE... YOU ARE A BEAUTIFUL FLOWER GROWING IN A WASTELAND.
WHAT ARE YOU LOOKING AT, FEELING, THINKING...? I DON'T KNOW. I DO NOT KNOW.
I GET THE FEELING THAT THAT I'M BEING WATCHED THESE DAYS.
THIS TREMBLING FEELING IS GONNA BECOME A HABIT.
OCCASIONALLY, SHE ENDS UP GETTING TOO ABSORBED IN WHAT'S GOING ON.
TREMBLE
TREMBLE
TREMBLE

SOBASSHI: HANGING BY A THREAD

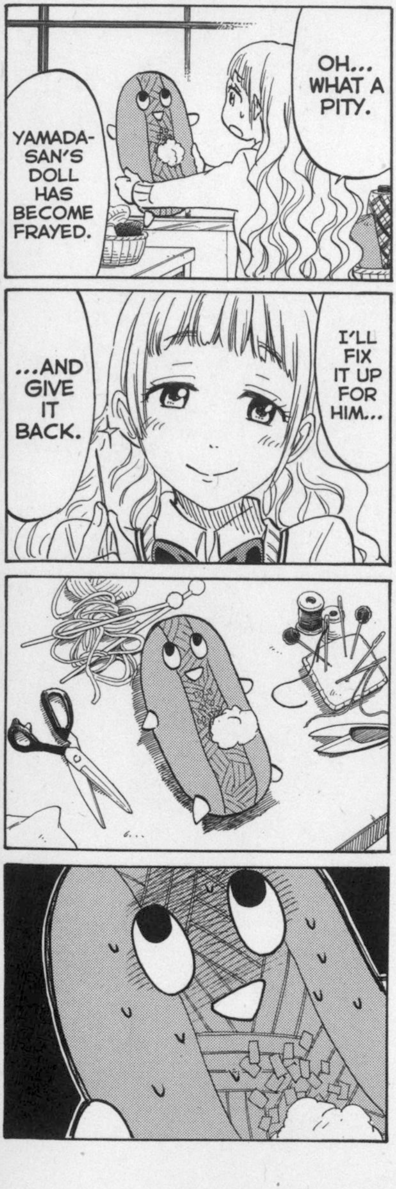
OH... WHAT A PITY.
YAMADA-SAN'S DOLL HAS BECOME FRAYED.
I'LL FIX IT UP FOR HIM...
...AND GIVE IT BACK.

CEREMONY MEMORY

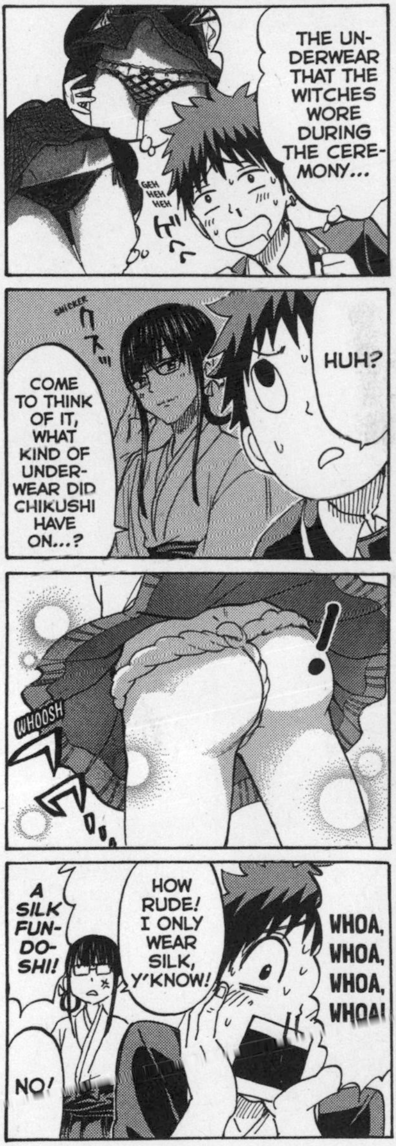
THE UN-DERWEAR THAT THE WITCHES WORE DURING THE CERE-MONY...
GEH HEH HEH
SNICKER
HUH?
COME TO THINK OF IT, WHAT KIND OF UNDER-WEAR DID CHIKUSHI HAVE ON...?
!
WHOOSH
WHOA, WHOA, WHOA, WHOA!
HOW RUDE! I ONLY WEAR SILK, Y'KNOW!
A SILK FUN-DO-SHI!
NO!

THE MOM OF THE SUPERNATURAL STUDIES CLUB

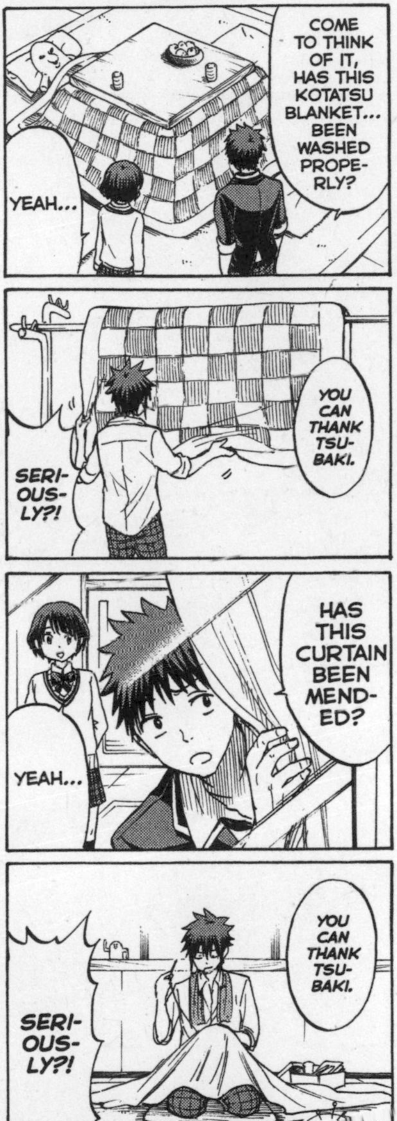
COME TO THINK OF IT, HAS THIS KOTATSU BLANKET... BEEN WASHED PROPE-RLY?
YEAH...
YOU CAN THANK TSU-BAKI.
SERI-OUS-LY?!
HAS THIS CURTAIN BEEN MEND-ED?
YEAH...
YOU CAN THANK TSU-BAKI.
SERI-OUS-LY?!

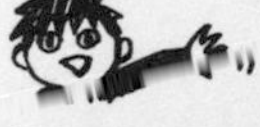

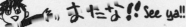

またな!! See ya!!

Translation Notes

Fundoshi, page 381

A traditional Japanese undergarment/loincloth that is made from cotton and is typically worn by men. You'll most often see people wearing fundoshi during traditional festivals and parades.

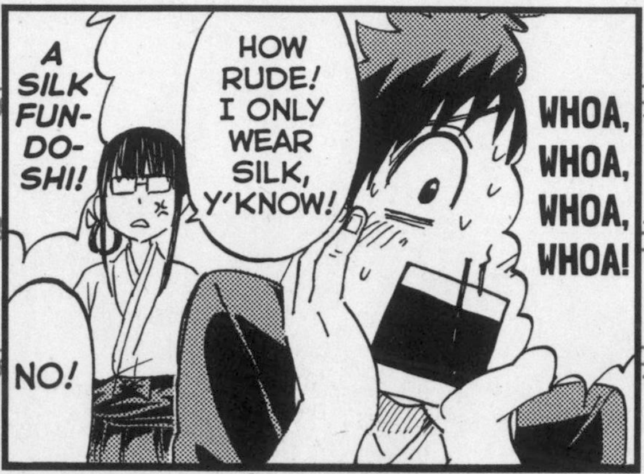
WHOA, WHOA, WHOA, WHOA!
HOW RUDE! I ONLY WEAR SILK, Y'KNOW!
A SILK FUN-DO-SHI!
NO!

Kotatsu, page 381

A type of Japanese table that includes a heating element on the bottom to warm your bottom half while relaxing or eating. Kotatsu are a centerpiece of Japanese home-life in the winter.

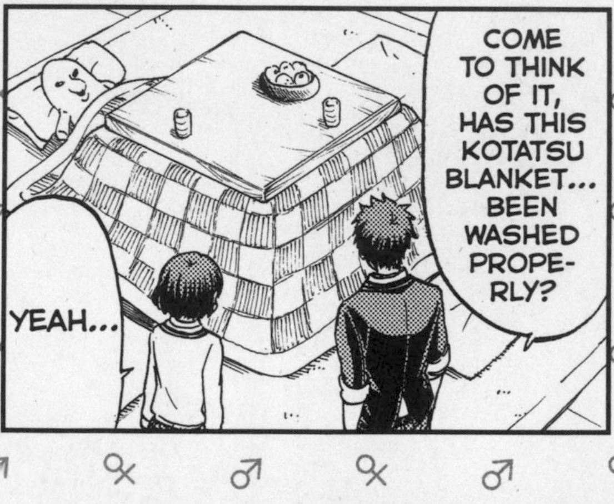
COME TO THINK OF IT, HAS THIS KOTATSU BLANKET... BEEN WASHED PROPE-RLY?
YEAH...

Bonus Gallery

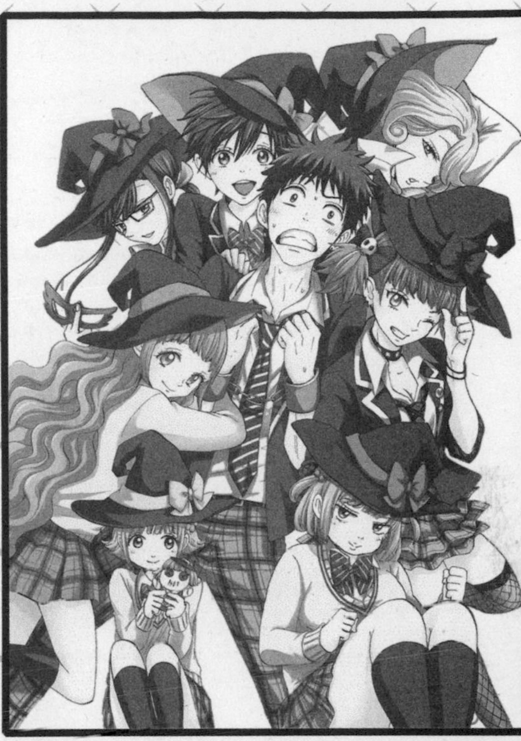

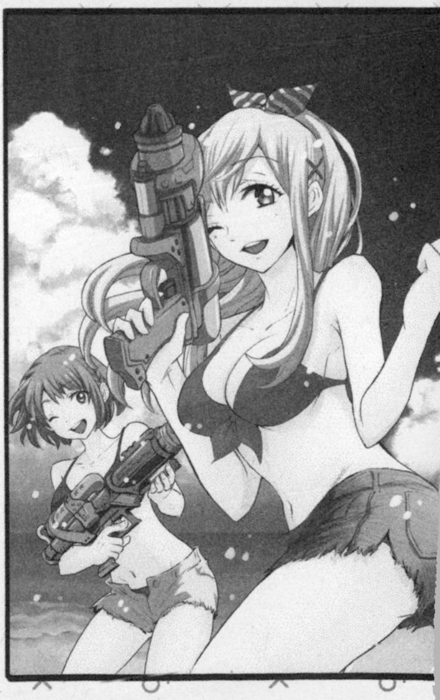

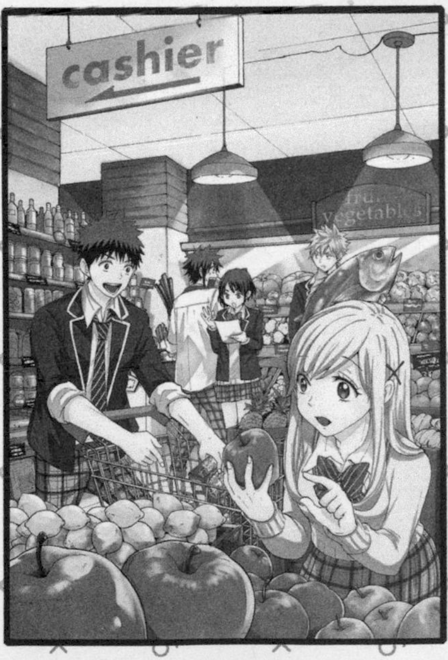
cashier

Yamada-kun and the Seven Witches volume 19-20 is a work of fiction. Names, characters, places, and incidents are the products of the author's imagination or are used fictitiously. Any resemblance to actual events, locales, or persons, living or dead, is entirely coincidental.

A Kodansha Comics Trade Paperback Original.

Published in the United States by Kodansha Comics,
an imprint of Kodansha USA Publishing, LLC, New York.

Publication rights for this English edition arranged through Kodansha Ltd., Tokyo.

First published in Japan in 2015 by Kodansha Ltd., Tokyo, as *Yamada-kun to Nananin no Majo* volumes 19 and 20.

ISBN 978-1-63236-632-0

Printed in the United States of America.

www.kodanshacomics.com

9 8 7 6 5 4 3 2 1

Translation: David Rhie
Lettering: Scott O. Brown
Editing: Ajani Oloye
Kodansha Comics edition cover design: Phil Balsman